THE GRASSES OF TEXAS

THE GRASSES
OF TEXAS

By

FRANK W. GOULD

With drawings by

VALLOO KAPADIA

and others

PUBLISHED FOR

The Texas Agricultural Experiment Station

BY

Texas A&M University Press

COLLEGE STATION

Library of Congress Cataloging in Publication Data
Gould, Frank W
    The grasses of Texas.

    Bibliography: p.
    Includes index.
    1. Grasses — Texas — Identification. I. Title.
QK495.G74G726   584'.9'097641   75-18688
ISBN 0-89096-005-4

Manufactured in the United States of America
First edition

Contents

Preface

This systematic treatment of Texas grasses has been prepared to provide the range scientist, the professional botanist and the amateur naturalist a ready means of identification of the native, introduced and adventive grasses of Texas. Only those grasses are included that occur regularly or occasionally outside of cultivation. Because of the large number of genera and species involved, it has been necessary to use technical terminology in distinguishing and describing species and varieties. An effort has been made to reduce the descriptive Latin adjectives to a minimum, and a complete glossary of scientific terms is provided.

This is the fourth book to deal specifically with the Texas grass flora, earlier publications being *Texas Grasses* by W. A. Silveus (1933), *Texas Range Grasses* by B. C. Tharp (1952) and *Grasses of the Texas Coastal Bend* by F. W. Gould and T. W. Box (1965). The most recent comprehensive treatment of Texas grasses is that presented in the *Manual of the Vascular Plants of Texas* by D. S. Correll and M. C. Johnston (1970). Other sources of information concerning grass taxonomy utilized in the preparation of this book were the revision of *Hitchcock's Manual of the Grasses of the United States* by Agnes Chase (1951), J. R. Swallen's treatment of Arizona grasses in *Arizona Flora* by T. H. Kearney and R. H. Peebles (1964) and two previous publications by the author, *Grasses of Southwestern United States* (1951) and *Grass Systematics* (1968).

The writer is deeply indebted to the numerous individuals who have directly or indirectly assisted in the preparation of this publication. Thanks are due the following for the treatments of the genera or subgenera indicated: Charlotte G. Reeder, *Muhlenbergia* and *Sporobolus*; Dennis Anderson, *Chloris* and *Eustachys*; LeRoy Harvey, *Eragrostis*; and Floyd R. Waller, *Panicum* section *Diffusum*. Derek Clayton of the Kew Botanic Gardens provides much of the information for the generic descriptions of *Coelorachis* and *Hemarthria*. Among those who have contributed significantly in the preparation of keys, species descriptions and patterns of distribution are Robert I. Lonard, John Bacon and Stephan L. Hatch. Special thanks are due Donna Bryant and John Strommer of the Texas Agricultural Experiment Station for editorial assistance.

The original line drawings of this publication were prepared by Valloo Kapadia. Many of the drawings by Kapadia were used first in *Grasses of the Texas Coastal Bend* and *Grass Systematics*. Several of the excellent line drawings prepared by Lucretia Breazeale Hamilton for *Grasses of Southwestern United States* also have been included. The figures from *Grass Systematics* are used with permission of the McGraw-Hill Book Company and those from *Grasses of Southwestern United States* are used with permission of the University of Arizona Press. Plates of some 32 of the fine illustrations in the *Manual of the Grasses of the United States* (Hitchcock, 1935, and Chase, 1951) were obtained through the courtesy of Gilbert Daniels, director of the Hunt Botanical Library.

The writer is especially indebted to Clarence Cottam and Caleb Glazener of the Rob and Bessie Welder Wildlife Foundation for financial assistance in this project and for the use of the Welder Refuge facilities during the preparation of this publication.

THE GRASSES OF TEXAS

Introduction

To fully appreciate the vast dimensions of Texas, one needs to traverse the 820 miles of fine state highways from Texarkana at the edge of the eastern Texas Pineywoods across the prairies, plains and broken woods of central Texas, through the Trans-Pecos with its dry valleys, mesas and rugged mountains, to historic El Paso on the banks of the Rio Grande some 600 miles upstream from its mouth. Equally enlightening is the 868 mile drive from Dalhart on the windswept plains of the Texas Panhandle to the tropical environs of Brownsville, at the southern tip of the state.

Because of its size and extreme variation in environmental conditions, Texas provides a habitat for nearly 5,000 species of flowering plants. Included are 523 species of grass, some of which are dominants in the vegetation over large areas of the State. The vegetation map used in this publication (Fig. 1) was developed on the basis of edaphic, topographic and climatic factors, as well as broad plant community similarities. The map is essentially the same as that presented by Gould in a preliminary checklist of Texas grasses (1957) and by Gould, Hoffman and Rechentin in their brief summary of the vegetational areas of the State (1960). The following discussions of the vegetational areas are based on and in part copied from the ecological summary of Texas vegetation by Gerald W. Thomas (in Gould, 1969).

VEGETATIONAL AREAS OF TEXAS

1. Pineywoods
2. Gulf Prairies and Marshes
3. Post Oak Savannah
4. Blackland Prairies
5. Cross Timbers and Prairies
6. South Texas Plains
7. Edwards Plateau
8. Rolling Plains
9. High Plains
10. Trans-Pecos, Mountains and Basins

Fig. 1.   Vegetational areas of Texas. From Gould, 1962.

1.   PINEYWOODS. For the most part an area of gently rolling or hilly country, averaging 200 to 500 feet in elevation and with numerous streams feeding into several large rivers, the Pineywoods region is characterized by extensive pine and pine-hardwood forests with numerous but not extensive swamp, marsh and bog areas. Rainfall averages 35 to more than 50 inches, rather uniformly distributed throughout the year. Frequent in and along forests are the cool-season grasses, *Elymus virginicus, E. canadensis* and *Stipa avenacea*, numerous warm-season grasses, including *Tridens flavus, Schizachyrium scoparium* var. *divergens, Chasmanthium latifolium* and *C. laxum*, and several species of *Paspalum, Panicum* and *Andropogon*. Characteristic of the Pineywoods are *Arundinaria gigantea*, the shrubby native bamboo, and the ever-present representatives of *Dichanthelium*, until recently grouped in the genus *Panicum*. Typical prairie vegetation is present on restricted clay prairie sites throughout the Pinewoods.

2.   GULF PRAIRIES AND MARSHES. There are two major divisions in this region, Coastal Prairie and Gulf Coastal Marshlands. The Coastal Prairie is a nearly level plain less than 150 feet in elevation, dissected by streams flowing into the Gulf. The Coastal Marsh is limited to narrow belts of

low wet marsh immediately adjacent to the coast. Soils of Coastal Prairie tend to be heavy-textured acid clays or clay loams, although there are some sandy loams. Soils of the Coastal Marsh are acid sands, sandy loams and clays. Average annual rainfall varies from about 50 inches in the northeast to less than 20 inches in the southwest. Although the climax vegetation of the Gulf Prairie is largely tall grass prairie or post oak (*Quercus stellata*) savannah, much of the area has been invaded by brush such as mesquite (*Prosopis glandulosa*), oaks, prickly pear (*Opuntia* spp.) and several acacias. The principal climax grasses are *Andropogon gerardii, Schizachyrium scoparium* var. *littoralis, Sorghastrum nutans, Tripsacum dactyloides* and *Panicum virgatum*. Frequent in moist shoreline sites and along borders of brackish marshes are *Spartina spartinae, S. patens, Distichlis spicata, Monanthochloë littoralis, Panicum amarum* and *Sporobolus virginicus.*

3.   POST OAK SAVANNAH. This region has been variously classified as savannah or as part of the oak-hickory or deciduous forest formation. Included are both the East and West Cross Timbers of northeastern Texas. Topography of the Post Oak Savannah is gently rolling to hilly. Elevations are from 300 to 800 feet. Annual rainfall is 35 to 45 inches, with most precipitation usually in May and June.

Climax grasses of the Post Oak Savannah are *Schizachyrium scoparium* var. *frequens, Sorghastrum nutans, Panicum virgatum, Tridens flavus, Bothriochloa saccharoides* var. *longipaniculata* and *Chasmanthium laxum*. The overstory primarily is *Quercus stellata* (post oak), *Q. marilandica* (blackjack oak) and species of *Carya* (hickory). Brush and tree densities have increased tremendously from the virgin condition.

4.   BLACKLAND PRAIRIES. The Blackland Prairies have a gently rolling to nearly level topography, with dark-colored calcareous clay soils developed under prairie grass - forb vegetation. Average annual rainfall varies from about 30 inches on the west to slightly more than 40 inches on the east. For the most part, the fertile Blackland Prairie soils have been brought under cultivation, but small acreages of meadowland remain in climax tall grass vegetation. Little bluestem, *Schizachyrium scoparium* var. *frequens*, has been determined to be the climax dominant. Other important grasses are *Andropogon gerardii, Sorghastrum nutans, Panicum virgatum, Bouteloua curtipendula, B. hirsuta, Sporobolus asper, Bothriochloa saccharoides* and *Stipa leucotricha.*

5.   CROSS TIMBERS AND PRAIRIES. This region comprises a large area of closely associated prairie and woodland sites. The topography is rolling to hilly, deeply dissected and with rapid surface drainage. Sharp changes in the vegetation cover are associated with differences in soils and topography. Soil types vary from slightly acid sandy or clay loams to dark-colored calcareous clays over limestone. Average annual rainfall is 25 to 40 inches.

The predominant tall grasses of this area are *Schizachyrium scoparium* var. *frequens, Andropogon gerardii, Sorghastrum nutans, Panicum virgatum, Sporobolus asper, Elymus canadensis* and *Stipa leucotricha.*

6.   SOUTH TEXAS PLAINS. The South Texas Plains are essentially the same as the Rio Grande Plain land resource area (Texas Agricultural Experiment Station, 1958) with the exception that the portion along the coast is included in the "Gulf Prairies and Marshes region." This area has a level to rolling topography and clay to sandy loam soil types that vary from calcareous to slightly acid. Elevations are from sea level to about 1,000 feet. Average annual precipitation is 16 to 35 inches, with most rainfall coming in May and June. Periodic drouths occur in this area, with annual rainfall totals below 5 inches being recorded. The South Texas Plains originally supported a grassland or savannah type climax vegetation. Although large acreages now are cultivated for crops, especially in the south, most of the area is range land. Long-continued heavy grazing and other factors have resulted in a general change from a grassland or savannah type climax vegetation to a cover of shrubs and low trees. Among the several species of shrubs and trees that have made dramatic increases are *Prosopis glandulosa* (mesquite), *Quercus virginiana* (live oak), *Q. stellata* (post oak), *Opuntia* spp. and *Acacia* spp.

Characteristic grasses of the sandy loam soils are *Schizachyrium scoparium* var. *littoralis, Heteropogon contortus, Bothriochloa saccharoides* var. *longipaniculata, Cenchrus myosuroides* and species of *Setaria, Paspalum, Chloris* and *Eragrostis*. The introduced *Cenchrus ciliaris* (buffelgrass) has become abundant almost throughout the area, both in pastures and as a casual weed of roadsides and waste places. Grass dominants on clay loam soils are *Bothriochloa saccharoides* var. *longipaniculata, Digitaria californica, Buchloë dactyloides, Hilaria belangeri* and species of *Setaria, Pappophorum* and *Bouteloua*.

7.   EDWARDS PLATEAU. Included in this "Hill Country" area is the granitic Central Basin, centered in Burnet, Llano and Mason counties, with the semi-arid Stockton Plateau on the west. On the east and south, the Balcones Escarpment forms a distinct boundary to the Edwards Plateau. Elevations range from slightly less than 100 feet to more than 3,000 feet. The surface is rough and well-drained. Average annual rainfall varies from less than 15 inches in the west to more than 33 inches in the east, with most precipitation usually in late spring and early autumn. Soils are mostly shallow with a wide range of surface textures. They are underlain by limestone or caliche on the Plateau proper and in the Central Basin by granite. The rough, rocky areas typically support a tall or mid-grass understory and a brush overstory complex made up of live oak, shinnery oaks, junipers and mesquite. Important climax grasses of the Plateau include *Panicum virgatum, Sorghastrum nutans, Bothriochloa barbinodis, B. saccharoides* var. *torreyana, Schizachyrium scoparium* var. *frequens, Bouteloua curtipendula, Elymus canadensis, Hilaria belangeri* and *Buchloë dactyloides*. The northwestern portion of the Plateau grades into "mesquite-tobosa country" similar to that of the Rolling Plains. The Stockton Plateau portion, with annual rainfall of 15 inches or less, supports the vegetation of semi-desert grasslands.

8.   ROLLING PLAINS. The Rolling Plains, the eastern portion of which is sometimes referred to as the Reddish Prairies, has a gently rolling to

moderately rough topography. Elevations are 800 to 3000 feet. Annual rainfall ranges from about 30 inches in the east to 22 inches in the west. May and September normally are the high rainfall months. Soils vary from coarse sands along outwash terraces adjacent to streams, to tight clays or red-bed clays and shales. The original prairie vegetation included tall- and mid-grasses, such as *Schizachyrium scoparium* var. *frequens, Andropogon gerardii* var. *gerardii* (big bluestem), *A. gerardii* var. *paucipilus* (sand bluestem), *Bouteloua curtipendula, B. gracilis, B. hirsuta, Sorghastrum nutans, Panicum virgatum, Elymus canadensis* and *Agropyron smithii.*

9. HIGH PLAINS. This is a part of the Great Plains region. It is a relatively level, high plateau separated from the Rolling Plains by the Cap Rock Escarpment and dissected by the Canadian River breaks. Elevations are from 3,000 to 4,500 feet, with a gentle slope towards the southeast. The surface is spotted with "playa lakes" which sometimes cover more than 40 acres and contain several feet of water after heavy rains. Average annual rainfall is 15 to 21 inches, with most precipitation coming in late spring and autumn. Soils range in surface texture from clays on hardland sites in the north to medium textures on mixed land sites and sands on the Southern High Plains. Surface soils are generally underlain by caliche at depths of 2 to 5 feet. Vegetation on the High Plains is variously classified as mixed-prairie, as short-grass prairie and, in some locations, as tall-grass prairie. The level, undissected portions of the High Plains are characteristically free of trees and shrubs, but *Artemisia filifolia* (sand sagebrush) and *Prosopis glandulosa* (mesquite) are common invaders, especially in the south. The most widespread and important grasses are *Buchloë dactyloides, Bouteloua gracilis* and *B. curtipendula.* Frequent in some areas are *Bouteloua eriopoda, Schizachyrium scoparium* var. *frequens, Panicum virgatum, Sorghastrum nutans, Agropyron smithii* and several species of *Sporobolus.*

10. TRANS-PECOS, MOUNTAINS AND BASINS. As the name implies, this area includes the region west of the Pecos River except for the Stockton Plateau. It is a land of mountains, plateaus and arid valleys. Elevations are from about 2,500 feet to more than 8,500 feet. Average annual rainfall over most of the area is less than 12 inches, although locally at the higher elevations it is as much as 20 inches. Soils and sites are extremely variable. Ponderosa pine (*Pinus ponderosa*) grows on a few slopes of the higher elevations, pinyon pines (*P. cembroides* and *P. edulis*) are associated with species of *Juniperus* and *Yucca* on the lower mountain slopes, and desert shrub formations are characteristic vegetation of dry valleys and basins. The grass vegetation, especially on the higher mountain slopes, includes many southwestern and Rocky Mountain species not present elsewhere in Texas. Included are *Piptochaetium fimbriatum, Lycurus phleoides* and *Poa fendleriana.* Grasses of the desert flats include *Panicum obtusum, Bouteloua eriopoda, Scleropogon brevifolius, Erioneuron pilosum, E. pulchellum, Muhlenbergia porteri* and several species of *Sporobolus* and *Aristida.*

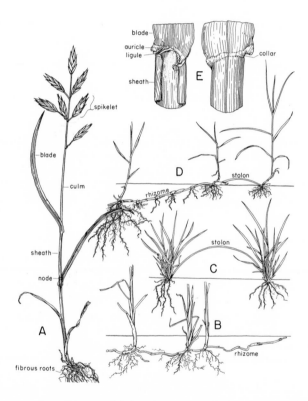

Fig. 2. The grass plant: (A) general habit, (*Bromus unioloides*); (B) rhizomes; (C) stolon; and (D) rhizome and stolon intergradation (*Cynodon dactylon*). From Gould, 1951.

The Grass Plant

Grasses are typical but highly specialized monocotyledonous plants.*
The earliest grasses probably grew in mesic habitats under tropical or subtropical climatic conditions. Modern grasses that inhabit the warmer regions
of the earth are extremely diverse both in respect to vegetative and reproductive characteristics. Adaptation of grasses to dry and cold habitats has been
accompanied by basic morphological and physiological changes.

The grass plant (Fig. 2) consists of roots, culms (stems), leaves and
inflorescences of small flowers borne in spikelets. The nature of these structures can best be explained by considering them separately.

ROOTS

Grass roots are fibrous (except for the prop roots discussed below), with
little or no increase in diameter after their original development from the root
tip meristem. Branching and rebranching is at irregular intervals, not at
regular nodes as in the stem. The *primary root system*, developed from the
primary root and other seminal roots, is short-lived, usually persisting only a

*This treatment follows closely the explanation of the grass plant structure in *Grasses of South-
western United States* (Gould, 1951).

few days to a few weeks. The root system of the mature grass plant is made up of *adventitious* roots developed at the lower nodes of the culm (stem). In many grasses, roots arise at all culm nodes that touch the ground. Grasses such as corn or maize, *Zea mays*, develop stout "prop roots" for mechanical support at the lower above-ground culm nodes.

CULMS (STEMS)

Grass culms generally are smooth and cylindrical with solid, often swollen nodes and elongated, hollow, solid or semi-solid internodes. Leaves, branches and adventitious roots are borne at the nodes. Most grasses have herbaceous culms, but those of the giant reed grasses become firm and "woody;" bamboo culms contain lignin and have a true woody structure.

In addition to the erect culms, *tillers, stolons* and *rhizomes* (Fig. 2) are developed by many grasses. Tillers or "suckers" are spreading basal branches usually associated with a "bunchgrass" habit. Stolons or "runners" spread or loop along the surface of the ground and often produce "new plants" by developing roots and upright culms at the nodes. Stolons may bear normal leaves or the leaves may be highly reduced. Rhizomes are underground stems with scale leaves and roots present at regular nodes, the roots not scattered along the primary axis as in a branching root system. A rhizomatous stem axis may become stoloniferous at the surface of the ground, or a stolon may become subterranean and rhizomatous.

Growth of the culm results from cell division and cell elongation at the *terminal* (apical) *meristem* and at *intercalary meristems* at the base of the internodes.

LEAVES

Grass leaves are borne in two ranks (rows) alternate at successive nodes of the culm. Nearly all grass leaves are differentiated into a well-defined basal *sheath* that tightly enfolds the culm for most or all of its length and a usually flattened *blade*. The sheath is attached just below the culm node, and characteristics of the node, for the most part, are characteristics of the sheath base rather than of the true culm node. The sheath usually has free margins to the base, but in a few grasses the margins are fused, forming a tubular structure. Most species of *Bromus, Melica* and *Glyceria* have closed or partially closed sheaths with the margins united at least below. The blade usually is flat and elongated but is highly modified in some grasses. Species of hot, dry areas tend to have narrow, involute blades or blades that are nearly terete. Many tropical grasses have broad, short, ovate or oblong blades, often with a petiole-like constriction at the base of the blade just above the sheath. The grass blade always has entire margins, but fine epidermal projections give some blades a saw-edge capable of inflicting deep cuts. In most but not all grasses, a membranous or hairy collar-like appendage or rim, the *ligule*, is present on the inner (adaxial) surface at the sheath-blade junction. Membranous projections of tissue termed *auricles* occasionally are present on either side, at the apex of the sheath or at the base of the blade.

The first leaf of the lateral shoot or branch is short and thin and consists usually of sheath only. This leaf, the *prophyll* (prophyllum) is always developed with its dorsal (back) surface tightly fitted against the culm axis and its margins infolded over the bud or base of the shoot. The prophyll has numerous fine nerves and a large, thick nerve on either side of the fold.

THE INFLORESCENCE

Grass flowers are borne in *spikelets* (Fig. 3 & 4), the basic units of the grass inflorescence. The spikelet usually consists of a short axis, the *rachilla*, bearing two "empty" bracts at the basal nodes and one or more *florets* above. Each floret usually consists of two bracts, the lemma (lower) and the *palea* (upper) which subtend and enclose a flower. The typical grass flower (Fig. 5) has two *lodicules* (vestigial perianth segments), three *stamens* and a *pistil*. Some flowers regularly are unisexual (imperfect), having only stamens (staminate) or only a pistil (pistillate). A few grasses, including cultivated corn or maize, *Zea mays*, and southern wildrice, *Zizaniopsis miliacea*, are monoecious, with staminate and pistillate spikelets borne on the same plant. Several other grasses, including buffalograss, *Buchloë dactyloides*, and burrograss, *Scleropogon brevifolius*, are dioecious, with staminate and pistillate spikelets usually borne on separate plants.

The dry, indehiscent, one-seeded grass fruit is commonly but not always a *caryopsis*, with the seed coat adherent to the ovary wall. The term "grain" is used in reference to the mature ovary alone or to the ovary enclosed by persistent glumes, lemmas or paleas. In *Stipa* and *Aristida* the ovary is permanently enclosed by the lemma and palea, and in most grasses of the Andropogon tribe, the ovary is permanently enclosed by firm glumes that are persistent over both the reduced and perfect florets.

The grass inflorescence is highly variable as to the number and size of spikelets and the disposition of the spikelets on the main axis or on branches. The inflorescence is delimited at the base by the uppermost culm leaf, which often is characterized by an enlarged sheath and a short, greatly reduced blade. Grass inflorescences are classified as spikes, racemes and panicles as follows:

SPIKE: All spikelets sessile on the main inflorescence axis.

RACEME: All spikelets borne on individual flower stalks (pedicels) developed directly on the main axis as in wheat, *Triticum aestivum*, or some spikelets sessile and some pediceled on the main axis as in little barley, *Hordeum pusillum*, or little bluestem, *Schizachyrium scoparium*.

PANICLE: Spikelets all or in part on rebranched branches. There are many types of panicles: some little-branched, some intricately much-branched and some with all spikelets sessile or short-pediceled on unbranched primary inflorescence branches.

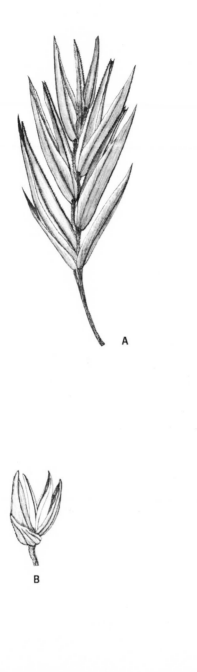

Fig. 3.   Spikelet types: (A) *Festuca arundinacea*
with several florets; (B) *Panicum hemitomon* with
two florets, the upper perfect, the lower staminate
or neuter; and (C) *Agrostis avenacea* with one floret.
From Gould, 1968.

10   THE GRASSES OF TEXAS

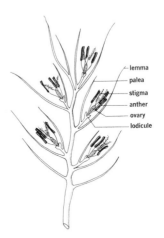

Fig. 4. Spikelet of *Bromus carinatus*, photograph and diagram, from GRASS SYSTEMATICS by Gould (copyright 1968 by McGraw-Hill, Inc.; used with permission of McGraw Hill Book Company).

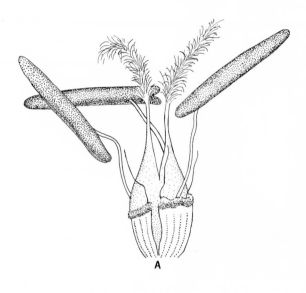

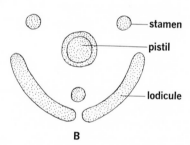

Fig. 5.   The grass flower: flower of *Sorghum halepense* (A) and diagram of the transverse section of the same flower (B). From GRASS SYSTEMATICS by Gould (copyright 1968 by McGraw-Hill, Inc.; used with permission of McGraw-Hill Book Company).

Grass Classification

In the first edition of *Species Plantarum* (1753), the designated point of origin for the binomial nomenclature of flowering plants, Linnaeus keyed and listed a total of 40 grass genera. The classification system of Linnaeus, based mainly on the number and arrangement of flower parts, was highly mechanical and resulted in the grouping together of some dissimilar plants and the separation of others that now are considered to be closely related. In the Linnaean system, grasses, for the most part, fall into the category TRIANDRIA (three stamens) MONOGYNIA (one pistil or ovary). *Zizania*, with stamens and pistils in separate flowers and the staminate flowers with six stamens, is referred to MONOECIA (monoecious) HEXANDRIA (six stamens).

Robert Brown (1810) was the first to understand the true nature of the grass spikelet and to recognize it as a reduced inflorescence branch. Linnaeus had interpreted it as a single flower. Brown recognized two major subdivisions of the grass family, the Paniceae and Poaceae, and noted the predominantly tropical-subtropical distribution of Paniceae, as contrasted with the cool-climate adaptations of Poaceae.

Many systems of grass classification were proposed in the 19th century, the most outstanding of which was that of the Englishman, George Bentham (1881). Like Brown, Bentham recognized two subfamilies, the Panicoideae and Festucoideae (Poaceae of Brown). Grasses of the Panicoideae were grouped in six tribes and those of the Festucoideae in seven tribes. Most of the early United States agrostologists patterned their classifications after that of Bentham. A. S. Hitchcock, in *The Genera of Grasses of the United States with special reference to the Economic Species* (1920) and *Manual of the Grasses of the United States* (1935; revised by A. Chase, 1951), followed the basic treatment of Bentham but shifted the tribes Oryzeae and Zoysieae from the Panicoideae to the Festucoideae and added another small tribe by splitting off the Zizanieae from the Oryzeae. Hitchcock thus recognized four tribes in the Panicoideae and 10 tribes in the Festucoideae (Pooideae).

Modern grass classification systems are based primarily on those proposed in the 1930's by a Russian, N. P. Avdulov, and a French-Canadian, H. Prat. In his system, Avdulov (1931) correlated data from chromosome studies with leaf anatomy, the nature of the starch grains in the fruit, geographical distribution and spikelet morphology. Prat, in 1932, reported on the significance of the grass leaf epidermis in classification and, in 1936, published a 93-page treatise entitled *La Systématique des Graminées.* In grouping tribes and genera, Prat correlated characters of leaf epidermis and anatomy; cytology; morphology of seedlings, embryos, fruits and the inflorescence; the nature of starch grains; physiology; ecology; and serology (Gould, 1968).

Numerous papers concerned with grass phylogeny were published in the 1950's and early 1960's, and six new subfamily groupings were proposed during this period. There is now general agreement that the Bambusoideae, Pooideae (Festucoideae), Eragrostoideae and Panicoideae comprise subfamilies. Four "recent" authors recognize two additional smaller subfamily groups, the Oryzoideae and the Arundinoideae. As presently interpreted, the Arundinoideae appears to be highly heterogeneous, and further segregation of this group can be expected.

The Grasses of Texas

The representation of grasses in the vegetation of Texas far exceeds that of any other state of the Union. Treated in the present publication are 122 genera and 523 species of native, introduced or adventive grasses. Based on modern concepts of phylogenetic relationships, the tribes and genera of Texas grasses are arranged as follows:

SUBFAMILY I. BAMBUSOIDEAE
  TRIBE 1. BAMBUSEAE
    1. *Arundinaria*
SUBFAMILY II. ORYZOIDEAE
  TRIBE 2. ORYZEAE
    2. *Oryza*
    3. *Leersia*
    4. *Zizania*
    5. *Zizaniopsis*
    6. *Hydrochloa*

SUBFAMILY III.   ARUNDINOIDEAE

TRIBE 3.   CENTOTHECEAE

    7. *Chasmanthium*

TRIBE 4.   ARUNDINEAE

    8. *Arundo*

    9. *Phragmites*

    10. *Cortaderia*

TRIBE 5.   DANTHONIEAE

    11. *Danthonia*

    12. *Schismus*

SUBFAMILY IV.   POOIDEAE (FESTUCOIDEAE)

TRIBE 6.   MELICEAE

    13. *Melica*

    14. *Glyceria*

TRIBE 7.   DIARRHENEAE

    15. *Diarrhena*

TRIBE 8.   STIPEAE

    16. *Stipa*

    17. *Oryzopsis*

    18. *Piptochaetium*

TRIBE 9.   POEAE

    19. *Bromus*

    20. *Brachypodium*

    21. *Vulpia*

    22. *Festuca*

    23. *Lolium*

    24. *Sclerochloa*

    25. *Catapodium*

    26. *Poa*

    27. *Briza*

    28. *Dactylis*

TRIBE 10.   AVENEAE

    29. *Koeleria*

    30. *Sphenopholis*

    31. *Trisetum*

    32. *Aira*

    33. *Avena*

    34. *Holcus*

35. *Limnodea*

36. *Agrostis*

37. *Polypogon*

38. *Gastridium*

39. *Phleum*

40. *Alopecurus*

41. *Phalaris*

42. *Cinna*

TRIBE 11. TRITICEAE

43. *Hordeum*

44. *Elymus*

45. *Agropyron*

46. *Triticum*

47. *Secale*

TRIBE 12. MONERMEAE

48. *Parapholis*

SUBFAMILY V. ERAGROSTOIDEAE
TRIBE 13. ERAGROSTEAE

49. *Eragrostis*

50. *Neeragrostis*

51. *Tridens*

52. *Triplasis*

53. *Erioneuron*

54. *Munroa*

55. *Eleusine*

56. *Dactyloctenium*

57. *Leptochloa*

58. *Trichoneura*

59. *Gymnopogon*

60. *Tripogon*

61. *Vaseyochloa*

62. *Redfieldia*

63. *Scleropogon*

64. *Blepharidachne*

65. *Calamovilfa*

66. *Lycurus*

67. *Muhlenbergia*

68. *Sporobolus*

69. *Blepharoneuron*

TRIBE 14. **CHLORIDEAE**

70. *Willkommia*

71. *Schedonnardus*

72. *Cynodon*

73. *Chloris*

74. *Eustachys*

75. *Bouteloua*

76. *Cathestecum*

77. *Buchloë*

78. *Spartina*

79. *Hilaria*

TRIBE 15. **ZOYSIEAE**

80. *Tragus*

TRIBE 16. **AELUROPODEAE**

81. *Distichlis*

82. *Allolepis*

83. *Monanthochloë*

TRIBE 17. **UNIOLEAE**

84. *Uniola*

TRIBE 18. **PAPPOPHOREAE**

85. *Pappophorum*

86. *Enneapogon*

87. *Cottea*

TRIBE 19. **ARISTIDEAE**

88. *Aristida*

SUBFAMILY VI. **PANICOIDEAE**

TRIBE 20. **PANICEAE**

89. *Digitaria*

90. *Leptoloma*

91. *Anthaenantia*

92. *Stenotaphrum*

93. *Brachiaria*

94. *Axonopus*

95. *Eriochloa*

96. *Panicum*

97. *Dichanthelium*

KEY TO THE GENERA

Leaf blades about 1 cm long; stoloniferous, mat-forming perennial with
    fascicled leaves and inconspicuous, unisexual spikelets
                              83. MONANTHOCHLOË

                                                      p. 375
Leaf blades more than 1 cm long; plants not as above

    Spikelets perfect or, if unisexual, then the staminate and pistillate
        spikelets not conspicuously different

        Spikelets with a single perfect floret, with or without reduced
            florets   A

        Spikelets with two or more perfect florets or, if unisexual, then
            with two or more staminate or pistillate florets   AA

    Spikelets unisexual, the staminate and pistillate conspicuously different

        Plants monoecious (staminate and pistillate spikelets on same plant)

            Staminate and pistillate spikelets in separate inflorescences
                                    122. ZEA
            Staminate and pistillate spikelets in same inflorescence   p. 622

                Pistillate spikelets becoming indurate and bony
                                  121. TRIPSACUM
                Pistillate spikelets not becoming indurate and bony   p. 622

                Inflorescence a spicate raceme
                              118. HETEROPOGON
                                          p. 614

                Inflorescence a panicle   GROUP III

        Plants usually dioecious; low, stoloniferous, mat-forming perennials

            Pistillate and staminate spikelets awnless, the pistillate spikelets
                in burlike clusters hidden in leafy portion of plant, the staminate
                spikelets sessile on 1-4 short, spicate branches of a well-exserted
                inflorescence   77. BUCHLOË
                                            p. 355

            Pistillate spikelets long-awned (each lemma 3-awned), the staminate
                spikelets awnless; both pistillate and staminate spikelets in
                contracted, usually spikelike racemes
                                   63. SCLEROPOGON
                                            p. 240

A (1 perfect floret)

Spikelets in pairs of 1 sessile or subsessile and 1 pediceled (2 pediceled
    at branch tips), infrequently both spikelets short-pediceled; pediceled
    spikelet like sessile one or more often reduced or rudimentary,

occasionally represented by pedicel alone; first glume large and firm, tightly clasping or enclosing second glume (tribe Andropogoneae)
GROUP I

Spikelets in pairs or not; when paired, then first glume not larger and firmer than lemma of perfect floret and not clasping or enclosing second glume

Reduced floret or florets (staminate or sterile) present below perfect one

Reduced floret 1; lemma of reduced floret similar to second glume in size and texture; disarticulation below glume or glumes (Tribe Paniceae) GROUP II

Reduced florets 1 or 2; lemma of reduced florets not similar to second glume in size and texture; disarticulation above glumes when glumes present GROUP III

Reduced florets absent or present above perfect one

Inflorescence a panicle or open raceme, the primary branches spreading or contracted but not spicate GROUP III

Inflorescence a spike, spicate raceme or with 2-several spicate primary branches

Inflorescence of 1-several unilateral spicate primary branches
GROUP V

Inflorescence a terminal, bilateral spike or spicate raceme
GROUP VI

AA (2 or more perfect florets)

Inflorescence an open or contracted panicle, or raceme with spikelets on well-developed pedicels GROUP IV

Inflorescence a spike, spicate raceme, or panicle with spicate primary branches

Inflorescence with 2 (infrequently 1) -several unilateral branches
GROUP V

Inflorescence a terminal, bilateral spike or spicate raceme
GROUP VI

GROUP I (Tribe Andropogoneae)

Spikelets all alike and with perfect florets B

Spikelets not all alike, the pediceled ones, or less frequently the sessile (or subsessile) ones, staminate or sterile BB

B

Pediceled spikelets present, like the sessile ones

  Spikelets falling in pairs together with sections of a disarticulating rachis   108. ERIANTHUS
p. 569

  Spikelets falling separately from a persistent rachis
107. IMPERATA
p. 567

Pediceled spikelets completely reduced, represented by pedicel only

  Spikelets mostly 7-9 mm long, borne on numerous scattered branches of a large terminal panicle   110. SORGHASTRUM
p. 577

  Spikelets 5 mm or less long, borne in small inflorescences on branchlets of a much-divided broomlike flowering culm
111. ANDROPOGON
p. 579

BB

Spikelet awnless

  Flowering culm terminating in a well-branched panicle
109. SORGHUM
p. 574

  Flowering culm or leafy branch terminating in a spicate raceme

    Rachis and pedicels glabrous; pediceled spikelet reduced, often rudimentary

    Sessile spikelet sunken in a thickened rachis

      Inflorescence flattened; first glume of sessile spikelet smooth on back; rachis not readily disarticulating
119. HEMARTHRIA
p. 618

      Inflorescence cylindrical; first glume of sessile spikelet with pits or irregular transverse ridges; rachis readily disarticulating
120. COELORACHIS
p. 620

    Sessile spikelet not sunken in a thickened rachis, the rachis slender
115. EREMOCHLOA
p. 611

    Rachis and pedicels puberulent or ciliate; pediceled spikelet well-developed   117. ELYONURUS
p. 612

Spikelet (lemma of upper floret) awned

  Awns 3-8 cm long

Perfect (awned) spikelets sessile; glumes and awn of perfect spikelet dark brown at maturity   118.   HETEROPOGON
p. 614

Perfect spikelets pediceled; glumes and awn of perfect spikelet light-
colored   116.   TRACHYPOGON
p. 612

Awns less than 3 cm long

Flowering culms much-branched above, the branches terminating in
numerous short, leafy branchlets, each bearing 1 to 6 pedunculate
spikelet clusters above the uppermost bract

Branchlets terminating in a spicate raceme
114.   SCHIZACHYRIUM
p. 605

Branchlets terminating in a panicle with 2 to 6 racemose branches
111.   ANDROPOGON
p. 579

Flowering culms not terminating in numerous short, leafy branchlets;
spikelets in small or large panicles

Pedicels, at least those above, and usually the upper rachis internodes,
with a central groove or membranous area
113.   BOTHRIOCHLOA
p. 591

Pedicels and rachis internodes flat or rounded, without a central
groove or membranous area

Panicle axis above lowermost branch usually 15 to 30 mm long;
panicle branches numerous, freely rebranched, not conspicuously spicate in appearance   109.   SORGHUM
p. 574

Panicle axis above lowermost branch less than 15 cm long; panicle
branches not or sparingly rebranched, conspicuously spicate in
appearance

Pediceled spikelet shorter or narrower than sessile one, tapering
to a narrow apex; native species   111.   ANDROPOGON
p. 579

Pediceled spikelet about as large as sessile one, broadly rounded
at the apex; introduced species   112.   DICHANTHIUM
p. 586

GROUP II (Tribe Paniceae)

Spikelets in involucres of bristles and/or flattened spines that disarticulate with the spikelets

Bristles or spines fused together, at least at the base
106.   CENCHRUS
p. 561

Bristles and spines not fused together   105.   PENNISETUM
p. 560

Spikelets not in bristly or spiny involucres that fall with the spikelets,
the bristles persistent when present

Spikelets all or in part (at least those terminating branchlets) subtended
by 1-several bristles   104.   SETARIA
p. 542

Spikelets not subtended by bristles

Inflorescence with spikelets partially embedded in a thick, flattened
rachis; first glume present   92.   STENOTAPHRUM
p. 422

Inflorescence not as above or, if so, then spikelets lacking the first
glume

Second glume awned; first glume awned or awnless

First glume minute; second glume and lemma of sterile floret
about equal, silky-villous   103.   RHYNCHELYTRUM
p. 542

First glume well developed; spikelets not silky-villous

First glume much shorter than the second, awnless or with
an awn shorter than the body   101.   ECHINOCHLOA
p. 529

First glume about as long as the second, with an awn to
3 times the length of the body   100.   OPLISMENUS
p. 529

Second and first glumes both awnless

Lemma of upper floret thin and flexible, the margins flat, membranous and not inrolled over palea; first glume minute or
absent   C

Lemma of upper floret relatively thick and rigid, the margins
most frequently inrolled over palea; first glume present
or absent   CC

C

Spikelets on long or short pedicels in an open or loosely contracted
panicle; panicle branches not spicate

Spikelets in a contracted panicle much longer than broad; pedicels mostly shorter than spikelets   91.   ANTHAENANTIA
p. 420

Spikelets in an open panicle about as broad as long at maturity; pedicels mostly 2-several times as long as spikelets
90.   LEPTOLOMA
p. 418

Spikelets subsessile or on short, appressed pedicels of a panicle with few to several spicate primary or secondary branches
89.   DIGITARIA
p. 406

CC

First glume absent on some or all spikelets

Lemma of upper floret mucronate or short-awned; a cuplike or disclike ring present at base of spikelet   95.   ERIOCHLOA
p. 430

Lemma of upper floret not mucronate or awned; cuplike or disclike ring not present at base of spikelet

Lemma of upper floret with rounded back turned away from the rachis; spikelets narrowly oblong, borne singly and widely spaced in 2 rows
94.   AXONOPUS
p. 427

Lemma of upper floret with rounded back turned towards the rachis; spikelets broadly ovate to oblong, closely placed and often paired in 2 or 4 rows   99.   PASPALUM
p. 500

First glume present on all spikelets

Second glume densely long-hairy; first glume glabrous, more than half the length of the spikelet   93.   BRACHIARIA
p. 422

Second glume not densely long-hairy; first glume less than half the length of the spikelet when second glume pubescent

Inflorescence of 2-several spicate, unbranched primary branches; spikelets in regular rows; first glume much shorter than second glume and lemma of lower floret

Second glume and lemma of lower floret scabrous-pubescent with short, stiff hairs   101.   ECHINOCHLOA
p. 529

Second glume and lemma of lower floret glabrous

Plants annual; rachis of inflorescence branches winged, 1-2 mm broad   93.   BRACHIARIA
p. 422

Plants perennial; rachis less than 1 mm broad
98.   PASPALIDIUM
p. 498

Inflorescence with some or all primary branches rebranched, or if not, then first glume about as long as second glume and lemma of lower floret

Second glume gibbous at base, thin, strongly 7-11-nerved, 3-4 times as long as first glume; upper floret on a short stipe
102.   SACCIOLEPIS
p. 539

Second glume not gibbous; upper floret not stipitate

Tip of lemma and palea of upper floret usually abruptly pointed; tip of palea free from lemma 101.   ECHINOCHLOA
p. 529

Tip of lemma and palea of upper floret usually rounded; tip of palea enclosed by lemma

Plants annual or perennial, not developing a rosette of short, broad basal leaves during the cool season; plants flowering in warm season only   96.   PANICUM
p. 433

Plants perennial, most species developing a rosette of short, broad basal leaves during the cool season; plants flowering first during the cool season; small axillary inflorescences commonly produced on much-branched and reduced lateral shoots during the warm season
97.   DICHANTHELIUM
p. 477

GROUP III (Panicle, with rebranched
primary branches; perfect floret 1)

Glumes absent or rudimentary

Spikelets perfect, strongly compressed laterally

Spikelets 7-10 mm long; annual, the cultivated rice
2.   ORYZA
p. 42

Spikelets less than 6 mm long; native perennials 3.   LEERSIA
p. 42

Spikelets unisexual, not strongly compressed laterally

Leaf blades 1-4 cm long; staminate and pistillate spikelets in separate, inconspicuous inflorescences; plants with trailing or floating culms and usually floating leaves   6.   HYDROCHLOA
p. 49

Leaf blades much more than 4 cm long; staminate and pistillate spikelets in same inflorescence; inflorescence large and conspicuous

Staminate spikelets pendulous on the spreading lower panicle branches, the pistillate spikelets erect on the stiffly erect upper branches   4. ZIZANIA
p. 48

Staminate and pistillate spikelets on the same branches, the pistillate at the tips, the staminate below   5. ZIZANIOPSIS
p. 49

Glumes, at least the second, well developed

Spikelets with 1 perfect floret and 1 or 2 staminate or rudimentary florets

Reduced floret 1, well-developed, above the perfect one; lemma of reduced floret with a short, straight or more often hooked, awn
34. HOLCUS
p. 135

Reduced florets 1 or 2, scale-like, rudimentary, awnless, borne below the perfect floret   41. PHALARIS
p. 150

Spikelets with 1 perfect floret and no reduced florets above or below

Glumes and lemmas awnless   D

Glumes or lemmas awned   DD

D (Glumes and lemmas awnless)

Lemma with a tuft of hair at base; spikelets 5 mm or more long
65. CALAMOVILFA
p. 243

Lemma without a tuft of hair at base when spikelets 5 mm or more long

Glumes both as long as or longer than lemma   36. AGROSTIS
p. 136

Glumes, at least the first, shorter than lemma

Lemma 3-nerved, the lateral nerves sometimes faint

Nerves of the lemma densely pubescent
69. BLEPHARONEURON
p. 311

Nerves of the lemma glabrous or scabrous
67. MUHLENBERGIA
p. 246

Lemma 1-nerved   68. SPOROBOLUS
p. 286

DD (Glumes or lemma awned)

First glume usually 2- or 3-awned, second glume usually 1-awned; spikelets in pairs, the lower of the pair sterile, the two falling together 66.   LYCURUS
p. 245

First and second glumes not as above, or if so, then spikelets not falling in pairs

Disarticulation below glumes; glumes equal or nearly so, as long as or longer than lemma

Glumes awned   37.   POLYPOGON
p. 145

Glumes awnless

Lemma awned from middle or below; inflorescence compact, cylindrical, spikelike   40.   ALOPECURUS
p. 148

Lemma awned from or near tip

Awn 2 mm or less long; strong perennial   42.   CINNA
p. 156

Awn 6 mm or more long; short-lived annuals
40.   ALOPECURUS
p. 148

Disarticulation above glumes

Lemma indurate, awned, permanently enclosing the palea and caryopsis, with a well-developed callus

Awn of lemma 3-branched, the lateral awns short or rudimentary in a few species   88.   ARISTIDA
p. 382

Awn of lemma unbranched

Awn straight or curved but not twisted, rarely more than 2-4 times as long as body of lemma, early deciduous; body of lemma broad, usually subglobose, with a short, blunt callus at base   17.   ORYZOPSIS
p. 79

Awn twisted and geniculate, usually several times as long as body of lemma, persistent or finally disarticulating

Margins of lemma not meeting at apex, the exposed tip of palea projecting as a short point; awn 1-2 cm long; floret subglobose, with a short callus at base
18.   PIPTOCHAETIUM
p. 81

Margins of lemma meeting or overlapping at apex, the tip of palea not exposed; awn 1.5-15 cm or more long; floret terete, slender, with a long, sharp-pointed, bearded callus   16. STIPA
p. 68

Lemma not indurate or permanently enclosing palea and caryopsis; spikelets with or without a well-developed callus

Glumes equal, broad, abruptly short-awned from an obtuse apex; lemma much shorter than glumes, awnless   39. PHLEUM
p. 148

Glumes not equal or, if nearly so, then not abruptly awned

Second glume 4-5 times as long as lemma; annual with densely contracted panicle   38. GASTRIDIUM
p. 147

Second glume shorter to slightly longer than lemma; annuals or perennials with contracted or open panicles

Lemma awned from back, base or cleft apex; glumes equaling or exceeding lemma   36. AGROSTIS
p. 136

Lemma awned from an entire or minutely cleft apex; glumes, at least the first, usually shorter than lemma   67. MUHLENBERGIA
p. 246

GROUP IV (Panicle with rebranched primary branches; perfect florets 2 or more)

Plants 2-6 meters tall

Spikelets mostly 3-7 cm long and 7-13-flowered   1. ARUNDINARIA
p. 40

Spikelets less than 2 cm long and with fewer than 7 florets

Leaves mostly basal, the blades 0.5-1.5 cm broad; culms densely clumped, without creeping rhizomes   10. CORTADERIA
p. 56

Leaves evenly distributed on the culm, blades 2-6 cm broad; culms with stout creeping rhizomes, forming large colonies

Lemmas villous; rachilla glabrous   8. ARUNDO
p. 54

Lemmas glabrous; rachilla villous   9. PHRAGMITES
p. 54

Plants less than 2 m tall

Lemmas with 3 nerves, these usually conspicuous   E

Lemmas, at least some, 5-15-nerved, the nerves conspicuous or obscure
                                                                    EE

E (Lemmas 3-nerved)

Nerves of lemma pubescent or puberulent, or base of lemma long-hairy

Palea densely long-ciliate on upper half; annual   52.   TRIPLASIS
                                                                    p. 215

Palea not densely long-ciliate on upper half; perennials

Panicle 1-8 cm long and contracted, ovoid or oblong; lemmas conspicuously long-hairy on nerves, at least below
                                         53.   ERIONEURON
                                                                    p. 215

Panicle open or contracted, 4-30 cm or more long; when panicle
less than 10 cm long, then lemmas inconspicuously puberulent
on nerves   51.   TRIDENS
                                                                    p. 203

Nerves of lemma not pubescent or puberulent; base of lemma not long-hairy

Lemmas 3-awned

Awns 4-10 cm long   63.   SCLEROPOGON
                                                                    p. 240

Awns less than 1 cm long   64.   BLEPHARIDACHNE
                                                                    p. 242

Lemmas awnless or with a single short, stout awn

Lemmas 6-10 mm long; second glume 3-5-nerved; caryopsis turgid,
beaked   15.   DIARRHENA
                                                                    p. 68

Lemmas less than 6 mm long; second glume 1-nerved; caryopsis not
turgid or beaked

Plants annual or perennial, not dioecious, the florets perfect; when
a stoloniferous and mat-forming annual, then anthers 0.5 mm
or less long, styles not exserted and lemmas 1.5-2 (occasionally
-2.3) mm long   49.   ERAGROSTIS
                                                                    p. 177

Plants annual, stoloniferous, mat-forming, dioecious; staminate
florets with anthers 1.2-2 mm long; pistillate florets with styles
long-exserted from lemma and palea, usually conspicuous long
after anthesis; lemmas 2.6 (occasionally 1.8) -3.3 mm long
                                         50.   NEERAGROSTIS
                                                                    p. 202

EE (Lemmas 5-13-nerved)

Lemmas awned   F

Lemmas awnless   FF

F (Lemmas awned)

Lemmas with 9 or more awns or awnlike lobes

Lemmas with 9 subequal, plumose awns   86. ENNEAPOGON
                                                                                         p. 380

Lemmas with 11 or more glabrous or scabrous awns of irregular lengths

Glumes 1-nerved; florets falling together
                                                                85. PAPPOPHORUM
                                                                                         p. 378

Glumes 5-many-nerved; florets falling separately
                                                                     87. COTTEA
                                                                                         p. 380

Lemmas with a single awn

Culms woody, perennial; spikelets mostly 3-7 cm long
                                                                     1. ARUNDINARIA
                                                                                         p. 40

Culms not woody or perennial; spikelets rarely as much as 3 cm long

Glumes 2 cm or more long; lemmas 1.5 cm or more long; introduced
     annual   33. AVENA
                                                                                         p. 132

Glumes less than 2 cm long or, if longer, then lemmas less than 1.5
     cm long

Lemmas awned from below middle of back   32. AIRA
                                                                                         p. 132

Lemmas awned from bifid or entire apex

First glume longer than lowermost floret; lemmas awned from a bifid
     apex

Awns 5-15 mm long; lemmas 3.5-10 mm or more long
                                                                11. DANTHONIA
                                                                                         p. 56

Awns 2 mm or less long; lemmas 2-3 mm long
                                                                12. SCHISMUS
                                                                                         p. 58

First glume about as long as or shorter than lowermost floret

First glume with 3 or 5 distinct nerves; glumes and lemmas
     rounded on back; lemmas 8-12 mm long, excluding awns

KEY TO THE GENERA   31

Plants perennial, palea not adherent to caryopsis

Plants perennial or annual; palea adherent to caryopsis

First glume with 1 or 3 distinct or indistinct nerves; glumes and lemmas keeled or rounded on back

Palea colorless

Second glume obovate, broadest above middle; disarticulation below glumes

Second glume broadest below middle; disarticulation above glumes

Palea green or brown, at least on nerves

Spikelets 1.5 (infrequently 1.2) cm or more long; lemma apex distinctly to minutely bifid

Spikelets less than 1.2 cm long

Lemmas awned from a distinctly bifid apex, the awn straight or geniculate; second glume equaling or exceeding lowermost floret

Plants perennial or, if annual, then spikelets disarticulating above glumes

Plants annual; spikelets disarticulating below glumes

Lemmas awned from an entire or minutely notched apex, the awn straight; second glume usually shorter than lowermost floret

Plants annual

Plants perennial

FF (Lemmas awnless)

Nerves of lemma strongly and uniformly developed and equally spaced

Nerves of lemma not strongly and uniformly developed or, if so, then not equally spaced

Glumes and lemmas spreading at right angles to rachilla, inflated and papery, resembling the rattles of a rattlesnake; spikelets on slender, delicate pedicels   27.   BRIZA
p. 122
Glumes and lemmas not as above

First glume distinctly longer than lowermost lemma
12.   SCHISMUS
p. 58
First glume about equaling or shorter than lowermost lemma

Lowermost 1-3 florets reduced, sterile, about half as long as those above

Disarticulation below the glumes, the spikelets falling entire; plants of coastal dunes   84.   UNIOLA
p. 375
Disarticulation above glumes and between florets; plants of woodland sites   7.   CHASMANTHIUM
p. 50
Lowermost florets not reduced, as large as those above

Palea colorless; lateral nerves of lemma indistinct

Second glume obovate, usually abruptly narrowing to an obtuse or broadly acute apex; disarticulation below glumes
30.   SPHENOPHOLIS
p. 127
Second glume not broadened above the middle or only slightly so, acute at apex; disarticulation above glumes
29.   KOELERIA
p. 124
Palea green or brown, at least on nerves

Lemmas 7-13-nerved   G

Lemmas 5-nerved (3-5 in *Diarrhena*)   GG

G (Lemmas 7-13-nerved)

Spikelets unisexual, the staminate and pistillate in separate inflorescences and usually on separate plants; glumes and lemmas thick, firm, indistinctly nerved

Plants without rhizomes but developing long, thick stolons

82.   ALLOLEPIS

p. 374

Plants strongly rhizomatous, usually without stolons

81. DISTICHLIS

p. 372

Spikelets perfect; glumes and lemmas relatively thin, the lemmas mostly
with distinct nerves and membranous margins

Margins of leaf sheath united to or near apex; caryopses oblong or
ovate, without persistent, hornlike styles

Palea adhering to caryopsis   19.   BROMUS

p. 82

Palea not adhering to caryopsis   13.   MELICA

p. 60

Margins of leaf sheath free to base; caryopses suborbicular with persistent hornlike styles   61.   VASEYOCHLOA

p. 238

GG (Lemmas 5-nerved, 3-5 in *Diarrhena*)

Lemmas thick, the nerves converging in a stout, beaked apex

15.   DIARRHENA

p. 68

Lemmas thin or firm but not thick, the nerves not converging in a stout,
beaked apex

Lemmas narrowly acute or attenuate at apex, not scarious on margins

22.   FESTUCA

p. 99

Lemmas obtuse or broadly acute at apex, usually scarious on margins

26.   POA

p. 110

GROUP V (Panicle with unbranched primary branches)

Glumes with hooked spines; spikelets deciduous in burlike clusters of
2-5   80.   TRAGUS

p. 370

Glumes without hooked spines; spikelets not in deciduous burlike clusters

Spikelets with 2 or more perfect florets   H

Spikelets with 1 perfect floret, with or without reduced florets above HH

H (2 or more perfect florets)

Inflorescence branches paired, verticillate or clustered at culm apex

Glumes and lemmas awnless 55. ELEUSINE
p. 222

Glumes or lemmas awned

Lemmas mostly 3-awned, lateral awns short and sometimes lacking; tall, cespitose perennials 73. CHLORIS
p. 316

Lemmas 1-awned; plants annual or perennial

Second glume short-awned or mucronate; rachis of branch projecting stiffly beyond terminal spikelet 56. DACTYLOCTENIUM
p. 223

Second glume not awned or mucronate; rachis not extended beyond terminal spikelet 73. CHLORIS
p. 316

Inflorescence branches distributed along culm axis, seldom more than one at a node

Lemmas 3-nerved

Glumes 8 mm or more long; lemmas ciliate on lateral nerves with stiff, spreading hairs 58. TRICHONEURA
p. 232

Glumes less than 8 mm long; lemmas glabrous or puberulent, not ciliate on lateral nerves with stiff, spreading hairs

Lemmas glabrous, acute and awnless; spikelets widely spaced on stiffly spreading branches
49. ERAGROSTIS (*E. sessilispica*)
p. 177

Lemmas glabrous or puberulent on nerves at base, usually awned or mucronate; spikelets closely placed on branches

Perennial, developing subterranean cleistogamous spikelets; awns 1 cm or more long 73. CHLORIS (*C. chloridea*)
p. 316

Perennial or annual without subterranean cleistogamous spikelets; when perennial, then the spikelets with awns much less than 1 cm long
57. LEPTOCHLOA (see also *Tridens ambiguus* and *T. buck-leyanus.*) p. 225

Lemmas with 5 or more nerves

Plants perennial, with tall culms and slender, flexuous inflorescence branches 14. GLYCERIA
p. 65

Plants annual, with short, tufted culms and short, stiff inflorescence branches

Spikelets 3-flowered; lowermost lemma about 5 mm long; upper
leaf sheaths broad and overlapping; disarticulation below glumes
24.   SCLEROCHLOA
p. 108

Spikelets more than 3-flowered; lowermost lemma about 2.5 mm
long; upper sheaths not large and overlapping; disarticulation
above glumes   25.   CATAPODIUM
p. 109

HH (1 perfect floret)

Spikelets on main inflorescence axis as well as on branches

Glumes absent; lemmas firm, boat-shaped; spikelets strongly compressed
laterally, closely imbricated on the branches   3.   LEERSIA
p. 42

Glumes, at least the second, present

Lemmas awned; leaf blades mostly 8-12 mm or more broad
59.   GYMNOPOGON
p. 234

Lemmas awnless; leaf blades 5 mm or less broad

Glumes stiff, the first narrowly acute or acuminate, strongly 1-nerved
71.   SCHEDONNARDUS
p. 313

Glumes soft, the first broad and irregularly lacerate or toothed
at apex, nerveless   70.   WILLKOMMIA
p. 313

Spikelets all on branches, none on main inflorescence axis, the latter
sometimes terminating in a single branch

Inflorescence branches 2 or more, digitate, clustered or in 2 or 3
verticils at culm apex

Rudimentary floret absent or represented by a minute scale; inflorescence branches slender, digitate, usually 2-6; spikelets awnless
72.   CYNODON
p. 316

Rudimentary floret or florets present above perfect one; inflorescence
branches few to numerous; spikelets usually awned

Glumes linear to lanceolate in side view, the upper obtuse to
acuminate or mucronate; lemma of perfect floret usually
conspicuously awned   73.   CHLORIS
p. 316

Glumes lanceolate to oblong in side view, the upper usually short-
awned from between obtuse lobes; lemma of perfect floret

mucronate or minutely aristate; spikelets becoming dark brown at maturity   74. EUSTACHYS
p. 333

Inflorescence branches 1-several, not digitate, clustered or in verticils

Spikelets 1-flowered, without rudimentary florets; inflorescence branches erect-appressed or somewhat spreading, mostly 3-12 cm long   78. SPARTINA
p. 358

Spikelets with 1 or more staminate or rudimentary florets above the perfect one; inflorescence branches spreading or reflexed, infrequently over 4 cm long

Spikelets in deciduous clusters of 3, the middle (terminal) spikelet, the lower 2 spikelets staminate or sterile
76. CATHESTECUM
p. 353

Spikelets not in deciduous clusters of 3 or, if so, then the lower two not staminate or sterile   75. BOUTELOUA
p. 335

GROUP VI (Spike or spicate raceme)

Spikelets in capitate clusters, these subsessile in leafy portion of plant; lemmas 3-nerved; low, tufted or sodforming grasses

Disarticulation below glumes, spikelets falling in burlike clusters; inflorescence axis and outer (second) glumes of spikelet cluster becoming thick and indurate; spikelets pistillate; plant strongly stoloniferous
77. BUCHLOË
p. 355

Disarticulation above glumes, spikelets not falling in clusters; glumes not becoming indurate; spikelets perfect

Lemmas with 3 stout, ciliate awns   64. BLEPHARIDACHNE
p. 242

Lemmas with a single awn

Glumes much longer than lemmas; lemmas deeply bifid at apex
53. ERIONEURON
p. 215

Glumes shorter than lemmas; lemmas acuminate at apex, not bifid
54. MUNROA
p. 220

Spikelets not in capitate clusters or, if so, then these elevated well above the basal cluster of leaves

Spikelets with a single floret

Spikelets single at each node

Plants annual, without stolons, not turf-forming

48.   PARAPHOLIS

Plants perennial, with stout stolons, turf-forming

92.   STENOTAPHRUM
p. 422

Spikelets 3 at each node   43.   HORDEUM
p. 158

Spikelets with 2 or more florets

Spikelets oriented edgewise to rachis, the first glume absent except
on terminal spikelet   23.   LOLIUM
p. 106

Spikelets not oriented edgewise to rachis, both glumes present on all
spikelets

Rachis mostly with two or more spikelets per node   I

Rachis mostly with one spikelet per node   II

I

Spikelets disarticulating in clusters from a persistent rachis

79.   HILARIA
p. 366

Spikelets disarticulating above the glumes or with sections of the rachis

44.   ELYMUS
p. 163

II

Lemmas thin, awnless, distinctly 3-nerved

Spikelets 1.5-3 cm long, staminate; stoloniferous perennial

63.   SCLEROPOGON
p. 240

Spikelets less than 1 cm long

Lemmas awnless; spikelets unisexual; stoloniferous annual

50.   NEERAGROSTIS
p. 202

Lemmas with a delicate awn; spikelets perfect; cespitose perennial
lacking stolons   60.   TRIPOGON
p. 237

Lemmas thick or thin, 5-several-nerved

Spikelets short-pediceled

38   **THE GRASSES OF TEXAS**

Culms woody, 2-8 m tall   1. ARUNDINARIA
                                                p. 40

Culms not woody, 1.5 m or less tall

  Lemmas awnless; upper sheaths enlarged or not; inflorescences
    well exserted or partially enclosed by sheaths

    Disarticulation below glumes

      Plants annual, with culms less than 20 cm tall; upper leaf sheaths
        enlarged, often partially enclosing the inflorescences
                                          24. SCLEROCHLOA
                                                p. 108

      Plants perennial, with culms mostly 60-100 cm tall; upper
        leaf sheaths not enlarged, not enclosing the inflorescences
                                          13. MELICA (M. mutica)
                                                p. 60

    Disarticulation above glumes; upper leaf sheaths not enlarged

      Culms not more than 30 cm tall; lower florets perfect, not
        reduced; annual   25. CATAPODIUM
                                                p. 109

      Culms 50 cm or more tall; lower 1-2 florets of spikelet empty,
        reduced in size; perennials   7. CHASMANTHIUM
                                                p. 50

  Lemmas awned; upper leaf sheaths not enlarged; inflorescences
    well exserted

      Glumes much longer than lemmas; lemmas with a geniculate
        awn from a bifid apex   11. DANTHONIA
                                                p. 56

      Glumes not longer than lemmas; lemmas with a straight awn from an
        entire apex   20. BRACHYPODIUM
                                                p. 94

Spikelets sessile

  Glumes narrow, rigid, setaceous; lemmas long-awned; cultivated
    annual   47. SECALE
                                                p. 175

  Glumes not setaceous, broadened at or above the base

    Glumes thick, indurate; annuals   46. TRITICUM
                                                p. 173

    Glumes thick or thin; perennials   45. AGROPYRON
                                                p. 167

SUBFAMILY I.   BAMBUSOIDEAE

Tribe 1. Bambuseae

1. ARUNDINARIA Michx.

A genus of about 100 species distributed mainly in southeastern Asia and adjacent islands, Japan to Madagascar.

1.   **Arundinaria gigantea** (Walt.) Muhl., Cat. Pl. 14. 1813. GIANT CANE. Fig 6. Shrubby perennial with much-branched woody culms 2-5 (infrequently -8) m tall from stout creeping rhizomes. *Nodes* puberulent or glabrous. *Leaves* extremely variable as to development of sheath and blade; lower leaves of main shoots with reduced, often rudimentary blades and short but broad, early deciduous sheaths; upper vegetative shoots with blades 2-4 cm broad and 15-25 cm long; flowering shoots with blades mostly 4 mm or less broad and 2-6 cm long. *Larger sheaths* auriculate and with an elevated collar, the auricles with usually 10-12 stiff bristles and the collar densely puberulent. *Ligule* firm, membranous, 1 mm or less long. *Larger blades* minutely reticulate or tesselate, with a short, petiole-like constriction at base; blades often deciduous from sheaths before sheaths fall from culms. *Inflorescences* numerous on slender, bracteate, floriferous branches developed on the leafy culms or on specialized flowering culms produced directly from rhizomes; inflorescence with 1-few large spikelets, the main axis terminating in a spikelet, the other spikelets pediceled below. *Spikelets* 4-7 cm long, mostly 6-12-flowered. *Rachilla* puberulent, disarticulating above glumes and between florets. *Glumes* irregularly developed, much shorter than lemmas, the lowermost glume sometimes absent. *Lemmas* 1.5-2.5 cm long, mostly 7-9 nerved, puberulent at least near base, attenuate and usually short awn-tipped. *Paleas* often nearly as large as lemmas, scabrous on nerves. *Chromosome number*, $2n=48$.

Distribution. Texas: Regions 1 and 2 in low, moist woodlands and along streams and swales. General: Southeastern United States, from Ohio and Missouri to Florida and eastern Texas.

Flowering period: Mostly April and May, flowering only at intervals of 4-6 years.

Arundinaria gigantea is closely related to and not always easily distinguished from the most easterly ranging *A. tecta* (Walt.) Muhl. McClure (1963) has shown that at least in some populations of *A. tecta* the rhizomes have large air canals, whereas in all rhizomes of *A. gigantea* examined air canals were completely lacking.

Fig. 6. *Arundinaria gigantea.* Sterile shoot and inflorescences. From Gould, 1968.

SUBFAMILY I. BAMBUSOIDEAE   41

SUBFAMILY II.   ORYZOIDEAE

Tribe 2. Oryzeae

2. ORYZA L.

A genus of 15-20 species widely distributed in moist or wet tropical-subtropical habitats of both the New and Old World but none native to the United States.

1. **Oryza sativa** L., Sp. Pl. 333. 1753. RICE. Fig. 7. Succulent, cespitose annual with stiffly erect, glabrous culms mostly 80-160 cm tall in small clusters or clumps. *Sheaths* rounded on back, glabrous or lower ones sparsely hirsute, usually with well-developed auricles; *auricles* rounded or elongate and attenuate, occasionally bearing 1-4 stiff hairs. *Ligules* large, thick, 2-lobed; on lower leaves the lobes mostly 5-15 mm long. *Blades* glabrous, 0.7-2 cm broad, flat or folded, those of the lower leaves often greatly thickened in vicinity of midrib with spongy mesophyll tissue. *Inflorescence* a somewhat contracted, drooping panicle of large, one-flowered spikelets. *Panicle branches and pedicels* glabrous or sparsely hirsute. *Disarticulation* below spikelet. *Spikelets* mostly 7-10 mm long, flattened laterally, with two short, acute or acuminate glume-like structures below lemma (these actually may be rudimentary lemmas of reduced florets). *Lemmas and paleas* firm, minutely reticulate, of equal length and both somewhat keel-shaped but the lemmas broader. *Lemmas* awnless or with a stout awn, 3- or 5-nerved, with 2 nerves on the margins. *Paleas* 2-nerved, the nerves on the extreme margins. *Chromosome numbers* reported, $2n = 12$ and 24.

Distribution. Texas: A crop plant in region 2, occasionally a weed of moist, disturbed soils in regions 1, 2 and 3. General: Coastal Plain, from Virginia to Florida and along the Gulf Coast west to Texas; cultivated throughout the warmer areas of the world.

Flowering period: June to December.

3.   LEERSIA Swartz

Perennials, mostly rhizomatous, with flat leaf blades and open or loosely contracted panicles. *Ligules* membranous, firm. *Spikelets* 1-flowered, laterally compressed and sharply keeled, awnless, subsessile and crowded at inflorescence branch tips, disarticulating at base in most species. *Glumes* absent. *Lemmas* firm or indurate, boat-shaped, 5-nerved, with lateral nerves on margins often indistinct, tightly enclosing margins of a firm, narrow, laterally compressed, 3-nerved palea, this also with lateral nerves on margins. *Stamens* varying in number from 1-6.

About 10 species in marshy or mesic woodland habitats of temperate and tropical regions of both hemispheres.

Fig. 7. *Oryza sativa*. Inflorescence and spikelet. From Gould and Box, 1965.

Panicle branches spikelet-bearing nearly to base; spikelets 3.2-4.5 mm long   1. *L. hexandra*

Panicle branches typically bare of spikelets on lower 1.5-4 cm; spikelets 1.5-5.5 mm long

SUBFAMILY II. ORYZOIDEAE   43

Spikelets 3-4 mm broad   2. *L. lenticularis*

Spikelets 2 mm or less broad

    Spikelets 4-5.5 mm long and 1.5-2 mm broad 3. *L. oryzoides*

    Spikelets 1.3-3.5 mm long and 1 mm or less broad

        Spikelets 2.2-3.5 mm long, oblong, finely hispid; culms decumbent
            at base; rhizomes well developed   *4. L. virginica*
        Spikelets 1.3-2 mm long, broadly ovate, glabrous; culms erect;
            rhizomes not developed   *5. L. monandra*

    1. **Leersia hexandra** Swartz, Prodr. Veg. Ind. Occ. 21. 1788.
CLUBHEAD CUTGRASS. Fig. 8. Perennial with decumbent or creeping
vegetative shoots and slender, erect, floriferous shoots from scaly rhizomes.
Erect culms mostly 50-100 cm tall. *Nodes* minutely retrorsely hispid. *Leaves*
minutely scabrous both on sheaths and blades. *Ligules* truncate or acute.
Blades thin but stiff, flat, mostly 3-7 mm broad. *Panicle* loosely contracted,
5-10 cm long, usually well exserted, with erect or erect spreading branches
mostly 1.5-3 cm long, branches spikelet-bearing nearly to base. *Spikelets*
3.2-4.5 mm long and 1-1.5 mm broad, the lemma and palea smooth or
minutely hispidulous, bristly-ciliate on keels. *Chromosome number,* $2n=48$.

Distribution. Texas: Regions 2 and 6 in moist or wet soils along ditches,
swamps, rivers and lakes, often in shallow water. General: Southeastern
United States, along the Coastal Plain from Virginia to Florida and Texas,
also reported from Tennessee; widely distributed in the tropics and subtropics
of both hemispheres.

Flowering period: April to November but mostly late summer and fall.

    2. **Leersia lenticularis** Michx., Fl. Bot. Amer. 1:39. 1803. CATCH-
FLYGRASS. Fig. 9. *Culms* mostly 90-150 cm long, decumbent at base,
produced singly or in small clusters from scaly, creeping rhizomes. *Sheaths*
roughly retrorsely scabrous to nearly glabrous. *Ligules* short, firm, truncate.
Blades mostly 5-15 (-20) mm broad, glabrous or scabrous. *Panicle* open,
mostly 10-20 cm long, with spikelets clustered towards the tips of flexuous,
often drooping branches, the longer branches bare of spikelets for the lower
1.5-4 cm and with or without a few short secondary branches above. *Spikelets*
imbricate, mostly 4-5 mm long, broadly oblong but slightly asymmetrical.
Keel and lateral nerves of lemma and keel of palea bristly-ciliate with stiff,
short hairs. *Chromosome number,* $2n=48$.

Distribution. Texas: Regions 1 and 2 in wet or marshy soil along streams,
lake shores and swales. General: Minnesota and Wisconsin, south to Florida
and eastern Texas.

Flowering period: Mostly July to November.

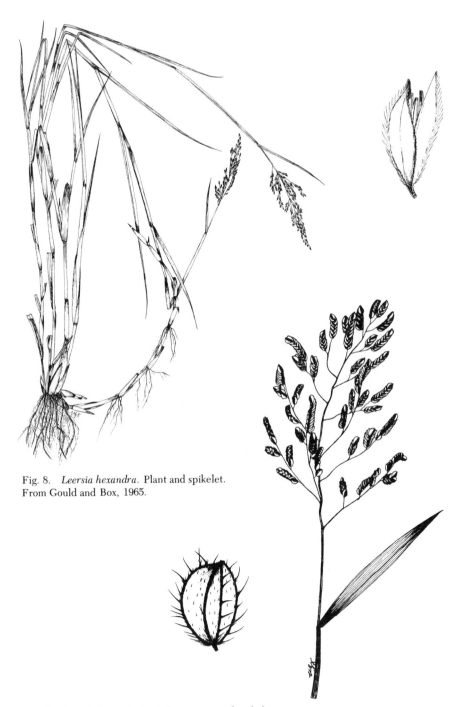

Fig. 8. *Leersia hexandra*. Plant and spikelet.
From Gould and Box, 1965.

Fig. 9. *Leersia lenticularis*. Inflorescence and spikelet.

3.   **Leersia oryzoides** (L.) Swartz, Prodr. Veg. Ind. Occ. 21. 1788. RICE CUTGRASS. Fig. 10. Perennial with culms mostly 80-150 cm tall from slender, creeping rhizomes, the culm bases often decumbent or stoloniferous. *Nodes* retrorsely hispid. *Sheaths and blades* usually strongly retrorsely scabrous, the margins and blade midnerve rather sharply serrate. *Ligules* short, firm, truncate. *Blades* mostly 7-10 mm broad, thin but firm. *Panicles* lax, drooping, mostly 10-20 cm long, often partially included in upper sheath, the long, slender lower branches bare of spikelets for the basal 1.5-4 cm. *Spikelets* narrowly oblong, asymmetrical. *Lemma and palea* short-hispid or scabrous, bristly-ciliate with stiff hairs on the keels. *Chromosome number,* 2n=48.

Distribution. Texas: Occasional throughout most of the State (no records from region 9), mostly in saturated soils along lakes, rivers, marshes and wet ditches. General: Southern Canada to southern United States, reported from all U. S. states except Montana, Wyoming and Nevada.

Flowering period: May to November but mostly autumn.

4.   **Leersia virginica** Willd., Sp. Pl. 1:325. 1797. WHITEGRASS. Fig. 11. Perennial with slender, weak, branching culms from rather stout, creeping, scaly rhizomes. *Culms* mostly 50-120 cm tall. *Culm nodes* hispidulous. *Sheaths* smooth, rounded. *Ligule* a short, stiff, truncate or 2-lobed membrane. *Blades* smooth or slightly scabrous, 3-8 mm broad and mostly 4-12 cm long. *Panicles* 5-18 cm long, with a few widely-spaced, long and slender branches as much as 8-12 cm long; branches with spikelets imbricate on upper half, the lower 2-5 cm bare. *Spikelets* mostly 2.2-3.5 mm long and about 1 mm broad. *Lemma and palea* hispid-ciliate on nerves, finely hispid laterally. *Chromosome number,* 2n=48.

Distribution. Texas: Regions 1, 2, 3 and 4 in moist or wet soils along streams and lakes and in marshes and moist ditches. General: Southeastern Canada and throughout the eastern half of the United States, west to Nebraska and Texas.

Flowering period: Mostly July to November.

5.   **Leersia monandra** Swartz, Prod. Veg. Ind. Occ. 21. 1788. BUNCH CUTGRASS. Fig. 12. Tufted perennial with stiffly erect, slender culms mostly 30-100 cm tall from a non-rhizomatous base. *Culm nodes* puberulent. *Sheaths and blades* smooth or nearly so. *Ligules* well-developed, laterally lobed, commonly 1.5-2.5 mm long. *Blades* mostly 2-5 mm broad and 5-18 cm long. *Panicles* 5-15 cm long, with small spikelets imbricate on the terminal one-third or one-half of long, slender, widely-spaced branches; branches erect or spreading, the basal ones sometimes reflexed. *Spikelets* 1.3-2 mm long, broadly ovate, glabrous. *Chromosome number,* 2n=48.

Distribution. Texas: Regions 2 and 6, infrequent, in wet ditches and swales, along shallow lakes and in moist, shaded woodland sites. General: southern Florida and the West Indies, Texas along the Gulf Coast and the South Texas Plains and northeastern Mexico.

Flowering period: March to October or November.

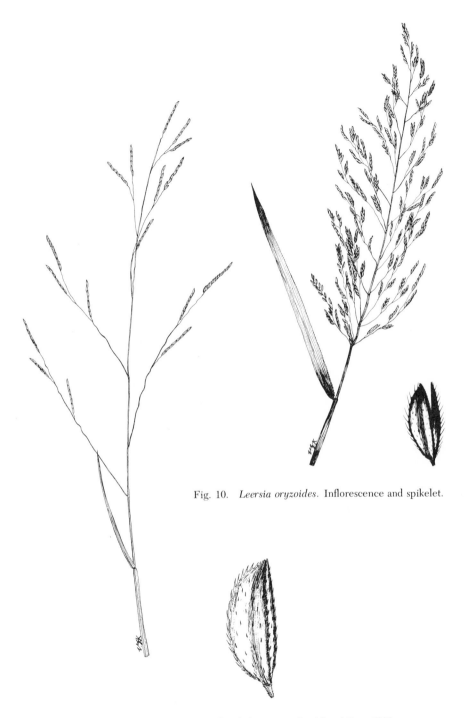

Fig. 10. *Leersia oryzoides*. Inflorescence and spikelet.

Fig. 11. *Leersia virginica*. Inflorescence and spikelet. From Gould and Box, 1965.

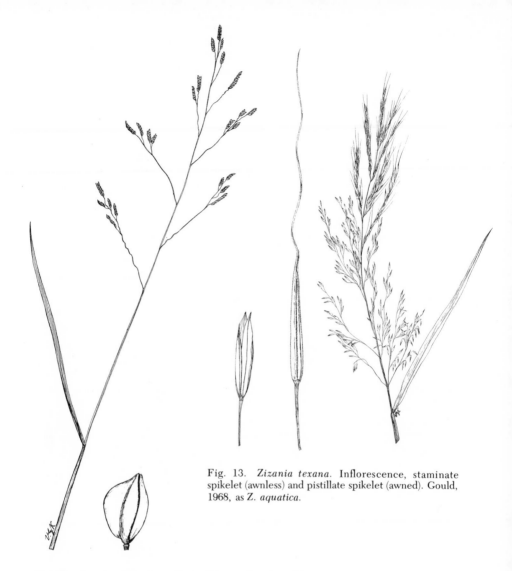

Fig. 13. *Zizania texana*. Inflorescence, staminate spikelet (awnless) and pistillate spikelet (awned). Gould, 1968, as Z. *aquatica*.

Fig. 12. *Leersia monandra*. Inflorescence and spikelet. From Gould and Box, 1965.

4. ZIZANIA L.

A genus of three species, two in the United States and one in Asia.

1. **Zizania texana** Hitchc., J. Wash. Acad. Sci. 23:454. 1933. TEXAS WILDRICE. Fig. 13. Succulent perennial with culms decumbent or stoloniferous at base and rooting at lower nodes, the erect portion mostly 1-1.7 m tall. *Culms and leaves* glabrous. *Ligules* membranous, 5-15 mm long; *blades* thin, flat, elongate, mostly 1-4 cm broad. *Panicles* mostly 20-30 cm long with spreading lower branches bearing awnless, one-flowered staminate spikelets

becoming pendulous at maturity and stiffly erect upper branches bearing long-awned, erect, one-flowered pistillate spikelets. *Staminate spikelets* mostly 7-9 mm long with a thin, papery, awnless, 5-nerved lemma, a 3-nerved palea of similar texture and nearly equal size and 6 stamens. *Pistillate spikelets* apparently glumeless but with an irregular, membranous cup or disc below the lemma and zone of disarticulation; body of lemma narrow, 3-nerved, about 1 cm long, clasping the palea by its margins and tapering into a stout awn 1-2 cm long; palea indistinctly 3-nerved. *Chromosome number*, $2n=30$.

Distribution. Texas: Known only from the vicinity of San Marcos, Hays County (region 7) where it grows in the cool, fast-flowing, spring-fed waters of the San Marcos River near its source. General: Known only from Texas.

Flowering period: At irregular intervals from April to November.

5. ZIZANIOPSIS Doell & Asch.

A New World genus of 3-4 species, one in the United States.

1. **Zizaniopsis miliacea** (Michx.) Doell and Asch., in Doell in Mart., Fl. Brasil 22:13. 1871. SOUTHERN WILDRICE. Fig. 14. Coarse, rhizomatous perennial with thick, glabrous culms mostly 2-3 m tall. *Sheaths* rounded on back, glabrous. *Ligules* membranous, with numerous fine nerves, mostly 6-20 mm long. *Blades* glabrous, mostly 8-22 mm broad and 1 m or more long, with coarsely serrate margins. *Panicles* 30-60 cm long with numerous, freely re-branched, erect-spreading branches bearing erect staminate and pistillate spikelets on the same branch or branchlet, the staminate ones below the pistillate ones. *Staminate and pistillate spikelets* 1-flowered, 6-8 mm long with a thin, 7-nerved lemma and a thin, 3-nerved palea and without glumes. Disarticulation immediately below spikelet. *Staminate spikelets* awnless, with 6 stamens. *Lemma of pistillate spikelet* mucronate or short-awned. *Ovary* with a single style and stigma, the style not centrally located and more or less persistent on the mature caryopsis. *Caryopses* globose, about 3 mm long, with an embryo about 1 mm long. Mature caryopsis only loosely enclosed by lemma and palea. *Chromosome number*, $2n=24$.

Distribution. Texas: Regions 1, 2, 3, 4, 6 and 7, growing in shallow water along streams, lakes and marshes. General: Southeastern United States, Maryland and Kentucky to Florida, Oklahoma and Texas.

Flowering period: Mostly April to July, occasionally later.

6. HYDROCHLOA Beauv.

A monotypic genus of southeastern United States.

1. **Hydrochloa caroliniensis** Beauv., Ess. Agrost. 135, 165, 182. pl. 3. f. 18; pl. 24. f. 4. Fig. 15. Aquatic, bottom-rooted perennial with slender, branching, floating or trailing culms mostly 30-100 cm long, these freely rooting at the nodes. *Sheaths* mostly 1-3 cm long, usually with 2-3 stiff bristles on either side of collar area. *Ligule* a membrane 1 mm or slightly less long. *Blades* flat, 2-4 (-6) cm long and 2-4 (-5) mm broad, acute or acuminate.

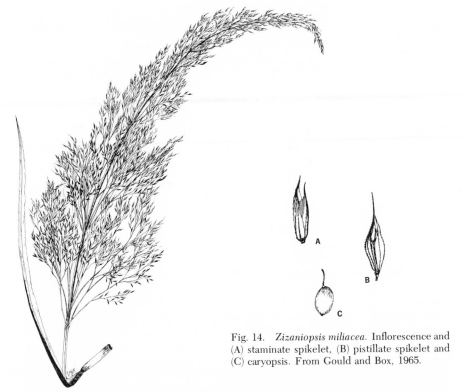

Fig. 14. *Zizaniopsis miliacea.* Inflorescence and (A) staminate spikelet, (B) pistillate spikelet and (C) caryopsis. From Gould and Box, 1965.

Spikelets unisexual, 1-flowered, awnless and lacking glumes; the staminate spikelets in small, few-flowered terminal panicles or racemes, the pistillate spikelets solitary or in few-flowered racemes in leaf axils. Disarticulation below the spikelet. *Staminate spikelets* about 2 mm long, with a thin 7-nerved lemma, a thin 2-nerved palea and 6 stamens. *Pistillate spikelets* ovate, about 4 mm long, with a thin 5-7-nerved lemma and a thin 4-7-nerved palea. *Stigmas* 2, long and slender. *Chromosome number,* $2n=24$.

Distribution. Texas: Region 1 in shallow water of lakes, ponds and marshes, infrequently collected but perhaps not uncommon in eastern Texas. General: North Carolina to Florida and Texas.

Flowering period: Late summer and fall.

SUBFAMILY III.   ARUNDINOIDEAE

Tribe 3. Centotheceae

7. CHASMANTHIUM Link

Moderately tall perennials, some rhizomatous, with broad, flat blades. *Ligule* a hyaline, ciliate membrane or fringe of hairs. *Inflorescence* an

Fig. 15. *Hydrochloa caroliniensis*. The plant, two views of the pistillate spikelet and the staminate spikelet. From Hitchcock, 1935.

open or contracted panicle or spikelike raceme, the spikelets long- or short-pediceled. *Spikelets* 2-many-flowered, the lower 1-4 sterile. *Disarticulation* above glumes and between florets. *Glumes* subequal, shorter than lemmas, acute to acuminate, 3-7 nerved, laterally compressed and keeled. *Paleas* shorter than to about as large as lemmas, 2-keeled, the keels serrate-winged. *Flowers* perfect, with a single stamen and two fleshy, cuneate, 2-4-nerved lodicules. *Caryopses* ovate to elliptic, laterally compressed, with an embryo slightly less than half the length of the endosperm.

A genus of 5 woodland species restricted for the most part to the southeastern United States.

Inflorescence open, the branches drooping, the spikelets long-pediceled, usually pendent; spikelets 20-50 mm long   1. *C. latifolium*

Inflorescence usually contracted, the branches erect or ascending, the
   spikelets subsessile or short-pediceled, not pendent; spikelets 5-18 mm
   long

Collar of sheath pubescent; sheaths, at least the lowermost, usually
   long-pubescent or hirsute, rarely glabrous   2. *C. sessiliflorum*

Collar of sheath glabrous; sheaths glabrous or nearly so   3. *C. laxum*

   1. **Chasmanthium latifolium** (Michx.) Yates, Southw. Naturalist
11:416. 1966. *Uniola latifolia* Michx. Fig. 16. Rhizomatous perennial with
usually unbranched culms to 1.5 m tall and leafy to four-fifths their height.
Nodes glabrous, often reddish-purple. *Leaf sheath and collar* glabrous. *Ligule*
a ciliate membrane 1 mm or less long. *Blades* thin, flat, glabrous or slightly
pilose near ligule, mostly 1-2 cm broad, gradually narrowing at both ends.
Inflorescence typically a panicle but occasionally a raceme, with large, flattened, many-flowered, awnless spikelets borne on slender pedicels. *Main
panicle axis, branches and pedicels* often drooping. *Spikelets* 6-17- (-26)
flowered, mostly 0.6-1.6 (-2) cm broad and 2-5 cm long, the glumes and
lemmas sharply keeled and laterally compressed. *Lower 1-2 florets* neuter.
Glumes 0.5-0.7 mm long, subequal, acute, 5-7-nerved. *Lemmas* entire or
bifid, 11-15-nerved. *Paleas* entire or bifid, shorter than the lemmas. *Anthers*
yellow, to 4 mm long. *Caryopses* 2-2.5 mm wide, 3-5 mm long, brown to
reddish-black or black. *Chromosome number,* 2n=48.

   Distribution. Texas: Regions 1, 2, 3, 4, 5, 6, 7 and 8, absent from the
Panhandle and the extreme western and southern portions of the State,
growing along streambanks and in moist woodland habitats.
General: Pennsylvania, Illinois and Nebraska, southward to northwestern
Florida and the Gulf Coast to Texas; also reported from Manitoba, New
Mexico and Nuevo Leon, Mexico.

   Flowering period: June to October.

   2. **Chasmanthium sessiliflorum** (Poir.) Yates, Southw. Naturalist
11:426. 1966. *Uniola sessiliflora* Poir. Fig. 17. Cespitose rhizomatous perennial with slender, erect, usually unbranched culms mostly 0.7-1.5 m tall from
short, knotty rhizomes. *Culms* leafy for less than half of their height, the
inflorescence exserted on a long peduncle. *Nodes* glabrous to minutely pubescent. *Sheaths* glabrous to densely hispid. *Leaf collar* pubescent. *Ligule* a
minute, short-ciliate membrane. *Blades* long and narrow, mostly 0.4-1.2
(-1.5) cm broad, gradually narrowing at both ends, usually sparsely pilose on
adaxial surface. *Inflorescence* a contracted, few-flowered panicle or spikelike
raceme mostly 15-50 cm long, the main axis stiffly erect, the branches widely
spaced, 0.5-9 cm long. *Spikelets* sessile or short pediceled, glabrous,
3-6-flowered, 3-5 mm broad and 5-8 mm long, with the lower 1-2 florets not
seed-bearing. *Glumes* 1-2.5 mm long, equal or subequal, glabrous.
Lowermost lemma only slightly larger than glumes and similar in appearance,
upper lemmas mostly 3-5 mm long, often beaked at apex. *Paleas* thick, acute,

Fig. 16. *Chasmanthium latifolium*. Plant, spikelet and floret. From Gould and Box, 1965, as *Uniola latifolia*.

Fig. 17. *Chasmanthium sessiliflorum*. Inflorescence and spikelet. From Gould, 1968.

slightly shorter than lemmas. *Anthers* 1.5-2 mm long, reddish-brown. *Caryopses* broadly ovate, 1-2 mm broad and 2-3 mm long, with a dull brown to reddish-black or black pericarp, the caryopsis exposed at maturity by the widely spreading lemma and palea. *Chromosome number*, $2n = 24$.

Distribution. Texas: Regions 1, 2, 3 and borders of 4 in moist pine and deciduous forests and adjacent prairie openings, often a dominant woodland grass. General: Throughout the southeastern states, from southeastern Virginia westward to eastern Oklahoma and southward to the Gulf, from Florida to eastern Texas; one record from eastern central Missouri.

Flowering period: June to November.

SUBFAMILY III. ARUNDINOIDEAE   53

3. **Chasmanthium laxum** (L.) Yates, Southw. Naturalist 11:433. 1966. *Uniola laxa* (L.) B.S.P. Cespitose, rhizomatous perennial, generally similar to *Chasmanthium sessiliflorum* but the leaf collar glabrous and the herbage more glabrous in general. Chromosome number, $2n=24$.

Distribution. Texas: Regions 1, 2, 3 and 4 in woodlands, meadows and marshy areas, apparently not common. General: Throughout the southeastern states, as far north as Long Island, west to southeastern Missouri, southeastern Oklahoma and eastern Texas.

Flowering period: June to November.

Chasmanthium laxum and *C. sessiliflorum* are similar in habit, general morphology, chromosome number and distribution. In his investigation of the genus, however, Yates (1966) found no evidence of hybridization between the two.

Tribe 4. Arundineae

8. ARUNDO L.

A genus of about 6 species, all native to Asia.

1. **Arundo donax** L., Sp. Pl. 81. 1753. GIANT REED. Fig. 18. Perennial with stout culms mostly 2-6 m tall from thick, knotty rhizomes. *Culms and leaves* glabrous. *Leaves* rather uniformly spaced and distichous on the culm; sheaths rounded. *Ligule* a ciliate membrane 1 mm or less long. *Blades* thick, flat, elongate, acuminate, scabrous on margins, mostly 4-7 cm broad on main culms. *Inflorescence* a dense, contracted, many-flowered panicle typically 30-60 cm long, the numerous, stiffly erect primary branches 15-25 cm or more long. *Panicle* branches and branchlets glabrous or nearly so. *Spikelets* mostly 2-4-flowered, 10-15 mm long with short, glabrous rachilla joints. *Glumes* broad, thin, nearly equal, irregularly 3-several-nerved, narrowly acute or acuminate. *Lemmas* thin, 3-5 nerved, 5-10 mm long, densely pilose with soft hairs 6-9 mm long, acuminate and often short-awned at apex, the tip sometimes notched on either side of the awn. *Paleas* broad, much shorter than lemmas, minutely ciliate on nerves. *Chromosome numbers* reported, $2n=110$ and ca. 120.

Distribution. Texas: Throughout the State except on the High Plains (region 9), for the most part established through highway plantings along culverts and ditches and apparently not setting fertile seed. General: An Old World species widely introduced in the southern United States.

Flowering period: Mostly September to November.

9. PHRAGMITES Adans.

A genus of two or three species.

1. **Phragmites australis** (Cav.) Trin. *ex* Steud., Nom. Bot. ed. 2, 2:324. 1841. *Phragmites communis* Trin. COMMON REED. Fig. 19. Stout peren-

Fig. 19. *Phragmites australis.* Spikelet. From Gould and Box, 1965, as *P. communis.*

Fig. 18. *Arundo donax.* Plant, spikelet and floret. From Hitchcock, 1935.

nial with culms 2-4 m tall from thick, creeping rhizomes; stolons also frequently developed. *Culms and leaves* glabrous. *Culms* leafy to base of inflorescence. *Sheaths* smooth, rounded. *Ligules* minute, ciliate, the hairs
longer than the membranous base. *Blades* flat, elongate, minutely scabrous on
margins, those of the main culms mostly 1.5-5 cm broad. *Inflorescence*
densely flowered, with spikelets borne on slender, wiry pedicels and
branchlets of a contracted but much-branched panicle. Disarticulation above
glumes and between florets. *Spikelets* 10-15 mm long, mostly with 4-8 florets.
Rachilla joints villous with hairs 1 cm or more long, the glumes, lemmas and
paleas glabrous. *First glume* one-half or two-thirds as long as second,
3-nerved. *Second glume* 3-5 nerved, mostly 6-8 mm long, acute or mucronate.

SUBFAMILY III. ARUNDINOIDEAE   55

Lower floret infertile with a 3-nerved, acuminate lemma mostly 11-14 mm long, much longer than lemmas of upper florets. *Chromosome numbers* reported, $2n = 48$ and 72.

Distribution. Texas: Occasional throughout the State but most frequent along the Gulf Coast (region 2), growing along stream and lake borders and in marshes. General: Widespread in temperate and tropical regions of both hemispheres, infrequent in the southeastern United States but reported from all the western and northern states.

Flowering period: Mostly July to November but occasionally flowering throughout the year.

This native reed grass has long been known in the United States and throughout the world as *Phragmites communis*. In a recent publication, however, Clayton (1968) noted that *P. communis* and *P. australis* comprise a single species and that *P. australis* is the oldest valid name for the taxon.

10. CORTADERIA Stapf

A South American genus of about 15 species.

1. **Cortaderia selloana** (Schult.) Aschers. & Graebn., Syn. Mitteleur. Fl. 2:325. 1900. PAMPASGRASS. Fig. 20. Cespitose, dioecious perennial with densely clustered culm bases and leaves forming clumps as much as a meter or more in diameter. *Sheaths* broad, rounded, smooth, glabrous or with a ring of hairs around the collar, abruptly narrowing into long, narrow, firm blades mostly 3-10 mm broad and often 1 m or more in length. *Blades* sharply serrate with stout spicules on margins and often on midnerve. *Ligule* a dense tuft of hairs 3-5 mm long. *Panicles* densely-flowered, silvery white, 25-100 cm long. *Spikelets* 2-3-flowered, disarticulating above glumes and between florets. *Glumes* thin, narrow, glabrous, 1-nerved and attenuate at apex. *Lemmas* thin, long and narrow, attenuate to an awnlike tip; lemmas of the pistillate inflorescences with long silky hairs on back and base, the lemmas of the staminate spikelets glabrous. *Chromosome numbers* reported, $2n = 72$, $72 + 1B$ and 76.

Distribution. Texas: Grown in regions 1, 2, 3 and 6 as a lawn ornamental, this hardy perennial occasionally persists as a weed of vacant lots and waste areas. General: Native to Brazil, to Argentina and Chile, now grown in many areas of the southern United States as an ornamental.

Flowering period: Mostly September to November.

Tribe 5. Danthonieae

11. DANTHONIA Lam. & DC.

Low to moderately tall, cespitose perennials with flat or involute blades. *Ligule* a short, ciliate membrane. *Inflorescence* a small panicle or raceme of usually large spikelets. *Glumes* about equal, 1-5-nerved, much longer than the lemmas. *Lemmas* rounded on back, indistinctly several-nerved, more or less

Fig. 20. *Cortaderia selloana.* Flowering plant. From Gould, 1968.

hairy all over, bifid at apex, with a well developed callus at base and with the midnerve extended into a stout geniculate awn, this flattened and twisted below. Disarticulation below lowermost floret.

Over 100 species throughout the temperate regions of the world but mostly in the Southern Hemisphere. Seven species are native to the United States.

Lemmas sparsely pubescent with hairs of uniform length; glumes 10-13 (occasionally -15) mm long; sheaths glabrous or inconspicuously pubescent   1.   *D. spicata*

Lemmas villous with long hairs on margins and shorter hairs on back; glumes 13-18 mm long; sheaths typically villous or conspicuously pubescent, infrequently sparsely pubescent or glabrous
2.   *D. sericea*

1. **Danthonia spicata** (L.) Beauv. *ex* Roem. & Schult., Syst. Veg. 2:690. 1817. POVERTY DANTHONIA. Fig. 21. Tufted perennial with culms 20-80 cm tall, stiffly erect and little-branched above base. *Nodes* glabrous. *Leaves* mostly basal. *Sheaths* glabrous or inconspicuously hispid, often with papilla-based hairs. *Collar* usually densely hispid, at least on margins. *Ligule* a minute, lacerate membrane. *Blades* short, filiform, infrequently more than 2 mm broad and 15 cm long, glabrous or variously hispid or hirsute on one or both surfaces. *Inflorescence* a narrow, few-flowered raceme or panicle 2-5 cm long, the spikelets mostly on pedicels 1-3 mm long. *Spikelets* 10-13 (occasionally -15) mm long, with 4-9 florets. Disarticulation above glumes. *Glumes* glabrous, acuminate, with 3-5 distinct nerves and sometimes additional indistinct nerves, about equal or first glume slightly longer, both much longer than florets. *Lemmas* 3.5-5 mm long, sparsely pubescent on back with hairs of uniform length, awned at the deeply cleft apex from between two acute or acuminate teeth; awn geniculate and twisted, mostly 5-7 mm long, with a flattened, dark-colored lower segment. *Chromosome numbers* reported, $2n=31$ and 36.

Distribution. Texas: Regions 1, 3 and 5, infrequent, mostly in and along pine and hardwood forests on dry, rather sterile sites. General: Throughout the United States, except in the Southwest (reported from New Mexico); also in Newfoundland and British Colombia.

Flowering period: May to July.

2. **Danthonia sericea** Nutt., Gen. Pl. 1:71. 1818. DOWNY DANTHONIA. Similar to *D. spicata* but culms to 100 cm tall, sheaths usually conspicuously pilose or hispid, panicle mostly 6-10 cm long, glumes 13-18 mm long and lemmas villous with long hairs on margins and shorter hairs on back. *Chromosome number* not reported.

Distribution. Texas: Region 1, rare, in pine and mixed pine-hardwood forests. General: Eastern and Gulf coastal plains of the United States and in Kentucky and Tennessee.

Flowering period: April to July.

12. SCHISMUS Beauv.

About five species native to Europe, Asia and Africa; two species adventive in the southwestern United States.

1. **Schismus barbatus** (L.) Thell., Bull. Herb. Boissier II. 7:391. 1907. Fig. 22. Tufted annual; culms glabrous, weak, mostly 5-35 cm tall. *Sheaths* rounded, the lowermost with broad hyaline margins near apex. *Collar* with a few long, stiff hairs on either side. *Ligule* a short, ciliate membrane. *Blades* weak, filiform 0.5-2 mm broad, glabrous or sparsely hirsute. *Panicles* dense, contracted, 1-6 cm long, with short, erect branches and spikelets borne on short pedicels. *Spikelets* mostly 5-7 mm long and 5-7-flowered, disarticulating above glumes and between florets. *Glumes* about equal, acute to acuminate, much longer than lemmas and almost equaling the spikelet in length. *Lemmas*

Fig. 21. *Danthonia spicata.*
Inflorescence and spikelet.
From Gould, 1968.

Fig. 22. *Schismus barbatus.* Plant and spikelet.
From Gould, 1968.

broad, rounded on the back, several-nerved, mostly 2-2.5 mm long, glabrous
or sparsely hairy on margins, occasionally with a few hairs on back; apex of
lemma broad and rounded, with a notch 2-3 mm deep, this often with a minute
seta, the terminal lobes broadly acute. *Palea* about equaling the lemma.
Caryopses shiny and translucent, oval to obovate, 0.6-1 mm long.
Chromosome number, $2n = 12$.

Distribution. Texas: Region 10, infrequent. General: Adventive from the
Mediterranean region, now frequent in southern California and Arizona and
occasionally east to the mountains and plains of western Texas.

Flowering period. February to May.

SUBFAMILY III. ARUNDINOIDEAE   59

SUBFAMILY IV. POOIDEAE

Tribe 6. Meliceae

13. MELICA L.

Cespitose, moderately tall perennials, frequently with swollen, corm-like culm bases. *Leaf sheaths* closed, the margins connate to or near the apex. *Ligule* membranous, continuous with sheath margins. *Inflorescence* a panicle, usually simple and contracted but open in a few species. *Spikelets* with 2 (rarely 1)-several perfect florets and 2-3 reduced, neuter florets above; neuter florets represented by successively smaller empty lemmas and collectively referred to as "the rudiment"; disarticulation above or below the glumes (below in most Texas species). *Glumes* large, broad, thin, not keeled, 3-5-nerved, with hyaline or papery margins and apices. *Lemmas* firmer than the glumes, not keeled, usually 7-nerved, awned or awnless (awnless in Texas species), with hyaline apices and upper margins. *Palea* usually three-fourths as long as lemma. *Caryopsis* smooth and shiny, free.

About 60 species in temperate and cool regions of both hemispheres, some ranging southward to the subtropics in North America as cool-climate grasses. In a monographic treatment by Boyle (1945), 17 species and 4 varieties of *Melica* were reported for the United States.

Culms bulbous at the base; disarticulation above glumes and between florets   1. *M. bulbosa*

Culms not bulbous at base; disarticulation below glumes, the spikelet falling entire

Rudiment (reduced upper florets) club-shaped or obconic, rarely narrowing above; perfect florets usually 1-3

Spikelets with 1 perfect floret; back of lemma with coarse, flat, twisted hairs   2. *M. montezumae*

Spikelets with 2-3 perfect florets; lemmas glabrous or scabrous

Panicle simple, rarely compound; rudiment usually bent at an angle to rachilla; apices of perfect florets nearly at same height   3.   *M. mutica*

Panicle usually compound, the branches spreading; rudiment never bent at an angle to rachilla; apices of perfect florets not at same height   4. *M. nitens*

Rudiment almost always narrowing above, not club-shaped or obconic; perfect florets usually 4-5   5.   *M. porteri*

1. **Melica bulbosa** Geyer, Porter and Coulter, Syn. Fl. Colo. 149. 1874. ONIONGRASS. *Culms* tufted, reaching 60 cm tall, usually bulbous at the base, the bulbs attached directly to a stout rhizome in older plants. *Sheaths* and *blades* glabrous, scabrous or pubescent; *ligules* 2-5 mm long; *blades* elongate, mostly 2-5 mm broad, flat or involute. *Panicles* usually narrow and with short, appressed branches. *Spikelets* 7-15 (6-24) mm long, with 2-5, usually 3, perfect florets. *Glumes* two-thirds to three-fourths as long as spikelet, acute to obtuse, the first glume 5-9 mm long, the second 6-10 mm long. *Lemmas* obtuse, the lowermost 6-11 mm long, purple-tinged below the scarious apex. *Anthers* about 4 mm long. *Rudiment* narrow, tapering above. *Chromosome number*, $2n = 18$.

Distribution. Texas: Reported from the Trans-Pecos (region 10) by Hitchcock (1935), Boyle (1945) and Chase (1951) but no Texas specimens seen in present study. General: British Columbia and Montana to Colorado, Utah, Nevada, California and Texas; not reported from New Mexico or Arizona.

Flowering period: Late spring and early summer.

2. **Melica montezumae** Piper, Proc. Biol. Soc., Wash. 18:144. 1905. MONTEZUMA MELIC. *Culms* 50-100 cm tall, loosely tufted. *Leaf sheaths* scaberulous. *Ligules* 5-10 mm long. *Blades* flat or involute, elongate, 2-3 mm broad. *Panicles* 8-16 (5-25) cm long, with short, widely-spaced, ascending or spreading branches; the branches simple, infrequently compound. *Spikelets* 7-8 mm long, with a single perfect floret and pale glumes and lemmas. *First glume* usually exceeding the perfect floret, broad, hyaline, shiny, rounded at apex, glabrous. *Second glume* usually slightly shorter and narrower than first, with a firm rugose body and broad, thin, hyaline margins and apex. *Lemma* of perfect floret about as long as second glume, with a firm, rugose, longitudinally striated body and thin, hyaline margins and apex; back of lemma with tuft of long, coarse, flattened hairs. *Palea of perfect floret* scaberulous or minutely pubescent, short-ciliate on nerves at apex. *Rudiment* obconic, knob-like, shorter than and more or less enclosed by the perfect floret. *Chromosome number* not reported.

Distribution. Texas: Region 10, Pecos and Brewster counties, rocky slopes, shaded canyons and in juniper or juniper-pinyon pine woods, reported by Correll and Johnston (1970) to be "locally abundant." General: Texas and northern Mexico.

Flowering period: March to May.

3. **Melica mutica** Walt., Fl. Carol. 78. 1788. TWOFLOWER MELIC. Fig. 23. *Culms* mostly 45-100 cm tall, tufted from slender, creeping rhizomes. *Sheaths* scabrous or pubescent, closed nearly to apex on upper leaves. *Ligules* short, mostly 1 mm or less long. *Blades* flat or folded, elongate, 2-6 mm broad, glabrous, scabrous or short-pubescent. *Inflorescence* usually a simple, narrow panicle or raceme 4-16 cm long, the primary branches infrequently rebranched. *Spikelets* 7-11 mm long, flat-topped and more or less triangular in outline, with 2 (rarely more) perfect florets, the lower longer than the upper

Fig. 23. *Melica mutica.* Inflorescence and spikelet.

and the apices of the two at about the same height; disarticulation below spikelet. *Florets* and *rudiment* spreading from rachilla at maturity. *Glumes* about equal in length or the second slightly longer, mostly 6-9 mm long, both usually thin and scarious, glabrous or scaberulous, with hyaline margins and apex. *Lemmas* firm, ridged on the nerves, minutely rugose and scaberulous, with narrow membranous margins and a broad membranous apex; lemma of lower perfect floret 6-10 mm long, the second shorter. *Paleas* scaberulous, ciliate on nerves at apex. *Anthers* about 3 mm long. *Caryopses* 2-3 mm long. *Rudiment* obconic, truncate, at maturity spreading at an angle from the rachilla. *Chromosome number,* $2n = 18$.

Fig. 24. *Melica nitens*. Plant and spikelets. From Hitchcock, 1935.

Distribution. Texas: Regions 1, 2 and 3 in moist woods openings, not infrequent but seldom abundant. General: Maryland to Iowa, south to Florida and Texas.

Flowering period: March to May.

4. **Melica nitens** (Scribn.) Nutt. *ex* Piper, Bull. Torrey Bot. Club 32:387. 1905. Fig. 24. *Culms* mostly 50-120 cm tall, in small clumps from a firm, often woody, rhizomatous base. *Sheaths* glabrous, scabrous or puberulent, closed nearly to the apex. *Ligules* mostly 3-6 mm long. *Blades* glabrous, scabrous or puberulent, flat, 3-10 (-15) mm broad. *Panicles* mostly 10-26 cm long but occasionally shorter, the lower branches usually compound, spreading or ascending. *Spikelets* much longer than broad, 8-15 mm long, with 1-4, usually 2-3 perfect florets; florets not spreading or only slightly so at maturity, apex of second floret exceeding apex of first by 1-2 mm; disarticulation below spikelet. *Glumes* shorter than spikelet, obtuse or acute, membranous on margins and at apex; first glume usually broad, 5-7 mm long, the second glume narrower, 7-9 mm long. *Lemmas* striated, minutely rugose and scabrous, with narrow hyaline margins and an acute or obtuse hyaline apex; lemma of lower floret 8-11 mm long. *Paleas* broad, ciliate on nerves. *Anthers* about 3 mm long. *Rudiment* oblong or obovate, usually broadest near apex, erect and not spreading at an angle from rachilla. *Chromosome number, 2n=18*.

Distribution. Texas: Regions 5, 7, 8, 9 and 10 on relatively undisturbed sites in open woodlands, moist canyon slopes and bottoms and rocky grasslands. General: Pennsylvania and Virginia to southern Wisconsin, Kansas and Texas.

Flowering period: Mostly April to June.

SUBFAMILY IV. POOIDEAE   63

Fig. 25. *Melica porteri.* Spikelet.

Melica nitens frequently is confused with *M. mutica* from which it differs in the more woody plant base, the generally taller and coarser culms, longer ligules, often broader blades, larger panicles with rebranched lower branches, narrower and longer spikelets and rudiment that is not obconic and does not spread at an angle from the rachilla. In Texas plants of both species, the spikelets quite regularly have 2 perfect florets. The vernacular name THREEFLOWER MELIC commonly applied to *M. nitens* thus is misleading and a source of confusion in the separation of this species from *M. mutica.*

5. **Melica porteri** Scribn., Proc. Acad. Nat. Sci. Philadelphia Monogr. 1885:44. 1885. Fig. 25. *Culms* loosely tufted, slender, reaching 100 cm, arising from a firm or hard rhizomatous base. *Sheaths* usually glabrous. *Ligules* mostly 3-7 mm long, often sparsely pubescent. *Blades* flat, glabrous, scabrous or hispid, elongate, mostly 2-5 mm broad. *Panicles* 13-25 cm long, narrow or open. *Spikelets* 8-15 mm long, with 4-5 perfect florets and a narrow rudiment; disarticulation below spikelet. *Glumes* thin, subequal, usually 4-8 mm long and one-half to two-thirds the length of the spikelet, with hyaline margins and apex. *Lemmas* glabrous, minutely rugose, tapering to a rounded or acute membranous apex. *Palea* ciliate on nerves. *Anthers* about 2 mm long. *Caryopses* 2-3 mm long. *Rudiment* narrow, broadest near base, tapering to apex. *Chromosome number, 2n* = 18.

Distribution. Texas: Regions 7 and 10 on rocky slopes and in mountain canyons, infrequently collected. General: Colorado and Texas to Arizona.

14. GLYCERIA R. Br.

Perennials, often rhizomatous or with culms decumbent at base and rooting at lower nodes. *Ligules* membranous. *Sheaths* closed or partially so, the margins completely or incompletely connate. *Inflorescence* an open or contracted panicle, occasionally reduced to a raceme. *Spikelets* several-flowered, awnless, disarticulating above glumes and between florets. *Glumes* unequal, short, broad, the first 1-nerved, the second 1- or obscurely 3-nerved. *Lemmas* rounded on back, with 7 usually strong nerves, these not converging above; apex of lemma acute, obtuse or truncate. *Palea* large, broad, often longer than lemma. *Anthers* 3 or 2.

About 35 species in moist or marshy habitats of cool, temperate and subtropical regions of both hemispheres.

Spikelets 5 mm or less long; panicle branches, at least the lower, typically
  long and flexuous   1. *G. striata*

Spikelets mostly 8-30 mm long; panicle branches usually short, stiffly
  erect or erect-spreading

  Lemmas 2.5-3.5 mm long, hirsute or hirtellous   3. *G. arkansana*

  Lemmas, at least some, 3.5-5 mm long, scabrous 2. *G. septentrionalis*

1. **Glyceria striata** (Lam.) Hitchc., Proc. Biol. Soc., Wash. 41:157. 1928. FOWL MANNAGRASS. Fig. 26. Perennial with slender culms 40-90 cm tall; plant often with short rhizomes. *Herbage* glabrous. *Sheaths* rounded, the uppermost with margins united almost to apex. *Ligules* 1.5-4 mm long. *Blades* flat, elongate, 2-8 mm broad. *Panicle* mostly 12-22 cm long with flexuous, glabrous or minutely scabrous, loosely contracted or more frequently spreading branches, the lowermost 6-12 cm long, bare of spikelets on lower one-third or one-half. *Glumes* broad, membranous on margins, minutely ciliolate at apex, the first 0.4-0.9 mm long, the second slightly longer. *Lemmas* strongly 7-nerved, obovate, mostly 1.5-2 mm long, broadly rounded and ciliolate-lacerate at apex. *Stamens* 2, the anthers 0.3-0.5 mm long. *Chromosome number*, $2n = 20$.

Distribution. Texas: Regions 3, 4, 7 and 10, not common, growing along streams and moist woods borders. General: Newfoundland to British Columbia, south throughout the United States to Florida, Texas and California.

Flowering period: April to August.

Fig. 26. *Glyceria striata*. Plant, spikelet and floret. From Gould, 1951.

66   **THE GRASSES OF TEXAS**

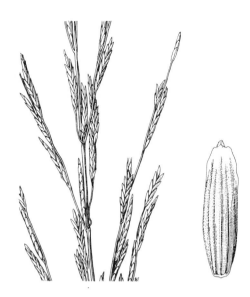

Fig. 27.   *Glyceria septentrionalis.*
Inflorescence and spikelet. From
Hitchcock, 1935.

2. **Glyceria septentrionalis** Hitchc., Rhodora 8:211. 1906. EASTERN MANNAGRASS. Fig. 27. Culms thick, 1-1.8 m tall, often rooting at lower nodes. *Herbage* glabrous. *Sheaths* closed almost to apex. *Ligules* mostly 3-6 mm long. *Blades* flat, elongate, 4-10 mm broad. *Panicles* 18-40 (-50) cm long with stiff, usually erect, few-flowered branches 3-12 cm long. *Spikelets* 0.8-3 cm long, with 7-20 imbricate but rather widely-spaced florets. *Glumes* thin, hyaline on margins, minutely erose at apex, the first glume 2-5 mm long, the second slightly longer. *Lemmas* typically 3.5-5 mm long, scabrous, broad and erose at apex. *Stamens* 3, the anthers about 1 mm long. *Chromosome number,* $2n=40$.

Distribution. Texas: Regions 1, 3 and northern portion of region 2, usually in moist or marshy ground, often in woodlands. General: Quebec to Minnesota, south to Georgia, Louisiana and eastern Texas.

Flowering period: March to June.

3. **Glyceria arkansana** Fern., Rhodora 31:49. 1929. ARKANSAS MANNAGRASS. Similar in general habit and spikelet characters to *G. septentrionalis* but spikelets slightly smaller (2.5-3.5 mm long) and lemmas hirsute or hirtellous rather than scabrous. *Chromosome number* not reported.

Distribution. Texas: Reported to occur in the eastern part of the State (region 1) but no Texas specimens examined. General: Arkansas, Louisiana and Texas.

Flowering period: March to May.

Glyceria arkansana is close to and weakly differentiated from *G. septentrionalis* and probably should be treated as a variety of that species.

15. DIARRHENA Beauv.

A monotypic genus of the northeastern and central United States.

1. **Diarrhena americana** Beauv., Agrost. 142. pl. 25. f. 2. 1812. BEAK-GRAIN. Fig. 28. Perennial with scaly, creeping rhizomes, stiffly erect culms, flat blades and well-exserted, spikelike racemes or panicles of a relatively few large spikelets. *Culms* single or in small clusters, mostly 50-120 cm tall, glabrous. *Sheaths* rounded on back, glabrous or scabrous. *Ligule* a minute, stiff, membranous collar. *Blades* linear, mostly 0.8-2 cm broad and 25-50 cm or more long, smooth or scabrous on the abaxial surface, scabrous or scabrous-hispid on the adaxial surface. *Inflorescence* a narrow, erect or drooping panicle or raceme usually 8-25 cm long, the spikelets short- or long-pediceled directly on the main axis or on short, erect branches. *Spikelets* mostly 10-18 mm long, with 3-5 florets rather widely spaced on a glabrous, slightly flattened rachilla. At maturity the spikelets spread or curve outward. Disarticulation above glumes and between florets. Uppermost floret usually rudimentary. *Glumes* firm, glabrous, unequal, acute, much shorter than lemmas, the first glume 1-nerved, the second 3-5-nerved, the nerves converging at apex. *Margins of lemma* broad, thin, nerveless; lemma apex with convergent nerves and more or less beaked. *Paleas* broad, obtuse, glabrous, strongly 2-nerved. *Stamens* 3 or 2. *Caryopses* large, turgid, broadly beaked above; at maturity, conspicuously exserted from between the spreading lemma and palea. *Chromosome number* not reported.

Distribution. Texas: Region 1, infrequent in the pine-hardwood forest in the northern portion of the region. General: Virginia, Michigan, Wisconsin and eastern South Dakota to Tennessee, Arkansas, eastern Oklahoma and eastern Texas.

Flowering period: Mostly July to October.

Tribe 8. Stipeae

16. STIPA L.

Cespitose perennials with long, narrow, mostly involute blades; blades usually in a basal clump. *Ligule* membranous. *Inflorescence* a narrow, contracted, often drooping panicle of 1-flowered spikelets. *Spikelets* disarticulating above the glumes. *Glumes* thin, several-nerved, acute, acuminate or infrequently aristate, longer than body of lemma. *Lemmas* firm or hard, relatively slender, usually terete, tightly enclosing the membranous palea and flower or caryopsis. *Lemma awn* commonly geniculate and twisted, scabrous or pubescent in many species, persistent or, at length, deciduous in a few species. *Base of lemma and rachilla* forming a usually sharp-pointed callus, this typically bearded with stiff hairs.

Fig. 28. *Diarrhena americana*. Plant, spikelet and floret. From Hitchcock, 1935.

A genus of about 150 species widely distributed in temperate and subtropical regions of the world. All but a few of the approximately 35 species in the United States are in the western states.

Lemmas 2-3 mm long   11. *S. tenuissima*

Lemmas 5 mm or more long (including the callus)

  Lemmas 8 mm or more long; lemma awns 4-20 cm long

    Apex of lemma with smooth, whitish neck 0.6-1 mm long and ring of stiff hairs around awn base   1. *S. leucotricha*

    Apex of lemma not with whitish neck, with or without a ring of hairs around awn base

      Terminal segment of lemma awn plumose with hairs mostly 0.6-1.5 mm long   5. *S. neomexicana*

      Terminal segment of awn glabrous, scabrous or minutely hairy, the hairs less than 0.6 mm long

        Lemmas 8-10 mm long (including callus), with a fringe of stiff hairs around awn base   2. *S. avenacea*

        Lemmas 10-15 mm long, glabrous at awn base   4. *S. comata*

  Lemmas less than 8 mm long or, if this long, then lemma awns less than 4 cm long

    Lemma awns 3.5-6 cm long; panicles open or contracted

      Ligules 1.5-6 mm long; panicles narrow but open, not dense; the branches and pedicels capillary, at least some elongate and spreading   6. *S. eminens*

      Ligules 1 mm or less long; panicles contracted, often dense, the branches and pedicels short and erect   7. *S. arida*

    Lemma awns 2-3.5, occasionally to 3.8, cm long; panicles contracted, usually dense

      Apex of lemma with membranous lobes 0.7-1.5 mm long on either side of awn base   8. *S. lobata*

      Apex of lemma without membranous lobes

        Lemmas plump, 1-1.5 mm thick, 7-8.5 mm long   3. *S. pringlei*

Lemmas slender or, if plump, then less than 7 mm long

Culms slender, 70-100 cm tall and 1.5-2.5 mm in diameter at base; widest blades 3 (rarely 4) mm broad
9. *S. columbiana*

Culms stout, 100- (70-) 150 cm tall and 3-6 mm in diameter at base; widest blades 5-8 mm broad   10. *S. robusta*

1. **Stipa leucotricha** Trin. & Rupr., Acad. St. Petersb. Mem. VI. Sci. Nat. 5:54. 1842. TEXAS WINTERGRASS. Fig. 29. Tufted perennial. *Culms* 30-70 (-90) cm tall, often geniculate-spreading at base. *Nodes* usually appressed hispid, glabrate in age. *Sheaths* variously pubescent to nearly glabrous, the collar with long hairs at least on sides. *Ligules* variable, from absent or minute to a thin truncate membrane as much as 1 mm long. *Blades* 10-30 (5-40) cm long and 1-4 (-5) mm broad, usually pubescent with short, stiff hairs on one or both surfaces, flat or loosely involute. *Panicles* mostly 6-25 cm long, usually with long, slender, flexuous lower branches. *Glumes* thin, glabrous, attenuate, about equal in length or the first longer, mostly 14-18 mm long. *First glume* 3-nerved, second glume 3-5-nerved. *Callus* sharp-pointed, densely hairy. *Lemma* 9-12 mm long, light brown, densely hairy at base, rugose on body above base, with a rounded, whitish neck 0.6-1 mm long; neck fringed on top with ring of stiff hairs but otherwise glabrous. *Awn of lemma* stout, loosely once- or twice-geniculate, scabrous-pubescent on the twisted lower portion, 4.5-10 cm long. *Chromosome number*, $2n=28$.

Distribution. Texas: Throughout the State, most frequent in open grassland sites of central and southern Texas, growing on both sandy and clayey soils. General: Oklahoma to Texas and northeastern Mexico.

Flowering period: Mostly March to May or June but occasionally later in cool sites.

Texas wintergrass thrives under conditions of moderate disturbance and is frequently abundant on roadsides and heavily grazed pastures. It is not highly shade-tolerant and is replaced in the woods areas of eastern Texas by *S. avenacea*. Although of considerable value for early spring green forage, the growing period for *S. leucotricha* generally is short.

2. **Stipa avenacea** L., Sp. Pl. 78. 1753. BLACKSEED NEEDLE-GRASS. Fig. 30. Tufted perennial. *Culms* slender, usually stiffly erect, 35-75 (-100) cm tall. *Culm nodes* glabrous. *Leaves* glabrous or the sheaths sparsely hairy without long hairs on collar. *Ligule* a firm, white membrane 1.5-4.5 mm long. *Blades* elongate, filiform, flat or involute, mostly 1 mm broad. *Panicles* 7-25 cm long, few-flowered. *Branches* slender, stiffly spreading or drooping at maturity. *Glumes* thin, glabrous, 10-15 mm long, attenuate, about equal, first glume 3-5 nerved, the second 5-nerved. *Callus* sharp-pointed, densely hairy with stiff brownish hairs. *Lemma* 8-10 mm long (to base of callus), hairy at base, smooth over most of body, papillose-scabrous just below awn, dark at

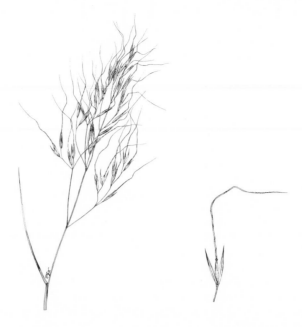

Fig. 29. *Stipa leucotricha.* Inflorescence and spikelet. From Gould and Box, 1965.

maturity, without a whitish, glabrous neck region, with a fringe of stiff, brownish hairs around base of awn. *Lemma awn* slender, twisted at base, weakly once- or twice-geniculate, 3.5-7 cm long. *Chromosome number,* $2n = 22$.

Distribution. Texas: Regions 1, 2 and 3, usually on sandy soils in shaded woodland habitats. General: Massachusetts and Michigan, south to Florida and Texas.

Flowering period: Mostly March to May.

Stipa avenacea and S. *leucotricha* are the two common stipas of eastern Texas. They frequently grow in the same vicinity but usually are segregated locally by the adaptation of S. *leucotricha* to open, often disturbed sites, while S. *avenacea* is restricted to shaded, little-disturbed sites.

3. **Stipa pringlei** Scribn.,in Vasey, Contr. U.S. Natl. Herb. 3:54. 1892. PRINGLE NEEDLEGRASS. Fig. 31. Cespitose perennial. *Culms* 40-100 (-120) cm long, often pubescent at nodes. *Ligules* 1-3 mm long. *Blades* 1-3 mm broad, flat or somewhat involute, those of basal tuft 20-35 cm long. *Panicles* 8-15 (-20)cm long, loosely contracted and narrow, occasionally the lower branches spreading or drooping. *Glumes* broad, about equal, mostly 9-11 mm long, 5-9-nerved, usually abruptly narrowing to an acuminate or short-awned apex. *Callus* short, blunt. *Lemmas* plump, 7-8.5 mm long, dark-colored at

Fig. 30. *Stipa avenacea*. Spikelet.

Fig. 31. *Stipa pringlei*. Spikelet. From Hitchcock, 1935.

maturity, finely rugose and more or less sparsely covered with reddish-brown hairs, the hairs forming a dense tuft at base. *Lemma awn* stout, 2-3 cm long, dark, finely scabrous, loosely twisted below, once- or indistinctly twice-geniculate. *Chromosome number,* $2n=42$ (one record).

Distribution. Texas: Region 10, in the Davis Mountains at 5,000 to 7,000 feet elevation on rocky, open slopes. General: Texas to Arizona and northern Mexico.

Flowering period: Summer.

Fig. 32. *Stipa comata*. Plant, glumes and floret. From Gould, 1951.

4. **Stipa comata** Trin. & Rupr., Acad. St. Petersb. Mem. VI. Sci. Nat. 5:75. 1842. NEEDLE-AND-THREAD. Fig. 32. Cespitose perennial. *Culms* 30-70 (-110) cm tall, in dense clumps, usually strictly erect. *Herbage* glabrous. *Ligules* thin, 1.5-4 mm long, developed as a continuation of sheath apex. *Blades* glaucous, filiform, flat, infolded or tightly involute, 1-2 mm broad, mostly 15-30 (-40) cm long in Texas. *Panicles* contracted, mostly 10-20 cm long, with a few large, long-awned spikelets, usually remaining partially included in sheath. *Glumes* 20-33 mm long, 5-7-nerved, about equal, with long, attenuate, membranous tips. *Lemmas* 10-15 mm long, the callus and base of body densely bearded with stiff hairs, the body sparsely pubescent with white hairs to nearly glabrous, the apex without hairs. *Lemma awns* 10-20 cm long, twisted and short-pubescent on lower half, glabrous or scabrous on terminal segment, flexuous and weakly twice-geniculate, persistent or deciduous. *Chromosome numbers* reported, $2n=44$ and 46.

Distribution. Texas: Regions 8, 9 and 10, frequent in open grasslands on the High Plains and infrequent in the mountains of region 10. General: Western Canada and in the United States from Michigan, Indiana, Kansas and Texas westward to the Pacific.

Flowering period: Mostly May to July.

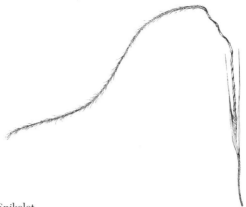

Fig. 33. *Stipa neomexicana.* Spikelet.

5. **Stipa neomexicana** (Thurb.) Scribn., U.S.D.A. Div. Agrost. Bull. 17:132. 1899. NEW MEXICO FEATHERGRASS. Fig. 33. Generally similar to *S. comata* but ligules less than 1.5 mm long, glumes to 4 cm long, lemmas mostly 15-18 mm long and terminal awn segment pubescent with hairs 0.5-1.5 mm long. *Chromosome number, 2n=44.*

Distribution. Texas: Regions 7, 8, 9 and 10, widespread on rocky, open slopes but never abundant. General: Colorado and Utah to Texas, Arizona and northern Mexico.

Flowering period: April to July.

Stipa neomexicana is similar to and perhaps not specifically distinct from the more widely ranging *S. comata.* Typical plants of the two species differ in the hairy terminal awn segment of *S. neomexicana*, but some plants appear intermediate in this character.

6. **Stipa eminens** Cav., Icon. Pl. 5:42. 1799. SOUTHWESTERN NEEDLEGRASS. Cespitose perennial. *Culms* mostly 50-120 cm tall, strictly erect from a hard base. *Leaves* long and narrow, uniformly distributed on culms. *Sheaths* glabrous or scabrous, usually with tufts of hair on the membranous margins on either side of ligule. *Ligules* 1.5-6 mm long. *Blades* flat or involute, 1-2 (-3) mm broad, at least some 20-35 cm long, usually short-pubescent on adaxial surface. *Panicles* narrow but loosely-flowered with long, capillary lower branches, at least some of which are curved and spreading. *Lower nodes of panicle axis* usually densely hairy. *Spikelets* on slender, long or short pedicels. *Glumes* thin, acuminate, membranous at the tip, with 3-5 long nerves and often additional short ones. *First glume* 8-15 (usually 10) mm long. *Second glume* narrower and usually 1-3 mm shorter. *Lemmas* 4.5-7 mm long, uniformly pubescent with silvery hairs. *Lemma awns* mostly 3.5-6 cm long, weakly twice-geniculate, with a flexuous terminal segment. *Chromosome numbers* reported, *2n=44 and 46.*

Distribution. Texas: Region 10, dry rocky slopes and valleys. General: Texas to Arizona and central Mexico.

Flowering period: June to October.

7. **Stipa arida** M. E. Jones, Proc. Calif. Acad. Sci. ser. 2, 5:725. 1895. MORMON NEEDLEGRASS. Cespitose perennial. *Culms* mostly 40-85 cm tall, stiffly erect, glabrous or sparsely pubescent at nodes. *Sheaths* glabrous or scabrous, pubescent at junction of ligule but not on collar. *Ligules* 1 mm or less long, short-ciliate. *Blades* flat or involute, 1-2.5 mm broad, at least some 15-25 cm long. *Panicles* 8-15 cm long, narrow and contracted, moderately dense with short, closely-flowered, mostly appressed branches. *Lower nodes of panicle axis* glabrous or scabrous-pubescent. *Glumes* acuminate, with hyaline margins and tips, 3- (occasionally 5-) nerved, the first glume mostly 9-15 mm long, slightly longer and broader than the second. *Lemmas* 4-6 mm long, slender, light-colored, uniformly pubescent from callus to apex with fine, short, silvery hairs of uniform length, occasionally glabrate above. *Lemma awns* mostly 4-7 cm long, scabrous and twisted below, indistinctly twice-geniculate, the non-twisted terminal segment mostly 3-5 cm long. *Chromosome number* not reported.

Distribution. Texas: Reported from region 10, a grass of dry, open, rocky slopes. General: Colorado and Utah, south to Texas, Arizona and southeastern California.

Flowering period: Summer.

8. **Stipa lobata** Swallen, J. Wash. Acad. Sci. 23:199. f. 2. 1933. LITTLEAWN NEEDLEGRASS. Cespitose perennial. *Culms* densely tufted, stiffly erect, scaberulous below panicle, 40-100 cm tall. *Leaf sheaths* rounded, glabrous. *Ligules* mostly 0.2-0.5 mm long. *Blades* flat or folded, narrow and elongate, 1-4 mm broad, the lower blades as much as 50 cm long. *Panicles* contracted, dense, mostly 12-25 cm long and 1-1.5 cm broad excluding the awns. *Glumes* thin, acuminate, 8-15 mm long, 3-5-nerved, the first glume usually 2-3 mm longer than the second. *Lemmas* 7-8 mm long with a short, puberulent callus and pubescent body, the hairs at apex and on upper portion longer than those below, mostly 1.5-2 mm long. *Lemma* with membranous lobes 0.7-1.5 mm long at base of awn. *Lemma awns* 10-20 mm long, somewhat twisted below, once- and sometimes obscurely twice-geniculate. *Chromosome number* not reported.

Distribution. Texas: Regions 9 and 10 at elevations to 9,000 feet on rocky, open slopes, infrequent. General: Texas and New Mexico.

Flowering period: May to August.

9. **Stipa columbiana** Macoun, Cat. Canada Pl. 2:191. 1888. COLUMBIA NEEDLEGRASS. Tufted perennial. *Culms* 40-80 (-100) cm tall, 2.5 mm or less in diameter at base. *Sheaths* glabrous or scabrous, occasionally pubescent on margins at apex. *Ligule* 0.5-2 mm long, truncate and ciliate. *Blades* 1-3 (-4)

mm broad, 10-30 cm long, conspicuously narrower at base than sheath apex, usually involute on drying, at least the long-attenuate tips tightly involute. *Panicles* narrow, contracted, usually dense and with appressed branches, 10-20 (-30) cm long. *Glumes* subequal, attenuate, 7-13 mm long, usually 3-nerved but occasionally 5-nerved. *Lemmas* slender, 5.5-7 mm long, sparsely appressed-hairy, the hairs at the apex mostly 0.7-1 mm long and longer than those below. *Lemma awns* 1.8-3.3 cm long, once- or indistinctly twice-geniculate, minutely scabrous and twisted below, the upper segment variable in length but often 1.5 cm or more long. Mature lemma reported to be typically dark brown but on most herbarium specimens the lemma is light brown or yellowish. *Chromosome numbers* reported, $2n=36$ and 44.

Distribution. Texas: Regions 7 and 10, reportedly occurring in mountains of the Trans-Pecos and one specimen seen from Kimble County (*Coleman*, 27 May 1969). It is possible that the Kimble County plant persisted from range-land seedings. General: Central Canada, south to Texas and California.

Flowering period: Late spring and (?) summer.

10. **Stipa robusta** (Vasey) Scribn., U.S.D.A. Div. Agrost. Bull. 5:23. 1897. SLEEPYGRASS. Cespitose perennial. *Culms* stout, 100- (70-) 150 cm tall and 3-6 mm in diameter at base. *Sheaths* with a tuft of hair on either side of collar and often with a line of hairs on collar. *Ligules* 0.5-4 mm long, mostly 1.5 mm or more long on main culm leaves. *Blades* flat or involute, the larger blades commonly 5-8 mm broad and 30-50 cm long, tapering from middle to base and apex. *Panicles* large, contracted, thick and dense, typically 25-50 cm long but occasionally shorter. *Glumes* subequal, attenuate, 3- (occasionally 5-) nerved, 8-13 mm long. *Lemmas* 6-8 mm long with a short, hairy callus and slender, sparsely hairy body, the hairs mostly 1-2 mm long. *Lemma awns* 2-3.8 cm long, loosely twice-geniculate, with a twisted, scabrous or short-pubescent lower segment and a straight or flexuous terminal segment usually 12-18 mm long. *Chromosome number*, $2n=64$.

Distribution. Texas: Reported from region 10, a grass of rocky slopes and mountain valleys. General: Southern Colorado to Texas, New Mexico, Arizona and northern Mexico.

Flowering period: June to September.

Stipa robusta is known to have a narcotic effect on horses and, to a lesser extent, on sheep and cattle when grazed. When eaten in sufficient amounts by horses it causes drowsiness and deep slumber. The effects are seldom fatal, and the sleepiness is usually of only a few hours duration, rarely as much as 48 hours. Sleepygrass is of low palatability and is generally avoided when better forage is available. Its narcotic effect apparently varies from region to region and also with the stage of growth when consumed.

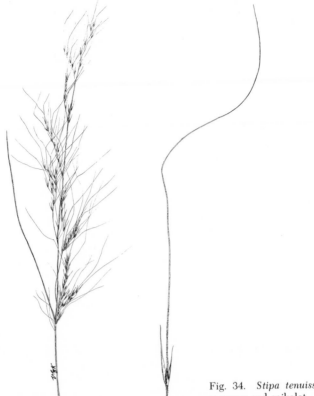

Fig. 34. *Stipa tenuissima.* Inflorescence and spikelet.

11. **Stipa tenuissima** Trin., Acad. St. Petersb. Mem. VI. Sci. Nat. 2:36. 1836. FINESTEM NEEDLEGRASS. Fig. 34. Tufted perennial. *Culms* slender, densely branched and stiffly erect, mostly 45-70 cm tall. *Culm nodes and leaf sheaths* glabrous or minutely puberulent or scabrous. *Margins of sheath* membranous near apex, continued upward to form a thin ligule 1-5 mm long. *Blades* long, stiff, filiform, involute, less than 1 mm broad. *Panicles* 8-20 (-30) cm long, narrow, few-flowered, with the small, delicately-awned spikelets on short, scabrous, flattened or angular pedicels. *Glumes* thin, long-attenuate, colorless or purple-tinged, faintly 1-3-nerved, 5-10 mm long, the first usually longer than the second. *Callus* short, rather blunt. *Lemmas* 2-3 mm long, the base with a tuft of long hairs, the body rugose, the apex with a fringe of stiff hairs around awn base. *Awn of lemma* slender, scaberulous, yellowish, untwisted and non-geniculate, mostly 4-8 cm long. *Chromosome numbers* reported, $2n=32$ (Texas) and $2n=40$ (Argentina).

Distribution. Texas: Region 10, locally abundant on open, rocky slopes at 5,000-7,000 feet elevation. General: Texas and New Mexico to central Mexico and also in Argentina.

Flowering period: June to September.

17. ORYZOPSIS Michx.

Cespitose perennials with narrow, flat or often involute blades and membranous ligules. *Inflorescence* an open or narrow panicle of 1-flowered, awned spikelets. Disarticulation above glumes. *Glumes* broad, obtuse to acuminate. *Lemmas* broad, subterete, firm or indurate, equaling or shorter than glumes in length, with a short, blunt callus and a straight or twisted and bent, deciduous awn from an entire apex. *Palea* and *caryopsis* completely enclosed by lemma.

About 20 species distributed in the cool and temperate regions of both hemispheres.

Spikelets excluding awns 2.5-4 mm long, subsessile or on pedicels 4 mm or less long; lemmas glabrous or infrequently puberulent
1.   *O. micrantha*

Spikelets excluding awns 5-8 mm long, on pedicels mostly 8-30 mm long; lemmas densely pubescent with long hairs   2.   *O. hymenoides*

1. **Oryzopsis micrantha** (Trin. & Rupr.) Thurb., Proc. Pennsylvania Acad. Sci. 1863:78. 1863. LITTLESEED RICEGRASS. Perennial with tufted, slender culms, filiform blades and small, short-pediceled spikelets in a delicate, contracted or loosely spreading panicle. *Leaves* glabrous. *Ligules* oblong, 4-5 mm long and about 1.5 mm broad, unequally rounded at apex on either side of awn, tightly investing the palea and caryopsis, light colored with silvery hairs when immature but dark brown with reddish hairs at lower ones mostly 2-6 cm long, bare of spikelets on lower half. *Spikelets* subsessile or appressed on very short, straight pedicels. *Glumes* thin and hyaline 2.5-4 mm long, acute to acuminate, 1-3-nerved, the lateral nerves short when present. *Lemmas* 2 mm or slightly more in length, 3-nerved, usually smooth and shiny but occasionally puberulent, yellowish-brown or dark-brown at maturity. *Lemma awns* more or less undulate, 5-10 mm long. *Chromosome number, 2n=22.*

Distribution. Texas: Region 9 on shaded canyon slopes just below the caprock. General: North Dakota and Montana, south to Nevada, Texas, New Mexico and Arizona.

Flowering period: Mostly May to July.

2. **Oryzopsis hymenoides** (Roem. & Schult.) Ricker, in Piper, Contrib. U.S. Natl. Herb. 11:109. 1906. INDIAN RICEGRASS. Fig. 35. Strong perennial with culms usually in large, dense clumps. *Culms* slender, glabrous, stiffly erect, mostly 30-70 cm tall. *Leaves* mostly in basal clump. *Sheaths* glabrous, rounded on the back, much shorter than the internodes. *Ligules* thin, rounded or lacerate, 3-7 mm long. *Blades* long, firm, filiform, tightly involute, not over 1.5-2 mm broad, the lower ones to 30 cm or more long. *Panicles* open, diffuse, with few to many 1-flowered spikelets on slender, spreading branchlets and long pedicels.

Fig. 35. *Oryzopsis hymenoides*. Plant, glumes and floret. From Gould, 1951.

Spikelets 5-8 mm long excluding the awn, on kinked or curved pedicels mostly 0.7-3 cm long. Disarticulation above glumes. *Glumes* subequal, broad, thin, 3-nerved, glabrous, scabrous or puberulent, 5-8 mm long, acuminate, sometimes short-awned. *Lemmas* 3-4 mm long, pubescent with hairs mostly 2-4 mm long, dark brown to nearly black at maturity, with a stout, straight, deciduous awn 3-6 mm long. *Chromosome number*, $2n=48$.

Distribution. Texas: Regions 9 and 10 on dry, sandy slopes. General: Throughout the western states from North Dakota and Washington to Texas and California.

Flowering period: May to July.

Fig. 36. *Piptochaetium fimbriatum*. Plant and spikelet. From Gould, 1951.

18. PIPTOCHAETIUM Presl

About 20 species, one in North America, the others in South America.

1. **Piptochaetium fimbriatum** (H.B.K.) Hitchc., J. Wash. Acad. Sci. 23:453. 1933. PINYON RICEGRASS. Fig. 36. Tufted perennial with stiffly erect culms, filiform, mostly basal leaves and small panicles of plump 1-flowered, awned spikelets. *Culms* 30-80 cm tall, glabrous. *Leaves* glabrous. *Sheaths* rounded. *Ligules* membranous, mostly 0.5-1 mm long. *Blades* involute, mostly 1 mm or less broad, the basal ones 5-30 cm or more long. *Panicles* mostly 6-15 cm long, few-flowered, open or loosely contracted. *Panicle branches* slender, spreading in age, the lower ones 2-10 cm long, bare of spikelets on lower half or two-thirds. *Pedicels* variable in length but mostly longer than glumes. Disarticulation above glumes. *Glumes* subequal, thin, broad, acuminate, faintly 3-several-nerved, mostly 5-6 mm long, with thin, hyaline borders and apex. *Lemmas* thick, firm, pubescent, oblong, 4-5 mm long and about 1.5 mm broad, unequally rounded at apex on either side of awn, tightly investing the palea and caryopsis, light colored with silvery hairs when immature but dark brown with reddish hairs at maturity. *Lemma awn* stout, mostly 12-18 mm long, weakly twice-geniculate, the lower segments twisted and scabrous. *Palea* as long as lemma and for the most part enclosed by it, the firm palea tip minutely protruding at apex. *Chromosome numbers* reported, $2n=22$ and 24.

Distribution. Texas: Regions 10 on dry, rocky slopes. General: Colorado, Texas, New Mexico, Arizona and Mexico.

Flowering period: July to October.

Tribe 9. Poeae

19. BROMUS L.

Annuals and perennials, the culms solitary or in clumps of few to numerous. *Leaves* with rounded sheaths, these united by margins to well above middle. *Ligule* membranous, usually prominent. *Blades* thin and flat, often broad. *Inflorescence* a panicle, infrequently a raceme, the spikelets all pediceled. *Spikelets* 13 to 45 mm or more long with 4-numerous florets. Disarticulation above glumes and between florets. *Glumes* unequal, usually acute and awnless, 1-5-nerved. *Lemmas* 5-13-nerved, 1-awned from the notch of a bifid apex or infrequently awnless. *Paleas* large, adnate to the caryopses. *Caryopses* with a tuft of hair at apex.

A genus of about 100 species present for the most part in temperate and cool regions of the world. In Texas, the bromes flower mostly from January to June at the lower elevations and into the summer months at high elevations.

Glumes and lemmas sharply keeled, the spikelets strongly compressed laterally

    Plants perennial; lemma awns 4-7 mm long   1. *B. polyanthus*

    Plants annual

      Lemma awns 4-15 mm long   2. *B. arizonicus*

      Lemmas awnless or with awns 1-3 mm long   3. *B. unioloides*

Glumes and lemmas not keeled, spikelets not strongly compressed laterally

    Plants perennial; culm bases firm

      Glumes glabrous, scabrous or minutely puberulous

        Hairs present on back as well as margins of lemmas, sometimes absent from upper half

          Lower sheaths glabrous or more or less villous; anthers about 2.5 mm long; blades mostly 2-5 mm broad; plants not robust
                6. *B. anomalus*

          Lower sheaths lanate; anthers 3.6-3.9 mm long; blades mostly 5-10 mm broad; plants robust   7. *B. lanatipes*

        Hairs of lemma restricted to margins or margins and base
                8. *B. richardsonii*

Glumes sparsely to densely hairy

Awns 5-11 mm long; blades mostly 5-10 mm broad; ligules 0.5-3 mm long   5. *B. pubescens*

Awn 1-4 (rarely -5) mm long; blades mostly 3.5-5 mm broad; ligules 1 mm or less long   6. *B. anomalus*

Plants annual, short-lived; culms with soft bases

Awns mostly 3-6 cm long; second glume 2-3.5 cm long   9. *B. diandrus*

Awns 2.5 cm or less long; second glume 1.5 cm or less long

First glume 1- or occasionally 3-nerved, gradually tapering to slender, usually acuminate, hyaline tip

Awns 10 mm or less long; teeth of lemma apex about 1 mm long   4. *B. texensis*

Awns 11-25 mm long; teeth of lemma apex mostly 2-5 mm long

Panicle branches and pedicels short, stout, erect or stiffly erect-spreading, mostly much less than 2 cm long   10. *B. rubens*

Panicle branches slender, flexuous and drooping, often much more than 2 cm long, the branchlets and pedicels capillary, frequently S-curved   11. *B. tectorum*

First glume 3-7-nerved, with an obtuse, acute or acuminate tip

Teeth of lemma apex mostly 3-5 mm long; lemmas densely long-pubescent; awns mostly 1.5-2.5 cm long   13. *B. macrostachys*

Teeth of lemma apex less than 3 mm long; lemmas pubescent or glabrous; awns less than 1.5 cm long

Glumes and lemmas pubescent   12. *B. mollis*

Glumes and lemmas glabrous

Paleas 1-2 mm shorter than lemmas; margins of mature lemmas not inrolled; basal sheaths typically retrorsely pilose with long, soft, somewhat matted hairs, but on some plants with hairs sparse and erect   14. *B. japonicus*

Paleas slightly shorter to slightly longer than lemmas; margins of mature lemmas inrolled; basal sheaths glabrous or inconspicuously hirsute   15.   *B. secalinus*

1. **Bromus polyanthus** Scribn., in Shear, U.S.D.A. Div. Agrost. Bull. 23:56. 1900. POLYANTHUS BROME. Perennial with culms mostly 80-100 cm tall. *Sheaths and blades* glabrous or the latter scabrous. *Panicles* 15-25 cm long, usually open. *Spikelets* mostly 2.5-4 cm long and with 6-9 florets. *Glumes and lemmas* laterally compressed and sharply keeled. *Glumes* glabrous or scabrous, first glume 3-nerved, the second 5-7-nerved. *Lemmas* glabrous, scabrous or puberulent on margins, with an awn 4-7 mm long. *Chromosome number, 2n=*56.

Distribution. Texas: Occasional in open grasslands of region 9 and mountain slopes of region 10. General: Montana to Washington, south to Texas, California and northern Mexico.

Flowering period: Spring and summer.

2. **Bromus arizonicus** (Shear) Stebbins, Proc. Calif. Acad. Sci. IV. 25:309. 1944. ARIZONA BROME. Tufted annual with culms mostly 30-70 cm tall. *Panicles* short, stiffly erect, relatively narrow. *Spikelets* mostly 2.5-3 cm long and with 5-8 florets, glumes and lemmas laterally compressed and sharply keeled. *Glumes* glabrous or minutely hirsute, the first glume usually 3-nerved, the second usually 5-nerved. *Lemmas* glabrous or more commonly sparsely hirsute, with an awn 7-15 mm long and apical teeth 0.7-2 mm long. *Chromosome number, 2n=*84.

Distribution. Texas: Region 10, infrequent on mountain slopes at medium altitudes. General: Western Texas, Arizona, southern California and south along the Pacific mountain ranges into Baja California.

Flowering period: Spring.

3. **Bromus unioloides** (Willd.) H.B.K., Nov. Gen. Sp. 1:151. 1815. RESCUEGRASS. Fig. 37. Tufted annual (in Texas) with culms mostly 50-80 cm tall. *Young shoots* soft and succulent, laterally flattened and usually somewhat keeled. *Sheaths* nearly glabrous to densely puberulent with fine, straight, spreading hairs. *Ligules* large, well developed. *Blades* mostly 5-12 mm broad, glabrous or hirsute with spreading hairs, with a yellowish band just above ligule. *Inflorescence* an open, drooping panicle of large, flattened spikelets; spikelets usually with 6-12 florets. *Glumes* awnless, the first glume usually 5-7-nerved, the second usually 7-9-nerved. *Lemmas* 7-11-nerved, laterally flattened and sharply keeled, glabrous or variously pubescent, awnless or with an awn 1-3 mm long. *Chromosome number, 2n=*28.

Fig. 37. *Bromus unioloides.* Plant, spikelet and floret. From Gould and Box, 1965,
as *B. wildenowii.*

Distribution. Texas: In all regions of the State. General: Native of South
America, now frequent in most of the southern states and reported as far north
as New York, South Dakota and Oregon.

Flowering period: Early spring to early summer.

Introduced as a forage grass, *B. unioloides* is now a common weed of
roadsides, field borders, vacant lots and other disturbed sites. This is one of
the first of the cool-climate grasses to flower in the spring. The Texas plants of
this species were referred to *Bromus catharticus* Vahl. by Hitchcock (1935)
and Chase (1951) and to *B. wildenowii* Kunth by Raven (1960), Gould (1962)
and Gould & Box (1965).

Fig. 38. *Bromus texensis.* Inflorescence and spikelet. From Gould and Box, 1965.

4. **Bromus texensis** (Shear) Hitchc., Contrib. U. S. Natl. Herb. 17:381. 1913. TEXAS BROME. Fig. 38. Short-lived annual with culms usually 40-75 cm tall. *Leaves* pubescent with soft, spreading hairs, glabrate in age. *Blades* soft, thin, 3-7 mm broad, uniformly pubescent on both surfaces with short hairs. *Inflorescence* a narrow panicle or raceme commonly 10-15 cm long, the short lateral branches stiffly erect or more frequently widely spreading. *Spikelets* about 2 cm long excluding the awns, usually with 6-8 florets. *First glume* 1-nerved. *Second glume* 3-nerved with broad membranous margins. *Lemmas* minutely to conspicuously scabrous or scabrous-pubescent, mostly 9-12 mm long and with an awn 6-10 mm long. *Paleas* about as long as lemmas. *Chromosome number,* $2n=28$.

Distribution. Texas: Regions 2, 6 and 7, reported from Travis, Bexar, Karnes, Goliad, Aransas, San Patricio, Nueces and Duval counties. General: Known only from Texas.

Flowering period: Spring.

This grass grows mainly in the shade of thickets and oak motts. Though frequently locally abundant, it is relatively inconspicuous and has a short life span.

5. **Bromus pubescens** Muhl. *ex* Willd., Enum. Pl. 120. 1809. Perennial with culms 70-140 cm tall. *Lower sheaths* typically pilose with spreading hairs, the upper sheaths pubescent or glabrous. *Blades* mostly 5-10 mm broad, glabrous or less frequently sparsely hirsute. *Panicles* usually 10-25 cm long with erect, spreading or even reflexed branches, the lowermost as much as 8 cm long. *Spikelets* mostly 2-3.5 cm long with 5-12 florets. *Glumes* sparsely hirsute, the first 1-nerved, the second 3-5-nerved. *Lemmas* rounded on back, uniformly pubescent or less frequently glabrous in midsection, with an awn 5-11 mm long. *Paleas* nearly as long as lemmas. *Chromosome number*, $2n=14$.

Distribution. Texas: Regions 1, 3, 4 and 7. General: Vermont to Wyoming, south to Georgia and Texas.

Flowering period: Spring.

This species grows in moist woodland sites, often along shaded streambanks. Wagnon (1952) referred Texas plants with 5-nerved glumes to *Bromus nottowayanus* Fern. The segregation of Texas plants into two species on the basis of glume nervation alone, however, does not appear justifiable.

6. **Bromus anomalus** Rupr. *ex* Fourn., Mex. Pl. 2:126. 1886. NODDING BROME. Fig. 39. Cespitose perennial with culms mostly 45-75 cm tall. *Culms* usually villous at and below nodes. *Sheaths and abaxial blade surfaces* more or less villous, the adaxial blade surfaces glabrous. *Ligules* 1 mm or less long. *Blades* 2-5 (occasionally -6) mm broad. *Panicles* mostly 10-15 cm long with slender, flexuous branches and pedicels. *Inflorescence branches and pedicels* minutely villous. *Spikelets* mostly 2.2-2.7 cm long and with 7-9 florets. *Glumes* glabrous or villous, the first glume 1-nerved, the second 3-nerved. *Lemmas* about 11 mm long, uniformly villous across the back, obtuse at the apex and bearing a scabrous awn 1-4 (rarely -5) mm long. *Paleas* about 9.5 mm long, puberulent between nerves. *Anthers* about 2.5 mm long, orange. *Chromosome numbers* $2n=14$ and 28.

Distribution. Texas: In the mountains of region 10. General: Colorado, western Texas, New Mexico, Arizona and south in Mexico to Oaxaca, Michoacan and Baja California.

Flowering period: Summer.

7. **Bromus lanatipes** (Shear) Rydb., Colorado Exp. Sta. Bull. 100:52. 1906. *Bromus porteri* var. *lanatipes* Shear, *B. anomalus* var. *lanatipes* (Shear) Hitchc. Cespitose perennial with stout culms mostly 1-1.3 m tall. *Culm nodes* and upper portion of the internodes usually villous. *Sheaths* densely retrorsely villous. *Ligules* glabrous, 1-2 mm long. *Blades* 5-10 mm broad, puberulent on both surfaces or glabrous. *Panicles* erect to drooping, 20-25 cm long, with 1-3 branches at the lower nodes. *Spikelets* about 3 cm long, usually with 7-9 florets. *Glumes* more or less villous, the first glume 1-nerved, the second 3-nerved. *Lemmas* villous on the back, obovate, 9-11 mm long, with an awn about 5 mm long. *Paleas* as long as or slightly longer than lemmas, puberulent or glabrous between nerves. *Anthers* 3.6-3.9 mm long, orange. *Chromosome number*, $2n=28$.

Fig. 39. *Bromus anomalus*. Inflorescence and spikelet. From Hitchcock, 1935, in part.

Distribution. Texas: In the mountains of region 10. General: Southern Rocky Mountains region, from Colorado to Western Oklahoma and Texas, New Mexico and northeastern Arizona.

Flowering period: Summer.

8. **Bromus richardsonii** Link, Hort. Berol. 2:28. 1833. Cespitose perennial with glabrous culms 50-110 cm tall. *Sheaths* pilose or glabrous. *Blades* mostly 4-7 (rarely 3-9) mm broad, entirely glabrous or with tufts of hair at the auricle positions. *Auricles* absent. *Ligules* 0.8-2 mm long, glabrous. *Panicles* 10-25 cm long, the lower branches as much as 14 cm long. *Spikelets* mostly 1.7-4 cm long, with 6-10 florets. *Glumes* glabrous, the first glume 1- or rarely 3-nerved, the second 3-nerved. *Lemmas* 10-14 mm long, hairy on margins and sometimes at base, glabrous on the back, with an awn 3-6 mm long. *Paleas* shorter than lemmas, ciliate on nerves and glabrous between nerves. *Anthers* mostly 2-3.5 mm long. *Chromosome number,* $2n=28$.

Distribution. Texas: Mountains of region 10, infrequent. General: Rocky Mountains, from British Columbia south to western Texas, southern Nevada and southern California.

Flowering period: Summer.

9. **Bromus diandrus** Roth, Bot. Abh.:44. 1787. RIPGUT BROME. Fig. 40. Short-lived annual with rather thick but weak culms mostly 20-70 cm tall. *Sheaths and blades* usually pubescent with spreading hairs. *Blades* flat, soft, mostly 4-7 mm broad. *Panicle* narrow, with stout, erect branches or less frequently with lower branches spreading. *Spikelets* large, mostly 3-4 cm long excluding awns. *Glumes* unequal, lanceolate-acuminate, with broad hyaline margins, the first glume 1-3-nerved, the second 3-5-nerved. *Lemmas* glabrous or scabrous, slender, with a body typically 2 cm or more long, with broad hyaline margins, apical teeth usually 4-5 mm long, and a stout awn 3-6 cm long. *Chromosome number,* $2n=56$.

Distribution. Texas: Occasional in regions 1, 3 and 7, growing as a weed of roadsides, field borders and waste places. General: A European species, now well-established in the western states and occasional in the south and east.

Fig. 40. *Bromus diandrus.* Spikelet.

Flowering period: Spring.

In the United States, *Bromus diandrus* commonly has gone under the name of *B. rigidus* Roth., a closely related Mediterranean species. Ripgut brome is a serious weed pest in semi-arid regions of the Southwest. The stout, sharp-awned florets are injurious to stock, frequently working their way into the eyes and nostrils of grazing animals.

10. **Bromus rubens** L., Cent. Pl. 1:5. 1755. FOXTAIL BROME. Tufted annual with culms usually 20-50 cm tall but on dry sites 15 cm or less tall. *Lower sheaths and blades* pubescent. *Blades* mostly 1.5-3 mm broad but occasionally as much as 7 mm broad. *Panicles* short, dense, bristly, mostly 4-8 cm long, typically dark brown or purple-tinged at maturity. *Spikelets* mostly 1.5-2.5 cm long excluding awns. *Glumes* unequal, lanceolate-acuminate, with broad membranous margins, the first glume 1-nerved, the second 3-nerved. *Lemmas* averaging about 1 cm long, scabrous to pubescent, with broad, membranous margins, slender apical teeth usually 3-5 mm long and an awn 1.5-2.2 cm long. *Paleas* about as long as lemmas, coarsely ciliate on nerves. *Chromosome number*, $2n = 28$.

Distribution. Texas: Occasional in regions 7 and 10 as weed of open, disturbed sites. General: A European species, adventive in the United States and now abundant over large areas of the western states, especially on overgrazed rangelands and dry roadsides.

Flowering period: Spring.

SUBFAMILY IV. POOIDEAE   89

11. **Bromus tectorum** L., Sp. Pl. 77. 1753. DOWNY BROME. Annual with weak, erect or spreading culms usually 25-60 cm tall. *Sheaths and blades* usually softly pubescent but occasionally glabrous or nearly so. *Blades* typically 2.5-6 mm broad. *Panicles* narrow and loosely contracted, the branches and pedicels slender, flexuous and often S-curved. *Spikelets* mostly 1.2-2 cm long excluding the awns, usually with 4-6 florets. *Glumes* unequal, thin, with broad hyaline margins, the first glume 1-3-nerved, narrowly acute to acuminate, the second 3-nerved, often notched at apex. *Lemmas* mostly 9-12 mm long with thin, membranous margins and slender apical teeth 2-3 mm long. *Lemma awns* 12-18 mm long. *Paleas* slightly shorter than lemmas, ciliate on nerves. *Chromosome number,* 2n=14.

Lemmas soft-pubescent   11A. *B. tectorum* var. *tectorum*

Lemmas glabrous or scabrous   11B. *B. tectorum* var. *glabratus*

11A. **Bromus tectorum** L. var. **tectorum.**

Distribution. Texas: Regions 5, 7, 8, 9 and 10. General: Native to Europe, adventive in the United States and now common throughout most of the country except in the southeast.

Flowering period: Spring and early summer (at higher elevations).

A weed of heavily grazed rangelands, roadsides and other open, disturbed sites.

11B. **Bromus tectorum** L. var. **glabratus** Spenner, Fl. Friburg. 1:152. 1825.

Distribution. Texas: Region 4 (no Texas collections examined). General: Throughout the range of the species with numerous intergradations.

Flowering period: Spring.

12. **Bromus mollis** L., Sp. Pl. ed. 2:112. 1762. SOFT BROME. Annual with weak, usually geniculate culms typically 20-40 cm tall. *Sheaths,* at least the lower ones, densely hirsute with spreading hairs. *Blades* soft, flat or folded, glabrous or sparsely hirsute, mostly 2-6 mm broad. *Inflorescence* a contracted, densely-flowered panicle or raceme 3-10 cm long; pedicels and branches typically all shorter than spikelets. *Spikelets* mostly 1.5-2 cm long, with 5-9 florets. *Glumes* large, broad, soft, hirsute, the first glume 3-5-nerved, the second 5-7-nerved. *Lemmas* hirsute (in Texas plants), similar to glumes in texture, mostly 7-10 mm long, with awn 5-9 mm long. *Paleas* usually 1.5-2 mm shorter than lemmas. *Chromosome number,* 2n=28.

Distribution. Texas: Regions 1, 3 and 4, infrequent in Texas and probably not persisting long in any locality (Tracy Herbarium specimens from Brazos and Crockett counties). General: A European species, now frequent as a weed of roadsides and waste places over much of the northern half of the United States and occasional in the southern states.

Flowering period: Spring.

In their manual of Texas plants, Correll and Johnston (1970) referred Texas collections of this species to *B. molliformis* Lloyd, stating, "Very likely no more than a form of *B. mollis.*"

13. **Bromus macrostachys** Desf., Fl. Atlant. 1:96. 1798. MEDITERRA-NEAN BROME. Annual with culms mostly 30-60 cm tall. *Sheaths and blades,* especially the lowermost, hirsute or hispid. *Blades* 2-7 mm broad. *Inflorescence* a narrow panicle or raceme of large, conspicuously pubescent spikelets with stout, spreading awns. *Spikelets* 3-4.5 cm long at maturity, mostly with 8-12 florets. *Glumes* awnless, acute or acuminate, pilose, the first glume 3-7-nerved, the second 5-9-nerved. *Lemmas* typically densely villous, several-nerved, with apical teeth or narrow lobes 3-5 mm long and a stout curved awn 1.5-2.5 cm long. *Paleas* large, longer than the apical notch of the lemmas but shorter than the teeth. *Chromosome number,* 2n=56.

Distribution. Texas: Region 3, known only from the vicinity of College Station, Brazos County. General: A Mediterranean species reported by Chase (1951) to occur in the United States only at College Station, Texas, and Yonkers, New York.

Flowering period: Spring.

The apparent restriction of the Texas distribution of this annual weed species is surprising, because it is locally abundant and widespread in the College Station area.

14. **Bromus japonicus** Thunb., Fl. Japon. 52. 1784. JAPANESE BROME. Fig. 41. Annual with slender, weak culms mostly 30-60 cm tall. *Sheaths,* at least the lowermost, typically shaggy-pilose with spreading or reflexed hairs. *Blades* usually pilose or puberulent, 2-7 mm broad. *Panicles* 8-20 cm long with slender, flexuous, often kinked branches and pedicels; branches spreading from the main axis and curving-erect at maturity. *Spikelets* 1.5-3 (averaging 2) cm long excluding the awns, with 6-11 florets. *Glumes* broad, glabrous, awnless, the first glume 3-5-nerved, the second 5-9-nerved. *Lemmas* glabrous, mostly 7-9 mm long, rounded on back and with thin, flat margins that do not become inrolled at maturity, with apical teeth mostly 1.5-2 mm long and with a slender, straight or flexuous awn 8-13 mm long on upper florets; at maturity the lemma relatively thin and margins not inrolled. *Paleas* ciliate on nerves, usually 1-2 mm shorter than lemmas. *Chromosome numbers,* 2n=14 and 28; Texas counts, 2n=14.

Distribution. Texas: Reported from all regions except region 1, a common weed of roadsides, field borders and pastures. General: Widespread in temperate regions of the Northern Hemisphere, adventive in the United States and reported from nearly all the states.

Flowering period: Spring.

Fig. 41. *Bromus japonicus.* Inflorescence and spikelet.

15. **Bromus secalinus** L., Sp. Pl. 76. 1753. RYE BROME. Fig. 42.
Annual with relatively thick culms mostly 30-90 cm tall. *Sheaths* glabrous or
inconspicuously hirsute. *Blades* mostly 3-8 mm broad, glabrous, scabrous, or
less frequently inconspicuously hirsute or pilose. *Panicles* typically 10-18 cm
long with slender, erect or spreading branches. *Spikelets* mostly 1.5-2.5 cm
long excluding the awns, with 6-11 florets. *Glumes* short, broad, stiff, awnless,
the first glume 3-7-nerved, the second 5-9-nerved. *Lemmas* mostly 6-7.5 mm
long, 7-11-nerved, with apical teeth about 1 mm long and an awn usually 4-9
mm long, infrequently awnless. At maturity the lemma thick, firm and with
inrolled margins. *Paleas* ciliate on keels, 1 mm shorter to slightly longer than
lemmas. *Chromosome numbers,* $2n = 14$ (?) and 28.

Distribution. Texas: Regions 1, 2, 3, 4, 5, 7, 8 and 9, a weed of roadsides,
ditches and other disturbed sites. General: Widespread in temperate regions
of the Northern Hemisphere, adventive in the United States and now widespread throughout.

Flowering period: Spring.

Bromus secalinus characteristically differs from *B. japonicus,* with which
it frequently grows, in the glabrous or inconspicuously hirsute lower sheaths,
the long paleas and the firm lemmas that become tough and inrolled at
maturity. *Bromus secalinus* plants tend to be taller and stouter, with thicker
culms and with generally shorter and stouter inflorescence branches. For the
most part, the lemmas of *B. secalinus* are firmer, less prominently nerved and

Fig. 42. *Bromus secalinus.* Plant, spikelet and floret. From Hitchcock, 1935.

have shorter apical teeth than those of *B. japonicus.* The rather conspicuous pubescence of the sheaths and blades of some plants referable to *B. secalinus* probably reflects natural hybridization between this species and *B. japonicus.* Texas plants of *B. secalinus* have been referred to *B. racemosus* L. by Shinners (1958) and by Gould (1962, 1969). A third species of this complex, *B. commutatus* Schrad., is reported by Correll and Johnston (1970) to occur in Texas. These authors note, however, that Texas plants of *B. commutatus* and *B. secalinus* possibly should be referred to a single species.

SUBFAMILY IV. POOIDEAE   93

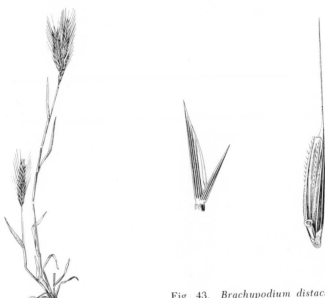

Fig. 43. *Brachypodium distachyon*. Plant, glumes and floret. From Chase, 1951.

20. BRACHYPODIUM Beauv.

A genus of about 15 species, none native to the United States but two indigenous to Mexico.

1. **Brachypodium distachyon** (L.) Beauv., Ess. Agrost. 101, 155. 1812. PURPLE FALSEBROME. Fig. 43. Tufted annual with culms mostly 20-50 cm tall. *Culm nodes* puberulent. *Sheaths* glabrous or sparsely ciliate on margins near apex. *Ligules* 1-2 mm long, erose at apex. *Blades* short, flat, mostly 2-4 mm wide, glabrous or sparsely hirsute on both surfaces, usually ciliate on margins below. *Inflorescence* a spike or spicate raceme of 1-5 large, awned, stiffly erect spikelets; spikelets 2-3.5 cm long, with usually 9-18 closely imbricated florets. Disarticulation above glumes and between florets. *Glumes* unequal, short, glabrous, narrowly acute and stiffly pointed, the first glume 3-7-nerved, the second 7-9-nerved. *Lemmas* firm, rounded on back, usually 7-nerved, 7-10 mm long, tapering to an awn 1-2 cm long from an entire apex. *Paleas* firm, rounded at apex, about as long as lemmas, with conspicuous, thick and stiff pectinate-ciliate hairs on nerves. *Chromosome number*, $2n=28$.

Distribution. Texas: Occasional in regions 5 and 7, growing as a weed of roadsides and disturbed field borders. General: A European species, adventive in the United States and now well established along the Pacific Coast and occasional at other United States locations.

Flowering period: Spring.

21. VULPIA K. S. Gmel.*

Tufted annuals (Texas species) with weak, erect or decumbent culms and narrow blades. *Ligule* a short membrane. *Inflorescence* a panicle or spicate raceme, the branches all erect-appressed or the lowermost spreading. *Spikelets* with 3-many florets. Disarticulation above glumes and between florets. *Glumes* narrow, subulate, first glume 1-nerved, the second 3-nerved. *Lemmas* rounded dorsally, inconspicuously 5-nerved, mucronate or awned. *Stamens* 1, infrequently 3, per flower. *Caryopses* cylindrical, elongate.

A genus of about 30 species, these for the most part short-lived, weedy annuals. The species are distributed widely in temperate regions of Europe and North and South America. In Texas, they are cool-climate grasses, flowering from March until early June. Hitchcock (1935, 1936) and Chase (1951) treated *Vulpia* as a section of *Festuca*. Fernald, in Gray's Manual (1950) gave *Vulpia* generic status, as do most European workers.

First glume one-eighth to less than one-half the length of second glume; panicle typically only partially exserted from upper sheath at maturity
1. V. myuros

First glume more than one-half the length of second glume; panicle well exserted from upper sheath at maturity

Spikelets with 5-17 florets; awn of lowermost floret 0.3-6 mm long
2. V. octoflora

Spikelets with 1-7 florets; awn of lowermost floret 3-12 mm long

Lemma of lowermost floret 2.5-3.5 mm long; caryopsis 1.5-2 mm long
3. V. sciurea

Lemma of lowermost floret 3.5-7.5 mm long; caryopsis 3.5-5.5 mm long
4. V. bromoides

1. **Vulpia myuros** (L.) K.C. Gmelin, Fl. Baden. 1:8. 1805. RATTAIL SIXWEEKSGRASS. Plants annual, 15-70 cm tall. *Sheaths* glabrous. *Ligules* 0.5-1 mm long. *Blades* mostly 15 cm or less long and 0.5-3 mm wide, flat or involute, glabrous. *Panicles* contracted, 3-25 cm long, usually only partially exserted from the sheath. *Spikelets* 5.5-12 mm long excluding the awns, with 3-7 florets. *Glumes* glabrous, the first one-eighth to one-half the length of second, the second 2.5-5.5 mm long. *Lemma of lowermost floret* 4.5-6.5 mm long, scabrous above or ciliate on upper margins, with an awn 7.5-22 mm long.

*Modified from *A Biosystematic Study of the Genus Vulpia (Gramineae)*, by R. I. Lonard, 1970, PhD Dissertation on file in the Texas A&M University Library.

Lemmas not ciliate on margins near apex   1A.   *V. myuros* var. *myuros*

Lemmas ciliate with long hairs on margins near apex
1B.   *V. myuros* var. *hirsuta*

1A. **Vulpia myuros** (L.) K.C. Gmelin var. **myuros.** *Festuca myuros* L.
Lemmas scabrous above. *Awn of lowermost floret* 7.5-17 mm long. *Chromosome numbers,* 2n = 14 and 42; Texas counts, 2n = 42.

Distribution. Texas: Northeastern portion of State, in northern portions of regions 1, 3 and 4. General: Probably native to central Europe, occurring as a common weed throughout southern Europe, Africa, Asia, Australia and North and South America.

Flowering period: Spring.

1B. **Vulpia myuros** (L.) K.C. Gmelin var. **hirsuta** Hack., Cat. Garm. Port. 24. 1880. *Festuca megalura* Nutt., *Vulpia megalura* (Nutt.) Rydb. Fig. 44. *Lemmas* sparsely to densely ciliate on margins. *Awn of lowermost floret* 9.5-22 mm long. *Chromosome number,* 2n = 42.

Distribution. Texas: Occasional in the northeast, regions 1 and 3, and the western portion of the Edwards Plateau, region 7. General: Widespread in the world and present in North America from Alaska and British Columbia to Mexico but probably not native to the continent.

Flowering period: Spring.

2. **Vulpia octoflora** (Walt.) Rydb., Bull. Torrey Bot. Club. 36:538. 1909. COMMON SIXWEEKSGRASS. Short-lived annual with slender, weak, erect or decumbent, solitary or loosely tufted culms mostly 10-60 cm tall. *Ligules* 0.5-1 mm long. *Blades* to 10 cm long and 0.5-1 mm broad, glabrous or pubescent. *Inflorescence* a panicle 1-20 cm long with short, appressed branches or sometimes reduced to a spicate raceme. *Spikelets* glabrous, scabrous or pubescent, 4-10 mm long excluding the awns, with 5-17 florets, the uppermost reduced. *First glume* 1.7-4.5 mm long, second glume 2.7-6.7 mm long. *Lemma of lowermost floret* 2.7-6.5 mm long with an awn 0.3-6 mm long. *Caryopses* brown at maturity, 1.7-3.3 mm long, with an embryo about 0.3 mm long.

Spikelet excluding awns usually 4.5-5 mm long; awn of lowermost floret
0.3-3 mm long   2B.   *V. octoflora* var. *glauca*

Spikelet excluding awns 5.5-10 mm long; awn of the lowermost floret
2.5-6.5 mm long

Lemma glabrous or slightly scabrous above
2A.   *V. octoflora* var. *octoflora*

Lemma sparsely to densely pubescent   2C.   *V. octoflora* var. *hirtella*

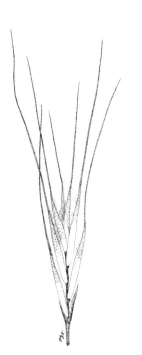

Fig. 44. *Vulpia myuros* var. *hirsuta.* Spikelet.

Fig. 45. *Vulpia octoflora* var. *octoflora.* Plant and spikelet. From Gould and Box, 1965.

2A. **Vulpia octoflora** (Walt.) Rydb. var. **octoflora.** *Festuca octoflora* Walt. Fig. 45. Lower branches of panicle often spreading. *Spikelets* 5.5-10 mm long, rather widely spaced and usually not overlapping. *Lemmas* glabrous or slightly scabrous on margins or near apex. *Lemma awn of lowermost floret* 3-6 mm long. *Chromosome number,* $2n = 14$.

Distribution. Texas: Regions 1, 2, 3 and 4. General: Native to North America and widespread throughout the continent. Adventive in South America, Europe and Asia.

Flowering period: Spring.

2B. **Vulpia octoflora** (Walt.) Rydb. var. **glauca** (Nutt.) Fern. Rhodora 47:104. 1945. *Festuca tenella* Willd., *F. tenella* Willd. var. *glauca* Nutt., *V. octoflora* (Walt.) Rydb. var. *tenella* (Willd.) Fern. *Vulpia tenella* (Willd.) Heynh. *Panicle branches* usually all appressed. *Spikelets* mostly 4-5.5 mm long excluding awns. *Lemmas* glabrous or scabrous. *Lemma awn of lowermost floret* 0.3-3 mm long.

Distribution. Texas: Central and northern portions of state, frequent in regions 1, 3, 4, 5 and 8. General: Widespread in North America but most frequent in southern Canada and northern United States.

Flowering period: Spring.

2C. **Vulpia octoflora** (Walt.) Rydb. var. **hirtella** (Piper) Henr., Blumea 2:320. 1937. *Festuca pusilla* Buckl., *Festuca octoflora* subsp. *hirtella* Piper. *Panicle branches* appressed, densely-flowered, the spikelets closely placed and overlapping. *Spikelets* mostly 5.5-10 mm long excluding awns. *Lemmas* strongly scabrous to densely pubescent. *Awn of lowermost lemma* 2.5-6.5 mm long.

Distribution. Texas: Occasional throughout Texas except in the extreme southern portion of the State. General: Western and southwestern United States, with a general range from British Columbia to eastern Texas and southward into northern Mexico from Coahuila to Baja California.

Flowering period: Spring.

This variety of *Vulpia octoflora* is most frequent in the western and southwestern states. It grades into V. *octoflora* var. *octoflora* through plants with strongly scabrous lemmas.

3. **Vulpia sciurea** (Nutt.) Henr., Blumea 2:323. 1937. *Festuca sciurea* Nutt. SQUIRREL SIXWEEKSGRASS. Fig. 46. Delicate, short-lived annual with weak culms, mostly 15-60 cm tall. *Culms and leaves glabrous. Ligules* 0.5-1 mm long. *Blades* usually less than 10 cm long and 0.5-1 mm broad. *Panicles* 5-20 cm long, contracted, with appressed branches. *Spikelets* 3.5-5 mm long excluding awns, with 3-7 florets. *Glumes* glabrous, the first 1.3-2.5 mm long, the second 2.5-4 mm long. *Lemma of lowermost floret* 2.5-3.5 mm long, pubescent on back, with an awn 4.5-9.5 mm long. *Stamens* 1, with a short filament. *Anthers* about 0.5 mm long. *Caryopses* 1.5-2 mm long. *Chromosome number, 2n*=42.

Distribution. Texas: Regions 1, 3, 4, 5 and 7. General: Virginia to central Oklahoma, south to Florida and the eastern half of Texas.

Flowering period: Spring.

Correll and Johnston (1970) have taken up the name *Vulpia elliotea* (Raf.) Fern. for this taxon.

4. **Vulpia bromoides** (L.) S.F. Gray, Natur. Arrange. Brit. Plants. 124. 1821. *Festuca bromoides* L., *Festuca dertonensis* (All.) Aschers. & Graebn., *Vulpia dertonensis* (All.) Gola. BROME SIXWEEKSGRASS. Annual with loosely tufted or solitary culms 5-50 cm tall. *Culms and leaves* glabrous. *Ligules* membranous, about 0.5 cm long. *Panicles* 5-15 cm long, well exserted above the uppermost leaf. *Pedicels* flattened or noticeably clavate above. *Spikelets* 5-10 mm long excluding the awns, with 4-7 florets. *Glumes* glabrous, the first 3.5-5 mm long, one-half to three-fourths the length of the second, the second 4.5-7 mm long. *Lemma of lowermost floret* 4-6.5 mm long, glabrous or puberulent, with a firm awn 3-12 mm long. *Caryopses* 3.5-5.5 mm long. *Chromosome number, 2n*=14.

Fig. 46. *Vulpia sciurea*. Spikelet.

Distribution. Texas: Regions 1 and 3, infrequent. General: Present in disturbed habitats throughout temperate regions of the world, *Vulpia bromoides* is adventive in North and South America. In North America it is most common in the western coastal region, where it ranges from British Columbia to northern Baja California.

Flowering period: Spring.

Vulpia bromoides is similar in general appearance to *V. myuros*. It can best be distinguished from *V. myuros* on the basis of glume length.

22. FESTUCA L.

Tufted perennials with flat or involute blades. *Ligules* membranous. *Spikelets* with 2-several florets, awned or awnless, in contracted or, less frequently, open panicles. Disarticulation above glumes and between florets. *Glumes* narrow, acute or acuminate, 1-3-nerved. *Lemmas* usually 5-7-nerved, rounded on back, obtuse or acute at apex, awned or awnless. *Stamens* 3, the anthers usually 2-3 mm or more long. *Caryopses* commonly ovoid or ellipsoid but occasionally fusiform, free from palea.

A genus of more than 100 species in temperate and cool regions of the world or as cool-season grasses in subtropical regions. None of the 7 species of *Festuca* that occur in Texas are of special economic significance, and most are infrequent or rare.

SUBFAMILY IV. POOIDEAE   99

Blades involute or folded, less than 3 mm broad; plants of the higher elevations in the Trans-Pecos region

Ligules 3-4 mm long; spikelets 2-3-flowered   1. *F. ligulata*

Ligules mostly 0.5-1.5 mm long; spikelets 4- (infrequently 3-) 8-flowered

    Culms densely tufted, mostly erect at base; basal sheaths brown or grayish, remaining entire and not shredding; blades usually glaucous   2. *F. arizonica*

    Culms not densely tufted, usually decumbent at base; basal sheaths reddish or purplish, typically shredding and fibrillose in age; blades not glaucous   3. *F. rubra*

Blades flat or flat and folded, usually at least some more than 3 mm broad; plants absent from or uncommon in the Trans-Pecos region

Spikelets mostly 10-15 mm or more long; florets mostly 5- (3-) 10 per spikelet; lower branches of inflorescence often floriferous to well below middle   4. *F. arundinacea*

Spikelets less than 10 mm long; florets 2-5 per spikelet; lower branches of inflorescence not spikelet-bearing below middle

    Longest glumes 4-7 mm long; lemmas 5-7 mm long   5. *F. versuta*

    Longest glumes 5 mm or less long; lemmas 3-4.5, rarely -5 mm long

        Spikelets not or only slightly overlapping, rather uniformly distributed on upper one-half or one-third of branch   6. *F. obtusa*

        Spikelets well imbricated and more or less densely clustered at branch tips   7. *F. paradoxa*

1. **Festuca ligulata** Swallen, Amer. J. Bot. 19:436. 1932. GUADALUPE FESCUE. Cespitose perennial. *Culms* mostly 50-80 cm tall, usually decumbent at base and often rhizomatous, scabrous below panicle. Sheaths glabrous. *Ligules* 3-4 mm long. *Blades* 1-2 mm broad, flat or involute, scabrous. *Panicle* 6-10 (-16) cm long, with 1-3 stiffly erect or spreading, scabrous branches; branches few-flowered and bare of spikelets on lower portion. *Spikelets* 2-3-flowered, awnless, on short, appressed pedicels. *Glumes* acute, scabrous, the first glume 1-nerved, about 3 mm long, the second 3-nerved, about 4 mm long. *Lemmas* 4-6 mm long, rounded on back, broadly acute, scaberulous, faintly-nerved, awnless. *Paleas* slightly longer than lemmas. *Chromosome number* not reported.

Distribution. Texas: Moist, shaded slopes in the higher mountains of the Trans-Pecos (region 10). General: Endemic to western Texas.

Flowering period: June to August.

2. **Festuca arizonica** Vasey, Contr. U. S. Natl. Herb. 1:277. 1893. ARIZONA FESCUE. Fig. 47. Culms densely tufted, mostly 45-90 cm tall, tough and wiry at maturity. *Leaves* usually glaucous. *Sheaths* much broader than blades, glabrous or scaberulous, the lower ones laterally lobed (auriculate) or truncate at apex, the lobes membranous, minutely ciliolate above, mostly 0.5-1.5 mm long. *Ligules* membranous, 0.5-1.5 mm long, ciliolate, formed by continuation of sheath margins across throat. *Blades* firm, filiform, folded or involute, usually scabrous, mostly 20-50 cm long and 1.5 mm or less broad. *Panicles* 8-18 cm long, contracted or open, the branches usually short and erect or spreading at a narrow angle but the lower ones occasionally slender and widely spreading. *Spikelets* 4- (3-) 8-flowered. *Glumes* lanceolate, narrowly acute and usually scabrous at apex, first glume 1-nerved, slightly shorter and narrower than second, the second 3-nerved, slightly shorter than lowermost lemma. *Lemmas* rounded on back, narrowly acute, awnless or with an awn to 2 mm long, usually scabrous at apex, the lowermost lemma 5.5-7 mm long. *Palea* about as long as lemma body, scabrous-ciliolate on nerves. *Anthers* 2-3 mm long. *Chromosome number*, $2n=42$.

Distribution. Texas: Open woods and grassy slopes at high elevation in the Trans-Pecos (region 10), not common. General: Colorado, Nevada, Texas, New Mexico and Arizona.

Flowering period: June to August.

3. **Festuca rubra** L., Sp. Pl. 74. 1753. RED FESCUE. Similar to *F. arizonica*, differing mainly in the smooth, reddish-purple or brownish basal sheaths that become shredded and fibrillous in age, the relatively soft, glabrous blades mostly 1.5-2.5 mm broad and the minute ligule, this usually 0.1-0.4 mm long. Numerous *chromosome numbers*, both euploid and aneuploid, have been reported for this widespread and polymorphic species. Euploid counts are $2n=14$, 28, 42, 56 and 70. The hexaploid $(2n=42)$ count has been reported by seven different investigators.

Distribution. Texas: On the highest slopes of the Davis Mountains in the Trans-Pecos (region 10), infrequent and in moist, shaded sites. General: Throughout the cooler regions of the world but most widespread in the Northern Hemisphere; throughout northern United States, south to Georgia and Missouri in the east and Texas, Arizona and California in the west; in the mountains of Mexico.

Flowering period: Summer.

4. **Festuca arundinacea** Schreb., Spic. Fl. Lips. 57. 1771. *Festuca elatior* L. *sensu stricto*, *F. elatior* L. var. *arundinacea* (Schreb.) Wimm. TALL FESCUE. Fig. 48. Cespitose perennial without rhizomes. *Culms* stout, erect

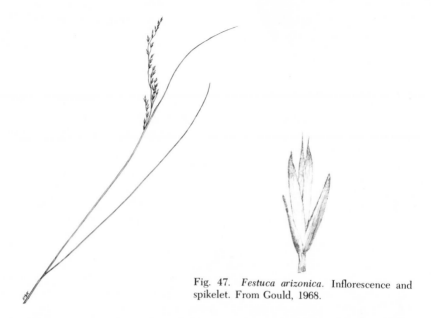

Fig. 47. *Festuca arizonica.* Inflorescence and spikelet. From Gould, 1968.

or curving-erect at base, 50-150 (-200) cm tall, often scabrous below panicle. *Sheaths* smooth or scabrous, rounded on back, usually with narrow, rounded auricles at apex, minutely hairy on auricles and at junction with blade. *Ligules* ranging from a minute ciliate rim to a membrane 2 mm long. *Blades* elongate, flat or folded, 3-12 mm broad, often scabrous on margins. *Panicles* mostly 10-30 cm long, erect or somewhat nodding, contracted and narrow or the lower branches long, spreading and bare of spikelets on lower one-third to one-half; shortest of lowermost branches usually with 3 or more spikelets. *Rachilla* glabrous to scabrous, disarticulating between florets. *Spikelets* short-pediceled and appressed, mostly 10-15 (-18) mm long, 5-7 (-10)-flowered. *Glumes* glabrous, lanceolate, acute, membranous on margins, the first glume 1-nerved, 4-6 mm long, the second 3-nerved, slightly longer than the first. *Lemmas* 6-9 mm long, rounded dorsally, 5-nerved, smooth or minutely rugose and scabrous on nerves, awnless or with an awn 1-4 mm long. *Paleas* as long as lemmas, scabrous on margins. *Chromosome number,* $2n = 42$.

Distribution. Texas: Occasional in the northern and eastern counties, regions 1, 3, 4, 5, 7, 8 and 9, mostly growing in seeded pastures or as an escape in the vicinity of such pastures. General: Native to Europe, now widely established in temperate and cool regions of North America.

Flowering period: Mostly April to June.

Festuca arundinacea and the closely related *F. pratensis* Huds. (*Festuca elatior auct. non* L. *sensu stricto*) are both referred to *F. elatior* L. by Correll and Johnston (1970). Terrell (1967) reported that the name *F. elatior* L. appeared to be a *"nomen ambiguum"* that has been rejected by most European workers in favor of *F. pratensis* for the grass commonly known as

Fig. 48. *Festuca arundinacea.* Plant, spikelet and floret. From Hitchcock, 1935, as *F. elatior.*

MEADOW FESCUE. *Festuca pratensis* is a European diploid ($2n=14$) that differs from *F. arundinacea* in several minor characteristics. It has become well-established in the United States but apparently does not occur in Texas except in experimental plantings.

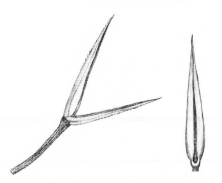

Fig. 49. *Festuca versuta*. Glumes and floret of spikelet.

5. **Festuca versuta** Beal, Grasses N. Amer. 2:589. 1896. TEXAS FES-CUE. Fig. 49. Tufted perennial with slender, glabrous culms 50-100 cm long. *Herbage* glabrous. *Sheaths* rounded on back, not auriculate. *Ligules* 0.5-1 mm long. *Blades* linear, flat or some flat and some loosely folded, mostly 2-5 mm broad. *Panicles* 8-30 cm long with long, flexuous lower branches; branches bare of spikelets on lower one-half to one-third. *Spikelets* mostly 6-9 mm long and 2-4-flowered, loosely aggregated at the branch tips. *Glumes* narrow, lanceolate, well-developed, unequal to nearly equal, spreading at maturity, the first glume 1-nerved and usually 4-7 mm long, the second 3-nerved and 5.5-7 mm long. *Lemmas* rounded on the back, narrowly acute or acuminate and somewhat beaked at apex, occasionally minutely awn-tipped; lowermost lemmas of spikelet 5-7 mm long. *Paleas* about as long as lemmas. *Chromosome number* not reported.

Distribution. Texas: Southeastern portion of region 7 in moist, partially shaded sites, infrequent. General: Arkansas, Oklahoma and Texas.

Flowering period: March to June.

6. **Festuca obtusa** Bieler, Pl. Nov. Herb. Spreng. Cent. 11. 1807. NODDING FESCUE. Fig. 50. Tufted perennial with slender culms mostly 50-100 mm tall; culms usually unbranched above base. *Sheaths* rounded on back, glabrous or sparsely hirsute, without auricles. *Ligules* 0.5-1 mm long. *Blades* flat, elongate, mostly 3-7 (-9) mm broad, tapering to a long, narrow tip, glabrous or sparsely pubescent on adaxial surface. *Panicles* 10-25 cm long, loose, open, relatively few-flowered, the lower branches long, flexuous, loosely erect or spreading. *Spikelets* mostly 5-8 mm long with 3-5 (-6) florets, widely spaced and not or only slightly imbricated on the upper one-half to one-third of the branches. *Glumes* well-developed, unequal to nearly equal, lanceolate, mostly 2-5 mm long, the first glume 1-nerved, the second 3-nerved. *Lemmas* rounded on back, lanceolate to narrowly oblong, acute to narrowly rounded at apex; *lowermost lemma* of spikelet 3.4-5 mm long. *Paleas* about as long as lemmas. *Chromosome number*, $2n=42$.

Distribution. Texas: Region 4 and northern portions of regions 1 and 3, in open forest and along woods borders, infrequent. General: Quebec and Manitoba, south to Florida and Texas.

Flowering period: April to June.

Fig. 50. *Festuca obtusa*. Inflorescence, glumes and floret of spikelet.

SUBFAMILY IV. POOIDEAE   105

7. **Festuca paradoxa** Desv., Opusc. 105. 1831. CLUSTER FESCUE.
Generally similar to *F. obtusa* but spikelets more clustered at branch tips and
lemmas often broader and more blunt at apex. *Chromosome number* not
reported.

Distribution. Texas: Northern portions of regions 1 and 3, in open forests
and along woods borders, infrequent. General: Pennsylvania and Wisconsin,
south to Georgia, Mississippi and Texas.

Flowering period: April to June.

Festuca paradoxa is close to and possibly not specifically distinct from the
more common and widely distributed *F. obtusa*.

23. LOLIUM L.

Annuals and short-lived perennials with usually succulent culms and
flat or folded blades. *Ligules* membranous. *Blades* often with thin, membranous auricles. *Inflorescence* a spike of several-flowered spikelets; spikelets solitary and oriented edgewise at the nodes of a continuous rachis.
Disarticulation above glume or glumes and between florets. *First glume*
absent except on terminal spikelet. *Second glume* usually large, broad,
several-nerved, awnless. *Lemmas* 5-9-nerved, rounded on back, awnless or
awned from a usually broad apex.

A group of a dozen or less species with natural distribution in the
temperate regions of Europe and Asia.

Glume shorter than spikelet; long-lived annual or short-lived perennial
1. *L. perenne*

Glume exceeding uppermost floret; short-lived annual 2. *L. temulentum*

1. **Lolium perenne** L., Sp. Pl. 83. 1753. RYEGRASS. Fig. 51.
Annual or short-lived perennial without rhizomes or stolons. *Culms* 25-70 cm
tall, glabrous, relatively thick and succulent when green. *Leaves* glabrous
or scabrous, dark green. *Sheaths* often with delicate, membranous auricles.
Upper margins of sheath thin, hyaline, merging at base of blade to
form a membranous ligule. *Blades* 2-10 mm broad, shrivelling and with
very little body when dry. *Spike* usually 10-20 cm long with 15-30 appressed
or somewhat spreading spikelets borne singly at the nodes. *Spikelets* mostly
5-12-flowered, oriented edgewise to the rachis, the first glume absent except
on terminal spikelet. *Glumes* mostly 5-10 mm long, one-third to two-
thirds as long as spikelet, with 3-7 strong nerves. *Lemmas* about as long
as glumes, with 5 nerves, these obscure except at margins and apex,
awnless and with a blunt, membranous tip or with an awn to 8 mm
long from a minutely notched tip. *Paleas* about as long as lemmas, scabrous
or short ciliate on nerves. *Chromosome number*, $2n=14$.

Fig. 51. *Lolium perenne*. Plant, inflorescences, spikelet and floret. From Hitchcock, 1935, as *L. multiflorum* in part.

Distribution. Texas: In all 10 regions but apparently absent from the southern portion of the South Texas Plains. Occasionally seeded in pastures and as a cool season lawn grass, Ryegrass is a common weed of roadsides, field borders and ditches throughout much of Texas. General: A European species, introduced into the United States as a pasture grass at an early date and now widespread throughout, especially in the northern states.

Flowering period: March to June.

Lolium perenne was the first pasture grass to be cultivated in Europe (Hitchcock, 1935). Closely related and probably not specifically distinct are populations referable to *L. multiflorum* Lam. As delimited by Chase in Hitchcock (1951), *L. multiflorum* differs from *L. perenne* in having taller and more robust culms, larger spikelets with more numerous florets and awned rather than awnless lemmas. Texas plants exhibit much variation in plant and spikelet size and may have awnless or awned lemmas. The grouping of these plants into more than one species does not appear justifiable, and even the recognition of two varieties is not satisfactory.

SUBFAMILY IV. POOIDEAE   107

2. **Lolium temulentum** L., Sp. Pl. 83. 1753. DARNEL. Annual with thick, weak culms mostly 30-70 cm tall. *Leaves* glabrous, typically with sheath auricles and a short, lacerate membranous ligule. *Blades* 2-8 mm broad. *Spike* 10-25 cm long, stiffly erect, the spikelets closely appressed to flattened and somewhat concave rachis internodes. *Rachis* thick, with internodes mostly 1-2 cm or more long. *Spikelets* laterally flattened and oriented edgewise to the rachis, mostly with 5-9 florets. *First glume* absent except on the terminal floret. *Second glume* 1.5- (1-) 2 cm long, broad, 5-13-nerved, acute or rounded at apex. *Lemmas* 4-7 mm long, smooth or scabrous, plump at maturity. *Chromosome number*, $2n = 14$.

Lemmas awned, the awns 5-15 mm long
2A. *L. temulentum* var. *temulentum*

Lemmas awnless
2B. *L. temulentum* var. *leptochaeton*

2A. **Lolium temulentum** L. var. **temulentum.**

Distribution. Texas: Regions 1, 2, 3, 4, 5, 7, 8 and 9, growing as a weed of roadsides, fields and waste places. General: A European species, adventive in the United States and now frequent in the eastern and western states and along the Gulf of Mexico.

Flowering period: March to May.

Darnel has been known as a poisonous weed of cultivated fields since the earliest historical periods. Like the classical cheat grass, *Bromus secalinus* L., it was thought to be a degenerate form of rye and other cereals. The poisonous properties of *Lolium temulentum* are now known to be due to the frequent presence in the grain of a fungus which produces a deadly poisonous alkaloid, temulin. Infected grains have been found in an Egyptian tomb believed to date from 2000 B.C.

2B. **Lolium temulentum** L. var. **leptochaeton** A. Br., Flora 1:252. 1834.

Distribution. Texas: Region 1. General: About the same distribution as the species in the United States but much less frequent.

Flowering period: March to May.

24. SCLEROCHLOA Beauv.

A monotypic European genus.

1. **Sclerochloa dura** (L.) Beauv., Ess. Agrost. 98, 174, 177. 1812. HARDGRASS. Low, tufted annual. *Culms* 4-10 (-18) cm long, freely branched at base. *Leaves* glabrous or minutely scabrous. *Sheaths* thin and rounded on back. *Ligule* a pointed membrane 1-2 mm long. *Blades* flat, blunt

at apex, mostly 2-7 cm long and 1-3 mm broad. *Inflorescence* a spicate raceme or contracted panicle 1-3 (-4.5) cm long, with spikelets subsessile and crowded on main inflorescence axis or some on short branches. *Spikelets* mostly 6-11 mm long, awnless, with 3-4 florets, the uppermost floret often reduced. *Glumes* unequal, broad, glabrous, with membranous margins, first glume usually 3-nerved, the second 5-7-nerved, obtuse or notched and apiculate. *Lemmas* 5-7-nerved, with narrow membranous margins, obtuse at apex, glabrous or minutely scabrous on midnerve. *Paleas* slightly shorter than lemmas. *Chromosome number,* $2n = 14$.

Distribution. Texas: Regions 4 and 7, infrequent as a weed of lawns, golf courses, ditches and other areas of disturbed, moist soil. General: Native to southern Europe, this inconspicuous, short-lived annual has been reported from widely scattered locations in the western United States and from New York state.

Flowering period: March to May.

25. CATAPODIUM Link

A genus of 2 annual species, these with natural distribution in western and southern Europe, northern Africa and western Asia.

1. **Catapodium rigidum** (L.) C.E. Hubb. *ex* Dony, Fl. Bedfordsh. 437. 1953. *Scleropoa rigida* (L.) Griseb. Fig. 52. Low, tufted annual with glabrous herbage and narrow, contracted panicles or spicate racemes. *Culms* 5-15 (-30) cm tall, branching below middle. *Sheaths* rounded on back, with thin membranous margins above that continue upward as lateral portions of ligule. *Ligule* a lacerate membrane 1.5-4 mm long. *Blades* flat, thin and soft, 1-3 (-4) mm broad and 2-8 (-12) cm long. *Inflorescence* typically 3-9 cm long and 5-15 mm thick but occasionally larger, with 5-9-flowered spikelets on short, stout pedicels. Disarticulation above glumes and between florets. *Spikelets* narrow, awnless, mostly 5-7 mm long. *Glumes* unequal, stiff, acute, the first 1-nerved, about 1 mm long, the second 3-nerved, about 2 mm long. *Florets* widely spaced on a zigzag rachilla; rachilla scabrous or rugose. *Lemmas* rounded on back, minutely rugose, obscurely 5-nerved, broadly acute and with hyaline margins at apex. *Paleas* about as long as lemmas, scabrous on nerves. *Chromosome number,* $2n = 14$.

Distribution. Texas: Regions 1, 2, 3, 4, 6 and 7, growing along roadsides, field borders, ditches and other disturbed sites. General: Adventive from Europe and now occasional at widely scattered locations throughout the United States.

Flowering period: March to May.

Catapodium rigidum has long gone under the name of *Scleropoa rigida* in this country. In general aspect it is similar to *Vulpia octoflora*, with which it commonly is associated.

Fig. 52. *Catapodium rigidum.* Plant and spikelet. From Gould, 1968.

26. POA L.

Low to moderately tall annuals and perennials, many with rhizomes. *Blades* flat or folded. *Ligule* membranous. *Inflorescence* an open or contracted panicle or occasionally reduced to a raceme. *Spikelets* relatively small, awnless, with 2-7 florets. Disarticulation above glumes and between florets. *Glumes* relatively broad, 1-3-nerved. *Lemmas* typically thin and broad, 5-nerved, keeled or rounded on back, with a membranous border, broadly acute or obtuse at apex. *Nerves of lemma* often puberulent and base of lemma often with long, kinky hairs. *Palea* glabrous, scabrous or ciliate.

About 250 species widespread in temperate and cold regions of the world, extending into the subtropics and tropics as montane grasses and as cool-season grasses at low altitudes.

Plants annual; lemmas pubescent on nerves

Panicle branches erect, the inflorescence narrow, contracted; sheaths scabrous   1. *P. bigelovii*

Panicle branches, at least the lowermost, spreading; sheaths glabrous

Lemmas with long, kinky hairs at base and with 3 strong nerves and 2 faint nerves   3. *P. chapmaniana*

Lemmas without long hairs at base and with 5 strong nerves
2. *P. annua*

Plants perennial; lemmas pubescent or glabrous on nerves

Culms swollen at base; florets often developing into bulblets with rudimentary leafy shoots 13. *P. bulbosa*

Culms not swollen at base; florets not developing into bulblets

Culms and basal sheaths strongly flattened; plants with rhizomes and a contracted panicle 11. *P. compressa*

Culms and basal sheaths terete or only slightly flattened; plants with or without rhizomes and with a contracted or open panicle

Spikelets, at least some, with few to many long, kinky hairs at base of lemmas or on rachilla just below lemmas

Plants with slender, well developed rhizomes

Plants dioecious; panicles narrow, densely-flowered
12. *P. arachnifera*

Plants not dioecious, the flowers perfect; panicles open, not dense 10. *P. pratensis*

Plants without rhizomes

Lower panicle branches widely spreading at maturity; eastern Texas 4. *P. sylvestris*

Lower panicle branches erect or somewhat spreading, not widely spreading at maturity; western Texas 5. *P. interior*

Spikelets without long, kinky hairs at base of lemmas or on rachilla just below lemmas

Spikelets unisexual, the pistillate flowers sometimes with minute, non-functional anthers; region 9 8. *P. fendleriana*

Spikelets with perfect flowers, the anthers 1-2 mm long

Lemmas glabrous on nerves; western Texas 7. *P. involuta*

Lemmas pubescent on either or both midnerve and lateral nerves

SUBFAMILY IV. POOIDEAE 111

Panicle branches spreading or reflexed, the lowermost bare
of spikelets for 3 cm or more; eastern Texas
6. *P. autumnalis*

Panicle branches erect, densely-flowered; western Texas
9. *P. arida*

1. **Poa bigelovii** Vasey and Scribn., in Vasey, Grasses U. S. Descr. Cat.
81. 1885. BIGELOW BLUEGRASS. Fig. 53. Tufted annual with culms
mostly 10-35 (-45) cm tall from an erect or geniculate base. *Leaves* glabrous.
Lowermost sheaths thin, membranous. *Ligules* 1.5-6 mm long, decurrent on
either side as membranous sheath margins. *Blades* thin, short, flat, mostly 2-5
mm broad. *Panicles* contracted, interrupted, 2-15 cm long, 0.5-1.5 cm thick,
the branches strictly erect or only slightly spreading. *Spikelets* broadly ovate,
mostly 4-5-flowered and 5-6 mm long. *Glumes* slightly unequal, glabrous, the
first glume 1-3-nerved, the second 3-nerved. *Lemmas* mostly 3-4 mm long,
5-nerved, intermediate nerves faint, densely pubescent with long, soft hairs
on midnerve and marginal nerves to near apex, usually also pubescent on
internerves near base, often with a tuft of long, kinky hairs at base.
Chromosome number not reported.

Distribution. Texas: Frequent at low to medium elevations in the mountains of region 10 and occasional in regions 8 and 9 and the northern portion of
region 7. General: Oklahoma, Colorado and Utah to Texas, southern California and northern Mexico.

Flowering period: February to April.

2. **Poa annua** L., Sp. Pl. 68. 1753. ANNUAL BLUEGRASS. Fig. 54.
Tufted annual with weak, usually geniculate culms mostly 6-30 cm long.
Leaves glabrous, bright green. *Ligules* 1.5-4 mm long, decurrent on either
side as membranous sheath margins. *Blades* thin, flat, mostly 1.5-4 mm broad
and 2-12 mm long. *Panicles* typically open, well exserted or hidden in the
basal tuft of leaves, mostly 3-8 cm long, the lower branches tending to be stiffly
spreading and bare of spikelets on lower one-third to one-half. *Glumes* thin,
broad, slightly unequal, the first glume 1-3-nerved, the second 3-nerved.
Lemmas broad, hyaline-margined, 3-3.5 mm long, all 5 nerves equally developed. *Lemmas* variously pubescent to nearly glabrous, the pubescence
commonly on the midnerve and marginal nerves but occasionally on the
intermediate nerves and marginal internerves. Basal tuft of long, kinky hairs
not developed. *Anthers* mostly 0.5-1 mm long. *Chromosome number*, $2n = 28$.

Distribution. Texas: Essentially throughout the State, mostly in lawns
and lawn borders. General: Introduced from Europe and now established as a
casual or weedy grass throughout North America, growing at high elevations
in tropical regions.

Flowering period: Mostly October or November to May. This usually is
the first cool-season grass to flower in the fall and winter.

Fig. 53. *Poa bigelovii*. Inflorescence and floret.

Fig. 54. *Poa annua*. Plant and spikelet. From Gould and Box, 1965.

SUBFAMILY IV. POOIDEAE 113

3. **Poa chapmaniana** Scribn., Bull. Torrey Bot. Club 21:38. 1894. CHAPMAN BLUEGRASS. Tufted annual similar to *Poa annua* but lemmas with long, kinky hairs at base and with 3 strong and 2 faint nerves and anthers 0.1-0.2 mm long.

Distribution. Texas: Reported from the eastern and north-central portions of the State (regions 1, 4 and 5) but no Texas collections seen by the author. General: Lawns, cultivated fields and roadsides of Massachusetts and New York to Nebraska, Florida and Texas.

Flowering period: Late fall to spring.

Populations referable to *P. chapmaniana* possibly are not specifically distinct from *P. annua*, and *P. chapmaniana* has been treated as a synonyn of *P. annua* by some authors.

4. **Poa sylvestris** A. Gray, Man. 596. 1848. WOODLAND BLUE-GRASS. Tufted perennial with culms 30-60 (-90) cm tall. *Sheaths* rounded, glabrous or the lower ones pubescent. *Ligules* mostly 2-3 mm long. *Blades* thin, flat, weak, 2-5 mm broad. *Panicles* open, 10-18 cm long; *panicle branches* widely spreading, loosely-flowered, 3.5-6 cm long, lower branches in verticils of 3-7, bare of spikelets on the lower one-half or two-thirds. *Spikelets* 2-4-flowered, laterally compressed, 3-4 mm long. *Lemmas* 2.5-3 mm long, thick nearly to margins and only moderately membranous at tip, with 5 nerves about equally developed; lemmas variously scabrous or pubescent, especially on marginal nerves, to nearly glabrous but with a tuft of long, kinky hairs at base. *Anthers* 1-1.5 mm long. *Chromosome number*, 2n=28.

Distribution. Texas: Region 1, infrequent. General: Moist, woodland sites from New York to Wisconsin and Nebraska, south to Florida and Texas.

Flowering period: Spring.

5. **Poa interior** Rydb., Bull. Torrey Bot. Club 32:604. 1905. INLAND BLUEGRASS. Tufted perennial with stiffly erect culms mostly 25-60 cm tall. *Ligules* 1-1.5 mm long. *Blades* thin, flat, weak, mostly 1-2 mm broad. *Panicles* usually narrow and rather dense, mostly 4-10 cm long, the branches short, stiff, scabrous, erect or erect-spreading, the basal node with 2 (rarely 3) branches. *Spikelets* mostly 3.5-5 mm long, 2-5-flowered, laterally flattened. *Lower lemmas* 2.5-3.5 mm long with inconspicuous lateral nerves, the mid-nerve and marginal nerves pubescent at least near base, a tuft of long, kinky hairs typically present at base but this lacking in some spikelets. *Anthers* 1-1.5 mm long. *Chromosome number*, 2n=28; aneuploid numbers also reported.

Distribution. Texas: Reported to occur in the western portion of the State (regions 9 or 10) but no Texas collections seen by the author. General: Southern Canada and northern United States, ranging southward in the Rocky Mountain area to Texas, New Mexico and Arizona.

Flowering period: Summer.

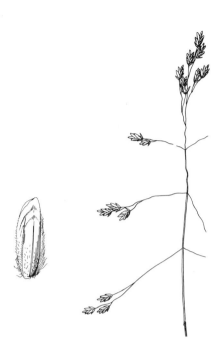

Fig. 55. *Poa autumnalis*. Inflorescence and floret. From Hitchcock, 1935.

6. **Poa autumnalis** Muhl. *ex* Ell., Bot. S.C. and Ga. 1:159. 1816.
AUTUMN BLUEGRASS. Fig. 55. Tufted perennial with slender, weak
culms mostly 30-70 cm tall. *Leaves* glabrous. *Ligules* 0.5-1 mm long. *Blades*
thin, flat, weak, 1-4.5 mm broad. *Panicles* mostly 8-18 cm long with slender,
usually paired branches mostly 4-8 cm long at the widely spaced lower nodes;
lower branches spikelet-bearing only near tips, often with only 1-3 spikelets;
panicle branches at first erect but usually spreading at maturity. *Spikelets* 5-7
mm long, 3-6-flowered. *First glume* usually about one-third as long as
spikelet, second glume about one-half as long as spikelet. *Lower lemmas*
mostly 3.5-4.5 mm long, with a broad, rounded, membranous apex and 5
well-defined nerves. *Lemmas* sparsely pubescent to nearly glabrous, often
hairy on midnerve and margins below middle, without a basal tuft of long,
kinky hairs. *Anthers* 1-1.5 mm long. *Chromosome number,* 2n=28.

Distribution. Texas: Region 1, mostly in pine or mixed pine-hardwood
forest, frequent in some areas. General: Throughout the eastern United
States, ranging westward to Michigan, Illinois, Arkansas and Texas.

Flowering period: March to May.

The common name, autumn bluegrass, is somewhat anomalous in view of
the fact that in Texas this species flowers only in the spring.

SUBFAMILY IV. POOIDEAE   115

7. **Poa involuta** Hitchc., Proc. Biol. Soc., Wash. 41:159. 1928. CHISOS BLUEGRASS. Fig. 56. Perennial with slender, weak culms 30-60 cm tall. *Leaves* scabrous. *Ligule* a pointed scale about 0.5 mm long. *Blades* firm, filiform, 1-2 mm broad and mostly 15-30 cm long (upper culm leaves shorter), involute or flat. *Panicles* 7-15 (-20) cm long with flexuous, loosely-spreading lower branches 3-8 cm long; lower branches usually bare of spikelets on lower half; lowermost node of panicle axis usually with 2-4 branches. *Spikelets* 4.5-6 mm long, 3-5-flowered. *Glumes* and *lemmas* glabrous or minutely scaberulous, with whitish, membranous margins and tips. *Lower lemmas* 2.5-3.5 mm long. *Anthers* about 1-2 mm long. *Chromosome number* not reported.

Distribution. Texas: Region 10, known only from rocky slopes in the Chisos Mountains at high elevations. General: Endemic to the Chisos Mountains.

Flowering Period: May to July.

Relationships of this species to *Poa albescens* Hitchc. (Contrib. U. S. Nat. Herb. 17(3):375. 1913.) should be checked.

8. **Poa fendleriana** (Steud.) Vasey, U.S.D.A. Div. Bot. Bull. 13(2):pl.74. 1893. MUTTON BLUEGRASS. Fig. 57. Tufted perennial, usually dioecious, occasionally with slender, creeping rhizomes. *Culms* 30-50 (15-80) cm tall. *Ligules* 1.5-3 mm long. *Blades* 1-4 mm broad, usually short, stiff and involute but not infrequently flat and basal blades occasionally 20-25 cm long. *Panicles* narrow, contracted, densely-flowered, 3-10 cm long, with short, erect or erect-spreading branches. Main panicle axis glabrous or scabrous. *Spikelets* 6-10 (rarely 5) mm long, 4-8-flowered, typically unisexual with staminate and pistillate spikelets similar but usually on separate plants and only rarely in the same inflorescence. *Glumes* broad, thin, glabrous or scabrous, with broad scarious margins, usually subequal and one-half to two-thirds as long as lowermost lemma. *Lemmas* mostly 4-5 mm long, thin, laterally compressed and keeled, with broad hyaline margins and rounded apex, glabrous or pubescent on midnerve and marginal nerves, the intermediate nerves evident but not pubescent; long, kinky hairs not developed at lemma base. *Palea* with greenish, ciliate nerves. *Flowers* typically unisexual but reported to be occasionally perfect. *Anthers* of male flowers about 2 mm long; rudimentary stamens less than 0.5 mm long present in some pistillate florets. *Chromosome number* not reported.

Distribution. Texas: Region 10 on rocky mountain slopes and canyons, infrequent. General: Manitoba and British Columbia, south through western South Dakota and Montana to Texas and southern California.

Flowering period: Late spring and summer.

Fig. 56. *Poa involuta*. Inflorescence and floret.

Fig. 57. *Poa fendleriana*. Plant, separate inflorescence, spikelet with glumes separated from florets and floret. From Gould, 1951.

SUBFAMILY IV. POOIDEAE   117

9. **Poa arida** Vasey, Contrib. U.S. Natl. Herb. 1:270. 1893. PLAINS
BLUEGRASS. Tufted perennial with culms 30-60 (20-80) cm tall and rhizomes to 15 cm long. *Leaves* glabrous, scabrous or puberulent at the sheath-
blade junction. *Ligule* a pointed membrane 2-4 (-6) mm long. *Blades* 1-3 mm
broad and mostly 3-12 cm long; the leaf of the single elevated culm node
usually with a blade 2-6 cm long. *Panicles* tightly or loosely contracted, 5-10
(-15) cm long, the lower branches floriferous to near base or bare of spikelets
on lower 2-4 cm; lowermost panicle node with usually 2-3 branches. *Spikelets*
4-8-flowered, the flowers perfect. *Glumes* unequal, the first usually 2.5-3.5
mm long, the second about as long as lower lemmas. *Lower lemmas* 3-4 mm
long with inconspicuous, equally developed lateral nerves, the midnerve and
lateral nerves pubescent below middle, the internerve region puberulent on
lower half or near base only. *Anthers* 1-2 mm long. *Chromosome number:*
Euploid and aneuploid numbers of $2n = 63, 64, 84$, ca. 90 and ca. 103 reported.

Distribution. Texas: Reported from the High Plains (region 9) but no
Texas specimens seen by the author. General: North Dakota and Montana to
New Mexico and Arizona.

Flowering period: Late spring and summer.

10. **Poa pratensis** L., Sp. Pl. 67. 1753. KENTUCKY BLUEGRASS. Fig.
58. Strongly rhizomatous perennial. *Culms* tufted, relatively slender and
wiry, 20-60 (-100) cm tall, mostly curving-erect from individual, prostrate and
rhizomatous bases. *Sheaths* glabrous or scabrous. *Ligules* 1-2 mm long. *Blades*
1-4 mm broad, firm, flat, usually short and dull green or glaucous. *Panicles*
mostly 5-8 (3-13) cm long and 3-5 cm broad, typically open, with slender,
flexuous branches, at least the lower ones spreading; panicle branches at
lowermost node of main axis mostly 4-6, bare of spikelets on lower one-half to
two-thirds. *Spikelets* 3-6 mm long, 3-6-flowered. *Glumes* broad, usually
strongly keeled, often scabrous on midnerve, slightly unequal in length.
Lemmas usually scabrous and pubescent on midnerve and pubescent on
margins, the intermediate nerves glabrous, the base with a tuft of long, silky
hairs. *Anthers* 1-2 mm long. *Chromosome number:* Euploid counts of $2n = 28$,
42, 56, 70 and 84 have been reported together with an extensive series of
aneuploid numbers from $2n = 21$ to 147.

Distribution. Texas: Occasional in the northern and western portions of
the State, reported from regions 1, 5, 9 and 10. In Texas, mostly occurring as a
weed of fields, gardens and other disturbed sites. General: Native to the Old
World and possibly to the northern, mountainous areas of North America;
various selections of lawn and pasture strains introduced into the United
States and present in all but the warmer areas of the country.

Flowering period: Mostly April to June.

11. **Poa compressa** L., Sp. Pl. 69. 1753. CANADA BLUEGRASS.
Rhizomatous perennial similar to *Poa pratensis* but culm bases and lower
sheaths strongly compressed laterally and sharply keeled, *panicle branches*
usually short and appressed or only slightly spreading and lemmas with or

Fig. 58. *Poa pratensis.* Plant, spikelet and floret. From Gould, 1951.

without a tuft of long, kinky hairs at base. *Chromosome numbers* reported, $2n=14$, 35, 42 and 56 and aneuploid counts from $2n=45$ to 50.

Distribution. Texas: Reported from regions 5, 6 and 9, seeded in various areas as a forage grass and probably not persisting outside of cultivation. General: Native to Europe, now widely introduced in the cooler portions of North America.

Flowering period: April to June.

12. **Poa arachnifera** Torr., in Marcy, Expl. Red Riv. 301. 1853. TEXAS BLUEGRASS. Fig. 59. Tufted dioecious perennial with long, slender rhizomes. *Culms* stiffly erect, 35-50 cm tall. *Leaves* glabrous. *Ligule* a short, pointed membrane, usually less than 0.5 mm long. *Blades* elongate, flat or less frequently involute, 1-4 (-5) mm broad. *Panicles* contracted, narrow, sometimes lobed, mostly 5-15 cm long, the lower branches 2-7 cm long, the lowermost culm node usually with 2-4 branches; branches floriferous to base or bare of spikelets on lower half. *Spikeles* with 3-6 (-10) florets, the pistillate spikelets densely woolly-pubescent with long kinky hairs attached at base of lemmas or on the rachilla joints immediately below lemmas. Staminate spikelets not conspicuously hairy but usually with a few long kinky hairs at base of floret. *Glumes* and *lemmas* broad, thin, papery, acute or acuminate. *Lemmas* of pistillate spikelets mostly 5-6 mm long; lemmas of staminate spikelets 3-5 mm long. *Anthers* 2-2.5 mm long. *Chromosome number*, $2n=84$; aneuploid numbers also reported.

Distribution. Texas: Regions 1, 2, 3, 4, 5, 7 and 8 in grasslands and woods borders. Also reported from region 10 but its occurrence in this area doubtful. General: Distribution reported by Chase in Hitchcock's Manual (1951) as ". . . southern Kansas to Texas and Arkansas; introduced eastward to North Carolina and Florida."

Flowering period: May to June.

13. **Poa bulbosa** L., Sp. Pl. 70. 1753. BULBOUS BLUEGRASS. Perennial with slender, weak culms mostly 25-60 cm tall from swollen, more or less bulbous bases. *Leaves* glabrous or puberulent. *Ligules* 1.5-3.5 mm long, decurrent downward as membranous sheath margins. *Blades* thin, weak, flat or folded, 0.5-3 mm broad. *Panicles* contracted, mostly 5-8 cm long. *Spikelets* glabrous, 3-6-flowered, usually proliferating early in their development to asexual bulbils with short, leafy, rudimentary shoot apices. Base of bulbils often purple-tinged. *Chromosome numbers* reported, $2n=14$, 28, 42 and 56 and aneuploid numbers from $2n=39$ to 58.

Distribution. Texas: Reported by Shinners (1958) to be spreading from cultivation at Denton (region 5). General: Native to Europe, introduced at many localities in the United States and generally persisting as a weed of roadsides, vacant lots and other areas of moist, disturbed soil.

Flowering period: Spring.

Fig. 59. *Poa arachnifera.* Panicle of pistillate spikelets, pistillate spikelet and floret (lower), staminate spikelet and floret (upper).

SUBFAMILY IV. POOIDEAE   121

27. BRIZA L.

Annuals and perennials, Texas species annual, with usually open panicles of several-flowered, awnless spikelets. *Ligules* membranous. Florets crowded and widely spreading from the rachilla. Disarticulation above glumes and between florets. *Glumes* subequal, broad, thin and papery, rounded on back, 3-9-nerved, spreading at right angles to rachilla. *Lemmas* similar to glumes, broader than long, broadly rounded at apex. *Paleas* short, rounded, with widely spaced nerves.

About 20 species, three native to Europe, one in Mexico and Central America and the remainder in South America.

Spikelets 2-6 mm long	1. *B. minor*
Spikelets mostly 12-25 mm long	2. *B. maxima*

1. **Briza minor** L., Sp. Pl. 70. 1753. LITTLE QUAKINGGRASS. Fig. 60. Delicate, short-lived annual with culms single or in small clumps, mostly 15-50 cm tall. *Herbage* glabrous or essentially so. *Ligule* 5-10 mm long, broadly pointed and with an inverted v-shaped area of attachment, continuing downward inside margins of the upper portion of sheath to become the sheath margins well below the apex. *Blades* thin, flat, mostly 2-8 mm broad and 4-18 cm long, merging rather imperceptibly into sheath on abaxial surface. *Panicles* 3-15 cm long, typically much-branched and open, the broad spikelets on long, capillary, spreading, usually kinked pedicels. *Spikelets* 2-6 mm long and about as broad, 3-12-flowered, glabrous, awnless. *Glumes* longer than the successively shorter lemmas, the spikelet somewhat pyramidal. *Lemmas* indistinctly nerved, with a firm, shiny, more or less pustulate or rugose central portion and broad, thin margins. *Caryopses* light brown, orbicular, flattened on one side, mostly 0.6-0.8 mm long. *Chromosome number*, $2n = 10$ ($2n = 14$ also reported for Texas plants but this count needs verification).

Distribution. Texas: Regions 1, 2 and 3 in moist woodland clearings and along semi-disturbed soils of roadsides and ditchbanks. General: Native to Europe, well established in the southeastern states and frequent in Oregon and California.

Flowering period: Mostly April and May.

2. **Briza maxima** L., Sp. Pl. 70. 1753. BIG QUAKINGGRASS. Annual with culms erect or decumbent at base, mostly 30-60 cm tall. *Herbage* glabrous or the blades minutely scabrous. *Ligule* of uppermost leaf usually 10 mm or more long. *Blades* flat, 2-8 mm broad and 5-15 (-20) cm long. *Panicle* few-flowered, often with only 1-6 spikelets but occasionally with a dozen or more. *Spikelets* 12-25 mm long and 8-12 mm broad, on long, slender, drooping pedicels. *Glumes* and often the lemmas with purple

Fig. 60. *Briza minor*. Inflorescence. From Gould, 1968.

or brown margins. *Lemmas* with 5-7 greenish nerves, usually hirsute over back and margins. *Chromosome number,* $2n=14$.

Distribution. Texas: Reported by Chase in Hitchcock's Manual (1951) as occurring in Texas but undoubtedly not persisting in the State; not listed by Correll and Johnston (1970) for Texas. General: A European species introduced into the United States as a garden ornamental and established as a casual weed in a few localities.

Flowering period: April and May.

28. DACTYLIS L.

A genus of about 5 species indigenous to temperate and cold regions of Europe and Asia.

1. **Dactylis glomerata** L., Sp. Pl. 71. 1753. ORCHARD GRASS. Fig. 61. Erect perennial with densely clumped culms and well exserted panicles. *Culms* glabrous, slender, 50-100 cm tall. *Sheaths* glabrous or essentially so, often keeled and laterally compressed. *Ligule* a membrane 2-5 mm long. *Blades* elongate, 2-8 mm broad, flat or folded, glabrous, scabrous or minutely hirsute on adaxial surface. *Panicles* 3-20 cm long, with or without elongated lower branches, the spikelets clustered on short pedicels at apex of main axis and on upper portion of branches. *Lower branches* often 6-10 cm or more long, bare of spikelets on lower half. *Spikelets* mostly 2-5-flowered, disarticulating above glumes and between florets. *Glumes* unequal to nearly equal, keeled, 1-3-nerved, glabrous or hispid-scabrous on midnerve, acute to acuminate or short-awned. *Lemmas* mostly 5-8 mm long, 5-nerved, usually keeled, hispid-scabrous on midnerve, acute, acuminate or short-awned at apex. *Paleas* slightly shorter than lemmas, scabrous-ciliate on nerves. *Chromosome number*, $2n=28$.

Distribution. Texas: Region 9; in Texas, an infrequent, adventive weed, growing mostly in ditches and on field borders. General: Native to the cooler parts of Europe and Asia, introduced as a forage grass in the central and northern United States and now common or occasional almost throughout the country.

Flowering period: April to July.

Tribe 10. Aveneae

29. KOELERIA Pers.

Annuals and perennials with narrow blades and shining, contracted panicles of 2-6-flowered, flattened spikelets. *Ligules* membranous. *Rachilla* disarticulating above glumes and between florets, extending as a bristle above uppermost floret. *Glumes* large, thin, acute, nearly equal in length, the first glume 1-nerved, the second indistinctly 3-5-nerved. *Lemmas* thin, shining, the lowermost usually slightly longer than the glumes, awnless or awned from a minutely bifid apex. *Paleas* large, scarious and colorless.

About 50 species, in the temperate regions of both hemispheres.

Plants perennial; spikelets scaberulous; on grassy uplands
1.   *K. pyramidata*

Plants annual; spikelets minutely pubescent; coastal region 2.   *K. gerardii*

Fig. 61. *Dactylis glomerata*. Plant, spikelet and floret. From Hitchcock, 1935.

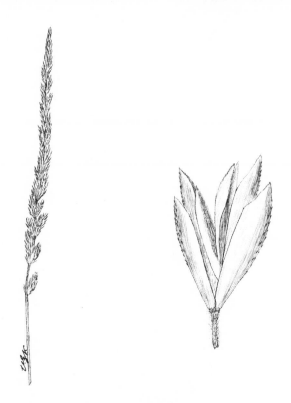

Fig. 62. *Koeleria pyramidata.* Inflorescence and spikelet.

1. **Koeleria pyramidata** (Lam.) Beauv., Ess. Agrost. pp. 84, 166 and 175. 1812. *Koeleria cristata* Pers. JUNEGRASS. Fig. 62. Tufted perennial. *Culms* 25-70 cm tall, usually minutely puberulent on inflorescence axis and in vicinity of nodes. *Leaves* mostly basal. *Sheaths* rounded on back or somewhat keeled, the lowermost hispid. *Ligules* 0.5-1 (-2) mm long. *Blades* elongate, 1-4 mm broad, flat, irregularly folded or involute, glabrous or sparsely hispid on adaxial surface to strongly hispid on both surfaces. *Panicles* contracted, 5-15 cm long, with short, erect, densely-flowered branches. *Main panicle axis and branches* puberulent. *Spikelets* 4-5 mm long. *Glumes* large, scabrous on midnerve and scaberulous on back, slightly unequal, the second glume obovate, about equaling lowermost lemma. *Lemmas* scabrous on midnerve, scaberulous or smooth and shiny on back, acute or minutely apiculate at apex. *Paleas* hyaline, translucent and shiny, as large as lemmas. *Chromosome numbers* reported, mostly $2n = 14$ and 28.

Distribution. Texas: Regions 7, 8, 9 and 10, occasional in grasslands of the High Plains and on rocky slopes of the mountainous or broken country, often in partial shade. General: Widespread in temperate regions of the Northern Hemisphere; almost throughout the United States except in the southeastern states.

Flowering period: Mostly May to July, occasionally as late as September.

2. **Koeleria gerardii** (Vill.) Shinners, Rhodora 58:95. 1956. *Koeleria phleoides* (Vill.) Pers. ANNUAL KOELERIA. Tufted annual with culms 10-30 (5-40) cm tall. *Culms* glabrous to sparsely hirsute, the hairs mostly in vicinity of nodes. *Leaves* nearly glabrous to sparsely or densely hispid on sheath and both blade surfaces. *Ligules* lacerate, about 1 mm long. *Blades* thin, soft, flat, 1-5 mm broad, mostly 2-15 cm long. *Panicle* dense, uninterrupted, mostly 2-7 cm long and 5-10 mm thick, with central axis and branches glabrous or nearly so. *Spikelets* 4-6-flowered, 4-5 mm long. *Glumes* and *lemmas* papillose or papillose-hispid on back, hyaline and shiny on margins, the second glume and lemmas 2.5-3 mm long, the lemmas with an awn to 2 mm long from a minutely bifid apex. *Paleas* narrow, hyaline, the 2 nerves awn-tipped. *Anthers* 5-8 mm long. *Chromosome number,* $2n = 26$.

Distribution. Texas: Region 2, reported by Correll and Johnston (1970) as a "rare waif in coastal areas near Galveston;" Chase in Hitchcock's Manual (1951) indicates a record from Cameron Country. General: Native to Europe. Adventive at a few coastal localities in the United States.

Flowering period: Spring.

30. SPHENOPHOLIS Scribn.

Low, tufted annuals or short-lived perennials with membranous ligules, flat or involute blades and elongate, mostly densely-flowered panicles. *Spikelets* with 2- (rarely 1-) 3 florets, disarticulating below glumes. *Rachilla* prolonged beyond terminal floret as a slender bristle. *Glumes* dissimilar in size and shape, first glume usually narrow, acute, 1- (rarely 3-) nerved, second glume wider and longer, obovate, 3- or occasionally 5-nerved. *Lemmas* firm, smooth or scabrous, rounded on back, faintly 5-nerved, the nerves sometimes not apparent, obtuse, acute or short-awned. *Paleas* hyaline, shorter than lemmas, narrowed towards base, slightly scabrous on nerves and slightly 2-toothed at apex. *Caryopses* round or slightly compressed in transverse section, oblong, abruptly narrowed to a short beak at apex. *Endosperm* liquid to semi-solid in consistency.

As treated by Erdman (1965), a North American genus of 5 species. The morphological descriptions and key are modified from those of Erdman.

First glume less than one-third the width of second glume; lemma of second floret smooth to scaberulous; inflorescence loose to dense

Lower leaf blades usually less than 10 cm long, 2-8 mm wide

1. *S. obtusata*

Lower leaf blades to 45 cm long, 1-2 mm wide   2. *S. filiformis*

First glume one-third to two-thirds the width of second glume; lemma of second floret strongly scabrous; inflorescence loose   3. *S. nitida*

1. **Sphenopholis obtusata** (Michx.) Scribn. Rhodora 8:144. 1906. Tufted annual (in Texas) with culms 20-70 (-120) cm tall. *Sheaths* and *blades* glabrous, scabrous or pubescent with spreading hairs, the sheaths rounded on back. *Ligules* 1.5-3 mm long, glabrous or ciliate. Blades flat, soft, mostly 2-8 mm broad and 4-10(-15) cm long. *Panicles* usually contracted and densely-flowered but sometimes open, mostly 5-25 cm long. *Pedicels* shorter than spikelets. *Spikelets* 1.5-5 mm long, 2-3-flowered. *Glumes* glabrous or scaberulous on nerves, first glume acute, 1-4 mm long, 0.1-0.3 (-0.4) mm broad, second glume 1.2-4.2 mm long, conspicuously obovate, 0.5-1 mm broad, with a rounded or acute apex. *Lemmas* acute to obtuse, mostly 1.4-4.4 mm long, glabrous to scaberulous. *Chromosome number*, $2n=14$.

Apex of second glume rounded; panicle dense, spikelike; second glume
    one-third to one-half as broad as it is long
                          1A. *S. obtusata* var. *obtusata*

Apex of second glume rounded to acute; panicle loose; second glume
    less than one-third as broad as it is long
                          1B. *S. obtusata* var. *major*

1A. **Sphenopholis obtusata** (Michx.) Scribn. var. **obtusata**. PRAIRIE WEDGESCALE. Fig. 63.

Distribution. Texas: Throughout the State except in the South Texas Plains (region 6) and the southern portion of region 2, growing mainly in moist prairies, along open streambanks and in swales. General: Throughout the United States; in southern Canada, Bermuda and the Caribbean; and occasional in Mexico, south to Puebla.

Flowering period: Mostly April and May.

Several chromosome counts of $2n=14$ have been reported for *Sphenopholis obtusata* with varieties unspecified.

1B. **Sphenopholis obtusata** (Michx.) Scribn. var **major** (Torr.) Erdman, Iowa State Coll. J. Sci. 39 (3):310. 1965. *Sphenopholis intermedia* (Rydb.) Rydb. *Sphenopholis longiflora* (Vasey) Hitchc.

Distribution. Texas: Regions 1, 2, 3 and 7, mostly in open woodlands but occasionally in prairies. General: From the Hudson Bay area, Alaska and northern British Colombia, south to Florida, Texas and Arizona; in the United States, infrequent west of the Rocky Mountains and absent from the Pacific Coast region.

Flowering period: Mostly April and May.

Fig. 63. *Sphenopholis obtusata* var. *obtusata*. Plant and spikelet. From Gould and Box, 1965.

SUBFAMILY IV. POOIDEAE   129

2. **Sphenopholis filiformis** (Chapm.) Scribn. Rhodora 8:144. 1906. LONGLEAF WEDGESCALE. Tufted perennial (often appearing annual) with culms 35-75 (20-100) cm tall; lower portion of culms, sheaths and blades often puberulent. *Lower leaves* with sheaths 1-3 cm long and blades to 45 cm long, blades 1-2 mm broad, involute. *Upper leaves* with longer sheaths and much shorter blades. *Panicle* narrow, with relatively few branches, these loosely ascending. *Spikelets* 2-3-flowered, mostly 3-4 mm long. *Glumes* spreading at maturity, broadly rounded or truncate at apex, occasionally scabrous on keel near apex, the first glume narrow, 1.1-2.5 mm long, the second much wider, 1.5-3.5 mm long. *Lemmas* glabrous or scabrous towards apex, rounded on back, the lowermost one 1.8-3.2 mm long, acute or minutely awned, the second shorter, awnless or occasionally awned, the third reduced and neuter when present. *Chromosome number, $2n = 14$.*

Distribution. Texas: Region 1 along woods borders and openings, road and railroad right-of-ways and moist meadows. General: Southeastern United States from southern Virginia and Tennessee to Florida and Texas.

Flowering period: March to May.

3. **Sphenopholis nitida** (Biehler) Scribn., in Fernald, Rhodora 47:198. 1945. SHINY WEDGESCALE. Tufted perennial (or annual ?) with slender culms mostly 30-70 cm tall. Culms, sheaths and blades usually pubescent but occasionally glabrous. *Leaves* clustered at base of plant or scattered on lower half of culm. Blades flat, 2-4 mm broad. *Panicles* open, few-flowered, mostly 9-20 cm long and 1-5 cm broad, with flexuous pedicels mostly 0.5-2 mm long. *Spikelets* mostly 2.5-4 mm long, 2-3-flowered, the florets spreading at maturity. *Glumes* smooth and thin, about equal in length, 1.5-3.5 mm long, the first one-third to two-thirds as wide as the second. *Lemmas* firm, rounded on back, minutely roughened or papillate, the first 2.6-3.3 mm long. Second lemma often with minute, appressed hairs on the papillae near apex. *Chromosome number, $2n = 14$.*

Distribution. Texas: Region 1, occasional in dense forest and in woods openings; the distribution map of Erdman (1965) also indicates a collection from the Edwards Plateau (region 7). General: Throughout the eastern United States from Connecticut, Michigan and Illinois south to Florida and Texas; apparently not present in the immediate coastal area of the Gulf of Mexico.

Flowering period: Mostly April and May.

31. TRISETUM Pers.

About 75 species, mostly in the temperate and cold regions of both hemispheres.

1. **Trisetum interruptum** Buckl., Proc. Acad. Nat. Sci. Philadelphia Monogr. 1862:100. 1862. PRAIRIE TRISETUM. Fig. 64. Tufted annual

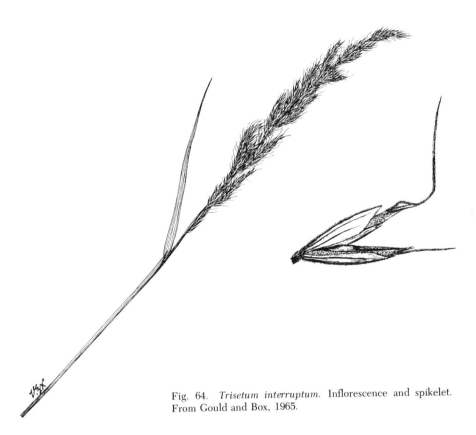

Fig. 64. *Trisetum interruptum.* Inflorescence and spikelet. From Gould and Box, 1965.

with weak, erect or geniculate-spreading culms 10-50 (-60) cm tall. *Culms* glabrous or minutely puberulent, especially just below nodes. *Sheaths* rounded, hispid with short, spreading or reflexed hairs, sometimes densely so. *Ligule* a rounded or lacerate, ciliate membrane 1.5-2 mm long. *Blades* thin, flat, mostly 1-4 mm broad and 2-10 (-15) cm long, nearly glabrous to densely hispid. *Panicle* narrow, contracted, 5-10 (2-15) cm long and 4-15 mm thick; main axis and branches of panicle glabrous or nearly so. *Spikelets* 4-6 mm long excluding the awns, 2-3-flowered, upper floret often reduced and sterile; disarticulation both between florets and below glumes. *Glumes* subequal but the second broader, about as long as lemmas, glabrous or scabrous, obovate, the first glume 3-nerved, the second 3-5-nerved. *Lemmas* glabrous, rounded on back, minutely rugose, obscurely nerved, 3.5-5 mm long excluding the awn but including the setaceous apical teeth. *Lemma awns* mostly 5-8 mm long, loosely twisted and twice-geniculate at maturity. *Paleas* hyaline, colorless, variable in length but usually two-thirds as long as lemma. *Chromosome number* not reported.

Distribution. Texas: Occasional throughout the State except in the extreme eastern and southern regions. General: Colorado, Texas, New Mexico and Arizona.

Flowering period: Late March to May.

SUBFAMILY IV. POOIDEAE   131

32. AIRA L.

A genus of about 10 species native to southern Europe but now widely distributed in the world.

1. **Aira elegans** Willd. *ex* Gaudin, Agrost. Helv. 1:130, 355. 1811. *Aira capillaris* Host. not Savi. ANNUAL HAIRGRASS. Fig. 65. Delicate, tufted annual with slender, erect culms mostly 10-35 cm long and thin, filiform, mostly basal leaves. *Culms* glabrous or minutely scabrous below nodes. *Sheaths* thin, scabrous. *Ligule* a whitish membrane 1.5-4 mm long, appearing as a continuation of sheath margins. *Blades* flat or involute, mostly 0.5 mm or less broad and 1-8 cm long. *Inflorescence* a delicate open panicle 4-12 cm long and about two-thirds as wide as it is long, spikelets borne at and near the tips of capillary branchlets and pedicels, the main branches bare of spikelets below middle. *Spikelets* 2-flowered, about 2 mm long excluding the awn. Disarticulation above glumes and between florets. *Rachilla* not extended beyond insertion of upper floret. *Glumes* about equal, longer than lemmas, thin, lanceolate, 1- or obscurely 3-nerved. *Lemmas* firm, brownish, rounded and minutely papillose-scabrous on back; lemma of lower floret awnless, lemma of upper floret with a delicate, short, usually geniculate awn from near middle of back, the awn about 2 mm long. *Palea* about as long as lemma, tightly clasped by the inrolled lemma margins. *Chromosome number*, $2n=14$.

Distribution. Texas: Regions 1 and 3, infrequent, in sterile, sandy woods openings. General: In the southeastern states from Maryland to Florida and Texas and in Washington and Oregon; native to Europe, adventive in the United States.

Flowering period: Mostly April to June.

33. AVENA L.

A genus of 15-20 species native to temperate Europe but widely cultivated elsewhere.

1. **Avena fatua** L., Sp. Pl. 80. 1753. Annual with thick, succulent culms and broad, flat blades. *Culms* glabrous, mostly 30-120 cm tall. *Sheaths* glabrous or hispid with spreading hairs. *Ligule* a whitish membrane mostly 2-4 mm long, appearing as the continuation of the membranous sheath margins. *Blades* flat, elongate, mostly 5-12 mm broad, glabrous or ciliate on lower margins, occasionally sparsely hispid. *Inflorescence* a loose panicle or raceme of usually 8-30 large, awned spikelets on slender, curved or kinked pedicels. *Spikelets* with 2-4 florets; when florets more than 2, the uppermost usually reduced and sterile. Disarticulation above glumes and between florets. *Glumes* large, broad, glabrous, acute to acuminate, with broad hyaline margins and tip, 7-9-nerved, the nerves not extending to the margins or tip. *Lemmas* firm or hard, rounded on back, the lowermost lemma usually 1.5-2 cm long. *Paleas* thin, slightly shorter than lemmas with widely-spaced, ciliate nerves. *Chromosome number*, $2n=42$.

Fig. 65. *Aira elegans.* Plant and spikelet. From Gould, 1968.

Lemmas with stiff, usually reddish-brown hairs on dorsal surface; spikelets usually 3-4-flowered; awn of lemma geniculate, mostly 2.5-4 cm long
1A.   A. *fatua* var. *fatua*

Lemmas glabrous; spikelets usually 2-flowered; awn of lemma not geniculate, irregularly developed or absent   1B.   A. *fatua* var. *sativa*

SUBFAMILY IV. POOIDEAE   133

Fig. 66. *Avena fatua.* Inflorescence of var. *fatua* (A) and spikelet of var. *sativa* (B).

1A. **Avena fatua** L. var. **fatua.** WILD OAT. Fig. 66A.

Distribution. Texas: Regions 2, 3, 7, 8 and 9, infrequent as a weed of roadsides and other areas of moist, disturbed soil. General: A European grass now present almost throughout the United States except in the southeastern states. It is especially abundant in coastal areas of California.

Flowering period: Mostly April and May.

1B. **Avena fatua** L. var. **sativa** (L.) Hausskn., Mitt. Geogr. Ges. Thuringen 3:238. 1885. *Avena sativa* L. COMMON OAT. Fig. 66B.

Distribution. Texas: Throughout the State, occasional as a cool-season weed of roadsides, field borders, vacant lots and ditchbanks. General: Introduced from Europe as a cultivated crop plant, now common as a cultivated plant and casual weed throughout the United States except in the southeastern states.

Flowering period: Mostly March to June but occasional during the winter months.

34. HOLCUS L.

About 8 species native to Europe and Africa; two species adventive in the United States.

1. **Holcus lanatus** L., Sp. Pl. 1048. 1753. Perennial (annual in Texas?) with thick, weak, puberulent culms mostly 25-100 cm tall. *Sheaths* rounded on back, puberulent or pubescent with spreading hairs, occasionally the lower ones closed at base or up to middle. *Ligule* a lacerate, ciliate membrane 1.5-3 mm long, appearing as the continuation of sheath margins. *Blades* soft, flat, elongate, mostly 5-10 mm broad, typically sparsely hispid or hirsute on both surfaces. *Inflorescence* irregularly contracted, densely-flowered, 4-15 cm long and 1.5-5 cm broad, with main axis and branches hispid. *Spikelets* 2-flowered, 4-6 mm long. Disarticulation below glumes. *Glumes* subequal, ciliate on midnerve and often scabrous-hispid on back, first glume 1-nerved, 3-4.5 mm long, the second much broader, 3-nerved. *Lower floret* about 2 mm long, perfect, with firm, smooth, shiny, awnless lemmas and paleas. *Upper floret* usually staminate, about as long as lower floret but more slender, the lemma with a short, stout, hooked, yellowish awn exserted from back near apex. *Chromosome number*, $2n = 14$.

Distribution. Texas: Listed in the Texas plant checklist (Gould, 1969) for regions 1 and 2 but no voucher specimens located. General: Adventive from Europe and widespread in the United States; Chase in Hitchcock's Manual (1951) indicates distribution along both coasts and in all southern states except Florida, Oklahoma, Texas and New Mexico.

Flowering period: May to June.

35. LIMNODEA L. H. Dewey

A monotypic North American genus.

1. **Limnodea arkansana** (Nutt.) L. H. Dewey, Contrib. U.S. Natl. Herb. 2:518. 1894. OZARKGRASS. Fig. 67. Short-lived annual with weak culms, thin, flat blades and a contracted panicle of 1-flowered spikelets. *Culms* in small clumps, mostly 20-60 cm tall. *Sheaths* rounded on back, often hispid. *Ligule* a lacerate membrane 1-2 mm long. *Blades* glabrous or more commonly hispidulous or hispid on both surfaces, 2-8 mm broad 3-12 cm long. *Panicles* narrow, contracted, 5-20 cm long, with few to several short branches; branches mostly floriferous to the base or nearly so. *Spikelets* 3.5-4 mm long excluding the awn. Disarticulating below glumes. *Glumes* equal, as long as spikelet, firm, obscurely 3-5-nerved, rounded and minutely rugose on back, usually hispid but becoming glabrous or scabrous, acute and awnless at apex. *Lemmas* about as long as glumes but thinner, glabrous and minutely rugose with a twisted and geniculate awn just below the acute or minutely bifid apex. *Lemma awn* mostly 8-11 mm long. *Paleas* hyaline, narrow, shorter than lemmas, nerved only at base. *Chromosome number*, $2n = 14$.

Fig. 67. *Limnodea arkansana.* Inflorescence and spikelet. From Gould and Box, 1965.

Distribution. Texas: Throughout the State, except in regions 9 and 10, a common grass of open woodlands, streambanks and ditchbanks and brushy grasslands. General: Arkansas and Oklahoma to Florida, Texas and northeastern Mexico.

Flowering period: Mostly late March to early June.

36. AGROSTIS L.

Annuals and perennials, several with rhizomes. *Ligule* membranous. *Blades* flat or involute. *Inflorescence* an open or contracted panicle. *Spikelets* small, one-flowered, disarticulating above glumes (except in *A. semiverticillata*). *Glumes* thin, lanceolate, acute to acuminate, nearly equal; first glume usually 1-nerved, the second 1-3 nerved. *Lemmas* thin, broad, 3- or 5-nerved, acute to obtuse or truncate at apex, awnless or awned from middle or below. *Paleas* present or absent.

136   THE GRASSES OF TEXAS

A genus of about 125 species mostly in temperate and cold regions of the world. A few species grow as cool-climate grasses of the subtropics and at high elevations in the mountains of the tropics.

Lemmas awnless or with an awn less than 3 mm long

Paleas present, 1 mm or more long; plants usually with rhizomes or stolons

Panicle branches not in dense verticils, the panicle contracted or open; glumes, at least some, more than 2 mm long

Panicles usually open and loose; loosely tufted perennial with stout, creeping rhizomes   1. *A. gigantea*

Panicles narrow, usually contracted except at anthesis; mat-forming perennial with extensive creeping stolons
2. *A. stolonifera* var. *palustris*

Panicle branches in dense verticils, the panicle contracted and densely-flowered; glumes 2 mm or less long
3. *A. semiverticillata*

Paleas absent or a nerveless scale 0.5 mm or less long; plants without rhizomes or stolons

Panicle tightly or loosely contracted, the branches short, erect-spreading or appressed, bearing spikelets to or nearly to base
4. *A. exarata*

Panicle open at maturity, at least some branches spreading or reflexed, without spikelets on lower portion

Spikelets 1.5-2.1 mm long

Plants weakly perennial; primary panicle branches rebranched 3.5-10 cm from base   5. *A. hiemalis*

Plants annual; primary panicle branches all rebranched 3 cm or less from base   8. *A. elliottiana*

Spikelets, at least some, 2.2-3.2 mm long

Panicle with long, slender branches rebranching only towards the tips, the spikelets clustered at the tips; mountains of western Texas, occasional as an introduction elsewhere
6. *A. scabra*

Panicle with primary branches rebranched below middle; eastern
Texas   7. *A. perennans*

Lemmas with awns 3-8 mm long

Spikelets 1.2-2.2 mm long; paleas absent or a nerveless scale
0.5 mm or less long; annual   8. *A. elliottiana*

Spikelets 3-4 mm long; paleas at least 0.8 mm long; perennial
9. *A. avenacea*

1. **Agrostis gigantea** Roth, Tent. Germ. 1:31. 1788. *Agrostis alba* of
authors, not L. REDTOP. Fig. 68. Loosely tufted perennial with extensive,
tough, creeping rhizomes. *Culms* stout, 40-120 (-150) cm tall, erect or ascending from a curved base. *Herbage* glabrous. *Sheaths* rounded on back. *Ligules*
1.5-6 mm long, usually erose at apex. *Blades* flat, firm, often scabrous, mostly
5-20 cm long and 2-8 mm broad. *Panicles* open but often rather closely-
flowered, 8-25 cm long, 4-10 (3-15) cm broad. *Panicle branches* spreading at
maturity, mostly in verticils of 3-8, the longer ones bare of spikelets on the
lower one-third to one-half but usually some branches of the lower verticil
short and spikelet-bearing to or near base. *Spikelets* 2-3 mm long, awnless.
Glumes broad, 1-nerved, slightly unequal, acute or acuminate, scabrous on
nerve near tip. *Lemmas* two-thirds to three-fourths as long as glumes, thin,
ovate to oblong, 3-5-nerved, minutely hairy at base. *Paleas* about two-thirds as
long as lemmas. *Anthers* 1-1.5 mm long. *Chromosome number, 2n=42.*

Distribution. Texas: Reported from regions 8 and 10, introduced as a
tame pasture grass and probably not persisting. General: Native to temperate
regions of Europe and Asia, introduced at numerous localities in the United
States.

Flowering period: Late spring and early summer.

2. **Agrostis stolonifera** L., Sp. Pl. 62. 1753. Mat- or turf-forming perennial, often with rhizomes but spreading by leafy stolons. *Culms* typically 8-40
cm tall from a curved or decumbent, stoloniferous base. *Leaves* glabrous or
scabrous. *Sheaths* rounded on back. *Ligules* 1-6 mm long. *Blades* flat, 1-5 mm
broad, seldom over 10 cm long. *Panicles* contracted, densely-flowered, linear
to lanceolate or oblong, often lobed, 2-15 cm long, 0.5-2.5 cm broad, open at
anthesis but then contracted and dense, at least above. *Spikelets* as in *A.*
gigantea. Chromosome numbers reported, 2n=28 and 42.

Agrostis stolonifera apparently is represented in Texas only by CREEP-
ING BENTGRASS, var. *palustris* (Huds.) Farw. (Rep. Mich. Acad. Sci.
21:351. 1920). This is given species status (*A. palustris* Huds.) by Correll and
Johnston (1970).

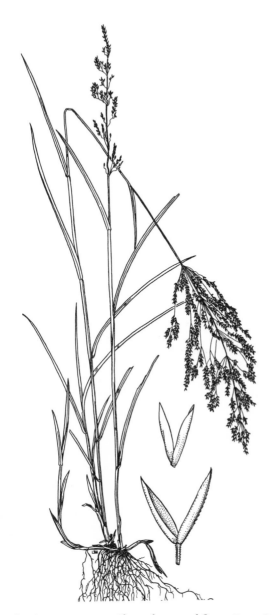

Fig. 68. *Agrostis gigantea*. Plant, glumes and floret. From Gould, 1951, as *A. alba*.

Distribution. Texas: Creeping bentgrass has been reported from the upper Gulf Coast (region 2) where it possibly has been introduced in forage grass trials. It grows in moist lowlands. General: Throughout Europe and temperate Asia, introduced in North America.

Flowering period: Late spring.

SUBFAMILY IV. POOIDEAE   139

3. **Agrostis semiverticillata** (Forsk.) Christ., Dansk. Bot. Arkiv. 4:12. 1922. WATER BENTGRASS. Tufted perennial. *Culms* succulent, decumbent and geniculate below, often stoloniferous and rooting at lower nodes, mostly 10-50 (-70) cm long. *Leaves* glabrous or the lower ones puberulent. *Ligules* 2-7 mm long. *Blades* thin, flat, 2-8 mm broad, usually short but elongate on vigorous plants. *Panicles* densely-flowered, contracted and lobed, 4-12 cm long and 1-3 cm thick. *Panicle branches* mostly verticiled, erect or erect-spreading, spikelet-bearing to the base, mostly 0.5-3 cm long. *Spikelets* 1.3-2 (-2.5) mm long, awnless, disarticulating below glumes. *Glumes* equal, as long as spikelet, scabrous, 1-nerved, narrowly acute. *Lemmas* 0.9-1.5 mm long, thin, hyaline, shiny. *Palea* hyaline, about as long as lemma. *Anthers* 0.4-0.7 mm long. *Caryopses* minutely rugose, ovate, pointed at apex, mostly 0.6-1 mm long. *Chromosome number*, $2n=28$.

Distribution. Texas: Regions 4, 6, 7, 8 and 10 in low, moist areas, especially streambanks and along swale areas. General: Texas and Colorado, west to Washington, Oregon and California and in northwestern Mexico. Introduced into North America from the Old World.

Flowering period: Mostly April to July but occasionally at other times of the year.

Agrostis semiverticillata frequently is treated as a species of *Polypogon* (*P. semiverticillata* (Forsk.) Hylander). It is the only species of *Agrostis* in which the spikelet disarticulates below the glumes.

4. **Agrostis exarata** Trin., Gram. Unifl. 207. 1824. SPIKE BENTGRASS. Tufted perennial, lacking rhizomes or stolons. *Culms* 30-90 (-120) cm tall. *Ligules* 3-6 mm long. *Blades* flat, mostly 4-15 cm long, 2-6 (-8) mm broad. *Panicles* contracted, usually dense, 10-18 (-30) cm long, mostly 1-3 cm broad. *Panicle branches* stiffly erect or erect-spreading, 1-4 cm long, some or all floriferous to the base. *Spikelets* 2.5-3.5 mm long. *Glumes* equal in length or the first slightly longer, scabrous on the nerve, acute or acuminate. *Lemmas* membranous, about 2 mm long, awnless (in Texas plants), often with a few long hairs at base. *Paleas* absent. *Anthers* about 0.6 mm long. *Chromosome number*, $2n=42$; one record of $2n=56$.

Distribution. Texas: At high elevations in the mountains of region 10, infrequent. General: Western United States, eastward to South Dakota, Nebraska and Texas.

Flowering period: Summer.

On the West Coast *Agrostis exarata* is extremely variable. It often develops culms over 100 cm tall, and in the var. *pacifica* Vasey, the lemmas are conspicuously awned.

5. **Agrostis hiemalis** (Walt.) B.S.P., Prel. Cat. N. Y. 68. 1888. WINTER BENTGRASS. Fig. 69. Weak perennial with tufted, usually stiffly-erect culms 15-70 cm tall. *Herbage* glabrous. *Ligules* mostly 1.5-4 cm long. *Blades* thin, linear, flat, 0.5-3 mm broad. *Panicles* loose and open at maturity, 7-30

Fig. 69. *Agrostis hiemalis.* Plant and spikelet. From Gould and Box, 1965.

(-40) cm long. *Panicle branches* slender, flexuous, at least some 5-15 cm or more long, branching at the middle or above and floriferous only near tips. *Spikelets* closely placed and overlapping, 1.5-2.1 mm long. *Glumes* acute or acuminate, usually scabrous on the nerve; first glume often slightly longer than second. *Lemmas* thin, hyaline, slightly shorter than glumes. *Paleas* absent. *Chromosome numbers* reported, $2n=14$, 28 and 42.

Distribution. Texas: Regions 1, 2, 3, 4, 5, 6, 7 and 10, frequent in pastures, on roadbanks and ditchbanks and in open woods, usually in moist, sandy soil. General: Throughout most of eastern United States, west to Iowa, Kansas, Oklahoma and Texas.

Flowering period: Mostly March to May but as late as August at the higher elevations in western Texas.

SUBFAMILY IV. POOIDEAE   141

Fig. 70. *Agrostis scabra*. Inflorescence, spikelet and floret. From Gould, 1951.

6. **Agrostis scabra** Willd., Sp. Pl. 1:370. 1797. ROUGH BENTGRASS.
Fig. 70. Tufted perennial without rhizomes or stolons. *Culms* slender, erect,
30-60 (-80) cm tall. *Ligules* 2-4 mm long. *Blades* thin, flat, 0.5-3 (-4) mm long.
Panicle and spikelets as in *A. hiemalis* but spikelets (at least some) 2.2-3 mm
long. *Anthers* about 0.6 mm long. *Chromosome number*, $2n=42$.

Distribution. Texas: At high elevations in the mountains of region 10.
Reported by Correll and Johnston (1970) to occur also in Dallas, Hardin and
Harris counties where it was probably introduced. General: Almost through-
out the United States except in the extreme southeast.

142   THE GRASSES OF TEXAS

Fig. 71. *Agrostis perennans.* Inflorescence.

7. **Agrostis perennans** (Walt.) Tuckerm., Amer. J. Sci. 45:44. 1843. AUTUMN BENTGRASS. Fig. 71. Tufted perennial with slender, weak culms mostly 30-80 (-100) cm tall. *Ligules* 2-5 mm long. *Blades* linear, flat, narrow, 1-6 mm broad, those of the basal tuft to 20 cm or more long, the culm leaves shorter. *Panicles* open, thinly-flowered, 10-20 cm long, the branches infrequently over 5 cm long and usually rebranched below the middle. *Spikelets* 2.2-2.8 (2-3.2) mm long. *Glumes* about equal, lanceolate, narrowly acute or acuminate, scabrous on the nerve. *Lemmas* slightly shorter than glumes, awnless (in Texas plants), with 5 fine nerves. *Paleas* absent. *Caryopses* slender, about 1.5 mm long and 0.2 mm thick. *Chromosome number,* $2n=42$.

Distribution. Texas: Regions 1 and 3, occasional along shaded streambanks and woods borders, usually in moist, sandy soil. General: Quebec to Minnesota, south to Florida and Texas and in Mexico.

Flowering period: August to October, occasionally in the spring.

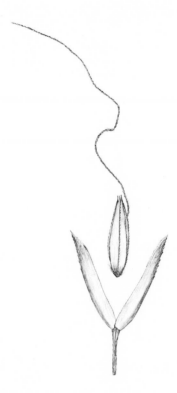

Fig. 72. *Agrostis elliottiana.* Spikelet with glumes separated from floret.

8. **Agrostis elliottiana** Schult., Mantissa 2:202. 1824. ELLIOTT
BENTGRASS. Fig. 72. Tufted annual with slender, weak culms 10-30
(-40) cm tall. *Leaves* glabrous. *Ligules* 1.5-5 mm long, rounded or broadly
pointed. *Blades* thin, weak, flat or folded, mostly 2-7 cm long and 1.6 mm
or less broad. *Inflorescence* a delicate, open panicle of small, usually
awned spikelets, mostly 5-20 cm long and one-third to one-half as broad.
Panicle branches capillary, bare of spikelets below, often paired or in
verticils of 3-5, with secondary branches 0.5-3.5 cm from base. *Spikelets*
1.2-2.2 mm long, clustered near branch tips, lateral ones appressed to
branch axis. *Glumes* about equal, as long as spikelet, with membranous
margins, often scabrous on midnerve and margins near tip. *Lemmas* thin,
5-nerved, slightly shorter than glumes, usually with a fine threadlike
dorsal awn 4-8 mm long just below tip but occasionally awnless. *Paleas*
absent or a nerveless scale. *Chromosome number* not reported.

Distribution. Texas: Regions 1, 3, 4, northern half of region 2 and eastern
portion of region 7 in open, grassy areas, along ditches, road right-of-ways and
woods borders. General: Throughout southeastern United States, north to
Maine, west to Kansas, Oklahoma and Texas, and in eastern Mexico (Yucatan).

Flowering period: March to May.

9. **Agrostis avenacea** J. F. Gmel., Syst. Nat. 2:171. 1791. PACIFIC BENTGRASS. Tufted perennial with slender, weak culms 20-60 cm tall. *Leaves* glabrous. *Ligules* 2-5 cm long. *Blades* short, flat or involute, mostly 1-2.5 mm broad. *Panicles* open, 15-30 cm long and usually 8-20 (-30) cm broad, with spikelets clustered near tips of sparingly rebranched primary branches. *Main panicle branches* usually bare of spikelets 4-12 cm above base. *Spikelets* 3-4 mm long. *Glumes* 1-nerved, about equal, narrowly lanceolate, acute or acuminate, scaberulous on midnerve near tip. *Lemmas* about 1.5 mm long, strigose-pubescent, with a once-geniculate awn 3-6 mm long from just above middle of back. *Paleas* hyaline, slightly shorter than lemmas. *Chromosome number* not reported.

Distribution. Texas: Apparently known in Texas only from a Tracy and Earle collection of 1902 made near the railroad at Kent in Culberson County (region 10). General: Known in the United States only from the Texas collection and from California where it has become established in several areas; introduced or adventive from the South Pacific.

Flowering period: April and May.

37. POLYPOGON Desf.

Annuals and perennials with usually weak, decumbent-erect culms, these often rooting at the lower nodes. *Ligules* membranous, margins continuing downward as sheath margins. *Inflorescence* a dense, contracted panicle of small spikelets. *Spikelets* 1-flowered, disarticulating below glumes and falling entire. *Glumes* about equal, 1-nerved, abruptly awned from an entire or notched apex. *Lemmas* broad, thin, smooth and shiny, mostly 5-nerved, much shorter than glumes, awnless or with a short, delicate awn from the broad, often minutely toothed apex.

About 10-15 species throughout the temperate regions of the world but mostly in Europe and Asia.

Glume awn usually 5-10 mm long, glistening, conspicuous; panicles uniformly dense, seldom interrupted; annual   1. *P. monspeliensis*

Glume awn usually 2-4 mm long, inconspicuous; panicles typically lobed and interrupted; perennial   2. *P. interruptus*

1. **Polypogon monspeliensis** (L.) Desf., Fl. Atlant. 1:67. 1798. RABBITFOOT GRASS. Fig. 73. Tufted annual with glabrous or scabrous herbage. *Culms* thick, weak, usually geniculate-erect and often rooting at lower nodes, 8-70 cm or more long. *Ligules* scabrous, many-nerved, 4-10 mm long. *Blades* flat, sharply scabrous on one or both surfaces, short or elongate, mostly 2-8 mm broad. *Inflorescence* dense, bristly with yellowish awns, often lobed but seldom interrupted, 2-15 cm or more long, 1-2.5 cm broad. *Spikelets* short-pediceled and densely congested on short, scabrous branches. *Glumes* thin, scabrous-pubescent, narrow, the body 1.5-2 mm

Fig. 73. *Polypogon monspeliensis.* Plant, spikelet and floret. From Hitchcock, 1935.

146   THE GRASSES OF TEXAS

long, usually minutely lobed at apex. *Lemma* and *palea* thin, hyaline, much shorter than glumes, the lemma usually with a delicate, deciduous awn about 1 mm long. *Caryopses* minutely rugose, brownish, 1 mm or less long. *Chromosome numbers* reported, $2n = 14$ and 28.

Distribution. Texas: Occasional throughout the State, along streams, swales, moist ditches and waste places, usually in sandy soils. General: A European species now widespread and weedy in North America.

Flowering period: Mostly March to July.

2. **Polypogon interruptus** H.B.K., Nov. Gen. et Sp. 1:134. 1815. DITCH POLYPOGON. Similar to *Polypogon monspeliensis* but perennial, usually with a more lobed and interrupted panicle, slightly longer glume body (2-3 mm long) and shorter glume awns. *Chromosome number*, $2n = 28$. Depauperate, short-awned plants of *P. monspeliensis* cannot always be satisfactorily distinguished from this species.

Distribution. Texas: Region 7, apparently known in the State only from a collection made under the old Devil's River bridge in Val Verde County, an area now under the waters of the Amisted Reservoir. General: British Columbia to Nebraska, California and Louisiana and south to Argentina.

Flowering period: April to May.

38. GASTRIDIUM Beauv.

A genus of 2 species, both native to the Mediterranean region.

1. **Gastridium ventricosum** (Gouan) Schinz and Thell. Vierteljahrs. Nat. Ges. Zurich 58:39. 1913. NITGRASS. Tufted annual with weak culms, flat blades, membranous ligules and a short, tightly-contracted panicle. *Herbage* glabrous or essentially so. *Ligule* a thin membrane mostly 3-4 mm long. *Blades* thin, flat, smooth or scabrous, mostly 2-6 mm broad and 3-10 cm long. *Panicles* pale green, mostly 5-8 cm long, with densely clustered, 1-flowered, awned spikelets. Disarticulation above glumes. *Glumes* narrow, lanceolate, 1-nerved, hyaline on margins, scabrous on nerve, first glume 3-5 mm long excluding the awn when present, the second about one-fourth shorter, both usually tapering to a stout, straight awn tip. *Lemma* and *palea* about 1 mm long, thin and hyaline, the lemma appressed-hispid, indistinctly nerved, with a straight or geniculate awn 4-5 mm long from just below apex. *Rachilla* prolonged behind palea as a minute, hispid bristle. *Chromosome numbers* reported, $2n = 14$ and 28.

Distribution. Texas: Region 10, infrequent as a casual weed. General: Native to the Mediterranean region, adventive at scattered localities in the United States and common in coastal and central California.

Flowering period: Spring.

39. PHLEUM L.

About 10 species in temperate and cold regions of both hemispheres; 4 species in the United States but only *P. alpinum* L. native.

1. **Phleum pratense** L., Sp. Pl. 59. 1753. TIMOTHY. Fig. 74. Perennial with thick culms, these solitary or in clumps from a firm, somewhat bulbous base. *Culms* decumbent below, 50-100 cm tall, glabrous. *Sheaths* glabrous, rounded on back, slightly shorter than nodes. *Ligules* membranous, 3-6 mm long. *Blades* flat, glabrous or scabrous, linear, mostly 4-10 mm broad. *Inflorescence* a contracted, cylindrical, spikelike panicle 5-9 (4-15) cm long and 5-9 mm thick. *Spikelets* 1-flowered, laterally flattened, disarticulating above glumes. *Glumes* equal, with 3 closely-placed nerves and broad, scarious margins, abruptly short-awned, coarsely ciliate on nerves, with a body 2-3.5 mm long and an awn 0.8-1.5 mm long. *Lemmas* thin, membranous, 5-7-nerved, broad and blunt, awnless, one-half to two-thirds as long as glumes. *Paleas* slightly shorter than lemmas and similar in texture. *Chromosome numbers* reported, $2n=42$ and 56 and aneuploid numbers.

Distribution. Texas: Reported by Correll and Johnston (1970) as occasional as a waif in the eastern half of the State; no Texas collections seen by the author. General: Frequent in the mountain meadows of the western United States and occasional as a cultivated grass or weedy escape from cultivation throughout the country.

Flowering period: Mostly April to June.

40. ALOPECURUS L.

Annuals and perennials with flat blades and membranous ligules, the margins of which continue downward as sheath margins. *Panicle* dense, slender, cylindrical, spikelike. *Spikelets* 1-flowered, disarticulating below glumes and falling entire. *Glumes* equal, awnless, laterally flattened and often dorsally keeled, 3-nerved, as long as spikelets, usually united by margins on the lower one-fourth to one-half. *Lemmas* about as long as glumes, firm, obtuse, 5-nerved, midnerve often separated from the body at or near base as an awn. *Paleas* usually absent. *Caryopses* laterally compressed, asymmetrically obovate.

About 25 species in the temperate regions of the Northern Hemisphere; 6 species native to the United States.

Spikelets 1.8-3 mm long; glumes hispid-ciliate on midnerve to apex; anthers 0.3-0.5 mm long   1. *A. carolinianus*

Spikelets 4.5-7 mm long; glumes glabrous, scabrous or minutely pubescent on midnerve near base; anthers 2-4 mm long   2. *A. myosuroides*

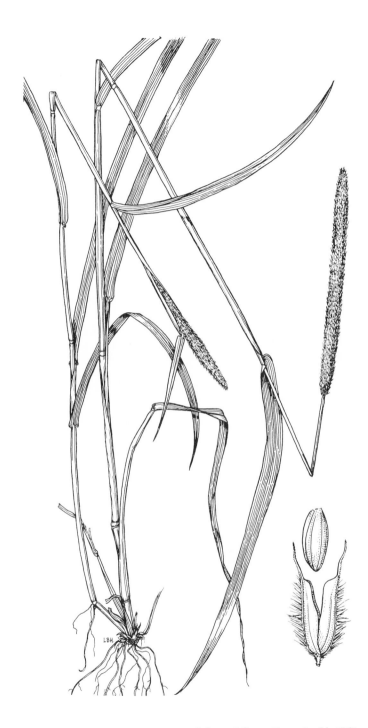

Fig. 74. *Phleum pratense*. Plant, spikelet and floret. From Gould, 1951.

1. **Alopecurus carolinianus** Walt., Fl. Carol. 74. 1788. CAROLINA FOXTAIL. Fig. 75. Tufted annual with glabrous culms mostly 10-50 cm long. *Sheaths* glabrous, usually much shorter than culm internodes. *Ligules* mostly 3.5-7 mm long. *Blades* glabrous or minutely scabrous, mostly 3-15 cm long and 1-4 (-5) mm broad. *Panicles* 2-6 cm long, 4-6 mm thick. *Glumes* 1.8-3 mm long, hispid-ciliate on the strong midnerve and margins. *Lemmas* glabrous, obtuse at apex, with midnerve projecting from base or near base as an awn 3-5 mm long. *Anthers* 0.3-0.5 mm long. *Caryopses* 1-1.4 mm long with an embryo about one-fourth the length of the endosperm. *Chromosome number* not reported.

Distribution. Texas: Regions 1, 2, 3, 4 and 5 in moist, often-disturbed soils along ditches, streams, woods borders and pasturelands. General: Throughout the United States, except in the extreme northeast.

Flowering period: March to June.

2. **Alopecurus myosuroides** Huds., Fl. Angl. 23. 1762. MOUSE FOXTAIL. Tufted annual with glabrous culms mostly 20-70 cm long. *Sheaths* smooth, shorter than culm internodes. *Ligules* 2-3 (-5) mm long. *Blades* 3-20 (-30) cm long, 2-8 mm broad, scabrous on both surfaces or smooth on abaxial side. *Panicles* 3-14 cm long, 4-8 mm thick. *Glumes* as long as spikelets, with a slightly winged dorsal keel, glabrous or scabrous on midnerve or midnerve sparsely short-pubescent near base. *Lemmas* about as long as glumes, awned from base, the awn slightly geniculate and twisted, 5-8 mm long. *Chromosome number,* $2n = 14$.

Distribution. Texas: Regions 1 and 2, infrequent, in moist soil. General: Native to Eurasia, adventive on the eastern and western coasts of the United States and occasionally reported at other locations in the country.

Flowering period: March to June.

41. PHALARIS L.

Annuals and perennials, the annuals with weak, soft culms, the perennials rather coarse, often with rhizomatous bases. *Leaves* mostly glabrous with membranous ligules and flat blades. *Inflorescence* a cylindrical, tightly-contracted panicle. *Spikelets* with one terminal, perfect floret and one or two rudimentary florets below. Disarticulation above glumes, the reduced florets falling with the perfect one. *Glumes* about equal, large, strongly 3-nerved, awnless, usually laterally flattened and dorsally keeled, the keel often with a membranous wing. *Lemma of perfect floret* awnless, coriaceous and shiny, shorter than glumes, often more or less appressed-pubescent, permanently enclosing a faintly 2-nerved palea and plump caryopsis.

About 15 species in temperate regions of the world. The following key and species concepts are based on the monographic treatment of the genus by Anderson (1961). Excluded is *Phalaris aquatica* L. which has

Fig. 75. *Alopecurus carolinianus.* Inflorescence and spikelet. From Gould, 1968.

SUBFAMILY IV. POOIDEAE   151

been grown under cultivation in Texas. In the United States this introduced perennial has been known as *P. stenoptera* Hack. and *P. tuberosa* L. var. *stenoptera* (Hack.) Hitchc.

Reduced florets 2

  Reduced florets subulate or scalelike, 1-4.5 mm long

    Reduced florets subulate, pointed, usually less than half as long as lemma of perfect floret

      Lateral nerves of glumes glabrous or scabrous, with 5 or less spicules; panicle usually 2-7 cm long; culms mostly 30-70 cm tall
                                                                1. *P. caroliniana*

      Lateral nerves of glumes scabrous with 9 or more spicules; panicle usually 6-15 cm long; culms mostly 0.6-1.5 m tall
                                                                2. *P. angustata*

    Reduced florets broad and chaffy, more than half as long as lemma of perfect floret   3. *P. canariensis*

  Reduced florets swollen and somewhat fleshy, 0.4-0.8 mm long
                                                                4. *P. brachystachya*

Reduced florets 1   5. *P. minor*

1. **Phalaris caroliniana** Walt., Fl. Carol. 74. 1788. CAROLINA CANARYGRASS. Fig. 76. Tufted annual with culms mostly 25-70 cm tall. Herbage glabrous. *Ligules* 3-5 mm long. *Blades* flat, 6-15 cm long, 3-10 mm broad. *Panicle* 2-7(-8) cm long, 8-13 mm broad. *Glumes* mostly 5-6 mm long, keel with a greenish wing 0.2-0.5 mm broad. *Lemma of perfect floret* 3-4 mm long, shiny, ovate-lanceolate, pointed, long, hirsute with whitish hairs. *Paleas* slightly shorter than lemmas. *Reduced florets* narrow, scalelike, somewhat unequal, one-third to one-half as long as lemma of perfect floret and closely placed at its base. *Caryopses* 1.7-2 mm long, brownish, oblong, minutely rugose, with an embryo about one-third as long as the endosperm. *Chromosome number*, 2n=14.

Distribution. Texas: In all regions of the State, in grasslands and open woodlands, especially abundant on roadsides, stream banks and ditchbanks and along fence rows. General: Virginia, Colorado and Oregon, south to Florida, Texas, California and northern Mexico.

Flowering period: March to June.

2. **Phalaris angustata** Nees, *ex* Trin., Gram. Icon. 1:pl. 78. 1827. TIMOTHY CANARYGRASS. Fig. 77. Annual with thick, succulent culms mostly 60-150 cm tall. *Herbage* glabrous. *Ligule* a broad, rounded, whitish

Fig. 76. *Phalaris caroliniana*. Plant, spikelet and floret. From Gould and Box, 1965.

Fig. 77. *Phalaris angustata.* Inflorescence and spikelet.

membrane 3-5 mm long. *Blades* flat, mostly 6-18 cm long and 5-12 mm broad. *Panicles* 6-15 cm long and 8-10 mm thick. *Glumes* 3.5-4 mm long, the keel scabrous and narrowly winged towards apex. *Lemma of perfect floret* thick, shiny, ovate-attenuate, hispid, with two subequal, scalelike reduced florets at base, the reduced florets about 1 mm long. *Caryopses* 2.6-3 mm long. *Chromosome number,* $2n = 14$.

Distribution. Texas: Regions 1, 2, 3, 6 and 10 along ditches, swales and other moist, open sites. General: Mississippi and Louisiana to Texas, Arizona and California and in southern South America.

Flowering period: March to June.

Fig. 78. *Phalaris canariensis.* Inflorescence and spikelet. From Gould and Box, 1965.

3. **Phalaris canariensis** L., Sp. Pl. 54. 1753. CANARYGRASS. Fig. 78. Tufted annual with culms 25-70 cm tall. *Herbage* glabrous. *Ligules* 2-6 mm long. *Blades* flat, 3-7 mm broad and 5-15 cm long, occasionally 20 cm or more long. *Panicles* short, thick, 1.5-3 (-4) cm long and 10-18 mm broad. *Glumes* 7-9 mm long, glabrous or sparsely hispid, pale with conspicuously dark green bands along the lateral nerves, the upper half of keel broadly winged, the wing to 1 mm broad. *Lemma of perfect floret* densely appressed-pubescent, narrowly acute or acuminate, 4.5-6.5 mm long. *Grain* 3.9-4.2 mm long. *Reduced florets* scalelike, subequal, 2.5-4.5 mm long. *Chromosome number* reported by several workers as $2n=12$; one count of $2n=28$.

Distribution. Texas: Regions 1, 2 and 3, infrequent as a plant of vacant lots, road right-of-ways and waste places. General: Native to the Mediterranean region, *P. canariensis* supplies all commercial bird seed. The occasional occurrence of this grass in our area probably results from the feeding of grains to canaries and other bird pets. It is doubtful that it persists for any considerable time from the chance seedings.

Flowering period: March to June.

4. **Phalaris brachystachya** Link, New J. Bot. Schrad. 13:134. 1806. SHORTSPIKE CANARYGRASS. Tufted annual similar to *P. canariensis* but glumes and lemma of perfect floret usually shorter and reduced florets not scalelike and much shorter. *Chromosome number* reported about equally as 2n=12 and 2n=14.

Distribution. Texas: Region 6, infrequent, probably growing only from chance seedings and not persisting in any one locality. General: Native to the Mediterranean region, introduced at scattered localities in the United States.

Flowering period: Spring.

5. **Phalaris minor** Retz., Obs. Bot. 3:8. 1783. LITTLESEED CANARYGRASS. Tufted annual generally similar to *P. canariensis* but panicle often longer (to 8 cm long), glumes narrower, with pale green lateral striations, lemma of perfect floret mostly 2.5-3.5 mm long and only one scalelike reduced floret present at base of lemma, this about 1 mm long. *Chromosome number*, 2n=28 (two reports of 2n=28+1).

Distribution. Texas: Reported by Chase in Hitchcock's Manual (1951) as occurring in Texas but no Texas collections seen. General: Native to the Mediterranean region and introduced at scattered locations in the United States from chance seedings and probably not persisting.

Flowering period: Spring.

42. CINNA L.

A genus of 3-4 species, one in North and South America and the others in Europe and Asia.

1. **Cinna arundinacea** L., Sp. Pl. 5. 1753. STOUT WOODREED. Fig. 79. Tall perennial with stout culms, flat blades and a contracted panicle of 1-flowered spikelets. *Culms* glabrous mostly 1-1.5 m tall but occasionally shorter, solitary or in small clumps, usually swollen and somewhat bulbous at base. *Leaves* glabrous or scabrous. *Sheaths* rounded on back, continued laterally at apex as the ligule. *Ligule* a lacerate, brownish membrane 2-5 mm or more long. *Blades* scabrous, elongate, flat, mostly 6-10 mm broad. *Panicle* narrow 15-25 (5-30) cm long with the short branches floriferous nearly to base. *Spikelets* 1-flowered, 5-6 mm long, disarticulating below glumes. *Glumes* nearly equal, scabrous, acute, the first glume 1-nerved, the second 3-nerved. *Lemmas* equaling second glume, minutely scabrous, 3-nerved, the midnerve usually projecting as a short, straight awn from a narrow, notched apex. *Paleas* shorter than lemmas, laterally compressed and apparently 1-nerved. *Chromosome number*, 2n=28.

Distribution. Texas: Region 1, infrequent in moist woodlands. General: Throughout the eastern and central United States, westward to South Dakota and Texas.

Flowering period: Mostly August to October.

Fig. 79. *Cinna arundinacea.* Inflorescence and spikelet. From Gould, 1968.

43. HORDEUM L.

Low to moderately tall annuals and perennials, mostly with weak culms and soft, flat blades. *Ligules* membranous. *Blade auricles* often present. *Inflorescence* a dense, spicate raceme with 3 spikelets at each node, the central spikelet usually perfect and sessile, the lateral ones usually pediceled and staminate or sterile (all sessile and perfect in *H. vulgare*). *Axis of inflorescence* fragmenting at maturity (except in *H. vulgare*), the short internodes falling attached to spikelets. *Spikelets* 1-flowered. *Rachilla* terminating in a bristle. *Lateral spikelets* often represented by glumes only. *Glumes* narrow, usually subulate or awned, mostly rigid. *Lemmas* firm, rounded on back and dorsally flattened, 5-nerved, nerves usually obscure. *Apex of lemma* usually with a strong awn. *Paleas* slightly shorter than lemmas.

A genus of about 25 species distributed in the temperate regions of both hemispheres (Covas, 1949).

Lemmas of lateral spikelets absent or much smaller than lemma of central spikelet

Awns of glumes and lemmas 1.5 cm or less long; annual
1.   *H. pusillum*

Awns of glumes and lemmas mostly 3.5-8 cm long; short-lived perennial
2.   *H. jubatum*

Lemmas of lateral spikelets as large as lemma of central spikelet

Rachis disarticulating at maturity; lateral spikelets pediceled; glumes of central spikelet and inner glumes of lateral spikelets ciliate
3.   *H. leporinum*

Rachis not disarticulating at maturity; lateral spikelets sessile; glumes glabrous or scabrous
4.   *H. vulgare*

1. **Hordeum pusillum** Nutt., Gen. Pl. 1:87. 1818. LITTLE BARLEY. Fig. 80. Tufted annual. *Culms* mostly 10-40 cm tall, usually geniculate at the base, with glabrous, dark-colored nodes. *Sheaths* glabrous or with short, spreading pubescence. *Ligules* truncate, about 0.5 mm long. *Blades* flat, glabrous or pubescent, mostly 3-12 cm long and 2-4 (-5) mm broad, with or without small auricles. *Inflorescences* narrow and dense, mostly 4-8 cm long and 4-8 mm broad excluding awns. *Outer glumes of lateral spikelets* awnlike, without expanded bodies, the other glumes broadened and flattened above base, scabrous, with awns mostly 7-15 mm long. *Lemma of lateral spikelets* short-awned, irregularly reduced, the body one-half to one-third as long as that of the central, perfect spikelet. *Lemma of central spikelet* with a body

Fig. 80. *Hordeum pusillum.* Plant and rachis joint with spikelet cluster. From Gould and Box, 1965.

usually 4-6 mm long and an awn 2-7 mm long. *Rachilla* extended behind palea as a stout bristle 2-4 mm long. *Chromosome number*, $2n=14$.

Distribution. Texas: Throughout the State, locally frequent in early spring on roadways, anthills and other disturbed sites, often associated with *Vulpia octoflora*. General: Throughout the United States except in a few of the north-central and northeastern states and in northern Mexico.

Flowering period: March to May, occasionally June.

Plants with especially broad inner glumes and pubescent lemmas are referable to *H. pusillum* var. *pubens* Hitchc. Glume width and lemma pubescence, however, appear to have only chance correlation.

2. **Hordeum jubatum** L., Sp. Pl. 85. 1753. FOXTAIL BARLEY. Tufted, short-lived perennial. *Culms* slender, 30-75 cm tall, erect or geniculate-spreading; nodes dark. *Ligules* truncate, mostly 0.2-0.5 mm long. *Blades* flat, scabrous, the lower ones sometimes finely pubescent, mostly 2-4 mm broad and 6-15 cm long. *Inflorescences* mostly 4-10 cm long and 4-6 mm broad excluding the long, spreading awns. *Lateral spikelets* greatly reduced, often represented only by the awnlike, scabrous, 3.5-8-cm-long glumes and a short rachilla. *Glumes* of central spikelet also awnlike and scabrous, about as long as those of lateral spikelets. *Floret of central spikelet* slender, the lemma mostly 4-7 mm long, tapering into an awn as long as those of glumes. *Rachilla* extended as a slender bristle back of palea. *Chromosome number*, $2n=28$.

Distribution. Texas: Regions 7, 8, 9 and 10, in moist, often-disturbed soils along ditches, streams and ravines. General: Labrador and Alaska, south to Mexico; throughout the United States except in the southeast.

Flowering period: Mostly May to July.

3. **Hordeum leporinum** Link, Linnaea 9:133. 1835. HARE BARLEY. Fig. 81. Tufted annual. *Culms* thick, succulent, mostly 15-60 cm tall, usually geniculate-spreading below. *Leaves* glabrous or more frequently hispid. *Ligules* truncate, about 1 mm long. *Blades* flat, weak, mostly 3-8 mm broad and 6-15 cm long, usually with well-developed, slender, pointed auricles. *Inflorescence* 4-8 cm long and about 1 cm broad excluding awns, often partially enclosed in the expanded uppermost leaf sheath. *Florets of lateral spikelets* large, usually equaling or exceeding that of central spikelet. *Floret of central spikelet* borne on an elongated rachilla joint about as long as pedicels of lateral spikelets. *Outer glumes of lateral floret* narrow, setaceous, long-awned. *Glumes of central spikelet and inner glumes of lateral spikelets* long-awned, more or less broadened and flattened below and coarsely ciliate on margins of flattened portion; glume awns scabrous, mostly 1-2.5 cm long. *Lemma body* 6-12 mm long, gradually tapering into an awn 10-35 mm long. *Paleas* of lateral florets pubescent. *Stamens of central florets* exserted at anthesis. *Chromosome number*, $2n=28$.

Distribution. Texas: Occasional throughout the State except the far eastern and southern portions (regions 1 and 6), growing as a weed of roadsides,

Fig. 81. *Hordeum leporinum*. Inflorescence and rachis joint with spikelet cluster. From Gould and Box, 1965.

ditches, vacant lots and other areas of disturbed soil. General: Maine and British Columbia southward to Texas, California and northern Mexico but infrequent in the central and eastern United States and absent from many states.

Flowering period: March to May or June.

Fig. 82. *Hordeum vulgare.* Inflorescence and spikelet cluster. From Gould and Box, 1965.

4. **Hordeum vulgare** L., Sp. Pl. 84. 1753. BARLEY. Fig. 82. Annual with thick, succulent culms 50-120 cm tall. *Sheaths* thin, rounded. *Ligules* truncate, mostly 1.5-3 mm long. *Blades* flat, elongate, mostly 5-15 mm broad, usually with firm, well-developed auricles at base. *Spikes* thick, closely-flowered, 2-10 cm long excluding the awns, with 3 sessile, perfect, closely-placed spikelets at each node of the non-disarticulating rachis. *Glumes* flattened and slightly broadened at base, glabrous or variously pubescent, tapering to a short or long awn. *Lemmas* shiny or glaucous, mostly 8-12 mm long, in the usual cultivated varieties tapering to a stout scabrous awn as much as 15 cm long. *Chromosome number,* $2n = 14$.

Distribution. Texas: Barley is planted as a crop plant in many areas of the State and occasionally is present as a weed of roadsides and field borders; it does not persist out of cultivation. General: An Old World species, now widely disseminated throughout the cooler regions of the world and in the subtropics as a cool-season grass.

Flowering period: Mostly April to June.

162   THE GRASSES OF TEXAS

44. ELYMUS L.

Cespitose or rhizomatous perennials with membranous ligules and usually flat blades. Slender, pointed *auricles* usually present on either side of the sheath-blade junction. *Inflorescence* a spike with 2-3 spikelets at a node (in Texas species), sometimes with a single spikelet at one or more of the upper nodes. Disarticulation between florets and above glumes or in nodes of rachis. *Glumes* firm or soft, narrow and setaceous to broad and blunt, 1-several-nerved, awned or awnless. *Lemmas* about as long as the glumes or longer, usually 5-7-nerved, rounded on the back, awned or awnless. *Paleas* usually obtuse or truncate, about as long as lemmas.

As presently interpreted, a genus of about 75 species widespread in the cooler regions of the Northern Hemisphere and to the southern United States as cool-season grasses; a few species also in southern South America. Included are the species referred to *Sitanion* Raf. by Hitchcock (1935, 1936) and Chase (1951).

Lemmas awnless or with awns 0.2 cm or less long; plants rhizomatous
1. *E. triticoides*

Lemmas with awns 0.3-8 cm or more long; plants not rhizomatous

Inflorescence axis (rachis) persistent at maturity, the disarticulation above glumes and between florets; glume awns 4.5 mm or less long.

Glumes strongly bowed out at base, indurate, thickened and shiny at base, mostly 1.2-2 mm broad 3. *E. virginicus*

Glumes not or only slightly bowed out at base

Glumes flat, not or only slightly thickened at base, 0.7-1.2 mm broad 2A. *E. canadensis* var. *canadensis*

Glumes terete or nearly so, indurate at least on lower portion, 0.2-0.5 mm broad 2B. *E. canadensis* var. *interruptus*

Inflorescence axis readily disarticulating at maturity, the spikelets falling with sections of rachis; glume awns 5-11 mm long
4. *E. longifolius*

1. **Elymus triticoides** Buckl., Proc. Acad. Nat. Sci. Philadelphia Monogr. 1862:99. 1862. CREEPING WILDRYE. Culms firm, erect, glabrous, usually glaucous, 40-120 cm tall, mostly single or in small clusters from slender, creeping rhizomes. *Ligules* truncate, ciliate, 1-1.6 mm long. *Blades* stiff, usually glaucous, flat or involute, elongate, mostly 3-6 mm broad. *Spikes* 6-20 cm long, spikelets usually paired at the lower and middle nodes of rachis and solitary at upper. *Spikelets* mostly 10-16 mm long and

4-6-flowered. *Glumes* slender, subulate, widely separated with the back of the lowermost lemma more or less centered between them; nerves of glumes often not evident. *Lemmas* smooth or slightly scabrous, acute or mucronate. *Chromosome number,* 2n=28.

Distribution. Texas: Reported by Chase in Hitchcock's Manual (1951) from region 10 and by Gould (1969) from regions 8 and 10 but no Texas specimens seen in the present study. A plant of moist, open valleys and flats. General: Western United States, from western Montana and (?) Texas to Washington and California and in Baja California.

Flowering period: Late spring and early summer.

2. **Elymus canadensis** L., Sp. Pl. 83. 1753. Tufted perennial lacking rhizomes. *Culms* usually decumbent at base, 80-150 cm tall, in small or occasionally large clumps. Slender, fragile auricles usually developed on either side of sheath-blade junction. *Ligule* a truncate membrane 0.5-1 mm long. *Blades* flat or folded, elongate, mostly 4-12 mm broad, glabrous or variously pubescent. *Spikes* erect or nodding, 8-20 cm long, spikelets paired or in threes at each node. *Spikelets* mostly 3-5-flowered. *Glumes* about equal, tapering to an awn usually longer than the body. *Lemmas* glabrous, hispid or scabrous, mostly 0.8-1 cm or more long, with flexuous awns 1.5-5 cm long, these usually outward-curving at maturity. *Chromosome number,* 2n=28.

2A. **Elymus canadensis** L. var. **canadensis**, CANADA WILDRYE. Fig. 83. *Glumes* flat, slightly broadened above the base. *Lemmas* glabrous or scabrous.

Distribution. Texas: Throughout the State except in the southern portion of the South Texas Plains (region 6), mostly in shaded sites, frequently along fence rows, woods borders and in moist ravines.

Flowering period: Mostly March to June, infrequently in summer and early autumn.

As presently interpreted, *E. canadensis* var. *canadensis* includes three forms that have been given varietal or even specific status (var. *robustus* (Scribn. & Smith) Mackenz., var. *brachystachya* (Scribn. & Ball) Farwell and var. *villosus* (Muhl.) Shinners).

2B. **Elymus canadensis** L. var. **interruptus** (Buckl.) Church, Rhodora 69:133. 1967. TEXAS WILDRYE. *Glumes* 15-30 mm long, equal, the base indurate and often terete, usually less than 0.5 mm wide at middle of body. *Lemmas* 8-9 mm long, glabrous, with a straight awn 15-20 mm long.

Distribution. Texas: Regions 7 and 10 in rocky, open woodlands and moist canyons, infrequent. General: Oklahoma, Texas and New Mexico.

Flowering period: April to August.

Fig. 83. *Elymus canadensis* var. *canadensis*. Plant, glumes and floret. From Gould, 1951.

In the interpretation of Hitchcock (1935), Chase (1951) and others, this taxon has a disjunct distribution, with populations in Texas, Tennessee, Oklahoma and New Mexico and also in Michigan, Wisconsin, Minnesota, North and South Dakota and Wyoming. Church (1967), however, believes the Texas plants have had a separate origin from those of the more northerly states.

Fig. 84. *Elymus virginicus.* Inflorescence. From Gould and Box, 1965.

3. **Elymus virginicus** L., Sp. Pl. 84. 1753. VIRGINIA WILDRYE. Fig. 84. *Culms* tufted, strictly erect or decumbent at base, mostly 60-120 cm tall, green or sometimes glaucous. *Sheaths* glabrous. *Ligule* a minute, truncate membrane. *Blades* flat, glabrous, scabrous or minutely pubescent, mostly 5-15 mm broad. *Spike* usually stiffly erect, often partly enclosed by upper sheath. *Glumes* strongly nerved, indurate, yellowish, nerveless and bowed out at base, the apex often somewhat curved, tapering into a straight awn shorter to longer than the body. *Lemmas* glabrous or sparsely hirsute with a straight or slightly curved awn 5-25 mm long. *Chromosome number*, $2n=28$.

Distribution. Texas: Occasional in all regions except regions 9 and 10, most abundant in the eastern half of the State. A grass of shaded banks, fence rows and open woodlands. General: Throughout the United States except in the extreme southwest. Apparently not reported from Oregon, Nevada or California.

166   THE GRASSES OF TEXAS

Flowering period: April to June, occasionally as late as September.

Several varieties of *E. virginicus* have been distinguished, but these do not appear to be especially significant or consistent. Reported for Texas are var. *australis* (Scrib. & Ball) Hitchc., var. *glabriflorus* (Vasey) Bush and var. *intermedius* (Vasey) Bush. *Elymus virginicus* apparently hybridizes freely with *E. canadensis* throughout its range, and these two species also hybridize with other *Elymus* species in the central, eastern and northern states.

4. **Elymus longifolius** (J. G. Smith) Gould, Brittonia 26:60. 1974. *Sitanion longifolium* J. G. Smith. LONGLEAF SQUIRRELTAIL. Plants tufted, usually much-branched at base. *Culms* geniculate or strictly erect, 25-60 cm tall. *Sheaths* usually glabrous and glaucous, occasionally puberulent or pubescent, the sheath subtending the spike, inflated and larger than those below; slender, pointed, fragile auricles usually developed laterally at apex of sheath. *Ligule* a minute membranous collar. *Blades* flat or involute, elongate, 2-5 (-6) mm broad, glabrous or less frequently puberulent or pubescent. *Spikes* 7-15 cm long, usually exserted, with 2 or occasionally 3 spikelets per node. *Rachillas* readily disarticulating above glumes and between florets. *Spikelets* 2-6-flowered, the terminal floret or florets often sterile. *Glumes* subulate, scabrous, usually 1-nerved, extending into an awn 5-11 cm long. *Lemmas* 7-12 mm long, glabrous, scabrous or pubescent, obscurely 3-5-nerved, the central nerve extending into a stout, spreading awn 5-10 cm long. *Chromosome number*, $2n=28$.

Distribution. Texas: Regions 7, 8, 9 and 10, on dry, open, often-disturbed areas. General: As interpreted by Wilson (1963), a species mainly of desert and montane habitats distributed from South Dakota, Montana and Oregon, south to Texas, Arizona, California and northern Mexico.

Flowering period: Mostly May to September.

Texas populations of *Elymus longifolius* were referred to the taxon *Sitanion hystrix* (Nutt.) J. G. Smith by Hitchcock (1935), Chase (1951) and Swallen (1964) and to *Sitanion longifolium* by Wilson (1963), Gould (1969) and Correll and Johnston (1970).

45. AGROPYRON Gaertn.

Annuals and perennials (Texas plants all perennial) similar to *Elymus* in general characteristics and variation pattern but spikes with 1, occasionally 2, spikelets per node.

As presently interpreted, a genus of about 100 species widely distributed in the cooler parts of the Northern Hemisphere, with a few species also in southern South America.

The separation of most or all species of *Agropyron* from *Elymus* is now generally recognized as artificial. The evolutionary reduction in the number of spikelets at the inflorescence nodes from 2 or 3 to 1 quite apparently has taken place independently in several lines of *Elymus* stock. Cytological and genetical studies have confirmed the close genetical relationships of these two groups. It is also known that species of the *Elymus-Agropyron* complex are closely related to *Hordeum* and that hybridization of species referable to the three recognized genera takes place in nature and can be readily repeated experimentally.

Lemmas with awns mostly 1.2-2.5 cm long   2. *A. arizonicum*

Lemmas awnless or with awns 3 mm or less long

    Internodes of rachis more than 2 mm long, the spikelets not closely placed and spreading on rachis

        Plants with well-developed, creeping rhizomes; herbage usually glaucous; spikelets well-imbricated, often overlapping as much as one-half their length   1. *A. smithii*

        Plants lacking creeping rhizomes; herbage typically not glaucous; spikelets not or only slightly imbricated, never overlapping as much as one-half their length

            Glumes mostly one-half or less as long as the spikelet; leaves usually strongly involute   3. *A. spicatum*

            Glumes two-thirds or more as long as the spikelet; leaves mostly flat   4. *A. trachycaulum*

    Internodes of rachis 2 mm or less long, the spikelets closely spaced and widely spreading on rachis   5. *A. cristatum*

    1. **Agropyron smithii** Rydb., Mem. New York Bot. Gard. 1:64. 1900. *Elymus smithii* (Rydb.) Gould. WESTERN WHEATGRASS. Fig. 85. Perennial with slender, firm culms mostly 30-90 cm tall, culms single or in small clusters from creeping rhizomes. *Leaves* glaucous. *Sheaths* glabrous or the lower ones puberulent, often short-ciliate along the upper margins and with or without slender, pointed auricles on either side of collar *Ligule* a truncate, minutely ciliate membrane about 1 mm long. *Blades* firm, stiff, glabrous or scabrous-hispid on adaxial surface, 2-7 mm broad, tapering to a long, slender tip, usually involute on drying. *Spikes* 6-20 cm long, often dense, the large, several-flowered spikelets typically one per node of the rachis but frequently paired at the lower and middle nodes. Disarticulation above glumes. *Internodes of rachis* flattened but thick, scabrous on the margins, averaging 7-10 mm long but sometimes much

Fig. 85. *Agropyron smithii.* Plant with rhizomes and spikelet.

longer. *Spikelets* mostly 1.5-2.5 cm long and 5-12-flowered, glaucous. *Glumes* slightly unequal, firm, narrowly lanceolate, with 3-7 coarse, rounded, often indistinct nerves, usually tapering from a broadened base to an acuminate or short-awned apex, second glume usually equaling or exceeding the lowermost lemma. *Lemmas* firm, pale, indistinctly several-nerved, glabrous or pubescent on margins. *Paleas* large, scabrous or ciliate on keels. *Chromosome numbers* reported, $2n=28$, 42 and 56.

Distribution. Texas: Regions 4, 7, 8, 9 and 10, usually in moist clay or clay-loam soils but also in sand, most frequent in low, moist flats and flood plains. General: New York to Alberta and Washington, south to Kentucky, Texas and California.

Flowering period: Mostly May to July, occasionally in August and September.

2. **Agropyron arizonicum** Scribn. & Smith, Bull. U.S.D.A. Div. Agrost. Bull. 4:27. 1897. *Elymus arizonicus* (Scrib. & Smith) Gould. ARIZONA WHEATGRASS. Fig. 86. Cespitose perennial. *Culms* mostly 60-100 cm tall. *Herbage* usually glaucous. *Sheaths of lower leaves* usually with slender auricles on either side of collar. *Ligules* membranous, mostly 2-4 mm long. *Blades* flat or folded, elongate, 2.5-6 mm broad, glabrous or the lower ones puberulent. *Spikes* flexuous, mostly 10-25 cm long, with large, widely-spaced, bristly spikelets. Disarticulation above glumes. *Rachis internodes* scabrous on margins, mostly 9-15 mm long. *Spikelets* solitary at nodes, usually with 4-6 florets. *Glumes* about equal, lanceolate, acute to acuminate or with an awn about 8 mm long. *Lemmas* firm, glabrous or slightly scabrous, the body about 1 cm long, tapering into a stout, curved, scabrous awn mostly 1.5-3 cm long. *Paleas* as long as lemmas. *Chromosome number*, $2n=28$.

Distribution. Texas: Region 10 in moist, shaded canyons at high elevations. General: Western Texas to California and northern Mexico.

Flowering period: Mostly July to September.

3. **Agropyron spicatum** Scribn. & Smith, Bull. U.S.D.A. Div. Agrost. Bull. 4:33. 1897. *Elymus spicatus* (Pursh) Gould. *Agropyron inerme* (Scribn. & Smith) Rydb. BLUEBUNCH WHEATGRASS. Perennial with slender, densely clustered culms mostly 50-80 cm tall. *Sheaths* glabrous, rounded, often with well-developed auricles. *Ligules* membranous, mostly 1-2 mm long. *Blades* filiform, 1-3 mm broad, usually involute, yellowish- or bluish-green but not glaucous, usually puberulent on the adaxial surface. *Spikes* stiffly erect, mostly 6-15 cm long and with 5-12 spikelets. *Rachis internodes* mostly 1-2 cm long. Disarticulation above glumes. *Glumes* short, acute or obtuse, awnless (in Texas plants), about half as long as spikelet at maturity. *Lemmas* mostly 0.8-1 cm long, faintly-nerved, acute to minutely awn-tipped (in Texas plants). *Paleas* as long as lemmas, scabrous-ciliate on keels. *Chromosome numbers* reported, $2n=14$ and 28.

Fig. 86. *Agropyron arizonicum.* Inflorescence and spikelet.

Distribution. Texas: Region 10 on rocky mountain slopes and dry canyons. General: Throughout western United States from western North Dakota and Texas, west to Washington and northern California.

Flowering period: Mostly July to September.

SUBFAMILY IV. POOIDEAE   171

The typical form of *A. spicatum* has long, curved lemma awns. Texas plants, with awnless lemmas, have been referred to *A. inerme*, but awnless plants frequently grow together with awned plants and the difference does not seem to be taxonomically significant.

4. **Agropyron trachycaulum** (Link) Malte, Canada Natl. Mus. Ann. Rep. 1930. Bull. 68:42. 1932. *Elymus trachycaulus* (Link) Shinners. SLENDER WHEATGRASS. Perennial with culms in large or small clumps. *Culms* glabrous, erect or decumbent at base, 40-110 (-150) cm tall. *Sheaths* glabrous or puberulent. *Ligules* membranous, about 1 mm long. *Blades* elongate, 2-6 (-8) mm broad, usually flat, glabrous or scabrous. *Spikes* slender, 8-18 (-25) cm long, the 4-7-flowered spikelets widely spaced on rachis. *Rachis* internodes mostly 6-20 mm long. *Spikelets* 12-20 mm long, usually overlapping less than one-half their length. Disarticulation above glumes and between florets. *Glumes* nearly equal, thin, broad, 3-7-nerved, acute or short awn-tipped, mostly 9-15 mm long, second glume usually about equaling lowermost lemma. *Lemmas* 8-13 mm long, obscurely nerved, glabrous, acute or with a short, straight awn. *Chromosome number, 2n=28.*

Distribution. Texas: Reportedly present in regions 8 and 9 but no Texas specimens seen. General: Labrador and Alaska, south through Canada and throughout the United States except in the Southwest.

Flowering period: Summer.

5. **Agropyron cristatum** (L.) Gaertn., Nov. Comm. Petrop. 14:540. 1170. CRESTED WHEATGRASS. Tufted perennial with culms to 1 m tall but usually shorter. *Sheaths* rounded, glabrous or the lower ones pubescent, often with slender sheath auricles. *Ligules* membranous, mostly 0.3-0.5 mm long. *Blades* of culm leaves mostly 5-15 mm long and 2-5 mm broad, flat or loosely infolded, pale green, mostly glabrous but basal ones sometimes pubescent. *Spikes* 2-5 (-8) cm long and 0.7-2 cm thick, the spikelets closely placed and typically spreading at a wide angle from rachis. *Rachis* scabrous-pubescent. Disarticulation above glumes and between florets. *Spikelets* 5-15 mm long, 4-8-flowered, upper florets usually sterile. *Glumes* narrow, with a strong midnerve and occasionally faint lateral nerves, first glume 4-5 mm long, the second 5-6 mm long, both twisted and short-awned. *Lemmas* 4-7 mm long, mucronate, often ciliate. *Chromosome numbers* reported, *2n=*14 and 28.

Distribution. Texas: Occasionally seeded as a pasture grass in regions 8 and 9, probably not persisting without reseeding. General: Native to Russia, seeded as a forage grass at widely scattered localities in the United States.

Flowering period: Late spring and summer.

46. TRITICUM L.

Annuals with erect or curving-erect, weak, glabrous culms, these freely branching at base. *Blades* thin, flat. *Ligule* membranous. *Inflorescence* a thick, bilateral spike with spikelets borne singly at the nodes of a continous or disarticulating rachis. *Spikelets* 2-5-flowered, laterally flattened and oriented flatwise to rachis or rounded and closely fitting into rachis joints. *Glumes* thick and firm, 3-several-nerved, usually somewhat asymmetrical, toothed, mucronate or 1-3-awned at apex. *Lemmas* similar to glumes in texture, keeled or rounded on back, awnless or 1-3-nerved.

A genus of about 30 species native to the cool and temperate regions of southern Europe and western Asia. Numerous varieties of cultivated wheat, *T. aestivum*, are grown throughout the central and western United States. Herein included in *Triticum* are the several weedy grasses referred to *Aegilops* by Chase (1951) and others.

Spikelets laterally flattened   1.   *T. aestivum*

Spikelets cylindrical or nearly so   2.   *T. cylindricum*

1. **Triticum aestivum** L., Sp. Pl. 85. 1753. WHEAT. Fig. 87. Annual with thick culms mostly 60-100 cm tall. *Sheaths* thin, rounded, glabrous or the lower ones puberulent, usually with slender auricles at apex on either side of collar. *Ligules* truncate, mostly 1-3 cm long. *Blades* elongate, 0.7-2 cm broad, glabrous or scabrous in Texas plants. *Spike* 5-12 cm long excluding the awns when present, the spikelets 2-ranked and closely imbricated on a stout, continuous rachis. *Spikelets* mostly 10-15 mm long excluding awns when present, 2-5-flowered, glabrous or pubescent, awned or awnless, disarticulating above glumes and between florets, laterally flattened and oriented flatwise to rachis. *Glumes* usually strongly keeled towards one side, the keel often mucronate or with a stout awn to 6 cm or more long. *Lemmas* keeled or rounded on back, awnless, mucronate or with a stout, scabrous awn to 15 cm or more long. *Paleas* well-developed, about as large as lemmas. *Caryopses* ovate or oblong, usually pubescent at apex, with an embryo one-fourth to one-third as long as endosperm. *Chromosome number, 2n=42.*

Distribution. Texas: Cultivated wheat has been collected as a weed of roadsides and waste places throughout the State. It is frequent as a wayside grass in agricultural areas but never actually becomes established outside of cultivation. General: Native to Eurasia, now widespread in the cooler regions of the world as a cultivated plant.

Flowering period: Mostly March to May.

Fig. 87. *Triticum aestivum.* Inflorescence. From Gould and Box, 1965.

Fig. 88. *Triticum cylindricum.* Inflorescence. From Gould, 1968.

Fig. 89. *Secale cereale.* Spikelet. From Gould, 1968.

174   THE GRASSES OF TEXAS

2. **Triticum cylindricum** (Host) Ces., Pass. and Gib., Comp. Fl. Ital. 86. 1867. *Aegilops cylindrica* Host. JOINTED GOATGRASS. Fig. 88. Tufted annual with slender culms mostly 30-60 cm tall. *Sheaths* glabrous or ciliate on margins with small, narrow auricles on either side of collar. *Ligules* short, truncate, less than 1 mm long. *Blades* mostly 3-12 cm long and 1-3 (-4) mm broad, often infolded when dry. *Spikes* cylindrical or nearly so, 5-10 cm long excluding awns, 2-5 mm thick, with the spikelets fitting into concavities in a stout, flattened, glabrous rachis; disarticulation usually first in the rachis at lowermost node, the spike falling entire. *Spikelets* mostly 8-12 mm long, excluding awns when present, 2-5-flowered but the upper florets reduced. Lower spikelets of spike with awnless or mucronate glumes and lemmas, the upper spikelets with awned glumes and lemmas, the awns stout, scabrous, straight, mostly 3-8 cm long. *Glumes* thick, asymmetrical, many-nerved, usually scabrous. *Lemmas* several-nerved, thin on back but with thick margins, slightly longer than the glumes. *Paleas* about as long as lemmas, ciliate on nerves. *Chromosome number*, $2n=28$.

Distribution. Texas: Regions 1, 3, 4, 5, 7, 8, 9 and 10, an occasional weed of open roadsides and waste places. General: Native to Europe, adventive in the United States and now established in many areas of the country.

Flowering period: Mostly May to June.

47. SECALE L.

Five species, distributed mainly in temperate Europe and Asia.

1. **Secale cereale** L., Sp. Pl. 84. 1753. RYE. Fig. 89. Annual with erect, weak culms mostly 50-120 cm tall, these branching only at base. *Sheaths* rounded on back, auriculate or not, glabrous or the lower sheaths hispid. *Ligule* a minutely ciliate membrane mostly 1-1.5 mm long. *Blades* thin, flat, glabrous or hirsute on one or both surfaces. *Inflorescence* a dense, bilateral spike mostly 5-12 cm long and about 1 cm thick. *Spikelets* awned, usually 2-flowered, borne singly and closely imbricated on a flattened rachis. *Rachis* densely hairy on margins, continued above upper floret as a short stipe. Disarticulation above glumes. *Glumes* narrow, acute or acuminate, apparently 1-nerved, glabrous or scabrous on the nerve, 6-10 mm long, subequal. *Lemmas* broad, firm, 5-nerved, usually asymmetrical, sharply serrate-ciliate on midnerve and exposed margins, tapering to a stout, straight, scabrous awn 1.5-6 cm or more long. *Paleas* hyaline with green nerves, about as long as lemma body. *Chromosome number* usually reported as $2n=14$.

Distribution. Texas: Regions 2, 7, 8 and 9, an occasional weed of roadsides and waste places, probably not persisting more than a year or two out of cultivation. General: Native to Europe, widely cultivated in the United States and frequent as a roadside weed in cereal-growing areas.

Flowering period: April to June.

Fig. 90. *Parapholis incurva*. Plant and spikelet with section of rachis. From Gould and Box, 1965.

Tribe 12. Monermeae

48. PARAPHOLIS C. E. Hubb.

A genus of 4 species, all native to temperate regions of the Old World.

1. **Parapholis incurva** (L.) C.E. Hubb., Blumea Suppl. 3 (Henrard Jubilee Vol.):14. 1946. *Pholiurus incurvus* (L.) Schinz. SICKELGRASS. Fig. 90. Low, tufted, much-branched annual with leafy, curving-erect or decumbent culms terminating in stiffly curved, cylindrical spikes. *Culms* mostly 5-35 cm long including inflorescences. *Leaves* glabrous. *Ligule* a glabrous membrane about 1 mm long. *Blades* thin, weak, soon withering, 2-8 (-12) mm long and 0.5-2 mm broad. *Inflorescence* a curved spike 3-10 cm long and 1.5-2.5 mm thick, occasionally broader at anthesis when glumes spread slightly. Disarticulation at nodes of thickened rachis. *Spikelets* 1-flowered, solitary at rachis nodes, partially embedded in and falling attached to rachis joints. *Glumes* subequal, 3-6 mm long, flattened but firm, several-nerved, somewhat asymmetrical, tapering to a point, placed in front of spikelet and appearing as halves of a single glume. *Lemmas* thin and hyaline, 1-nerved, awnless, shorter than glumes but longer than the narrow, hyaline paleas. *Chromosome numbers* reported, $2n=32$, 36, 38 and 42.

Distribution. Texas: Region 2, roadsides, coastal grasslands and along brackish swales, mostly in heavy, black, calciferous clayey soils. General: Native to Europe, adventive on both the eastern and western coasts of the United States, common along the California coast.

Flowering period: March to June.

SUBFAMILY V.   ERAGROSTOIDEAE

Tribe 13. Eragrosteae

49. ERAGROSTIS von Wolf*

Annual or perennial bunch grasses. *Sheaths* free on margins. *Ligules* ciliate. *Spikelets* in open or contracted, sometimes spicate panicles, 2-many-flowered, laterally compressed, disarticulating above glumes, the rachilla and/or the palea sometimes persistent. *Glumes* usually hyaline, one-nerved, deciduous. *Lemmas* usually membranous, three-nerved, the nerves sometimes inconspicuous. *Paleas* commonly hyaline, shorter than lemmas, 2-keeled, usually ciliolate on keels, longitudinally bowed out by mature grain. *Grain* lenticular or subellipsoidal and tapering to apex or cylindrical and tending to be truncate at both ends, usually somewhat laterally compressed, sometimes grooved on adaxial surface, smooth to reticulate, typically reddish-brown and translucent. *Basic chromosome number*, x= 10.

Several *Eragrostis* species have been introduced into this country for hay or pasture grasses particularly in semi-arid regions. They may be found as ephemeral escapes along roadsides, in railroad yards and in similar places. Unless they have become established in Texas, they are not included in this treatment.

Plants annual, without innovations or buds in the basal sheaths

    Paleas ciliate on keels, the cilia 0.4-0.8 mm long   18. *E. ciliaris*

    Paleas scabrous or ciliolate on keels, if ciliate then the cilia less than 0.1 mm long

        Plants with prostrate culms rooting at the nodes; sheaths with a ring of very short hairs at base   19. *E. hypnoides*

        Plants with culms sometimes decumbent at base and rooting at nodes but never prostrate and rooting at nodes; sheaths glabrous at base

            Spikelets 2-3 mm long, 2-5-flowered; panicles usually about two-thirds the length of the culm   20. *E. capillaris*

            Spikelets usually over 4 mm long and more than 5-flowered, if shorter or fewer-flowered then panicles less than half the length of the culm

                Spikelets broadly ovate, broadly lanceolate or linear, when linear and less than 2 mm wide then lower panicle branches not verticillate

*Contributed by LeRoy Harvey.

Spikelets linear, almost as thick as wide   25. *E. barrelieri*

Spikelets ovate to lanceolate, much wider than thick

Glumes and lemmas usually with glandular pits in the keels
24. *E. cilianensis*

Glumes and lemmas without glandular pits in the keels
21. *E. mexicana*

Spikelets narrowly ovate, narrowly lanceolate or linear, usually less than 2 mm wide, if linear the lower panicle branches verticillate

Lower panicle branches capillary, usually verticillate; spikelets usually less than 1 mm wide   23. *E. pilosa*

Lower panicle branches solitary or in bunches of 2 or 3, if some-what verticillate then not capillary; spikelets over 1 mm wide   22. *E. diffusa*

Plants perennial, with innovations, with or without buds in the basal sheaths

Panicles dense and spicate   2. *E. spicata*

Panicles open, or if dense, then not spicate

Spikelets sessile; panicle branches simple   1. *E. sessilispica*

Spikelets pedicellate, if sessile, then panicle branches with at least some primary branchlets

Panicle branches densely-flowered; spikelets in imbricate groups
14. *E. secundiflora*

Panicle branches loosely-flowered; spikelets not imbricate

Plants with a knotty, rhizomatous base

Culms, sheaths, blades, rachis and upper panicle branches viscid   16. *E. silveana*

Culms, sheaths, blades, rachis and upper panicle branches not viscid   15. *E. spectabilis*

Plants without a knotty, rhizomatous base

Spikelets on pedicels appressed to stiffly spreading branchlets
17. *E. curtipedicellata*

Spikelets on ascending to spreading pedicels on spreading and flexuous primary or secondary branchlets

Spikelets 10-30- (mostly over 15-) flowered; panicle branches stiffly spreading or flexuous, capillary, strongly scabrous

Spikelets sessile or subsessile   13. *E. refracta*

Spikelets long-pedicellate   12. *E. elliottii*

Spikelets 2-12- (mostly less than 10-) flowered; panicle branches not capillary and strongly scabrous when spreading

Plants with a glandular ring below nodes and usually on pedicels   9. *E. swallenii*

Plants without glandular tissue

Panicle oblong, at least 3 times as long as wide, with most branches about the same length

Blades, particularly the basal, long-attenuate, arching over towards the ground, more than 30 cm long, about 1 mm wide; grain about 1.4 mm long; lemma nerves conspicuous   10. *E. curvula*

Blades, if attenuate, attenuate only at tip and less than 30 cm long or, if blades attenuate and over 30 cm long, then grains less than 1 mm long; lemma nerves only faintly evident

Blades 2-10 cm long; culms frequently branched at lower nodes   11. *E. lehmanniana*

Blades 20-35 cm long; culms branching only at base
6. *E. palmeri*

Panicles ovate, the longest branches at base or below middle, those branches above progressively shorter

Lemmas usually over 2.4 mm long

Grains about 1 mm long; rachilla persistent; lemmas reddish-tinged   8. *E. trichodes*

Grains about 1.6 mm long; rachilla disarticulating; lemmas greenish with golden tips

7. *E. erosa*

Lemmas 1.5-2.4 mm long

Spikelets 2-6-flowered; blades 4-8 mm wide

3. *E. hirsuta*

Spikelets 5-11-flowered; blades 1-3 mm wide

Spikelets linear, 1 mm or less wide; lemmas 1.5-1.6 mm long; grain without adaxial groove or with only a shallow one; blades mostly less than 15 cm long, usually completely involute; branches, branchlets and pedicels capillary and strongly flexuous; lower panicle branches usually verticillate   5. *E. lugens*

Spikelets ovate to narrowly lanceolate, 1.6-1.8 mm wide; lemmas 1.8-2.2 (rarely 1.6) mm long; grain with strong adaxial groove; blades over 15 cm long or, if shorter, then usually flat at base; primary branches and branchlets stiffly flexuous, the pedicels capillary; lower panicle branches usually in bunches of 2 or 3

4. *E. intermedia*

1. **Eragrostis sessilispica** Buckl., Proc. Acad. Nat. Sci. Philadelphia Monogr. 1862:97. 1862. TUMBLE LOVEGRASS. Fig. 91. Perennial. *Culms* tufted, 30-90 cm tall, with few innovations. *Sheaths* overlapping below, pilose at throat. *Blades* flat to involute, usually glabrous, 10-30 cm long, 1-3 mm wide. *Panicles* ovate, open, few-flowered, 25-65 cm long, 10-25 cm wide, the rachis finally twisted in a loose spiral, deciduous and becoming a tumble weed. *Panicle branches* distant, flat, tough, stiffly spreading, scabrous, simple, 3-30 cm long. *Spikelets* sessile, appressed, somewhat distant, oblong to oblanceolate, compressed, 5-12.5 mm long, 2-3 mm wide, 5-12-flowered, the rachilla disarticulating but tough. *Glumes* indurate, persistent, acuminate, first glume 2-6 mm long, the second 3-6 mm long. *Lemmas* indurate, barely imbricate, straw-colored to purplish-tinged, acuminate, 3-5 mm long, 2-4 mm wide, the lateral nerves conspicuous. *Paleas* indurate, conspicuously bowed out, ciliolate on keels. *Grains* ellipsoidal, tapering toward apex, about 1.25 mm long. *Chromosome number, 2n=40.*

Distribution. Texas: Southern portion of region 2, western portion of regions 4 and 5 and eastern portion of regions 6, 8 and 9, in sandy prairies.

Fig. 91. *Eragrostis sessilispica.* Inflorescence and spikelet. From Gould and Box, 1965.

General: Southwest Kansas, western Oklahoma, central Texas and northern Tamaulipas, Mexico.

Flowering period: April through September.

2. **Eragrostis spicata** Vasey, Bot. Gaz. 16:146. 1891. SPICATE LOVEGRASS. Perennial. *Culms* tufted, 75-100 cm tall, with few innovations. *Sheaths* overlapping, glabrous. *Blades* glabrous, flat to involute, 20-30 cm long, 4-8 mm wide. *Panicles* dense, narrow, spicate, 30-35 cm long, 4-5 mm wide. *Branches* appressed, densely-flowered, about 5 mm long. *Spikelets* subsessile, ovate, compressed, 1.5-2 mm long, about 1 mm wide, 2-3-flowered, the rachilla disarticulating. *Glumes* hyaline, ovate, obtuse, persistent, the first glume about 1.25 mm, the second about 1 mm long. *Lemmas* hyaline, imbricate, greenish-white, ovate, somewhat obtuse, about 2 mm long and 0.5 mm wide, the lateral nerves evident. *Paleas* hyaline, ciliolate on keels. *Grains* narrowly ellipsoidal, about 1 mm long. *Chromosome number*, $2n=40$.

SUBFAMILY V. ERAGROSTOIDEAE   181

Distribution. Texas: Region 6, infrequent in low areas. General: Lower Rio Grande Valley, Texas and eastern Tamaulipas and extreme southern Baja California, Mexico. *Eragrostis spicata* is easily mistaken for similar-appearing, widely-distributed species of *Sporobolus*, from which it differs principally in the 2-3-flowered spikelets.

Flowering period: Summer and fall.

3. **Eragrostis hirsuta** (Michx.) Nees, Agrost. Bras. 508. 1829. BIGTOP LOVEGRASS. Perennial. *Culms* tufted, stout, 45-100 cm tall. *Sheaths* overlapping, hirsute or papillose-hirsute at throat and on margins and sometimes on collar and back, rarely glabrous. *Blades* flat to involute at the long-attenuate tip, 25-40 cm long, 4-8 mm wide. *Panicles* broadly ovate, open, 25-60 cm long, 15-25 cm wide. *Branches* ascending to spreading, lanceolate, much-compressed, 2-4 mm long, 1-1.2 mm wide, 2-6-flowered, the rachilla persistent. *Glumes* membranous, lanceolate, acuminate, the first glume 1.4-2 mm long, the second 1.6-2.2 mm long. *Lemmas* membranous, loosely if at all imbricate, greenish with reddish-purple splotches, ovate, acute, 2-2.4 mm long and about 1.2 mm wide, the lateral nerves usually inconspicuous. *Paleas* hyaline, ciliolate on the keels, persistent. *Grains* short, cylindrical, about 0.8 mm long. *Chromosome number, 2n=100.*

Distribution. Texas: Regions 1, 3 and 4 in sand and sandy loam in woods and river bottoms. General: Maryland and Florida to southern Missouri, eastern Oklahoma and Texas, mostly on the Coastal Plain; also in British Honduras and Guatemala.

Flowering period: September to November.

4. **Eragrostis intermedia** Hitchc., J. Wash. Acad. Sci. 23:450. 1931. PLAINS LOVEGRASS. Fig. 92. Perennial. *Culms* tufted, 55-90 cm tall. *Sheaths* glabrous except for pilose throat and usually pilose margins. *Blades* usually glabrous except for hairs above ligule, 15-20 cm or more long, 2-3 mm wide. *Panicles* ovate, open, 20-40 cm long, 15-30 cm wide. *Branches* ascending to spreading, scabrous, 10-25 cm long. *Pedicels* shorter than the spikelets. *Spikelets* ovate, acute to narrowly lanceolate, compressed, 4-7 mm long, 1.6-1.8 mm wide, 5-11-flowered, the rachilla usually persistent. *Glumes* membranous, the first lanceolate, acute, 1.2-1.8 mm long, the second glume ovate, acute, 1.4-2 mm long. *Lemmas* membranous, loosely imbricate, grayish-green to reddish-purple-tinged, ovate, acute, 1.8-2.2 mm long, about 1.2 mm wide, the lateral nerves inconspicuous. *Paleas* hyaline, ciliolate on keels. *Grains* oblong, about 0.8 mm long with strong adaxial groove. *Chromosome numbers* reported, 2n=ca. 54, 60, 72, ca. 74, 80, 100 and 120.

Distribution. Texas: Regions 2, 3, 4, 5, 6, 7 and 10 on sand, clay and rocky ground, often in disturbed soil. General: Southern Arizona through the southern and eastern half of Texas, Alabama to southwest Arkansas and also in the mountainous portions of Mexico and Guatemala.

Flowering period: June through November.

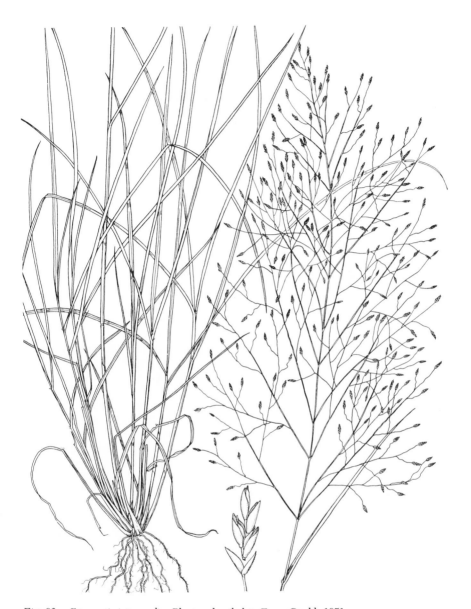

Fig. 92. *Eragrostis intermedia*. Plant and spikelet. From Gould, 1951.

Eragrostis intermedia, E. erosa, E. hirsuta, E. lugens and *E. palmeri* belong to a group of polymorphic species which are sometimes difficult to separate. The key characters and descriptions fit the majority of mature specimens. *Eragrostis trichocolea* Hack. & Arech., which also belongs to this group, has been reported from Texas, but no authentic specimens from the State have been seen.

SUBFAMILY V. ERAGROSTOIDEAE   183

5. **Eragrostis lugens** Nees, Agrost. Bras. 505. 1829. MOURNING LOVEGRASS. Perennial. *Culms* tufted, erect or ascending, 35-70 cm tall. *Sheaths* usually overlapping, pilose at throat. *Blades* usually involute, attenuate, glabrous, 8-20 cm long, 1-2 mm wide. *Panicles* ovate to pyramidal, open, 18-28 cm long, 10-18 cm wide. *Branches* slender, the lower mostly verticillate, with primary branchlets only, 9-15 cm long. *Spikelets* pedicellate, longer than the pedicels, linear-lanceolate, compressed, 3-4.5 mm long, 0.5-1 mm wide, 5-7-flowered, the rachilla persistent. *Glumes* hyaline, ovate, acute to subacuminate, first glume 0.6-1 mm long, the second 1.1-1.4 mm long. *Lemmas* membranous, barely if at all imbricate, usually shiny-plumbeous, ovate, acute, 1.5-1.6 mm long, 1-1.2 mm wide, the lateral nerves inconspicuous. *Paleas* hyaline, ciliolate on keels, persistent. *Grains* subellipsoidal, with weak or no adaxial grooves, 0.5-0.6 mm long. *Chromosome number* not reported.

Distribution. Texas: Southern portion of region 1 and eastern portion of region 6, mostly on sand dunes and other sandy areas. General: Texas, Mexico and northeastern Argentina to southeastern Brazil along the coast.

Flowering period: Mostly November to January, but also in the spring.

Plants herein referred to *E. lugens* are infrequent but quite distinct from *E. intermedia* in morphology and flowering period. They match the concept of the species held by Hitchcock as well as a fragment of the type in the National Herbarium. Exactly what populations belong to *E. lugens* Nees is difficult to determine as the type for the species no longer exists and the original description is not definitive.

6. **Eragrostis palmeri** S. Wats., Proc. Amer. Acad. Sci. 18:182. 1883. RIO GRANDE LOVEGRASS. Perennial. *Culms* tufted, 70-80 cm tall from a somewhat knotty base. *Sheaths* overlapping below, usually pilose at throat and on front of collar, sometimes on back. *Blades* involute, attenuate, glabrous, 20-35 cm long, 1-2 mm wide. *Panicles* oblong, open, 15-30 cm long. *Spikelets* pedicellate, narrowly ovate to linear-lanceolate, compressed, 4-6 mm long, 1-2 mm wide, 6-12-flowered, rachilla tardily disarticulating. *Glumes* hyaline, ovate, acute to acuminate, the first glume 1.2-1.8 mm long, the second 1.8-2.2 mm long. *Lemmas* membranous with hyaline tips, imbricate, grayish-green, ovate, acute, 2-2.4 mm long, about 0.8 mm wide, the lateral nerves evident. *Paleas* hyaline, somewhat persistent, glabrous on keels. *Grains* subovate, 0.6-0.8 mm long. *Chromosome number* not reported.

Distribution. Texas: Rio Grande Valley of region 6. General: From the Rio Grande Valley of Texas to Tamaulipas and northern Sonora, Mexico.

Flowering period: September through November.

7. **Eragrostis erosa** Scribn., in Beal, Grasses N. Amer. 2:483. 1896. CHIHUAHUA LOVEGRASS. Perennial. *Culms* tufted, 70-110 cm tall. *Sheaths* overlapping, pilose at throat and sometimes down margins. *Blades* flat to involute and attenuate at the tip, scattered-pilose at the base, 15-30 cm long, about 2 mm wide. *Panicles* ovate, open, 30-45 cm long, about 15 cm

wide. *Branches* slender, flexuous, ascending to spreading, 8-18 cm long. *Spikelets* pedicellate, lanceolate to linear-lanceolate, compressed, 6-9 mm long, 1-3 mm wide, 6-12-flowered, the rachilla persistent. *Glumes* membranous, ovate, acute to acuminate, the first glume 2-2.4 mm long, the second 2.4-2.6 mm long. *Lemmas* membranous, hyaline at margins, loosely imbricate, greenish with golden tips, ovate, acute to subacute, 2.8-3 mm long, about 1.6 mm wide, the lateral nerves inconspicuous. *Paleas* hyaline, ciliolate on the keels, persistent. *Grains* subellipsoidal, about 1.6 mm long. *Chromosome number* not reported.

Distribution. Texas: Occasional in regions 7 and 10 on rocky slopes of hills and mountains. General: Western Texas to New Mexico and southern Arizona and northern Chihuahua and Sonora, Mexico.

Flowering period: October and November.

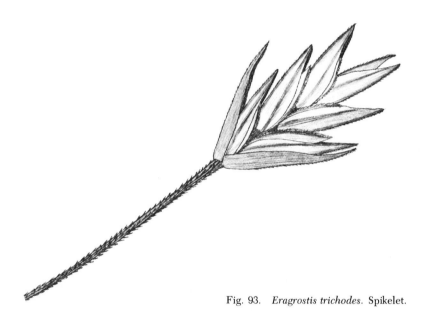

Fig. 93. *Eragrostis trichodes.* Spikelet.

8. **Eragrostis trichodes** (Nutt.) Wood, Class Book. 796. 1861. *Eragrostis pilifera* Scheele. SAND LOVEGRASS. Fig. 93. Perennial. *Culms* tufted, 60-160 cm tall. *Sheaths* overlapping, pilose at throat, sometimes villous on back or papillose-villous on margins. *Blades* usually flat with an involute tip, glabrous except for hairs above ligule, 15-40 cm long, 1-8 mm wide. *Panicles* oblong to ovoid, open, 35-55 cm long, 7-30 cm wide. *Branches* ascending to spreading 7-20 cm long. *Spikelets* pedicellate, ovate to lanceolate, compressed, 4-10 mm long, 1.5-3 mm wide, 4-18-flowered, the rachilla persistent. *Glumes* membranous, lanceolate, acuminate to ovate, acute, the first glume 1.8-4 mm long, the second 1.8-3.4 mm long. *Lemmas* membranous, scarcely imbricate, darkish straw-colored with reddish-tinged splotches, ovate, acute,

2.4-3.4 mm long, about 1.6 mm wide, the lateral nerves inconspicuous. *Paleas* hyaline, deciduous with the lemmas, ciliolate on keels. *Grains* cylindrical, about 1 mm long, with adaxial groove. *Chromosome number* not reported.

Distribution. Texas: Regions 1, 3, 4, 5, 6, eastern portion of region 7 and 8 and northern portion of region 9, in sandy prairies and open woods. General: Illinois and Nebraska to southwestern Arkansas and central Texas.

Flowering period: July to December and sporadically in the spring.

9. **Eragrostis swallenii** Hitchc., J. Wash. Acad. Sci. 23:451. 1933. SWALLEN LOVEGRASS. Perennial. *Culms* tufted, 40-70 cm tall, with a glandular band below the nodes. *Sheaths* overlapping, usually glabrous. *Blades* flat to involute towards tip, glabrous except for hairs above ligule, 10-20 cm long, 2-4 mm wide. *Panicles* ovate, open, 15-25 cm long, 10-15 cm wide. *Branches* mostly simple, ascending to spreading, stiffly flexuous, 3-12 cm long. *Pedicels* frequently with a glandular band. *Spikelets* pedicellate, linear-lanceolate, compressed, 6-16 mm long, 1.5-2.5 mm wide, 8-25-flowered; *rachilla* disarticulating tardily if at all. *Glumes* hyaline, ovate, acute, the first glume about 1.4 mm long, the second about 1.8 mm long. *Lemmas* membranous, imbricate, dull green, ovate, acute, about 2 mm long and 1.2 mm wide, the lateral nerves conspicuous. *Paleas* hyaline, somewhat persistent, scabrous on keels. *Grains* subellipsoidal, flattened, about 1 mm long. *Chromosome number,* $2n = 84$.

Distribution. Texas: Southern portion of region 2 in sandy soil. General: Southern Coastal Plain of Texas and also in Cardenas, San Luis Potosi; Mendoza, Veracruz; and Tehuacan, Puebla, Mexico.

Flowering period: Mostly fall.

10. **Eragrostis curvula** (Schrad.) Nees, Fl. Afr. Austr. 397. 1841. WEEPING LOVEGRASS. Perennial. *Culms* in large tufts, 75-150 cm tall. *Sheaths* shorter than culm internodes, the basal ones densely villous on back near base and less so on margins, the upper sheaths pilose only at throat. *Blades* involute, setaceous, those of the culm leaves 20-30 cm long, 1-1.4 mm wide, the basal leaf blades much longer and arching towards the ground. *Panicles* oblong to ovate, open, 25-40 cm long, 8-12 cm wide. *Branches* slender, ascending to spreading, mostly 5-7 cm long. *Spikelets* pedicellate, linear-lanceolate, compressed, 6-10 mm long, 1.4-1.6 mm wide, 6-12-flowered, the rachilla disarticulating. *Glumes* membranous, ovate, acute, the first glume about 1.8 mm long, the second about 2.8 mm long. *Lemmas* membranous, imbricate, grayish-green, ovate, acute, 2.2-2.6 mm long, about 1.4 mm wide, the lateral nerves conspicuous. *Paleas* hyaline, scabrous on keels. *Grains* ellipsoidal, about 1.4 mm long, the adaxial surface flattened and grooved. *Chromosome numbers* reported, $2n = 40$ and 50.

Distribution. Texas: In regions 3, 4, 5, 7, 8 and 9 on roadsides, in fields and in sandy areas. General: Native of South Africa, introduced in the southern United States.

Flowering period: Spring and fall.

11. **Eragrostis lehmanniana** Nees, Fl. Afr. Austr. 402. 1841. LEHMANN LOVEGRASS. Perennial. *Culms* tufted, commonly geniculate and branched (often fasciculate) at the nodes, 50-75 cm tall. *Sheaths* shorter than culm internodes, pilose at throat. *Blades* involute, stiffly spreading, glabrous, mostly 2-10 cm long, about 1 mm wide. *Panicles* oblong, somewhat open, 7-18 cm long, 3-8 cm wide. *Branches* stiffly ascending to spreading, 4-8 cm long. *Spikelets* pedicellate, linear, compressed, 12-14 mm, long, about 0.8 mm wide, 8-12-flowered, the rachilla tardily disarticulating. *Glumes* membranous, ovate, acuminate, the first glume about 1.6 mm long, the second about 1.8 mm long. *Lemmas* membranous, imbricate, dull grayish-green, narrowly ovate, obtuse, about 1.6 mm long and 1.2 mm wide, the lateral nerves evident. *Paleas* hyaline, scaberulous on keels, somewhat persistent. *Grains* oblong, flattened on adaxial surface, about 0.7 mm long. *Chromosome number* not reported.

Distribution. Texas: Rio Grande Valley in regions 6 and 10, in mesquite brush and along roadsides. General: Native of South Africa introduced and persisting in Oklahoma, Texas, New Mexico and Arizona and in Sonora, Mexico.

Flowering period: July through October.

12. **Eragrostis elliottii** S. Wats., Proc. Amer. Acad. Sci. 25:140. 1890. ELLIOTT LOVEGRASS. Fig. 94. Perennial. *Culms* tufted, 25-75 cm tall. *Sheaths* overlapping, bearded at throat, otherwise glabrous. *Blades* flat, glabrous, 6-30 cm long, 2-4 mm wide. *Panicles* ovate, open, 30-60 cm long, 15-40 cm wide. *Branches* capillary, scabrous, stiffly ascending to spreading, fragile, 8-15 cm long. *Spikelets* long pedicellate, linear-oblong, strongly compressed, 4.5-18 mm long, 1.5-3 mm wide, 6-30-flowered, the rachilla tardily disarticulating. *Glumes* membranous, acuminate, first glume 1.2-3.4 mm long, the second 1.6-3.4 mm long. *Lemmas* membranous, barely imbricate, greenish-white to reddish-tinged, ovate, acute to acuminate, 1.8-4.4 mm long, 1.2-1.6 mm wide, the lateral nerves conspicuous. *Paleas* membranous, scabrous on keels, somewhat persistent. *Grains* subellipsoidal, slightly flattened, about 0.75 mm long. *Chromosome number* not reported.

Distribution. Texas: Regions 2 and 3 in low sandy pinelands. General: North Carolina to Florida and southeastern Texas on the Coastal Plain, on the Coastal Plain of Mexico and British Honduras and in the West Indies.

Flowering period: Fall.

Fig. 94. *Eragrostis elliottii.* Inflorescence.

13. **Eragrostis refracta** (Muhl.) Scribn., Mem. Torrey Bot. Club. 5:49. 1894. COASTAL LOVEGRASS. Fig. 95. Perennial. *Culms* tufted, 35-80 cm tall. *Sheaths* overlapping at base, usually glabrous. *Blades* flat, those of the innovations densely hairy above ligule, 10-25 cm long, 2-5 mm wide. *Panicles* ovate, open, few-flowered, 30-60 cm long, 25-40 cm wide. *Panicle branches* capillary, stiff but not straight, scabrous, spreading to reflexed, 10-20 cm long. *Spikelets* sessile to subsessile, appressed, somewhat distant, linear, strongly compressed, 5-16 mm long, 1.5-2 mm wide, 10-28-flowered, the rachilla disarticulating. *Glumes* membranous, acuminate, persistent, first glume 0.8-1

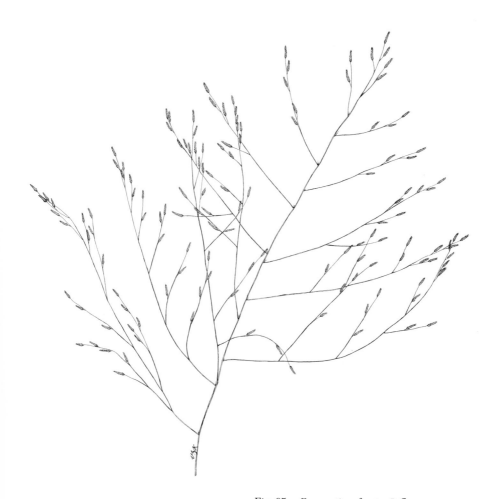

Fig. 95. *Eragrostis refracta.* Inflorescence.

mm long, the second 1.4-1.8 mm long. *Lemmas* membranous, imbricate, greenish to reddish-purple-tinged, ovate, acute to acuminate, 1.4-2.2 mm long, 0.8-1.2 mm wide, the lateral nerves conspicuous. *Paleas* scabrous on keels. *Grains* short, ellipsoidal, 0.6 mm long. *Chromosome number* not reported.

Distribution. Texas: Regions 1, 2 and 3 in sandy pineland. General: On the Coastal Plain, Delaware to Florida and extreme eastern Texas.

Flowering period: August through October.

SUBFAMILY V. ERAGROSTOIDEAE   189

Fig. 96. *Eragrostis secundiflora*. Inflorescence and spikelet. From Gould and Box, 1965, as *E. oxylepis*.

14. **Eragrostis secundiflora** Presl, Rel. Haenk. 1:276. 1820. *Eragrostis beyrichii* J. G. Smith, *E. oxylepis* (Torr.) Torr. RED LOVEGRASS. Fig. 96. Perennial. *Culms* tufted, 30-75 cm tall. *Sheaths* overlapping, pilose at the throat and sometimes down margins. *Blades* flat to involute with long hairs above ligule, usually 10-15 cm long and 2-2.5 mm wide. *Panicles* usually contracted, spicate or sometimes open, 5-30 cm long, 1-15 cm wide, the spikelets in dense clusters on branches and branchlets. *Panicle branches* usually appressed, at least the lowest somewhat distant, 1-14 cm long. *Spikelets* pedicellate, linear-oblong to ovate, strongly compressed, 6-20 mm long, 3-5 mm wide, 10-24-flowered, the rachilla disarticulating. *Glumes*

membranous, acuminate, the first glume 2.5-3 mm long, the second 3-4 mm long. *Lemmas* membranous, closely imbricate, broadly ovate, usually abruptly acute, straw-colored to reddish-purple-tinged, 1.6-2.4 mm long, about 1.2 mm wide, the lateral nerves conspicuous. *Paleas* membranous, falling with the lemmas, ciliolate on keels. *Grains* ellipsoidal about 1 mm long. *Chromosome number,* 2n=40.

Distribution. Texas: Regions 1, 2, 3 and 4 and uncommon in regions 6, 7, 8 and 9, often somewhat weedy. General: Florida and the Panhandle and Gulf Coast of Texas to eastern Colorado and New Mexico and south to Veracruz, Mexico.

Flowering period: May through June and August through December.

Included here in *Eragrostis secundiflora* is *E. beyrichii,* a population that typically differs in having acuminate and longer lemmas, shorter glumes and narrower leaf blades. The spikelets also tend to be pinkish instead of reddish-purple-tinged as in *E. secundiflora.* The name *E. oxylepis* has been used for this species by Chase (1951), Gould (1969) and Correll and Johnston (1970).

15. **Eragrostis spectabilis** (Pursh) Steud., Nom. Bot. Ed. II. 1:564. 1840. PURPLE LOVEGRASS. Fig. 97. Perennial. *Culms* tufted from a knotty rhizomatous base, 40-75 cm tall. *Sheaths* overlapping, usually pilose on collar and upper margins, sometimes densely so on back. *Blades* flat, with hairs above ligule, sometimes also pilose on both surfaces, 15-40 cm long, 3-7 mm wide. *Panicles* ovate to oblong, open, 25-45 cm long, 15-30 cm wide. *Branches* capillary, wiry, very scabrous, stiffly ascending to spreading, 9-15 cm long. *Spikelets* pedicellate, linear-oblong, compressed, 5-7 mm long, 1.5-2 mm wide, 7-11-flowered, the rachilla disarticulating. *Glumes* chartaceous, ovate, acute, the first glume 1.4-2 mm long, the second 1.6-2.2 mm long. *Lemmas* chartaceous, scarcely if at all imbricate, reddish-purple, ovate, acute, 1.8-2.2 mm long, with conspicuous lateral nerves. *Paleas* chartaceous, ciliolate on keels. *Grains* broadly ellipsoidal, flattened, about 0.8 mm long. *Chromosome number,* 2n=42.

Distribution. Texas: Regions 1, 2, 3 and 4, eastern portion of regions 5, 6 and 7 and rare in northern portion of regions 8 and 9, on sandy and disturbed soil. General: Maine and Minnesota to Nebraska, northern Florida and eastern Texas and northeastern Mexico and the British Honduras.

Flowering period: August through October.

This species apparently intergrades somewhat with *E. silveana.* See note under that species.

16. **Eragrostis silveana** Swallen, Amer. J. Bot. 19:438. 1932. SILVEUS LOVEGRASS. Perennial. *Culms* tufted from a knotty, rhizomatous base, 45-60 cm tall, usually viscid in long, rectilinear strips. *Sheaths* overlapping, viscid as on culm, pilose on front of collar and upper margins, rarely pilose elsewhere. *Blades* flat to involute, sometimes viscid below, 8-25 cm long, 2-4

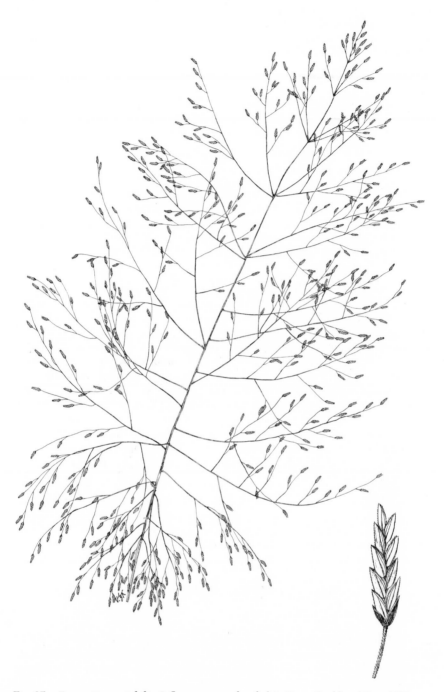

Fig. 97. *Eragrostis spectabilis.* Inflorescence and spikelet. From Gould and Box, 1965.

192   THE GRASSES OF TEXAS

mm wide. *Panicles* ovate, open, 20-30 cm long, about 15 cm wide, commonly viscid above. *Branches* capillary, ascending to spreading, viscid above, 6-12 cm long. *Spikelets* pedicellate, linear to oblong, compressed, 3.5-5 mm long, about 1 mm wide, 4-9-flowered, the rachilla disarticulating. *Glumes* chartaceous, ovate, acute, the first about 1 mm long, the second 1-1.2 mm long. *Lemmas* chartaceous, imbricate, reddish-purple, ovate, acute, about 1.4 mm long and 1 mm wide, the lateral nerves conspicuous and sometimes double. *Paleas* hyaline, ciliate on the keels. *Grains* broadly ellipsoidal, about 0.6 mm long. *Chromosome number* not reported.

Distribution. Texas: Infrequent, in region 2, on clay to sandy soils. General: San Patricio to Brazoria counties, Texas, and Cardenas, San Luis Potosi, Mexico.

Flowering period: August through November.

This species seems to be intermediate between *E. spectabilis* and *E. curtipedicellata* and occurs where their distributions overlap.

17. **Eragrostis curtipedicellata** Buckl., Proc. Acad. Nat. Sci. Philadelphia Monogr. 1862:97. 1862. GUMMY LOVEGRASS. Fig. 98. Perennial. *Culms* tufted, viscid, 20-60 cm tall. *Sheaths* overlapping, pilose at throat and sometimes down margins, frequently viscid. *Blades* flat, glabrous except sometimes with a few hairs above ligule, about 10 cm long and 4 mm wide. *Panicles* ovate, open, 30-45 cm long, 10-25 cm wide, with branches and pedicels viscid and scabrous. *Branches* stiffly ascending to spreading, 3-15 cm long. *Spikelets* subsessile, linear to oblong, compressed, 4-5 mm long, 1-1.5 mm wide, 4-10-flowered, the rachilla disarticulating. *Glumes* membranous, ovate, subacuminate, the first glume 1.25-1.5 mm long, the second 1.8-2 mm long. *Lemmas* membranous, barely if at all imbricate, greenish to reddish-tinged to straw-colored, ovate, acute, about 2 mm long, about 1 mm wide, the lateral nerves conspicuous. *Paleas* membranous, ciliate on keels. *Grains* ellipsoidal, tapering to apex, about 1 mm long. *Chromosome number*, $2n = 40$.

Distribution. Texas: In all regions except region 10, in sandy and clay soil. General: Southeastern Arkansas and southern Kansas, to eastern New Mexico, Texas and extreme northeastern Mexico.

Flowering period: Spring and fall.

This species appears to intergrade with *E. silveana*. See note under that species.

18. **Eragrostis ciliaris** (L.) R. Br. in Tuckey, Narr. Exp. Congo. 478. 1818. GOPHERTAIL LOVEGRASS. Annual. *Culms* tufted, 10-55 cm tall. *Sheaths* overlapping, usually pilose at throat and down margins. *Blades* flat, 4-10 cm long and about 2 mm wide, with hairs above ligule. *Panicles* densely spicate or somewhat open, interrupted at base and occasionally above, 4-10

Fig. 98. *Eragrostis curtipedicellata*. Inflorescence and spikelet. From Gould and Box, 1965.

194   THE GRASSES OF TEXAS

cm long, 2-6 mm wide. *Branches* usually appressed but sometimes spreading, densely-flowered, 1-5 cm long. *Spikelets* subsessile, broadly ovate, compressed, 2-3 mm long, 1-1.2 mm wide, 6-12-flowered, the rachilla disarticulating. *Glumes* hyaline, narrowly acute to acuminate, the first glume 0.8-1 mm long, the second 1.2-1.5 mm long. *Lemmas* hyaline, loosely imbricate, greenish-white, linear-oblong, obtuse to subtruncate, 1-1.8 mm long, about 0.8 mm wide, the lateral nerves conspicuous. *Paleas* hyaline, long-ciliate (0.4-0.8 mm) on keels. *Grains* ellipsoidal, about 0.5 mm long. *Chromosome number*, 2n=20.

Distribution. Texas: In Waller and Washington counties in region 3, introduced but not persistent. General: Tropics of the Old and New Worlds, in the United States introduced along the Gulf Coast from Florida to Mississippi and Texas.

Flowering period: Fall and winter.

A closely related species, *Eragrostis tenella* (L.) Beauv., has been reported from Texas (as *E. amabilis*), but no specimens have been seen. It differs from *E. ciliaris* in having an open panicle and shorter cilia. (0.2-0.4 mm long) on the palea keels.

19. **Eragrostis hypnoides** (Lam.) B.S.P., Prelim. Cat. N.Y. City. 69. 1888. TEAL LOVEGRASS. Fig. 99. Annual. *Culms* creeping, rooting at the nodes, forming mats, the erect, floriferous culms 10-25 cm tall. *Sheaths* much shorter than culm internodes, usually with a ring of hairs at base, pilose at throat and usually down margins. *Blades* flat, sparsely appressed-pilose below, more densely so above, 0.5-2.5 cm long, 0.5-1.5 mm wide. *Panicles* ovate, open, few-flowered, 2-5 cm long, 1-3.5 cm wide. *Branches* ascending to spreading, glabrous to pubescent, 0.5-2.5 cm long. *Spikelets* short-pedicellate, lanceolate to narrowly ovate, compressed, 5-12 mm long, 1.5-2.5 mm wide, 8-22-flowered, the rachilla persistent. *Glumes* hyaline, acuminate, the first glume about 0.8 mm long, the second 1.2-1.8 mm long. *Lemmas* membranous, barely if at all imbricate, greenish-white, ovate, acute to acuminate, 1.8-2 mm long, about 1 mm wide, the lateral nerves conspicuous. *Paleas* hyaline, persistent, ciliolate on keels. *Grains* discoid, about 0.6 mm long. *Chromosome number* not reported.

Distribution. Texas: Occasional in regions 1, 2, 3, 4, 5 and 7 on mud and sand bars in streams and rivers and on lakes and pond margins. General: Occasional, Vermont and Virginia to the eastern portion of the Dakotas and eastern Texas, scattered in the western portion of the Intermountain Region and on the West Coast and in Mexico, the West Indies and adjacent South America.

Flowering period: Mostly fall, sparser in the spring and occasionally in the summer.

Fig. 99. *Eragrostis hypnoides*. Plant, spikelet and floret.

20. **Eragrostis capillaris** (L.) Nees, Agrost. Bras. 505. 1829. LACE-GRASS. Fig. 100. Annual. *Culms* tufted, 40-50 cm tall. *Sheaths* overlapping, hispid at throat and down margins. *Blades* mostly flat, scattered papillose-hispid above, 15-30 cm long, 2-4 mm wide. *Panicle* narrowly ovate, open, 15-40 cm long, 9-25 cm wide. *Branches* capillary, ascending to spreading, 5-15 cm long. *Spikelets* pedicellate, lanceolate to ovate, compressed, about 2 mm long and 1 mm wide, 2-5-flowered, the rachilla persistent. *Glumes* hyaline, usually acuminate, the first glume about 1.2 mm long, the second 1.2-1.4 mm long. *Lemmas* membranous, not imbricate, greenish to plumbeous, ovate, acute, about 1.5 mm long, about 1 mm wide, the lateral nerves inconspicuous. *Paleas* hyaline, about one-half the length of lemmas, ciliolate on keels, persistent. *Grains* short-cylindric, about 0.6 mm long. *Chromosome numbers* reported, $2n = 50$ and 100.

Distribution. Texas: Infrequent, in regions 2, 3 and 8, on dry, open ground in woods. General: Maine to Iowa, south to Virginia and eastern Texas.

Flowering period: Summer.

196   THE GRASSES OF TEXAS

Fig. 100. *Eragrostis capillaris.* Spikelet. From Gould and Box, 1965.

21. Eragrostis mexicana (Hornem.) Link, Hort. Berol. 1:190. 1827. *Eragrostis neomexican* Vasey. MEXICAN LOVEGRASS. Annual. *Culms* tufted, sometimes geniculate, decumbent and branched at lower nodes, sometimes with a partial or complete ring of glands below nodes, 15-120 cm tall. *Sheaths* overlapping below, often with glandular pits in keel or nerves, pilose or papillose-pilose. *Blades* lanceolate, flat, glabrous above, sometimes papillose-pilose below, often with glandular pits in nerves below, 5-10 cm long, 3-6 mm wide. *Panicles* narrowly to broadly ovate, open to densely-flowered, 10-18 cm long and 4-8 cm wide. *Branches* ascending to spreading, flexuous, sometimes with glandular pits, 4-6 cm long. *Spikelets* pedicellate, ovate, acute, compressed, 6-9 mm long, 1.8-2 mm wide, 7-15-flowered, the rachilla persistent. *Glumes* membranous, ovate, acute, first glume 1.6-1.8 mm long, the second 1.8-2 mm long. *Lemmas* membranous, hardly imbricate, grayish-green to green and red mottled, broadly ovate, acute, 2-2.2 mm long, about 1.2 mm wide, the lateral nerves conspicuous. *Paleas* hyaline, ciliolate on keels, persistent. *Grains* cylindric, flattened, with an adaxial groove, 0.4-0.6 mm long. *Chromosome number*, $2n=60$.

Distribution. Texas: Region 10 on disturbed ground. General: Southern California to western Texas and also in Mexico and Central America.

Flowering period: July to September.

Plants with large panicles, large spikelets and wide leaf blades were referred to *Eragrostis neomexicana* by Hitchcock (1935) and Chase (1951), but there is complete intergradation in these characters.

SUBFAMILY V. ERAGROSTOIDEAE   197

22. **Eragrostis diffusa** Buckl., Proc. Acad. Nat. Sci. Philadelphia Monogr. 1862:97. 1862. SPREADING LOVEGRASS. Fig. 101. Annual. *Culms* tufted, sometimes geniculate and branching at lower nodes, 30-55 cm tall. *Sheaths* shorter than culm internodes, glabrous except at the pilose throat. *Blades* lanceolate, flat to folded, 8-18 cm long, 3-7 mm wide. *Panicles* much-branched, oblong to ovate, open, 12-30 cm long and 6-20 cm wide. *Branches* 4-9 cm long, ascending to spreading, the branchlets appressed and appearing few-flowered. *Spikelets* pedicellate, narrowly lanceolate, compressed, 5-8 mm long, 1-2 mm wide, 8-14-flowered, the rachilla persistent. *Glumes* hyaline, ovate, acute to acuminate, the first glume 1-1.2 mm long, the second 1.4-1.6 mm long. *Lemmas* membranous, only slightly imbricate, grayish-green, narrowly ovate, acute, 1.8-2.2 mm long, about 1.2 mm wide, the lateral nerve evident. *Paleas* hyaline, ciliolate on keels, persistent. *Grains* ellipsoidal, about 1 mm long. *Chromosome number,* 2n=60.

Distribution. Texas: In all regions except region 1, on disturbed ground. General: Georgia and the upper Mississippi Valley to Kansas, Texas and southern California and also in Mexico.

Flowering period: June through November.

Eragrostis diffusa intergrades northeastward with *E. pectinacea* (Michx.) Nees, which does not reach Texas. A form with spreading pedicels and branchlets has been differentiated as *E. arida* Hitchc. *Eragrostis tephrosanthos* Schult. may be distinct or only a smaller form with less imbricate lemmas. Spreading lovegrass has been confused with *E. mexicana* (Hornem.) Link but is easily separated from it on grain characteristics.

23. **Eragrostis pilosa** (L.) Beauv. Ess. Agrost. 71, 162, 175. 1812. INDIA LOVEGRASS. Annual. *Culms* tufted, branched at base or above, 15-45 cm tall. *Sheaths* overlapping below, pilose at throat. *Blades* flat to folded, glabrous, 5-15 cm long, 2-3 mm wide. *Panicles* ovate, open, 5-20 cm long, 2.5-10 cm wide. *Branches* 2-10 cm long, capillary, flexuous, ascending to spreading, commonly verticillate below. *Spikelets* pedicellate, linear-lanceolate, compressed, 2-6 mm long, 0.6-1 mm wide, 4-10-flowered, the rachilla persistent. *Glumes* hyaline, the first glume acuminate, 0.8-1 mm long, the second ovate, acute, 1.2-1.6 mm long. *Lemmas* membranous with a hyaline tip, scarcely if at all imbricate, grayish-green with reddish tips, ovate, acute, 1.2-1.6 mm long, the lateral nerves conspicuous. *Paleas* hyaline, persistent, ciliolate on keels. *Grains* ellipsoidal, 0.6-0.8 mm long. *Chromosome number,* 2n=40.

Distribution. Texas: Regions 2, 3, 4, 5, 6 and 9 on disturbed ground. General: Introduced from the Old World, now distributed from Maine and Florida westward to Colorado and Texas and also in Mexico, the West Indies and South America.

Flowering period: June through August.

Eragrostis perplexa L. H. Harvey, reported from Texas (Texline), probably is not specifically distinct from *E. pilosa.*

Fig. 101. *Eragrostis diffusa*. Inflorescence and spikelet.

SUBFAMILY V. ERAGROSTOIDEAE   199

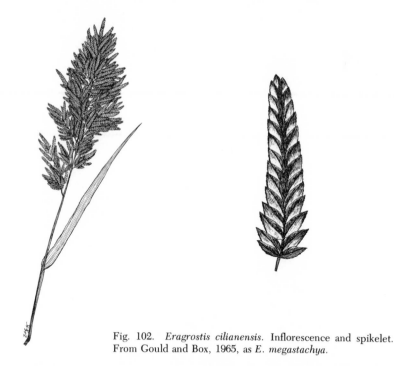

Fig. 102. *Eragrostis cilianensis*. Inflorescence and spikelet. From Gould and Box, 1965, as *E. megastachya*.

24. **Eragrostis cilianensis** (All.) E. Mosher, Ill. Agr. Exp. Sta. Bull. 205:381. 1918. *Eragrostis megastachya* Link. STINKGRASS. Fig. 102. Annual. *Culms* tufted, 10-60 cm tall, branching at base and above, frequently geniculate, usually with a ring of glands below the nodes. *Sheaths* overlapping, glabrous except the pilose throat, usually with glandular pits in the keel and sometimes in the other nerves. *Blades* lanceolate, flat, sometimes folded, glabrous, with glandular pits in midrib on lower surface, 10-20 cm long, 2.5-7 mm wide. *Panicles* ovate to oblong, densely-flowered to open, 5.5-16 cm long, 2-8.5 cm wide. *Branches* stiffly ascending to spreading, 2.5-5 cm long. *Spikelets* pedicellate, ovate, acute to linear-oblong or lanceolate, slightly compressed, 6-20 mm long, 2-4 mm wide, 12-40-flowered, the rachilla persistent. *Glumes* membranous, broadly to narrowly ovate, acute to subacute, keels with glandular pits, the first glume 1.2-2.2 mm long, the second 1.2-2.5 mm long. *Lemmas* membranous, closely imbricate, dull grayish-green, ovate, acute to obtuse, 2.2-2.8 mm long, about 1.2 mm wide, the lateral nerves conspicuous, usually glandular-pitted on keels. *Paleas* hyaline, ciliolate on keels, persistent. *Grains* ellipsoidal, 0.5-0.8 mm long. *Chromosome number*, $2n = 20$.

Distribution. Texas: In all regions, in disturbed ground. General: Native of Europe and a cosmopolitan weed in the United States, Mexico, Central America, most of the West Indies and South America.

Flowering period: Mostly August through October.

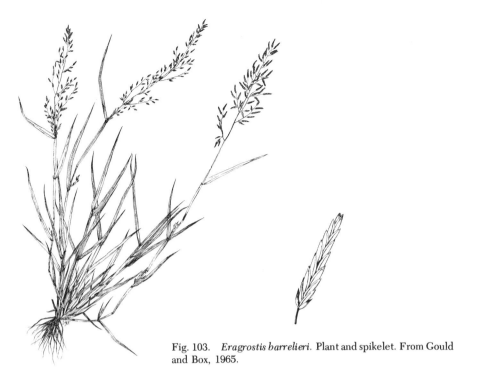

Fig. 103. *Eragrostis barrelieri*. Plant and spikelet. From Gould and Box, 1965.

25. **Eragrostis barrelieri** Daveau, J. Bot. (Morot) Paris. 8:289. 1894. MEDITERRANEAN LOVEGRASS. Fig. 103. Annual. *Culms* tufted, 20-55 cm tall, decumbent and branching at lower nodes, usually with a complete or partial ring of glandular tissue below nodes. *Sheaths* shorter than culm internodes, pilose at throat, otherwise glabrous. *Blades* lanceolate, flat to involute at tips, glabrous except for scattered hairs above, 3-10 cm long, 1-5 mm wide. *Panicles* ovate, open, frequently with glandular areas or rings on rachis below branches, 5-16 cm long, 2-8 cm wide. *Branches* ascending to spreading, frequently with glandular spots or rings, 1.5-5.5 cm long. *Spikelets* pedicellate, linear to oblong, little compressed, 5-11 mm long, 1-1.5 mm wide, 6-15-flowered, the rachilla persistent. *Glumes* hyaline, ovate, acute to acuminate, the first glume 1-1.4 mm long, the second 1.4-1.8 mm long. *Lemmas* membranous, scarcely imbricate, grayish-green, sometimes with reddish splotches, ovate, obtuse, 1.8-2 mm long, about 1.2 mm wide, the lateral nerves conspicuous. *Paleas* hyaline, ciliolate on upper half of keels, persistent. *Grains* ellipsoidal, about 1 mm long. *Chromosome number*, $2n=60$.

Distribution. Texas: In all regions except region 1, in disturbed soil. General: Native of the Mediterranean Basin, now distributed in the United States from Kansas to Texas and New Mexico and on the Florida Panhandle, in the lowlands of eastern and southern Mexico and in the West Indies.

Flowering period: April through November.

SUBFAMILY V. ERAGROSTOIDEAE   201

Fig. 104. *Neeragrostis reptans.* Two pistillate florets (A), the upper with the lemma removed, and two staminate florets (B), the upper with the lemma removed. From Gould and Box, 1965.

50. NEERAGROSTIS Nicora

A monotypic North American genus.

1. **Neeragrostis reptans** (Michx.) Nicora, Revista Argent. Agron. 29:1-11. 1962. *Eragrostis reptans* (Michx.) Nees. CREEPING LOVEGRASS. Fig. 104. Annual with creeping, branching, mat-forming culms, the erect, floriferous tips mostly 5-10 (-20) cm tall including the inflorescence. *Culms* wiry, with numerous nodes and short internodes, glabrous or conspicuously pubescent, especially below the inflorescence. *Sheaths* glabrous or pubescent, much shorter than culm internodes, mostly 0.5-1 cm long. *Ligule* a ring of hairs usually 0.5 mm or less long. *Blades* flat or folded, 1-4 cm long, 1-2 mm broad, glabrous or frequently pubescent on both surfaces. *Staminate and pistillate inflorescences* similar, capitate, with a short, glabrous or pubescent main axis, this usually equaled or exceeded in length by the many-flowered spikelets. *Spikelets* ovate to linear, extremely variable in size, shape and number of florets but mostly 0.8-2 cm long with 16-40 florets, occasionally to over 2.5 cm long with 60 florets. *Glumes* thin, translucent, 1-nerved, glabrous or sparsely hirsute, irregularly reduced, the first glume one-third to two-thirds as long as the second, the second slightly shorter than lemmas. *Florets of pistillate spikelets* with feathery stigmas exserted and conspicuous until the caryopses are completely developed. *Lemmas* ovate, acute, acuminate or short-awned, 2.6-(occasionally 2-) 3.3 mm long, 3-nerved, similar to glumes in texture, glabrous or hirsute. *Lemmas of pistillate spikelets* eventually deciduous from rachilla, the lemmas of staminate spikelets apparently persistent. *Paleas of pistillate spikelets* about half as long as lemmas, paleas of staminate spikelets nearly as long as lemmas. *Anthers* mostly 1.5-2 mm long. *Caryopses* brownish, about 0.5 mm long, little if at all compressed, with an embryo one-third to one-half as long as the endosperm. *Chromosome number,* $2n = 60$.

Distribution. Texas: Regions 1, 2, 3, 4, 5, 6, 7 and 8 along the shores of lakes, streams and marshy areas, most frequent and abundant on the exposed beds of lakes and streams following periods of drouth, usually in tight, clayey soils. General: Central United States from Kentucky and South Dakota to Louisiana and Texas and also in Florida and northeastern Mexico.

Flowering period: April through November, under favorable conditions for growth.

Correll and Johnston (1970) have followed Hitchcock (1935) and Chase (1951) in recognizing this grass as a species of *Eragrostis* (*E. reptans*). Nicora (1962) reviewed the characteristics of the taxon and concluded that it was distinct from *Eragrostis*. Differences in ovary and epidermal characters were noted, as well as the dioecious nature of *N. reptans*. Nicora indicated probably close relationships between *Neeragrostis* and the genera *Distichlis* and *Monanthochloë*.

51. TRIDENS Roem. & Schult.

Perennials with stiffly erect culms, flat blades and open or contracted panicles of several-flowered spikelets. *Ligule* a glabrous ciliate membrane. Disarticulation above glumes and between florets. *Glumes* mostly thin and membranous, the first 1-nerved, the second 1-3- (rarely 5-7-) nerved. *Lemmas* broad, thin, 3-nerved, short-hairy on the nerves below (except in *T. albescens*), rounded on back, mostly bidentate at apex, the mid-nerve and often the lateral nerves minutely mucronate. *Palea* equaling or slightly shorter than lemma, the nerves glabrous or hairy. *Caryopses* dark brown, the embryo about two-fifths the length of the caryopsis.

A genus of about 16 species present for the most part in the eastern and southern United States and northern Mexico. As treated by Hitchcock (1935) and Chase (1951), *Tridens* included those species now referred to *Erioneuron*.

Panicle open, more or less loosely-flowered, not spikelike

Pedicels of lateral spikelets less than 1 mm long   3. *T. ambiguus*

Pedicels of lateral spikelets, at least some, more than 1 mm long

Lateral nerves of lemmas commonly excurrent as short points

Blades mostly 1-3 mm wide; panicles mostly 5-16 cm long
                                                      1. *T. texanus*

Blades mostly 3-10 mm wide; panicles mostly 15-35 cm long
                                                      2. *T. flavus*

Lateral nerves of lemmas rarely excurrent as points

Lemmas 4-6 mm long; ligule a minute fringed membrane, the membrane less than 0.5 mm long   4. *T. buckleyanus*

Lemmas 2-3.2 mm long; ligule a membrane 1.2-3 mm long
     5. *T. eragrostoides*

Panicle contracted, densely-flowered or elongate and spikelike

Nerves of lemma glabrous or hairy at extreme base   6. *T. albescens*

Nerves of lemma ciliate or puberulent to well above base

Glumes slightly longer to shorter than lemmas, much shorter than spikelets

Midnerve of lemma pubescent on lower one-third to one-half, excurrent at apex as a short awn (mucro)   7. *T. congestus*

Midnerve of lemma usually pubescent to well above middle, not excurrent at apex as an awn   9. *T. muticus*

Glumes much exceeding lemmas in length,. usually as long as spikelets
     8. *T. strictus*

1. **Tridens texanus** (S. Wats.) Nash, in Small, Fl. Southeast. U. S., 142. 1903. TEXAS TRIDENS. Tufted perennial without rhizomes or stolons. *Culms* slender, strictly erect, 20-75 cm tall; nodes glabrous but the internodes often pilose with soft, spreading hairs. *Sheaths* glabrous or pilose on back, densely pubescent on collar and on upper margins. *Ligule* a fringed scale, usually 0.5 mm or less long. *Blades* thin, flat or becoming inrolled, attenuate to a long, narrow tip, mostly 7-20 cm long and 1-5 mm broad, more or less hispid, with long hairs on adaxial surface just above ligule. *Inflorescence* an open or loosely contracted panicle 5-16 cm long, with scattered, slender, flexuous branches, these bare of spikelets near base and not or only moderately rebranched. *Panicle axis and branches* hispid. *Spikelets* large, mostly 6-13 mm long and with 6-12 florets, usually purple or rosy-purple at maturity, borne on short lateral pedicels or on rather long, pedicel-like branch tips. *Glumes, lemmas* and *paleas* thin and papery. *Glumes* 1-nerved, nearly equal, mostly more than half as long as lemmas, the single nerve strong, bright green. *Lemmas* broad, pubescent on nerves below middle, the midnerve minutely mucronate from a slightly notched apex, at least some of lateral nerves excurrent as minute mucro. *Paleas* glabrous, slightly shorter than lemmas, abruptly broadened and bowed-out below. *Chromosome number, 2n = 40.*

Distribution. Texas: Regions 2, 6 and 7, not infrequent in the area of distribution on both clayey and sandy loam soils, often in protection of shrubs and along fenced road right-of-ways. General: Southern Texas and Tamaulipas, Nuevo Leon and Coahuila, Mexico.

Flowering period: Mostly May to early June and again in late August to November.

2. **Tridens flavus** (L.) Hitchc., Rhodora 8:210. 1906. Perennial bunchgrass with a firm, often knotty and somewhat rhizomatous base. *Culms* mostly 0.6-1.8 m tall, glabrous. *Sheaths* pubescent on the collar, otherwise glabrous, the lower sheaths laterally compressed and keeled. *Ligule* a minute ciliate membrane, less than 0.5 mm long. *Blades* elongate, mostly 3-10 mm broad, typically long-attenuate and inrolled at tip, glabrous or sparsely hispid, usually with hairs in vicinity of ligule. *Panicles* open, 15-35 cm or more long and with erect-spreading or widely spreading lower branches 10-25 cm long; lower panicle branches bare of spikelets for the basal one-third to one-half of their length. *Spikelets* 5-9 mm long, 4-8-flowered, short pediceled and loosely imbricate or clustered on branchlets and branch tips. *Glumes* firm, shiny, 1-nerved, acute or obtuse, often mucronate. *Lemmas* thin but firm, 3-5 mm long, the lower ones longer than the upper ones, the lateral nerves puberulent or ciliate to well above middle; lemma apex usually notched and mucronate, the lateral nerves of at least some lemmas also excurrent as minute mucro. *Paleas* about as long as lemmas, broadened below. *Chromosome number, 2n=40.*

Panicles drooping, the main axis and branches flexuous; pulvini at base of branches on upper side of branch only, inconspicuously hairy or glabrous   2A.   *T. flavus* var. *flavus*

Panicles erect, not drooping, the branches and branchlets stiffly spreading; pulvini at base of branches extending entirely around branch base, conspicuously hairy   2B.   *T. flavus* var. *chapmanii*

2A. **Tridens flavus** (L.) Hitchc. var. **flavus.** PURPLETOP. Fig. 105.

Distribution. Texas: Frequent in open woods and on roadsides in regions 1 and 3 and occasional but less common in regions 2, 4, 5, 7, 8 and 9. General: Throughout the eastern United States, westward to Nebraska and Texas.

Flowering period: Late August to November.

2B. **Tridens flavus** (L.) Hitchc. var. **chapmanii** (Small) Shinners, Rhodora 56:27. 1954. CHAPMAN PURPLETOP.

Distribution. Texas: Region 1, infrequent, in piney woods.

Flowering period: Late summer and fall.

Fig. 105. *Tridens flavus* var. *flavus*. Inflorescence and spikelet. From Gould and Box, 1965.

206   THE GRASSES OF TEXAS

3. **Tridens ambiguus** (Ell.) Schult., Mantissa 2:333. 1824. PINE BAR-REN TRIDENS. Tufted perennial with a firm, knotty base. *Culms* glabrous, stiffly erect, mostly 60-125 cm tall. *Sheaths* glabrous except for a few hairs on either side of collar, rounded or basal ones slightly keeled. *Ligule* to 1 mm long, the membranous base minute. *Blades* firm, elongate, attenuate and often infolded at apex, mostly 2-5 mm broad, glabrous except for a few hairs above ligule. *Inflorescence* a narrow but loose panicle 8-20 cm long, with scattered, stiffly erect-spreading branches to 10 cm long, these sparsely rebranched or occasionally none of primary branches rebranched. *Spikelets* 4-6 mm long and about 4 mm broad at maturity, 4-6-flowered; spikelets not terminating branches on pedicels mostly less than 1 mm long. *Glumes* thin, glabrous, 1-nerved, acute, the second glume about as long as the lowermost lemma, the first slightly shorter. *Lemmas* 3-4 mm long, ciliate on nerves to middle or above, slightly notched at apex and with midnerve and often lateral nerves excurrent as minute mucro. *Paleas* about as long as lemmas, ciliolate on nerves, enlarged and bowed out at base. *Chromosome number, 2n=40.*

Distribution. Texas: Regions 1 and 2 in piney woods and road right-of-ways bordering woods areas, infrequent.

Flowering period: September to November.

4. **Tridens buckleyanus** (L.H. Dewey) Nash, in Small, Fl. Southeast. U. S., 143. 1903. BUCKLEY TRIDENS. Tufted perennial with erect culms 40-80 cm tall from a firm, non-rhizomatous base. *Culms* glabrous or the lower nodes hispid. *Sheaths* rounded and scabrous on back, without hairs at collar. *Ligules* 0.4-1 mm long, the membranous base about as long as the fringe of hairs. *Blades* long, flat, 1-4 mm broad, scabrous or pubescent with short hairs. *Panicles* 10-28 cm long with a few, widely-spaced, stiffly erect or erect-spreading branches; main axis and branches roughly scabrous, the branches sparsely-flowered, little if at all rebranched, mostly 4-13 cm long. *Spikelets* 3-5-flowered, 7-10 mm long, mostly 2-3 mm broad. *Glumes* thin but firm, 1-nerved, acute or rounded at apex, the first glume typically 5-6 mm long, the second slightly shorter. *Lemmas* 4-6 mm long, pubescent on nerves and back below middle, the lateral nerves pubescent to well above middle, rounded and usually notched at apex, occasionally minutely mucronate; lateral nerves often faint, usually not extending to lemma margins. *Paleas* about 1 mm shorter than lemmas, pubescent on nerves below. *Caryopses* oblong, finely reticulate, about 2.5 mm long. *Chromosome number* reported as *2n=32* but this may be erroneous.

Distribution. Texas: Southeastern portion of region 7 on shaded stream banks and woods borders, not common. General: Endemic to Texas.

Flowering period: Late summer and fall.

5. **Tridens eragrostoides** (Vasey & Scribn.) Nash, in Small, Fl. South-east. U. S., 142. 1903. LOVEGRASS TRIDENS. Fig. 106. Densely tufted perennial. *Culms* slender, stiffly erect, mostly 50-100 cm tall; nodes glabrous

Fig. 106. *Tridens eragrostoides*.   Inflorescence and spikelet. From Gould and Box, 1965.

or sparsely bearded with long, soft hairs. *Sheaths* glabrous, scabrous or sparsely pilose. *Ligule* a thin membrane 1.2-3 mm long, the tip usually lacerate and glabrous. *Blades* elongate, mostly 1.5-5 mm broad, scabrous and occasionally sparsely pilose, narrowing both at base and apex, with a long, slender, attenuate tip. *Panicles* open, mostly 10-30 cm long, the usually lax and drooping lower branches bare of spikelets at base, typically 6-12 cm long, rebranched or remaining simple. *Spikelets* 3-7 mm long, 5-12-flowered, usually on pedicels 1.5 mm or more long. *Glumes* and *lemmas* thin, often purple-colored. *Glumes* glabrous, acute or acuminate, 1-nerved, the second glume 2-3 mm long, the first slightly shorter. *Lemmas* puberulent on nerves often to well above middle; lemma apex rounded or notched, the midnerve usually excurrent as a mucro, the lateral nerves rarely reaching the margins and minutely mucronate; lowermost lemma of spikelet 2-3.2 mm long, those above successively shorter. *Paleas* shorter than lemmas, not enlarged and bowed-out at base, glabrous or scabrous on nerves. *Caryopses* 1-1.3 mm long. *Chromosome number*, $2n=40$.

Distribution. Texas: Regions 2, 6, 7 and eastern portion of 10, most frequent in brushy grasslands of the South Texas Plains, usually growing in partial shade. General: Florida (and Cuba), Texas, Arizona and northern Mexico.

Flowering period: Mostly September to November but not infrequently flowering in May and June.

6. **Tridens albescens** (Vasey) Woot. & Standl., New Mex. Col. Agric. Bull. 81:129. 1912. WHITE TRIDENS. Fig. 107. Tufted perennial with culms from a hard, often knotty and rhizomatous base. *Culms* mostly 30-90 cm tall, glabrous or the lowermost nodes sparsely bearded. *Sheaths* glabrous, rounded or the lower ones somewhat compressed laterally. *Ligule* a minute, fringed membrane, usually 0.5 mm or less long. *Blades* firm, glaucous, glabrous, elongate or rather short, 1-4 mm broad, often loosely infolded or involute on drying, with long, attenuate, involute tips. *Panicle* contracted, dense, 8-25 cm long, 0.6-1.5 cm thick, with short, appressed branches, the lowermost 2-6 cm long. *Spikelets* short-pediceled, 4-10 mm long, 4-11-flowered, mostly straw-colored but lemma tips usually purple and spikelets thus appearing banded. *Glumes* thin, broad, 1-nerved, subequal, about as long as lower lemmas, acute or apiculate. *Lemmas* thin and papery, glabrous or with a few short hairs on lateral nerves at extreme base, usually purple-tinged at the broad, slightly notched and minutely mucronate tips; lower lemmas of spikelet 3-4 mm long. *Paleas* slightly shorter than lemmas, glabrous, broadened and somewhat bowed-out at base. *Chromosome number* reported as $2n=60$, 64 and 72.

Distribution. Texas: Throughout the State except in region 1, usually growing in clayey soils along ditches, swales and other areas that periodically receive an abundance of drainage water.

Flowering period: March to November.

Fig. 107. *Tridens albescens*. Plant, spikelet and floret. From Gould and Box, 1965.

210   **THE GRASSES OF TEXAS**

Fig. 108. *Tridens congestus*. Inflorescence and spikelet. From Gould and Box, 1965.

7. **Tridens congestus** (L. H. Dewey) Nash, in Small, Fl. Southeast. U. S. 143. 1903. PINK TRIDENS. Fig. 108. Tufted perennial with firm, often hard and rhizomatous base. *Culms* 30-75 cm tall, glabrous, unbranched above base. *Leaves* glabrous, firm, the sheaths rounded on back, the blades elongate, 1.5-5 mm broad, with long, attenuate, inrolled tips. *Ligule* a minute ciliate membrane, 0.5 mm or less long. *Panicles* contracted, congested, mostly 5-8 (-10) cm long and 1.2-2.5 cm broad, panicle axis and branches glabrous, the branches mostly 0.5-3 cm long. *Pedicels* all much shorter than spikelets. *Spikelets* mostly 5-10 mm long and 5-11-flowered, with thin, papery, usually pink-tinged glumes and lemmas. *Glumes* broad, 1-nerved, glabrous, the second glume about as long as the lower lemmas, the first slightly shorter. *Lemmas* 3-4 mm long, pubescent on lower one-third to one-half of midnerve and margins, notched and mucronate at the broadly obtuse or rounded apex, the lateral nerves usually not reaching the margins. *Paleas* 0.5-1 mm shorter than lemmas, scabrous on nerves, broadened below, becoming firm and bowed out on lower half at maturity. *Chromosome number* not reported.

SUBFAMILY V. ERAGROSTOIDEAE   211

Distribution. Texas: Regions 2 and 4, adapted to moist depressions, ditches and low flats in regions of black, clayey soils. General: Endemic to Texas.

Flowering period: April to November.

Tridens congestus is generally similar to *T. albescens* and occupies similar habitats. It differs mainly in the usually shorter panicles, the more pubescent lemmas, the more deeply cleft lemma apex and the slightly stouter and longer mucro at the lemma apex. The lemmas are pink-tinged rather than purple or rosy-purple, and the coloration is not confined to the tip as in *T. albescens*.

8. **Tridens strictus** (Nutt.) Nash, in Small, Fl. Southeast. U. S. 143. 1903. LONGSPIKE TRIDENS. Fig. 109. Stout perennial with culms usually in small clumps from a hard base. *Culms* stiffly erect, glabrous, 50-170 cm tall. *Sheaths* firm, rounded on back, glabrous except for a few hairs on either side of collar. *Ligule* a ciliate rim of tissue, about 0.5 mm long. *Blades* firm, glabrous except for hairs just above the ligule, elongate, 2-8 mm broad, flat or loosely infolded, the tips long-attenuate and involute. *Panicles* narrow, contracted, mostly 10-36 cm long and 1-2 cm thick. *Panicle axis, branches* and *pedicels* glabrous or nearly so, the branches to 6 cm long, strictly erect-appressed, the pedicels very short and stout. *Spikelets* mostly 4-7 mm long, 5-11-flowered, with glumes usually conspicuously longer than the rest of the spikelet. *Glumes* subequal, 1-nerved, glabrous, narrow and usually tapering to an acuminate apex, 4-7 mm long. *Lemmas* ciliate or pubescent on nerves to well above middle, notched and mucronate at apex, the lateral nerves also often excurrent as mucro; lower lemmas of a spikelet 2-3 mm long, the upper ones successively shorter. *Paleas* broad but not bowed out at base, nearly as long as lemmas. *Caryopses* obovate, flattened, about 1 mm long. *Chromosome number*, 2n = 40.

Distribution. Texas: Regions 1, 2, 3 and 4, mostly on sandy soils but also on clay, in open woods, old fields, road and railroad right-of-ways and coastal grasslands. General: Southeastern United States, Illinois, North Carolina and Georgia, west to Kansas, Oklahoma and Texas.

Flowering period: July to November.

9. **Tridens muticus** (Torr.) Nash, in Small, Fl. Southeast. U. S. 143. 1903. Tufted perennial. *Culms* mostly 20-80 cm tall, stiffly erect; culm nodes often bearded with long, soft hairs. *Sheaths* rounded on back, the upper ones glabrous or scabrous, the lower ones often strigose or pilose, usually longer than the internode. *Ligule* a ciliate membrane 0.5-1 mm long. *Blades* 6-25 cm long, 1-4 mm broad, usually involute or loosely infolded on drying, gradually tapering to a long-attenuate tip, glabrous, scabrous or sparsely pilose. *Panicles* elongate and narrow, mostly 7-20 (-25) cm long and 3-8 mm thick, the spikelets short-pediceled and imbricate but usually not crowded or congested. *Spikelets* 8-13 mm long, 5-11-flowered, usually purple-tinged. *Glumes* glabrous, acute, 1-7-nerved, equal

Fig. 109. *Tridens strictus.* Spikelet. From Gould and Box, 1965.

or the first glume shorter than the second, the second slightly shorter to longer than the lower lemmas. *Lemmas* 3.5-5.5 mm long, ciliate-pubescent on midnerve to about the middle and on lateral nerves to well above the middle, obtuse or slightly notched at apex, infrequently the midnerve minutely mucronate. *Paleas* 1-2 mm shorter than lemmas, pubescent on margins. *Caryopses* oblong, finely reticulate, mostly 2-2.3 mm long.

Second glume 1-nerved, typically but not always 5 mm or less long
9A. *T. muticus* var. *muticus*

Second glume 3-7-nerved, typically 6-8 mm long
9B. *T. muticus* var. *elongatus*

9A. **Tridens muticus** (Torr.) Nash var. **muticus.** SLIM TRIDENS. Fig. 110. *Culms* mostly 20-50 cm tall. *Blades* typically 1-2 mm broad. *Glumes* relatively thin, usually markedly unequal in length and less than 5 mm long. *Chromosome number,* 2n=40.

Distribution. Texas: Mostly in regions 6, 7, 10 and southern portion of 2 but occasional in regions 3, 4, 5, 8 and 9, most frequent on dry, open slopes in sandy or clayey soils. General: Texas to southern Utah, Nevada and California and south through northern, central and northwestern Mexico.

Flowering period: Mostly August to November but occasionally flowering as early as May.

9B. **Tridens muticus** (Torr.) Nash var. **elongatus** (Buckl.) Shinners. Rhodora 56:28. 1954. *Tridens elongatus* (Buckl.) Nash. ROUGH TRIDENS. Similar to the typical variety but culms mostly 40-80 cm tall, blades often 3-4 mm broad and glumes relatively firm, the second glume 3-7-nerved, usually 5.5-10 mm long. *Chromosome number,* 2n=40.

Distribution. Texas: Regions 5, 7, 8, 9 and northern portions of 3 and 4, usually in clayey soils but sometimes on sandy sites and often on well-drained sandy or gravelly-clay sites.

Flowering period: April to November.

SUBFAMILY V. ERAGROSTOIDEAE 213

Fig. 110. *Tridens muticus* var. *muticus*. Plant and spikelet with glumes separated from florets. From Gould, 1951, in part and Gould, 1968, in part.

214　THE GRASSES OF TEXAS

52. TRIPLASIS Beauv.

A North American genus of two species.

1. **Triplasis purpurea** (Walt.) Chapm., Fl. Southeast. U. S. 560. 1860. PURPLE SANDGRASS. Fig. 111. Tufted annual, sometimes appearing perennial. *Culms* mostly 45-80 cm long, spreading-erect or even decumbent at base on margins of clumps, with numerous nodes and short internodes, the nodes hirsute; culms eventually with 1-flowered, cleistogamous spikelets in the axils of enlarged sheaths, these falling with the culm sections which readily break at the nodes in age. *Sheaths* rounded, glabrous or hispid with long hairs. *Ligule* a dense ring of hairs. *Blades* flat or involute, usually ciliate with papilla-based hairs and sometimes hispid, mostly 1-3 mm broad and 4-8 cm long, the upper blades greatly reduced. *Panicle* 3-11 cm long, with a few sparingly rebranched primary branches, the lower branches spreading, bare of spikelets on the lower one-third or one-half. *Spikelets* 6-10 mm long, with usually 2-4 florets widely spaced on slender, terete, readily disarticulating rachilla. *Glumes* glabrous or scabrous, 1-nerved, tapering to a blunt, often notched apex, first glume about 3 mm long, the second slightly longer. *Lemmas* 3-4 mm long, 3-nerved, villous on nerves, broad, notched and mucronate or awned at apex, the notch 0.5-1 mm deep, rounded lobes on either side, the awn slightly shorter to slightly longer than the notch; palea narrow, 2-keeled, silky-villous on nerves. *Chromosome number,* $2n=40$.

Distribution. Texas: Occasional in sandy soils throughout the State except in region 10, mostly along woods borders, moist streambanks and open sandy areas. General: Scattered throughout the eastern and central United States, ranging southward from southern Canada (Ontario) and Maine, Minnesota and eastern Colorado to Florida and Texas, and reported from Central America.

Flowering period: Mostly September and October but occasionally July to November.

53. ERIONEURON Nash

Low, tufted perennials, some stoloniferous, with narrow, often involute, cartilaginous-margined leaf blades. *Ligule* a short, ciliate membrane. Inflorescence a short, often capitate raceme or panicle. *Spikelets* large, several-flowered, disarticulating above glumes and between florets. *Glumes* large, subequal, membranous, glabrous and shiny, 1-nerved. *Lemmas* broad, rounded on back, 3-nerved, conspicuously long-hairy along nerves or at least below, bilobed at apex (except in *E. pilosum*), the midnerve short-awned, the lateral nerves often prolonged as short mucro. *Paleas* slightly shorter than lemmas, ciliate or puberulent on keels, long-hairy below between nerves. *Caryopses* oblong, glossy and translucent, with an embryo more than half as long as the caryopsis.

Fig. 111. *Triplasis purpurea*. Inflorescence and spikelet. From Gould and Box, 1965.

A genus of 5 species distributed in low rainfall areas of the south-western United States and Mexico.

Spikelets in leafy fascicles, not or scarcely surpassing the pungent, spine-tipped leaf blades; plants often developing slender, wiry stolons
1. *E. pulchellum*

Spikelets on an elongated, leafless floral axis; plants not or rarely stolon-iferous

Tip of lemma acute or with a notch 0.5 mm or less deep
2. *E. pilosum*

Tip of lemma with a notch 1-2.5 mm deep   3. *E. avenaceum*

1. **Erioneuron pulchellum** (H.B.K.) Tateoka, Amer. J. Bot. 48:572. 1961. *Tridens pulchellus* (H.B.K.) Hitchc. FLUFFGRASS. Fig. 112. Tufted peren-nial with or without slender stolons, often appearing annual. *Culms* numerous in a tuft, 2-15 cm tall, scabrous below the nodes. *Leaves* fascicled at all culm nodes, with broad, short sheaths and short, tightly involute, aciculate blades 1 mm or less broad. *Sheaths* often with a tuft of long hairs at base. *Ligule* a ciliate membrane about 0.5 mm long. *Spikelets* sessile or short-pediceled in capitate clusters or short racemes, these exceeded in length by leaves of fascicle. *Spikelets* mostly 7-13 mm long with 6-12 florets. *Glumes* subequal, acuminate or short-awned, scarious, about as long as spikelet. *Lemmas* mostly 3-5 mm long, densely long-ciliate on nerves, deeply cleft to just above middle and with a stout, straight or curved awn slightly shorter to slightly longer than apical lobes. *Paleas* broad, pubescent on margins and between nerves, puberulent on nerves. *Chromosome number*, $2n = 16$.

Distribution. Texas: Regions 8, 9, 10 and the western portion of 7, on dry rocky slopes and desert flats. General: Utah and Nevada to Texas, Arizona and northern Mexico.

Flowering period: June to November.

2. **Erioneuron pilosum** (Buckl.) Nash, in Small, Fl. Southeast. U. S. 144. 1903. *Tridens pilosus* (Vasey) Hitchc. HAIRY TRIDENS. Fig. 113. Tufted perennial without creeping or looping stolons. *Culms* mostly 10-30 cm tall, typically with only one node elevated above the basal clusters of leaves. *Lower sheaths* laterally compressed and keeled. *Ligule* a fringe of hairs about 0.5 mm long. *Blades* thick, narrow, flat, glabrous, 2-8 (-11) cm long and 1-2 mm broad, with a thick white margin and an abruptly pointed but not spinescent tip. *Inflorescence* a contracted panicle or raceme mostly 2-3 (-4) cm long and 1.5-2 cm broad, with usually 4-9 (-12) large, pale spikelets. *Spikelets* mostly 10-16 mm long and with 7-18 closely imbricated florets. *Glumes* acuminate, 4.5-6

Fig. 112. *Erioneuron pulchellum*. Plant. From Gould, 1951.

mm long. *Lower lemmas* about as long as the glumes, densely ciliate-
pubescent with long silvery hairs on nerves and also on margins and internerves near base, with an entire or minutely notched apex and an awn 1-2 mm
long. *Caryopses* 1.3-1.5 mm long. *Chromosome number*, $2n = 16$; one count of
$2n = 32$ from Mexican plants.

Distribution. Texas: Throughout the State except in the far eastern
portion (regions 1 and 3 and the northern half of region 2), on open rangelands
and pastures and frequent along road right-of-ways. General: Kansas to
Nevada and south to Texas, Arizona and central Mexico.

Flowering period: Mostly April to July but occasionally to October.

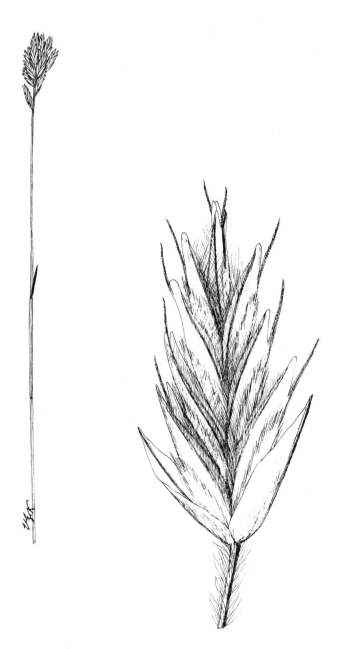

Fig. 113. *Erioneuron pilosum*. Inflorescence and spikelet. From Gould and Box, 1965.

SUBFAMILY V. ERAGROSTOIDEAE 219

3. **Erioneuron avenaceum** (H.B.K.) Tateoka, Amer. J. Bot. 48:572. 1961. *Tridens avenaceus* (H.B.K.) Hitchc. *Culms* 15- (5-) 60 cm tall, tufted and with leaves basally clustered, the single elevated culm node with a much-reduced leaf. *Stolons and rhizomes* lacking (in Texas plants). *Leaves* mostly in a basal tuft, the blades 2-12 cm long, 1-3 mm broad, usually sparsely pilose and minutely spine-tipped. *Inflorescence* dense, well exserted above the leaves. *Leaves* glabrous or sparsely pilose. *Basal sheaths* laterally compressed and keeled. *Ligule* a short fringe of hairs. *Blades* thick, flat, abruptly pointed at apex, with thick, whitish margins and midrib, mostly 1-2 mm broad.

Spikelets of vigorous plants 10-15 mm long, usually silvery or only slightly
　　purple-tinged; lemmas copiously hairy at base
　　　　　　　　　　　　3A.　*E. avenaceum* var. *grandiflorum*

Spikelets seldom over 1 cm long, usually purple-tinged or brownish-
　　purple; lemmas not copiously hairy at base
　　　　　　　　　　　　3B.　*E. avenaceum* var. *nealleyi*

3A. **Erioneuron avenaceum** (H.B.K.) Tateoka var. **grandiflorum** (Vasey) Gould, Brittonia 26:60. 1974. *Culms* mostly 10-50 cm tall, glabrous or pubescent on the nodes. *Inflorescence* ovate or oblong, often broadly so. *Chromosome numbers* reported, $2n= 16$ and 32.

Distribution. Texas: Region 10 on dry, rocky slopes. General: Western Texas to southern Arizona and northern Mexico.

Flowering period: Mostly July to October.

3B. **Erioneuron avenaceum** (H.B.K.) Tateoka var. **nealleyi** (Vasey) Gould, Brittonia 26:60. 1974. *Culms* mostly 15-60 cm tall, glabrous or pubescent on nodes. *Inflorescence* narrowly oblong, relatively longer and narrower than in var. *grandiflorum*. *Chromosome number,* $2n= 16$.

Distribution. Texas: Region 10 on dry, rocky slopes. General: Western Texas, southern New Mexico and northern Mexico.

Flowering period: Mostly July to October.

54. MUNROA Torr.

A genus of three species, one in western North America and two in Argentina.

1. **Munroa squarrosa** (Nutt.) Torr., U. S. Rep. Expl. Miss. Pacif. 4:158. 1857. FALSE BUFFALOGRASS. Fig. 114. Low, mat-forming annual with decumbent, much-branched culms and slender stolons 2-8 cm long. *Erect floriferous culms* seldom more than 10-15 cm tall. *Culms* and *leaves* harshly scabrous and often minutely puberulent. *Leaves* short and fascicled. *Sheaths*

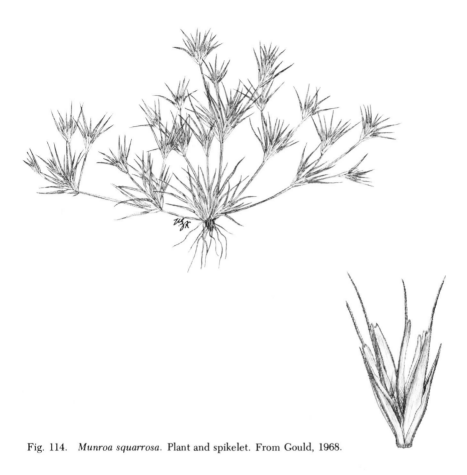

Fig. 114. *Munroa squarrosa.* Plant and spikelet. From Gould, 1968.

broad, mostly 4-7 mm long, ciliate on upper margins and with a tuft of long hairs on either side of collar. *Ligule* a dense ring of hairs. *Blades* stiff, flat or folded, mostly 1-5 cm long and 1-2.5 mm broad, with an acuminate, sharp-pointed tip. *Inflorescence* a small cluster of subsessile spikelets; spikelets mostly 2-3-flowered and 7-10 mm long. Disarticulation above glumes and between florets. *Glumes* of lower 1-2 spikelets equal, 1-nerved, acute, slightly shorter than the lemmas, glumes of the upper florets unequal, the first reduced or absent. *Lemmas* prominently 3-nerved, more or less scabrous, those of lower spikelets with tufts of hair on margins near middle. *Midnerve of lemma* extended as a stout, scabrous awn 0.5-1.5 mm long, the lateral lemma nerves occasionally mucronate. *Chromosome number,* $2n = 16$.

Distribution. Texas: Regions 7, 8, 9 and 10 on dry, open sites, often associated with anthills or other areas of recently disturbed soils. General: Alberta, Canada, south through North Dakota and Montana to Texas, Arizona and Chihuahua, Mexico.

Flowering period: Mostly July to November but occasionally earlier.

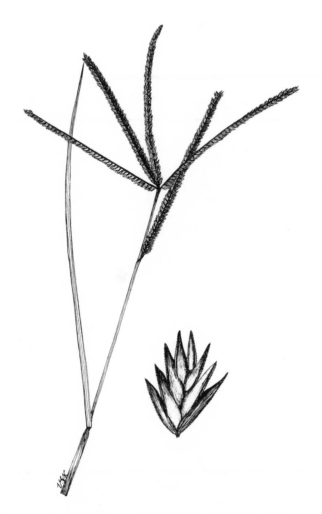

Fig. 115. *Eleusine indica.* Inflorescence and spikelet. From Gould and Box, 1965.

55. ELEUSINE Gaertn.

A genus of about six species, one native to South America, the others in the warmer regions of the Eastern Hemisphere.

1. **Eleusine indica** (L.) Gaertn., Fruct. and Sem. 1:8. 1788. GOOSE-GRASS. Fig. 115. Succulent, leafy annual. *Culms* erect or spreading, occasionally stoloniferous at base, mostly 15-70 cm long but much shorter on mowed, grazed or otherwise disturbed plants. *Sheaths* compressed laterally and strongly keeled, glabrous or sparsely long-hispid on margins. *Ligule* a lacerate, ciliate membrane about 1 mm long. *Blades* elongate, linear, mostly

222   THE GRASSES OF TEXAS

3-8 cm broad, flat or folded and keeled at base, glabrous or hispid with long hairs along margins and sometimes on adaxial surface near ligule. *Inflorescence* with 2- (1-) 8 spreading, spicate branches, these mostly digitate at culm apex but frequently 1-2 branches present 1-4 cm below apical whorl. *Inflorescence branches* 3-15 cm long, with a flattened winged rachis bearing closely imbricate awnless spikelets in two rows. *Spikelets* 3-6 mm long, 3-6-flowered. *Glumes* acute, glabrous or scabrous, the first glume 1-nerved, the second larger, 3-7-nerved. *Lemmas* glabrous or scaberulous, somewhat laterally compressed and keeled, acute or obtuse, occasionally slightly mucronate. *Paleas* shorter than lemmas. *Grains* 1-2 mm long, plump, transverse ridged and rugose, the seed loosely enclosed by a thin pericarp. *Chromosome number,* $2n = 18$.

Distribution. Texas: Throughout the State as a weed of lawns, gardens, ditches and other areas of disturbed soils. General: A common weed of the warmer regions of both hemispheres, adventive in the United States and established almost throughout the country but absent or infrequent in the Northwest.

Flowering period: Mostly late summer and autumn, occasionally flowering in late spring.

56. DACTYLOCTENIUM Willd.

1. **Dactyloctenium aegyptium** (L.) Willd., Enum. Pl. 1029. 1809. DURBAN CROWFOOTGRASS. Fig. 116. Tufted or mat-forming annual with thick, weak, usually spreading-erect culms mostly 10-60 cm tall, these often rooting at the lower nodes. *Sheaths* laterally compressed and keeled. *Ligule* a truncate membrane 0.5-1 mm long fringed with hairs shorter than to about as long as the membrane. *Blades* thin, flat or irregularly folded, mostly 2-8 mm broad, usually ciliate on margins with long, papilla-based hairs and often hispid on one or both surfaces. *Inflorescence* with 2-6 or more thick, digitately arranged spicate branches mostly 1.5-6 cm long; branch rachis minutely but densely hispid near the point of attachment to main axis, bearing two rows of closely-placed, tightly-compressed and pectinately-spreading spikelets from near base to near tip; rachis tip projecting beyond terminal spikelet as a sharp point 1-7 mm long. *Spikelets* mostly 3-4 mm long, 3-5-flowered, disarticulating between or above glumes. *Glumes* firm, glabrous, keeled, 1-nerved, subequal and about as large as lemmas. *First glume* acute or with a minute, nearly straight awn. *Second glume* usually with a short, stout, curved and crooked awn. *Lemmas* similar to glumes, usually with a short, crooked awn. *Paleas* about as large as lemmas, with widely separated, minutely scabrous nerves. *Anthers* 0.5 mm or less long. *Grain* plump, reddish-brown, 1 mm or slightly less long, coarsely rugose and transversely ridged, with an embryo two-fifths to one-half as long as the endosperm. *Chromosome numbers* reported, $2n = 20$, 36, 40, 45 and 48.

Distribution. Texas: Regions 1, 2, 3, 4, 6 and 7, a weed of loose, sandy soils, often along intermittent creek beds, moist ravines and in disturbed soils

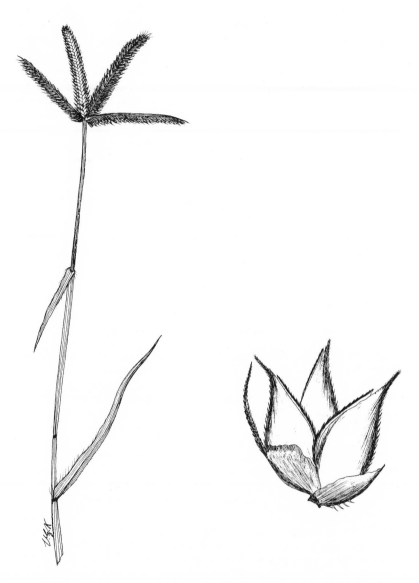

Fig. 116. *Dactyloctenium aegyptium.* Inflorescence and spikelet. From Gould and Box, 1965.

of cultivated fields. General: Native to the Old World tropics, now widespread as an introduced weed in the southern United States, especially on the Atlantic and Gulf of Mexico coastal plains; occasionally but probably not persisting in Illinois, Colorado and other more northerly states.

Flowering period: Mostly September to December, occasionally as early as July.

57. LEPTOCHLOA Beauv.

Cespitose annuals and perennials with leafy culms and flat, linear blades. *Ligules* membranous, glabrous or ciliate. *Inflorescence* with few to numerous spicate primary branches scattered along main axis or clustered near tip. *Spikelets* 2-12-flowered, overlapping and closely-spaced on the branches, disarticulating above glumes and between florets. *Glumes* thin, 1-nerved or the second glume occasionally 3-nerved, acute, awnless or mucronate, the second usually longer than the first. *Lemmas* 3-nerved, frequently puberulent on nerves. *Apex of the lemma* acute to obtuse or notched, awnless or awned. *Paleas* well developed, occasionally puberulent on nerves.

A genus of about 70 species in the warmer parts of both hemispheres.

Apex of lemmas broad, truncate, usually notched, awnless; lowermost lemma
    3.5-5 mm long   1. *L. dubia*

Apex of lemmas broad or narrow; if broad and truncate then lowermost
    lemma less than 3 mm long

    Inflorescence branches 10-15 cm long, clustered on upper 3-5 cm of
        main axis; perennial of well-drained, usually dry sites
                  8. *L. chloridiformis*

    Inflorescence branches 3-15 cm long, when clustered on upper 3-5 cm
        of main axis then less than 10 cm long

        Lemmas, at least some, with awns more than 0.5 mm long

            Spikelets 2-4 mm long; perennial   2. *L. virgata*

            Spikelets 5-10 mm long; annual   3. *L. fascicularis*

        Lemmas awnless or with a mucro 0.5 mm or less long

            Spikelets, at least some, 5.5 mm or more long; inflorescence branches
                mostly 10-35 per panicle

                Second glume 3-4.2 mm long   3. *L. fascicularis*

                Second glume less than 3 mm long   4. *L. uninervia*

            Spikelets mostly 2-5.5 mm long, when 5 mm or more long then the
                inflorescence branches 40-60 per panicle

                  Spikelets 4-7-flowered, 4-5 mm long; largest lemmas 2-2.8 mm
                long   5. *L. panicoides*

SUBFAMILY V. ERAGROSTOIDEAE   225

Spikelets mostly 2-4-flowered and 2-3 mm long; largest lemmas
1-1.6 mm long

Inflorescence axis 25-50 cm long, bearing numerous, closely-
placed, short, stiffly erect branches, these mostly 2-4 cm long
6. *L. nealleyi*

Inflorescence axis short or long, when 20 cm or more long then
the lower branches 8 cm or more long; inflorescence
branches slender and more or less flexuous
7. *L. filiformis*

1. **Leptochloa dubia** (H.B.K.) Nees, Syll. Pl. Ratisb. 1:4. 1824.
GREEN SPRANGLETOP. Fig. 117. Tufted perennial with a firm base but
without stolons or rhizomes. *Culms* mostly 30-110 cm tall, unbranched
above base. *Sheaths* glabrous or the lower ones pilose; lower sheaths,
especially those of sterile shoots, often laterally flattened and sharply keeled.
Ligule a fringed membrane about 0.5 mm long. *Blades* dull bluish-green,
glabrous, scabrous or sparsely pilose, mostly 5-30 cm long and 2-6 (-8)
mm broad, often inrolled on drying. *Inflorescence* with 2-15 unbranched
primary branches mostly 4-12 cm long, these flexuous, loosely erect or spreading, well spaced on the upper 5-20 cm of culm. *Spikelets* subsessile and
loosely to closely imbricated on branch, solitary at nodes, with 3- (2-) 8
florets. *Glumes* lanceolate, awnless, the second glume usually 4-5 mm long,
the first slightly shorter. *Lemmas* broad, rounded on back, truncate and
usually notched at apex, glabrous or puberulent on margins, the lowermost
lemma 3.5-5 mm long. *Chromosome numbers* reported, $2n = 40$, 60 and 80.

Distribution. Texas: Occasional or frequent in all regions except regions
1 and 3, most common in the western and southern portions of the State.
General: Oklahoma to Arizona, south through Texas and Mexico and reported
from southern Florida and Argentina.

Flowering period: May to November.

Plants of *Leptochloa dubia* regularly develop perfect cleistogamous
spikelets in the axils of the lower sheaths. This is the best forage species
of the Texas sprangletops. It is widespread and highly palatable but usually
is present in mixed stands with other grasses and seldom is abundant.

2. **Leptochloa virgata** (L.) Beauv., Ess. Agrost. 71, 161, 166, pl. 15.
f. 1. 1812. TROPIC SPRANGLETOP. Fig. 118. Tufted perennial with erect
culms 30-100 cm or more tall, the culm bases sometimes moderately geniculate and spreading at base. *Leaves* well distributed on culm, glabrous,
scabrous or pilose. *Sheaths* rounded on back, shorter than the internodes.
Ligule a minute fringed membrane. *Blades* long, linear, 3-10 mm broad,
flat or inrolled, glabrous or somewhat hairy towards base. *Inflorescence*
with usually 5-16 slender, spicate branches 3-14 cm long, these scattered
on upper 3-23 cm of main axis, occasionally paired or in threes. *Spikelets*

Fig. 117. *Leptochloa dubia.* Plant and spikelet. From Gould, 1951.

2-4 mm long, 3- (2-) 8-flowered, the upper florets successively reduced in size and the uppermost usually rudimentary. *Glumes* glabrous, 1-nerved, 1.2-3.2 mm long. *Lemmas* 1.5-2.8 mm long, ciliate or pubescent on margins, awnless or with an awn to 3 mm long; lemma when awned usually slightly notched at apex. *Chromosome number,* $2n=40$.

Distribution. Texas: Region 6 and lower portion of region 2, in moist coastal prairie soils and along swales, ditches, marshes and similar sites. General: Southern Florida and Texas, south through the warmer parts of the Americas.

Flowering period: May to November.

Fig. 118. *Leptochloa virgata.* Inflorescence and spikelet. From Gould and Box, 1965.

Most Texas plants of *L. virgata* have awned lemmas and thus have been referred to *L. domingensis* (Jacq.) Trin. Relationships and variation patterns in this series are uncertain, however, and recognition of *L. domingensis* must await additional supportive evidence.

3. **Leptochloa fascicularis** (Lam.) A. Gray, Man. 588. 1848. BEARDED SPRANGLETOP. Fig. 119. Annual with coarse, somewhat succulent culms typically 50-100 cm tall, moderately branched and usually in rather large clumps; under adverse conditions of extreme salinity, alkalinity, trampling or drought, flowering culms may develop in tufts not over 10-15 cm tall. *Culm leaves* well-developed, the uppermost usually sheathing the inflorescence at base and with a long blade often overtopping the inflorescence. *Lower sheaths* usually keeled, the upper rounded on back. *Ligules* well-developed, hyaline, 2-6 mm long, lacerate but not ciliate, with lateral lobes appearing as sheath auricles. *Blades* firm, glabrous or sparsely hispid, elongate, 2-7 mm broad, usually loosely involute on drying. *Inflorescence* 10-30 cm long, with usually 8-35 stiffly erect or erect-spreading branches scattered on the upper 6-25 cm of the culm axis, the branches mostly 4-12 cm long. *Spikelets* 5-10 mm long and 6-12-flowered, maturing with a bluish, grayish or occasionally violet coloration. *Glumes* usually unequal, broad or narrow, 1-nerved, scabrous on the nerve, the second glume mostly 3-4.2 mm long, acute or lobed, the midnerve often extending as a short awn. *Lemmas* ovate to oblong, usually pubescent on margins and midnerve below middle, acute or acuminate but often with a slightly notched apex, the central nerve usually projecting as an awn 0.5-1.5 mm long, the lateral nerves often exserted as minute mucro; body of lowermost lemma 3-5 mm long, infrequently shorter. *Chromosome number,* $2n=20$.

Distribution. Texas: Nearly throughout the State, in muddy or wet clayey soils along lakes and ponds, swales and shores of sluggish streams, frequent in brackish marshes along the coast. General: Widely distributed throughout the United States, south through Central and South America to Argentina.

Flowering period: March to November but mostly June to September.

4. **Leptochloa uninervia** (Presl) Hitchc. & Chase, Contr. U.S. Natl. Herb. 18:363. 1917. MEXICAN SPRANGLETOP. Fig. 120. Generally similar to *L. fascicularis* but inflorescence branches averaging shorter (3-6 cm long), spikelets usually more darkly colored at maturity and lower lemmas 2-3 mm long, obtuse and awnless or abruptly mucronate at apex. *Chromosome number,* $2n=20$.

Distribution. Texas: Regions 2, 6, 7 and 10 along streams, ditches, swales and muddy ponds. General: Southern and southwestern United States, West Indies, Mexico and South America to Peru and Argentina.

Flowering period: March to December under favorable conditions.

5. **Leptochloa panicoides** (Presl) Hitchc., Amer. J. Bot. 21:137. 1934. AMAZON SPRANGLETOP. Tufted annual with stiffly erect, rather coarse culms 40-100 cm or more tall. *Sheaths* glabrous or scabrous, tightly compressed at base, the lowermost sheaths keeled. *Ligule* a truncate, erose, glabrous membrane 1-4 mm long. *Blades* linear, 6-12 mm broad, scabrous on

Fig. 119. *Leptochloa fascicularis*. Inflorescence and spikelet. From Gould and Box, 1965.

Fig. 120. *Leptochloa uninervia*. Spikelet. From Gould and Box, 1965.

the margins, flat or loosely involute on drying. *Inflorescence* 12-30 cm long, mostly 4-8 cm broad, with 40-90 short, crowded, erect-spreading branches 3-6 (2-8) cm long. *Spikelets* pediceled, 4-7-flowered, 4-5 mm long. *Glumes* acute or acuminate, the first narrow, 1-nerved, the second much broader, 1-3-nerved, 1.6-2 mm long. *Lemmas* 2-2.8 mm long, pubescent on margins near the base, usually mucronate at the broadly acute, minutely lobed apex. *Chromosome number* not reported.

Distribution. Texas: Region 1 and possibly the northeastern tip of region 2, infrequent, growing on muddy shores, in swamps and in swales. General: Brazil, introduced into the United States and now established from Indiana and Missouri south to Mississippi, Louisiana and Texas.

Flowering period: Spring to autumn.

230   THE GRASSES OF TEXAS

Fig. 121. *Leptochloa nealleyi*. Inflorescence and spikelet. Gould and Box, 1965.

6. **Leptochloa nealleyi** Vasey, Bull. Torrey Bot. Club. 12:7. 1885. NEALLEY SPRANGLETOP. Fig. 121. Coarse, tufted annual with stout, stiffly erect culms mostly 60-150 cm tall. *Sheaths* scaberulous, the lower ones sharply keeled and laterally compressed. *Ligules* 1-3 mm long, truncate, lacerate, glabrous. *Blades* long, linear, 3-10 mm broad, rather thick, folded or loosely involute, at least at the long slender tips. *Inflorescence* commonly 20-50 cm long, with 25-75 or more stiffly erect or erect-spreading branches 2-6 (1-10) cm long, the branches scattered or the lower ones irregularly verticiled. *Spikelets* closely placed, laterally compressed, 3-4-flowered, 2-3 mm long. *Glumes* 1-nerved, glabrous or scabrous, 1-1.5 mm long, the first glume acute, the second longer and broader, with a broad, often slightly notched apex. *Lemmas* slightly keeled, pubescent on nerves, the lowermost lemma of the spikelet 1-1.6 mm long; apex of lemma broad, awnless, occasionally slightly notched and apiculate. *Paleas* broad, slightly shorter than lemmas. *Caryopses* oblong, about 1 mm long, with an embryo about two-fifths as long as the endosperm. *Chromosome number,* $2n=40$.

Distribution. Texas: Regions 2 and 6, mostly along the coast in wet, muddy or clayey soils of marshes, swales and river and pond borders, often in saline sites. General: Gulf Coast, Louisiana, Texas and Tamaulipas, Mexico.

Flowering period: April to November.

7. **Leptochloa filiformis** (Lam.) Beauv., Ess. Agrost. 71, 161, 166. 1812. RED SPRANGLETOP. Fig. 122. Weedy annual with slender, decumbent-spreading culms from less than 10 to over 80 cm tall. *Leaves* usually papillose-hispid or pilose. *Sheaths* rounded on back. *Ligules* lacerate, ciliate, 1-2 mm long. *Blades* thin, flat, linear, 1-10 mm broad. *Inflorescence* mostly 8-35 cm long, usually one-third to one-half the entire culm length. *Inflorescence branches* few to numerous, scattered, slender, flexuous, mostly 3-8 (2-15) cm long and 1-2 mm thick, erect-spreading or often widely spreading at maturity. *Spikelets* 2-4-flowered, 1.5-3 mm long, widely spaced on the rachis and only slightly overlapping. Glumes acute, the first narrower and usually slightly shorter than the second, the second as long as the spikelet. *Lemmas* mostly 1-1.6 mm long, usually but not always hairy on nerves below middle, obtuse or truncate at apex. *Caryopses* ovate or obovate, usually 0.7-0.8 mm long. *Chromosome number,* $2n=20$.

Distribution. Texas: Throughout Texas except in region 9, growing mostly as a weed of disturbed soils of gardens, ditches, pastures and road right-of-ways. General: Frequent in the southeastern United States, north to Virginia and southern Indiana and west to Arizona and southern California.

Flowering period: Mostly July to November but occasionally as early as May.

8. **Leptochloa chloridiformis** (Hack.) Parodi, Physis 4:184. 1918. ARGENTINE SPRANGLETOP. Stout perennial with stiffly erect culms mostly 60-150 cm tall. *Sheaths* scaberulous, mostly rounded on the back but the basal ones occasionally keeled. *Ligule* a dense fringe of white hairs 1-2 mm long on a minute membranous base. *Blades* firm, scabrous, elongate, 2-7 mm broad. *Inflorescence* long-exserted, with 5-20 stout branches clustered or subdigitate at culm apex. *Inflorescence branches* mostly 10-16 cm long and about 3 mm thick, the 3-4-flowered spikelets short-pediceled and closely imbricated. *Glumes* 1-nerved, acute, 1.5-3 mm long, the first glume shorter than the second. *Lemmas* ciliate on the margins with rather long hairs, notched and usually with an awn to 0.6 mm long at apex; lowermost lemmas 2.5-3.5 mm long. *Chromosome number* not reported.

Distribution. Texas: Introduced and infrequent in the southern portion of region 2, usually present in disturbed soil of dry sites. General: Native to Argentina and Paraguay.

Flowering period: Mostly late summer and fall.

58. TRICHONEURA Anderss.

About 10 species, mostly in Africa, one in Texas and two in South America.

1. **Trichoneura elegans** Swallen, Amer. J. Bot. 19:439. f. 4. 1932. SILVEUSGRASS. Fig. 123. Tufted annual with many-noded culms mostly 30-110 cm long. *Culms* erect or more commonly decumbent below and rooting at the

Fig. 122. *Leptochloa filiformis*. Inflorescence and spikelet. From Gould and Box, 1965.

SUBFAMILY V. ERAGROSTOIDEAE   233

lower nodes, branching mostly near base. *Sheaths* rounded, minutely scabrous but otherwise glabrous. *Ligule* a truncate, lacerate membrane 1.5-3 mm long, present below collar region and appearing as a continuation of sheath. *Blades* glabrous or slightly scabrous, mostly 6-30 cm long and 3-8 mm broad, flat or loosely involute on drying, the lower blades deciduous in age just above ligule. *Panicle* narrow but usually loose, mostly 5-20 cm long, with 5-20 or more erect or erect-spreading unbranched primary branches 1-6 cm long, these floriferous to base. *Panicle* axis strongly angled, scabrous on angles, often puberulent below. *Spikelets* short-pediceled, 5-8-flowered, 7-10 mm long. Disarticulation above glumes. *Glumes* 1-nerved, firm, scabrous, acuminate or short-awned, the second glume longer than the first and about equaling the spikelet in length. *Lower florets* perfect, mostly 4-5 mm long, the upper florets successively shorter, the terminal 1-3 staminate or sterile. *Lemma* ciliate with long hairs on the mid-sections of the lateral nerves, the nerves bare both below and above. *Apex of lemma* notched, often minutely apiculate. *Chromosome number* not reported.

Distribution. Texas: Regions 2 and 6, from Victoria County south along the Gulf Coast and in sandy areas of the South Texas Plains region, often locally abundant. General: Southern Texas and northern Tamaulipas, Mexico.

Flowering period: Mostly late summer and autumn but occasionally in the spring.

59. GYMNOPOGON Beauv.

About fifteen species, in the American tropics and subtropics.

1. **Gymnopogon ambiguus** (Michx.) B.S.P., Prel. Cat. N. Y. 69. 1888. BEARDED SKELETONGRASS. Fig. 124. Perennial with culms usually stiffly erect from a hard, knotty, rhizomatous base and numerous short, overlapping leaves with spreading or deflexed blades. *Culms* slender, many-noded, 25-60 cm tall, often branching at the upper nodes. *Sheaths* rounded on back, glabrous except for a few hairs in vicinity of collar. *Ligule* a minute membrane or rim of callus tissue. *Blades* stiff, lanceolate, flat or folded, mostly 4-15 mm broad and 3-10 cm long, abruptly narrowed at base, glabrous except for a few hairs at base. *Panicles* large, open, mostly 10-25 cm long and broader than long. *Spikelets* pediceled and appressed on numerous, slender, widely spaced and widely spreading spicate branches. *Panicle branches* mostly 10-20 cm long, single or occasionally paired at the nodes of an axis mostly 5-18 cm long, the axis terminating in a floriferous branch. Branches floriferous to base or bare of spikelets on lower 2-5 cm, the lower spikelets successively more widely spaced and the lowermost 1-2 spikelets often rudimentary. *Callus* at branch base commonly hirsute but occasionally nearly glabrous. *Spikelets* with a perfect lower floret and a rudimentary upper floret, this usually reduced to a stipitate awn. Disarticulation above glumes, the two florets falling together. *Glumes* about equal, narrow, 1-nerved, scabrous on the nerve, 4-6 mm long, tapering to a narrow point. *Lemmas* thin, 3-nerved,

Fig. 123. *Trichoneura elegans*. Inflorescence and spikelet. From Gould and Box, 1965.

slightly shorter than the glumes, glabrous or scabrous at apex and on back, ciliate with a few long hairs on margins near middle and with a tuft of hairs at base, with an awn usually 4-8 mm long from a minutely notched apex. *Paleas* as long as or slightly longer than lemmas. *Rudimentary floret* usually reduced to an awn 2-5 mm long on a slender stipe. *Chromosome number*, $2n = 40$.

SUBFAMILY V. ERAGROSTOIDEAE   235

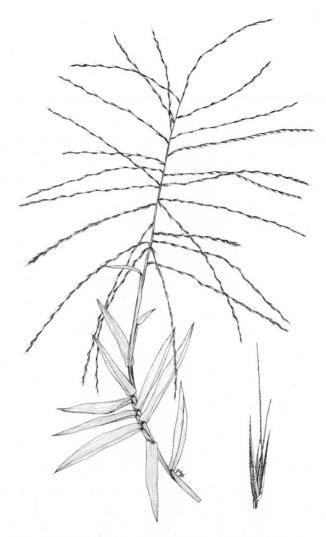

Fig. 124. *Gymnopogon ambiguus*. Culm tip with inflorescence and spikelet.

Distribution. Texas: Regions 1, 2, 3 and occasionally in 5, in sand or sandy clay soils, usually in shade of shrubs or forest trees. General: Eastern United States, north to Pennsylvania and Indiana, west to eastern Kansas and south to Florida and Texas.

Flowering period: Mostly late August to November.

Correll and Johnston (1970) recognize the presence of *Gymnopogon brevifolius* Trin. in Texas. The characters by which the species are distinguished in Texas, however, do not appear sufficiently consistent to warrant the recognition of more than one species.

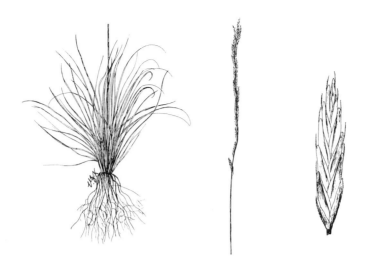

Fig. 125. *Tripogon spicatus.* Plant base, inflorescence and spikelet. From Gould, 1968.

60. TRIPOGON Roth.

About 10 species, one in the Americas and the others in Africa and the East Indies.

1. **Tripogon spicatus** (Nees) Ekman, Ark. Bot. 11 (4):36. 1912. AMERI-CAN TRIPOGON. Fig. 125. Low tufted perennial with filiform leaves, these mostly in a basal clump. *Culms* 10-30 cm tall, slender, stiffly erect. *Sheaths* rounded, glabrous except for tufts of hair on either side of collar. *Ligule* a minute, truncate, erose, ciliate membrane, not over 0.2-0.3 mm long. *Blades* filiform, mostly involute on drying but some remaining flat, 1 mm or less broad and mostly 3-10 cm long, glabrous or sparsely hirsute with long hairs. *Inflorescence* a slender, glabrous spike or spicate raceme 4-10 cm long, with several-flowered spikelets appressed to and loosely imbricated in two rows along a flattened but narrow rachis. *Spikelets* 5-10 mm long, 6-12-flowered, sessile or on stout pedicels to 0.3 mm long, disarticulating above glumes and between florets. *Glumes* narrow, 1-nerved, acute or acuminate, the first one-half to two-thirds as long as the second. *Lemmas* 3-nerved, glabrous except for a tuft of hair at base, shallowly notched and short-awned, the awns mostly 0.2-0.5 mm long. *Paleas* thin, slightly shorter than lemmas. *Caryopses* narrow and elongate, triangular, reddish-brown, about 1.5 mm long, with an embryo slightly less than one-fourth as long as the endosperm. *Chromosome number,* $2n=20$.

Distribution. Texas: Eastern portion of region 7, usually in shallow pockets of soil on granitic rocks. General: Texas, Mexico, Cuba and South America.

Flowering period: Mostly April through July but occasionally late summer.

SUBFAMILY V. ERAGROSTOIDEAE　　237

61. VASEYOCHLOA Hitchc.

A monotypic North American genus.

1. **Vaseyochloa multinervosa** (Vasey) Hitchc., J. Wash. Acad. Sci. 23:452. 1933. TEXASGRASS. Fig. 126. Cespitose perennial with culms mostly 50-100 cm tall. Plants with or without slender, creeping rhizomes. *Culm nodes* glabrous or the lower ones hairy. *Upper sheaths* glabrous but the lower ones hirsute or hispid on margins near collar and also frequently hirsute at base. *Ligule* a short, fringed membrane. *Blades* elongate, flat or involute, mostly 2-5 mm broad and 15-35 cm long, essentially glabrous. *Panicles* 6-20 cm long, at first loosely contracted but at maturity the slender branches spreading and drooping under the weight of the caryopses. *Spikelets* awnless, mostly 10-18 mm long and with 6-11 florets. *Glumes* broad, firm, obtuse or slightly notched at apex, somewhat unequal and shorter than lemmas, glabrous or scabrous, the first glume 3-5-nerved, the second 7-9-nerved. *Lemmas* 5-7 mm long, broad, firm, rounded on the back, more or less hirsute, especially below, strongly 7-9-nerved, obtuse or slightly notched at apex. *Paleas* shorter than lemmas, keeled and winged on margins, splitting down the center at maturity. *Caryopses* oval, 2.5-3 mm long, concave-convex, dark brown or black, with two persistent horn-like style bases. *Chromosome numbers* reported, $2n=56$, 60 and 68.

Distribution. Texas: Regions 2 and 6, occasional on sands of river banks, coastal dunes and sandy open pastures. General: Reported only from southeastern Texas but probably also present along the coast of Tamaulipas, Mexico.

Flowering period: April to November.

An interesting endemic with no apparent close relatives. Reported as "rare" by Chase in Hitchcock's Manual (1951), this species periodically is locally abundant on sandy sites in San Patricio and Kleberg counties (region 2). It also is reported from Padre Island, Nueces County, and probably is occasional on sands throughout the central and southern portion of the Coastal Bend area.

62. REDFIELDIA Vasey

A monotypic North American genus.

1. **Redfieldia flexuosa** (Thurb.) Vasey, Bull. Torrey Bot. Club. 14:133. 1887. BLOWOUT GRASS. Fig. 127. Perennial with long, slender rhizomes. *Culms* firm, glabrous, mostly 50-100 cm tall. *Sheaths* smooth, rounded, the basal ones becoming fibrous in age. *Ligule* a short, densely ciliate membrane. *Blades* long, firm, involute, 1.5-4 mm broad, the terminal 10-25 cm, filiform and flexuous. *Panicles* large and open, as much as half the length of the culm, with spikelets borne on slender, flexuous pedicels. Disarticulation above glumes and between florets. *Spikelets* awnless, 5-8 mm long, 2- (1-) 6-flowered, the florets closely placed and spreading at maturity. *Glumes* thin,

Fig. 126. *Vaseyochloa multinervosa*. Plant, spikelet, floret and caryopsis. From Gould and Box, 1968.

narrow, lanceolate, slightly unequal to nearly equal, 2-5 mm long, the first glume 1-nerved, the second 3-nerved. *Lemmas* firm, lanceolate, 4-5 mm long, 3-nerved, glabrous or scabrous above base, with a tuft of long hairs at base, narrow at the apex, occasionally with a short mucro. *Chromosome number* not reported.

Distribution. Texas: Region 9, infrequent in sandy areas of the High Plains. General: North Dakota, Colorado and Utah, south to Texas, New Mexico and Arizona.

Flowering period: July to October.

SUBFAMILY V. ERAGROSTOIDEAE   239

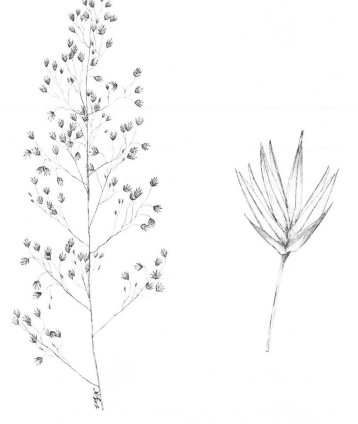

Fig. 127. *Redfieldia flexuosa.* Inflorescence and spikelet. From Gould, 1968.

63. SCLEROPOGON Phil.

A monotypic genus of the New World.

1. **Scleropogon brevifolius** Phil., Anales Univ. Chile 36:206. 1870. BURROGRASS. Fig. 128. Dioecious or, less frequently, monoecious perennial with wiry, creeping stolons and tufted flowering culms mostly 10-25 cm tall. *Leaves* mainly in a basal cluster. *Sheaths* short, strongly nerved, the upper sheaths glabrous, but those at base of plant often hispid or villous. *Ligule* a minute fringe of hairs. *Blades* firm, flat or folded, 1-2 mm broad and mostly 2-8 cm long. *Florets* mostly imperfect, the staminate and pistillate on different plants or less frequently on the same plant. *Perfect flowers* occasionally produced. *Spikelets* large, in few-flowered spicate racemes or contracted panicles, the staminate spikelets awnless, the pistillate spikelets long-awned. *Staminate spikelets* with 5-10, occasionally as many as 20, florets. *Glumes* and *lemmas of staminate spikelets* similar, thin, pale, lanceolate, usually 3-nerved, the glumes separated by a short internode, the florets widely spaced and persistent on the rachilla. *Pistillate spikelets* mostly with 3-5 perfect florets and 1-several awn-like rudimentary florets above, the

Fig. 128. *Scleropogon brevifolius*. Staminate plant, staminate spikelet (awnless) and pistillate spikelet (awned). From Gould, 1968.

SUBFAMILY V. ERAGROSTOIDEAE   241

florets disarticulating together. *Glumes of pistillate spikelets* unequal, lanceolate, awnless, 3-nerved, occasionally with additional fine lateral nerves. *Lemmas of pistillate spikelets* firm, rounded on the back, 3-nerved, the nerves extending into awns 5-10 cm long. *Lowermost lemma* with a bearded, sharp-pointed callus at base. *Paleas* narrow, the two nerves extending into short awns. *Chromosome number, 2n=40.*

Distribution. Texas: Regions 7, 8, 9 and 10 on open, dry flats and valleys. General: Colorado to Texas, Arizona and central Mexico and in Chile and Argentina.

Flowering period: Mostly late summer and autumn but occasionally also in the spring.

A range grass of low palatability, often developing in large dense stands and apparently spreading in heavily grazed areas.

64. BLEPHARIDACHNE Hack.

A genus of three species, two in the United States and one in Argentina.

1. **Blepharidachne bigelovii** (S. Wats.) Hack., in DC., Monogr. Phan. 6:261. 1889. BIGELOW DESERTGRASS. Fig. 129. Low, tufted perennial with culms branching from a firm, often knotty base. *Culms* 6-20 cm long, covered by the closely imbricate leaf sheaths, freely branching above as well as at base. *Sheaths* broad, short, mostly 0.5-1 mm long, usually with a tuft of hairs on either side of collar, often puberulent on back. *Ligule* a minute fringed membrane. *Blades* firm, involute, harshly puberulent, stiffly curved, spine-tipped, mostly 1-2 cm long; lower blades deciduous from sheaths. *Inflorescence* a contracted panicle of 5-10 spikelets, these little if at all ex-serted from upper leaf sheaths; main axis and branches of panicle harshly puberulent. *Spikelets* mostly 5-7 mm long, with 4 florets, the first and second sterile, the third perfect and the fourth reduced to a 3-awned rudiment. Disarticulation just above glumes, the florets falling together. *Glumes* large, thin, translucent, nearly equal in length to body of the lower lemma, acute at apex, glabrous except the nerve often minutely scabrous. *Lemmas* 3-nerved, 3-lobed and 3-awned, the awns conspicuously plumose; lemma deeply cleft between the nerves, villous along central lobe and lateral nerves. *Palea* of perfect floret membranous, awnless, slightly longer than body of lemma, laterally compressed and with the two nerves very close together; palea of lower floret reduced to a narrow membrane. *Chromosome number* reported as 2n=14 but this count needs confirmation.

Distribution. Texas: Region 10 on open, dry, limey slopes, mesas and desert flats, infrequently collected, though reported to be locally abundant in some areas. General: Known only from western Texas and adjacent areas in Coahuila, Mexico.

Flowering period: Spring and early summer.

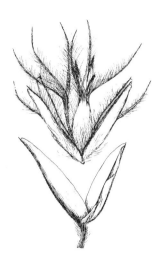

Fig. 129. *Blepharidachne bigelovii.* Plant and spikelet with florets separated from glumes. From Gould,
1968.

65. CALAMOVILFA Hack.

A genus of four species, all North American.

1. **Calamovilfa gigantea** (Nutt.) Scribn. & Merr., U.S.D.A. Div. Agrost.
Cir. 35:2. 1901. BIG SANDREED. Fig. 130. Large, coarse perennial with
stout, creeping rhizomes. *Culms* mostly solitary at the rhizome nodes, usually
1-2 m tall and 4-15 mm or more thick near base. *Sheaths* rounded, glabrous or
occasionally puberulent near collar. *Ligule* a fringe of hairs mostly 1-2 mm
long. *Blades* elongate, firm, glabrous, flat or folded, 5-12 mm long near base,
tapering to a long, narrow involute apex. *Panicles* large and open, mostly
30-60 cm long and with stiffly ascending or spreading branches to 20 cm or
more long, the longer branches bare of spikelets or secondary branches on
lower 2.5-6 cm. *Spikelets* 1-flowered, awnless, mostly 7-10 mm long, clustered at the branch tips on very short pedicels. Disarticulation above glumes.
Glumes firm or papery, glabrous, 1-nerved, acute, the second glume equaling
or exceeding the lemma, the first slightly shorter. *Lemma* similar to the
glumes in texture, 1-nerved, narrow above, acute at apex, pubescent on back
below middle, with a tuft of silvery hairs 3-5 mm long at base. *Palea* narrow,
usually slightly longer than lemma and of similar texture, pubescent on nerves
below middle. *Chromosome number,* $2n=40$.

Distribution. Texas: Regions 8, 9 and 10 on open, sandy hills and dunes.
General: Kansas, Colorado and Utah, south to Texas, New Mexico and
Arizona.

Flowering period: Mostly June to October.

Fig. 130. *Calamovilfa gigantea*. Base of plant, inflorescence, glumes and floret.

244   THE GRASSES OF TEXAS

Fig. 131. *Lycurus phleoides*. Plant, separate inflorescence and spikelet with floret separated from glumes. From Gould, 1951.

66. LYCURUS H.B.K.

A genus of six species, distributed in southwestern North America and northern South America.

1. **Lycurus phleoides** H.B.K., Nov. Gen. et Sp. 1:142. 1815. WOLF-TAIL. Fig. 131. Tufted perennial. *Culms* 20-60 cm tall, straight or slightly geniculate, flattened or angled below, scabrous to pubescent, especially in vicinity of nodes. *Leaves* mostly in a basal clump. *Sheaths* laterally compressed and sharply keeled, much shorter than internodes. *Ligule* a whitish, 3-lobed membrane, the acuminate lobes mostly 3-5 mm long, the lateral lobes decurrent downward as sheath margins. *Blades* pale, usually grayish-green,

SUBFAMILY V. ERAGROSTOIDEAE   245

0.5-2 (-3) mm broad, flat or folded, usually with a whitish midnerve and margins. *Inflorescence* a slender, bristly, spicate panicle, 3-8 (-12) cm long and 5-8 mm thick. *Spikelets* 1-flowered, short-pediceled, deciduous in pairs with the pedicels, the lowermost spikelet of the pair usually sterile or staminate, the upper perfect. *Body of glumes* about 2 mm long, shorter than lemma, the first glume 2-3-nerved and with 2-3 awns mostly 3-5 mm long, the second glume similar but 1-nerved and with a single short awn. *Lemmas* 3-nerved, puberulent at least on the margins, mostly 3-4 mm long, tapering to an awn 0.5-3 mm long. *Paleas* puberulent, similar to the lemmas and as long but awnless, enclosed by lemma only near base. *Chromosome number*, $2n = 40$.

Distribution. Texas: Regions 9 and 10 and the western portion of region 7, in desert grasslands and on rocky slopes at medium to high elevations. General: Colorado and Utah to Texas, New Mexico, Arizona and Mexico.

Flowering period: Mostly June to October.

67. MUHLENBERGIA Schreb.*

Plants of diverse habit, from delicate annuals to large, coarse perennials, several species with scaly, creeping rhizomes. *Culms* simple or variously branched. *Leaves* with flat, folded or involute blades, usually with a well-developed membranous ligule (firmer below in some species). *Inflorescence* varying from an open, diffuse panicle to a loosely or tightly contracted spikelike inflorescence. *Spikelets* typically 1-flowered, a second floret occasionally produced in some species. Disarticulation above glumes in almost all species. *Glumes* usually 1-nerved or nerveless, rarely 3- (5-) nerved, mostly shorter than the lemma, obtuse, acute, acuminate or short awned. *Lemma* as firm as or firmer than the glumes, with 3 (very rarely 5) distinct or inconspicuous nerves, usually with a single flexuous awn at apex but sometimes mucronate or awnless, in a few species awned from between the lobes of a minutely bifid apex. *Culms* short and rounded, often hairy. *Palea* well-developed, of the same texture as the lemma, 2-nerved. *Caryopses* elongate, cylindrical, fusiform or slightly dorsally compressed, usually not falling free from the lemma and palea.

As presently interpreted, a genus of over 125 species, these mostly in the Americas with the center of distribution in Mexico but also a few species in the Old World. Chase in Hitchcock's Manual (1951) reports some 70 species in the United States.

References: Soderstrom, 1967; Pohl, 1969; Pinson & Batson, 1971.

Panicles open, loosely flowered, usually 2-10 cm or more wide, the
    branches bare of spikelets near the base   A

Panicles contracted, usually densely flowered and less than 2 cm wide (1-3
    cm wide in *M. montana*), the branches often floriferous to or nearly

*Contributed by Charlotte G. Reeder.

to the base (the panicles often more open during anthesis than otherwise)   AA

A

Culms widely spreading, much-branched, with wiry, widely divergent
  branches   6. *M. porteri*

Culms erect or curving-erect at base, the culm branches when present
  not widely divergent

  Plants annual

    Glumes glabrous; ligule with short auricles   40. *M. fragilis*

    Glumes minutely pilose, at least near apex; ligule without auricles

      Lemmas 1-1.7 mm long, awnless or with an awn up to 0.8 mm long
        (rarely longer); pedicels spreading, 2-5 mm long
                                                      39. *M. minutissima*

      Lemmas 2-2.5 mm long with an awn 1.5-3.5 mm long; pedicels
        appressed, commonly not over 2 mm long   41. *M. eludens*

  Plants perennial

    Plants rhizomatous and often decumbent at base

      Spikelets awnless; panicle branches ascending or spreading

        Ligules truncate with pointed auricles 1-2 mm long; culms scabrous
          and striate; blades with thickened white midnerve and margins
                                                        1. *M. arenacea*

        Ligules truncate, without lateral lobes; culms glabrous and smooth;
          blades without thickened white margins and midnerve
                                                        2. *M. asperifolia*

      Spikelets with awns 1-1.5 (-2) mm long; panicle branching in fascicles
                                                        5. *M. pungens*

    Plants cespitose, tufted, without scaly, creeping rhizomes

      Sheaths compressed-keeled; blades flat or folded

        Ligules 10-25 mm long; spikelets 2.5-3 (-3.2) mm long; lemmas
          pubescent on midnerve and margins on the lower half;

SUBFAMILY V. ERAGROSTOIDEAE   247

lemma awns to 15 mm long (rarely awnless)
15.   M. emersleyi

Ligules 3-12 mm long; spikelets 3-4 mm long; lemmas glabrous
except pubescent on margins at the very base; lemma awns
0.5-2 mm long   13.   M. involuta

Sheaths rounded, not keeled; blades becoming involute

Awn of lemma mostly 5-30 mm long (rarely less in M. capillaris)

Panicles mostly not over 4 cm wide

Lemmas purple, scaberulous near the apex; glumes 1-1.3 mm
long   7.   M. rigida

Lemmas stramineous, smooth and shining; glumes 1.5-2.1
(-2.5) mm long   8.   M. setifolia

Panicles mostly over 8 cm wide, open and diffuse

Glumes obtuse or subacute, not awned   7.   M. rigida

Glumes, at least the second, awned

Second glume with an awn to 1.5 (-2.5) mm long; lemmas
without conspicuous setaceous teeth; awn of lemma
mostly 5- (2-) 13 mm long   9.   M. capillaris

Second glume usually with an awn 5-19 mm long; lemmas
with evident setaceous teeth (0.5-2.5 mm long); awn of
lemma mostly 11-26 mm long   10.   M. filipes

Awn of lemma 0-3 (rarely as much as 5) mm long (see also M.
capillaris)

Lemmas less than 3.5 mm long, finely pubescent on midnerve
and margins on lower half

Blades strongly arcuate, less than 1 mm wide; no culm nodes
exposed; leafy portion equal to one-eighth to one-sixteenth
of the plant   4.   M. torreyi

Blades rather straight; about 1-2 mm wide; 1 or more culm
nodes exposed; leafy portion equal to one-third to one-half
of the plant   3.   M. arenicola

Lemmas 4- (3.5-) 5 mm long, glabrous except for a few short, appressed hairs on callus

Glumes 3-3.5 mm long, acute or acuminate; basal sheaths becoming fibrous   11. *M. expansa*

Glumes 2- (1.5-) 2.5 mm long, subacute to erose; basal sheaths not fibrous   12. *M. reverchonii*

AA

Plants annual

Glumes about equaling lemma; spikelets 2.5-3.5 mm long; awn of lemma 0.5-5 (rarely -10) mm long   37. *M. depauperata*

Glumes usually half as long as lemma or less; spikelets 4-5 (-6) mm long; awn of lemma 5-15 mm long   38. *M. brevis*

Plants perennial

Glumes minute, mostly 0.1-0.3 mm long, the first often absent; culms decumbent, often stoloniferous and rooting at lower nodes
23. *M. schreberi*

Glumes, at least the second, 0.5 mm long or more; culms erect or somewhat decumbent, rarely stoloniferous

Plants without scaly, creeping rhizomes   B

Plants with scaly, creeping rhizomes   BB

B

Second glume 3-nerved and 3-toothed   22. *M. montana*

Second glume usually 1-nerved, entire or irregularly erose

Sheaths compressed-keeled

Lemmas minutely scaberulous or glabrous, awnless
14. *M. lindheimeri*

Lemmas pubescent on midnerve and margins on lower half, with an awn usually 10-20 mm long (very rarely awnless)
15. *M. emersleyi*

SUBFAMILY V. ERAGROSTOIDEAE   249

Sheaths rounded

Lemma awns mostly less than 10 mm long (see also *M. pauciflora*)

Ligules 1-2 mm long; lemmas about 3 mm long, mucronate
16. *M. rigens*

Ligules 4-15 mm long; lemmas 4-5 mm long, short-awned

Panicles gray or greenish, to 1 cm wide; glumes 2-3 mm long
17. *M. dubia*

Panicles purplish, to 2 cm wide; glumes 1.5-2 mm long
18. *M. metcalfei*

Lemma awns 10 mm or more long

Glumes obtuse, 0.5-1 (-1.4) mm long; awn of lemma 20-40 mm long
21. *M. parviglumis*

Glumes acute or awn-pointed or, if truncate, the glumes mostly over 1.5 mm long; awn of lemma flexuous, mostly less than 25 mm long

Lemmas essentially glabrous, with only a very few closely appressed hairs on the callus; ligules 0.5-1 mm long with lateral projections (auricles) 1.5-3 mm long
19. *M. pauciflora*

Lemmas pubescent on lower half; ligules thin, lacerated, 1.5-3 (-5) mm long   20. *M. monticola*

BB

Leaf blades mostly 1-2 cm long, 0.5-1 (-2) mm wide

Lemmas short pubescent on lower half; culms nodulose-roughened
26. *M. villosa*

Lemmas glabrous or scaberulous near apex; culms glabrous and smooth

Lemmas 3-3.5 mm long; plants of dry, rocky or sandy, open (often alkaline) soil   24. *M. repens*

Lemmas about 2 mm long; plants of moister soil, along ditches and streams   25. *M. utilis*

Leaf blades mostly 4 cm or more long, 1-3 mm or more wide

Panicles terminal only

Anthers pale, yellowish; blades 2-5 (-7) mm wide

Glumes attenuate or aristate, the tips exceeding the floret in length
29. *M. racemosa*

Glumes pointed, equaling or shorter than the floret

Panicle densely flowered, 2-5 cm long; lemmas with copious white
hairs as long as the floret; internodes just below nodes glabrous
or minutely antrorsely puberulent   31. *M. andina*

Panicle slender, loosely flowered, 6-21 cm long; lemmas short-
pilose on callus; internodes retrorsely scabrous below nodes
36. *M. sylvatica*

Anthers orange; blades mostly 1-2 mm wide

Lemmas awnless, mucronate or with an awn 1-3 mm long
27. *M. glauca*

Lemmas with an awn 6-10 mm long   28. *M. polycaulis*

Panicles terminal and axillary

Culms glabrous

Glumes overlapping at base, abruptly tapering to an awn tip;
panicles usually long exserted on peduncles up to 11 cm long
30. *M. sobolifera*

Glumes not overlapping at base, lanceolate, gradually tapering to
an awn tip; panicles on peduncles 1-2 cm long

Glumes 1.4-2 mm long; ligules 0.2-0.6 mm long
33. *M. bushii*

Glumes 2-4 mm long; ligules 0.8-1.4 mm long
34. *M. frondosa*

Culms scabrous or pubescent below the nodes

Lemmas glabrous   35. *M. glabriflora*

Lemmas pilose on callus   32. *M. mexicana*

SUBFAMILY V. ERAGROSTOIDEAE   251

1. **Muhlenbergia arenacea** (Buckl.) Hitchc., Proc. Biol. Soc. Wash. 41:161. 1928. EAR MUHLY. Fig. 132. Low perennial with extensive creeping rhizomes and leaves mostly in a basal clump. *Culms* striate, scabrous, 10-20 (-40) cm tall, decumbent, spreading and sod-forming. *Sheaths* rounded, shorter than the internodes. *Ligules* hyaline, 0.5 mm long, mostly with lateral points 1-2 mm long, these longer than the lacerate central portion and appearing as hyaline sheath auricles. *Blades* flat, folded or loosely involute, often somewhat twisted, mostly 1-3 (-6) cm long and 0.5-1.5 mm wide, with a thick, white midnerve and usually thickened whitish margins, tapering to a slender, often firm and sharp-pointed tip. *Panicles* open, diffuse, loosely flowered, mostly 5-15 cm long and 4-12 cm wide. *Pedicels* capillary, flexuous, longer than the spikelets. *Spikelets* 1.5-2 mm long. *Glumes* glabrous or slightly scabrous, subequal, acute, occasionally slightly toothed or minutely mucronate, 0.9-1.3 mm long, about half as long as lemmas. *Lemmas* 1.5-2 mm long, thin, glabrous, purple-tinged at maturity, rounded and awnless at apex, rarely minutely mucronate. *Paleas* as long as or slightly longer than lemmas. *Chromosome number* not reported.

Distribution. Texas: Regions 7, 9 and 10 on sandy plains, valley flats and along washes. General: Colorado, Texas to Arizona and south to Zacatecas, Mexico.

Flowering period: May to November.

2. **Muhlenbergia asperifolia** (Nees & Mey.) Parodi, Revista Univ. Buenos Aires Publ. Fac. Agron. Vet. 6:117. 1928. ALKALI MUHLY. Perennial with spreading, decumbent culms from extensive creeping, scaly rhizomes. *Culms* smooth and shining, the erect portion mostly 15-30 (-60) cm tall. *Leaves* usually not in a basal tuft but tending to be rather uniformly distributed along the culms. *Ligules* membranous, truncate, minutely ciliate, 0.2-0.5 mm long, without lateral projections (auricles). *Blades* scabrous, flat or folded, mostly 2.5-8 (-14) cm long, and 1-3 mm wide. *Panicles* open, diffuse, 5-15 cm long and about as wide. *Pedicels* slender, capillary, much longer than the spikelet. *Spikelet* about 1.5 (-2) mm long, not infrequently 2-flowered, and often infected with a smut fungus. *Glumes* acute, 0.6-1 (-1.7) mm long. *Lemmas* 1.2-1.5 (-2) mm long, glabrous, rounded or very short mucronate. *Paleas* of the same length and texture as lemmas. *Anthers* pale, 1-1.2 mm long. *Chromosome numbers* reported, $2n=20$, 22 and 28.

Distribution. Texas: Regions 7, 8, 9 and 10, mostly in canyon bottoms, low flats and marshy or moist meadows. General: Minnesota to British Columbia, south throughout the midwestern and western United States and Mexico and in southern South America.

Flowering period: June to November.

3. **Muhlenbergia arenicola** Buckl., Proc. Acad. Nat. Sci. Philadelphia Monogr. 1862:91. 1862. SANDY MUHLY. Densely tufted perennials with culms 20-60 cm tall from a firm, somewhat decumbent base. *Culms* hispidulous below nodes, 1 or more nodes evident. *Blades* 4-14 cm long, 1-2

Fig. 132. *Muhlenbergia arenacea*. Plant, spikelet and leaf showing ligule.

mm wide, mostly basal but the culm leaves with well-developed blades, usually glaucous and minutely scabrous, not strongly arcuate. *Ligules* mostly 2-7 (-9) mm long, hyaline with somewhat firmer margins which may separate, thus appearing as sheath auricles. *Panicles* mostly 12-25 (-30) cm long and 5-15 cm wide, with stiffly erect-spreading primary branches. *Branchlets and pedicels* often remaining appressed or ascending at a narrow angle, the lateral pedicels commonly shorter than the spikelets. *Glumes* 1.5-2 (-2.5) mm long, scabrous, lanceolate, acute, acuminate or occasionally irregularly toothed at the apex, often awn-tipped. *Lemmas* stramineous or purple-tinged, 2.5-3.5 mm long, scabrous above, short-pubescent on the midnerve and margins on the lower half, with a slender awn, 0.5-2.5 (-3.5) mm long. *Paleas* as long as lemmas, the nerves usually extended as very short mucros. *Anthers* 1.7-1.9 mm long, often greenish-tinged. *Chromosome number* not reported.

Distribution. Texas: Regions 7, 8, 9 and 10 on dry, sandy mesas and valleys. General: Kansas and Colorado to Texas and Arizona and in northern Mexico.

Flowering period: May to October.

SUBFAMILY V. ERAGROSTOIDEAE   253

4. **Muhlenbergia torreyi** (Kunth) Hitchc. *ex* Bush, Amer. Midl. Naturalist. 6:84. 1919. RING MUHLY. Densely tufted perennial with culms mostly 15-30 (-40) cm tall, curving-erect from a mass of slender culm bases, no culm nodes in evidence. *Leaves* mostly in a dense tuft, the short, fine, arcuate blades forming a compact cushion 2-5 cm in depth. *Ligules* membranous, glabrous, 2-5 (-7) mm long, acute or becoming split and then appearing as continuations of the sheath (auricles). *Blades* 0.3-0.5 mm wide, tightly involute or folded, mostly 1-3 cm long (rarely over 4 cm long), rather strongly arcuate and sharp-pointed. *Panicles* mostly 7-20 cm long and 4-12 cm wide, the main branches widely spreading, the branchlets and pedicels appressed or at maturity spreading, the pedicels equaling or longer than the spikelets. *Glumes* 1.5-2.5 (-3) mm long, acute or acuminate to short awn-tipped or irregularly toothed, glabrous or scaberulous. *Lemmas* 2.5-3.5 mm long, minutely bifid at the apex, scabrous above, very short appressed-pubescent on midnerve and margins of lower half, with an awn 1-2 (-3) mm long. *Paleas* minutely bifid at apex. *Anthers* about 1.4-1.7 mm long, often greenish-tinged. *Chromosome number* not reported.

Distribution. Texas: Regions 7, 8, 9 and 10 on dry, sandy mesas and valleys. General: Kansas and Colorado to Texas and Arizona, southward into northern Mexico.

Flowering period: May to October.

Closely related to *Muhlenbergia arenicola* but with more slender culms and culm bases, generally shorter culms, finer, shorter and more densely massed arcuate blades and smaller panicles. Ring muhly derives its name from its peculiar growth habit. As the base of the plant grows and enlarges the center dies out, leaving a "fairy ring" several inches to a few feet in diameter.

5. **Muhlenbergia pungens** Thurb. in A. Gray, Proc. Acad. Nat. Sci. Philadelphia Monogr., 1863. 78. 1863. SANDHILL MUHLY. Fig. 133. Perennial with coarse, scaly rhizomes and usually scabrous or cinerous-puberulent herbage. *Culms* mostly 20-50 (-60) cm tall, often in dense clumps. *Sheaths* short, rounded, with membranous margins often terminating in rounded auriculate appendages. *Ligules* 0.5-1 mm long, densely ciliate. *Blades* stiff, involute, mostly 2-4 cm long, about 1 mm wide, spinescent at apex. *Panicles* usually long exserted, open, mostly 8-18 cm long, usually with 3-5 short primary branches, these moderately rebranched thus appearing fascicled or directly bearing clusters of long pediceled spikelets. *Spikelets* 3-4, borne on capillary pedicels mostly 10-25 mm long. *Glumes* 1.5-2.5 mm long, slightly unequal, broad, thin, erose or irregularly toothed, with an awn-tip 0.5-1 mm long, scaberulous. *Lemmas* dark purple, 3-4 mm long, with an awn 1-1.5 (-2) mm long, scaberulous at tip and on lateral margins. *Paleas* about as long as lemmas, the nerves extended as two short teeth. *Anthers* purple, 2-2.5 mm long. *Chromosome numbers* reported, $2n=42$ and 60.

Distribution. Texas: Region 9, in loose, sandy and sandy clay soils and dunes areas. General: South Dakota, Wyoming and Utah to Texas, New Mexico and Arizona.

Fig. 133. *Muhlenbergia pungens*. Plant, separate inflorescence and spikelet with floret separated from glumes. From Gould, 1951.

Flowering period: September to November.

Plants of this species form large dense clumps. In time the center often dies, leaving a "fairy ring" of considerable size.

SUBFAMILY V. ERAGROSTOIDEAE   255

Fig. 134. *Muhlenbergia porteri*. Plant and spikelet with floret separated from glumes. From Gould, 1951.

6. **Muhlenbergia porteri** Scribn. *ex* Beal, Grasses North Amer. 2:259. 1896. BUSH MUHLY. Fig. 134. Perennial with slender, wiry, geniculate, much branched culms from a hard, knotty base. *Culms* mostly 30-100 cm long, striate, minutely puberulous or scabrous below the many nodes, the internodes 1.5-6 cm long. *Sheaths* mostly shorter than the internodes. *Ligule* a

lacerate membrane 1-2 (-2.5) mm long, the outer edges often a bit longer. *Blades* thin, flat, becoming involute, mostly 2-5 cm long and 0.5-2 mm broad. *Panicles* numerous, terminal on the branches, mostly 4-10 cm long and nearly as broad, usually purple. *Spikelets* widely spaced on pedicels 5-20 mm long. *Glumes* thin, glabrous, narrowly lanceolate or acuminate, subequal, about 2-3 mm long, the second glume two-thirds to nearly as long as lemma. *Lemmas* thin, usually sparsely and minutely puberulous between nerves and on lateral margins, with a body 3-4 mm long and an awn 5-10 (-13) mm long. *Paleas* about as long as lemmas, acuminate at apex. *Anthers* 1.7-2 mm long. *Chromosome numbers:* euploid counts of $2n = 20$ and 40 and aneuploid counts of $2n = 23$ and 24 have been reported.

Distribution. Texas: Frequent in region 10, occasional in region 7 and the southern part of region 9, on dry, rocky slopes, brushy flats and along dry arroyos, usually in the protection of shrubs or cacti. General: Colorado and Nevada to western Texas, Arizona, southern California and central Mexico.

Flowering period: June to November.

7. **Muhlenbergia rigida** (H.B.K.) Kunth, Rev. Gram. 1:63. 1829. PURPLE MUHLY. Perennial with culms in dense, cespitose clumps. *Culms* 50-100 cm tall, firm and slender, stiffly erect, the nodes obscure. *Sheaths* rounded. *Ligules* thin above, often firmer below, 3-9 (-15) mm long, usually frayed and lacerated, the edges extending as rather firm sheath auricles. *Blades* 12-35 cm long and 1-3 mm broad, usually involute. *Panicle* dark purple, 10-35 cm long, mostly 2-4 cm broad but occasionally as much as 9-10 cm wide, loose but appearing densely-flowered when contracted. *Panicle branches* capillary, spreading to ascending or not infrequently rather closely appressed. *Pedicels* slender, variable but at least some 5-15 mm long. *Glumes* subequal, broad, glabrous, rounded, obtuse or acute, mostly 1-1.3 (-1.5) mm long. *Lemmas* with few short appressed hairs on the callus, the slender body 4-(3.5-) 5 mm long, with an awn 10-22 mm long. *Paleas* about as long as lemmas. *Anthers* 1.8-2.3 mm long, usually purple. *Chromosome number:* most counts $2n = 40$, one report of $2n = 44$.

Distribution. Texas: Region 10, locally abundant on rocky mountain slopes at medium and high elevations. General: Texas to Arizona and Mexico.

Flowering period: Mostly July to September.

Panicles of this species may be open and diffuse or rather contracted; usually they open up to some extent at anthesis but maintain a quite distinct narrow form.

8. **Muhlenbergia setifolia** Vasey, Bot. Gaz. 7:92. 1882. CURLYLEAF MUHLY. Cespitose perennial with firm, slender culms 50-80 cm tall. *Sheaths* broader than the involute blades, extended upward into a broad, rather firm ligule mostly 4-7 (-10) mm long (the tip may be membranous, soon becoming frayed). *Blades* mostly 6-18 (-25) cm long and about 1 mm wide but tightly involute and 0.2-0.5 mm wide as inrolled, rather markedly curved to curly.

Panicles mostly 8-20 (-25) cm long and 2-4 cm wide, usually loosely contracted, the branches capillary, ascending, naked below. *Glumes* broad, obtuse or irregularly truncate at apex, 1.5-2 (-2.5) mm long, the second glume often mucronate. *Lemmas* stramineous, less frequently pale purple-tinged, 3.5-5 mm long, glabrous and shining except for a few short, appressed hairs on the callus, with an awn 10-28 mm long. *Paleas* about as long as lemmas. *Anthers* about 2 mm long. *Chromosome number,* 2n=40.

Distribution. Texas: Region 10 and western portion of region 7, mostly in calcareous soil on open, rocky slopes at medium to high elevations. General: Western Texas, New Mexico and northern Coahuila.

Flowering period: August to November.

9. **Muhlenbergia capillaris** (Lam.) Trin., Gram. Unifl. 191. 1824. HAIRYAWN MUHLY. Fig. 135. Densely cespitose perennial. *Culms* erect, rather slender, puberulent below the nodes, 60-100 cm tall. *Sheaths* rounded, glabrous or somewhat scaberulous above. *Ligules* firm, prominent, strongly decurrent, 2-5 mm long, those of the upper blades as much as 8 mm long. *Blades* elongate, flat or becoming involute on drying, 20-50 cm long, mostly 1-2 (-4) mm wide, often curved outward near base exposing the firm ligule. *Panicles* open, diffuse, purple, as much as 35 (-40) cm long, 8-17 (-20) cm wide, the branches and pedicels capillary and widely spreading at maturity. *Spikelets* purple, 3.5-4.5 mm long. *Glumes* 1-1.5 (-2) mm long, acute to acuminate, irregularly erose at apex, or the second glume frequently with an awn as much as 1.5 (-2.5) mm long. *Lemmas* 3.5-4.5 mm long, scaberulous especially near apex, with a few very short, appressed hairs on callus. *Awn* of lemma variable, flexuous, 5- (2-) 13 mm long. *Paleas* acuminate, scaberulous between nerves. *Anthers* mostly purplish, 1.5-2 mm long. *Chromosome number* not reported.

Distribution. Texas: Regions 1 and 3 (Walker County and Bastrop State Park) in rocky or sandy woodlands. General: Massachusetts to Indiana and eastern Kansas, southward to Florida and eastern Texas. Also in eastern Mexico and the West Indies.

Flowering period: September and October.

10. **Muhlenbergia filipes** M. A. Curtis, Amer. J. Sci. I. 44:83. 1843. [*Muhlenbergia capillaris* (Lam.) Trin. var. *filipes* (M. A. Curtis) Chapm. *ex* Beal] [cf. Pinson & Batson, Jour. Elisha Mitchell Sci. Soc. 87 (4):188-191. 1971.] Densely cespitose perennial. *Culms* glabrous, 70-160 cm tall. *Sheaths* rounded, glabrous. *Ligules* firm, prominent, strongly decurrent, 1-2 mm long on the lower blades, 5-8 (-10) cm long on the upper blades. *Blades* mostly involute, 40-100 cm long, 1-2 mm wide, curved outward at the base exposing the firm ligule. *Panicles* purple, open, diffuse, 30-70 cm long, 20-30 cm wide when mature; the branches and pedicels long, capillary and widely spreading. *Spikelets* mostly purplish, 4-5 mm long. *Glumes* awned, the first glume 0.5-1 mm long with an awn 1-5 mm long; the second glume 1-1.5 m long with an awn 5-19 mm long. *Lemmas* 3-4 (-5) mm long, awned from between two small

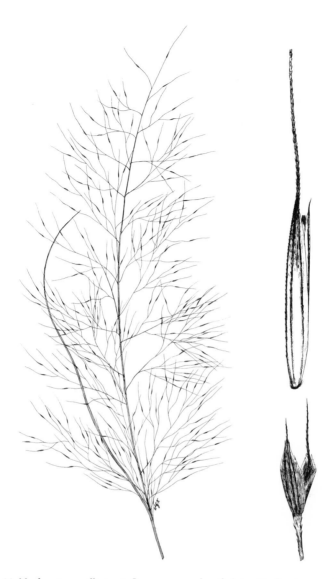

Fig. 135. *Muhlenbergia capillaris*. Inflorescence and spikelet with floret separated from glumes. From Gould and Box, 1965.

setaceous teeth 1-3 mm long. *Awn of lemma* flexuous, 11-26 mm long. *Paleas* 3-4 mm long, distinctly 2-nerved, the nerves extended as two short teeth (as much as 0.5 mm long). *Anthers* purplish, 1.5-2 mm long. *Chromosome number* not reported.

Distribution. Texas: Region 2 in sand dunes and open coastal woodlands. General: Coastal Plains of North Carolina to Florida, Alabama, Mississippi and eastern Texas.

SUBFAMILY V. ERAGROSTOIDEAE   259

Flowering period: October and November.

Similar to *Muhlenbergia capillaris* but with culms tending to be stouter, with blades mostly involute, with both glumes awned, lemmas and paleas with setaceous teeth and with lemma awn usually longer. The flowering period for *M. filipes* is later (October and November).

11. **Muhlenbergia expansa** (Poir.) Trin., Gram. Pan. 26. 1826. Densely cespitose perennial. *Culms* erect, slender, glabrous, 60-100 cm tall. *Sheaths* rounded, glabrous, the older ones becoming fibrous at the base. *Ligules* rather firm, prominent, strongly decurrent, 2-4 (-5) mm long, those of the upper blades longer than the lower. *Blades* elongate, flat or becoming involute, reaching 30-50 cm long, 2-3 mm wide, curved outward at the base exposing the firmish ligule. *Panicles* open, oblong, 20-30 (-50) cm long, 4-7 (-10) cm wide, the branches flexuous and spreading, the pedicels slender, mostly longer than the spikelets. *Spikelets* 3.5-4 (-5) mm long. *Glumes* nearly equal, one-half to two-thirds as long as the lemma, acute to acuminate or very short aristate, 2.5-3.5 mm long. *Lemmas* brownish or bronze, acuminate, 3.5-4 (-5) mm long, scaberulous near apex and with a few very short appressed hairs on callus. *Awn of lemma* mostly 0.5-1 (-1.5) mm long. *Chromosome number* not reported.

Distribution. Texas: Southern portion of region 1 and eastern portion of region 2 (Buna and in Liberty County) in sandy pine woods of the Coastal Plain. General: Coastal Plain of North Carolina to Florida and eastern Texas.

Flowering period: August to October.

Although Correll and Johnston (1970) consider *Muhlenbergia expansa* and *M. filipes* as no more than synonyms of *M. capillaris*, which, indeed, both resemble, closer inspection shows both *M. expansa* and *M. filipes* to have characters sufficiently distinct to warrant specific recognition. *Muhlenbergia expansa* may be distinguished by the fibrous sheaths at the base of the culms, the short lemma awns and the acute to acuminate glumes which are one-half to two-thirds as long as the lemma.

12. **Muhlenbergia reverchonii** Vasey & Scribn., Contr. U. S. Natl. Herb. 3:66. 1892. SEEP MUHLY. Densely tufted perennial with stiffly erect culms 40-80 cm tall. *Sheaths* scaberulous, rounded on back. *Ligule* 2-4 mm long (upper to 6-9 mm long), firm at base, thin and lacerate at apex. *Blades* filiform and elongate, arcuate to broadly curving, mostly 8-35 cm long and 1-2 mm wide, flat or more commonly tightly involute when dried or mature. *Panicles* 10-20 (-30) cm long (rarely longer) and 4-10 (-15) cm wide, open but not diffuse, with stiffly erect-spreading primary branches mostly 3-8 (-10) cm long. *Spikelets* stramineous, brownish, or slightly purple-tinged. *Glumes* subequal, 1-2.5 (-3) mm long, broadly acute or obtuse, often abruptly mucronate or minutely awned, usually stramineous or light bronze. *Lemmas* glabrous or scabrous, with a few short appressed hairs at base, 3.5-5 mm long,

tapering to a minutely scabrous awn 0.5-3 (-6) mm long. *Paleas* slightly shorter than body of lemma. *Chromosome numbers* reported, 2n=20 and 40.

Distribution. Texas: Regions 4, 5, 7 and 8, mostly on calcareous soils. General: Southern Oklahoma and Texas.

Flowering period: August to November.

13. **Muhlenbergia involuta** Swallen, Amer. J. Bot. 19:436. fig. 2. 1932. CANYON MUHLY. Fig. 136. Perennial with densely tufted, stiffly-erect culms 60-140 cm tall. *Sheaths*, at least the lower, laterally compressed and somewhat keeled. *Ligules* 3-12 mm long, firm and brown at base, membranous above. *Blades* mostly 10-40 (-45) cm long and 2-5 mm broad, mostly tightly folded. *Panicles* narrow but open and loosely flowered, mostly 18-40 cm long and 2-5 (-7) cm wide. *Panicle branches* slender, stiffly erect-spreading, the lower mostly 3-10 (-15) cm long, naked below. *Spikelets* 3-4 mm long, stramineous, less frequently purple-tinged. *Glumes* glabrous or at times scaberulous, subequal, mostly 2-2.5 (-3) mm long, acute or obtuse and somewhat erose, infrequently minutely awned. *Lemmas* 3-4 mm long, glabrous or sparsely pubescent on margins at the very base, with an awn 0.5-2 mm long from between the teeth of a minutely bifid apex. *Paleas* glabrous, about as long as lemmas. *Chromosome number*, 2n=24.

Distribution. Texas: Edwards Plateau (regions 4, 5 and 7) and most frequent in southern portion of region 7, in rocky prairie openings and along canyons. The type specimen was collected 20 miles northeast of San Antonio. General: Endemic to Texas.

Flowering period: Mostly September to December.

This is a member of the *Epicampes* group of species.

14. **Muhlenbergia lindheimeri** Hitchc., J. Wash. Acad. Sci. 24:291. 1934. LINDHEIMER MUHLY. Fig. 137. Strongly cespitose perennial with stout, stiffly erect culms 80-100 (50-150) cm tall. *Sheaths* firm, the basal ones compressed-keeled. *Ligules* firm and brown below, membranous above, 8-15 mm long (rarely more), decurrent and continuous at base with margins of sheath. *Blades* firm, elongate, pale green or glaucous, folded or the tip becoming involute when dry, mostly 10-45 (-50) cm long and 2-3 (-5) mm wide, short-pubescent on upper surface. *Panicle* tightly or loosely contracted, densely-flowered, the branches floriferous almost to base, mostly 20-40 (15-50) cm long and 1-1.5 (0.6-3) cm wide. *Panicle axis and branches* often purple-tinged, this contrasting with the light grayish spikelets, glumes and lemmas. *Glumes* subequal, glabrous or scabrous, 2-3.5 mm long, acute or slightly notched at apex, occasionally mucronate. *Lemmas* about as long as glumes, glabrous, scabrous or rarely puberulent, awnless or infrequently with awns to 3 (-4) mm long. *Paleas* slightly shorter than lemmas. *Anthers* about 1.5 mm long. *Chromosome number*, 2n=20.

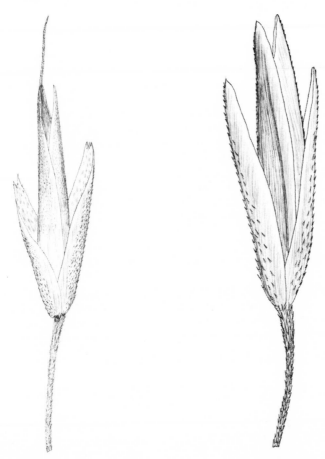

Fig. 136. *Muhlenbergia involuta*. Spikelet. Fig. 137. *Muhlenbergia lindheimeri*. Spikelet.

Distribution. Texas: Regions 4, 5, 6 and 7 on rocky, usually limestone soils in canyons and open areas. General: South-central Texas and northern Coahuila, Mexico. The type specimen was collected near Fredericksburg, in Gillespie County.

Flowering period: September to December.

Not infrequently specimens of *Muhlenbergia lindheimeri* are confused with the closely related *M. longiligula* Hitchc., which they resemble in habit and general appearance. However, in *M. longiligula* the basal sheaths are rounded and never keeled.

Fig. 138. *Muhlenbergia emersleyi*. Spikelet.

15. **Muhlenbergia emersleyi** Vasey, Contr. U. S. Natl. Herb. 3:66. 1892.
BULLGRASS. Fig. 138. Coarse, densely cespitose perennial. *Culms* erect,
stout, 100-150 (-200) cm tall, with 3 or 4 nodes, glabrous or puberulent below
the nodes. *Basal sheaths* laterally compressed and sharply keeled; sheath
auricles lacking. *Ligules* thin, deeply lacerate, mostly 10-25 mm long. *Culm
blades* firm, 23-40 (20-47) cm long, 2-5 (-6) mm wide, flat or folded, scabrous at
least on lower surface, coarsely scabrous on margins. *Panicles*
densely-flowered, narrowly pyramidal or cylindrical, light purple to
purplish-tan, 20-40 cm long, 4-7 cm wide. *Panicle branches* densely-flowered,
appressed, loosely ascending, or spreading-erect, usually naked below.
Spikelets 2.5-3 (2.2-3.2) mm long. *Glumes* obscurely 1-nerved, broadly acute
or obtuse, subequal or the second glume 1-2 mm longer than the first, usually
scaberulous to scabrous. *Lemma* slightly shorter than second glume, pubescent on midnerve and margins on lower one-half to two-thirds, usually awned
from just below the acute bifid tip, with a flexuous, purplish awn to 15 mm
long, this often deciduous. *Paleas* slightly shorter than lemmas, pubescent
between the two keels. *Chromosome numbers* reported, most counts $2n=40$;
records of $2n=42$, 60 and 64 also published.

Distribution. Texas: Region 10, frequent on rocky mountain slopes, rock
ledges and along canyons and arroyos, at medium to high elevations. General:
Texas to Arizona and southward in Mexico to Oaxaca.

Flowering period: July to November.

An extremely variable species in which the panicles may be somewhat
contracted or quite open; the awn on the lemma may be long and flexuous or
absent. In some specimens, the awns are readily deciduous; thus, some
spikelets of an inflorescence may appear to be awned, others awnless.

SUBFAMILY V. ERAGROSTOIDEAE   263

Fig. 139. *Muhlenbergia rigens.* Inflorescence and spikelet with floret separated from glumes. From Gould, 1968.

16. **Muhlenbergia rigens** (Benth.) Hitchc., J. Wash. Acad. Sci. 23:453. 1933. DEERGRASS. Fig. 139. Densely cespitose perennials. *Culms* firm and coarse, 50-150 cm tall, 1.5-4 mm thick near base. *Sheaths* rounded, often becoming flat in age, broader than the blades. *Ligules* firm, truncate or with short rounded auricles 0.5-2 mm long. *Blades* firm, pale green, 10-50 cm long, 1.5-4 mm wide, usually folded or involute in age, long attenuate. *Panicles* dense, contracted, spikelike, mostly 8-40 (-60) cm long and 0.5-1 cm wide, with short, appressed branches which are floriferous to base. *Spikelets* grayish green, awnless, 2.5-3.5 mm long. *Glumes* scabrous, broadly acute, occasionally minutely mucronate, mostly 2-3 mm long and often nearly as long as lemma. *Lemmas* 2.5-3.5 mm long, smooth or scabrous, acute, occasionally minutely mucronate, sparingly pilose on callus, occasionally with an awn to 1 mm long. *Paleas* as long as lemmas and similar in texture. *Chromosome number,* $2n = 40$.

Distribution. Texas: Region 10, gravelly or sandy canyon bottoms and washes, often in moist soil. General: Texas to southern California and northern Mexico.

Flowering period: August to November.

17. **Muhlenbergia dubia** Fourn. *ex* Hemsley, Biol. Centr. Amer. Bot. 3:540. 1885. PINE MUHLY. Densely cespitose perennial. *Culms* erect, 30-100 cm tall, faintly puberulent to scaberulous below the nodes. *Sheaths* rounded, glabrous or scaberulous. *Ligules* firmer below, membranous above, 4-12 mm long, those of the lowermost blades shorter. *Blades* elongate, gray-green, 25-60 cm long, 1-2 mm wide, involute, scabrous. *Panicles* densely-flowered, narrow-contracted, 10-30 cm long, about 1 cm wide, often interrupted below, the branches mostly 1-2 cm long, closely appressed or ascending. *Spikelets* 4-5 mm long. *Glumes* obtuse, scaberulous, 2-3 mm long. *Lemmas* 4-5 mm long, scabrous above with a few short closely appressed hairs on callus, awnless or with an awn to 4 mm long (rarely longer). *Anthers* about 2 mm long. *Chromosome number* not reported.

Distribution. Texas: Region 10, confined to the Guadalupe Mountains. A variable species of canyons and rocky hills at higher elevations. General: Western Texas and New Mexico to northern Mexico.

Flowering period: September to November.

Similar to *Muhlenbergia metcalfei*, which usually has purplish panicles, the branches of which may reach 5 cm long, glumes 1.5-2 mm long and a lemma awn mostly 5- (3-) 10 mm long.

18. **Muhlenbergia metcalfei** M. E. Jones, Contr. W. Bot. 14:12. 1912. *Culms* densely cespitose, 40-80 cm tall, puberulous below the nodes. *Sheaths* rounded, scaberulous. *Ligule* membranous toward apex, firmer below, 4-15 mm long, those on the lower portion of culms shorter than the upper. *Panicles* purplish, narrow-contracted, densely-flowered, 20-40 cm long, about 2 cm wide. *Panicle branches* appressed or stiffly ascending, to 5 cm long. *Glumes* 1.5-2 mm long, scabrous toward the obtuse apex. *Lemmas* 4-5 mm long, scabrous or scaberulous near apex with a few closely appressed short hairs on callus. *Awn of lemma* 5-10 (rarely 3) mm long. *Anthers* 2-2.2 mm long. *Chromosome number* not reported.

Distribution. Texas: Region 10, confined to rocky hillsides in the Davis and Guadalupe Mountains of southwestern Texas. General: Rocky hills of Texas and New Mexico. The type specimen was collected in the Santa Rita Mountains of New Mexico.

Flowering period: September to November.

Muhlenbergia metcalfei is often confused with *M. dubia*, and, in fact, Correll and Johnston (1970) consider *M. metcalfei* as no more than a synonym of *M. dubia*, which differs in having greenish panicles with shorter branches (-2 cm long), longer glumes (2-3 mm long) and lemma awns that are mostly shorter (0-4 mm long).

19. **Muhlenbergia pauciflora** Buckl., Proc. Acad. Nat. Sci. Philadelphia Monogr. 1862:91. 1862. NEW MEXICO MUHLY. Tufted perennial with firm, wiry culms from a hard, knotty base, the culms often geniculate below

and rooting at the lower nodes. *Culms* mostly 20-70 cm tall, often branching freely below middle. *Sheaths* rounded, shorter than the internodes. *Ligules* mostly 0.5-1 mm long, with lateral auriculate projections 1.5-3 mm long. *Blades* scabrous, filiform, mostly 4-12 cm long and 0.5-1 mm broad, flat or involute. *Panicles* narrow, contracted, densely-flowered, occasionally lobed, mostly 5-12 cm long and 4-10 (-15) mm wide. *Panicle branches* appressed, to 6 cm long, spikelet-bearing nearly to the base. *Spikelets* mostly on pedicels 0.2-1.5 mm long. *Glumes* 1-nerved, subequal, lanceolate, 1.5-3.5 mm long. *Lemmas* 3-4.5 mm long, glabrous or scabrous, the callus often with a few short, appressed hairs, the midnerve extending into a straight or undulant awn (5-) 7-25 mm long. *Paleas* about as long as lemmas. *Chromosome number* not reported.

Distribution. Texas: Region 10 on rocky, open slopes at medium to high elevations. General: Colorado and Utah to Texas, Arizona and northern Mexico.

Flowering period: August to October.

20. **Muhlenbergia monticola** Buckl., Proc. Acad. Nat. Sci. Philadelphia Monogr. 1862:91. 1862. MESA MUHLY. Fig. 140. Tufted perennial with slender, wiry culms from a usually firm, knotty base. *Culms* mostly 20-60 cm tall, scabrous to scaberulous below the nodes. *Sheaths* rounded, shorter than the internodes. *Ligules* membranous, 1.5-3 (-5) mm long, lanceolate. *Blades* loosely involute, mostly 3-12 cm long and 1-1.5 (-2) mm wide, scabrous. *Panicles* typically narrow, contracted, often interrupted, 5-20 cm long and 3-6 mm wide with appressed branches and spikelets; at anthesis, however, the branches often spread and the panicle becomes more or less open. *Spikelets* on pedicels mostly 0.2-3 (-4) mm long. *Glumes* 1-nerved, glabrous, subequal to very unequal, acute, short-aristate or erose and mucronate, occasionally somewhat truncate, the first glume 1- (0.5-) 1.9 mm long, the second 1.8-2.3 (-2.8) mm long. *Lemmas* 2.5-3.5 (-4) mm long, scaberulous above, pubescent on the lower one-third to one-half with short, straight, spreading hairs, the midnerve extended as a slender, flexuous awn 10-15 (-20) mm or more long. *Paleas* as long as lemmas. *Anthers* 1-1.5 mm long. *Caryopses* 1.8-2.2 mm long. *Chromosome numbers* reported, $2n=20$ and 40.

Distribution. Texas: Region 10 and western portion of region 7, on dry slopes and rocky ledges. General: Texas, New Mexico and Arizona to northern Mexico.

Flowering period: July to November.

21. **Muhlenbergia parviglumis** Vasey, Contr. U. S. Natl. Herb. 3:71. 1892. LONGAWN MUHLY. Perennial with slender, erect, wiry culms from a hard, cespitose base. *Culms* 25-80 cm tall, freely branching at base and lower nodes. *Ligules* membranous, mostly 1-3 mm long, often deeply lacerate. *Blades* flat or becoming involute on drying, scabrous to hispidulous on the adaxial surface, mostly 4-15 cm long, and 1-2.5 mm broad. *Panicles*

Fig. 140. *Muhlenbergia monticola*. Plant, glumes and floret. From Gould, 1951.

contracted, dense but usually interrupted, with appressed branches and spikelets, mostly 8-20 cm long and 4-10 mm thick. *Spikelets* 2.3-3 mm long, on pedicels mostly 0.5-1.5 (-3) mm long. *Glumes* mostly obtuse, often slightly toothed at apex, 0.5-1 mm long. *Lemmas* 3-4 mm long, uniformly scabrous, often with short, appressed, straight hairs on callus, and with an awn 20 (10-) 40 mm long. *Anthers* about 1 mm long. *Chromosome number*, $2n=40$.

Distribution. Texas: Region 10 on dry, rocky slopes. General: Texas, New Mexico, northern Mexico and Cuba.

Flowering period: July to October.

SUBFAMILY V. ERAGROSTOIDEAE   267

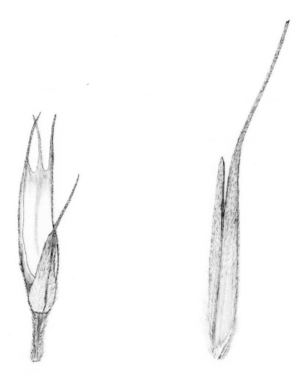

Fig. 141. *Muhlenbergia montana*. Glumes and floret.

22. **Muhlenbergia montana** (Nutt.) Hitchc., U.S.D.A. Bull. 722:145, 147. 1920. MOUNTAIN MUHLY. Fig. 141. Perennial with densely cespitose culms 25-75 (-80) cm tall. *Sheaths* glabrous, rounded, the lower ones often becoming flat and spreading. *Ligules* thin, hyaline, pointed, not auriculate, mostly 4-12 (-20) mm long. *Blades* flat or becoming involute, scabrous on adaxial surface, mostly 6-25 cm long and 1-2 mm wide. *Panicles* 8-20 (-25) cm long, mostly 1-3 cm broad, dense and contracted, interrupted or the lower branches erect-spreading and rather loosely flowered. *Primary panicle branches* usually floriferous to within 1 cm or less of base. *Spikelets* mostly on pedicels 0.2-1.5 mm long. *Glumes* thin, scabrous to nearly glabrous, lead-colored, the first glume 1 (rarely 3) -nerved, 0.5-1.5 mm long, usually acute or mucronate, the second glume 1-2.2 mm long, 3-nerved and 3-toothed, the teeth often short-aristate. *Lemmas* greenish or yellowish, with dark green or purple blotches or bands, scabrous above, pubescent on margins and midrib on lower half, 3-4.5 mm long, with a flexuous awn 6-25 mm long. *Chromosome number*, $2n=40$.

Distribution. Texas: Region 10 at medium and high elevations on rocky mountain slopes, especially in the Davis Mountains. General: Western Montana to Texas, California and southwestern Mexico, to Guatemala.

Flowering period: Mostly August to October.

23. **Muhlenbergia schreberi** Gmel., Syst. Nat. 2:171. 1791. NIMBLE-WILL. Fig. 142. Perennial with slender, rather lax, much-branched culms, these decumbent below, often stoloniferous and rooting at lower nodes. *Flowering culms* slender, mostly 10-40 (-60) cm tall. *Sheaths* shorter than the internode, typically glabrous except for a few long hairs on upper margins and near throat. *Ligules* minute, erose or lacerate, ciliolate, not over 0.5 mm long. *Blades* thin, flat, glabrous or with a few hairs above ligule, mostly 3-8 cm long and 1-3 (-4) mm broad. *Panicles* contracted, usually lobed or interrupted, mostly 4-12 (-15) cm long and 1-3 (-6) mm wide, the short branches appressed or sometimes slightly spreading. *Pedicels* scabrous-hispidulous, appressed, mostly shorter than the spikelets. *Glumes* rounded, scabrous, frequently erose at apex, the first glume often rudimentary or absent, the second 0.1-0.3 mm long. *Lemmas* 2-2.5 mm long, with an awn about 1.5-5 mm long, the body usually more or less pubescent at the base with rather coarse hairs. *Paleas* scabrous, often with a few hairs at base, about as long as lemmas. *Anthers* 0.1-0.4 mm long. *Chromosome number*, $2n=40$; one count of $2n=42$ reported.

Distribution. Texas: Regions 1, 2, 3, 4, the eastern portions of region 7 and the northern portion of region 6. General: Throughout the eastern United States, west to Wisconsin, eastern Nebraska, Kansas, Oklahoma and Texas; also reported from northern Arizona and eastern Mexico.

Flowering period: May to November.

24. **Muhlenbergia repens** (Presl) Hitchc. in Jepson, Flora California 1:111. 1912. *Muhlenbergia abata* I. M. Johnston. CREEPING MUHLY. Fig. 143. Low perennial with hard, shining, scaly, creeping rhizomes. *Culms* freely branched, tufted, the main ones often decumbent below, glabrous below the nodes. *Erect flowering branches* mostly 6-25 (-35) cm tall. *Sheaths* mostly glabrous. *Ligules* membranous, 0.5-1 mm long, usually truncate or split down middle. *Blades* short, mostly 1-2 mm broad, those of floriferous shoots 1-3 (-5) cm long, typically tightly involute and arcuate-spreading, those of sterile shoots as much as 9 cm long and often flat below. *Panicles* few-flowered, mostly 1-4 cm long and 2-3 mm wide, the spikelets appressed and short pediceled but often rather widely spaced. *Glumes* broad, glabrous or scabrous, subequal, more than half as long as lemma (mostly 1.5-3 mm long), usually acute, occasionally mucronate. *Lemmas* 2.5-4 mm long including the awn, minutely scabrous, lead-colored, gradually tapering to a short awn-tip. *Paleas* equaling lemmas and similar in texture. *Anthers* 1.2-1.4 mm long. *Caryopses* 1.3-1.5 mm long. *Chromosome number*, $2n=72$; count of $2n=70$ also reported.

Distribution. Texas: Regions 9 and 10, forming rather large stands on open, low ground. General: Texas to Arizona and south through Mexico.

Flowering period: May to November.

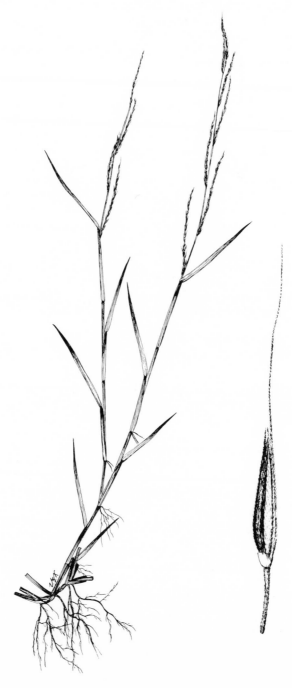

Fig. 142. *Muhlenbergia schreberi*. Plant and spikelet. From Gould and Box, 1965.

270 THE GRASSES OF TEXAS

Fig. 143. *Muhlenbergia repens*. Flowering culm and spikelet.

SUBFAMILY V. ERAGROSTOIDEAE   271

25. **Muhlenbergia utilis** (Torr.) Hitchc., J. Wash. Acad. Sci. 23:453. 1933. APAREJOGRASS. Fig. 144. Low perennials with slender, scaly, creeping rhizomes. *Culms* slender, glabrous below the nodes, 20-40 cm long. *Sheaths* glabrous. *Ligules* membranous, truncate, about 0.5 mm long. *Blades* slender, filiform, often involute, not infrequently spreading widely from the culms, 5-20 mm long, 0.4-0.6 (-1) mm wide. *Blades of innovations* often longer (-35 mm long). *Panicles* narrow, interrupted, loosely-flowered, 1-4 cm long. *Spikelets* about 2 mm long. *Glumes* subequal, about half as long as lemma, 0.6-1 (-1.3) mm long. *Lemmas* 1.6-2 mm long, acute or abruptly short pointed, scaberulous on nerves near apex. *Paleas* similar to lemmas in size and texture. *Anthers* purplish, about 1.4 mm long. *Chromosome number,* $2n=20$.

Distribution. Texas: Region 7, Edwards Plateau, occasional on calcareous or alkaline soils along streams and in marshy meadows. General: Texas to Nevada, southern California and northwestern Mexico.

Flowering period: Mostly late summer and fall.

Similar in general habit to *Muhlenbergia repens,* in which the culms are 6-25 (-35) cm long and typically more robust and the blades are 1-2 mm wide. The spikelets of *M. repens* are longer (2.5-4 mm long), the lemmas generally taper abruptly to an awn tip and the glumes are usually more than half as long as the lemma (1.5-3 mm long).

26. **Muhlenbergia villosa** Swallen, J. Wash. Acad. Sci. 31:350. fig. 2. 1941. HAIRY MUHLY. Rhizomatous perennial, branching to form small tufts. *Culms* wiry, striate, somewhat hispidulous below nodes, the internodes nodulose-roughened, freely-branched, mostly 10-26 cm tall. *Ligule* membranous, erose, mostly 0.5-1.7 mm long. *Blades* narrow, firm, involute, arcuate-spreading, puberulent on abaxial surface, mostly 1.5-3.5 (-4.5) cm long and less than 1 mm wide as inrolled. *Panicles* 1-4 cm long, narrow, loosely-flowered, the branches to 11 mm long, and the short pedicels appressed or sometimes slightly spreading. *Glumes* about equal, broadly acute, 1-1.5 (-1.6) mm long, prominently 1-nerved. *Lemmas* 2.2-2.7 mm long, villous on lower half, acute or mucronate. *Paleas* about as long as lemmas, villous between nerves below middle. *Anthers* 1.4-1.5 mm long. *Chromosome number,* $2n=20$.

Distribution. Texas: Northwestern portion of region 7, southern portion of region 9 and northeastern portion of region 10, in extremely localized sites where it appears to be confined to gypsum soil. General: Endemic to Texas.

Flowering period: July to August.

This species is closely related to the Mexican *M. villiflora* Hitchc., of which it may be no more than a slightly larger northern form.

27. **Muhlenbergia glauca** (Nees) Mez, Repert. Spec. Nov. 17:214. 1921. DESERT MUHLY. Perennial with slender creeping rhizomes, these branching to produce erect culms in small or large tufts. *Culms* mostly 25-60 cm tall, slender, moderately stiff, retrorsely hispid below the nodes. *Sheaths*

Fig. 144. *Muhlenbergia utilis*. Plant, glumes and floret. From Hitchcock, 1935.

rounded, longer than culm internodes, minutely pubescent. *Ligule* 0.5-1 (-2) mm long, truncate, erose or lacerate. *Blades* usually flat, tapering into an involute point, thin, scabrous, mostly 4-12 cm long and 2 (-2.5) mm wide. *Panicles* contracted, often interrupted, mostly 4-10 cm long and 3-6 mm wide, with short, scabrous, appressed branches and pedicels. *Glumes* about equal, prominently 1-nerved, scabrous on the nerve, attenuate into a narrow, usually short-awned tip, mostly 1.5-3.5 mm long including the awn. *Lemmas* 3-4 mm long, equaling or slightly longer than glumes, pubescent with long hairs on lower one-half to two-thirds, mucronate or with an awn to 1.5-3 mm long. *Anthers* orange, about 2 mm long. *Chromosome number*, $2n=60$.

Distribution. Texas: On rocky slopes of the mountains of region 10 at medium elevations. General: Western Texas to southern California and northern Mexico.

Flowering period: July to October.

SUBFAMILY V. ERAGROSTOIDEAE 273

28. **Muhlenbergia polycaulis** Scribn., Bull. Torrey Bot. Club 38:327. 1911. CLIFF MUHLY. Tufted perennial with slender, wiry culms from a firm or hard, knotty, rhizomatous base. *Culms* 15-40 cm tall, freely branched at the lower nodes, strigose below nodes. *Sheaths* rounded, glabrous to scaberulous. *Ligules* membranous, erose or lacerate, 0.5-1 mm long. *Blades* flat, folded or involute, 3-8 (-10) cm long and about 1 mm wide, scaberulous. *Panicles* narrow, contracted, densely-flowered, mostly 3-9 cm long and 3-6 mm wide, often lobed and interrupted. *Glumes* subequal, prominently 1-nerved, scabrous to hispidulous on the nerve, abruptly narrowed to an acuminate or short-awned apex, with a body 1.5-2.5 mm long and an awn 0.2-1.5 mm long. *Lemmas* 2.3-3.5 mm long, villous on lower one-half or two-thirds, with a slender, flexuous awn 10-20 (-25) mm long. *Paleas* about as long as lemmas, villous on lower half. *Anthers* orangish, 1.5-2 mm long. *Caryopses* 1.5-2 mm long. *Chromosome numbers* reported, $2n = 20$ and 40.

Distribution. Texas: Region 10, on dry, rocky slopes at medium to high elevations. General: Texas, New Mexico, Arizona and northern Mexico.

Flowering period: June to October.

29. **Muhlenbergia racemosa** (Michx.) B.S.P., Prelim. Cat. New York Pl. 67. 1888. GREEN MUHLY. Fig. 145. Perennial with culms tufted from scaly, creeping rhizomes, 1-2 mm thick. *Culms* erect, 25-60 (-100) cm tall, often branching at middle nodes, with well-developed leaves up to the base of the inflorescence. *Internodes* shining, glabrous or puberulent below nodes. *Sheaths* more or less keeled, glabrous or scabrous. *Ligules* truncate, lacerate or erose, 0.5-1.5 mm long. *Blades* flat or loosely involute, 4-10 (-16) cm long and 3-5 (-7) mm wide. *Panicles* terminal on main culm or on elongated leafy branches, contracted, interrupted or lobed, densely-flowered, mostly 3-10 (-17) cm long and 4-10 (-18) mm wide. *Glumes* about equal, 1-nerved, acuminate or gradually tapering to a stiff, minutely scabrous awn, 4.5-7.5 mm long including the awn. *Lemmas* acute, acuminate or short-awned, 2.2-4.5 mm long, pubescent below middle with soft hairs not over 1 mm long. *Paleas* shorter than lemmas and of similar texture, pilose on lower half. *Anthers* yellowish, 0.5-0.9 mm long. *Caryopses* 1.4-2.3 mm long, fusiform. *Chromosome number*, $2n = 40$.

Distribution. Texas: Northern portion of region 9, infrequent, on grassy plains and along ditches. General: Manitoba to Alberta and south through the United States from Michigan and eastern Washington, south to Texas and Arizona.

Flowering period: Mostly August to October.

Apparently known in Texas only from collections made in Deaf Smith, Ochiltree, Hartley and El Paso counties (regions 9 and 10).

30. **Muhlenbergia sobolifera** (Muhl.) Trin., Gram. Unifl. 189. pl. 5. fig. 4. 1824. ROCK MUHLY. Fig. 146. Perennial with numerous, widely creeping, scaly rhizomes, 1-3 mm thick. *Culms* slender, somewhat wiry, scaberul-

Fig. 145. *Muhlenbergia racemosa*. Inflorescence, glumes and floret.

SUBFAMILY V. ERAGROSTOIDEAE 275

Fig. 146. *Muhlenbergia sobolifera*. Spikelet.

ous below nodes, mostly 40-85 (-100) cm tall, branching rather freely from upper nodes to produce numerous, slender, long-pedunculate panicles. *Sheaths* rounded, glabrous. *Ligules* membranous, truncate, erose, mostly 0.3-1 mm long. *Blades* thin, flat, glabrous or sparsely puberulent near base, mostly 4-15 cm long and 2-8 mm broad. *Panicles* terminal and axillary, very slender, somewhat nodding, usually interrupted, mostly 5-15 cm long and 1-3 (-4) mm wide. *Glumes* about equal, scabrous, 1-nerved, broader below, overlapping at base, acute, acuminate, or abruptly awn-tipped, mostly 1.2-2.3 mm long and one-half to three-fourths as long as lemmas. *Lemmas* scabrous, minutely pubescent near base, 2-3 mm long, acute or with an awn to 1 mm long. *Paleas* about as long as lemmas. *Anthers* 0.4-0.8 mm long. *Caryopses* fusiform, 1.8-2.1 mm long, with an embryo about half as long as the endosperm. *Chromosome number*, 2n=40; one count of 2n=42.

Distribution: Texas: Regions 1 and 4, infrequent, usually in partial shade on rocky slopes or along rock outcrops. General: New Hampshire and Virginia to Wisconsin, eastern Nebraska and Texas; absent or infrequent in the southeastern states.

Flowering period: August to November.

Included here is *M. sobolifera* f. *setigera* (Scribn.) Deam, Grasses of Indiana 163. 1929, a minor variant of this widespread taxon, found in Arkansas and Texas. The type specimen was collected by J. Reverchon (No. 70) in Texas, probably in the vicinity of Dallas. This form is distinguished by the short lemma awns (2-4 mm long) and more scabrous foliage.

31. **Muhlenbergia andina** (Nutt.) Hitchc., U.S.D.A. Bull. 772:145. 1920. FOXTAIL MUHLY. Perennial with erect culms from rather coarse, scaly, creeping rhizomes, 2-4 mm thick. *Culms* simple or sparingly branched, 35-60 (-80) cm tall, internodes glabrous or minutely puberulent below the nodes. *Sheaths* puberulent, at least the lowermost. *Ligules* membranous, ciliolate at the apex, 0.6-1.3 mm long. *Blades* flat, scaberulous, 4-16 cm long, 2-3 mm wide. *Panicles* terminal, densely-flowered, variously lobed, silvery green or purplish-tinged, 4-10 (-13) cm long and 5-15 mm wide. *Glumes* narrowly lanceolate, scabrous on the prominent nerve, 2-4 mm long, equaling or exceeding the floret. *Lemma* 2-3.2 mm long, scabrous on nerves, with copious silky white hairs as long as the floret and with an awn 4-8 mm long. *Anthers* yellowish, 0.4-1.5 mm long. *Caryopses* fusiform, about 1 mm long. *Chromosome number*, $2n=20$.

Distribution. Texas: Known from a single specimen collected by W. A. Silveus (no. 3428—TEX) near Sierra Blanca, Hudspeth County (region 10). General: In moist thickets, river banks and similar habitats from the western United States as far east as western Montana, eastern Kansas and the westernmost portion of Texas.

Flowering period: July and August.

32. **Muhlenbergia mexicana** (L.) Trin., Gram. Unifl. 189. 1824. Perennial from extensively creeping, coarse rhizomes, 1-2.5 mm thick. *Culms* 30-90 cm tall, much branching from the upper nodes, internodes dull and puberulent. *Blades* mostly glabrous, rather lax, flat, 5-15 cm long, 2-6 mm wide. *Ligules* membranous, 0.4-1 mm long. *Panicles* terminal and axillary, rather slender, often lobed below, 7-21 cm long, 2-10 mm wide, the branches densely flowered, the inflorescence exserted on peduncles 2-12 cm long. *Spikelets* about 2-4 (-4.4) mm long. *Glumes* narrow, equal to or a bit shorter than the floret, scabrous on the prominent nerve, awn-tipped, the awn up to 1.5 mm long. *Lemma* 1.3-3.4 mm long, awnless or with an awn tip to 0.5 mm long, pilose on the callus. *Paleas* similar in texture and length to the lemmas. *Anthers* yellowish, 0.3-0.5 mm long. *Chromosome number*, $2n=40$.

Distribution. Texas: Reported by Pohl as occurring in Granbury, Hood County (region 5), based on a specimen collected by Reverchon (4110). General: Quebec to British Columbia, Canada, southward through the United States to North Carolina, New Mexico and California.

Flowering period: Fall.

Muhlenbergia mexicana, obviously rare in Texas, resembles *M. frondosa* from which it differs in being pubescent below the culm nodes. *M. mexicana* is closely related to *M. glabriflora*, which has glabrous florets.

SUBFAMILY V. ERAGROSTOIDEAE   277

33. **Muhlenbergia bushii** Pohl, Amer. Midl. Naturalist. 82:534. 1969. *Muhlenbergia brachyphylla* Bush. NODDING MUHLY. Perennials with extensively creeping, coarse, scaly rhizomes, 1-3 mm thick. *Culms* 30-90 cm tall, at first erect, becoming bushy and much-branched from the upper nodes. *Internodes* glabrous and shining, mostly covered by the glabrous sheaths. *Ligules* membranous, 0.2-0.6 mm long. *Blades* flat, glabrous or scaberulous, 5-10 (-15) cm long, 2-5 mm wide. *Panicles* numerous, terminal and axillary, slender, 4-15 cm long, 1-4 mm wide, the few branches appressed. *Spikelets* 2.5-3.3 mm long. *Glumes* acute to acuminate, 1.4-2 (-2.5) mm long. *Lemma* 2.6-3.3 mm long, awnless or short awn-tipped (awn rarely as much as 7 mm long), pilose at base. *Anthers* yellowish, 0.3-0.6 mm long. *Chromosome number*, $2n = 40$.

Distribution. Texas: Region 4, infrequent in black clay-loam along shaded creek banks and in low grasslands. General: Maryland to North Carolina, Indiana and Wisconsin to Nebraska and central Texas.

Flowering period: July to October.

Similar to *Muhlenbergia frondosa* in having terminal and axillary panicles from culms which are bushy and much-branched from the upper nodes. The internodes are smooth and shining. In *M. frondosa*, however, the ligules are longer (0.8-1.4 mm long), as are the glumes (2-4 mm long).

34. **Muhlenbergia frondosa** (Poir.) Fernald, Rhodora 45:235. *pl. 750.* 1943. WIRESTEM MUHLY. Fig. 147. Perennial with extensive scaly, creeping rhizomes, 2-3 mm thick. *Culms* slender, firm, typically with numerous nodes and short, glabrous, shining internodes, often becoming decumbent, prostrate or sprawling, as much as 1 meter long. *Sheaths* glabrous, rounded, mostly shorter than culm internodes. *Ligules* membranous, erose-ciliate, 0.8-1 (-1.4) mm long. *Blades* thin, flat, 4-12 cm long and 1-7 mm wide, glabrous. *Panicles* numerous, terminal and axillary, dense, contracted, often lobed, mostly 3-10 cm long and 1-6 (-9) mm wide, the densely-flowered branches erect-spreading. *Glumes* usually about equal, acute, acuminate, or short-awned, 2-4 mm long, equaling or often exceeding the lemma, rarely shorter. *Lemmas* 2.9-3.6 mm long, awnless or with an awn 1-2 mm long, pubescent on callus. *Anthers* yellowish, 0.3-0.6 mm long. *Chromosome number*, $2n = 40$; one report of $2n = 42$.

Distribution. Texas: Region 4, infrequent, reported by Correll and Johnston (1970) as occurring in Dallas and Grayson counties. General: New Brunswick and Maine to North Dakota, south to Georgia and Texas.

Flowering period: Fall.

No specimens of this taxon from Texas localities are in the Tracy Herbarium.

35. **Muhlenbergia glabriflora** Scribn., Rhodora 9:22. 1907. INLAND MUHLY. Perennials with coarse, scaly, creeping rhizomes, 1.5-3 mm thick.

Fig. 147. *Muhlenbergia frondosa.* Plant and spikelet with floret separated from glumes. From Chase, 1951.

Culms 30-95 cm tall, becoming much-branched from the upper nodes. *Internodes* glabrous except puberulent just below nodes. *Ligules* truncate, 0.5-1.5 mm long, membranous. *Blades* rather stiff, mostly flat, glabrous, 3-4 (-8) cm long, 1.5-4 mm wide. *Panicles* numerous, terminal and axillary, densely-flowered, 2-5 cm long, 3-5 mm wide, exserted on peduncles 1-4 cm long. *Glumes* acute, acuminate or short-aristate, 2-3 mm long, more or less equaling the floret. *Lemmas* 2.2-3 mm long, awnless, glabrous. *Anthers* yellowish, 0.3-0.5 mm long. *Chromosome number,* $2n=40$.

Distribution. Texas: Region 4, infrequent, in moist woodlands. General: Maryland to North Carolina, Indiana to Illinois and south to Texas.

Flowering period: Fall.

This species, the type of which was collected by Reverchon probably in the Dallas area, is closely related to *Muhlenbergia frondosa,* from which it differs primarily in having glabrous florets.

SUBFAMILY V. ERAGROSTOIDEAE   279

36. **Muhlenbergia sylvatica** (Torr.) Torr. in A. Gray, North Amer. Gram. Cyp. 1:13. 1834. FOREST MUHLY. Fig. 148. Perennial with scaly, creeping rhizomes, 1.5-3 mm wide. *Culms* slender, wiry, mostly 40-100 cm long, usually decumbent or sprawling below, in age branching freely at the middle nodes; the internodes puberulent and retrorsely scabrous below the nodes. *Sheaths* rounded, glabrous. *Ligules* membranous, erose, ciliate, 0.5-1.5 (-2.5) mm long. *Blades* thin, flat, bright green, mostly 4-18 cm long and 2-8 mm broad. *Panicles* terminal, slender, contracted, often interrupted, mostly 5-15 (-21) cm long and 3-6 mm wide, on peduncles to 8 cm long. *Glumes* scabrous on nerve, about equal, 1.9-3 mm long, as long as or slightly shorter than lemmas, the body gradually tapering to an attenuate or short-awned tip. *Lemmas* 2.2-3.2 mm long, short pilose on callus, with an awn 3-10 (-18) mm long. *Anthers* 0.5-0.7 mm long. *Chromosome number*, 2n=40.

Distribution. Texas: Regions 4, 5 and eastern portion of 7, infrequent in woodlands and along shaded streambanks. General: Widespread through the eastern United States, west to South Dakota and eastern Texas; also reported in northern Arizona.

Flowering period: Mostly August to October.

37. **Muhlenbergia depauperata** Scribn., Bot. Gaz. 9:187. 1884. SIXWEEKS MUHLY. Fig. 149. Tufted annual 3-15 cm tall, much-branched at the lower nodes. *Culms* strigose below the nodes. *Sheaths* keeled, striate, glabrous or scabrous, with conspicuous scarious margins. *Ligules* membranous, lacerated, 1.5-4.5 mm long, decurrent laterally and with lateral, pointed, auriculate projections. *Blades* flat, scabrous to strigose, with whitish, thickened margins and midrib, 1-2 (-3) cm long, 0.5-1 (-1.5) mm wide, often somewhat twisted. *Inflorescence* contracted, dense, 2-7 cm long and mostly 2-5 mm thick, with short branches bearing 2 or 3 appressed spikelets, the spikelets tending to fall as a unit with the branch. *Spikelets* 2.5-3.5 mm long. *Glumes* subequal, as long as or longer than lemma, scabrous on nerves; first glume 2-nerved and usually bifid, second glume 1-nerved, lanceolate, acuminate or attenuate. *Lemmas* scabrous above and with short appressed hairs between nerves on lower half, awnless or with an awn to 10 mm long, the lemmas of the lower spikelets on a panicle branch commonly with reduced awns (0-2.5 mm) and the upper spikelet of each branch usually longer-awned. *Paleas* about as long as lemmas and similar in texture. *Anthers* pale, 0.5-0.8 mm long. *Caryopses* narrowly fusiform, about 2 mm long. *Chromosome number*, 2n=20.

Distribution. Texas: Region 10, in the Davis and Chisos Mountains, infrequent, on rocky mountain slopes at moderately high elevations. General: Colorado to Texas, New Mexico, Arizona and south into Mexico.

Flowering period: Mostly July to September.

Fig. 148. *Muhlenbergia sylvatica*. Flowering branch, two views of spikelet and floret. From Hitchcock, 1935.

SUBFAMILY V. ERAGROSTOIDEAE   281

38. **Muhlenbergia brevis** C. O. Goodding, J. Wash. Acad. Sci. 31:505. 1941. SHORT MUHLY. Fig. 150. Tufted annual, much-branched from lower nodes. *Culms* slender, erect or spreading, 3-20 cm tall, scabrous to hispidulous below nodes. *Sheaths* keeled, striate, usually longer than the internodes, with scarious margins. *Ligules* 1-3 (mostly about 2) mm long, membranous, lacerate, often somewhat auriculate. *Blades* flat to involute, sometimes somewhat twisted, 0.5-4 cm long, 1-2 mm wide, scabrous or puberulent above, scabrous below, with white, thickened margins and midrib. *Panicles* narrow, contracted, rather densely flowered, pale green tinged with purple, 1-12 cm long, less than 0.5 cm wide, often the lower portion included within the subtending sheath, the short branches with 2 or 3 spikelets disarticulating and falling as a unit. *Spikelets* 4-5 mm long, slender. *Glumes* scabrous, shorter than lemmas, the first glume 1-2 mm long, 2-nerved, minutely to deeply bifid; second glume 1.5-4 mm long, 1-nerved, acuminate to setaceous. *Lemma* 4-5 mm long, prominently 3-nerved, scabrous especially on nerves, sparsely to rather densely appressed-pubescent between nerves on lower half. *Awn* of lemma 10-20 mm long, rarely less, slightly flexuous. *Anthers* 0.5-0.8 mm long. *Caryopses* narrowly fusiform, 2-2.5 mm long. *Chromosome number*, $2n=20$.

Distribution. Texas: Region 10, apparently known only from Mt. Livermore at about 8,000 ft. General: Colorado and Texas to Arizona and south into Mexico.

Flowering period: August to September.

This species is closely related to *Muhlenbergia depauperata* which differs in having a shorter lemma (3-3.5 mm long), a shorter lemma awn (5-10 mm long) and glumes which are about as long as the floret.

39. **Muhlenbergia minutissima** (Steud.) Swallen, Contr. U. S. Natl. Herb. 29:207. 1947. *Muhlenbergia texana* Buckl. LEAST MUHLY. Fig. 151. Annual with weak, simple or branched culms 5-40 cm tall. *Culms* strigose below nodes. *Ligules* membranous, hyaline, lacerate, 1-3 mm long. *Blades* thin, scabrous to short hirsute, especially on adaxial surface, flat or loosely involute on drying, 2-6 cm long and about 1 mm wide. *Panicles* open, diffuse, to 20 (rarely 40) cm long, usually two-thirds to three-fourths the entire height of plant. *Pedicels* capillary, spreading, 2-5 mm long. *Spikelets* 1.2-1.8 mm long, tawny, purplish or pale green. *Glumes* subequal, acute to obtuse, pilose especially near apex, 0.5-1 mm long. *Lemma* 1-1.7 mm long, short appressed-pubescent along midnerve and margins below, obtuse or bifid at apex, awnless or with a mucro to 0.8 mm long (commonly 0.1-0.2 mm). *Paleas* obtuse, as long as lemmas. *Anthers* 0.3-0.5 mm long. *Caryopses* 0.6-1 mm long. *Chromosome number*, $2n=60$.

Distribution. Texas: Region 10, infrequent on rocky slopes at high elevations. General: Montana to Washington, south to Texas, Arizona, California and northern Mexico.

Flowering period: August and September.

Fig. 149. *Muhlenbergia depauperata.*
Spikelet.

Fig. 150. *Muhlenbergia brevis.* Plant
and spikelet.

SUBFAMILY V. ERAGROSTOIDEAE   283

Fig. 151. *Muhlenbergia minutissima.* Spikelet.

40. **Muhlenbergia fragilis** Swallen, Contr. U. S. Natl. Herb. 29:206. 1947. DELICATE MUHLY. Annual with culms mostly 10-35 cm tall, much-branched below or nearly simple, forming small or large tufts. *Culms* strigose below nodes. *Ligules* hyaline, with conspicuous auriculate lateral projections (auricles) 1.5-2.5 mm long. *Blades* thin, flat or folded, scabrous to short hirsute, mostly 2-5 (-6) cm long and 1.5-2 mm wide, with whitish, thickened margins and midnerve. *Panicles* open, diffuse and loosely-flowered, usually two-thirds to three-fourths the entire height of plant, readily breaking off at maturity. *Pedicels* capillary, spreading, 2.5-8 mm or more long, enlarged below spikelet. *Spikelets* 0.9-1.3 mm long, awnless. *Glumes* obtuse to broadly acute, glabrous, 0.6-0.9 mm long. *Lemmas* 0.9-1.2 mm long, usually acute, usually short appressed-pubescent along midnerve and margins below but in some cases appearing glabrous. *Paleas* as long as lemmas. *Anthers* 0.4-0.5 mm long. *Caryopses* elliptic, 0.6-0.9 mm long, reddish brown. *Chromosome number* not reported.

Distribution. Texas: Region 10, on open, rocky slopes at medium to high elevations, infrequent. General: Western Texas, New Mexico, Arizona and south to central Mexico.

Flowering period: Mostly August and September.

41. **Muhlenbergia eludens** C. G. Reeder, J. Wash. Acad. Sci. 39:365. fig. 1B. 1949. Fig. 152. Annual with culms 10-35 (-40) cm tall, simple or branched at base. *Culms* with 2 to 4 nodes, strigose below nodes. *Sheaths* keeled, minutely scabrous to sparsely puberulent. *Ligules* membranous, lacerate, 1.5-2.5 mm long. Blades thin, 1-8 (mostly 2-5) cm long and about 1 mm broad, scabrous or puberulent on abaxial surface, pubescent on adaxial surface. *Panicle* open, narrowly pyramidal, usually two-thirds or more the height of

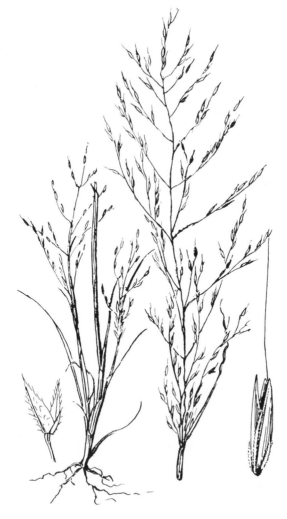

Fig. 152.   *Muhlenbergia eludens*. Glumes, plant, separate inflorescence and floret. From Chase, 1951.

the plant, to 7 cm broad. *Panicle branches* capillary, ascending or widely spreading. *Pedicels* slender, appressed along branches, enlarged below spikelet, 0.5-2 mm long. *Spikelets* 2-2.5 mm long, short-awned. *Glumes* subequal, 1-nerved, acute to acuminate, 1-2 mm long, pubescent at least at apex. *Lemmas* 2-2.5 mm long, short appressed-pubescent along midnerve and margins, prominently 3-nerved, bifid at apex and with an awn 1.5-3.5 mm long. *Paleas* about as long as lemmas. *Anthers* 0.5-0.6 mm long. *Caryopses* about 1.5 mm long. *Chromosome number* not reported.

Distribution. Texas: Region 10, on rocky slopes at medium elevations, infrequent. General: Texas, New Mexico and Arizona to central Mexico.

Flowering period: Late summer and early autumn.

SUBFAMILY V. ERAGROSTOIDEAE   285

68. SPOROBOLUS R. Br.*

Plants of diverse habit, from delicate annuals to large, robust, cespitose or rhizomatous perennials. *Leaves* mostly in a basal tuft, the blades linear, flat, folded or involute. *Ligule* usually a minute, densely pilose or ciliate membrane. *Inflorescence* an open or less frequently a contracted panicle of small, awnless, 1-flowered spikelets. Disarticulation above glumes. *Glumes* 1-nerved, usually unequal and at least the first shorter than the lemma. *Lemmas* 1-nerved (rarely faintly 3-nerved in *S. ozarkanus* and *S. vaginaeflorus*), thin, awnless. *Paleas* well developed, often splitting at maturity exposing the caryopsis, mostly as long as or slightly longer than the lemma. *Grain* obovate, somewhat asymmetrical, often laterally flattened, usually falling free from the lemma and palea. *Grain* not a true caryopsis, the seed coat not fused to ovary wall, slipping away readily or becoming gelatinous when moistened.

About 100 species, in temperate and tropical regions of both hemipheres. *Sporobolus* appears closely related to *Muhlenbergia* but differs in having thinner 1-nerved, consistently awnless lemmas, obovate, flattened grains with a free pericarp and usually ciliate ligules.

Plants annual

    Spikelets all less than 2 mm long; glumes very unequal; panicles becoming open, the lower branches in whorls   2. *S. pulvinatus*

    Spikelets, at least some, over 2 mm long; glumes equal or subequal; panicles narrow, densely-flowered, often included within the somewhat inflated subtending sheath

        Florets glabrous

        Lemmas 1-nerved, 2-3 mm long; lower sheaths not papillose-pilose   16. *S. neglectus*

        Lemmas with 1 midnerve and two less evident lateral nerves; lower sheaths papillose-pilose   17. *S. ozarkanus*

        Florets pubescent

        Glumes as long as or longer than floret; lemmas 3-nerved (1 midnerve and 2 less conspicuous lateral nerves); lower sheaths and blades papillose-pilose; floret length/width ratio 1.6-3.3 (-3.8)   17. *S. ozarkanus*

*Contributed by Charlotte G. Reeder.

Glumes shorter than floret; lemmas with 1 or 3 nerves (the lateral nerves less conspicuous); lower sheaths and blades not papillose-pilose; floret length/width ratio 2.2-5.7 (-7.5)

19. *S. vaginaeflorus*

Plants perennial

Pedicels 5-25 mm long

Spikelets 2-3 mm long; ligule about 0.5 mm long; second glume 1-nerved

14. *S. texanus*

Spikelets 5-6 mm long; ligule about 0.1 mm long; second glume 3-nerved

23. *S. silveanus*

Pedicels 4 mm or less long

Plants with evident creeping, scaly rhizomes

Spikelets not over 3.2 mm long; plants of the seashore; leaves often distichous

3. *S. virginicus*

Spikelets 4-5 mm long; plants of moist pinelands; leaves not distichous

15b. *S. asper* var. *macer*

Plants mostly cespitose, without extensive scaly, creeping rhizomes

Spikelets 1-2 (-2.9) mm long

Lower sheaths strongly laterally compressed and keeled

10. *S. buckleyi*

Lower sheaths rounded

Glumes about equal, one-third to one-half shorter than the floret

4. *S. indicus*

Glumes unequal, the first short, the second about as long as the floret

Panicles spikelike

Culms robust, 1-2 meters tall; lower culms 2-7 mm in diameter at base

7. *S. giganteus*

Culms not robust, commonly less than 1 meter tall; lower culms 1.5-3.5 mm in diameter at base

6. *S. contractus*

SUBFAMILY V. ERAGROSTOIDEAE 287

Panicles open, at least toward apex, the lower portion often
enclosed within subtending sheath (see also S. *tharpii*)

Panicles 10-25 (-30) cm wide, open, subpyramidal

Sheaths with many long hairs at corners
5.   S. *cryptandrus*

Sheaths glabrous or with only a few long hairs at corners

Panicles purplish, 20-45 cm long, 15-25 cm wide;
branchlets naked below, the pedicels 0.5-2 mm
long, spreading   11.   S. *airoides*

Panicles pale, tawny, 20-60 cm long, 12-26 cm wide;
branchlets densely flowered to base; pedicels less
than 0.5 mm long, appressed to branches with
spikelets seeming to overlap   12.   S. *wrightii*

Panicles mostly less than 10 cm wide

Base of plant knotty; blades stiff, spreading at right angles
to culm   8.   S. *nealleyi*

Base of plant cespitose; blades erect or ascending

Panicles 3-15 (-18) cm long, lower branches in whorls;
culms 10-30 (-50) cm tall   1.   S. *pyramidatus*

Panicles 10-30 (-40) cm long, the lower branches not
in distinct whorls; culms 35-120 cm tall

Hairs at the sheath corners 1-1.5 mm long; first
glumes 1-1.3 mm long; panicles nodding, with
upper branches as long as lower, divaricate and
flexuous; spikelets loosely arranged on branchlets   9.   S. *flexuosus*

Hairs at the sheath corners 2-4 mm long; first
glumes 0.5-1.1 (-1.5) mm long; panicles mostly
included within sheath, the upper branches
shorter than the lower, ascending; spikelets on
short appressed pedicels, densely crowded on
the branchlets   5.   S. *cryptandrus*

Spikelets, at least some, 3 mm or more long

Panicle branches in distinct whorls

Panicles cylindrical, 0.8-1.6 cm wide, the branches appressed
and densely flowered to base   21. S. *purpurascens*

Panicles elongated, pyramidal, 3-6 cm wide, the lower branches
widely spreading, naked near base   20. S. *junceus*

Panicle branches not in whorls

Panicles contracted, spikelike, the branches appressed along
main axis

Panicles elongate, 15-50 cm long (or rarely, more); coarse
cespitose perennials; sheaths with conspicuous hairs at
corners

Culms 2-7 mm wide at the base; plants robust, over 1
meter tall; exserted portion of panicle 8-25 mm wide
7. S. *giganteus*

Culms 1.5-3.5 mm wide at the base; plants usually less
than 1 meter tall; exserted portion of the panicle
4-7 mm wide   6. S. *contractus*

Panicles usually less than 10 cm long, terminal and axillary,
mostly included within the somewhat inflated subtending
sheath; sheaths not conspicuously hairy at corners

Lemma pubescent; pericarp of grain loose when moistened
18. S. *clandestinus*

Lemma glabrous; pericarp of grain gelatinous when moistened   15. S. *asper*

Panicles open or ellipsoidal, not spikelike, the branches ascending or spreading

Spikelets about 3 mm long; blades 3-6 mm wide; grain oblong
13. S. *tharpii*

Spikelets 4-6 mm long; blades 1-2 mm wide; grain globose,
indurate, nut-like   22. S. *heterolepis*

SUBFAMILY V. ERAGROSTOIDEAE   289

1. **Sporobolus pyramidatus** (Lam.) Hitchc., U.S.D.A. Misc. Publ. 243:84. 1936. *Sporobolus argutus* (Nees) Kunth. WHORLED DROPSEED. Fig. 153. Tufted perennial. *Culms* numerous, glabrous, mostly 10-50 cm tall, ascending, branching only near base. *Sheaths* shorter than culm internodes, glabrous except for long white hairs on either side of collar. *Ligule* a short, densely ciliate membrane, 0.5-0.7 mm long. *Blades* flat, mostly basal, 3-12 (-20) cm long and usually 2-4 mm wide, mostly ciliate on lower margins and often sparsely hispid on adaxial surface. *Panicles* 3-15 (-18) cm long, contracted at first, but becoming pyramidal at maturity, with branches successively shorter from base upward; lower branches in whorls, naked on lower one-third to one-half. *Spikelets* 1.5-2 mm long. *Glumes* thin, acute, the first usually 0.3-0.8 mm long, the second mostly 1.2-2 mm long. *Lemmas* acute, 1.2-2 mm long. *Paleas* subacute or obtuse, translucent, about as long as lemmas, splitting as grains mature. *Grains* usually 0.6-0.9 mm long, broadly oblong, flattened laterally, pale orange and translucent, pericarp finely striate. *Anthers* 0.3-0.4 mm long. *Chromosome numbers*, several counts of $2n=24$, two reports of $2n=36$ and one report of $2n=54$.

Distribution. Texas: Throughout the State except in region 1, in open, usually disturbed sites on a wide variety of soil types, frequent on coastal sands and on sandy or saline clay or alkaline inland soils. General: Kansas to Colorado, south to Texas, Louisiana and Arizona, in southern Florida and throughout tropical America.

Flowering period: Mostly March to November.

The closely related West Indian species, *Sporobolus domingensis* (Trin.) Kunth, has been collected at least once in the shell debris along the causeway in Aransas Pass, Nueces County, but probably has not persisted there. It differs from S. *pyramidatus* in having erect culms and an elongated narrowly elliptical panicle 12-20 mm wide, the branches of which commonly are not verticillate, although occasionally the lowermost may be in whorls.

2. **Sporobolus pulvinatus** Swallen, J. Wash. Acad. Sçi. 31 (8):351. fig. 4. 1941. Tufted annual. *Culms* 5-30 cm tall, decumbent-spreading at base, glabrous. *Sheaths* shorter than culm internodes, glabrous, more or less pubescent at throat. *Ligules* ciliate, about 0.5 mm long. *Blades* mostly 4-7 cm long and 2-5 mm wide, scabrous on both surfaces and on the thickened white margins. *Panicles* 2-5 (-8) cm long, pyramidal, the branches verticillate, naked at base, densely-flowered, appressed at first but spreading at maturity, with prominent glandular areas and conspicuous pulvini. *Spikelets* 1.5-1.7 mm long, short-pedicellate, appressed on the branchlets. *First glume* minute; second glume about as long as spikelet, abruptly acute or subobtuse. *Lemma* similar to second glume but more narrow. *Palea* broad, as long as lemma, minutely dentate. *Anthers* pale, 0.3 mm long. *Grains* about 1 mm long, pale tannish, the embryo conspicuous, greenish-black. *Chromosome number* not reported.

Fig. 153. *Sporobolus pyramidatus.* Inflorescence and spikelet. From Gould and Box, 1965.

Distribution. Texas: Region 10, known only from sandy, gravelly slopes in the vicinity of El Paso. General: Extreme western Texas, New Mexico, and Arizona, south throughout the Mexican highlands to Oaxaca.

Flowering period: Summer and early autumn.

Similar in general appearance to *Sporobolus pyramidatus,* which is a densely tufted perennial with stiff erect blades and spikelets up to 2 mm long. Correll and Johnston (1970) treat *S. pulvinatus* as a synonym of *S. pyramidatus* and refer the annual plants of western Texas to *S. patens* Swallen.

SUBFAMILY V. ERAGROSTOIDEAE   291

3. **Sporobolus virginicus** (L.) Kunth, Rev. Gram. 1:67. 1829. SEASHORE DROPSEED. Fig. 154. Plants perennial, strongly rhizomatous, with culms of several to many nodes rising singly or in small clusters from widely spreading, usually yellowish rhizomes. *Culms* smooth and shining, 10-50 (-65) cm tall, 1-2 mm near base. *Sheaths* mostly overlapping, striate, glabrous except for a few long hairs on either side of collar. *Ligule* a minute, ciliate membrane, 0.2-0.5 mm long. *Blades* firm, usually tightly involute, at least on drying, mostly 3-10 (-15) cm long and 1.5-4 (-5) mm wide, often conspicuously distichous. *Panicles* contracted, spicate, densely-flowered, mostly 2-8 cm long and 6-7 (-10) mm wide. *Spikelets* straw-colored, grayish or purple-tinged, glabrous, shining, 1.8-3.2 mm long. *First glume* one-third shorter than to as long as second glume. *Second glume* 1.8-3.2 mm long, equaling or often slightly longer than lemma. *Paleas* of same size and texture as lemmas. *Chromosome numbers* reported, $2n = 20$ (Texas) and $2n = 30$ (Yucatan, Mexico and South Africa).

Distribution. Texas: Region 2, frequent on sandy beaches and at bases of sand dunes. General: Along the coast, Virginia to Florida and Texas, southward through the West Indies and the Caribbean to Brazil and in South Africa.

Flowering period: May to October, occasionally to December.

4. **Sporobolus indicus** (L.) R. Br., Prodr. Flora Nov. Holl. 170. 1810. *Sporobolus poiretii* (Roem. & Schult.) Hitchc. SMUTGRASS. Fig. 155. Cespitose perennial with tough, fibrous roots and glabrous culms and leaves. *Culms* stiffly erect, mostly 30-100 cm tall, unbranched above the base. *Leaves* mostly in a basal tuft. *Ligule* a minute ciliate membrane, 0.2-0.5 mm long. *Blades* flat, folded or more commonly involute, mostly 10-30 cm long or longer and 1-5 mm broad at base, tapering to a long, flexuous, filiform tip. *Panicle* narrowly contracted or with a few of the lower branches erect-spreading, 10-30 (-40) cm long and averaging 0.6-1 cm wide. *Panicle branches* densely flowered to base, mostly 1-2 cm long but occasionally as much as 3-5 cm long. *Spikelets* 1.4-2 mm long. *Glumes* subequal, thin, translucent, the first less than one-half as long as lemma, the second glume acute, one-half to two-thirds as long as lemma. *Lemmas* of same texture as glumes, essentially glabrous. *Paleas* of same texture as glumes and lemmas, broad, slightly shorter than lemmas. *Anthers* pale, about 0.5 mm long. *Grains* obovate, flattened laterally, the apex somewhat truncate, reddish brown. *Chromosome numbers* reported, $2n = 18$, 24 and 36.

Distribution. Texas: Regions 1, 2, 3, 4 and the southeastern portion of region 7, mostly on moist clay soils but also in sand, often in trampled or otherwise disturbed sites. General: Virginia to Tennessee and Oklahoma, south to Florida and Texas, southward throughout Central and South America to Argentina and on ballast in Oregon and New Jersey. Apparently introduced into the Americas from tropical Asia.

Flowering period: Collected in flower March to December and probably flowering throughout the year under favorable growing conditions.

Fig. 154. *Sporobolus virginicus.* Plant and spikelet. From Gould and Box, 1965.

Correll and Johnston (1970) followed Clayton (1965) in reducing *Sporobolus poiretii* to synonymy under *S. indicus.* The species is often infected with a smut fungus.

SUBFAMILY V. ERAGROSTOIDEAE   293

Fig. 155. *Sporobolus indicus*. Inflorescence and spikelet. From Gould and Box, 1965.

294   THE GRASSES OF TEXAS

5. **Sporobolus cryptandrus** (Torr.) A. Gray, Man. 576. 1848. SAND DROPSEED. Fig. 156. Tufted perennial. *Culms* erect, mostly 35-120 cm tall but occasionally shorter, 1-3.5 mm in diameter at base. *Sheaths* rounded, usually with tufts of long white hairs (2-4 mm long) on either side of collar and often ciliate-pubescent on upper margins. *Ligule* a minute, ciliate membrane, 0.5-1 mm long. *Blades* mostly 8-25 cm long and 2-5 mm wide, usually flat but often folded or involute on drying, glabrous or scabrous, not stiffly divergent from culm. *Panicles* 15-30 (-40) cm long and 2-12 (-15) cm wide, usually partially enclosed by the elongated upper sheath. *Main panicle axis* slender but often stiffly erect, the primary branches borne singly at the nodes, appressed or spreading, floriferous nearly to base or naked on lower 5-10 mm. *Secondary branches and branchlets* appressed to primary branches. *Spikelets* short pediceled, often subsessile, light brown, lead-colored or purple-tinged, 1.5-2.3 (-2.8) mm long. *Glumes* thin, membranous, acute, the first about half as long as the second, the second glume equaling or slightly shorter than the lemma. *Lemmas* as long as spikelet. *Paleas* well-developed, slightly shorter than lemmas. *Grain* reddish orange, oblong, flattened laterally, about 1 mm long. *Chromosome numbers* reported, $2n = 36$, 38 and 72.

Distribution. Texas: Throughout the State except in region 1, frequent on sandy soil and one of the most common roadside perennial grasses. General: Maine to Ontario and Washington, south throughout most of the United States to Mexico but not reported in the southeastern United States.

Flowering period: Mostly May to November.

6. **Sporobolus contractus** Hitchc., Amer. J. Bot. 2:303. 1915. SPIKE DROPSEED. Fig. 157. Cespitose perennial. *Culms* mostly 40-110 cm tall, 2-3.5 mm in diameter at base, in small to moderately large clumps. *Sheaths* rounded, glabrous on back, usually with long white hairs on collar and often ciliate-pilose on margins of sheath. *Ligule* a minute, fringed membrane, 0.5-1 mm long. *Blades* elongate, 4-35 cm long, flat or becoming involute, 3-8 mm wide, tapering to a long slender tip. *Panicle* green or pale, densely contracted and spikelike, mostly 15-50 cm long and 0.5-0.7 (-1) cm wide, usually partially enclosed within the sheath. *Spikelets* similar to those of S. *cryptandrus*, 2.5-(2.2-) 3.2 mm long. *Glumes* unequal, the first 1-2 mm long, the second mostly 2-2.7 mm long. *Lemmas* glabrous, 2.4-3.2 mm long. *Paleas* slightly shorter than lemmas. *Caryopses* about 1 mm long, 0.6 mm wide, opaque, yellowish brown or orangish, the embryo conspicuous, about one-half as long as the endosperm. *Chromosome number*, $2n = 36$.

Distribution. Texas: Regions 8, 9 and 10, occasional on open sandy or gravelly slopes. General: Colorado to Texas, southeastern California and Sonora, Mexico and adventive in Maine.

Flowering period: Mostly July to November.

Plants referable to *Sporobolus contractus* differ from the widespread and variable S. *cryptandrus* primarily in having a pale green, narrow-contracted panicle as much as 50 cm long.

Fig. 156. *Sporobolus cryptandrus.* Plant, glumes and floret. From Gould, 1951.

7. **Sporobolus giganteus** Nash, Bull. Torrey Bot. Club 25:88. 1898. GIANT DROPSEED. Tall, robust, glabrous perennial with clumps of few to several erect culms mostly 100-200 cm tall and 3-6 (-7) mm in diameter at base. *Sheaths* rounded, striate, firm, often ciliate on margins near top. *Ligule* a short, ciliate membrane, 1-1.5 mm long. *Blades* firm, mostly involute or folded, 20-50 cm long, 3-8 (-13) mm wide, tapering to a long slender point. *Panicles* dense, contracted, spikelike, pale and shining, mostly 25-70 cm long and 0.8-2.5 (-4) cm wide, the branches appressed, the lower portion frequently enclosed within the sheath. *Spikelets* similar to those of *Sporobolus*

296   **THE GRASSES OF TEXAS**

Fig. 157. *Sporobolus contractus*. Plant, glumes and floret. From Gould, 1951.

cryptandrus, 2.6-3.2 (-4) mm long, at least some 3 mm long. *Glumes* unequal, 1-nerved, the first glume 1-2 mm long; the second 2.6-3.2 mm long. *Lemmas* 2.5-3.1 mm long, the palea about as long. *Caryopses* about 1.5 mm long, 0.8 mm wide, orangish. *Chromosome number,* $2n=36$.

Distribution. Texas: Regions 9 and 10, open sandy or gravelly sites, frequent in the dune areas of Ward, Crane and Winkler counties. General: Oklahoma and western Texas to Colorado and Arizona.

Flowering period: Mostly August to October.

SUBFAMILY V. ERAGROSTOIDEAE   297

8. **Sporobolus nealleyi** Vasey, Bull. Torrey Bot. Club 15:49. 1888, name only; Contr. U. S. Nat. Herb. 1:57. 1890. GYPGRASS. Tufted perennial with erect culms from a hard, knotty base. *Culms* slender, mostly 10-40 cm tall, typically 0.8-1 mm in diameter at base. *Sheaths* pubescent with soft, kinky hairs on margins and collar. *Blades* 2-5 (-7) cm long and 1-1.5 mm wide, stiffly divergent from culm, usually tightly involute on drying. *Panicle* delicate, few-flowered, mostly 3-10 cm long, usually with at least some short, erect-spreading branches exposed, but occasionally almost entirely enclosed within upper leaf sheath. *Spikelets* 1.6-2.2 mm long. *Glumes* acute, the first 0.5-1.2 mm long, the second slightly shorter to as long as spikelet. *Lemma* equaling the second glume or slightly longer. *Paleas* about as long as lemmas. *Caryopses* pale orange, 0.7-1 mm long, 0 3-0.5 mm wide. *Chromosome number*, single record is $2n = 40$.

Distribution. Texas: Region 10, apparently confined to gypsum soils, locally abundant. General: Western Texas, New Mexico, Arizona, Nevada and into Mexico as far south as San Luis Potosi.

Flowering period: June to November.

9. **Sporobolus flexuosus** (Thurb.) Rydb., Bull. Torrey Bot. Club 32:601. 1905. MESA DROPSEED. Fig. 158. Cespitose perennial, similar to *Sporobolus cryptandrus* but the lead-colored panicles always open, about 10-30 cm long, 4-9 cm wide, with the main axis drooping or recurved above and the primary branches widely spreading, divaricate, or reflexed, with curved, pubescent pulvini in their axils. *Lower branches* as long as upper. *Panicle branchlets* loosely flowered, usually widely spreading from primary branches, with short, spreading or appressed pedicels. *Sheaths* rounded, with long white hairs (1-1.5 mm long) at corners. *Spikelets* 1.9-2.5 mm long, lead-colored. *Glumes* unequal, the first 1-1.3 mm long, the second 0.9-2.5 mm long. *Lemma and palea* equal to or slightly shorter than second glume. *Caryopses* about 1 mm long, 0.5-0.8 mm wide, the pericarp minutely striate or roughened. *Chromosome number*, $2n = 38$.

Distribution. Texas: Regions 9, 10 and the western portion of region 7, on open sandy or gravelly sites. General: Southern Utah to western Texas, southern California and northern Mexico.

Flowering period: Mostly May to November.

10. **Sporobolus buckleyi** Vasey, Bull. Torrey Bot. Club 10:128. 1883. BUCKLEY DROPSEED. Tufted perennial. *Culms* slender, erect, strongly compressed below, unbranched, 40-100 cm tall, 0.7-2 mm in diameter at the base. *Sheaths* striate, laterally compressed and keeled, the lower ones pubescent on margins on upper half. *Collar* of short hairs in a line broken only by the midnerve. *Ligule* a minute ciliate membrane, 0.2-0.4 mm long. *Blades* flat or folded, glabrous, the lowermost short, the upper elongate, 12-30 cm long and 4-12 mm wide. *Panicles* open, mostly 15-40 cm long, 7-17 cm wide, with slender, gracefully spreading branches, the lower 5-15 cm long and naked on the lower 2-5 cm. *Spikelets* purplish 1.3- (1-) 2 mm long. *Glumes* unequal, the

Fig. 158. *Sporobolus flexuosus.* Plant, glumes and floret. From Hitchcock, 1935.

first glume 0.6-1 mm long, the second glume, lemma and palea about equal; the palea broader than the lemma and often splitting as the grain matures. *Grain* about 1 mm long, flattened laterally. *Chromosome number,* $2n=40$.

Distribution. Texas: Southern portion of region 2 (Cameron and Hidalgo counties) on loamy soil in shaded habitats. General: Southern Texas and northeastern Mexico.

Flowering period: September to November.

11. **Sporobolus airoides** (Torr.) Torr., U. S. Report Expl. Miss. Pacific 7:21. 1856. ALKALI SACATON. Fig. 159. Coarse perennial with numerous erect, firm, tough culms arising from a hard base. *Culms* glabrous, shining, 50-150 cm tall, 1-2 (-3.5) mm in diameter at base. *Sheaths* rounded, glabrous, often with a few long white hairs (2-4 mm long) on margins on either side of collar. *Ligule* a short ciliate membrane. *Blades* flat or becoming involute, 15-45 cm long, 2-6 mm wide. *Panicles* variable, 20-45 cm long, 15-25 cm wide, usually open, diffuse and subpyramidal. *Spikelets* purplish or greenish, 1.3-2.5 (-2.8) mm long, mostly on spreading pedicels 0.5-2 mm long, the branchlets naked at base. *Glumes* unequal, the first 0.4-1.8 (-2) mm long, acute, the second 1-2.2 (-2.8) mm long. *Lemma and palea* similar to second glume in length. *Anthers* yellowish, 1.5- (1-) 1.7 mm long. *Caryopses* about 1 mm long, 0.7 mm wide, opaque, with a reddish or blackish striated pericarp. *Chromosome numbers* reported, $2n=$ ca. 80, ca. 90, 108 and 126.

SUBFAMILY V. ERAGROSTOIDEAE   299

Fig. 159. *Sporobolus airoides*. Plant, glumes and floret. From Gould, 1951.

Distribution. Texas: Regions 7, 8, 9 and 10 on dry sandy or gravelly slopes and along saline or alkaline flats. General: Nebraska, Missouri, South Dakota and Texas, west to eastern Washington and southern California and in northern Mexico as far south as San Luis Potosí.

Flowering period: June to November.

12. **Sporobolus wrightii** Munro *ex* Scribn., Bull Torrey Bot. Club 9:103. 1882. *S. airoides* (Torr.) Torr. var. *wrightii* (Munro *ex* Scribn.) Gould. BIG ALKALI SACATON. Robust, erect perennial with numerous firm, tough culms rising from a hard, densely cespitose base. *Culms* 90-250 cm tall, 2-9 mm in diameter near base. *Sheaths* rounded, glabrous, except rarely a few long white hairs on either side of collar. *Ligule* a ciliate membrane, 1-2 mm long, rarely longer. *Blades* flat, becoming involute or drying, 20-70 cm long, 3-6 (-10) mm wide. *Panicle* tawny or pale, 20-60 cm long, 12-26 cm wide, broadly lanceolate in outline, the secondary branchlets densely flowered for most of their length. *Spikelets* 1.5-2.1 (-2.5) mm long, on pedicels about 0.5 mm long, crowded, appressed and slightly overlapping. *Glumes* unequal, the first 0.5-1 mm long, the second 0.8-1.8 mm long. *Lemma and palea* rather obtuse, 1.2-2.1 (-2.5) mm long. *Caryopses* about 1.3 mm long and 0.7 mm wide, the pericarp reddish or blackish striate, loose, frequently slipping off at maturity. *Chromosome number*, $2n = 36$.

Distribution. Texas: Regions 6, 7 and 10 on moist clay flats, on borders of alkaline or saline areas and in western Texas on rocky slopes. General: Texas and Oklahoma to southern California and northern Mexico.

Flowering period: May to December.

13. **Sporobolus tharpii** Hitchc., Proc. Biol. Soc., Wash. 41:161. 1928. PADRE ISLAND DROPSEED. Fig. 160. Stout cespitose perennial with culms 60-170 cm tall from a thick, erect or somewhat decumbent base. *Sheaths* smooth, firm, shining, the upper margins glabrous or pubescent with long silvery hairs. *Ligule* a minute, short ciliate membrane. *Blades* long, narrow, usually involute, 30-60 cm long, 3- (1-) 6 mm wide, the base of the blade immediately behind ligule with silvery hairs 3-10 mm long. *Panicles* open, mostly 20-45 cm long, typically with stiffly erect-spreading branches 8-15 cm long. *Spikelets* glabrous, 2.8-3.5 mm long, at least some 3 mm long, crowded and appressed to the stiffly spreading secondary and tertiary branchlets. *Glumes* narrowly acute or acuminate, the first glume 1-2 mm long, the second 2-2.9 mm long, only slightly shorter than the lemma and palea. *Chromosome number* not reported.

Distribution. Texas: Regions 2 and 6 along the coast from Aransas County southward and frequent in the sands of Padre Island, the locality from which the type specimen was collected. General: Endemic along the southern Texas coast and probably also along the coast of Tamaulipas, Mexico.

Flowering period: May to November.

A specimen with widely divergent primary panicle branches from the Welder Refuge in San Patricio County is tentatively referred to this species.

14. **Sporobolus texanus** Vasey, Contr. U. S. Natl. Herb. 1:57. 1890. TEXAS DROPSEED. Tufted erect perennial. *Culms* slender, 30-70 cm tall, often somewhat decumbent at base. *Sheaths* rounded, glabrous or pubescent

Fig. 160. *Sporobolus tharpii*. Inflorescence and spikelet. From Gould and Box, 1965.

302   THE GRASSES OF TEXAS

with long papillose-pilose hairs. *Ligule* a minute, short ciliate membrane, seldom over 0.5 mm long. *Blades* flat or folded, rather stiff, 2.5-10 cm long, 1-4 mm wide, scabrous on the adaxial surface, often with a few long hairs at base on either side of ligule. *Panicle* diffuse, 15-30 cm long and about as wide, with widely spreading branches and branchlets. *Spikelets* mostly 2.3-3.3 mm long, widely spaced on spreading pedicels or pedicel-like branchlets mostly 5-25 mm long. *First glume* narrow, one-third to one-half as long as spikelet. *Second glume* equal to or slightly shorter than lemma and palea. *Palea* frequently splitting as the grain matures. *Grains* light brown, translucent, oblong, laterally flattened, 1-1.5 mm long, with a darker brown embryo about half as long as the endosperm. *Chromosome number* not reported.

Distribution. Texas: Regions 8, 9 and 10, infrequent, mostly in low, moist, somewhat saline or alkaline areas. The type specimen was collected near Screw Bean, Presidio County. General: Western Kansas and eastern Colorado to Texas, New Mexico and Arizona.

Flowering period: August to November.

15. **Sporobolus asper** (Michx.) Kunth, Rev. Gram. 1:68. 1829. Perennial with spikelets in contracted terminal panicles and often with cleistogamous spikelets in shorter axillary panicles, these partially or entirely enclosed within the subtending sheaths. *Culms* slender, erect, solitary or in small clumps, mostly 60-120 cm tall. *Sheaths* glabrous or the lower ones pilose near collar. *Ligule* a minute, short ciliate membrane. *Blades* elongate, flat or folded, glabrous or the lower ones pilose, mostly 1-4 mm wide. *Inflorescence* spikelike, 5-30 cm long and 4-10 (-16) mm wide, often almost entirely enclosed within the somewhat inflated subtending sheath. *Spikelets* 4-6 (-7) mm long, mostly densely crowded on the branches, these appressed along the main axis. *Glumes* silvery, pale green or purplish, usually with a bright green midnerve, keeled, the first glume slightly more than one-half as long to nearly as long as second glume. *Lemmas* somewhat rounded at apex, usually longer than second glume, glabrous. *Paleas* well-developed, conspicuous, slightly shorter to a little longer than lemmas. *Grains* mostly 1.6-2 mm long, about 1 mm wide, semitranslucent, reddish brown, plump; embryo about three-fourths as long as endosperm; pericarp becoming mucilaginous when moistened.

Plants with scaly rhizomes   15b. *S. asper* var. *macer*

Plants cespitose, without rhizomes

    Culms 1-2 (-2.5) mm wide near the base; terminal sheath 0.8-2 (-2.5) mm wide when folded; primary panicle branches 8-18, lax
                15c. *S. asper* var. *drummondii*

    Culms 2- (1.4-) 5 mm wide near the base; terminal sheath 1.5- (1.3-) 6 mm wide when folded; primary panicle branches 12-35, crowded
                15a. *S. asper* var. *asper*

15a. **Sporobolus asper** (Michx.) Kunth var. **asper.** TALL DROPSEED. Fig. 161. *Culms* 2- (1.4-) 5 mm wide near the base. *Terminal sheaths* 1.5- (1.3-) 6 mm wide when folded. *Panicles* dense, crowded, with 12-25 primary branches. *Chromosome numbers* reported, $2n=54$, 88 and 108.

Distribution. Texas: Regions 1, 2, 3, 4, 5, 6, 7 and 8, frequent in grasslands, borders of woods and road right-of-ways. General: Vermont to eastern Washington, south to Mississippi, Louisiana, Texas and Arizona.

Flowering period: Mostly September to November.

15b. **Sporobolus asper** (Michx.) Kunth var. **macer** (Trin.) Shinners, Rhodora 56:29. 1954. MISSISSIPPI DROPSEED. Similar to *Sporobolus asper* var. *asper*, but the culms mostly 50-70 cm tall, rising from short scaly rhizomes. *Blades* flat, 10-20 cm long, 1-2 mm wide, often pilose on the upper surface near base. *Spikelets* 4-5 mm long.

Distribution. Texas: Region 1 in open pine woods and grassy borders of woods. General: Mississippi, Louisiana, Arkansas and eastern Texas.

Flowering period: August to November.

15c. **Sporobolus asper** (Michx.) Kunth var. **drummondii** (Trin.) Vasey, Contr. U. S. Natl. Herb. 3:60. 1892. *S. asper* var. *hookeri* (Trin.) Vasey; *S. pilosus* Vasey. MEADOW DROPSEED. Similar to *Sporobolus asper* var. *asper* except that the culms are more slender, 1-2 (-2.5) mm in diameter at base, and the terminal sheaths are smaller, 0.8-2 (-2.5) mm wide when folded. *Blades* mostly 1-2 mm wide, glabrous or infrequently sparsely pilose. *Panicles* rather lax, with 8-18 primary branches. *Spikelets* 4-5 mm long, fewer in number and less crowded on the branches than in *S. asper* var. *asper*. *Anthers* purplish, 2-3 mm long.

Distribution. Texas: Regions 1, 2, 3, 4, 5, 6, 7 and 8, frequent in grasslands, borders of woods and along road right-of-ways. General: Alabama to Texas, Oklahoma, Kansas and Missouri.

Flowering period: Mostly August to November.

16. **Sporobolus neglectus** Nash, Bull. Torrey Bot. Club 22:464. 1895. PUFFSHEATH DROPSEED. An erect or partially decumbent annual. *Culms* slender, branching at base, 10-40 cm tall. *Sheaths* shorter than the internodes, somewhat inflated. *Lower sheaths* 0.5-1.5 (-2) mm wide when folded. *Ligule* a short ciliate membrane. *Lower blades* flat, 3-12 cm long, about 2 mm wide, tapering to a slender point, often sparsely pilose; the upper blades shorter. *Terminal panicles* narrow, contracted, 2-5 cm long, often only the apical portion exserted from sheath; axillary panicles shorter, almost entirely enclosed within sheath. *Spikelets* 1.6- (1.3-) 2.8 mm long, on short pedicels. *Glumes* about equal, rather acute, shorter than floret. *Lemmas* acute, 1-nerved, glabrous, white or purple-tinged. *Paleas* acute, about as long as lemmas, splitting as the grain matures. *Grains* brownish orange, about 1.5 (-2.5) mm long, 0.7 (-1) mm wide, plump, the embryo about three-fourths the

Fig. 161. *Sporobolus asper* var. *asper*. Plant and spikelet.

SUBFAMILY V. ERAGROSTOIDEAE 305

length of the endosperm, the pericarp finely striate, becoming gelatinous when moistened. *Chromosome number* reported, $2n=36$.

Distribution. Texas: Region 7 on dry ground and sandy fields. General: New England and Quebec to Montana, south to Virginia, Tennessee and Texas and in Washington and Arizona.

Flowering period: Mostly August to November.

17. **Sporobolus ozarkanus** Fernald, Rhodora 35:109. 1933. OZARK DROPSEED. Loosely tufted annual with slender, erect or rather widely spreading culms 4-50 cm tall and about 0.5-0.7 mm in diameter near base. *Sheaths* ciliate at throat. Lower sheaths sparsely papillose-pilose, 1.5- (1-) 3 mm wide when folded. Terminal sheaths as much as 1.1-2.5 mm wide when folded. *Ligule* a short ciliate membrane; often some long white hairs on upper margins of sheath. *Lower blades* 8- (5.5-) 26 cm long, 1-1.5 mm wide, flat or becoming somewhat involute on drying, tapering to a slender point, sparsely papillose-pilose on upper surface. *Inflorescences* narrow, contracted, 3-5 cm long, partially to almost entirely enclosed within sheath. *Spikelets* 2.3-3.8 (-4.2) mm long. *Glumes* about equal to unequal, 3-4 mm long, scaberulous, longer than floret. *Lemmas* acutish, 3-nerved, 3-3.5 mm long, pale yellow and irregularly mottled with dark purplish spots, glabrous or pubescent with scattered short appressed hairs. *Paleas* equal to or slightly longer than lemmas. *Floret* length/width ratio 1.6-3.3 (-3.8). *Anthers* 2-2.8 mm long.

Distribution. Texas: Region 7 and the southern portions of regions 4 and 5, often in rather dense stands. General: Missouri, Arkansas and Texas. The type specimen was collected in limestone barrens in Jasper County, Missouri.

Flowering period: Late August to October.

18. **Sporobolus clandestinus** (Bieler) Hitchc., Contr. U. S. Natl. Herb. 12:150. 1908. *Sporobolus canovirens* Nash. Stout to somewhat slender perennial. *Culms* erect or somewhat spreading, glabrous or glaucous below nodes, 50-100 cm tall, 1-2 mm in diameter near base. *Sheaths* rounded, often with long white hairs on either side of collar. *Lower sheaths* often papillose-pilose. *Ligule* a minute, ciliate membrane, 0.2-0.3 mm long. *Blades* flat, becoming involute on drying, tapering to a long point, the lower blades 20 cm long or longer. *Inflorescences* terminal and axillary, spikelike, 5-10 cm long, at least partly enclosed within the terminal sheath which is 1.5-2 mm wide when folded. *Spikelets* 5-7 (-10) mm long, flattened laterally, often purple-tinged. *Glumes* unequal, shorter than floret, keeled, acute or subacute, scaberulous, first glume 2-3.5 mm long, second glume 3-4.2 mm long. *Lemmas* mottled with purple, acute to acuminate, appressed pubescent, 4-5 mm long. *Paleas* appressed pubescent, especially between nerves, pointed, longer than lemma and occasionally to 10 mm long. *Anthers* orangish, 2.5-2.8 mm long. *Grains* 2-3 mm long, about 0.7-1 mm wide, translucent, reddish brown, the embryo obvious, about one-half as long as the endosperm; pericarp smooth, becoming loose when moistened. *Chromosome number* not reported.

Distribution. Texas: Regions 1, 2, 3, 4, 5, 6, 7 and 8, frequent in grasslands, borders of woods and road right-of-ways. General: New England to Wisconsin, Iowa and Kansas, south to Florida and Texas.

Flowering period: August to October.

Sporobolus clandestinus is the only perennial species in the *Sporobolus asper* complex which has a pubescent lemma and a pericarp which becomes loose when moistened.

19. **Sporobolus vaginaeflorus** (Torr. *ex* A. Gray) Wood, Class Book ed. 1861. 775. 1861. Fig. 162. Tufted annual. *Culms* spreading-erect, with several nodes and short internodes, mostly 15-55 (-70) cm long. *Sheaths* mostly shorter than culm internodes, glabrous, usually with tufts of short hairs on either side of collar. *Lower sheaths* 0.8-1.7 mm wide when folded. *Ligule* a minute ciliate membrane, not more than 0.3 mm long. *Blades* glabrous or less frequently hispid or pilose, flat or involute, mostly 1-2 mm wide, those of the upper nodes mostly 1-5 cm long, the basal blades 4.5-11 (-13) cm long. *Panicles* terminal and axillary, contracted, mostly 1-4 cm long and 2-5 mm wide, frequently partially or entirely enclosed within the subtending, often inflated, sheath. *Panicles* commonly produced at the upper 3-5 culm nodes, the terminal one developing first. *Glumes* usually shorter than the floret, acute or acuminate, glabrous, equal or the first glume slightly shorter, 1.8-4.5 mm long. *Lemmas* 1- or faintly 3-nerved, acute or acuminate, often mottled with dark purple, short appressed-pubescent. *Paleas* variable in length, shorter than to longer than the lemmas, also sparsely short appressed-pubescent. *Floret* length/width ratio 2.2-5.7 (-7.5). *Caryopses* about 2 mm long, 0.7 mm wide, translucent, with an embryo at least one-half as long as the endosperm. *Chromosome number*, $2n = 54$.

Distribution. Texas: Regions 1, 3, 4, 5, 6, 7 and 8 in a wide variety of habitats and soil types but most frequently found in sandy clays. In the plateau country, common on limestone outcrops. General: Throughout the eastern United States, west to Minnesota, Nebraska and Texas and occasionally farther west in Mexico and Arizona.

Flowering period: Mostly September to November.

20. **Sporobolus junceus** (Michx.) Kunth, Rev. Gram. 1:68. 1829. *Sporobolus gracilis* (Trin.) Merr. PINEYWOODS DROPSEED. Cespitose perennial with long basal leaves. *Culms* slender, stiffly erect, mostly 50-100 cm long, unbranched above base. *Sheaths* glabrous or sparsely hispid-ciliate on margins, with long white hairs at throat. *Ligule* a minute ciliate membrane about 0.2 mm long. *Blades* glabrous or sparsely hispid, flat or involute, mostly 1-2 mm wide. Lower blades broad and mostly 13-30 cm long, the upper blades short. *Panicle* narrow but open, mostly 10-25 cm long and 3-6 cm wide at base, gradually tapering upward. *Panicle branches* usually simple, in rather widely-spaced verticils, the lower ones usually 2-3.5 cm long, naked on about

Fig. 162. *Sporobolus vaginaeflorus*. Plant and spikelet.

308   THE GRASSES OF TEXAS

the lower half. *Spikelets* appressed along branches, brownish or bronze-purple, 3-3.8 mm long. *Glumes* unequal, glabrous, narrowly acute or acuminate, the first glume 1.2-3 mm long, the second 3-3.8 mm long. *Lemma and palea* glabrous, slightly shorter than the second glume. *Anthers* 1.5-2 mm long. *Grains* plump, brownish, minutely rugose, asymmetrically oblong, about 1.5 mm long, with an embryo two-thirds to three-fourths the length of the grain. *Chromosome number* not reported.

Distribution. Texas: Regions 1 and 2 as far south as San Patricio and Atascosa counties, mostly in pine and hardwood forests but also associated with tall prairie grasses in sandy soils of the upper Texas coastal plain. General: Southeastern Virginia to Florida and eastern Texas.

Flowering period: Mostly September to November, occasionally flowering in early spring.

21. **Sporobolus purpurascens** (Swartz) Hamilt., Prodr. Pl. Ind. Occ. 5. 1825. PURPLE DROPSEED. Cespitose perennial with leaves mostly in a basal tuft. *Culms* stiffly erect, unbranched above the base, 25-90 cm tall. *Sheaths* rounded, glabrous or hispid-ciliate on margins, usually with long white hairs on either side of collar. *Ligule* a ciliate membrane mostly 0.2-0.5 mm long. *Blades* of basal leaves flat or involute, mostly 8-15 (-22) cm long and 2-5 mm wide at least near base, tapering to a long slender point. *Panicles* 10-25 (7-30) cm long and 0.8-1.6 cm wide, somewhat cylindrical, not pyramidal in outline but interrupted below, typically with branches 0.8-1.5 cm long, the lower occasionally to 2-3 cm long. *Panicle branches* in well defined verticils, appressed or narrowly spreading, densely flowered nearly to base. *Spikelets* purple- or bronzy-tinged, similar to those of *S. junceus. First glume* 1.6-2.5 mm long, acute; second glume 3-4.5 mm long, acute. *Lemma and palea* equal to second glume, the palea frequently splitting as the grain matures. *Anthers* 1.5-1.6 mm long. *Caryopses* 2-2.2 mm long, about 1 mm wide, reddish brown, the embryo about one-half the length of the endosperm, the pericarp becoming gelatinous when moistened. *Chromosome number,* $2n=60$.

Distribution. Texas: Region 6 and the southern portion of region 2, in sandy soils, mostly in coastal prairie or oak motts. General: Southern Texas to eastern Mexico, the West Indies and Central America to Brazil.

Flowering period: Mostly October and November but not infrequently flowering in the spring.

Sporobolus purpurascens is closely related to *S. junceus* from which it differs in the broader, shorter blades, the narrower panicles and the short branches which are floriferous to the base or nearly so. Some specimens from Wilson and Atascosa counties with long, narrow blades and rather open panicles appear to be intermediate.

22. **Sporobolus heterolepis** (A. Gray) A. Gray, Man. 576. 1848. PRAIRIE DROPSEED. Fig. 163. Perennial with culms in densely cespitose clumps. *Culms* slender, glabrous, 30-70 (-100) cm tall, unbranched above base.

Fig. 163. *Sporobolus heterolepis.* Plant, spikelet and floret with caryopsis and split palea. From Hitchcock, 1935.

Sheaths rounded, glabrous or pubescent with long hairs on back of lower sheaths, often also with long hairs on either side of collar and the throat sometimes pubescent. *Ligule* minute, ciliate, usually 0.1-0.3 mm long. *Blades* filiform, folded or involute, 1-2 mm wide, the basal ones mostly 12-30 (-50) cm long, the upper ones shorter, 6-12 cm long. *Panicles* narrowly pyramidal or ellipsoidal, commonly 5-20 (-25) cm long and 2-4 (-7) cm wide. *Panicle branches* spreading or somewhat erect, loosely-flowered, often naked on the lower one-fourth to one-half, not in regular verticils but 2 or 3 branches may develop at same node. *Spikelets* 4-6 mm long, lead-colored. *Glumes* unequal, glabrous, shining, long-acuminate, the first glume narrow, usually two-thirds to three-fourths as long as the second, the second broader, 3.5-5 (-6) mm long, often tapering to a point 1-1.5 mm long. *Lemma* slightly shorter than the second glume, broadly acute. *Palea* about as long as second glume, splitting between nerves as grain matures. *Grains* globose, smooth and shining, indurate, mostly 1.5-1.8 (1-2) mm in diameter, the embryo demarcation obscure. *Chromosome number,* $2n=72$.

Distribution. Texas: Regions 1 and 3, infrequent, in sandy soil of woodlands and borders of woods. General: Quebec to Saskatchewan, Canada, southward throughout the central United States to Arkansas, Oklahoma and Texas, and in Colorado and Wyoming.

Flowering period: Mostly September to November.

23. **Sporobolus silveanus** Swallen, J. Wash. Acad. Sci. 31:350. fig. 3. 1941. SILVEUS DROPSEED. Densely cespitose perennial with slender, erect culms mostly 90-120 cm tall, scabrous at least below nodes. *Sheaths* rounded, often sparsely pubescent with long hairs on margins and near collar. *Lower sheaths* firm, shining, becoming flat and papery with age. *Ligule* erose-ciliate, mostly 0.1-0.8 mm long. *Blades* mostly basal, firm, involute or loosely folded, 1-2 mm wide, 15-30 (-45) cm long, curved or flexuous. *Panicles* somewhat open, 30-40 (20-50) cm long and typically 10-12 (-15) cm wide, the few-flowered branches ascending, 6-12 (-15) cm long, naked below, *Spikelets* purple, 5-6 (-7.2) mm long, the pedicels 5-8 mm long, appressed or somewhat spreading. *Glumes* acuminate or narrowly acute, subequal, the first glume 3-4.5 mm long, 1-nerved. *Second glume* 4-6 (-7) mm long, about as long as lemma and palea, 3-nerved. *Lemmas* 5-6 mm long, subacute. *Paleas* about as long as lemmas. *Grains* oblong, 2-2.5 mm long and about 0.8 mm wide, with an embryo slightly over one-third as long as the endosperm. *Anthers* dark purple, about 3-4 mm long. *Chromosome number* not reported.

Distribution. Texas: Regions 1 and 3, infrequent, in pine and hardwood forests. Only two records in the Tracy Herbarium: *Gould 11028* from Hardin County and *Lonard 2504* from Brazos County. The type specimen was collected near Orange, Texas. General: Western Louisiana and eastern Texas.

Flowering period: September to November.

69. **BLEPHARONEURON** Nash

A monotypic North American genus.

1. **Blepharoneuron tricholepis** (Torr.) Nash, Bull. Torrey Bot. Club 25:88. 1898. PINE DROPSEED. Fig. 164. Tufted perennial with culms 30-(15-) 70 cm tall. *Culm nodes* glabrous. *Leaves* usually but not always basally clustered. *Sheaths* glabrous, rounded on back. *Ligule* a rounded, minutely ciliate membrane 0.3-0.5 mm long. *Blades* glabrous or scabrous, filiform, involute, 2 mm or less broad, mostly 8-15 cm long. *Panicles* loosely contracted or moderately open, 7-15 (4-20) cm long and one-fourth to one-third as broad. *Spikelets* 1-flowered, awnless, 2.5-3.8 mm long, bluish-gray, borne on slender erect-spreading branchlets and short pedicels. Disarticulation above glumes. *Glumes* glabrous, broad, rounded on back, broadly acute or obtuse and often minutely apiculate at apex; first glume faintly 5-nerved, equal to or slightly shorter than the second, second glume faintly 3-nerved, slightly shorter to slightly longer than lemma. *Lemma* firm, 3-nerved, densely puberulent on

Fig. 164. *Blepharoneuron tricholepis*. Plant and spikelet. From Gould and Box, 1965.

midnerve to above middle and on margins nearly to apex, the apex broad, rounded, occasionally apiculate. *Palea* equaling or slightly exceeding lemma in length, puberulent between the rather closely-placed nerves. *Chromosome number, 2n=16.*

Distribution. Texas: Region 10 on rocky, open slopes and in dry woodlands at medium to high elevations, most records from the Chisos Mountains. General: Colorado, Utah, Texas, New Mexico and Arizona and northwestern Mexico.

Flowering period: Mostly July to October.

Tribe 14. Chlorideae

70. WILLKOMMIA Hack.

A genus of four species, one in Texas and Argentina and three in South Africa.

1. **Willkommia texana** Hitchc., Bot. Gaz. 35:283. f. 1. 1903. WILLKOMMIA. Fig. 165. Tufted perennial with culms in small clumps from a firm base. *Culms* 20-40 cm tall, glabrous. *Leaves* thick, firm, mostly basal. *Sheaths* rounded, glabrous or the lowermost sparsely hairy. *Ligule* a minute fringed membrane. *Blades* glabrous, flat or more commonly infolded or involute, mostly 4-10 cm long and 1-3 mm broad, serrate on margins. *Inflorescence* a spikelike panicle 7-18 cm long and 4-10 mm broad, with 5-10 (4-20) appressed spicate branches mostly 2-3 cm long and 1-2 mm thick. *Spikelets* 1-flowered, sessile, appressed and imbricated in 2 rows along the slender, triangular branch rachis. *Glumes* thin, glabrous, 1-nerved, the first glume acute, one-half to two-thirds as long as the second, the second mostly 4-5 mm long, slightly exceeding the lemma in length, with a thin, rounded, membranous tip. *Lemmas* 3-nerved, the lateral nerves obscure, pubescent on back and margins. *Palea* pubescent, slightly shorter and narrower than lemma. *Chromosome number, 2n=60.*

Distribution. Texas: Regions 1 and 2, Tracy Herbarium records from San Patricio and Kleberg counties, restricted to relatively bare, clayey soils. General: Endemic to southern Texas (Chase, 1950, reports the species also from "central" Texas).

Flowering period: Mostly April to June.

71. SCHEDONNARDUS Steud.

A genus of a single species, this with distribution in central United States, Mexico and Argentina.

1. **Schedonnardus paniculatus** (Nutt.) Trel., in Branner and Coville, Geol. Survey Ark. Rep. 1888:236. 1891. TUMBLEGRASS. Fig. 166. Low, tufted perennial with slender, stiffly curving-erect culms. *Culms* mostly 8-50 (-70) cm long, often decumbent-spreading at base. *Leaves* glabrous. *Sheaths*

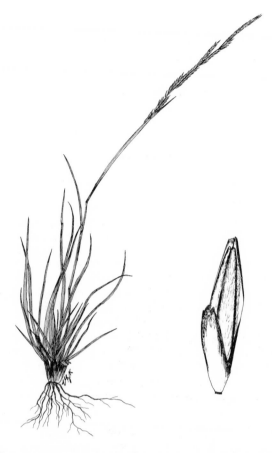

Fig. 165. *Willkommia texana*. Plant and spikelet. From Gould and Box, 1965.

laterally compressed and keeled, with broad hyaline margins that are continued at apex as a membranous, rounded ligule. *Ligules* mostly 1-3 mm long. *Blades* 0.6-2 (-3) mm broad and 2-12 cm long, scabrous on margins, often folded on the strong midnerve and spirally twisted on drying. *Panicles* with a curved main axis equaling or much longer than leafy portion of culm, with a few, widely-spaced, spicate branches 2-10 (-20) cm long, the panicle eventually breaking off at the base and rolling before the wind as a tumbleweed. *Spikelets* slender, sessile, 3-4 mm long, widely-spaced (not or only slightly overlapping) and appressed on the branches and tip of panicle axis. Disarticulation above glumes and at base of inflorescence. *Glumes* narrow, lanceolate or acuminate, 1-nerved; the second glume about as long as the lemma, the first

314   THE GRASSES OF TEXAS

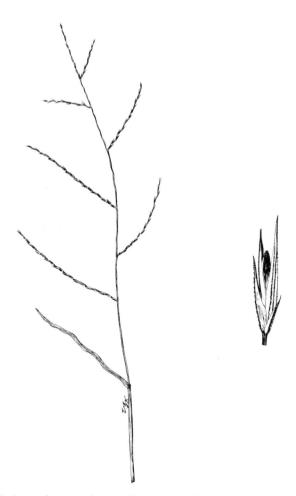

Fig. 166. *Schedonnardus paniculatus*. Inflorescence and spikelet. From Gould and Box, 1965.

shorter. *Lemmas* narrow, rigid, 3-nerved, narrowly acute or with a minute awn tip, glabrous or scabrous. *Paleas* about as long as lemmas, glabrous. *Caryopses* narrow, 2.5-3.5 mm long, with an embryo about one-third as long as the endosperm. *Chromosome number,* $2n = 20$.

Distribution. Texas: Throughout the State, at least occasional in all regions, most frequently on clay or clay loam soils. General: Central North America, Saskatchewan, Canada, to Illinois and Montana, south to Louisiana, Texas and Arizona and reported from Argentina.

Flowering period: Throughout the year under favorable conditions.

Though widespread throughout the central grasslands of the United States, this grass contributes little forage for cattle and horses.

SUBFAMILY V. ERAGROSTOIDEAE   315

72. CYNODON L. Rich

About 10 species, mostly native to Africa and Australia.

1. **Cynodon dactylon** (L.) Pers., Syn. Pl. 1:85. 1805. BERMUDA-GRASS. Fig. 167. Low, mat-forming stoloniferous and rhizomatous perennial, the rhizomes stout, creeping, extensive. *Culms* weak, mostly stoloniferous, only the floriferous shoots or shoot tips erect, these 10-50 cm tall. *Sheaths* rounded, glabrous except for tufts of hair on either side of collar and into ligular area. *Ligule* a ciliate membrane mostly 0.2-0.5 mm long. *Blades* linear, flat or folded, 1-3 (-4) mm broad, mostly 3-8 (-14) cm long, glabrous. *Inflorescence* of usually 3-5 (2-7) digitately arranged spicate branches, the branches glabrous or scabrous, mostly 2-6 cm long, floriferous to the base, with numerous awnless spikelets closely imbricated in 2 rows on a narrow, flattened or triangular rachis. *Spikelets* with a single perfect floret, the rachilla prolonged behind the palea and often bearing a rudimentary floret. *Glumes* lanceolate, subequal, 1-nerved, about two-thirds as long as lemma. *Lemmas* mostly 2-2.5 mm long, firm, shiny, awnless, acute, laterally compressed and keeled, 3-nerved, the lateral nerves near the margins, the midnerve obscurely pubescent or scabrous. *Palea* narrow, slightly shorter than lemma, with 2 closely-placed nerves. *Chromosome number*, $2n=36$ for Texas plants; counts of $2n=18$ and 40 also reported.

Distribution. Texas: Throughout the State, commonly cultivated as a lawn and pasture grass but frequent as a weed of ditches, vacant lots and roadways and along streams, lakes and marshy swales. General: Widespread in the southern United States, where it is one of the most important forage grasses, occasional to Canada in the northeast as a casual weed, infrequent or absent in Wisconsin, Nebraska, Montana, Washington and northward. Native to tropical-subtropical Africa, this species now is widespread through the warmer parts of the world.

Flowering period: Throughout the year under favorable growing conditions.

73. CHLORIS Swartz*

Fibrous rooted annuals or rhizomatous, stoloniferous or cespitose perennials with erect culms and open to contracted panicles of few to several digitately to subdigitately arranged one-sided spicate branches. *Leaves* with rounded to flattened, overlapping sheaths, often restricted to lower portions of culm, usually glabrous or scabrous, rarely pilose. *Ligule* often a ciliate crown, sometimes wanting. *Spikelets* imbricate to distant, usually pale to tawny, sometimes brown, with 1, rarely 2, perfect florets; disarticulation above glumes. *Glumes* usually unequal in length, lanceolate, glabrous with scabrous nerves, acute or sometimes acuminate, shorter than florets. *Lemma of lower (perfect) floret* lanceolate, 3-nerved,

Contributed by Dennis Anderson.

Fig. 167. *Cynodon dactylon*. Plant, separate inflorescence, spikelet with floret separated from glumes and caryopsis. From Gould, 1951.

with shortly to prominently pubescent margins, glabrous to scabrous inter-nerves and usually scabrous nerves, awned either from the tip or between two teeth. *Reduced florets* sometimes 2 or 3, varying from rudimentary to cylindrical or inflated-obovoid, acute to truncate, awned or awnless. *Caryopses* brown, ovoid to trigonous, the embryos usually one-third to one-half the length of the caryopses. *Basic* chromosome numbers, $x=9$ and 10.

A genus of 56 species widely distributed in the tropical to warm temperate regions of the world. In the United States the greatest number of species is found in Texas.

SUBFAMILY V. ERAGROSTOIDEAE   317

Following Clayton (1967), the genus *Trichloris* is here merged with *Chloris*. While the New World species of *Trichloris* are readily distinguished from New World species of *Chloris* by their 3-awned lemmas, this distinction breaks down in Australia where no sharp lines of generic separation can be maintained. *Eustachys*, treated as a section of *Chloris* by Hitchcock (1935) and Chase (1951), herein is recognized as a distinct genus.

Lemma of lower floret 4.5-7.5 mm long, dorsally compressed; plants with modified, cleistogamous underground spikelets at the tips of rhizome branches   12. *C. chloridea*

Lemma of lower floret less than 4.5 mm long, laterally compressed; plants without cleistogamous underground spikelets

Lemma of lower floret awned from between 2 lobes

Lobes of lemma prominently awned, the lateral awns about equal in length to central awn   14. *C. crinita*

Lobes of lemma short-awned, the lateral awns one-fifth or less as long as central awn

Second glume abruptly tapering to a prominent awn; inflorescence branches 7-20, inserted along panicle axis for several cm
13. *C. pluriflora*

Second glume narrowly lanceolate, attenuate, awnless; inflorescence branches 3-9, digitate   11. *C. divaricata*

Lemma of lower floret not awned from between 2 lobes

Neuter or staminate floret 1

Panicle branches typically in several verticils along an axis 20 mm or more long   3. *C. verticillata*

Panicle branches in a single verticil or if in several verticils, then crowded near apex of panicle axis

Inflorescence branches bearing spikelets to base, the lower spikelets mostly less than 3 mm apart

Lower lemma 2 mm or less long, with an awn 1.5 mm or less long, appressed-pilose on keel, otherwise glabrous; sterile floret inflated, about as wide as long
6. *C. cucullata*

Lower lemma more than 2 mm long, with an awn more than 1.5 mm long; sterile floret inflated or not

Lower lemma prominently gibbous, the upper margins with a
prominent tuft of cilia to 2 mm long; annual
2. *C. virgata*

Lower lemma not gibbous, the upper margins with short,
appressed hairs; perennial   7. *C. subdolichostachya*

Inflorescence branches mostly not spikelet-bearing to base, the
lower spikelets 3 mm or more apart

Lower lemma less than 3 mm long, with an awn less than 6
mm long; panicle branches bearing spikelets along most of
the length   4. *C. andropogonoides*

Lower lemma more than 3.5 mm long, with an awn more than
7 mm long; panicle branches not bearing spikelets on lower
one-fourth to one-third   5. *C. texensis*

Neuter or staminate florets 2 or more

Lowermost neuter or staminate floret more than 2 mm long; stoloniferous perennial with culms often more than 75 cm tall
1. *C. gayana*

Lowermost neuter or staminate floret less than 2 mm long; annuals
or tufted perennials, frequently with culms less than 60 cm tall

Awn of lowermost neuter or staminate floret 5 mm or more
long; all florets awned; annual   8. *C. inflata*

Awn of lowermost neuter or staminate floret less than 3.5 mm
long; upper reduced florets lacking awns; perennials

Lowermost floret less than 3 mm long; upper florets with awns
less than 1.5 mm long   9. *C. ciliata*

Lowermost floret more than 3 mm long excluding awn; upper
florets with awns 1.5-3.5 mm long   10. *C. canterai*

1. **Chloris gayana** Kunth, Rev. Gram. 1:89. 1829. RHODESGRASS.
Fig. 168. Perennial. *Culms* generally tall, often over 1 m, erect, usually
stoloniferous, occasionally tufted, glabrous. *Sheaths* glabrous to scabrous.
Ligule a ciliate fringe. *Blades* flat, scabrous, to 30 cm long and 1.5 cm wide.
Panicles with 9-30 digitate, somewhat divaricate branches 8-15 cm long.
Spikelets imbricate, with about 10 spikelets per cm of rachis, pale to tawny.
Glumes narrowly lanceolate, glabrous with scabrous nerves, the first glume
1.4-2.8 mm long, the second 2.5-4.3 mm long. *Lemma of lower floret* ovate to
obovate or elliptic, somewhat gibbous, with a body 2.5-3.2 mm long and awn

Fig. 168. *Chloris gayana*. Plant and spikelet. From Gould and Box, 1965.

1.5-6.5 mm long, the margins usually with a prominent tuft of hairs near apex, occasionally appressed pilose. *Sterile florets* 2-4, rarely 1, similar to perfect floret but smaller, the lowest 2.2-3.2 mm long and with an awn 0.8-3.2 mm long, the upper awnless or awn-tipped, progressively smaller with the uppermost reduced to a turbinate cup. *Chromosome numbers* reported, $2n=20$, 30 and 40.

Distribution. Texas: Regions 2 and 6, an important cultivated forage grass in south Texas, commonly escaped along roadsides, generally in loamy soils;

less common in southeastern parts of state. General: Worldwide in tropics and warm temperate regions. Probably originally native to tropical east Africa.

Flowering period: May through December.

2. **Chloris virgata** Sw., Fl. Ind. Occ. 1:203. 1797. SHOWY CHLORIS. Fig. 169. Annual, extremely variable in size and habit, usually tufted, with glabrous culms from a few cm to over 1 m tall, often decumbent and stoloniferous at base. *Sheaths* usually glabrous, occasionally densely pilose near ligule. *Ligule*, a ciliate fringe or wanting. *Blades* flat, usually glabrous, occasionally pilose, to 30 cm long and 1.5 cm wide. *Panicles* with 4-20 digitate, more or less erect branches, 5-10 cm long. *Spikelets* tawny, tightly imbricate, with about 10 spikelets per cm of the rachis. *Glumes* narrowly lanceolate, hyaline, glabrous with scabrous midnerve, the first glume 1.5-2.5 mm long, the second 2.5-4.3 mm long. *Lemma of lower floret* ovate to elliptic, prominently gibbous dorsally, with keel, midnerves and lower margins variously pubescent, the upper margins long-ciliate, 2.5-4.2 mm long; awn usually 5-15 mm long. *Sterile florets* 1, rarely 2, similar in shape to the perfect one but 1.4-2.9 mm long and with awns 3-9.5 mm long. *Chromosome numbers* reported, $2n=20$, 26 and 40.

Distribution. Texas: Throughout the State as a roadside and wasteground weed. General: Worldwide in tropics to warm temperate regions.

Flowering period: May through November.

3. **Chloris verticillata** Nutt., Trans. Amer. Philos. Soc. 5:150. 1837. WINDMILLGRASS. Fig. 170. Perennial. *Culms* erect to decumbent, glabrous, 15-40 cm tall. *Sheaths* glabrous. *Ligule* a ciliate crown with hairs to 2 mm long. *Blades* glabrous to scabrous, to 15 cm long and 2-3 mm wide. *Panicle* with 10-16 laterally spreading branches 5-15 cm long, well distributed in 2-5 verticils often separated by 5 mm or more, the panicle axis usually terminating in an upright branch. *Spikelets* appressed, tawny, widely spaced, with about 4-7 spikelets per cm of rachis. *Glumes* lanceolate, membranous, glabrous except for the scabrous midnerve, the first glume 2-3 mm long, the second 2.8-3.5 mm long. *Lemma of the lower floret* elliptic to lanceolate, 2-3.5 mm long, with glabrous keel and appressed-pubescent margins, the apex acute to obtuse; awn 4.8-9 mm long. *Sterile floret* 1, oblong, somewhat inflated, truncate, glabrous, 1.1-2.3 mm long, with an awn 3.2-7 mm long. *Chromosome number*, $2n=40$.

Distribution. Texas: Regions 5, 7, 8, 9 and 10 in heavy sandy or gravelly soils of disturbed areas, roadsides, lawns and parks. General: Central United States, Nebraska and Iowa to Colorado, Texas, New Mexico and Arizona.

Chloris verticillata hybridizes extensively with *Chloris cucullata* where the two grow together, often forming extensive populations of intermediate plants.

Flowering period: May through September.

SUBFAMILY V. ERAGROSTOIDEAE   321

Fig. 169. *Chloris virgata*. Plant and spikelet. From Gould, 1951.

322   THE GRASSES OF TEXAS

Fig. 170. *Chloris verticillata.* Plant and spikelet. From Gould, 1951.

SUBFAMILY V. ERAGROSTOIDEAE   323

4. **Chloris andropogonoides** Fourn., Mex. Pl. 2:143. 1886. SLIMSPIKE WINDMILLGRASS. Fig. 171. Perennial. *Culms* erect, tufted to shortly stoloniferous, glabrous, 10-40 cm tall. *Sheaths* glabrous, somewhat flattened and keeled. *Ligule* a short naked crown. *Blades* glabrous or scabrous except sparsely pilose basally, to 20 cm long, 2-4 mm wide. *Panicle* branches 6-13, mostly 4-15 cm long, usually radiating in a single series, occasionally a second poorly-developed verticil produced above. *Spikelets,* pale to tawny, appressed to and widely spaced on the branch rachis, with about 4-7 spikelets per cm of rachis. *Glumes* narrowly lanceolate, acute, thin; glabrous except for the scabrous midnerve, the first glume 2-2.3 mm long, the second 3-3.3 mm long. *Lemma of lower floret* narrowly lanceolate to elliptic, the margins and keel appressed-pilose, otherwise glabrous, 1.9-2.7 mm long, acute at apex and with an awn 1.9-5.2 mm long. *Sterile floret* 1, narrowly cylindrical, more or less flattened, glabrous, 0.9-1.7 mm long, with an obtuse apex and an awn 2.5-3.5 mm long. *Chromosome number,* $2n=40$.

Distribution. Texas: Region 2 in open pastures and lawn areas and along roadsides. General: Texas and northern Mexico.

Flowering period: April through October.

This species hybridizes with *Chloris cucullata* and *C. verticillata* where their ranges overlap, sometimes forming rather large hybrid populations, especially in disturbed areas.

5. **Chloris texensis** Nash, Bull. Torrey. Bot. Club. 23:151. 1896. Cespitose perennial. *Culms* erect, glabrous, 30-45 cm tall. *Sheaths* glabrous to sparsely pilose. *Ligule* a low membranous crown. *Blades* scabrous, to 15 cm long, about 4 mm wide. *Panicle* with 8-10 branches to 20 cm long; branches radiate, occasionally in two verticils, floriferous on distal one-half to three-fourths only. *Spikelets* widely spaced, mostly 3-4 per cm of rachis, tawny. *Glumes* lanceolate, glabrous except for the scabrous midnerve, the first glume 2.7-3 mm long, the second 3.5-3.8 mm long. *Lemma of lower floret* lanceolate, 3.7-4.3 mm long, the upper margins sparsely appressed-ciliate, otherwise glabrous; awn 7-11 mm long. *Sterile floret* 1, narrowly elliptical, acute, glabrous, 2-2.5 mm long, with an awn 4.5-6.5 mm long. *Chromosome number* not reported.

Distribution. Texas: Regions 2 and 3 (Brazoria, Brazos and Harris counties), endemic, rare. Few specimens have been collected and most of these were collected over 30 years ago.

Flowering period: October through November.

6. **Chloris cucullata** Bisch., Ann. Sci. Nat. Bot. III. 19:357. 1853. HOODED WINDMILLGRASS. Fig. 172. Perennial. *Culms* erect, tufted, glabrous, 15-60 cm tall. *Sheaths* glabrous. *Ligule* a short-ciliate crown. *Blades* glabrous to scabrous, to 20 cm long, 2-4 mm wide. *Panicles* with 10-20 branches 2-5 cm long, these flexuous or arcuate, borne in several close-radiating verticils. *Spikelets* at first straw-colored and later becoming tawny,

Fig. 171. *Chloris andropogonoides.* Inflorescence and spikelet. From Gould and Box, 1965.

closely-spaced and widely divergent, with about 14-18 spikelets per cm of rachis. *Glumes* lanceolate to obovate, glabrous except for the scabrous midnerve, membranous, the first glume 0.5-0.7 mm long, the second 1-1.5 mm long. *Lower lemma* broadly elliptic, glabrous except for the appressed-pilose keel and margins, 1.5-2 mm long, awn 0.3-1.5 mm long, with an obtuse apex. *Sterile floret* 1, markedly inflated, with the upper margins inrolled, 1-1.5 mm long, unawned or with an awn to 1.5 mm long. *Chromosome number*, 2n=40.

Distribution. Texas: Regions 2, 6, 7, 8, 9 and 10, frequent in the central and western portions of the State, mainly in pastures and along roadsides and in lawns, parks and waste areas. General: Texas, New Mexico and Nuevo Leon and Tamaulipas, Mexico.

Flowering period: May through September.

Chloris cucullata hybridizes with *C. verticillata* and *C. andropogonoides* in areas where their ranges overlap, sometimes forming rather large hybrid populations. The hybrids are mostly morphologically intermediate between the parents.

SUBFAMILY V. ERAGROSTOIDEAE   325

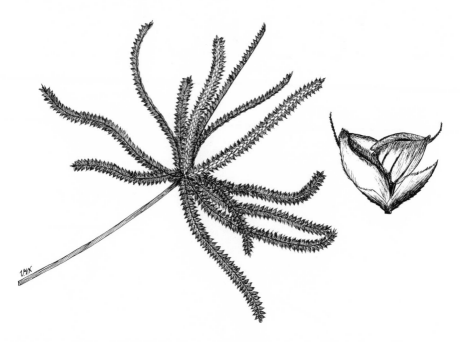

Fig. 172. *Chloris cucullata.* Inflorescence and spikelet. From Gould and Box, 1965.

*7. **Chloris subdolichostachya** Muller, Bot. Ztg. 19:341. 1861. *Chloris latisquamea* Nash, Bull. Torrey Bot. Club 25:439. 1898. SHORTSPIKE WINDMILLGRASS. Strongly stoloniferous perennial, with culms 30-70 (-90) cm tall. *Leaves* glabrous, crowded towards culm base, with keeled and laterally compressed sheaths. *Blades* linear, 10-20 (-30) cm long and 1.5-3 (-4) mm broad. *Inflorescence* highly variable in length, thickness and arrangement of branches. *Branches* 5-numerous, 3-17.6 cm long, bearing closely-placed spikelets to the base. *Spikelets* with a single rudiment. *Lemma of lower floret* 2.2-2.9 mm long, appressed-pilose on midnerve and margins, with an awn 2-5 mm long. *Rudiment* variable in length and width, usually 0.5-1.4 mm wide and with a truncate, cuneate or rounded apex. *Mature florets* black or remaining light-colored at maturity. *Chromosome* number, $2n=40$-84.

Distribution. Texas: Regions 2, 3, 4, 5, 6 and 7 on sand and clay but mostly on slightly disturbed, sandy sites. General: Texas and northeastern Mexico.

Flowering period: May to October.

*This species has been amended to the *Chloris* treatment by F. W. Gould and was not included in the manuscript prepared by Dr. Anderson. Characterization of the *C. subdolichostachya* taxon has largely been taken from that of L. E. Brown (A Biosystematic Study of the *Chloris cucullata* - *Chloris verticillata* complex, Texas A&M University PhD dissertation, 1969). Further investigation is needed to more accurately determine the status of populations referable to this taxon.

Chloris subdolichostachya apparently is made up largely or possibly entirely of hybrid derivatives of *C. cucullata* X *C. verticillata* crosses and *C. cucullata* X *C. andropogonoides* crosses. Tetraploid ($2n=40$) populations with regular meiosis and good seed set have been sampled in San Patricio and Brazos counties, but these may represent stabilized tetraploid hybrids. Plants referable to *C. subdolichostachya* are exceedingly abundant in the southeastern portion of the State. In the Bryan-College Station area of Brazos County this is perhaps the most common native warm-season perennial grass of roadsides, vacant lots, golf courses, pastures and other disturbed sites.

8. **Chloris inflata** Link., Enum. Pl. 1:105. 1821. Annual. *Culms* slender, erect to decumbent and rooting at lower nodes. *Sheaths* glabrous. *Ligule* short, often pilose, occasionally short-ciliate. *Blades* flat, often glabrous, occasionally pilose toward the base, to 15 cm long, 3-6 mm wide. *Panicle* with 7-15 digitate, more or less erect branches 3-8 cm long. *Spikelets* tawny, closely imbricate, with about 14 spikelets per cm of rachis. *Glumes* narrowly lanceolate, hyaline, glabrous except for the scabrous midnerve, the first glume 1.2-2.1 mm long, the second 2.3-2.7 mm long. *Lemma of lower floret* ovate to elliptic, 2-2.7 mm long, pilose, the keel glabrous to pilose, the internerves usually glabrous, occasionally sparsely pilose; lemma awn 4-7.7 mm long. *Sterile florets* usually 2, occasionally 3, the lower enclosing the upper, narrowly turbinate, inflated, truncate, usually glabrous, the lower floret(s) 0.9-1.3 mm long, with an awn 5-7 mm long, the upper floret(s) similar but smaller. *Chromosome number,* $2n=20$.

Distribution. Texas: Extreme southern portion of region 6 (Hidalgo County), a roadside weed. General: Worldwide in tropical to warm temperate regions.

Flowering period: June through October.

9. **Chloris ciliata** Sw., Prodr. Veg. Ind. Occ. 25. 1788. FRINGED CHLORIS. Fig. 173. Tufted perennial. *Culms* erect, slender, 25-60 cm tall, glabrous. *Sheaths* glabrous. *Ligule* wanting or a short ciliate crown. *Blades* long-acuminate, 10-20 cm long and about 5 mm wide, glabrous or scabrous. *Panicles* with 3-5 (rarely 6-7) digitate, somewhat flexuous or spreading branches 3.5-6 cm long. *Spikelets* brown, closely inserted and appressed on the scabrous to hirsute rachis. *Glumes* narrowly lanceolate, glabrous except for the scabrous midnerve, with hyaline margins, the first glume 1.3-1.7 mm long, the second 2-2.5 mm long. *Lower lemma* strongly flattened, elliptic, 1.8-2.8 mm long, awn 0.9-2.7 mm long, the margins and keel strongly ciliate. *Sterile florets* 2, the lower enclosing the upper, truncate, glabrous, 1.3-1.8 mm long, with an awn 0.9-1.4 mm long; upper sterile floret similar but smaller, awnless. *Chromosome number,* $2n=40$.

Distribution. Texas: Regions 2 and 6 on heavy loam, sometimes in silty or sandy soils, often along highway right-of-ways. General: Texas, northern Mexico, Yucatan, Cuba and other Caribbean Islands, Argentina and Uruguay.

Flowering period: March through October.

Fig. 173. *Chloris ciliata.* Spikelet. From Gould and Box, 1965.

10. **Chloris canterai** Arech., Anales Mus. Nac. Montevideo 5:386. 1896. Fig. 174. Tufted perennial. *Culms* erect, slender, glabrous, to 1 m tall. *Sheaths* glabrous. *Ligule* long-ciliate with hairs to 7 mm long. *Blades* narrow, often inrolled and appearing filiform, to 25 cm long, 1-5 mm wide. *Panicles* with usually 3-6 (occasionally 2-9) erect to arcuate, digitate branches 4-14 cm long, bearing about 11 spikelets per cm of rachis. *Spikelets* brown, densely imbricate. *Glumes* narrowly lanceolate, glabrous except for the scabrous midnerve, the margins hyaline, the first glume 1.6-2.4 mm long, the second 2.3-3.8 mm long. *Lemma of lower floret* flattened, narrowly ovate, 3- (2.7-) 3.7 mm long, with a densely ciliate keel and an awn 2.4-5.5 mm long. *Sterile florets* 2-3, turbinate, flattened, glabrous, 1.1-1.8 mm long, the lowermost with an awn 1.5-3.5 mm long; upper sterile floret or florets similar but smaller and enclosed by the lower. *Chromosome number* $2n=36$.

Distribution. Texas: Regions 2 and 6, primarily in Atascosa, Bexar, Jackson, Milam and Wharton counties as a naturalized introduction on sandy to clay or loamy soils, especially on low lying right-of-ways. General: Native to northern Argentina, Paraguay and Uruguay.

Flowering period: April through September.

Texas plants of this species were referred to *C. polydactyla* (L.) Swartz by Gould and Box (1965).

11. **Chloris divaricata** R. Br., Prodr. Fl. Nov. Holl. 1:186. 1810. Perennial. *Culms* to 50 cm tall but usually shorter, stoloniferous, sometimes mat-forming. *Sheaths* glabrous. *Ligule* a short ciliate crown. *Blades* glabrous to scabrous, usually 5-10 cm long, 1-1.5 mm wide. *Panicles* with 3-9 widely diverging branches 4-17 cm long. *Spikelets* widely spaced, with 3-7 spikelets per cm of rachis, appressed, tawny. *Glumes* narrowly lanceolate, thin and membranous, glabrous except for the scabrous midnerve, the first glume 0.9-1.8 mm long, the second 2-2.9 mm long. *Lemma of lower floret* linear to

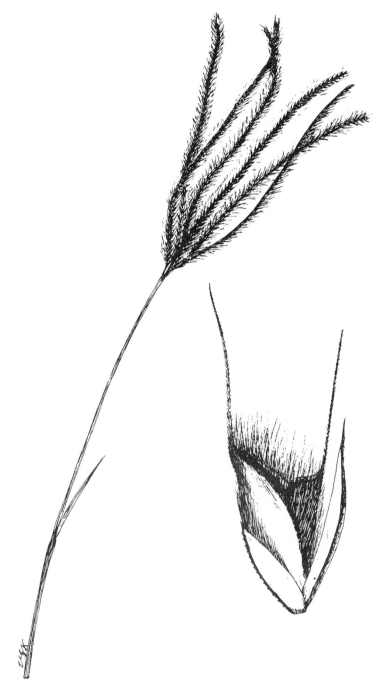

Fig. 174.   *Chloris canterai*. Inflorescence and spikelet. From Gould and Box, 1965, as *C. poly-dactyla*.

SUBFAMILY V. ERAGROSTOIDEAE   329

narrowly lanceolate, 2.9-4 mm long, with glabrous to scabrous or sparsely pubescent margins, the keel and internerves scabrous, the apex acute, bilobed, with lobes to one-half the lemma length; awn 7.5-17 mm long. *Sterile floret* one, narrowly elliptic, bilobed, the lobes to one-half the floret length, with an awn 4.5-9.5 mm long. *Chromosome number* unknown.

Distribution. Texas: Adventive in region 2, known only from isolated collections in Nueces and Refugio Counties. General: Native to Australia, Fiji and the Tonga Islands.

Flowering period: May through July.

12. **Chloris chloridea** (Presl) Hitchc., Proc. Biol. Soc., Wash. 41:162. 1928. BURYSEED CHLORIS. Fig. 175. Perennial with cleistogamous spikelets at the tips of long, scaly, branched rhizomes. *Culms* erect, glabrous, to 1 m tall. *Sheaths* mostly glabrous, occasionally sparsely long-pilose near apex. *Ligules* strongly ciliate on lower leaves, those of the upper leaves reduced to a low crown. *Blades* scabrous, occasionally pilose, to 30 cm long and 1 cm wide. *Panicles* with 3-15 (usually less than 10) branches 6-10 cm long; branches in several well-separated verticils, occasionally single at the nodes. *Spikelets* tawny, appressed and widely spaced on the rachis, with about 4 spikelets per cm of rachis. *Glumes* markedly unequal, lanceolate, glabrous except for the scabrous midnerve, the first glume 1-2 mm long, the second 2-3.5 mm long. *Lemma of lower floret* linear to narrowly lanceolate, dorsally compressed, acuminate, with ciliate margins but otherwise glabrous, 4.5-7.5 mm long; lemma awns 6.5-15 mm long, arising between two setae. *Sterile floret* 1, compressed, scabrous to short-pilose, 1.4-3 mm long, with an awn 2-8 mm long. *Chromosome number*, $2n=80$.

Distribution. Texas: Regions 2, 4 (Brazos County) and 6, occasional in grasslands, brushy areas and old fields. General: Texas and southern Arizona, northern Mexico and Honduras.

Flowering period: October through November.

The underground cleistogamous spikelets are an unusual and interesting feature of *Chloris chloridea*, the only species of the genus to have this character.

13. **Chloris pluriflora** (Fourn.) Clayton, Kew Bull. 21:102. 1967. *Trichloris pluriflora* Fourn. MULTIFLOWERED FALSE-RHODES-GRASS. Perennial. *Culms* to 1.5 m tall, stoloniferous or tufted, glabrous. *Sheaths* glabrous to sparsely hirsute. *Ligule* prominently ciliate. *Blades* scabrous to sparsely hirsute, to 30 cm long, 1 cm wide. *Panicle* with 7-20 somewhat divaricate branches to 20 cm long, these in a few rather distant verticils. *Spikelets* pale to tawny, imbricate, with 7-9 spikelets per cm of rachis. *Glumes* lanceolate, glabrous except for the scabrous midrib, the first glume 2-3 mm long, the second 3-5 mm long. *Perfect florets* 1-2, occasionally a third with rudimentary pistils and stamens. *Lemma of lowermost floret* narrowly lanceolate, 3-5 mm long, 3-awned, the margins short-ciliate near

Fig. 175. *Chloris chloridea.* Base of plant showing cleistogenes on rhizomes, leafy culm with inflorescence, aerial spikelet (left), caryopsis of aerial spikelet (left center) and large caryopsis of subterranean spikelet (center). From Gould and Box, 1965.

middle, the upper portions sparsely scabrous, otherwise glabrous; central awn 8-12 mm long, lateral awns 0.5-1.5 mm long. *Sterile florets* 2-3, rarely 1, narrowly lanceolate, 1.5-3 mm long, with central awn of upper sterile florets to 8 mm long, the lateral awns 0.2-1 mm long. *Chromosome number,* $2n = 60$.

Distribution. Texas: Regions 2 and 6 in silt or clay, generally in low areas. General: Southern Texas, Mexico and Central and South America.

Flowering period: July to September.

Fig. 176. *Chloris crinita*. Plant and spikelet with florets separated from glumes. From Gould, 1951, as *Trichloris mendocina*.

14. **Chloris crinita** Lag., Nov. Gen. et. Sp. 5. 1816. *Trichloris crinita* (Lag.) Parodi. FALSE-RHODESGRASS. Fig. 176. Perennial. *Culms* to 1 m tall, glabrous, tufted or stoloniferous. *Sheaths* glabrous to sparsely hirsute. *Ligules* prominently ciliate. *Blades* scabrous, to 20 cm long, 5-10

mm wide. *Panicles* with 6-20 branches, these to 15 cm long in several close verticils. *Spikelets* imbricate, with 7-9 spikelets per cm of rachis, pale to tawny. *Glumes* narrowly lanceolate, glabrous except for the scabrous midnerve, the first glume 0.8-1.1 mm long, the second 2-2.5 mm long. *Lower lemma* dorsally flattened, narrowly lanceolate to elliptic, scabrous especially above middle, 2.4-3.8 mm long, 3-awned, the central awn 8-12 mm long, the lateral awns usually shorter. *Sterile floret* usually 1, occasionally 2, greatly reduced, cylindrical, 1-1.5 mm long, gradually narrowing into subequal awns 5-7 mm long. *Chromosome number*, $2n=40$.

Distribution. Texas: Primarily region 10, occasional in region 7 and rare elsewhere in scattered localities, mostly in heavy alluvial soils near streams. General: Texas, Arizona, New Mexico, Chihuahua, Coahuila, Durango, Argentina, Bolivia, Paraguay and Venezuela.

Flowering period: May through September.

74. EUSTACHYS Desv.*

Rhizomatous, stoloniferous or cespitose perennials with erect culms and panicles of a few to many digitately to subdigitately arranged one-sided branches. *Leaves* glabrous, with flattened, overlapping sheaths and acute to blunt blade apices, the blades often folded. *Ligule* a naked to ciliate crown, sometimes wanting. *Spikelets* with 1 perfect floret, usually dark brown or nearly black, occasionally tawny; disarticulation above glumes. *Glumes* unequal, the first lanceolate, acute, the second nearly linear, bilobed at apex, with a short awn arising between the lobes. *Lemma* of perfect floret, ovate to elliptic, 3-nerved, scabrous or pubescent, with obscure nerves, bearded callus, shortly to prominently pubescent margins, glabrous to scabrous or sparsely appressed-pilose internerves, and glabrous nerves; lemma apex mucronate to short-awned. *Paleas* shorter than lemmas, the nerves scabrous. *Sterile floret* usually 1, mostly neuter but sometimes staminate, cylindrical to rudimentary, awnless to short-awned. *Caryopses* brown, ovoid to trigonous, the embryos one-third to one-half the length of the caryopses. *Basic chromosome number*, $x=10$.

A genus of 12 species widely distributed in tropical and warm-temperate regions. In the United States the greatest number of species is found in Florida.

Hitchcock (1935) and Chase (1951) treated *Eustachys* as a section of *Chloris*. The two genera differ most conspicuously in the bilobed, short-aristate glumes of *Eustachys* as contrasted with the lanceolate or acuminate glumes of *Chloris*.

Lemma midnerve densely appressed-pubescent; spikelets generally dark brown; on coastal strand   1. *E. petraea*

*Contributed by Dennis Anderson.

Fig. 177. *Eustachys petraea*. Inflorescence and spikelet. From Gould and Box, 1965.

Lemma midnerve glabrous; spikes pale to tawny; mostly inland in distribution   2. *E. retusa*

1. **Eustachys petraea** (Sw.) Desv., Nouv. Bull. Soc. Philom. Paris
2:189. 1810. *Chloris petraea* Sw. Fig. 177. Stoloniferous to tufted perennial. *Culms* erect, glabrous, leafless in upper portions, 20-120 cm tall.
Sheaths glabrous. *Ligule* a short ciliate crown. *Blades* scabrous, usually
obtuse; to 20 cm long, 0.8-1 cm wide. *Panicles* with 2-8 erect or spreading-
erect branches 4-12 cm long. *Spikelets* widely divergent, closely imbricate, with usually 15-30 spikelets per cm of rachis. *Glumes* unequal, glabrous except for the scabrous midnerve; first glume narrowly lanceolate,
0.9-1.5 mm long, the second nearly linear, 1.1-1.7 mm long, short-awned
from the obtusely lobed apex. *Lemma of lower floret* ovate-lanceolate,
obtuse to acute, dark brown at maturity, 1.1-2.5 mm long and 0.2-0.5 mm
wide, pilose on upper one-half to three-fourths with hairs 0.1-0.4 mm
long; lemma apex awnless or mucronate. *Sterile floret* 1, cylindrical, truncate, glabrous below, scabrous above, 0.8-1 mm long, awnless or short-
mucronate. *Chromosome number*, 2n=40.

Distribution. Texas: Region 2, common in beach sand. General: Coastal
strand, North Carolina to Florida and Texas and also in Mexico.

Flowering period: March through December.

2. **Eustachys retusa** (Lag.) Kunth, Rev. Gram. 1:88. 1829. Tufted perennial. *Culms* erect, 25-90 cm tall. *Sheaths* glabrous, strongly flattened. *Ligule* a small scale. *Blades* flat to somewhat folded, glabrous with scabrous margins, to 20 cm long, about 1 cm wide. *Panicle* with 3-14 digitate, more or less erect branches 4-9 cm long. *Spikelets* divergent, closely imbricate, with about 21 spikelets per cm of rachis. *Glumes* unequal, glabrous except for the scabrous midnerve, the first glume inequilateral, lanceolate, 1.1-1.2 mm long, the second linear, 1.5-1.8 mm long, short-awned from an obtusely lobed apex. *Lemma of lower floret* ovate-elliptic, acute, pale brown, 1.9-2.7 mm long, mostly 0.7-0.9 mm wide, glabrous except for the strongly ciliate margin and bearded callus, the marginal hairs to 1 mm long. *Sterile floret* 1, cylindric to narrowly obdeltoid-truncate, glabrous below, scabrous above, awnless or mucronate, 1.2-1.8 mm long and 0.6-0.8 mm wide. *Chromosome number*, $2n = 40$.

Distribution. Texas: Regions 3 and 4 on disturbed roadsides. General: Adventive in Texas from South America.

Flowering period: May through September.

This species has been confused with *E. distichophylla* (Lag.) Nees. The latter has much longer, flexuous spikes and acute sterile florets.

75. BOUTELOUA Lag.

Tufted annuals and perennials of diverse habit, some with rhizomes or stolons. *Leaves* mostly basal, with flat or folded, usually narrow blades. *Ligule* commonly a ring of hairs. *Inflorescence* of 1-numerous short, spicate branches, these closely or distantly spaced along the main axis. *Inflorescence branches* with 1-numerous sessile spikelets in 2 rows along the margins of an angular or flattened rachis. Disarticulation at base of the branch rachis or above glumes. *Spikelets* with 1 perfect floret and 1-3 staminate or sterile florets above. *Glumes* lanceolate, 1-nerved, unequal to nearly equal, awnless or short-awned. *Lemmas* 3-nerved, the midnerve often extending into an awn, the lateral nerves occasionally short-awned. *Paleas* membranous, the 2 nerves occasionally awn-tipped.

About 40 species, mostly in North America but several in Central and South America.

Inflorescence branches deciduous as a whole; spikelets mostly 1-9 per branch (section *Bouteloua*) **A**

Inflorescence branches persistent, the spikelets disarticulating above the glumes; spikelets mostly 15-60 per branch (section *Chondrosioides*) **AA**

A

Inflorescence branches usually 20-50 or more per culm

SUBFAMILY V. ERAGROSTOIDEAE 335

Inflorescence branches all or mostly bearing 2-9 spikelets

Leaf blades, at least some, more than 2.5 mm broad; anthers usually red, orange or yellow, rarely blue or purple   1.   *B. curtipendula*

Leaf blades 1-2 (-2.5) mm broad, usually involute on drying; anthers purple   2.   *B. warnockii*

Inflorescence branches all or mostly bearing 1 spikelet   3.   *B. uniflora*

Inflorescence branches less than 20, usually less than 15

Plants annual; branch rachis densely hirsute, at least near base
4.   *B. aristidoides*

Plants perennial; branch rachis hirsute or glabrous

Glumes hairy, the hairs not confined to midnerve

Glumes and branch rachis densely and conspicuously hairy; western Texas   5.   *B. chondrosioides*

Glumes and branch rachis usually sparsely and inconspicuously hairy; spikelets with a single 3-awned rudiment; frequent in eastern and central Texas, absent from far western Texas
6.   *B. rigidiseta*

Glumes glabrous or with spicules or short, stiff hairs on the midnerve

First glume usually 4.5-6 mm long, nearly as long and broad as second glume; southern Texas   7.   *B. repens*

First glume usually 2-3 mm long, much shorter and narrower than second glume; western Texas   2.   *B. warnockii*

AA

Plants annual

Inflorescence a unilateral spike (actually a single spicate branch)
8.   *B. simplex*

Inflorescence (of at least some culms) with 2-4 spicate branches
9.   *B. barbata*

Plants perennial

Outer (second) glume without papilla-based hairs, hispid or not

Culm internodes, at least the lower, woolly-pubescent
                                                    12. *B. eriopoda*

Culm internodes not pubescent

  Inflorescence branches mostly 3-20

    Inflorescence branches 3-8   10. *B. trifida*

    Inflorescence branches 12-20   11. *B. kayii*

  Inflorescence branches 1-3 (-4)

    Culms usually with 4-10 nodes; base of plant firm and relatively
      "woody"   13. *B. breviseta*

    Culms usually with 2-3 nodes; base of plant firm but not woody
                                                    14. *B. gracilis*

Outer (second) glume with papilla-based hairs

  Rachis ending with a spikelet, this often reduced and pointed
                                                    14. *B. gracilis*

  Rachis projecting beyond insertion of terminal spikelet, the tip often
    long-extended

    Tuft of hairs not present at base of lowermost rudiment; anthers
      2-2.5 mm long; culms mostly 15-40 cm tall
                                                    15. *B. hirsuta*

    Tuft of hairs present at base of lowermost rudiment; anthers about
      3 mm long; culms 35-75 cm tall   16. *B. pectinata*

    1. **Bouteloua curtipendula** (Michx.) Torr., in Emory, Notes Mil. Reconn. 154. 1848. SIDEOATS GRAMA. Perennial with flat, linear leaf blades. *Herbage* mostly glabrous, infrequently the leaves puberulent. *Lower margins of blades* usually sparsely ciliate with papilla-based hairs. *Ligule* a short, dense fringe of hairs seldom over 0.5 mm long. *Inflorescence* usually with 30-80 short, pendant branches, these 1-3 (-4) cm long, bearing 1-12 or more sessile spikelets. *Mean number of spikelets per inflorescence branch* 2-7, the number of spikelets per branch less at culm apex than at base. *Glumes* glabrous or scabrous, the first glume two-thirds or more as long as the second, the second usually 5.5-8 mm long. *Lemma* usually slightly shorter than second glume, glabrous or scabrous-strigose, often minutely rugose, acute or slightly 3-toothed at apex, with the nerves extending as short mucro. *Paleas* slightly shorter than the lemmas and similar in texture.

Rudiment variable but usually comprised of a lemma with a short, membranous base and 3 unequally-developed awns, the terminal awn occasionally to as much as 7 mm long.

Plants with creeping rhizomes; culms not in large clumps, decumbent
at base or stiffly erect
1A.   *B. curtipendula* var. *curtipendula*

Plants without creeping rhizomes, the base "knotty" in some forms; culms
in large or small clumps, stiffly erect
1B.   *B. curtipendula* var. *caespitosa*

1A. **Bouteloua curtipendula** (Michx.) Torr. var. **curtipendula.** Fig. 178. *Culms* single or in small clusters from slender or stout creeping rhizomes. *Leaves* mostly glabrous but infrequently puberulent, the blades flat, usually 3-7 mm broad and bluish-green but variable in width and color, usually with a few papilla-based cilia on lower margins. *Inflorescence* typically large, with a stout axis bearing 40-70 or more reflexed branches, these bearing an average of 3-7 spikelets. *Glumes* and *lemmas* typically purple or purple-tinged. *Anthers* red or red-orange, infrequently orange, yellow or purple. *Chromosome number* tetraploid ($2n=40$) or aneuploid from $2n=41$ to $2n=66$.

Distribution. Texas: Throughout the State in open grasslands, woods borders and road right-of-ways, generally in the better soils and on little-disturbed sites. Less frequent in western Texas than var. *caespitosa*. General: Southeastern Canada through the prairie and plains regions of the central United States to Colorado, southern Utah, Texas, New Mexico, Arizona and north central Mexico.

Flowering period: Mostly June through November.

This rhizomatous mid-grass provides excellent forage throughout its range. Genetically it is closely interrelated with *B. curtipendula* var. *caespitosa*, which for the most part has a different range and occupies a different ecological niche. Relationships of these varieties and other species of the *B. curtipendula* complex are discussed by Gould & Kapadia (1962, 1964) and Kapadia & Gould (1964a, 1964b).

1B. **Bouteloua curtipendula** (Michx.) Torr. var. **caespitosa** Gould & Kapadia, Brittonia 16:203. 1964. *Culms* stiffly erect, from ca. 0.5-1 m tall, usually stout and in large clumps, often from a hard "knotty" base; stolons and creeping rhizomes not developed. *Leaf blades* variable in width but most frequently narrow, typically thick and stiff. *Inflorescence* highly variable, with few to numerous branches, an average of 2-7 spikelets per branch. *Spikelet color* from bronze, yellowish-brown or straw-colored to green or various shades of purple. *Anthers* usually yellow or orange, infrequently red or purple. *Chromosome number* aneuploid, varying from $2n=58$ to 103.

Distribution. Texas: Regions 5, 6, 7 and 10, mostly on loose, limey soils, most common in western Texas and the western portion of the Edwards

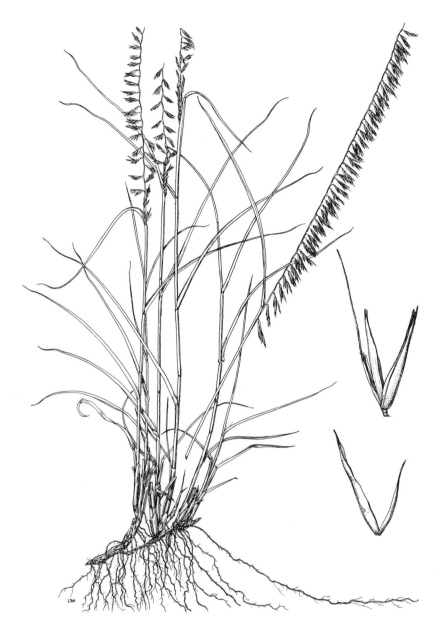

Fig. 178. *Bouteloua curtipendula* var. *curtipendula*. Plant and spikelet with glumes separated from florets. From Gould, 1951.

Plateau. General: Oklahoma, southern Colorado, Utah, Texas, New Mexico, Arizona and southern California through the highlands of northern and central Mexico to Oaxaca and in Venezuela, Bolivia, Uruguay, Argentina and Peru.

Flowering period: Mostly June to November.

SUBFAMILY V. ERAGROSTOIDEAE   339

2. **Bouteloua warnockii** Gould & Kapadia, Southw. Naturalist 7:176. 1962. WARNOCK GRAMA. Plants perennial, cespitose, with culms in tufts mostly 4-10 cm in diameter. *Culms* 20-35 (-50) cm tall, stiffly erect. *Leaves* bluish-green, more or less glaucous, glabrous except for long and short hairs in ligular area and a few long papilla-based hairs on basal margins of blades. *Ligule* a ring of hairs 1-1.5 mm long. *Blades* 1-1.5 (-2.5) mm broad, 5-15 (-25) cm long, stiffly erect or stiffly curving, tapering to a fine tip, involute on drying. *Inflorescence* well exserted, usually 5-10 cm long and with 9-15 (-25) rather widely-spaced branches. *Rachis of inflorescence branch* scabrous, 4-5.5 mm long, bearing usually 2-6 spikelets on the basal one-fourth to one-third. *Spikelets* 5-6.5 mm long. *Glumes and lemma* green, often with a purplish or brownish cast. *First glume* slightly shorter than second, both usually shorter than lemma. *Anthers* dark purple. *Rudiment* well-developed, usually about as long as lemma, awned but the awns only slightly or not at all exserted. *Chromosome numbers* reported, $2n = 21$, 22, 23, 24, 25, 28, 38 and 40.

Distribution. Texas: Region 10 on limestone ledges and dry slope below limestone outcrops. General: Texas, southern New Mexico and north-central Mexico.

Flowering period: June to August.

Bouteloua warnockii was observed to be growing with *B. curtipendula* var. *caespitosa* at three localities, and this close association probably is consistent throughout its range. Hybridization between the two is suspected and may be at least partially responsible for the aneuploidy in *B. warnockii* populations.

3. **Bouteloua uniflora** Vasey, Bot. Gaz. 16:26. 1891. NEALLEY GRAMA. Tufted perennial, lacking rhizomes or stolons. *Culms* glabrous, slender, stiffly erect. *Leaves* essentially glabrous or minutely scabrous, usually with a few long hairs in the vicinity of the ligule and on the blade margins. *Ligule* a minute fringe of hairs. *Blades* narrow and flat but usually involute on drying, 1-2 mm broad. *Inflorescence branches* bearing 1 spikelet (rarely 2) near the base of a stiff narrow rachis about 5 mm in length. *Glumes* broad, thin, acute or slightly notched and minutely apiculate, usually scabrous on midnerve, the first glume 3-4 mm long, the second 7-8 mm long. *Lemma* slightly shorter than second glume, acute or minutely notched, awnless. *Palea* similar to lemma in texture but slightly shorter. *Anthers* bright lemon yellow, 2.5-3 mm long. *Rudiment* absent or minute and represented by 1 or 3 short bristles. *Chromosome number,* $2n = 20$.

Distribution. Texas: Regions 7 and 10 on fertile soils, rather frequent in rocky, limey soils of the central Edwards Plateau, infrequent in western Texas. General: Texas and New Mexico; one doubtful record from southern Utah.

Flowering period: July to November.

All Texas plants of the species are referable to var. *uniflora*. A rather distinct taxon of northern Mexico with short, tufted leaves, short culms and relatively few inflorescence branches has been named *B. uniflora* var. *coahuilensis* Gould & Kapadia.

4. **Bouteloua aristidoides** (H.B.K.) Griseb., Fl. Brit. West Indies 537. 1864. NEEDLE GRAMA. Fig. 179. Tufted, short-lived annual. *Culms* 6-50 cm or more long, weak, slender, the lateral ones of a tuft geniculate and curving erect from a decumbent base. *Sheaths* usually much shorter than the internodes. *Ligule* a minute, puberulent rim. *Blades* short, thin, flat or folded, 1-2 mm broad, mostly glabrous but often with a few long hairs at the base. *Inflorescences* uinilateral, mostly 2.5-10 cm long, usually with 4-15 short, loosely-spaced and spreading, readily deciduous branches. *Inflorescence branches* mostly 1-2 cm long and with 1-4 spikelets, with a sharp-pointed hairy basal callus. *Branch rachis* flattened, densely pubescent at least near base, the curved tip extended 5-10 mm beyond insertion of terminal spikelet. *Lowermost spikelet* closely appressed to rachis, usually without a rudiment and with an awnless or minutely awned lemma. *Upper spikelets* with a 3-awned lemma and a rudiment reduced to an awn column and awns mostly 2-6 mm long. *Glumes* very unequal, narrowly acute or acuminate, the larger one often spreading from the floret. *Lemma* about as long as upper glume, with short or long awns. *Caryopses* brownish, narrow, flattened, mostly 2.5-3 mm long. *Chromosome number,* $2n = 40$.

Distribution. Texas: Regions 6, 7 and 10 on dry, open slopes and along washes, often on graded roadsides. General: Texas to southern California and Mexico and widespread in drier parts of South America.

Flowering period: Mostly August to October but occasionally May to November.

5. **Bouteloua chondrosioides** (H.B.K.) Benth. *ex* Wats., Proc. Amer. Acad. Sci. 18:179. 1883. SPRUCETOP GRAMA. Tufted perennial with culms from a firm but not rhizomatous base. *Culms* mostly 30-60 cm tall, erect or slightly spreading at base. *Sheaths* rounded, often with a few long hairs on upper margins. *Ligule* a minute, ciliolate rim. *Blades* short, flat, glaucous, 1-2.5 mm broad, usually ciliate on lower margins with long, papilla-based hairs and often with a few hairs on either or both surfaces. *Inflorescence axis* 2.5-6 cm long above the lowermost branch, with 3-8 densely-flowered, deciduous branches mostly 1-15 cm long excluding awns. *Branch rachis* mostly 6-15 mm long, densely pubescent, with a narrow, persistent base 1-2 mm long and a broad, flattened rachis above the point of disarticulation. *Tip of rachis* extending as a point well beyond insertion of uppermost spikelet. *Spikelets* closely placed, mostly 8-12 per branch, with 1 perfect floret and a single, awned rudiment above. All exposed structures of the spikelet more or less hairy. *Lemma of perfect floret* shallowly 3-cleft, the divisions muticous or short-awned. *Lemma of rudiment* 3-awned, the body cleft nearly to base or reduced to a slender awn-column. *Anthers* 3.5-4 mm long. *Chromosome counts* reported, $2n = 20, 22$ and 40.

SUBFAMILY V. ERAGROSTOIDEAE   341

Fig. 179. *Bouteloua aristidoides.* Plant and inflorescence branch with two spikelets and lowermost spikelet. From Gould, 1951.

Distribution. Texas: Region 10 on dry rocky slopes and grassy plateaus. All Texas collections are from Brewster County. General: Texas to Arizona and south through Mexico to Honduras.

Flowering period: Mostly August to October but occasionally earlier.

6. **Bouteloua rigidiseta** (Steud.) Hitchc., J. Wash. Acad. Sci. 23:453. 1933. TEXAS GRAMA. Fig. 180. Tufted perennial with slender, weak culms 15-40 (10-50) cm tall, densely clustered in small clumps. *Ligule* a minute fringe of short hairs. *Blades* narrow, flat or somewhat involute, mostly 4-12 (-17) cm long and 1-2 mm broad, usually sparsely pilose. *Inflorescence axis* 3-6 cm long above the lowermost branch. *Inflorescence branches* with their spikelets wedge-shaped, mostly 0.8-1.6 mm long including the awns, with 3- (2-) 5 closely placed, spreading spikelets, readily deciduous as a single unit. *Branch rachis* sparsely hispid above the hairy base, 4-7 mm long, deeply forked or trifurcate at apex, disarticulating about 0.5 mm above base, leaving a

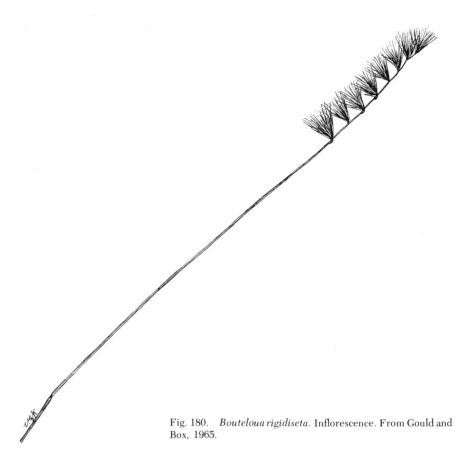

Fig. 180. *Bouteloua rigidiseta*. Inflorescence. From Gould and Box, 1965.

persistent, short stub on the main axis. *Spikelet* with 1 perfect floret and 1 greatly reduced floret. *Glumes* very unequal, the second large, sparsely appressed-pubescent, with a stout midnerve, this extending into a short, stout awn from between 2 thin, narrow, pointed apical lobes. *Lemma of perfect floret* with a glabrous or sparsely hairy body mostly 2.5-4 mm long, this divided above into 2 stout, short, spreading lateral awns and a slightly longer terminal awn extending from between the teeth of a notched apex. *Upper floret* rudimentary, usually reduced to an awn column and 3 awns 5-10 mm long. *Caryopses* narrowly obovate, flattened, with an embryo about two-thirds as long as the endosperm. *Chromosome number*, $2n=40$.

Distribution. Texas: Throughout, except in region 1 and the extreme western portion of the State, in grasslands, grassy woods openings, road right-of-ways and moist slopes. General: Oklahoma and Texas, south to Coahuila and Tamaulipas, Mexico.

Flowering period: April to November under favorable growing conditions.

SUBFAMILY V. ERAGROSTOIDEAE 343

7. **Bouteloua repens** (H.B.K.) Scribn. & Merr., U.S.D.A. Div. Agrost. Bull. 24:26. 1901. *Bouteloua filiformis* (Fourn.) Griffiths. SLENDER GRAMA. Fig. 181. Tufted perennial with slender, weak culms 20-45 cm tall. *Ligule* a minute fringed membrane. *Blades* thin, flat or the tips infolded, mostly 5-16 cm long and 1-3 mm broad, usually sparsely ciliate on margins below middle with long, papilla-based hairs. *Inflorescence* mostly 3-7 cm long, with 4-9 short, spicate branches on a flattened rachis. *Inflorescence branches* 1-2 cm long excluding the awns, with 4-7 (2-8) spikelets, readily deciduous as a unit. *Branch rachis* angular, glabrous or scabrous except at the puberulent base, projecting 2-6 mm above insertion of uppermost spikelet, disarticulating near base, leaving a persistent stub about 0.5 mm long on inflorescence axis. *Spikelets* with a perfect lower floret and a well-developed staminate or neuter floret above. *Glumes* only slightly unequal, 3.5-6 mm long, scabrous on the strong midnerve but otherwise glabrous. *Lemmas* glabrous, usually mucronate or short-awned at apex. *Rudiment* usually staminate, with a well-developed lemma and palea, the lemma with 3 stout awns mostly 3-7 mm long. *Anthers* orange, about 4 mm long. *Chromosome number*, $2n=20$ in Texas plants; other plants of the species with $2n=40$ and 60. A few aneuploid numbers also reported.

Distribution. Texas: Region 6 and southern margin of region 7, in open or brushy pastures and road right-of-ways and along streambanks. General: Southern Texas, New Mexico and Arizona, south through Mexico, Central America and islands of the Caribbean to Venezuela and Colombia.

Flowering period: April to November or December.

8. **Bouteloua simplex** Lag., Var. Cienc. 4:141. 1805. MAT GRAMA. Tufted annual with weak, decumbent-spreading, less frequently erect, culms 3-20 (-35) cm long. *Sheaths* glabrous. *Ligule* a minute, fringed membrane. *Blades* mostly 2-10 cm long and 0.5-1.5 mm broad, flat or involute, often pilose on adaxial surface and ciliate on margins above ligule. *Inflorescence* typically a unilateral spike (actually a single terminal branch) 1-2.5 cm long and with 30-80 closely-placed, pectinate spikelets. Rarely a pair of branches produced at culm apex. *Spikelets* with a perfect floret below and 2 (occasionally 1) rudimentary florets above. *Rachilla* with tufts of hair below lower floret and first rudiment. Disarticulation at a rounded, knob-like callus at base of lower floret. *Glumes* often scabrous near tip, otherwise glabrous, the first glume about one-half as long as the second. *Second glume* 3.5-5 mm long. *Lemma body* 2.5-3.5 mm long, silky-pubescent on nerves, with 3 short, stout awns. *Lower rudiment* with 3 stiff, scabrous awns 1-2 mm long and a stout awn column, the membranous body vestigial or entirely lacking. *Upper rudiment*, when present, a fan-shaped scale. *Chromosome numbers* reported, $2n=20$ and 40.

Distribution. Texas: Region 10 on rocky, open slopes at relatively high altitudes. General: Southern Colorado and Utah to western Texas, New Mexico and Arizona, south through Mexico to Guerrero and widespread in South America from Colombia to Argentina.

Fig. 181. *Bouteloua repens*. Plant. From Gould, 1951, as *B. filiformis*.

Flowering period: Mostly late summer.

9. **Bouteloua barbata** Lag., Var. Cienc. 4:141. 1805. SIXWEEKS GRAMA. Fig. 182. Low, tufted annual with usually geniculate or decumbent-spreading culms. *Leaves* short, mostly basal. *Sheaths* with a tuft of long hairs on either side of collar. *Ligule* a short membrane fringed with hairs to 1 mm long. *Blades* 1.5-7 mm long and 1-1.5 (rarely -3) mm broad, flat or involute, often scabrous and sparsely strigose on adaxial surface with a few long hairs just above ligule. *Inflorescence* with 4-6 (2-9) pectinate, persistent branches, these typically 1-3 cm long and with 25-40 closely-placed spikelets. *Branch rachis* glabrous or minutely scabrous. *Spikelets* 2.5-4 mm long including the short awns, with usually 2 rudiments above the perfect floret. *Glumes* glabrous, the first 1.5-2 mm long, acute or acuminate, the second slightly longer, acute, acuminate or slightly notched and mucronate at apex. *Rachilla* with a tuft of silvery hairs below the awned rudiment. *Lemma of perfect floret* lobed and 3-awned, the awns from shorter than the lobes to 3 mm long. *Body of lemma* densely pubescent, at least on margins. *Lower rudiment* with rounded lobes and 3 awns about as long as those of lemma. *Upper rudiment* reduced to a minute, inflated, awnless vestige. *Chromosome numbers* reported, $2n = 20$ and 40.

Distribution. Texas: Frequent in regions 6, 7, 9 and 10, occasional elsewhere in the State but not recorded from regions 1 and 3, in dry grasslands, roadsides and waste places, usually in sandy soils. General: Southern Colorado and Utah, southward to Oaxaca and Guerrero, Mexico and in Argentina.

Flowering period: April to November.

10. **Bouteloua trifida** Thurb., in Wats., Proc. Amer. Acad. Sci. 18:177. 1883. RED GRAMA. Fig. 183. Perennial with slender, wiry culms mostly 10-30 (8-40) cm long, densely tufted from a firm, often somewhat rhizomatous base. *Leaves* mostly in a basal clump, glabrous, scabrous or puberulent. *Ligule* a minute, fringed membrane. *Blades* flat or loosely infolded. *Basal blades* mostly 4-8 cm long and 1.5 mm or less broad, the upper culm leaves greatly reduced. *Inflorescence* 3-9 cm long with 2-7 slender, persistent branches mostly 12-25 mm long including the awns and with 8-24 (-32) spikelets. *Branch rachis* puberulent at base, scabrous or glabrous above. *Spikelets* with a perfect lower floret and an awned rudimentary floret above. *Glumes* slightly unequal, glabrous, acute, acuminate or mucronate from a slightly bifid apex. *Lemma body* about 2 mm long, glabrous or minutely hairy at base, the hairs not over 0.5 mm long. *Awn of lemma* about twice as long as body. *Rudimentary floret* with awns mostly 3.5-6 mm long and a short awn column. *Chromosome number,* $2n = 20$.

Distribution. Texas: Reported from all regions except regions 1 and 4, frequent in the western half of the State. A grass of dry, often rocky sites, persistent under heavy grazing by livestock. General: Texas, southern Utah, Nevada and California, southward through northern Mexico.

Flowering period: Mostly April to November, flowering whenever growing conditions are favorable.

Fig. 182. *Bouteloua barbata*. Plant. From Gould, 1951.

Plants of *Bouteloua trifida* flowering the first year are sometimes confused with the annual *B. barbata*. The latter has a conspicuously hairy lemma,
relatively short lemma awns and decumbent-spreading culms.

SUBFAMILY V. ERAGROSTOIDEAE   347

Fig. 183. *Bouteloua trifida*. Plant and spikelet with florets separated from glumes. From Gould, 1951.

348   THE GRASSES OF TEXAS

11. **Bouteloua kayii** Warnock, Field and Lab. 23:15-16. 1955. KAY GRAMA. Cespitose perennial. *Culms* stiffly erect and unbranched above base, mostly 20-40 (-50) cm tall, scaberulous in lines (on internerves). *Nodes* all basal or 1, infrequently 2, elevated on elongated internodes, the basal nodes sparsely hispid with long, straight hairs during the growing period but glabrate. *Leaves* glaucous, mostly basal, scaberulous to glabrous. *Ligule* a minute, fringed membrane. *Blades* involute, scaberulous on the adaxial surface, 1-1.5 mm broad. *Inflorescence* with 3-20, usually 7-15 slender, erect branches mostly 1.5-3 cm long and with 6-20, usually 7-14, widely-spaced (2.5-3.5 mm) spikelets on pedicels 0.6-0.8 mm long. *Spikelets* 6-8 mm long including the awns, with a perfect floret below and 1 rudimentary floret above. *Disarticulation* above glumes. *Glumes* about equal, glabrous, 2.5-4 mm long, acute or bidentate at the apex, awnless or the stout midnerve extending as a mucro or short awn. *Lemma* with 3 stout, nearly equal awns, these mostly 3-4 mm long and one-third to one-fourth longer than the glabrous or sparsely strigose body, the central awn from between 2 teeth 0.4-0.6 mm long. *Rudiment* a reduced lemma with stout awns similar in size to those of the lower floret and with a minutely lobed, much reduced membranous base; rudiment and stipe glabrous. *Chromosome number* not reported.

Distribution. Texas: Region 10, known only from the type locality in Brewster County where it grows on limestone. General: Endemic to Texas.

Flowering period: Summer.

A species close to *Bouteloua trifida* but differing in numerous characters. *B. kayii* has stouter, strictly erect culm bases and fewer expanded culm internodes and elevated nodes. The inflorescence branches usually are more numerous and longer, the lemma awns are generally shorter and the lemma body is longer.

12. **Bouteloua eriopoda** (Torr.) Torr., U. S. Rep. Expl. Miss. Pacif. 4:155. 1856. BLACK GRAMA. Fig. 184. Perennial with wiry culms mostly 20-60 cm long from a knotty base. *Culms* typically decumbent and often stoloniferous below, woolly-pubescent on lower internodes. *Leaves* inconspicuous, short, the sheaths much shorter than the internodes. *Ligule* a minute fringed membrane. *Blades* thin, flat or infolded, 0.5-2 mm broad. *Inflorescence* with 3-8 slender, persistent, widely-spaced floriferous branches, these mostly 2-5 cm long and with 8-18 loosely-spaced, non-pectinate spikelets. *Branch rachis* densely white-woolly at base, scabrous or inconspicuously hairy above. *Spikelets* with 1 perfect floret and a single awned rudiment on a long stipe. *Glumes* unequal, glabrous or scabrous, acute or acuminate, the second glume mostly 6-9 mm long. *Lemmas* usually bearded at base and otherwise glabrous but occasionally sparsely puberulent, tapering above to a stout terminal awn mostly 1.5-3 mm long and much-reduced, setaceous lateral awns. *Rudiment* usually bearded at base, with 3 awns 4-8 mm long and a firm, non-membranous base. *Chromosome number*, $2n=20$.

Fig. 184. *Bouteloua eriopoda*. Plant and spikelet with florets separated from glumes. From Gould, 1951.

Distribution. Texas: Regions 7, 8, 9 and 10 on dry slopes and plains, often associated with shrubs and subshrubs on heavily grazed rangelands. General: Colorado and Utah, south to Texas, Arizona and northern Mexico.

Flowering period: June to October.

13. **Bouteloua breviseta** Vasey, Contrib. U. S. Natl. Herb. 1:58. 1890. *Bouteloua ramosa* Vasey. CHINO GRAMA. Perennial with firm or hard, knotty or subrhizomatous base. *Culms* wiry, slender, several- to many-noded, freely branching below middle, mostly 25-70 cm long. *Nodes* pubescent or glabrous. *Prophylls of lateral shoots* (branches) woolly-pubescent with long hairs. *Leaves* small, inconspicuous. *Sheaths* shorter than internodes. *Ligule* a minute, hairy collar. *Blades* flat or inrolled, mostly 0.5-2 mm broad and 1-5 (-7) cm long. *Inflorescences* with 1-4 (usually 2) branches, these 1-3.5 cm long, densely-flowered with 25-45 (-60) pectinately spreading spikelets. *Branch* persistent, attached to main axis by a slender, curved, pubescent peduncle. *Branch rachis* scabrous, terminated by a spikelet but this often greatly reduced and needle-like. *Spikelets* with 1 perfect floret and 1 or 2 reduced florets above, the rachilla with tufts of long hair at the base of perfect and lowermost reduced florets. *Glumes* glabrous or sparsely short-hairy, acute or acuminate, the second glume 2-3.5 mm long. *Lemmas* sparsely to rather densely hairy, with a body 2.5-4 mm long and scabrous awns slightly shorter than the body. *Lower rudiment* with 3 stout awns 3-5 mm long, the upper rudiment, when present, a fan-shaped scale. *Chromosome number*, $2n=40$.

Distribution. Texas: Northwestern portion of region 6, southern portion of region 7 and region 10, on dry slopes and along dry washes, in gypsum sands and on calcareous outcrops. General: Western Texas, New Mexico and northern Mexico.

Flowering period: July to October.

Correll and Johnston (1970) followed Griffiths (1912) in recognizing *B. ramosa* as distinct from *B. breviseta*. Plants of gypsum flats do tend to have a different growth habit from those of other areas.

14. **Bouteloua gracilis** (H.B.K.) Lag. *ex* Steud., Nom. Bot. ed. 2. 1:219. 1840. BLUE GRAMA. Fig. 185. Tufted perennial, frequently with short, stout rhizomes. *Culms* mostly 25-60 (-70) cm long but occasionally much shorter, erect or somewhat geniculate at base. *Nodes* glabrous or puberulent. *Sheaths* rounded, glabrous or sparsely long-hirsute. *Ligule* a fringe of short hairs, often with marginal tufts of long hairs. *Blades* short, flat at base, 1-2.5 mm broad, usually scabrous or short-pubescent on the axial surface and often sparsely hirsute. *Inflorescences* with 1-3 (-4) branches, these broad and densely-flowered, 1.5-5 cm long. *Spikelets* commonly 40-90 or more per branch, closely-placed and pectinately spreading. *Branch rachis* scabrous on back, terminated at apex by a spikelet, this usually reduced and often appearing as a continuation of the rachis. *Glumes* glabrous or scabrous to hirsute on midnerve with papilla-based hairs. *Lemmas* mostly 4-5.5 mm long, pubescent at least below, 3-awned from apical and lateral clefts, the awns mostly 1-3 mm long. *Tufts of hair* at base of perfect floret and base of awned rudiment. A second rudiment (awnless) occasionally produced. *Chromosome numbers* reported, $2n=20$, 40 and 60 for most populations but aneuploid numbers also recorded.

Fig. 185. *Bouteloua gracilis.* Plant and spikelet with florets separated from glumes. From Gould, 1951.

Distribution. Texas: Regions 5, 7, 8, 9 and 10 on rocky slopes and in extensive stands on open grassy plains. General: Wisconsin to Alberta, Canada, south to Missouri, Texas, southern California and Mexico. Also reported from some eastern states and South America where it was probably introduced.

Flowering period: Mostly June to October.

15. **Bouteloua hirsuta** Lag., Var. Cienc. 4:141. 1805. HAIRY GRAMA. Fig. 186. Cespitose, short-lived perennial. *Culms* mostly 15-40 cm tall, spreading-erect, usually with 4-6 nodes, freely branching below. *Nodes* glabrous. *Leaves* well distributed on culm. *Sheaths* glabrous or the lowermost thinly pubescent, pilose at throat. *Ligule* a short, ciliate membrane. *Blades* 1-2 mm broad, flat or subinvolute, sparsely ciliate on lower margins with papilla-based hairs. *Inflorescence* 10-30 cm long to basal node of main axis, with 1-4 branches, these mostly 2.5-4 cm long with 20-50 closely-placed and pectinately arranged spikelets. *Branch rachis* projecting as a point 5-8 mm or more beyond terminal spikelet. *Spikelets* about 6 mm long. *Glumes* unequal, the first 1.5-3 mm long, minutely hispid, the second 3-5 mm long, with papilla-based hairs 1-2 mm long on midnerve and minutely awned at apex. *Lemma of perfect floret* 5-6 mm long, more or less puberulent on back. *Paleas* about as long as lemmas. *Rudimentary florets* 2, the lower with 3 hispid awns about 4 mm long, the upper a minute scale. *Rachilla* not hairy below lower rudiment. *Anthers* usually yellow, 2-2.5 mm long. *Caryopses* ovate, 1.5-2 mm long, 0.5-0.8 mm broad. *Chromosome numbers* reported, $2n = 20$, 40 and 60; numerous aneuploid numbers also reported.

Distribution. Texas: Throughout the State on a wide variety of soil types, in forested areas only in grassy openings and woods borders. General: Wisconsin and Illinois to North Dakota and south to Louisiana, Texas, New Mexico, Arizona, southern California and south through Mexico to Oaxaca and Chiapas. Also reported from Florida.

Flowering period: June to November.

16. **Bouteloua pectinata** Featherly, Bot. Gaz. 91:103. 1931. TALL GRAMA. Perennial with culms 35-75 cm tall from a firm or hard base. *Culms* strictly erect, unbranched, usually with 3 nodes. *Leaves* mostly in a basal clump, those of the upper culm nodes greatly reduced. *Lower sheaths* pubescent, pilose at throat. *Ligule* a short, ciliate membrane. *Blades* firm, curved, attenuate, involute, 15-30 cm long and 1.5-2 mm broad, ciliate on the lower margins with papilla-based hairs. *Inflorescence axis* 25-45 cm long from the uppermost culm node, with usually 3-5 spicate, pectinate branches. *Branches* mostly 3-4 cm long and with 40-50 spikelets. *Branch rachis* glabrous on back or with a few scattered hairs, infrequently with a few papilla or papilla-based hairs, projecting as a point beyond terminal spikelet. *Spikelets* as in *B. hirsuta* but anthers about 3 mm long and caryopses 2-3 mm long. *Chromosome number*, $2n = 20$.

Distribution. Texas: Regions 5 and 7 on limestone outcrops and hilltops. General: Southeastern Oklahoma to Texas.

Flowering period: July to November.

76. CATHESTECUM Presl

About 6 species, all but one limited to Mexico in their distribution.

Fig. 186. *Bouteloua hirsuta*. Plant. From Gould, 1951.

354   THE GRASSES OF TEXAS

1. **Cathestecum erectum** Vasey & Hack., Bull. Torrey Bot. Club 11:37. 1884. Fig. 187. Low, tufted perennial with wiry, spreading, stoloniferous culms and slender, erect, flowering culms mostly 25 cm or less tall. *Sheaths* rounded on back, those at plant base scale-like, papery, woolly-pubescent at least in part, those of the elevated culm nodes glabrous except for a few hairs on upper margins. *Ligule* a dense ring of hairs about 0.5 mm long. *Blades* firm, flat or folded, mostly 1.4 mm or less broad and 2-10 cm long, the adaxial surface scabrous and usually sparsely hirsute. *Inflorescences* 3-7 cm long, with mostly 4-8 spicate branches 4-7 mm long; branch rachis short, pubescent above base, readily disarticulating near base at maturity leaving a short stub attached to main axis; branch with congested cluster of 3 spikelets, the upper one with a perfect floret, the lower 2 with staminate or neuter florets (occasionally the rudiment of a fourth spikelet present above the perfect one). *Upper spikelet* with 1 perfect floret and 1 or more reduced florets above. *Glumes* 1-nerved, unequal, the second much longer than the first; second glume usually hairy on back and short-awned from a truncate or notched apex. *Lower spikelets of cluster* with a large neuter floret below and a slightly smaller staminate floret above, these mostly 2-3 mm long. *Lemmas* of all spikelets similar, membranous or papery, usually 3-nerved but occasionally 5-7-nerved, irregularly lobed at apex, the nerves usually extended into short awns. *Paleas* slightly shorter than lemmas and similar in texture, the 2 nerves usually excurrent as short awns. *Chromosome numbers* reported, $2n=20$, 40 and 60.

Distribution. Texas: Region 10, apparently known only from the dry mountains of Brewster County. General: Western Texas, southern Arizona and northern Mexico, on dry plains and rocky slopes at low elevations.

Flowering period: August to October.

77. BUCHLOË Engelm.

A monotypic North American genus.

1. **Buchloë dactyloides** (Nutt.) Engelm., Trans. Acad. Sci. St. Louis 1:432. 1859. BUFFALOGRASS. Fig. 188. Low, mat-forming, dioecious or occasionally monoecious perennial with extensive, wiry stolons and tufted leaves. *Sheaths* rounded on back, glabrous except for a few marginal hairs in vicinity of collar. *Ligule* a ciliate membrane about 0.5 mm long. *Blades* flat, glabrous or thinly hispid on one or both surfaces, mostly 1-2.5 mm broad, commonly 2-12 cm long but occasionally 20 cm or more in length. *Staminate inflorescences* elevated above basal leaves on slender, erect culms mostly 8-25 cm tall, the inflorescence with 1-4 spicate, unilateral branches mostly 6-14 mm long. *Branch rachis* narrow, flattened, scabrous on margins, bearing usually 6-12 closely-placed and moderately pectinate spikelets, these mostly 4-5.5 mm long. *Staminate spikelets* 2-flowered, both anther-bearing. *Glumes* broad, unequal, shorter than the lemmas, 1-2-nerved, the nerves occasionally excurrent as short awns. *Lemmas* thin, 3-nerved, typically glabrous and awnless. *Anthers* orange-red, mostly 2.5-3.5 mm long. *Pistillate spikelets* 1-flowered, in bur-like clusters of 3-5 (-7), more or less hidden in leafy portion

Fig. 187. *Cathestecum erectum*. Plant, spikelet cluster (inflorescence branch) and central spikelet of cluster.

of plant. *Bur* on a short stout rachis, partially enclosed in the broad, bracteate leaf sheath, falling as a unit with the indurate rachis united with the indurate second glumes of the spikelets. *Glumes* glabrous or puberulent, unequal, the first glume usually reduced, the second broad and hard below, abruptly narrowing to 3 rigid, pointed lobes. *Lemmas* thin but firm, glabrous, 3-nerved, the nerves extending into short, awn-tipped lobes. *Paleas* about as large as lemmas and similar in texture, the 2 nerves slightly scabrous above. *Caryopses* ovate or oblong, brownish, mostly 2-2.5 mm long, with a broad embryo almost as long as the endosperm. *Chromosome numbers* reported, $2n = 20$, 40 and 60.

Distribution. Texas: Occasional in all regions, most frequent in short-grass prairies and heavily grazed tall-grass regions and on mowed roadsides of the central and north-central portions of the State. General: Minnesota and Montana, south to Texas, Nevada, Arizona and northern Mexico, usually on heavy clayey soils.

Fig. 188. *Buchloë dactyloides*. Staminate plant (lower) and staminate spikelet with floret separated from glumes; pistillate plant (upper) with separate floriferous branch, spikelet cluster and floret. From Gould, 1951.

Flowering period: April to December under favorable growing conditions.

Buchloë is the most widespread of five closely-related, monotypic, dioecious North American genera of the tribe Chlorideae. These mostly are grasses of the semi-arid plains of Mexico and only *Buchloë dactyloides* ranges northward into the United States.

SUBFAMILY V. ERAGROSTOIDEAE   357

78. SPARTINA Schreb.

Perennials with slender or coarse, moderately tall to tall culms, these usually from a rhizomatous base. *Leaves* tough and firm, the blades long, flat or involute. *Ligule* a ring of long or short hairs. *Inflorescences* of few to numerous, racemosely arranged, short, usually appressed branches bearing closely-placed, sessile spikelets. Disarticulation below glumes. *Spikelets* 1-flowered, laterally flattened. *Glumes* unequal, keeled, usually 1-nerved or the second with 2-3 closely-placed nerves, acute or the second short-awned. *Lemmas* firm, keeled, strongly 1- or 3-nerved and often with additional indistinct lateral nerves, tapering to a narrow but rounded, awnless tip. *Paleas* as long as or longer than lemmas, with broad, membranous margins on either side of 2 closely-placed nerves.

A genus of about 16 species, one native to Europe, the others American.

Inflorescence branches short (typically 1.5-4 cm long), numerous (15-30 or more) and tightly appressed to the main axis; plants densely cespitose, without creeping rhizomes; culms usually 0.6-1 m tall
1. *S. spartinae*

Inflorescence branches short or long, appressed to the main axis or spreading, when 12 or more in number then at least some 5-10 cm long; plants cespitose or culms in small clusters from creeping rhizomes

Glumes both awn-tipped, the awn of the second glume 4-10 mm long; culms typically 1.5-2.5 m tall; plants of low grassland and swales in northern Texas
2. *S. pectinata*

Glumes, at least the first, awnless; culms 0.5-3 m or more tall, plants of saline coastal and south-Texas sites

Inflorescence branches 10 or more, appressed to the stout main axis; second glume glabrous, smooth on keel (in Texas)
3. *S. alterniflora* var. *glabra*

Inflorescence branches few to numerous, appressed or erect-spreading from main axis; second glume strongly scabrous on keel, rough to the touch

Culms 2-3.5 m tall; lower leaf blades remaining flat on drying, 1-2.5 cm broad
4. *S. cynosuroides*

Culms 0.5-2 m tall; leaf blades involute on drying, much less than 1 cm broad

Plants 0.5-1.5 m tall, the culms produced singly or in small clusters from creeping rhizomes or in clumps from bases lacking rhizomes; inflorescence branches mostly 2-7; blades 1-4 mm broad   5. *S. patens*

Plants typically 1.5-2 m tall, the culms in large clumps; creeping rhizomes not developed; inflorescence branches mostly 9 or more; blades as much as 7 mm broad   6. *S. bakeri*

1. **Spartina spartinae** (Trin.) Merr., U.S.D.A. Bur. Pl. Industr. Bull. 9:11. 1902. GULF CORDGRASS. Fig. 189. Stout perennial with culms in dense clumps from a non-rhizomatous base. *Herbage* glabrous or essentially so. *Sheaths* broad, rounded. *Ligule* a dense fringe of short hairs. *Blades* stiff, short, narrower than the sheaths, inrolled on drying, with a sharp-pointed apex. *Inflorescences* stout, spikelike, mostly 15-25 cm long and with usually 15-30 short branches, these typically 1.5-4 cm long but occasionally longer, closely crowded and appressed along the main axis. *Spikelets* 6-8 mm long. *Glumes* scabrous or hispid-ciliate on keel, the first narrow, usually about one-half or slightly less as long as the second. *Second glume* blunt or slightly notched, often short-awned. *Lemmas* blunt, scabrous on keel, awnless or abruptly short-awned, slightly shorter than paleas. *Chromosome number*, $2n = 40$ (records of $2n = 28$ by Mobberly [1956] and $2n = 42$ by Church [1940] probably are inaccurate).

Distribution. Texas: Regions 2, 3, 6 and 7, frequent on coastal flats and along brackish marshlands and occasional in salt flats and marshes at interior locations in the southern half of the State. General: Florida to Texas and eastern Mexico.

Spartina spartinae forms extensive meadows along the coastal salt flats and other lowland areas. It grows in soils that occasionally are submerged but which most of the time are above sea level.

2. **Spartina pectinata** Link, Jahrb. Gewachsk. I. 3:92. 1820. PRAIRIE CORDGRASS. Fig. 190. *Culms* mostly 1.5-2.5 m tall, solitary or in small clusters from stout, widely-spreading rhizomes. *Sheaths* smooth. *Ligule* a ring of hairs 1-3 mm long. *Blades* flat, becoming involute on drying, as much as 1.5 cm broad. *Inflorescence* with usually 8-40 appressed to somewhat spreading branches 4-15 cm long. *Spikelets* mostly 10-25 mm long, including awns. *Glumes* tapering to a scabrous awn tip, the first glume 5-10 mm long, the second 10-25 mm long including the 4-10-mm-long awn. *Lemmas* glabrous, with a deeply bilobed, usually apiculate apex. *Paleas* thin, slightly longer than the lemmas, bilobed at apex. *Anthers* 4-6 mm long. *Chromosome number*, $2n = 40$ (records of $2n = 28$, 42 and 84 by Church [1929, 1940] and $2n = 42$ and 70 by Mobberly [1956] probably are inaccurate).

Distribution. Texas: Regions 4, 5, 8 and 9 in marshy meadows and along swales and ditches. General: Prairies and plains of southern Canada and northern and central United States, extending south as far as North Carolina, Arkansas, northern Texas and New Mexico.

Flowering period: Mostly late summer and fall.

SUBFAMILY V. ERAGROSTOIDEAE   359

Fig. 189. *Spartina spartinae*. Inflorescence and spikelet.

360   THE GRASSES OF TEXAS

Fig. 190. *Spartina pectinata*. Plant, spikelet and floret. From Hitchcock, 1935.

SUBFAMILY V. ERAGROSTOIDEAE 361

3. **Spartina alterniflora** Loisel. var. **glabra** (Muhl.) Fern., Rhodora 18:178. 1916. SMOOTH CORDGRASS. Fig. 191. Strong perennial with culms mostly 1-2 m tall, solitary or in small clusters from thick but rather soft, whitish rhizomes. *Lower sheaths* broad and inflated. *Ligular hairs* 1-2 mm long. *Blades* mostly 5-12 mm broad, the broader blades flat, at least near base. *Panicle* 15-35 cm long, with appressed branches often partially enclosed in sheath. *Panicle branches* 9-20, loosely imbricated on a stout axis 5-15 cm long. *Spikelets* 8-14 mm long. *Glumes* glabrous, awnless or abruptly apiculate, the first glume often more than one-half as long as the second. *Nerve of glumes* usually smooth, occasionally with 1-few small spicules. *Lemmas* glabrous, slightly shorter than paleas. *Anthers* mostly 4-6 mm long. *Chromosome number*, $2n = 62$ (counts of $2n = 56$ and 70 by Church [1940] may be inaccurate). Counts of $2n = 40$ and 60 by Gould (1968) were based on plants referable to *S. bakeri* and *S. patens*).

Distribution. Texas: Region 2, usually in standing water or saturated, muddy soils of tideflats and bayou margins. General: In North America, along the Atlantic and Gulf coasts from Newfoundland to Florida and Texas; introduced on the Pacific Coast in Washington. Also present along the eastern coast of South America and in Europe along the coast of England and France.

Flowering period: Mostly July to November.

Spartina alterniflora in Texas differs from all other species of the genus in the glabrous and smooth keels of the glumes. Plants of the Atlantic Coast, especially at the more northerly localities, tend to have rough-scabrous glume keels. One readily recognizable characteristic of the species is the disagreeable odor of fresh, crushed herbage which persists for some time on herbarium specimens.

4. **Spartina cynosuroides** (L.) Roth., Cat. Bot. 3:10. 1806. BIG CORD-GRASS. Robust perennial with culms 2-3.5 m tall, produced singly from stout, widely creeping rhizomes. *Ligule* a ring of hairs 1-3 mm long. *Blades* 1-2.5 cm broad, for the most part remaining flat on drying. *Inflorescences* large, with usually 12-25 or more loosely contracted or spreading branches, the branches 4-9 cm long. *Spikelets* 10-14 mm long, awnless. *Glumes* acute to acuminate, sharply scabrous on keel, the first glume usually less than one-half as long as the second. *Second glume* irregularly 2-3-nerved. *Lemmas and paleas* blunt at apex, the lemma midnerve usually scabrous above. *Anthers* 4-6 mm long. *Chromosome number* not definitely known; the reports of $2n = 42$ by Church (1936, 1940) and $2n = 28$ and 42 by Mobberly (1956) probably are in error.

Distribution. Texas: Region 2, known only from the Port Arthur-Orange area at the mouth of the Sabine River, growing mainly in shallow water along bayous and tideland flats. General: Along the eastern coast of the United States, from Massachusetts to Florida and Texas.

Flowering period: Early- or mid-summer.

Fig. 191. *Spartina alterniflora* var. *glabra*. Inflorescence and spikelet. From Gould and Box, 1965.

This tall marsh grass has somewhat the aspect of *Arundo* or *Phragmites* and in the vegetative state could easily be mistaken for these reed-grasses.

SUBFAMILY V. ERAGROSTOIDEAE   363

5. **Spartina patens** (Ait.) Muhl., Desc. Gram. 55. 1817. MARSHHAY CORDGRASS. Fig. 192. *Culms* 0.5-1.5 m tall, single or in small clusters from creeping rhizomes or in dense tufts or clumps from non-rhizomatous bases. *Ligule* a minute fringe of hairs. *Blades* narrow, tightly involute on drying, 1-2 mm broad on the more slender, rhizomatous plants, 2-4 mm broad on coarse, cespitose plants. *Inflorescences* on the slender, rhizomatous plants with 2-3, infrequently -5 branches, on the coarser cespitose plants the inflorescences with usually 4-7 branches. *Inflorescence branches* slender, 3-8 cm long. *Spikelets* mostly 7-12 mm long. *Glumes* awnless, scabrous on nerve, at least above, the first glume usually less than one-half the length of the spikelet, the second glume as long as the spikelet. *Lemmas and paleas* blunt, the palea slightly longer than the lemma. A *chromosome number* of $2n = 40$ has been reported for the slender, rhizomatous type plant (Gould, 1968) and a $2n = 60$ count has been reported for a more robust but rhizomatous plant (*Gould, 1968; for Gould 11980*, incorrectly identified as *S. alterniflora*). Counts of $2n = 28$ and 42 by Church (1936, 1940), and $2n = 28$, 35 and 42 by Mobberly (1956) probably are in error.

Distribution. Texas: Frequent along the coast throughout region 2, the slender, rhizomatous form widespread and common on beaches, sandy flats and low dunes, the coarse, cespitose form along muddy bayous and marshlands of the northeastern Texas coast, usually in the tidewater zone. General: In North America, along the coast from Quebec to Florida, Texas and the eastern coast of Mexico. Present in a few localities in Michigan and New York and on islands in the Caribbean. Also known in Europe from France, Corsica and Italy.

Flowering period: Mostly May to September, but occasionally flowering throughout the growing season.

Many populations of diverse aspect are herein referred to *Spartina patens*, and this and related species are greatly in need of further study. For the most part the species is represented in Texas by rhizomatous plants with slender culms 0.5-0.8 m tall, narrow, tightly involute blades and slender inflorescences with 2-4 branches. Such plants are frequent on sandy beaches and low dunes throughout the Texas coast. Populations of cespitose plants with relatively tall, coarse culms in large clumps are frequent along the muddy bayous and marshlands of the northeastern Texas coast. These plants more or less link *S. patens* with *S. bakeri* as represented in Texas.

6. **Spartina bakeri** Merr., U.S.D.A. Bur. Pl. Industr. Bull. 9:14. 1902. *Culms* 1.5-2 m tall, in large, dense clumps from hard, knotty bases. *Ligule* a fringe of short hairs. *Leaf blades* mostly 3-7 mm broad, involute on drying or remaining partially flat. *Inflorescences* of usually 9-15 widely spaced, erect-spreading branches, these mostly 5-9 cm long. *Spikelets* 9-12 mm long. *Glumes* acute, acuminate or abruptly short-awned, scabrous on keel, the first glume usually slightly less than one-half as long as the second. *Lemmas* rounded at apex, slightly shorter than paleas. *Chromosome number*, $2n = 40$

Fig. 192. *Spartina patens.* Inflorescence. From Gould and Box, 1965.

(based on count for *Gould 11988,* reported as *S. alterniflora* [Gould, 1968]). The count of $2n = 42$ reported by Mobberly (1956) probably is in error.

Distribution. Texas: Occasional along the northeastern Gulf Coast (region 2), in marshes and bayous. General: South Carolina, Florida, Georgia and Texas.

Flowering period: Mostly June to September.

Spartina bakeri grows with and probably is closely related to *Spartina patens.* The latter has narrower blades, fewer inflorescence branches and, for the most part, shorter culms. *Spartina bakeri* has not previously been reported from Texas. The Texas plants generally are characteristic except that the inflorescence branches are longer and more spreading than on east coast plants. Further investigations may show that the Texas populations represent an undescribed species. Texas specimens of *S. bakeri* examined are from Orange County, 0.5 mile south of Bridge City, *Gould 11988* (Tracy Herbarium) and 1.5 miles south of Bridge City, *Gould 11994* (Tracy Herbarium) and *12910* (Tracy Herbarium).

SUBFAMILY V. ERAGROSTOIDEAE   365

79. HILARIA H.B.K.

Perennials, mostly rhizomatous or stoloniferous. *Leaf blades* narrow, usually short, flat or involute. *Ligule* a lacerate, often ciliate membrane. *Inflorescence* a slender, dense, bilateral spike, the spikelets in clusters of 3 at each node of a zigzag rachis, the clusters deciduous as a whole. *Spikelets* of the cluster dissimilar, the 2 lateral ones 2-flowered, staminate and the central one 1-flowered, perfect. *Glumes* firm, flat, usually asymmetrical, bearing an awn on one side from about the middle. *Lemmas* thin, 3-nerved, awned or awnless. *Paleas* about as large as lemmas and similar in texture.

About seven species, mostly in southern North America, one ranging southward to Venezuela.

Base of plant thick and hard, with stout scaly rhizomes; stolons not produced; blades relatively thick, flat or involute

Glumes of the lateral spikelets broadened and flabellate at the apex
1. *H. mutica*

Glumes of the lateral spikelets not broadened and flabellate at the apex, usually narrowing from middle to tip   2. *H. jamesii*

Base of plant not thick and hard, stout scaly rhizomes not produced; slender, looping stolons typically present; blades thin and flat

Glumes pale, without black glands or with only a few scattered glands; spikelet clusters 5-6 mm long   3. *H. belangeri*

Glumes dark, at least below the middle, densely beset with minute black glands; spikelet clusters 6.5-8 mm long   4. *H. swallenii*

1. **Hilaria mutica** (Buckl.) Benth., J. Linn. Soc., Bot. 19:62. 1881. TOBOSA. Fig. 193. Perennial with culms from a firm or hard, usually rhizomatous base, the thick scaly rhizomes usually short and much-branched. *Culms* slender, tough or wiry, mostly 30-75 cm tall, glabrous or scabrous-puberulent at nodes. *Leaves* glabrous, scabrous or occasionally with a few long hairs. *Sheaths* rounded on back. *Ligule* a fringed membrane 1 mm or less long. *Blades* firm, flat or more often involute, 2-4 (-5) mm broad. *Spikes* mostly 4-8 cm long and 6-8 mm thick, with 8-25 closely placed, sessile spikelet clusters. *Spikelet clusters* mostly 6-9 mm long, the 3 spikelets subequal in length, with a tuft of hairs mostly 2-3 mm long at base. *Glumes of lateral (staminate) spikelets* broadened upward to a fan-shaped, rounded or truncate apex, densely or sparsely ciliate on margins, the medial glumes with a lateral, scabrous or hairy awn 0.5-3 mm long. *Glumes of central spikelet* narrow, usually short, irregularly cleft and with awn-tipped nerves. *Lemmas* thin, entire or irregularly erose and ciliate at apex, awnless or minutely awn-tipped. *Lemma and palea of central spikelet* mostly 5-6 mm long,

Fig. 193. *Hilaria mutica.* Plant, spikelet cluster (upper) and spikelet cluster with one lateral spikelet removed (lower). From Gould, 1951.

SUBFAMILY V. ERAGROSTOIDEAE 367

with lateral margins more or less inrolled to form a tube through which the dark colored stigmas protrude at anthesis. *Anthers* 3-4 mm long. *Chromosome number:* Euploid numbers of 2*n*=36, 54, 72 and 180 reported, aneuploid numbers of 2*n*=38 and 74 also recorded.

Distribution. Texas: Regions 6, 7, 8, 9 and 10 on dry, rocky slopes and on level plains and plateaus. General: Oklahoma and Texas to Arizona and northern Mexico.

Flowering period: April to August, occasionally to October.

2. **Hilaria jamesii** (Torr.) Benth., J. Linn. Soc., Bot. 19:62. 1881. GALLETA. Fig. 194. Similar to *H. mutica* in general characteristics. *Culm nodes* often hairy. *Hairs* at base of spikelet cluster mostly 3.5-5 mm long. *Glumes of lateral spikelets* narrowing from the middle upward, not fan-shaped, the medial glumes with a lateral awn usually 3-6 (-8) mm long. *Chromosome number*, 2*n*=18.

Distribution. Texas: Regions 8, 9 and 10 on dry rocky ledges, rolling slopes and valley flats. General: Wyoming and Nevada, southward to Texas, Arizona and southern California.

Flowering period: June to September.

3. **Hilaria belangeri** (Steud.) Nash, N. Amer. Flora 17:135. 1912. COMMON CURLYMESQUITE. Fig. 195. Low tufted perennial, with erect, floriferous culms from small clumps and also at the tips of wiry, widely spreading rhizomes. *Erect culms* mostly 10-30 cm tall. *Culm nodes,* especially the lower ones, densely bearded with spreading hairs. *Ligule* membranous, lacerate, mostly 0.5-1 mm long. *Blades* short, flat or less commonly involute, scabrous, often sparsely pilose, 1-2 (-3) mm long. *Spikes* mostly 2-3.5 cm long, well exserted on slender, almost filiform peduncles, with usually 4-8 spikelet clusters. *Spikelet clusters* typically 4.5-6 mm long. *Glumes of lateral spikelets* pale, scabrous, united below, usually shorter than lemmas, the outer glume slightly broadened above, notched or lobed, the inner shorter and narrower, both frequently with the midnerve extended into a mucro less than 1 mm long. *Glumes of central spikelet* subequal, glabrous or scabrous, slightly broadened above, with scabrous awns mostly 2.5-5 mm long. *Lemmas* thin, narrowed above, awnless. *Chromosome numbers* reported, 2*n*=36, 72 and several aneuploid numbers.

Distribution. Texas: In all regions except regions 1 and 3 but absent from the northeastern portion of region 2. On rocky slopes, dry hillsides and grassy or brush plains. General: Texas to Arizona and the adjacent tier of Mexican states.

Flowering period: Mostly August to October but occasionally March to November.

Fig. 194. *Hilaria jamesii*. Two views of spikelet cluster.

Fig. 195. *Hilaria belangeri*. Plant and two views of spikelet cluster. From Gould, 1951, in part and Gould and Box, 1965, in part.

SUBFAMILY V. ERAGROSTOIDEAE   369

4. **Hilaria swallenii** Cory, Wrightia 1:215. 1948. SWALLEN CURLY-MESQUITE. Generally similar to *H. belangeri* but plants often larger and coarser, the erect culms to 35 cm tall. *Spikelet clusters* often 7-8 mm long, the glumes densely beset with minute black glands and usually tinged with purple. *Glume nerves* prominent, often excurrent as awns 1-3 mm long. *Chromosome number*, $2n = 72$ (90 and 120 also reported).

Distribution. Texas: Region 10 on dry slopes and plains. General: Texas and northern Coahuila, Mexico.

Flowering period: June to October.

Tribe 15. Zoysieae

80. TRAGUS Hall

Low annuals with weak stems, soft, flat blades and slender, spikelike inflorescences of bristly "burs" of 2-5 spikelets. *Ligule* a ring of short, woolly hairs. *Disarticulation* at the base of each spikelet cluster, the inflorescence axis persistent. *Spikelets* 1-flowered. *First glume* small, thin, much reduced or wanting. *Second glume* of the lower 2 spikelets of a cluster large and firm, bearing three rows of stout, hooked spines. *Lemmas of the lower spikelets* thin and flat. Upper 1-3 spikelets of inflorescence sterile, the uppermost usually rudimentary.

A genus of three weedy annuals widely distributed in the tropics and subtropics of the world but none native to the United States.

Spikelets 2-3 mm long; burs with peduncles 0.3-0.4 mm long
1. *T. berteronianus*

Spikelets 3.5-4.5 mm long; burs with peduncles mostly 0.6-1.5 mm long
2. *T. racemosus*

1. **Tragus berteronianus** Schult., Mant. 2:205. 1824. SPIKE BUR-GRASS. Fig. 196. *Culms* geniculate, spreading, 5-30 (-40) cm long. *Sheaths* usually shorter than culm internodes, glabrous or with a few long hairs on either side of collar. *Ligule* a thin, hyaline membrane fringed with fine, soft hairs. *Blades* short, flat or folded, 1.5-5 mm broad, usually with thickened, whitish, coarsely hispid-ciliate margins. *Inflorescence* 4-9 (2-12) cm long and 5-7 mm thick, with numerous burs closely placed on a stout, puberulent axis. *Peduncle of bur* mostly 0.3-0.4 mm long, the spikelets (and longest glumes) 2-3 mm long. *Chromosome number*, $2n = 20$.

Distribution. Texas: Regions 6, 7 and 10, usually in loose sandy soil, often in disturbed sites. General: An Old World species, now well-established in Texas, southern New Mexico and Arizona and Mexico; also present in South America.

Flowering period: April to November.

Fig. 196. *Tragus berteronianus.* Plant and spikelet cluster. From Gould, 1951.

2. **Tragus racemosus** (L.) All., Fl. Pedem. 2:241. 1785. STALKED BURGRASS. Closely similar to *T. berteronianus* but spikelets larger, burs with longer peduncles and with *chromosome number,* $2n = 40$.

Distribution. Texas: Regions 2 and 10, infrequent, in the same habitats as *T. berteronianus* but rarely collected. General: Native to the Old World, sparingly introduced in southern North America.

Flowering period: Mostly summer.

SUBFAMILY V. ERAGROSTOIDEAE   371

Tribe 16. Aeluropodeae

81. DISTICHLIS Raf.

A genus of 3-4 species with distribution in North and South America.

1. **Distichlis spicata** (L.) Greene, Calif. Acad. Sci. Bull. 2:415. 1887. SALTGRASS. Low, dioecious (rarely monoecious) perennial with stout, creeping rhizomes and short, overlapping, 2-ranked distichous leaves. *Culms* 10-60 cm tall, with several to many nodes and short internodes. *Culm nodes* glabrous. *Leaves* thick, firm, the lowermost reduced to scale-like sheaths. *Sheaths* rounded on the back, glabrous or puberulent. *Ligule* a minute membranous collar less than 0.5 mm long. *Blades* mostly 1-4 mm broad and 2-8 (-20) cm long, involute on drying. *Inflorescence* a contracted panicle or spikelike raceme 2.5-8 cm long, with large, several-flowered, awnless spikelets on short, stout branches and pedicels. *Pistillate panicles* with spikelets more congested and irregularly spreading than in the staminate panicles. *Spikelets* mostly 5-15-flowered, and 6-18 (-28) mm long, laterally flattened. Disarticulation above glumes and between florets. *Glumes* slightly unequal, firm, glabrous, acute, 3-9-nerved, the lateral nerves often indistinct. *Lemmas* similar to glumes but longer and broader, 5-11-nerved, laterally compressed and keeled, mostly 3-6 mm long, acute and often boat-shaped at apex. *Paleas* as long as lemmas or slightly shorter, the 2 nerves keeled and slightly to strongly winged, at maturity the paleas of pistillate florets bowed out at base. *Chromosome number,* 2n=40.

Culms 10-60 cm tall; leaf blades not over 15 cm long; pistillate inflo-
    rescences, and usually the staminate, congested, the short pedicels not
    readily visible; pistillate spikelets 5-9-flowered, staminate spikelets
    7-11-flowered; coastal plants   1A.   *D. spicata* var. *spicata*

Culms 10-35 cm tall; leaf blades to 20 cm long; pistillate and staminate
    inflorescences not congested, the pedicels readily visible; pistillate
    and staminate spikelets 5-20 flowered; inland plants
                                                      1B.   *D. spicata* var. *stricta*

1A. **Distichlis spicata** (L.) Greene var. **spicata.** COASTAL SALT-GRASS. Fig. 197.

Distribution. Texas: Region 2 in saline marshes and low, moist flats along the coast, often in dense, extensive colonies. General: Seashores and coastal marshes, Nova Scotia to Florida, Texas, Mexico and the West Indies and on the west coast, Washington to Baja California and Sinaloa.

Flowering period: Throughout the year under favorable growing conditions.

Fig. 197. *Distichlis spicata* var. *spicata*. Plant and separate inflorescence. From Gould and Box, 1965.

1B. **Distichlis spicata** (L.) Greene var. **stricta** (Torr.) Beetle, Bull. Torrey Bot. Club 70:645. 1943. *Distichlis stricta* (Torr.) Rydb. INLAND SALTGRASS.

Distribution. Texas: Regions 7, 8, 9 and 10, locally abundant in moist or wet alkaline or saline areas. General: Western United States, from Minnesota, Arkansas and Texas west to inland areas of the coastal states.

Flowering period: Mostly May to October.

This variety appears to represent little more than a variable series of inland populations of *Distichlis spicata* growing under a wide range of soil and climatic conditions. In general, plants of var. *stricta* differ from those of var. *spicata* in having shorter, more slender and more strictly erect culms, slightly longer blades and less congested panicles with fewer spikelets.

82. ALLOLEPIS Soderstrom & Decker

A monotypic North American genus.

1. **Allolepis texana** (Vasey) Soderstrom & Decker, Madroño 18:34. 1965. *Distichlis texana* (Vasey) Scribn. Dioecious perennial with long, creeping stolons and with or without rhizomes. *Culms* loosely ascending or spreading as stolons, the erect portion mostly 25-65 cm tall, glabrous. *Sheaths* rounded on back, the lower ones shorter than the internodes, glabrous except for a few long hairs on either side of collar. *Ligule* a short-ciliate membrane 0.5-1.4 mm long. *Blades* flat or loosely folded, 2.5-6 mm broad, to 30 cm or more long, glabrous above and below or scabrous towards the tip, roughly scabrous on margins. *Panicles* narrow, mostly 5-20 cm long, with appressed or stiffly ascending branches 1-6 cm long, these usually floriferous to base. *Spikelets* apparently not disarticulating. *Staminate spikelets* ovate-lanceolate to linear, shiny, 9-23 mm long, 3-8 mm wide, with 4-14 (-20) florets per spikelet. *Glumes* broadly ovate, hyaline, glabrous, the midnerve scabrous. *First glume* 1-nerved, 4-5 mm long, a little shorter than the second. *Second glume* 1- or 3-nerved. *Lemmas of lower florets* 5-5.5 mm long, strongly 3-nerved, glabrous, shiny. *Palea* equal to or a little longer than lemma, linear, the keels minutely ciliolate. *Anthers* yellow, 3-3.5 mm long. *Pistillate spikelets* ovate-lanceolate, terete or slightly compressed, 1-2 cm long, 2.5-3.5 mm wide, with up to 8-9 closely imbricated florets. *Glumes* broadly ovate, coriaceous, with broad, scarious margins, the midnerve scabrous. *First glume* slightly shorter than second, 7-9 mm long, with a strong midnerve and often 4-5 indistinct lateral nerves. *Second glume* with 3 strong nerves and occasionally 2-4 indistinct intermediate nerves. *Lemmas of lower florets* 7.5-10 mm long, broadly ovate, coriaceous, with irregular scarious margins, strongly 3-nerved, the midnerve scabrous above. *Paleas* slightly shorter than lemmas, narrow above, strongly bowed out below, the margins overlapping, the keels ciliolate. *Chromosome number*, $2n=40$.

Distribution. Texas: Region 10 in Presidio and Brewster counties, infrequent, in sandy, open bottomlands. General: Texas and the Mexican states of Coahuila, Chihuahua and Durango.

Flowering period: Mostly July to October.

83. MONANTHOCHLOË Engelm.

A genus of 3 species, one in southern North America, the other two in Argentina.

1. **Monanthochloë littoralis** Engelm., Trans. Acad. Sci. St. Louis. 1:437. 1859. SHOREGRASS. Fig. 198. Low, mat-forming, dioecious perennial with wiry, decumbent and stoloniferous, much-branched culms, the erect floriferous branches mostly 8-15 cm tall. *Leaves* mainly clustered and distichous on unexpanded lateral shoots 0.5-1.5 cm long and at the main branch tips. *Sheaths* rounded, glabrous or puberulent at base, smooth and shiny, mostly 0.4-0.6 mm long. *Ligule* a minute ciliate membrane. *Blades* thick, firm, uniformly several-nerved, mostly folded or involute, 1-2 (-3) mm broad and seldom over 1 cm long, glabrous or with a few hairs near ligule, bluish-green. *Spikelets* borne singly in the axils of fascicled leaves, in pistillate spikelets eventually disarticulating at the lower rachilla node. *Spikelets* 3-5-flowered, the uppermost florets rudimentary. *Glumes* apparently absent. *Lemmas* rounded on back, several-nerved, those of the pistillate spikelets like the leaf blades in texture. Paleas narrow, 2-nerved, enfolding the caryopses. *Chromosome number* not reported.

Distribution. Texas: Region 2 on saline flats and in marshlands along the ocean, from Orange County to Cameron County; also reported from Gonzales County. General: Florida to Texas, Cuba and the northern half of Mexico, both on the east and west coasts.

Flowering period: March to May and possibly later.

Tribe 17. Unioleae

84. UNIOLA L.

A genus of 2 species, one along the Atlantic and Gulf coasts of the southern United States and Mexico, the other along both coasts of Mexico and south to Equador.

1. **Uniola paniculata** L., Sp. Pl. 71. 1753. SEAOATS. Fig. 199. Perennial with tall, stout culms in small clumps or single from long, thick rhizomes. *Culms* glabrous, mostly 1-2.2 m tall, branching only at the base. *Leaves* firm and tough in texture, a few of the basal ones reduced and scalelike. *Sheaths* rounded or the lowermost slightly keeled, glabrous. *Ligule* a dense ring of hairs 1.5-3 mm long. *Blades* linear, flat, folded or involute at the base, involute at the elongated, filiform tips, to 80 cm or more long and 5-10 mm broad at the

Fig. 198. *Monanihochloë littoralis.* Plant, staminate spikelet (lower) and pistillate spikelet (upper). From Gould and Box, 1965.

base. *Panicles* contracted, typically 20-50 cm long and 5-100 cm broad, with relatively short, slender branches, the lower ones drooping at maturity under the weight of the large spikelets. *Spikelets* broad, laterally compressed, for the most part smooth and shiny, with 12-20 florets, the lower few sterile, 1.5-3.5 cm long; spikelets not readily disarticulating but at length breaking off below glumes and falling as a whole. *Glumes* firm, subequal, acute, awnless or mucronate, indistinctly 3-5-nerved, the keeled midnerve serrulate. *Lemmas* broad, keeled, acute, awnless or mucronate, 3-9-nerved, serrulate on the keels and often minutely ciliolate on the margins. *Paleas* about as long as lemmas, 2-keeled, the keels winged and serrate to ciliolate. *Caryopses* elongate, 3-5 mm long, with an embryo less than one-half the length of the endosperm. *Chromosome number*, $2n = 40$.

Distribution. Texas: Region 2 on dunes and sandy flats along the ocean. General: Along the ocean, Virginia to Florida and Texas, northern West Indies and eastern Mexico.

Flowering period: June to December but mostly late summer and early autumn.

Fig. 199. *Uniola paniculata*. Plant in natural habitat (upper) and inflorescence (lower). From Gould, 1968.

SUBFAMILY V. ERAGROSTOIDEAE   377

Tribe 18. Pappophoreae

85. PAPPOPHORUM Schreb.

Erect, cespitose perennials with slender, contracted, usually spikelike panicles of bristly spikelets. *Ligule* a ring of hairs. *Blades* long, narrow, flat or folded. *Spikelets* 3-6-flowered but only the lower 1-3 perfect; disarticulation above glumes, the florets falling together. *Glumes* subequal, thin and membranous, 1-nerved. *Lemmas* firm, rounded on the back, indistinctly many-nerved, the nerves extending into 11 or more unequal, glabrous or scabrous awns. *Paleas* about as long as body of lemma.

A small genus of North and South American grasses, two species in the United States.

Panicles pink or purple-tinged at maturity, contracted and narrow but often with some erect-spreading branches; perfect florets usually 2; body of lemma of lowermost floret 3-4 mm long   1. *P. bicolor*

Panicles white or tawny, tightly contracted; perfect floret usually 1; body of lemma of lowermost floret 2-3 mm long   2. *P. vaginatum*

1. **Pappophorum bicolor** Fourn., Mex. Pl. 2:133. 1886. PINK PAPPUS-GRASS. Fig. 200. *Culms* 30-80 (-100) cm tall, stiffly erect or somewhat geniculate below, glabrous. *Sheaths* with a tuft of long hairs on either side of collar, the hairs deciduous in age. *Ligule* a ring of short hairs but base of blade immediately above ligule with hairs 2-4 mm long. *Blades* flat or involute, scabrous on adaxial surface above base, smooth on the adaxial surface, 10-20 (-30) cm long and 1.5-5 mm broad. *Panicle* tightly or loosely contracted, most frequently with short but somewhat erect-spreading branches, pink or purple-tinged at maturity, mostly 12-20 cm long. *Spikelets* short-pediceled, appressed, 6-8 mm long, with 2-3 perfect florets and 2 reduced florets above. *Glumes* broad, glabrous, acute or minutely notched and mucronate at apex, usually 3-4 mm long. *Lemmas* with a broad, firm, rounded, many-nerved body, pubescent on midnerve and margins from base to middle, dissected into 11-15 awns of irregular lengths, the longest 2.5-5 mm long. *Body of lower lemmas* 3-4 mm long. *Paleas* slightly longer than lemma body, 2-nerved but tapering to an acute or acuminate apex. *Rudimentary florets* similar to perfect ones but smaller. *Chromosome number,* $2n = 100$.

Distribution. Texas: Regions 2, 6, 7, 8 and 10 on grassy plains, moist road right-of-ways and open valleys. General: Texas to Arizona and northern Mexico.

Flowering period: April to November.

2. **Pappophorum vaginatum** Buckl., Prelim. Rep. Geol. Agr. Survey Tex. App. 1. 1866. *Pappophorum mucronulatum* auct., not Nees. WHIP-LASH PAPPUSGRASS. Fig. 201. Perennial, similar in vegetative characters to *P. bicolor*. *Panicle* narrow, tightly contracted, whitish or tawny, only rarely

Fig. 200. *Pappophorum bicolor*. Inflorescence, spikelet and floret. From Gould and Box, 1965.

SUBFAMILY V. ERAGROSTOIDEAE   379

with a slight purple tinge, mostly 12-25 cm long and averaging longer than in *P. bicolor*. *Spikelets* with 1, rarely 2, perfect florets and 2 reduced florets above. *Lemma of lower floret* with a body 2-3 mm long and awns to 5 mm long. *Chromosome number*, $2n=60$.

Distribution. Texas: Regions 6 and 10 and southern portion of region 2. General: Texas, southern Arizona and northern Mexico.

Flowering period: April to November.

North American plants of this species have long gone under the name of *Pappophorum mucronulatum* Nees, a species which Rosengurtt has determined to be restricted to South America. The type of *P. mucronulatum* is from Brazil whereas that of *P. vaginatum* is from Texas.

86. ENNEAPOGON Desv. *ex* Beauv.

A genus of about 35 species, these mostly in Australia, Africa and Asia, with one species in North and South America.

1. **Enneapogon desvauxii** Beauv., Ess. Agrost. 82, 161. 1812. *Pappophorum wrightii* S. Wats. FEATHER PAPPUSGRASS. Fig. 202. Low, tufted perennial with narrow, spikelike panicles. *Culms* 10-50 cm tall, usually pilose at least at the nodes. *Leaves* well distributed on culm; sheaths rounded on back, usually pilose, much shorter than culm internodes; ligule a ring of fine hairs 0.5 mm or less long; blades filiform, hirsute at least on adaxial surface, 0.5-2 mm broad and mostly 2-12 cm long, involute or folded on drying. *Panicles* densely contracted, 2-9 cm long and 6-10 (-15) mm thick, grayish or lead-colored. *Spikelets* mostly 5-7 cm long including the awns, usually 3-flowered with only the lower floret perfect. *Glumes* subequal but the first usually broader, lanceolate, thin and membranous, puberulent, the first glume 3-5 mm long, 5-7-nerved, the second similar but with nerves reduced to 3-4 in some spikelets. *Lemmas* pubescent, broad, much shorter than glumes, firm, rounded on back, the body mostly 1.5-2 mm long, with 9 strong nerves and 9 equal, plumose awns mostly 3-4 mm long. *Palea* about as long as the lemma body, with widely divergent nerves. *Chromosome number*, $2n=20$.

Distribution. Texas: Regions 7, 8, 9 and 10, frequent on dry, open slopes in the western part of the State. General: Utah to Texas and Arizona and in Mexico, Bolivia, Peru and Argentina.

Flowering period: July to November, occasionally earlier.

87. COTTEA Kunth

A monotypic New World genus.

1. **Cottea pappophoroides** Kunth, Rev. Gram. 1:84. 1829. Fig. 203. Tufted short-lived perennial without rhizomes or stolons. *Culms* 30-70 cm

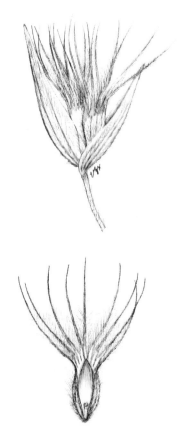

Fig. 201. *Pappophorum vaginatum*. Inflorescence. From Gould and Box, 1965, as *P. mucronulatum*.

Fig. 202. *Enneapogon desvauxii*. Spikelet (upper) and floret attached to section of rachilla (lower).

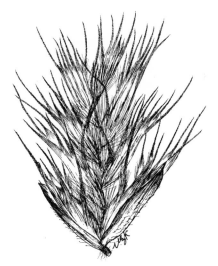

Fig. 203. *Cottea pappophoroides*. Spikelet and floret.

tall, strictly erect or geniculate-spreading below, soft-pilose with glandular hairs at least below nodes, uniformly leafy. *Sheaths* rounded on back, pilose. *Ligule* a ring of stiff hairs about 0.5 mm long. *Blades* mostly flat below and involute at the narrow, attenuate tips, finely pilose on both surfaces, 3-6 mm broad, mostly 8-20 cm long. *Cleistogamous spikelets* often developed on reduced panicles in the axils of the lower leaves. *Terminal panicles* loosely contracted 10-20 cm long and 4-6 cm broad, with stiffly erect-spreading branches, the branches and main axis densely glandular pubescent with long and short spreading hairs. *Spikelets* mostly 7-10 mm long and 4-6 mm thick, with 6-10 florets, the upper 1-2 usually sterile. Disarticulation above glumes and between florets. *Glumes* minutely hispid-scabrous, subequal, about as long as lemmas, broadly lanceolate, with 7-13 distinct nerves, the midnerve sometimes excurrent as a short awn. *Lemmas* broad, irregularly cleft and lobed with the two most lateral clefts much deeper than the others, long-hairy below, with 9-13 strong nerves, these extended into scabrous awns of irregular lengths but mostly 1-3.5 mm long. *Palea* broad, slightly longer than the body of the lemma, the nerves ciliate, widely divergent. Caryopses oblong, about 1.5 mm long. *Chromosome number* not reported.

Distribution. Texas: Region 10, infrequent on rocky slopes and desert flats. General: Texas to Arizona and central Mexico and Equador to Argentina and Peru.

Flowering period: Mostly late August to November.

Tribe 19. Aristideae

88. ARISTIDA L.

Low to moderately tall annuals and perennials, these lacking rhizomes or stolons. *Blades* narrow, usually involute. *Ligule* a ring of hairs or a minute, ciliate membrane. *Inflorescence* an open or contracted panicle of usually large, 1-flowered spikelets. Disarticulation above glumes. *Glumes* thin, lanceolate, with a strong central nerve and occasionally 2 lateral nerves. *Lemma* indurate, terete, 3-nerved, with a hard, sharp-pointed callus at base, tapering gradually or, less frequently, abruptly to an awn column bearing usually 3 stiff awns, the lateral awns partially or totally reduced in a few species. In some African taxa the awns are plumose and feathery. *Caryopses* long and slender, permanently enclosed by the firm lemma.

About 200 species, in the warmer parts of the world, mostly in the sub-tropics.

Lateral awns of lemma greatly reduced, one-third or less as long as central awn and often rudimentary

Central awn with a semicircular bend or spiral coil at base; plants annual

Lemmas 13-25 mm long to base of awns; central awn 15-25 mm long
2. *A. ramosissima*

Lemmas mostly 4-6 mm long; central awn 5-9 mm long
4. *A. dichotoma*

Central awn not with a semicircular bend or spiral coil at base; plants perennial

Awn column straight or only slightly twisted   14. *A. ternipes*

Awn column strongly twisted   15. *A. orcuttiana*

Lateral awns more than one-third as long as central awn

Awns, at least the central one, with a semicircular bend or spiral coil at base

Awn column jointed at base, disarticulating at the joint at maturity; lemmas 7-10 mm long to base of awns   3. *A. desmantha*

Awn column not jointed at base, persistent on the mature floret; lemmas 4-7 mm long to base of awns   5. *A. basiramea*

Awns without a semicircular bend or spiral coil at base

Lemmas 16 mm or more long to base of awns; annual
1. *A. oligantha*

Lemmas 15 mm or less long to base of awns; annuals and perennials

Sheaths, at least the lower ones, lanate pubescent   6. *A. lanosa*

Sheaths not lanate pubescent

Panicle open or loose, at least the lower branches spreading   A

Panicle contracted, the branches usually all stiffly appressed along the main axis   AA

A (Panicle open)

Main panicle branches stout, stiffly spreading, often widely so; awns not more than 2.5 cm long

Pedicels and branchlets mostly spreading, the latter usually with calluses in the axils   10. *A. barbata*

SUBFAMILY V. ERAGROSTOIDEAE   383

Pedicels and branchlets mostly appressed, the latter without calluses in their axils

Main panicle branches spreading at a narrow angle; spikelets typically small and delicate, the awns short and slender   12. *A. pansa*

Main panicle branches mostly spreading at an angle of 40° or more at maturity

Awn column strongly twisted, usually slender and long
11. *A. divaricata*

Awn column not or only slightly twisted, usually short and stout
13. *A. hamulosa*

Main panicle branches slender and short, 1-4 cm long, at least some curving in a "U" or "S" shape under weight of mature spikelets; awns mostly 3-8 cm long

Lemmas usually 10-16 mm long to base of awns; awns mostly 3-10 cm long

Awns 5-10 cm or more long; second glume usually 16-25 mm long but occasionally shorter; lemmas mostly 13-16 mm long including the short but slender awn column   21. *A. longiseta*

Awns 3-4.5 (-6) cm long; second glume usually 15 mm or less long; lemmas mostly 10-12 mm long including the short, stout awn column   22. *A. purpurea*

Lemmas 6-9 mm long to base of awns; awns 1.5-2.8 (-3.5) cm long
23. *A. roemeriana*

AA (Panicle contracted)

Lemma narrowing into a slender, usually twisted awn column 3-6 mm long

Glumes equal or nearly so, the second mostly 13-18 mm long; leaf blades narrow but usually flat, often curled   16. *A. arizonica*

Glumes unequal, the second mostly 10-14 mm long, as much as twice as long as first; blades strongly involute   17. *A. glauca*

Lemma thick nearly to base of awns, not or only slightly twisted at apex

Awns 4-9 cm long   21. *A. longiseta*

Awns 3.5 cm or less long

Plants annual

Central awn mostly 5-15 mm long, sharply reflexed on at least some
spikelets; lateral awns one-third to slightly over one-half as long
as central awn   9A. *A. longespica* var. *longespica*

Central awn 15- (12-) 36 mm long, typically not reflexed; lateral awns
usually two-thirds to three-fourths as long as central awn

First glume slightly shorter to slightly longer than second glume;
panicles mostly 15-35 cm long, slender, the lower panicle
branches with 1-5 closely appressed spikelets
9B. *A. longespica* var. *geniculata*

First glume distinctly shorter than second glume; panicles 6-15
(-20) cm long, relatively thick, the lower panicle branches
with 6-20 spikelets when panicle more than 10 cm long
20. *A. adscensionis*

Plants perennial

First glume slightly shorter to slightly longer than second glume

Awns 24-35 mm long; lemmas 7-10 mm long   7. *A. affinis*

Awns 15-28 mm long; lemmas 5-7 mm long
8. *A. purpurascens*

First glume one-half to two-thirds as long as second glume

Leaves mostly in a short, dense basal tuft, the blades mostly 4-10
cm long; panicles typically 5-10 cm long excluding the awns
18. *A. fendleriana*

Leaves distributed on culms to well above base, the basal blades
mostly 10-25 cm long; panicles typically 10-25 cm long
19. *A. wrightii*

1. **Aristida oligantha** Michx., Fl. Bor. Amer. 1:41. 1803. OLDFIELD
THREEAWN. Fig. 204. Tufted annual. *Culms* wiry, glabrous, much-
branched at base and freely branched above base in age, 15-80 cm long.
Sheaths rounded on back, glabrous or with a few hairs on either side of collar.
Ligule a minute fringed membrane, less than 0.5 mm long. *Blades* glabrous or
sparsely hispid above, filiform, with long-attenuate, involute tips, the basal
blades 10-25 cm long and 1-2 mm broad near base, the upper blades short.
Inflorescence a few-flowered, purplish panicle or raceme mostly 5-14 cm long,
with large, widely spaced spikelets at the branch tips and on short, scabrous or
pubescent pedicels. *Glumes* narrowly lanceolate, with subequal bodies

Fig. 204. *Aristida oligantha*. Plant. From Gould and Box, 1965.

mostly 18-25 mm long, the first glume usually 3-7-nerved and awnless or short-awned, the second usually 1-nerved, with an awn to 1 cm or more in length from between two slender teeth 1-2 mm long. *Lemmas* slender, scabrous above, 6-28 mm long to base of awns, with a very short, poorly-defined awn column; awns abruptly spreading, 3-7 cm long, nearly equal or the central one longer. *Chromosome number*, $2n = 22$.

Distribution. Texas: Reported from all regions but infrequent in the extreme eastern, southern and northern portions of the State. A common and abundant weedy species of the prairie regions of central and northern Texas, most common on sandy soils but also on tight, clayey soils. General: Frequent throughout the eastern United States and westward to South Dakota and Texas; occasional in California and other western states.

Flowering period: Mid-August to November.

2. **Aristida ramosissima** A. Gray, Man., ed. 2. 550. 1856. S-CURVE THREEAWN. Slender, branching annual with culms mostly 25-50 cm tall. *Sheaths* rounded, glabrous, much shorter than the internodes. *Ligule* a ciliate membrane 0.5 mm or less long. *Blades* flat or involute, mostly 1 mm or less broad, often with a few long hairs on the adaxial surface. *Inflorescence* a narrow, contracted, few-flowered panicle or raceme 5-12 cm long, the large 1-flowered spikelets terminal or on short, stout pedicels. *First glume* usually 3-7-nerved, shorter than the second, acute or acuminate, mostly 13-20 mm long. *Second glume* 1-3-nerved, with an awn 2-6 mm or more long from between the thin, setaceous teeth of a deeply bifid apex, body of second glume mostly 18-22 mm long. *Lemmas* 16- (13-) 25 mm long to base of awn, without a well-defined awn column; central awn mostly 18-28 mm long, with a semicircular curve or coil at base; lateral awns mostly 0.5-4 mm long, occasionally lacking. *Chromosome number* not reported.

Distribution. Texas: Reportedly in eastern Texas (region 1) but no Texas collections seen by the author. A grass of relatively sterile, clayey or, less frequently, sandy loam soils, often in old fields and eroded slopes. General: Central United States from southern Indiana, Illinois and Iowa south to Louisiana and (?) eastern Texas.

Flowering period: Late summer and autumn.

3. **Aristida desmantha** Trin. & Rupr., Acad. St. Pétersb. Mém. VI. Sci. Nat. 5:109. 1842. Fig. 205. Tufted, slender annual, the culms stiffly erect, branching above base, the branches erect or only slightly spreading. *Culms* wiry, mostly 45-100 cm tall. *Sheaths* rounded, shorter than the internodes, glabrous or variously hispid, pilose or woolly. *Ligule* a minute, fringed membrane, mostly 0.2-0.3 mm long. *Blades* long and narrow, flat or involute, the basal ones 2-4.5 mm broad and 25-40 cm or more long, those of the upper culm leaves 10-30 cm or more long; blades smooth on abaxial surface and scabrous on adaxial surface. *Panicle* loosely contracted, 8-20 cm long, with short, stiffly erect-spreading, few-flowered branches. *Spikelets* light yellowish- or golden-brown, the lemmas with 3 nearly equal, spreading awns. *Glumes*

Fig. 205. *Aristida desmantha.* Inflorescence and spikelet. From Gould and Box, 1965.

1-nerved, awn-tipped, glabrous or hispid, about equal or the second slightly longer, the body usually 10-13 mm long, the awn mostly 2-4 mm long. *Lemmas* 7-10 mm long to base of awns, densely bearded on the sharp-pointed basal callus, purple-mottled at maturity, with a well-defined joint at base of the short awn column. *Awns* mostly 2-3.5 cm long. *Chromosome number* not reported.

Distribution. Texas: Regions 1, 2, 3 and 4 and the northern portion of region 6, in sandy soil, mostly in open woods or woods borders. General: Locally abundant in eastern Texas and also reported in Illinois and Nebraska.

Flowering period: Mostly September to November, occasional in June.

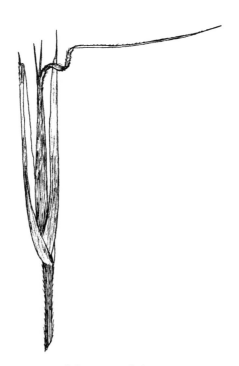

Fig. 206. *Aristida dichotoma* var. *dichotoma.* Spikelet.

4. **Aristida dichotoma** Michx., Fl. Bor. Amer. 1:41. 1803. CHURCH-MOUSE THREEAWN. Fig. 206. Delicate annual with slender, wiry culms, these generally developing short, erect branches at the middle and upper nodes. *Culms* 15-75 cm tall, sharply bent at the branched middle nodes, the branch usually erect and the main culm pushed to a lateral position. *Sheaths* rounded, much shorter than the internodes, glabrous. *Ligule* a ciliate membrane 0.2-0.3 mm long. *Blades* thin, narrow, mostly filiform, the lowermost 8-15 cm long and 1-2 (-3) mm broad, glabrous or with a few long, soft hairs. *Inflorescence* a delicate, contracted panicle or spikelike raceme, the inflorescences terminating main culms mostly 4-15 cm long, those terminating lateral branches usually shorter. *Glumes* thin, glabrous, 1-nerved, about equal or the second larger, acute or short awn-tipped, mostly 4-10 mm long including the awn. *Lemmas* 4-6 mm long to base of awns, usually blotched with purple. *Central awn* 5-9 mm long, spirally coiled at base and deflexed; lateral awns mostly 1-2 mm long, straight. *Chromosome number* not reported.

Distribution. Texas: Northern portions of regions 1, 3 and 4, mostly in sandy woods openings, old fields and open, sandy or sandy clay banks and ditches. General: Throughout the eastern United States, westward to Wisconsin, eastern Nebraska, Kansas, Oklahoma and Texas.

Flowering period: August to November.

5. **Aristida basiramea** Vasey, Bot. Gaz. 9:76. 1884. Slender, tufted annual, similar to *A. dichotoma* but the spikelets slightly larger, the lateral awns of lemma mostly 4-7 mm long and the central awn 9-15 mm long. *Chromosome number* not reported.

Distribution. Texas: Infrequent, apparently known only from Dallas and Red River counties (regions 3 and 4) and Bastrop County (region 3). General: Northeastern and central United States, from Maine and North Dakota to Kentucky, Colorado, Oklahoma and Texas.

Flowering period: Autumn.

6. **Aristida lanosa** Ell., Bot. S.C. and Ga. 1:143. 1816. WOOLLYLEAF THREEAWN. Perennial with culms tufted from a firm, often knotty base. *Culms* 70-150 cm tall, usually branching only near base. *Sheaths* rounded on back, densely lanate with soft, kinky hairs, glabrate in age. *Ligule* a minute ciliate collar, 0.2-0.5 mm long including the cilia. *Blades* elongate, filiform, flat or involute, 1-3 (-4) mm broad, the lowermost often as much as 50 cm or more long, scabrous, often sparsely hispid. *Panicles* narrow, with appressed or somewhat spreading branches, typically 15-40 (-55) cm long and 2-8 cm broad, with stiffly erect-spreading or flexuous branches below, these bare of spikelets near base, the lowermost 6-15 cm long. *Glumes* glabrous or somewhat scabrous, awnless or short awned, 9-15 mm long including the awn when present, the second glume slightly shorter than the first. *Lemmas* mostly 8-9 mm long to base of awns, untwisted above and without a well-defined awn column; *lemma awns* flexuous, at length somewhat twisted below, the lateral ones mostly 10-15 mm long, the central one 15-25 (-32) mm long, strongly deflexed at maturity. *Chromosome number* not reported.

Distribution. Texas: Regions 1, 2 and 3 and woods borders of region 4, frequent in open forest, mostly in sandy soil. General: Southeastern United States, along the Coastal Plain from New Jersey to Florida and Texas, also in Missouri, Arkansas and Oklahoma.

Flowering period: Late August or September to November.

7. **Aristida affinis** (Schult.) Kunth, Rev. Gram. 1:61. 1829. LONGLEAF THREEAWN. Tufted perennial with stiffly erect culms, long, narrow, flat blades and long, contracted inflorescences. Similar to *A. lanosa* in vegetative and inflorescence characteristics but sheaths glabrous. *Chromosome number* not reported.

Distribution. Texas: Region 1, infrequent. General: On the Coastal Plain, North Carolina to Florida and Texas; also reported from Kentucky.

Flowering period: Autumn.

8. **Aristida purpurascens** Poir., in Lam., Encyl. Sup. 1:452. 1810. ARROWFEATHER THREEAWN. Fig. 207. Tufted perennial with slender, stiffly erect, little-branched culms to 2 mm in diameter and 35-80 (-100) cm tall from a knotty base; several buds and short, slender, curving-erect rhizomes

Fig. 207. *Aristida purpurascens.* Inflorescence and spikelet.

usually present at plant base. *Sheaths* rounded, glabrous or sparsely hirsute. *Ligule* a minute fringed collar or membrane 0.2-0.3 mm long. *Blades* usually sparsely hirsute on adaxial surface near base, flat or involute, linear, elongate, mostly 1-2.5 mm broad, the lower ones 15-30 cm or more long. *Panicles* narrow, contracted but usually rather thinly-flowered, mostly 15-35 cm long. *First glume* scabrous, at least on nerve, tapering to a narrow, pointed apex, mostly 7-10 (-12) mm long. *Second glume* similar to first but usually 1-3 mm shorter. *Lemmas* purple or mottled with purple at maturity, mostly 5-7 mm long to base of awns, without a well-defined awn column. *Awns* moderately spreading to widely divergent, not twisted at base, the central awn usually spreading more than the laterals, mostly 15-28 cm long; lateral awns 2-10 mm shorter than the central one, usually not as divergent. *Chromosome number* not reported.

Distribution. Texas: Regions 1, 2, 3, 4 and 7, usually in sandy woods openings or woods borders. General: Throughout most of the eastern United States westward to Wisconsin, Kansas, Oklahoma and Texas.

Flowering period: September to November.

Chase (1951), Gould (1969) and Correll and Johnston (1971) all report the occurrence of *Aristida virgata* Trin. in eastern Texas, but it is probable that this taxon is not specifically distinct from *A. purpurascens*. All Texas collections of the complex examined appeared well within expected variation limits of *A. purpurascens*.

SUBFAMILY V. ERAGROSTOIDEAE 391

9. **Aristida longespica** Poir., in Lam., Encycl. Sup. 1:452. 1810. Tufted annual with slender, wiry, often geniculate culms 20-60 (-80) cm tall, these freely branched at the lower nodes. *Leaves* not in a conspicuous basal tuft. *Sheaths* glabrous or the lower ones hispid and often with a few long hairs in vicinity of ligule. *Ligule* a minute fringed membrane. *Blades* filiform, flat or involute, mostly 0.5-1 mm broad. *Inflorescence* a slender, contracted panicle with spikelets appressed on main axis and on short branches. *Glumes* usually about equal, narrowly acute or acuminate, the second occasionally slightly 3-lobed. *Lemmas* slender, often mottled or barred with purple.

9A. **Aristida longespica** Poir. var. **longespica.** SLIMSPIKE THREEAWN. Fig. 208. *Inflorescences* mostly 10-20 cm long, usually with few and widely spaced spikelets. Glumes 3-7 mm long. *Lemmas* 4-7 (-8) mm long, with a sharply reflexed middle awn mostly 6-15 cm long and much shorter, reflexed or erect lateral awns. *Chromosome number* not reported.

Distribution. Texas: Regions 1, 2, 3 and 4, most frequent in loose, sandy soils. General: Throughout the eastern United States, westward to Iowa, Kansas, Oklahoma and Texas.

9B. **Aristida longespica** Poir. var. **geniculata** (Raf.) Fern., Rhodora 35:318. 1933. *Aristida intermedia* Scribn. & Ball. KEARNEY THREEAWN. Fig. 209. *Inflorescence* mostly 15-35 cm long. *Glumes* mostly 6-9 mm long. *Lemmas* 7-9 mm long to base of awns. *Lemma awns* spreading (infrequently some reflexed), the central awn 15-36 mm long, the lateral awns slightly shorter.

Distribution. Texas: Regions 1, 2, 3, 4, 5 and 6 and the eastern portion of region 7, usually in sandy soil, often in woods clearings and along woods borders. General: Michigan, western Florida and Mississippi westward to Nebraska and Texas.

Flowering period: Late August to December.

For the most part, plants of *A. longespica* var. *geniculata* tend to be larger and to have larger spikelets and longer awns than do those of var. *longespica*. Chase (1951) and Correll and Johnston (1970) use the name *A. intermedia* for this taxon. Intermediacy between the two varieties of *A. longespica* may be observed in many localities.

10. **Aristida barbata** Fourn., Mex. Pl. 2:78. 1886. HAVARD THREEAWN. Low perennial with densely tufted culms often forming large clumps. *Culms* slender, stiffly erect mostly 15-40 cm tall, glabrous. *Sheaths* rounded, usually hairy on collar, at least on margins. *Ligule* a fringed membrane, about 0.5 mm long. *Blades* narrow, involute, mostly 5-15 cm long and 1.5 mm or less broad. *Panicles* mostly 6-18 cm long, relatively few-flowered, the primary branches short, widely spreading, sparingly rebranched. *Secondary branches and pedicels* typically spreading and with calluses in their axils, the spikelets widely spreading or even reflexed, appearing uniformly distributed throughout the panicle. *Glumes* subequal, mostly 8-13 mm long.

Fig. 208. *Aristida longespica* var. *longespica*. Inflorescence and spikelet.

Lemma gradually narrowing into a scabrous, usually twisted awn column, the body mostly 5-7 mm long including the long, stiffly bearded callus, the awn column 2-5 mm long; awns subequal, 8-22 mm long. *Chromosome number,* $2n = 22$.

Distribution. Texas: Regions 9 and 10 but infrequent in region 9, on open, sandy or rocky, dry slopes and flats. General: Western Texas to Arizona and central Mexico.

Flowering period: Mostly September to October but occasionally as early as July.

Included in this species is *A. dissita* I. M. Johnston which Correll & Johnston (1970) treated as distinct.

SUBFAMILY V. ERAGROSTOIDEAE   393

Fig. 209. *Aristida longespica* var. *geniculata*. Inflorescence and spikelet. From Gould and Box, 1965, as *A. intermedia*.

11. **Aristida divaricata** Willd., Enum. Pl. 1:99. 1809. POVERTY THREEAWN. Tufted perennial with slender, wiry culms mostly 25-70 cm tall. *Sheaths* rounded on back, usually with short or long soft hairs on collar. *Ligule* a fringed membrane, 0.5-1 mm long. *Blades* scabrous or short scabrous-pubescent on adaxial surface, 6-20 cm long, 1-3 mm broad, usually involute but those of the upper leaves often remaining flat at least near base. *Panicles* mostly 10-30 cm long, with widely spreading, often long primary branches, these typically bare of spikelets on lower one-half or one-third; secondary branches and pedicels appressed along the primary branches, usually without well-developed calluses in their axils. *Spikelets* similar to those of *A. barbata*, with a twisted awn column. *Chromosome number*, $2n = 22$.

Distribution. Texas: Regions 9 and 10, infrequent in region 9 but more common in region 10 where it grows on open, gravelly or sandy slopes and plains at the higher elevations. General: Kansas to southern California and south to Texas, Mexico and Guatemala.

Flowering period: Mostly September and October but occasionally as early as June.

Aristida divaricata is closely related to *A. barbata* from which it differs in the appressed branchlets and spikelets, in the frequently larger panicles, and in general habit. Hitchcock noted the close relationships of the two, stating (North Amer. Flora 17 (5):388, 1935) "This species (*A. barbata*) is closely allied to *A. divaricata*, but is distinguished by the hemispheric habit of growth and the flexuous or implicate branches and pedicels. In *A. divaricata* the culms are often prostrate or nearly so but do not form hemispheric tufts; the main branches are naked at the base and the pedicels usually appressed along the upper part of the branches. In *A. barbata* the branches are shorter and bear a basal branch, so that the spikelets are evenly distributed through the panicle."

12. **Aristida pansa** Woot. & Standl., Contr. U. S. Natl. Herb. 16:112. 1913. WOOTON THREEAWN. Fig. 210. Tufted perennial with stiffly erect culms mostly 20-50 cm tall. *Sheaths* hairy on collar, at least on the margins, the lower sheaths usually coarsely scabrous or with a fine, dense covering of short, appressed hairs. *Blades* usually involute but occasionally flat, to 15 cm long, 0.7-1.5 mm broad, scabrous or scabrous-pubescent on adaxial surface. *Panicles* narrow but not densely-flowered, 10-20 cm long, with stiffly erect-spreading branches, the lowermost 2-8 cm long. *Spikelets* closely appressed to branchlets, the pedicels usually without calluses in their axils. *Glumes* unequal, the first usually 5-7 mm long, the second 7-12 mm long. *Lemma* equaling or slightly shorter than second glume, pubescent on the stout callus, narrowing above to a straight or slightly twisted awn column about 2 mm long; awns subequal, 10-20 (-25) mm long. *Chromosome number*, $2n = 22$.

Distribution. Texas: Region 10 and western portion of region 7, on dry, rocky slopes and plains. General: Texas, New Mexico, Arizona and northern Mexico.

Flowering period: June to October.

Aristida pansa appears closely related to *A. divaricata* but typically has a more contracted panicle and lemmas with less twisted awn columns. This species also seems to grade into *A. roemeriana* but differs in the twisted awn column and the usually longer and stiffer lower inflorescence branches.

13. **Aristida hamulosa** Henr., Meded Rijks. Herb. 54:219. 1926. HOOK THREEAWN. Fig. 211. Tufted perennial with culms 30-75 cm tall from a firm base. *Sheaths* usually with tufts of hair on either side of collar. *Ligule* a ciliate membrane, about 0.5 mm long. *Blades* involute or some remaining flat, the lower ones 10-30 cm long and 1-3 mm broad, scabrous and often with a few long hairs on adaxial surface above ligule. *Panicles* mostly 18-40 cm long, with

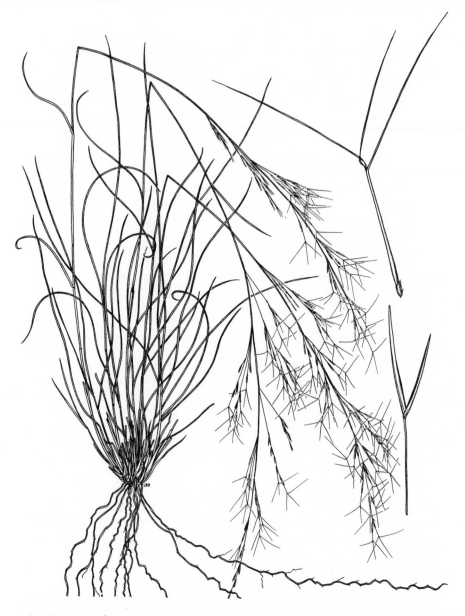

Fig. 210. *Aristida pansa.* Plant and spikelet with floret separated from glumes. From Gould, 1951.

stiffly spreading or reflexed branches, these often to 15 cm or more long and bare of spikelets on the lower one-half or two-thirds. *Primary* branches sparingly rebranched, with spikelets typically appressed to the branchlets and clustered near their tips. *Glumes* about equal or the second slightly shorter than the first, mostly 9-15 mm long. *Lemmas* 10-15 mm long to base of awns, with a bearded callus about 1 mm long and a stout, coarsely scabrous body;

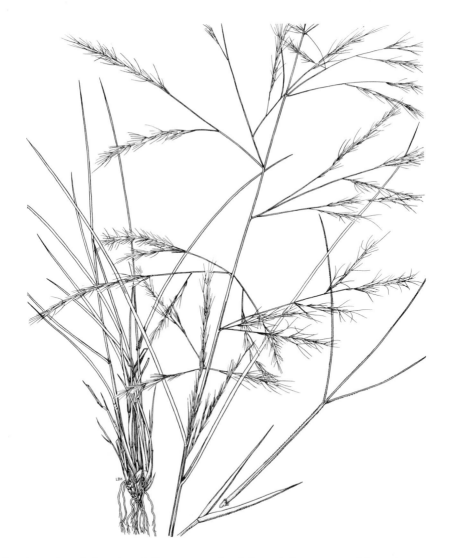

Fig. 211. *Aristida hamulosa.* Inflorescence and spikelet with floret separated from glumes. From Gould, 1951.

neck of lemma not or only slightly twisted. *Awns* usually about equal or the lateral ones shorter than the middle one, 8-25 (-30) mm long, not widely spreading. *Chromosome number,* $2n = 44$.

Distribution. Texas: Region 10 on dry slopes and plains. General: Texas to southern California and south to Guatemala.

Flowering period: Mostly July to September.

Aristida hamulosa is similar to *A. divaricata* but typically is more robust and has an untwisted or very slightly twisted lemma awn column.

14. **Aristida ternipes** Cav., Icon. Pl. 5:46. 1799. SPIDERGRASS. Coarse perennial with tufted culms 30-100 cm tall, generally similar to *A. hamulosa* but central awn of lemma 4-12 mm long and lateral awns absent or rudimentary, infrequently as much as 2 mm long. *Chromosome number, 2n = 22.*

Distribution. Texas: Region 10 on dry, open, rocky or sandy slopes and plains. General: Texas, New Mexico, Arizona, the West Indies and northern South America.

Flowering period: May to October.

15. **Aristida orcuttiana** Vasey, Bull. Torrey Bot. Club 13:27. 1886. SINGLEAWN ARISTIDA. Fig. 212. Tufted perennial with culms in small or large clumps. *Culms* 30-100 cm tall, unbranched except at base. *Sheaths* rounded on back or the basal ones flattened in age, glabrous or occasionally scabrous-pubescent, short- or long-hairy on the collar, at least on margins. *Ligule* a ciliate membrane, 0.5-1 mm long. *Blades* involute, at least at tips, mostly 8-30 cm long and 1-2 mm broad. *Panicles* loosely contracted or open, all or only the lower branches spreading or reflexed in age; lower branches 7-15 cm or more long, usually bare of spikelets below the middle or lower two-thirds. *Spikelets* appressed on the branchlets, the branchlets and pedicels typically without calluses in their axils. *Glumes* usually unequal, the second 8-12 mm long, the first 1.5-5 mm shorter. *Lemmas* 7-11 mm long including the bearded callus and tightly-twisted, scabrous awn column; the body usually minutely rugose and dark violet or blotched with violet at maturity. *Central awn* rather delicate, mostly 6-14 mm long; *lateral awns* absent or minute, rarely 2 mm or more long. *Chromosome number* not reported.

Distribution. Texas: Region 10 on rocky slopes at moderately high elevations, not common. General: Western Texas to southern California and northwestern Mexico.

Flowering period: July to October.

This probably is the best *Aristida* forage species in North America. It is nowhere abundant but most frequent at medium altitudes in grasslands of the southwestern mountain ranges.

16. **Aristida arizonica** Vasey, Bull. Torrey Bot. Club 13:27. 1886. ARIZONA THREEAWN. Tufted perennial. *Culms* in small clumps, stiffly erect, 30-100 cm or more tall. *Sheaths* rounded on back, glabrous or hairy on upper margins and on either side of collar. *Ligule* a fringed membrane, 0.5 mm or less long. *Blades* mostly 10-25 cm or more long, 1-3 (-4) mm broad, flat or involute, the basal blades often remaining flat, loosely curled and shaving-like. *Panicles* 10-25 cm long, contracted, few-flowered, with typically erect-appressed lower branches 2-6 cm long. *Glumes* equal or the first slightly shorter, brownish or bronze-tinged, usually narrow at apex and often short-aristate; second glume mostly 13-18 mm long. *Lemmas* mostly 13-16 mm long to base of awns, with a slender, twisted awn column 3-6 mm long; central awn mostly 2-3.5 cm long, slightly longer than the lateral awns. *Chromosome number, 2n = 22.*

Fig. 212. *Aristida orcuttiana.* Plant, separate inflorescence and spikelet with floret separated from glumes. From Gould, 1951.

Distribution. Texas: Region 10, on the higher mountain slopes, not frequent. General: Colorado to Texas, Arizona and Mexico.

Flowering period: July to October.

Aristida arizonica is a relatively distinct species but is closely related to *A. glauca* which generally occupies lower and drier sites. It is characterized by the narrow panicle, equal or nearly equal brownish- or bronze-tinged glumes, long, twisted awn column and the often flat, shavinglike lower blades.

SUBFAMILY V. ERAGROSTOIDEAE   399

17. **Aristida glauca** (Nees) Walp., Ann. Bot. 1:925. 1849. BLUE THREEAWN. Low tufted perennial with slender, erect culms. *Culms* mostly 15-50 (-65) cm tall, glabrous or rarely the lower thinly puberulous. *Sheaths* glabrous, scabrous or minutely puberulent on back, usually with tufts of long, soft hairs on either side of collar. *Ligule* a fringed membrane, 0.2-0.5 mm long. *Blades* long or short, basally clustered or well-scattered on the culms, typically glabrous and galucous, tightly involute and stiffly curved, mostly 0.7-1.5 mm broad. *Panicles* usually 6-18 cm long, characteristically slender and contracted, with tightly erect-appressed branches and spikelets; occasionally with a few slender, curved and spreading lower branches. Glumes narrowly acute or slightly acuminate, unequal, the first glume mostly one-half to two-thirds as long as the second, the second usually 7-12 mm long. *Lemmas* to base of awns mostly 1-3 mm longer than second glume, the slender body gradually tapering into a delicate, somewhat twisted awn column 1-4 mm long. *Awns* subequal or the middle one slightly longer than the laterals, characteristically 15-20 mm long but occasionally to 35 mm long. *Chromosome number*, $2n = 44$.

Distribution. Texas: Regions 5, 6, 7, 8, 9 and 10, abundant on dry slopes and plains in the western portion of the State, infrequent in the northern portions of regions 5, 8 and 9 and in the southern portion of region 6. General: Utah and southern Nevada, south to Texas, Arizona, southern California and northern Mexico.

Flowering period: Mostly May to October but flowering almost throughout the year under favorable climatic conditions.

As herein interpreted, *A. glauca* is somewhat of a "catch-all" taxon, including plants that show intermediacy between this and closely related species including *A. purpurea, A. roemeriana, A. fendleriana, A. wrightii* and *A. arizonica.* Characteristically, *A. glauca* has basally tufted leaves with rather short blades, a short, tightly-contracted inflorescence, unequal glumes, a slender lemma with a long, narrow, twisted neck and rather short awns.

18. **Aristida fendleriana** Steud., Syn. Pl. Glum. 1:420. 1855. FENDLER THREEAWN. Fig. 213. Low tufted perennial with wiry culms mostly 10-35 cm tall. *Leaves* numerous, short, mostly in a dense basal tuft. *Blades* fine, firm, tightly involute, usually 2-6 cm long and seldom over 10 cm long. *Inflorescences* slender, few-flowered, mostly 3-13 cm long, often reduced to a raceme with 2-6 spikelets but usually a simple panicle. *Spikelets* appressed to main axis or some on slender, S-curved branches. *Glumes* unequal, the second usually 11-15 mm long, the first one-half to two-thirds as long as the second. *Lemmas* mostly 11-13 mm long to base of awns, glabrous or scabrous in lines above, with a short, straight or slightly twisted, poorly-defined awn column; awns widely spreading, mostly 2-3.5 cm long, the central awn slightly longer than the lateral awns. *Chromosome number* not reported.

Distribution. Texas: Regions 9 and 10 on dry, open, sandy or gravelly slopes and flats, infrequent. General: North Dakota and Montana, south to Texas, Arizona and southern California.

Fig. 213. *Aristida fendleriana*. Plant. From Hitchcock, 1935.

Flowering period: July to September.

19. **Aristida wrightii** Nash, in Small, Fl. Southeast. U. S. 116. 1903.
WRIGHT THREEAWN. Tufted perennial with rather coarse and tough
culms mostly 35-80 cm tall. *Leaves* glaucous, distributed to well above the
base. *Sheaths* glabrous, scabrous or puberulent, the collar often short-hairy on
the back with tufts of long hairs on the sides. *Ligule* a fringed membrane, 0.5
mm or less long. *Blades* firm, involute or mostly so, the lower ones 10-25 cm
long and 1-2 mm broad, scabrous or scabrous-pubescent on adaxial surface.
Panicles contracted, 12-27 cm long, occasionally with rather long, stiff and

slightly spreading lower branches. *Glumes* rather broad, unequal, the second 11-15 mm long, the first one-half to three-fourths as long as the second. *Lemmas* stout, with a thick, scabrous, straight or slightly twisted awn column, equal to or slightly longer than second glume. *Awns* equal or the central one longer, mostly 15-30 mm long, the central awn occasionally as much as 40 mm long. *Chromosome number*, $2n=66$.

Distribution. Texas: Regions 5, 6, 7, 8, 9 and 10 and the northwestern portion of region 4, most frequent in regions 7 and 10, on dry, gravelly or sandy slopes and flats. General: Oklahoma to Utah and south to Texas, Arizona, southern California and northern Mexico.

Flowering period: Mostly May to October but occasionally as late as December.

Aristida wrightii is close to *A. fendleriana* but does not have the short, basally clustered leaves of that species and usually has a longer inflorescence.

20. **Aristida adscensionis** L., Sp. Pl. 82. 1753. SIXWEEKS THREEAWN. Fig. 214. Tufted annual, extremely variable in size, growth habit and longevity. *Culms* wiry, erect and unbranched or geniculate, spreading and freely branched, mostly 15-50 cm tall but occasionally from less than 10-80 cm or more tall. *Sheaths* rounded on back, glabrous, often much shorter than internodes. *Ligule* a fringed membrane 0.5-1 mm long. *Blades* flat or involute, 1-2.5 mm broad, variable in length but usually short, scabrous or finely hispid on adaxial surface. *Panicles* contracted, 6-15 (-20) cm long, often interrupted below, with the spikelets aggregated on short, widely-spaced branches. *Glumes* unequal, the first 4-8 mm long, the second 7-11 mm long. *Lemmas* 6-9 mm long to base of awns, usually scabrous in lines above. *Awns* scabrous, flattened at base, spreading but usually not widely so, the middle awn 7-15 (-20) mm long, the lateral awns slightly shorter (occasionally much shorter). *Chromosome number*, $2n=22$.

Distribution. Texas: Regions 6, 7 and 10 and occasional in the southern portions of regions 8 and 9, on dry, clayey or rocky slopes and flats. General: Western Missouri, Kansas and Texas to southern Nevada and California, southward through Mexico and South America, also in Africa.

Flowering period: Mostly June to October.

21. **Aristida longiseta** Steud., Syn. Pl. Glum. 1:420. 1855. RED THREEAWN. Fig. 215. Low to moderately tall, densely tufted perennial. *Culms* 10-35, occasionally -50, cm tall. *Leaves* short and in a dense tuft at base of plant or longer and well-distributed on the lower portion of the culms. *Sheaths* rounded on back, pubescent on collar and with tufts of long, soft hairs on either side of collar. *Ligule* a ciliate membrane 0.5 mm or less long. *Blades* firm, involute, 2 mm or less broad; in some plants the blades all less than 8 cm long, in others the blades to 15 cm long. *Inflorescences* narrow, flexuous or stiffly erect, contracted or open and with slender, spreading or drooping, few-flowered branches, usually paniculate but occasionally reduced to a

Fig. 214. *Aristida adscensionis*. Plant. From Hitchcock, 1935.

3-6-flowered raceme. *Spikelets* on short or long pedicels. *Glumes* broad, unequal, the first one-half to two-thirds as long as the second, the second typically 16-25 mm long. *Lemmas* mostly 13-15 mm long to base of awns, thick and straight or slightly twisted above, without a well-defined neck or awn column. *Awns* nearly equal, mostly 4-10 cm long, relatively stout when 5 cm or less long. *Chromosome number*, $2n = 22$.

Distribution. Texas: Regions 2, 4, 5, 6, 7, 8, 9 and 10 on well-drained roadbanks and ditchbanks, dry, open slopes and flats and washes. General: Western United States from North Dakota, Iowa, Oklahoma and Texas westward to Washington, Oregon, Utah and Arizona; also in northern Mexico.

Flowering period: Mostly April to November but collected in flower from March to December.

A widespread, variable species frequent on sterile soils over a wide range and seeming to intergrade with *Aristida purpurea*, *A. fendleriana* and possibly *A. glauca* and *A. wrightii*.

SUBFAMILY V. ERAGROSTOIDEAE   403

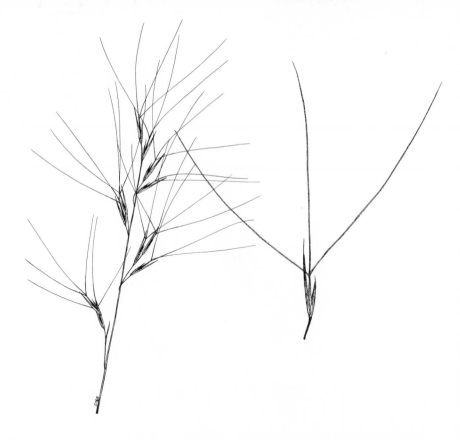

Fig. 215. *Aristida longiseta.* Inflorescence and spikelet. From Gould and Box, 1965.

22. **Aristida purpurea** Nutt., Trans. Amer. Philos. Soc. n. s. 5:145. 1837. PURPLE THREEAWN. Fig. 216. Low perennial with slender, tufted culms 25-70 (-90) cm tall. *Leaves* in a dense basal cluster or more frequently well-distributed on lower portion of culms. *Sheaths* glabrous, scabrous or puberulent, often with tufts of hair on either side of collar. *Ligule* a ciliate membrane 0.3-0.6 mm long. *Blades* variable in length, mostly 3-18 cm long, 0.7-2 mm broad, typically involute but the basal ones often remaining flat. *Panicles* 10-25 cm long, loosely- or closely-flowered but usually not appearing dense, the main axis flexuous and curving at maturity, the branches and pedicels slender, often capillary, spreading and curving under the weight of the mature grain but mostly erect when spikelets are immature and after they have shattered. *Glumes* unequal, the second mostly 11-15 mm long, as much as twice the length of the first. *Lemma* typically 10-12 mm long to base of awns, usually scabrous in lines above, straight or slightly twisted above; awns mostly 3.5-4.5 cm long, occasionally -6 cm long. *Chromosome numbers*, $2n = 22$ and 44.

Distribution. Texas: Throughout the State, except in regions 1 and 3, on both sandy and clayey soils, frequent in almost solid stands on road right-of-

Fig. 216. *Aristida purpurea.* Plant and spikelet. From Gould and Box, 1965.

ways in many areas. General: Arkansas and Kansas to southern Utah, south and west New Mexico, Arizona, southern California and northern Mexico.

Flowering period: Mostly April to October but occasionally flowering throughout the year.

A highly variable, poorly understood species that apparently intergrades with both *A. longiseta* and *A. roemeriana.*

23. **Aristida roemeriana** Scheele, Linnaea 22:343. 1849. ROEMER THREEAWN. Fig. 217. Plants vegetatively similar to *A. purpurea,* the erect or branching culms 15-70 cm tall. *Panicles* narrow but loose, mostly 5-18 cm long, with relatively small and delicate spikelets, some nearly sessile but many on capillary branchlets and pedicels, these U- or S-curved when grains mature and heavy. *Glumes* narrow, unequal, the first 3-6 mm long, the second usually twice as long or longer. *Lemmas* 6-8 (-9) mm long to base of awns, not twisted at apex. *Awns* nearly equal, usually not widely divergent, mostly 1.5-2.8 cm long but occasionally to 3.5 cm long. *Chromosome number,* $2n=44$.

Distribution. Texas: Frequent in sandy or clayey soils in region 6 and in the southern portion of region 2; also present in regions 7 and 10 and possibly

Fig. 217. *Aristida roemeriana*. Inflorescence and floret. From Hitchcock, 1935.

in the southern portion of regions 5, 8 and 9 but plants of these areas less typical and very similar to small forms of *A. purpurea*. General: Texas and northeastern Mexico and reported from New Mexico by Chase (1951) and Correll and Johnston (1970).

Flowering period: Commonly flowering in early spring and throughout the year under favorable conditions.

SUBFAMILY VI. PANICOIDEAE

Tribe 20. Paniceae

89. DIGITARIA Heister

Annuals and perennials, with erect or decumbent-spreading culms, membranous ligules and usually thin, flat blades. *Inflorescence* a panicle with few to numerous slender, spikelike branches, these unbranched or sparingly branched near the base with spikelets subsessile or short-pediceled in two rows on a flat or 3-angled, often winged rachis. *Spikelets* 2-flowered, the lower floret staminate or neuter, the upper perfect. Disarticulation below the glumes. *First glume* minute or absent. *Second glume* well-developed but usually shorter than lemma of lower floret. *Lemma of upper floret* relatively narrow, acute or acuminate, firm and cartilaginous but not hard, the margins thin and flat, not inrolled over the palea.

A genus of about 300 species distributed in temperate and tropical regions throughout the world.

Rachis of inflorescence branch winged, the wings often as broad as the body; annuals with weak, usually decumbent or trailing culms, these rooting at the lower nodes

Spikelets 2.2-3.5 mm long; lemma of upper floret light brown or grayish

Lemma of lower floret of lower spikelet of a pair glabrous or inconspicuously pubescent on margins, 5-nerved, the nerves not equidistant, the lateral ones crowded to the margins; first glume of lowermost spikelet of a pair obtuse or acute, often more than 0.3 mm long; glabrous or inconspicuously pubescent on margins

Second glume 1.0-1.7 mm long; spikelets 2.2-3 (occasionally -3.2) mm long; lemma of lower floret scabrous-hispid on the lateral nerves; leaves rather densely covered with papilla-based hairs, the blades usually pubescent on both surfaces for their entire length   1. *D. sanguinalis*

Second glume 1.6-2.7 mm long; spikelets 2.8 (occasionally 2.5) -3.5 mm long; lemma of lower floret not scabrous-hispid on the lateral nerves; leaves glabrous or sparsely pubescent with papilla-based hairs   2. *D. ciliaris*

Lemma of lower floret of lower spikelet of a pair, densely villous on margins, with 5 equidistant nerves; first glume of lower spikelet rounded or truncate, 0.3 mm or less long   3. *D. bicornis*

Spikelets 2 mm or less long; lemma of upper floret dark brown at maturity

Spikelets about 1.5 mm long   4. *D. violascens*

Spikelets about 2 mm long   5. *D. ischaemum*

Rachis of inflorescence branch not winged or obscurely so; annuals and perennials

Spikelets silky-pubescent with long, whitish hairs; leaf blades 2-4 mm broad; perennials

Inflorescence contracted, the branches appressed, closely-flowered; grain abruptly pointed   7. *D. californica*

Inflorescence open, the branches stiffly erect-spreading, with widely-spaced spikelets; grain gradually tapering to a point
                                                      8. *D. patens*

Spikelets variously pubescent but the hairs not silvery or purple-tinged when long; leaf blades 2-10 mm broad; perennials and annuals

Hairs of lemma of lower floret 2-4 mm long   6. *D. insularis*

Hairs of lemma of lower floret not over 1 mm long

Inflorescence branches few, mostly 2-4 cm long   9.   *D. hitchcockii*

Inflorescence branches few to numerous, some or all 6-12 cm or more long

Lemma of upper floret dark brown at maturity; culms erect or somewhat decumbent at base, never stoloniferous or rooting at lower nodes

Second glume and lemma of lower floret densely villous on margins; plant perennial, with short, hard, "knotty", rhizomatous culm bases   8.   *D. patens*

Second glume and lemma of lower floret puberulent on margins; plant annual, without hard, "knotty" culm bases

Spikelets 1.5-1.9 mm long; inflorescence branches mostly 8-13 cm long   10.   *D. filiformis*

Spikelets 2-2.6 mm long; inflorescence branches mostly 13-25 cm long   11.   *D. villosa*

Lemma of upper floret light brown or grayish at maturity; culms decumbent-erect, often somewhat stoloniferous and rooting at lower nodes

Spikelets 2-2.5 mm long, sparsely villous to glabrous
12.   *D. texana*

Spikelets 2.8-3.6 mm long, usually densely villous
13.   *D. runyoni*

1. **Digitaria sanguinalis** (L.) Scop., Fl. Carn. ed 2. 1:52. 1772. HAIRY CRABGRASS. Fig. 218. Annual with soft, weak stems, these decumbent-spreading and branching at base, often rooting at lower nodes. *Sheaths* pubescent with papilla-based hairs. *Ligules* glabrous, irregularly dissected, mostly 1-2.5 mm long. *Blades* 5-10 mm broad, usually pubescent on both surfaces with papilla-based hairs. *Inflorescence* with usually 4-9 primary branches, these digitate at culm apex or at the apex and in 1 or 2 verticils below, the branches slender, unbranched, mostly 6-14 cm long. *Branch rachis* strongly 3-angled and slightly winged, 1-1.4 mm broad, with spikelets in unequally pediceled pairs, the members of a pair essentially similar. *Spikelets* 2.2-3 (occasionally 3.2) mm long. *First glume* minute, scalelike, obtuse or acute. *Second glume* 1-1.7 mm long, puberulent on margins. *Lemma of lower floret* with 5 strong nerves, the lateral nerves scabrous at least above. *Palea* of lower floret minute or absent. *Lemma of upper floret* light brown, about as long as spikelet. Mean pollen size, 32.2-34.5 microns. *Chromosome number*, 2n=36.

Fig. 218. *Digitaria sanguinalis*. Plant, two views of spikelet and a floret. From Hitchcock, 1935.

Distribution. Texas: Regions 1, 3, 4, 5, 7, 8, 9 and 10. General: Major distribution in North America from Canada southward to Virginia, Kentucky and Texas and westward to California; reportedly adventive from Europe. A common weed of roadsides, lawns, field borders and gardens.

Flowering period: July to November.

2. **Digitaria ciliaris** (Retz.) Koel., Descr. Gram. 27. 1802. *Digitaria adscendens* (H.B.K.) Henrard. *Digitaria sanguinalis* var. *ciliaris* (Retz.) Parl. SOUTHERN CRABGRASS. Decumbent, spreading annual, similar to *D. sanguinalis* in general habit but differing in the following characteristics: *Leaves* glabrous or sparsely pubescent with papilla-based hairs. *Spikelets* 2.8 (occasionally 2.5) -3.5 mm long. *Second glume* 1.6-2.7 mm long. *Lemma of lower floret* not scabrous on lateral nerves. *Mean pollen size* 36.2-40.9 microns. *Chromosome number,* $2n=54$.

Distribution. Texas: Throughout the State in all regions but more frequent in the south, growing as a weed of road right-of-ways, lawns, gardens and field borders. General: Southern Virginia to southeastern Nebraska and south through Mexico and Central America to South America; presumably introduced from the Old World.

Flowering period: June to November.

Chase in Hitchcock's Manual (1951) referred plants of *Digitaria ciliaris* to the typical variety of *D. sanguinalis*. Fernald (1950) used the name *D. sanguinalis* var. *ciliaris* for this taxon. As pointed out by Ebinger (1962) and Gould (1963), the morphological, cytological and distributional differences indicated above show this species to be relatively distinct from *D. sanguinalis*.

3. **Digitaria bicornis** (Lam.) R. & S., Syst. 2:470. 1817. *Digitaria diversifolia* Swallen. Annual with decumbent-spreading culms, these often stoloniferous at base and rooting at lower nodes. Generally similar to *Digitaria sanguinalis* and *D. ciliaris* but differing in the key characters and also in having the octoploid $(2n=72)$ chromosome number rather than being tetraploid $(2n=36)$ as *D. sanguinalis* or hexaploid $(2n=54)$ as *D. ciliaris*.

Distribution. Texas: Regions 2 and 6. General: Tropics and subtropics of the world, apparently introduced in North America, a weed of roadsides, cultivated areas and waste places.

Flowering period: June to November.

4. **Digitaria violascens** Link, Hort. Berol. 1:229. 1827. VIOLET CRABGRASS. Tufted annual, the culms branched at the base and spreading-erect, mostly 30-50 cm tall. *Leaves* essentially glabrous except for a few cilia on sheath and blade margins in vicinity of sheath-blade junction. *Ligules* truncate, glabrous, usually 1-1.5 mm long. *Blades* 2-6 mm broad. *Inflorescence branches* 3-9 cm long, mostly 2-6 per culm, commonly all digitate at culm apex or with 1-2 branches below the apical cluster. *Spikelets* 1.3-1.7 mm long. *First glume* minute or absent. *Second glume* about three-fourths as long as lemma of upper floret, puberulent. *Lemma of lower floret* as long as that of upper floret, irregularly 5-7-nerved, pubescent with non-glandular hairs. *Lemma* of upper floret dark brown at maturity. *Chromosome number,* $2n=36$.

Distribution. Texas: Region 1 in partial shade in open pine or mixed pine-hardwood forest. General: Georgia and Florida to Arkansas, Texas and south into Central America; also present in tropical Asia.

Flowering period: August to November.

5. **Digitaria ischaemum** (Schreb.) Schreb. *ex* Muhl., Muhl., Cat. Pl. 9. 1813. SMOOTH CRABGRASS. Fig. 219. Tufted annual, similar to *Digitaria violascens* in size, general habit and inflorescence characters, except the spikelets mostly 1.9-2.2 mm long, the hairs of second glume and lemma of lower floret often minutely capitellate and the second glume more than three-fourths as long as lemma of upper floret. *Chromosome number*, $2n=36$.

Distribution. Texas: Region 1, infrequent in open pine forest. General: Widespread throughout temperate and subtropical North America and widely distributed in Europe and Asia.

Flowering period: August to November.

6. **Digitaria insularis** (L.) Mez *ex* Ekmann, Ark. Bot. 13:22. 1913. *Trichachne insularis* (L.) Nees, SOURGRASS. Fig. 220. Perennial with firm culms mostly 70-150 cm tall, stiffly erect from a hard, knotty base. *Lowermost leaf sheaths* densely pubescent, the herbage otherwise essentially glabrous. *Ligules* glabrous, 2-3 mm long. *Blades* elongate, mostly 0.4-1 cm broad (in Texas). *Panicle* contracted, rather densely-flowered, 15-30 cm long, the lower branches long but appressed along main axis. *Spikelets* mostly 3.6-4.2 mm long excluding the hairs. *First glume* minute. *Second glume and lemma of lower floret* densely shaggy-hirsute with long, brownish hairs, the hairs exceeding the spikelet in length. *Lemma of lower floret* usually pubescent on back as well as on margins. *Lemma* of upper floret dark brown, lanceolate-acuminate, gradually tapering to a point or short awn, as long as the spikelet. *Chromosome number*, $2n=36$.

Distribution. Texas: Regions 2, 6 and 10 and the southern portion of regions 3 and 7, rather frequent along ditches and moist or wet depressions. General: Florida to Arizona and south through Mexico and the West Indies to Argentina.

Flowering period: August to November.

The most northerly records in Texas are from Ward County (*Reeves* & *Morrow G-106*) and southern Caldwell County (*Silveus 5730*). The reported collection date of the Caldwell County collection, 28 April (1940), casts some doubt on the validity of this record.

7. **Digitaria californica** (Benth.) Henr., Blumea 1:99. 1934. *Trichachne californica* (Benth.) Chase, J. Wash. Acad. Sci. 23:455. 1933. CALIFORNIA COTTONTOP. Fig. 221. Cespitose perennial with stiffly erect culms mostly 50-100 cm tall from a firm, knotty base covered with densely pubescent scale leaves. *Leaves* glabrous, except for the felty-pubescent lower sheaths, or

Fig. 219. *Digitaria ischaemum.* Inflorescence and spikelet.

Fig. 220. *Digitaria insularis.* Inflorescence and spikelet. From Gould and Box, 1965.

sparsely hairy. *Blades* mostly 2-5 mm, occasionally -7 mm, broad, those at the middle and upper culm nodes 2-12 cm long. *Panicles* narrow, densely-flowered, usually 8-12 (occasionally -15) cm long, typically with appressed, mostly simple branches. *Spikelets* 3-4 mm long excluding the hairs. *Second glume* and margins of lemma of lower floret densely hirsute with silvery or purple-tinged hairs 2-4 mm long. *Lemma of lower floret* glabrous on back. *Lemma of upper floret* ovate-lanceolate, abruptly narrowing to a short awn tip. *Chromosome numbers* reported, $2n=36$, 54, 70 and 72.

Distribution. Texas: Regions 2, 4, 5, 6, 7, 8, 9 and 10 on open, well-drained soils. General: Colorado to Texas, Arizona and northern Mexico.

Flowering period: July to November.

Fig. 221.   *Digitaria californica*. Plant and spikelet. From Gould, 1951, as *Trichachne californica*.

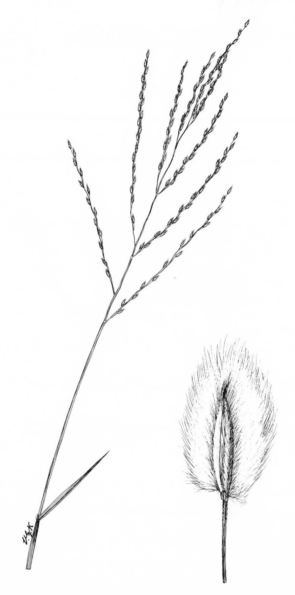

Fig. 222. *Digitaria patens.* Inflorescence and spikelet. From Gould and Box, 1965.

8. **Digitaria patens** (Swallen) Henr., Blumea 1:99. 1934. *Trichachne patens* Swallen, Amer. J. Bot. 19:442. 1932. TEXAS COTTONTOP. Fig. 222. Cespitose perennial, generally similar to *Digitaria californica* but the inflorescence branches stiffly spreading, frequently as much as 12 cm long, and the spikelets widely spaced, not or only slightly imbricated. Hairs of second glume and lemma of lower floret generally shorter than the spikelet. *Chromosome number,* $2n=72.$

Distribution. Texas: Regions 6 and 7 and the southern portion of region 2, on well-drained, usually sandy soil. General: Southern Texas and northern Mexico.

Flowering period: May to November.

Digitaria patens appears to be an octoploid derivative of *D. californica* stock. It differs from the latter species in having a more open, often slightly larger panicle, the spikelets often with shorter hairs and the caryopses gradually tapering to a point rather than abruptly pointed. It is the earliest flowering of the Texas species.

9. **Digitaria hitchcockii** (Chase) Stuck., Annuaire Conserv. Jard. Bot. Geneve 17:287. 1914. *Trichachne hitchcockii* (Chase) Chase. SHORTLEAF COTTONTOP. Low, tufted perennial with culms mostly 30-50 cm tall from a hard knotty, much-branched base. *Basal scale-leaves* felty-pubescent. *Upper leaves* glabrous or variously puberulent, ciliate or sparsely hirsute. *Blades* mostly 2-3 mm broad and 2-5 cm long. *Inflorescence* slender, mostly 6-10 cm long, with usually 3-6 appressed branches, these 2-4 cm long. *Spikelets* 2.5-3 mm long, villous with grayish hairs 1 mm or less long. *Chromosome number* not reported.

Distribution. Texas: Regions 6 and 10. General: Southwestern Texas and adjacent areas of northern Mexico. A relatively rare species of open, dry, gravelly slopes and plains.

Flowering period: August to November.

10. **Digitaria filiformis** (L.) Koel., Descr. Gram. 26. 1802. SLENDER CRABGRASS. Tufted annual with slender, erect culms 50-80 cm tall. *Lower sheaths* and *blades* sparsely to densely hirsute, the upper culm leaves pubescent or glabrous. *Ligules* mostly 1 mm or less long. *Blades* long and narrow, 2-6 mm broad and 10-25 cm or more long. *Primary inflorescence branches* slender, erect, unbranched, mostly 7-13 cm long. *Spikelets* 1.5-1.9 mm long. *First glume* absent. *Second glume* about three-fourths as long as lemma of lower floret, puberulent at least on the margins, the hairs usually capitellate. *Lemma of lower floret* strongly 7-nerved, puberulent on margins and sometimes dorsally, the hairs usually capitellate. *Lemma of* upper floret dark brown, finely reticulate, ovate-oblong, tapering to an acute apex. *Chromosome number,* $2n = 36$.

Distribution. Texas: Regions 1, 2 and 3, usually in sandy soil and partial shade. General: Eastern United States, New Hampshire and Iowa south to Florida and Texas, and northeastern Mexico.

Flowering period: August to November.

11. **Digitaria villosa** (Walt.) Pers., Syn. Pl. 1:85. 1805. Fig. 223. *Digitaria filiformis* (L.) Koel. var. *villosa* (Pers.) Fern. SHAGGY CRABGRASS. Cespitose annual with erect culms from a much-branched but not "knotty" base.

Fig. 223. *Digitaria villosa*. Section of culm, inflorescence and spikelet.

416   THE GRASSES OF TEXAS

Similar in general aspect to *D. filiformis* but plants often as much as 125 cm or more tall, blades often longer, inflorescence branches usually 15-25 cm long, spikelets larger (2-2.6 mm long), second glume usually more than three-fourths as long as lemma of upper floret, and second glume and lemma of lower floret usually more pubescent and with longer hairs. *Chromosome number*, $2n=36$.

Distribution. Texas: Regions 1, 2 and 3. General: Maryland and Illinois south to Florida, Texas, Mexico and islands of the Gulf.

Flowering period: August to November.

Digitaria villosa has about the same range as *D. filiformis* but in Texas is much more abundant. It grows in somewhat weedy stands on disturbed, sandy soil, especially along woods borders.

12. **Digitaria texana** Hitchc., Proc. Biol. Soc., Wash. 41:162. 1928. TEXAS CRABGRASS. Perennial with usually spreading, decumbent-based culms, these branching and often rooting at lower nodes, 30-70 cm tall. *Lower sheaths*, and sometimes the upper, villous-pubescent. *Ligules* 1.5-2 cm long. *Blades* hirsute to nearly glabrous, short, mostly 2-5 mm broad. *Inflorescence* with usually 4-12 branches, these scattered at the culm apex and typically not digitate or verticilled. *Inflorescence branches* mostly 6-10 cm, occasionally -13 cm, long; the branch rachis angled but not winged. *Spikelets* 2-2.5 mm long, narrowly ovate-oblong, acute. *First glume* absent. *Second glume and lemma of lower floret* about equal and nearly as long as lemma of upper floret, green or purple-tinged, pubescent with soft hairs on margins and sometimes over back. *Lemma of upper floret* gray, sometimes purple-tinged, as long as spikelet. *Caryopses* narrowly oblong, with an embryo about one-third as long as the endosperm. *Chromosome number* not reported.

Distribution. Texas: Regions 2 and 6 in sandy soil. General: Known only from Texas.

Flowering period: September through November.

13. **Digitaria runyoni** Hitchc., J. Wash. Acad. Sci. 23:455. 1933. DUNE CRABGRASS. Perennial with culms 40-80 cm tall from stout, decumbent or stoloniferous bases. Generally similar to *D. texana* but blades to 7 mm broad, spikelets 2.8-3.6 mm long and second glume and lemma of lower floret usually villous on margins. *Chromosome number* not reported.

Distribution. Texas: Region 2, in coastal sands, usually on or at the base of dune formations. General: Endemic to coastal southern Texas.

Flowering period: September through November.

Correll and Johnston (1970) do not recognize *D. runyoni* as being distinct from *D. texana*.

90. LEPTOLOMA Chase

Four species, one in North America and three in Australia.

1. **Leptoloma cognatum** (Schult.) Chase, Proc. Biol. Soc., Wash. 19:192. 1906. Perennial with a knotty, felty-pubescent, rhizomatous base and open panicles of spikelets on slender, spreading branches and pedicels. *Culms* mostly 30-80 cm tall, much-branched at the base and developing many secondary panicles in addition to the primary one. *Ligule* a short, truncate membrane. *Blades* short, flat, usually crisped on the margins. Disarticulation at base of spikelet and at base of panicle, the inflorescence breaking off to become a "tumbleweed". *Spikelets* 2.5-4 mm long, 2-flowered, the lower floret staminate or neuter, the upper perfect. *Glumes* and *lemmas* awnless, the first glume absent or vestigial, the second 3-5-nerved, about equaling the 5-7-nerved lemma of lower floret. *Second glume and lemma of lower floret* densely villous between nerves and on margins to nearly glabrous. *Lemma of upper floret* dark brown, smooth, cartilaginous, narrow acute at the apex, with thin, flat (not inrolled) margins.

Slender creeping rhizomes absent; widespread in state
1A. L. cognatum var. cognatum

Slender creeping rhizomes developed; in coastal sands
1B. L. cognatum var. arenicola

1A. **Leptoloma cognatum** var. **cognatum.** FALL WITCHGRASS. Fig. 224. Plants "knotty" at base but creeping rhizomes not produced. Spikelets 2.5-4 mm long, nearly glabrous to densely villous. *Chromosome numbers* reported, $2n = 36$, 70 and 72; most records $2n = 72$.

Distribution. Texas: Throughout the State in all regions. General: Eastern Canada and the United States, west to Minnesota, Nebraska and Arizona and south to Northern Mexico.

Flowering period: Mostly May to November, but flowering as early as February.

Plants of the southwestern United States and northern Mexico tend to have strongly villous-pubescent spikelets.

1B. **Leptoloma cognatum** var. **arenicola** (Swallen) Gould, Southw. Naturalist, 15:391. 1971. *Leptoloma arenicola* Swallen. SAND WITCH-GRASS. Generally similar to var. *cognatum* but with slender rhizomes. *Spikelets* about 4 mm long. *Second glume* and *lemma of lower floret* densely villous. *Chromosome number* not reported.

Distribution. Texas: Region 2, the range reported by Chase in Hitchcock's Manual (1951) as "Sand hills, Kennedy County." General: Known only from Texas.

Flowering period: Mostly September to November.

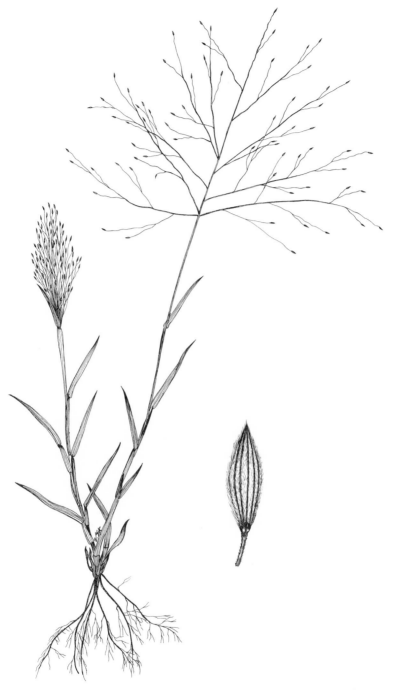

Fig. 224. *Leptoloma cognatum* var. *cognatum.* Plant and spikelet. From Gould and Box, 1965.

SUBFAMILY VI. PANICOIDEAE   419

91. ANTHAENANTIA Beauv.

Cespitose perennials with short rhizomes, stiffly erect culms and firm, narrow, flat blades. *Ligule* a short, fringed membrane. *Inflorescence* of awnless, conspicuously villous spikelets, these short-pediceled in a small, loosely contracted panicle. *Spikelets* 3-4 mm long, 2-flowered, the lower floret staminate or sterile, the upper perfect. Disarticulation below the spikelet. *First glume* absent, the second glume and lemma of lower floret about equal, 5-nerved, obovate, rounded at the apex, villous with appressed or erect hairs. *Lemma and palea of upper floret* dark brown, at maturity slightly separating to expose the globose-ovate caryopsis. *Lemma of upper floret* 3-nerved, cartilaginous, much narrower than the second glume, with thin, flat margins. *Palea* narrow, the 2 nerves nearly parallel.

A North American genus of 2 species.

Spikelets purplish, conspicuously hirsute with usually spreading hairs 0.6-1
    mm long; blades mostly 3-5 mm broad   1. A. *rufa*

Spikelets greenish, inconspicuously hirsute with mostly appressed hairs 0.5
    mm or less long; blades mostly 5-10 mm broad   2. A. *villosa*

1. **Anthaenantia rufa** (Ell.) Schult., Mantissa 2:258. 1824. PURPLE SILKYSCALE. Fig. 225. *Culms* mostly 70-110 cm tall, in small clusters from firm, knotty rhizomes. *Leaves* glabrous or the lower ones sparsely hirsute or inconspicuously pubescent. *Blades* relatively long and narrow, mostly 3-5 mm broad. *Panicles* 8-16 cm long, mostly 2-3 (-5) cm broad, the branches spreading-erect. *Spikelets* 3-4 mm long. *Hairs of second glume and lemma of lower floret* long, shaggy, usually purple or purple-tinged and spreading in age. *Caryopses* 1.2-1.4 mm long, with a broad, rounded embryo about one-half as long as the endosperm. *Anthers* 2.6-2.8 mm long. *Chromosome number* not reported.

Distribution. Texas: Region 1, the northern half of region 2 and the central portion of region 3. Collected in Jasper, Hardin, Victoria, Refugio, Brazos and Robertson counties. General: North Carolina and along the Coastal Plain to Florida and Texas.

Flowering period: July to October.

2. **Anthaenantia villosa** (Michx.) Beauv., Ess. Agrost. 48, 151, pl. 10, f. 7. 1812. GREEN SILKYSCALE. Perennial from scaly rhizomes, generally similar to *A. rufa* but blades mostly 5-10 mm broad, the inflorescence more contracted, usually 1-2 cm broad and with stiffly erect branches, the spikelets greenish, villous but typically with appressed or appressed and spreading hairs 0.5 mm or less long, the hairs not conspicuous to the naked eye. *Chromosome number* not reported.

Fig. 225. *Anthaenantia rufa.* Inflorescence and spikelet. From Gould, 1968.

Distribution. Texas: Occasional in southern portion of regions 1 and 3 and the northern portion of region 2. General: North Carolina and along the Coastal Plain to Florida and Texas.

Flowering period: August to October.

92. STENOTAPHRUM Trin.

A genus of 7 species, in tropical and subtropical regions of Africa, the Americas, Hawaii and other Pacific islands and Australia.

1. **Stenotaphrum secundatum** (Walt.) Kuntze, Rev. Gen. Pl. 2:74. 1891. ST. AUGUSTINEGRASS. Fig. 226. Low, mat-forming, stoloniferous perennial. *Culms* decumbent, creeping, much-branched, with erect flowering branches 10-30 cm tall. *Leaves* glabrous except for the ciliate ligule or the sheaths sparsely ciliate on upper margins. *Ligule* a minute membrane fringed with stiff hairs. *Blades* thick, flat, 4-10 mm broad, mostly 3-15 mm long but longer on sterile shoots, blunt and rounded at apex. *Inflorescence* spikelike, 5-10 cm long, with short, stout, closely-placed and appressed branches bearing 1-3 sessile or subsessile spikelets; *spikelets* partially embedded in one side of the broad, thick, flattened inflorescence rachis. Disarticulation at nodes of rachis, the spikelets falling attached to the sections. *Spikelets* 4-5 mm long, 2-flowered, the lower floret staminate or neuter, the upper perfect. *First glume* short but well-developed, irregularly rounded. *Second glume* and *lemma of lower floret* about equal, glabrous, awnless, faintly-nerved, pointed at apex. *Lemma of upper floret* chartaceous, ovate, awnless, pointed, with thin flat margins. *Chromosome number,* $2n = 18$.

Distribution. Texas: Regions 1, 2, 3, 4, 6 and 7, frequently grown as a lawn grass and also spontaneous in moist soil along stream courses, lake shores and swales. General: South Carolina to Florida and Texas and occasional throughout the tropics and subtropics of the world. St. Augustinegrass probably is not native to the United States but was present along the eastern coast before 1800 (Sauer, 1972).

Flowering period: Summer.

93. BRACHIARIA Griseb.

Low annuals and perennials with decumbent or stoloniferous culm bases. *Ligule* a minute membrane fringed with relatively long, stiff hairs. *Inflorescence* a small panicle, the spikelets solitary and subsessile and in two rows along the short, widely-spaced, unbranched primary branches. *Branch rachis* broad, flattened, slightly 3-angled. *Spikelets* 2-flowered, the lower floret staminate or neuter, the upper perfect, oriented with the first glume towards the rachis and the rounded back of the upper lemma away from the rachis. Disarticulation below glumes. *First glume* one-fourth to three-fourths as long as spikelet, *second glume* and *lemma of lower floret* about equal, acute, 5-9-nerved. *Lemma of upper floret* indurate, glabrous, obtuse or broadly acute at apex, rarely short-awned, usually rugose on the rounded back, with margins inrolled over palea.

About 15 species in tropical and subtropical regions of both hemispheres.

Fig. 226. *Stenotaphrum secundatum.* Plant and spikelet. From Gould and Box, 1965.

Second glume and lemma of lower floret conspicuously hairy; plants
    perennial   1.   *B. ciliatissima*

Second glume and lemma of lower floret glabrous; plants annual

    Branch rachis 1.6-2.3 mm wide; second glume and lemma of lower floret
        reticulate-veined, flattened and broadly acute or rounded at apex,
        usually extended 0.8-1 mm or more beyond tip of upper floret
                                          2.   *B. platyphylla*

SUBFAMILY VI. PANICOIDEAE   423

Branch rachis 0.3-1.5 mm broad; second glume and lemma of lower floret not or faintly reticulate-veined, with the apex acute, not flattened, less than 0.8 mm longer than tip of upper floret

Spikelets 4-4.5 mm long   3. *B. plantaginea*

Spikelets 1.8-2 mm long   4. *B. reptans*

1. **Brachiaria ciliatissima** (Buckl.) Chase, in Hitchc., U.S.D.A. Bull. 772:221. 1920. FRINGED SIGNALGRASS. Fig. 227. Perennial, the erect culms mostly 15-40 cm tall, produced singly or in small clumps at the nodes of long, freely-branched stolons. *Sheaths* variously hirsute and hispid with long and short spreading hairs, densely hirsute at base. *Blades* short, flat, scabrous, narrowly acute to acuminate at tip, 2-7 mm broad and 3-8 cm long. *Inflorescences* few-flowered, 3-7 cm long, with short, erect or spreading branches, these spikelet-bearing to base. *Spikelets* 3.5-4.5 mm long, awnless. *First glume* acute, three-fourths as long as the spikelet, glabrous. *Second glume* and *lemma of lower floret* about equal, 5-nerved, densely villous on margins and pubescent with shorter hairs on back. *Lemma* and *palea of upper floret* firm, finely reticulate-rugose. *Embryo* ovate-oblong three-fourths as long as the endosperm. *Chromosome number*, 2n=36.

Distribution. Texas: Widespread through central Texas on sandy soils, mostly in regions 2, 5, 6 and 7, occasional in regions 3 and 8. General: Arkansas, Oklahoma and Texas.

Flowering period: Mostly April to June, occasionally July to November.

2. **Brachiaria platyphylla** (Griseb.) Nash, in Small, Fl. Southeast. U.S. 1327. 1903. BROADLEAF SIGNALGRASS. Fig. 228. Coarse annual with decumbent and spreading culm bases, these rooting at lower nodes. *Sheaths* glabrous or sparsely hirsute, ciliate on margins near apex. *Blades* glabrous on both surfaces, mostly 6-13 mm broad. *Inflorescence* of 2-6 (usually 3-5) unbranched, widely-spaced, erect or erect-spreading branches. *Branches* 3-6 cm long, with a winged rachis 1.6-2.3 mm broad. *Spikelets* 4-4.5 mm long, ovate, glabrous. *First glume* one-fourth to one-third as long as spikelet. *Second glume and lemma of lower floret* about equal, with strong transverse veinlets at least near apex, usually extended 0.8-1.2 mm beyond tip of upper floret. *Lemma and palea of upper floret* firm, finely rugose, the lemma with thickened, inrolled margins. *Embryo* oblong, slightly more than half as long as endosperm. *Chromosome number*, 2n=36.

Distribution. Texas: Regions 1, 2, 3, 4, 6 and 7 along woods openings, swales, ditches, field borders and other areas of disturbed, moist soil. General: Georgia and Florida to Oklahoma and Texas; also in Mexico and Cuba.

Flowering period: April to November.

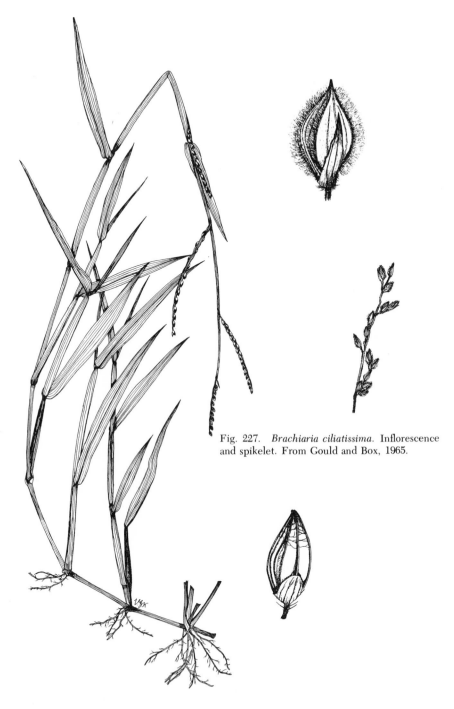

Fig. 227. *Brachiaria ciliatissima.* Inflorescence and spikelet. From Gould and Box, 1965.

Fig. 228. *Brachiaria platyphylla.* Plant and spikelet. From Gould and Box, 1965.

SUBFAMILY VI. PANICOIDEAE   425

3. **Brachiaria plantaginea** (Link) Hitchc., Contr. U. S. Natl. Herb. 12:212. 1909. *Brachiaria extensa* Chase. PLANTAIN SIGNALGRASS. Coarse annual with decumbent-spreading culms, similar to *B. platyphylla* but inflorescence branch rachis narrower and second glume and lemma of lower floret not or faintly reticulate-veined and with an acute, non-flattened tip less than 0.8 mm longer than tip of upper floret. *Chromosome number* not reported.

Distribution. Texas: Reported by Gould (1969) for region 1, presumably based on *Shinners 15714*, but the Tracy Herbarium specimen annotated by Shinners in 1953 as *B. plantaginea* appears referable to *B. platyphylla*. General: Mexico to Brazil and Bolivia, introduced at scattered localities in the eastern United States.

Flowering period: Presumably April to October in Texas.

4. **Brachiaria reptans** (L.) Gard. & C. E. Hubb. in Hook., Icon. Pl. 3363:3. 1938. *Panicum reptans* L. Fig. 229. Mat-forming annual with widely creeping and branching culms, these rooting at the nodes. *Culms* with erect floriferous branches mostly 10-35 cm tall; *culm nodes* glabrous or puberulent. *Sheaths* glabrous or hispid on back, usually with a fringe of hairs on margins. *Ligule* a minute fringed membrane, the hairs 0.5-1 mm long. *Blades* short, flat, lanceolate, coarsely crisped or undulant on margins, cordate at base, mostly 1.5-7 cm long and 4-12 mm broad, ciliate on lower margins but otherwise glabrous. *Panicles* 1.5-6 cm long, with spikelets subsessile to short-pediceled, mostly in unequally pediceled pairs and closely imbricated on simple or nearly simple, short, erect-spreading primary branches, these usually 4-10 (-16) in number. *Panicle axis, branches* and *pedicels* scabrous or scabrous-pubescent, often with a few long hairs at base of spikelets. *Spikelets* uniformly 1.8-2 mm long. *First glume* broadly rounded or truncate, one-fifth to one-fourth as long as spikelet. *Second glume* and *lower lemma* about equal, broad and slightly apiculate or beaked at apex. *Lower floret* often staminate, with a palea about as long as the lemma. *Lemma* and *palea of upper floret* transverse-rugose. *Chromosome number,* $2n = 14$.

Distribution. Texas: Regions 1, 2 and 6 in low, moist, often-shaded sites, frequent and somewhat weedy on disturbed soils. General: Tropical-subtropical regions of the world, probably introduced in Texas.

Flowering period: Mostly August to October but flowering as early as May.

Three separate investigators have reported the chromosome number $2n = 14$ for this species which in the United States commonly has gone under the name of *Panicum reptans.* Two of the chromosome records are for Texas plants. This is the only New World panicoid grass known to have $2n = 14$ chromosomes, a complement characteristic of pooid grasses.

Fig. 229. *Brachiaria reptans.* Inflorescence and spikelet. From Gould and Box, 1965, as *Panicum reptans.*

94. AXONOPUS Beauv.

Stoloniferous or cespitose perennials (the United States species) with thick, flat or folded, rounded or pointed blades. *Ligules* short, membranous, ciliate. *Inflorescence* with 2-several slender, spicate branches, the spikelets solitary at the nodes and rather widely spaced in 2 rows on 2 sides of a triangular, often somewhat winged rachis. *Spikelets* awnless, 2-flowered, the lower floret staminate or neuter, the upper perfect, with back of lemma of upper floret oriented away from rachis. Disarticulation at base of spikelets. *First glume* absent, the *second glume* and *lemma of lower floret* about equal, narrowly ovate or oblong. *Lemma* and *palea* of upper floret indurate, oblong, glabrous, usually obtuse at apex.

SUBFAMILY VI. PANICOIDEAE   427

A genus of about 100 species, all native to the American tropics and subtropics.

Spikelets 1.8-2.6 mm long; second (and only) glume and lemma of lower floret sparsely pubescent; midnerve of glume and lemma of lower floret obscure   1.   *A. affinis*

Spikelets 4-5.5 mm long; glume and lemma of lower floret glabrous; midnerve of glume and lemma of lower floret evident
                                                                   2.   *A. furcatus*

1. **Axonopus affinis** Chase, J. Wash. Acad. Sci. 28:180 f 1., 2. 1938. COMMON CARPETGRASS. Fig. 230. Cespitose or stoloniferous perennial with laterally flattened culms and sheaths. *Erect culms* 20-70 cm tall, glabrous or minutely puberulent on nodes. *Leaves* glabrous except for the minute, ciliate ligule or margins of sheath and blade sparsely ciliate in vicinity of ligule. *Blades* 1.5-7 mm broad. *Inflorescence* 2-4 (usually 2 or 3) slender branches on a slender axis, the upper 2 branches usually paired and spreading at the culm apex. *Inflorescence branches* mostly 2.5-8 cm long, bearing 2 rows of appressed spikelets on a 3-angled, slightly winged rachis. *Spikelets* mostly 1.8-2.6 mm long. *Glume and lemma of lower floret* sparsely pubescent, narrowly ovate-oblong, flattened and nerveless in middle, abruptly pointed at apex, slightly longer than lemma of upper floret. *Lemma of upper floret* minutely rugose, with thickened, inrolled margins. *Chromosome numbers* reported, $2n=20$, 40 and 80.

Distribution. Texas: Regions 1, 2 and 3, mostly in moist, sandy woods openings or on the borders of streams, lakes and marshy areas. General: North Carolina and Oklahoma, south to Florida and Texas and through Mexico, Central America and the Carribean to Argentina.

Flowering period: Mostly May to November, occasionally April to December.

Axonopus affinis appears very close to *Axonopus compressus* (Swartz) Beauv. and may not be specifically distinct. The latter, with a similar but slightly more restricted distribution, reportedly has usually densely pubescent culm nodes, broader blades (8-12 mm broad) and smaller spikelets (2.2-2.8 mm long) whose apices are more elongate and pointed.

2. **Axonopus furcatus** (Flugge) Hitchc., Rhodora 8:205. 1906. BIG CARPETGRASS. Stoloniferous perennial with the same general characteristics as *A. affinis* but culms to 100 cm tall, blades to 10 mm broad and spikelets 4-5.5 mm long. Also, the elongated second glume and lemma of the lower floret have a strong midnerve and pointed apex that extends 1.5-2 mm beyond the tip of the upper lemma.

Distribution. Texas: Regions 1, 2 and 3, with the same habitat adaptation as *A. affinis* but less frequent in Texas. General: Virginia and Florida, west to Arkansas and eastern Texas.

Fig. 230. *Axonopus affinis.* Plant and spikelet. From Gould and Box, 1965.

Flowering period: Mostly May to November.

SUBFAMILY VI. PANICOIDEAE   429

95. ERIOCHLOA H.B.K.

Cespitose annuals and perennials, with thin, flat blades. *Ligule* a minute membranous rim or ridge densely fringed with short, soft or stiff hairs. *Inflorescence* a contracted or somewhat open panicle, with sessile or short-pediceled spikelets borne singly or in pairs on erect or slightly spreading, unbranched primary branches. Disarticulation below spikelet. *Spikelets* 2-flowered, the lower floret staminate or neuter, the upper perfect. *First glume* reduced and fused with the rachis node to form a cup or disc. *Second glume and lemma of lower floret* about equal, usually scabrous, hispid or hirsute, acute or acuminate at apex. *Lemma of upper floret* indurate, glabrous, finely rugose, with slightly inrolled margins, abruptly apiculate or short-awned at apex.

About 20 species, in the tropics and subtropics of the world.

Pedicels glabrous or minutely puberulent; lemma of upper floret with an awn 0.5-1.5 mm long

    Spikelets 4-5 mm long; awn of lemma 1-1.5 mm long; plants perennial
                                                        1. *E. punctata*

    Spikelets 3.5-4 mm long; awn of lemma mostly 0.5-0.8 mm long; plants annual
                                               2. *E. contracta*

Pedicels with at least some hairs one-half as long to as long as spikelet; lemma of upper floret awnless or with an awn usually less than 0.5 mm long

    Plants annual, the culms weak, usually decumbent or geniculate below
                                          3. *E. lemmonii*

    Plants perennial, the culms stiffly erect from a firm base
                                            4. *E. sericea*

1. **Eriochloa punctata** (L.) Desv. *ex.* Hamilton, Prodr. Pl. Ind. Occ. 5. 1825. LOUISIANA CUPGRASS. Cespitose perennial with erect or spreading-erect culms 60-100 cm tall. *Culm nodes* minutely puberulent. *Sheaths* glabrous, rounded. *Blades* glabrous or scabrous, 4-10 mm broad. *Inflorescence* 8-18 cm long with usually 8-15 or more branches, these 2-6 cm long. *Inflorescence axis, branches and pedicels* puberulent or pubescent. *Spikelets* 4-5 mm long. *Glume and lemma of lower floret* sparsely appressed-pilose, the glume often short-awned. *Lemma of upper floret* abruptly tipped with an awn 1-1.5 mm long. *Chromosome number*, $2n=36$.

Distribution. Texas: Regions 2 and 6, growing in moist swales and ditches and along water courses. General: Southwestern Louisiana to southeastern Texas and south in eastern Mexico and the Caribbean to South America.

Flowering period: Late March to November.

2. **Eriochloa contracta** Hitchc., Proc. Biol. Soc., Wash. 41:163. 1928. PRAIRIE CUPGRASS. Fig. 231. Tufted annual with erect or geniculate, spreading culms mostly 30-70 cm tall. *Culm nodes* puberulent. *Sheaths and blades*, at least the lower, pubescent with minute, spreading or reflexed hairs. *Blades* mostly 2-7 mm broad. *Inflorescence* 6-15 cm long, with usually 6-15 erect-appressed branches 1-2 cm long, these densely hirsute with short, stiff hairs. *Spikelets* 3.5-4 mm long. *Glume and lemma of lower floret* appressed-hispid, short awn-tipped. *Lemma of upper floret* with an awn usually 0.5-0.8 mm long. *Chromosome number*, $2n=36$.

Distribution. Texas: Reported from all regions of the State except region 10. A somewhat weedy plant of moist soils, often occurring along ditches, low field borders, swales and water courses. General: Missouri and Nebraska to Louisiana, Texas and Arizona and in northern Mexico.

Flowering period: April to November.

3. **Eriochloa lemmonii** Vasey & Scribn., Bot. Gaz. 9:185. Pl. 2. 1884.

Leaf blades typically pubescent but occasionally glabrous; glume usually 4 mm or less long, abruptly acuminate; hairs of panicle branches dense, tending to be long (to 4 mm) or long and short
3A.   E. lemmonii var. lemmonii

Leaf blades typically glabrous but pubescent in some populations; glume usually 4.5-6 mm long, gradually tapering to an acuminate or aristate apex; hairs of panicle branches typically short and not dense
3B.   E. lemmonii var. gracilis

3A. **Eriochloa lemmonii** Vasey & Scribn. var. **lemmonii**. *Eriochloa gracilis* (Fourn.) Hitchc. var. *minor* (Vasey) Hitchc. SMALL SOUTH-WESTERN CUPGRASS. Tufted annual. *Culms* 20-60 (-100) cm long, weak and usually decumbent or geniculate below. *Blades* thin, flat, 3-10 mm broad. *Panicle* 6-18 cm long, with appressed or erect-spreading branches 2-5 cm long, these more or less densely pubescent with hairs to 4 mm long, the long hairs often interspersed with shorter, sometimes glandular hairs. *Glume and lemma* of lower floret 3-4 mm long, appressed-pubescent, usually awnless. *Lemma of upper floret* oblong, finely reticulate, abruptly awn-tipped, the awn usually less than 0.5 mm long. *Chromosome number* not reported.

Distribution. Texas: Regions 8 and 10, infrequent, typically a grass of open plains, road right-of-ways, fields and ditches, often growing as a weed. General: Western Texas to Arizona and northern Mexico.

Flowering period: June to November.

Reported by Chase in Hitchcock's Manual (1951) to occur in Texas (as *E. gracilis* var. *minor*) but no Texas collections examined by the writer.

Fig. 231. *Eriochloa contracta*. Plant, spikelet and floret. From Gould and Box, 1965.

432   THE GRASSES OF TEXAS

3B. **Eriochloa lemmonii** var. **gracilis** (Fourn.) Gould, Leafl. W. Bot. 6:50-51. 1950. *Eriochloa gracilis* (Fourn.) Hitchc. SOUTHWESTERN CUPGRASS. Tufted annual, differing from the typical variety in the long and dense hairs of the inflorescence branches, the larger, acuminate rather than blunt spikelets and the typically glabrous herbage. *Chromosome number*, $2n=36$.

Distribution. Texas: Regions 7 and 10, infrequent, in the same habitats as the typical variety. General: Oklahoma and southern California south to western Texas and northern Mexico. The single Texas collection examined by the author, *Silveus 2377* from near Marfa, is a specimen with small spikelets and only moderately hairy inflorescence branches.

Flowering period: June to November.

In the characteristic form, *E. lemmonii* var. *gracilis* differs conspicuously from *E. lemmonii* var. *lemmonii*. However, spikelet size and shape and pubescence of the leaves and inflorescence branches frequently are not correlated, and the two taxa cannot be satisfactorily segregated as separate species.

4. **Eriochloa sericea** (Scheele) Munro, in Vasey, U.S.D.A. Div. Bot. Bull. 12. pl. 1. 1890. TEXAS CUPGRASS. Fig. 232. Cespitose perennial, with culms 50-100 cm tall, strictly erect from a firm, non-rhizomatous base. *Culm nodes* pubescent. *Sheaths*, at least the lower, finely pubescent. *Blades* elongate, mostly 2-3 mm broad, flat or more frequently involute, glabrous or finely pubescent. *Inflorescence* narrow, contracted, usually a panicle with 4-10 widely-spaced and strictly erect branches 1.5-3 cm long. *Inflorescence* axis and branches ciliate or villous, with at least some hairs 2-4 mm long. *Spikelets* ovate, the glume and the lemma of lower floret appressed-hirsute, awnless, 3.6-4.2 mm long. *Lemma of upper floret* firm, finely rugose, with a minute awn tip. *Chromosome number*, $2n=54$.

Distribution. Texas: Regions 2, 4, 5, 6, 7 and 8 in prairies and grassy openings. General: Oklahoma, Texas and northern Mexico.

Flowering period: April (occasionally March) to November.

Eriochloa sericea is a highly palatable forage plant that survives only under moderate grazing pressure and persists on the more heavily utilized pastures only in the protection of shrubs.

96. PANICUM L.*

Annuals and perennials of diverse habit. *Ligule* a membrane, a fringe of hairs or absent. *Inflorescence* an open or contracted panicle. *Spikelets* awnless, 2-flowered, the lower floret neuter or staminate, the upper perfect.

*The treatment of the species belonging to *Panicum* section *Diffusa* (P. diffusum, P. ghiesbreghtii, P. capillarioides, P. hirsutum, P. hallii, P. pilcomayense) has been contributed by Floyd R. Waller.

Fig. 232. *Eriochloa sericea*. Plant, spikelet and floret. From Gould and Box, 1965.

Disarticulation below the glumes. *Glumes* usually both present, the first commonly short. *Lower floret* with a lemma similar to the glumes in texture and usually equaling or slightly longer than the second glume. *Lemma of the upper floret* shiny and glabrous in our species, smooth or rugose, firm or indurate, tightly clasping the palea with thick, usually inrolled margins. *Palea of upper floret* like lemma in texture, with 2 strong, widely separated nerves.

Panicum is the largest of the grass genera, with about 500 species distributed throughout the warmer parts of the world.

Plants annual   A

Plants perennial   AA

A. Plants annual

Spikelets 1-1.4 mm long   13. *P. trichoides*

Spikelets 1.8 mm or more long

  Second glume and lemma of lower floret verrucose or tuberculate-hispid

  Spikelets 2.8-3.1 mm long, glabrous   11. *P. verrucosum*

  Spikelets 3.2-3.6 mm long, hispid   12. *P. brachyanthum*

  Second glume and lemma of lower floret not verrucose or tuberculate-hispid

  Lemma of perfect floret transversely rugose; spikelets subsessile or short-pediceled on simple or nearly simple primary inflorescence branches

  Spikelets 5-6 mm long   1. *P. texanum*

  Spikelets 4 mm or less long

  Spikelets 2.4-3.8 mm long; culms in tufts; leaf blades, at least some, more than 8 cm long, not crisped on margins

  Spikelets 3.5-3.8 mm long, pubescent (in Texas plants)
                                                                    3. *P. arizonicum*

  Spikelets 2.4-3 mm long, glabrous   2. *P. fasciculatum*

  Spikelets about 2 mm long; leaf blades 1.5-7 cm long, crisped on margins   SEE *Brachiaria reptans*

  Lemma of perfect floret smooth; spikelets short- or long-pediceled in an open, usually freely rebranched panicle

  First glume about one-fourth as long as spikelet, obtuse or rounded; plant with coarse, trailing culms as much as 1 m or more long
                                                                    4. *P. dichotomiflorum*

First glume more than one-fourth as long as spikelet, acute or acuminate

Spikelets mostly 4.5-5 mm long   10.   *P. miliaceum*

Spikelets 4 mm or less long

Spikelets acute to slightly acuminate at tip, 1.5-2 (-2.2) mm long   7.   *P. philadelphicum*

Spikelets long-acuminate at tip, 1.8-3.5 mm long

Pulvini in axils of lower panicle branches pubescent; panicles one-half to one and one-half times as long as broad

Palea of lower floret usually absent; lemma of upper floret without a scar at base; leaves yellow-green; upper floret 0.5-0.9 mm wide   5.   *P. capillare*

Palea of lower floret present; lemma of upper floret with a raised crescent-shaped scar at base; leaves blue-green; upper floret 1.1-1.3 mm wide   6.   *P. hillmanii*

Pulvini in axils of lower panicle branches glabrous; panicles 2-10 times as long as broad

Palea of lower floret absent; culm internodes solid; spikelets scattered, on long pedicels; blades 1-7 mm broad
                                          8.   *P. flexile*

Palea of lower floret present; culm internodes hollow; spikelets closely placed, on short pedicels; blades 5-27 mm broad   9.   *P. hirticaule*

AA. Plants perennial

First glume about as long as second, broad at apex; spikelets short-pediceled on the simple primary inflorescence branches; long stolons developed   14.   *P. obtusum*

First glume shorter than second, if nearly as long then acute or acuminate at apex

Panicles 3-6 cm long; spikelets 3.5-4 mm long; leaf blades 3-9 cm long

Spikelets about 4 mm long, obovate or obpyriform
                                SEE *Dichanthelium nodatum*

Spikelets 3.5-3.7 mm long, oblong

SEE *Dichanthelium pedicellatum*

Panicles more than 6 cm long or, if this short, then spikelets less than 3 mm long; leaf blades, at least some, more than 9 cm long

Second glume and lemma of lower floret greatly elongated, more than twice the length of the grain

32. *P. capillarioides*

Second glume and lemma of lower floret not greatly elongated, less than twice the length of the grain

Spikelets 4-8 mm long; plants with rhizomes or stolons   B

Spikelets less than 4 mm long; plants with or without rhizomes or stolons   BB

B

Plants of coastal sands; panicle narrow, tightly contracted

17. *P. amarum*

Plants not of coastal sands; panicle broad or narrow but not tightly contracted

Spikelets 4-5 mm long; culms in dense clumps   16. *P. virgatum*

Spikelets 6-8 mm long; culms not in dense clumps

Plants with long, stout rhizomes and no stolons; ligule ciliate with hairs 1-3 mm long; western Texas   18. *P. havardii*

Plants without rhizomes, the culms decumbent and stoloniferous; ligule not ciliate; eastern Texas   21. *P. gymnocarpon*

BB

Palea of lower floret enlarged and inflated, firm, obovate   22. *P. hians*

Palea of lower floret not enlarged, inflated, firm and obovate

Culms hard and somewhat woody in age, becoming much-branched above; spikelets 2.5-3 mm long; first glume one-third to one-half as long as the spikelet, obtuse or broadly acute   20. *P. antidotale*

Culms not branching above when hard or firm in age

Spikelets appressed and usually closely clustered on simple or nearly simple primary panicle branches or on short spur branches; lemma of upper floret smooth and shiny   C

Spikelets not appressed and closely clustered on short, simple or nearly simple panicle branches and short spur branches; lemma of upper floret smooth or rugose   CC

C

Culm nodes densely pubescent; lemma of upper floret minutely rugose
23. *P. purpurascens*

Culm nodes not densely pubescent; lemma of upper floret smooth

Scaly, creeping rhizomes developed

Lemma of upper floret thin, scarcely thicker than glumes and lemma of lower floret; spikelets 2.4-2.6 mm long; lower culm internodes and sheaths not compressed-keeled; plants of wet or marshy habitats   24. *P. hemitomon*

Lemma of lower floret thick and firm; spikelets 2.8-3.5 mm long; lower culm internodes and sheaths compressed-keeled; plants of moist but usually not wet or marshy habitats   26. *P. anceps*

Scaly, creeping rhizomes not developed

Lower sheath sharply keeled and laterally compressed
27. *P. rigidulum*

Lower sheaths not sharply keeled or laterally compressed

Lower floret staminate   15. *P. coloratum*

Lower floret neuter

Inflorescence branches erect, not spreading; spikelets 2.2-2.8 mm long   25. *P. tenerum*

Inflorescence branches, at least the lower, spreading; spikelets 2.2-3.9 mm long   34. *P. hallii*

CC

Lemma of upper floret finely or coarsely rugose

Culm nodes glabrous; ligules 0.5-2 mm long; first glume acute at apex; culms usually swollen and cormlike at base   28. *P. bulbosum*

Culm nodes hirsute; ligules 4-6 mm long; first glume obtuse at apex; culms not swollen and cormlike at base   29. *P. maximum*

Lemma of upper floret smooth, not rugose

Plants with stout, scaly rhizomes

First glume acute, more than one-half as long as spikelet
16. *P. virgatum*

First glume broadly rounded or truncate, one-fourth to one-third as long as spikelet   19. *P. repens*

Plants without rhizomes

Leaf blades 1.5 to 4 cm wide; culms robust, 1-1.5 meters tall
33. *P. hirsutum*

Leaf blades less than 1.5 cm wide; culms less than 1 meter tall

Lower panicle branches in verticils of 3-5 (-7), pilose in the axils
35. *P. pilcomayense*

Lower panicle branches usually solitary, glabrescent in the axils

Sheath margins often ciliate with a line of ascending hairs; nodes spreading-pilose; plants green

Spikelets 2-2.8 mm; plants prostrate or ascending
30. *P. diffusum*

Spikelets 2.8-3.4 mm; plants erect   31. *P. ghiesbreghtii*

Sheath margins glabrous or with a tuft of hairs at the summit, not ciliate; nodes appressed-pubescent or glabrous; plants glaucous   34. *P. hallii*

1. **Panicum texanum** Buckl., Prelim. Rep. Geol. and Agr. Survey Tex. App. 3. 1866. TEXAS PANICUM. Fig. 233. Coarse annual, frequently forming large clumps. *Culms* mostly 40-120 cm or more long, tufted and erect from base or more commonly decumbent, creeping and rooting at the lower nodes, soft-pubescent at least on and immediately below the nodes. *Leaves* usually pubescent or hispid with short or long hairs, occasionally nearly glabrous. *Ligule* a short, densely ciliate membrane, the hairs 1-1.5 mm long. *Blades* lanceolate, firm, flat or folded, mostly 8-20 cm long and 7-20 mm broad, usually soft-pubescent on both surfaces with short, fine hairs. *Panicles* 7-18, occasionally -25 cm long, with short, usually simple, erect-appressed or

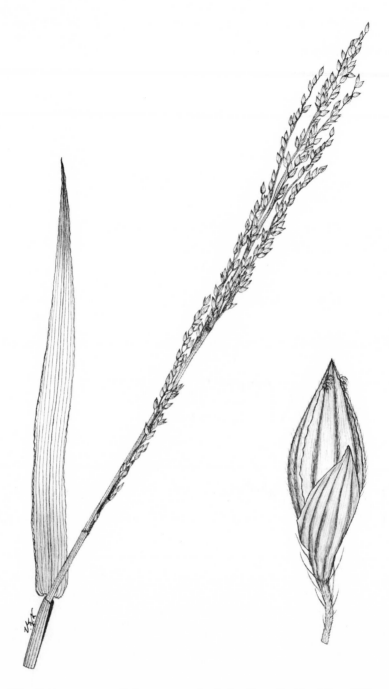

Fig. 233. *Panicum texanum*. Inflorescence and spikelet. From Gould and Box, 1965.

440   THE GRASSES OF TEXAS

slightly spreading branches. *Panicle branches* and pedicels usually densely pubescent with fine hairs and with a few silvery seta. *Spikelets* 5-6 mm long, usually sparsely pubescent. *First glume* about two-thirds as long as spikelet, strongly 5-7-nerved. *Second glume and lower lemma* strongly 5-nerved, about equal. *Lower floret* staminate, with a thin, silvery palea about as long as the lemma. *Lemma and palea of upper floret* transverse rugose, the lemma slightly beaked or apiculate, mostly 3.5-4 mm long. *Chromosome number*, $2n = 54$.

Distribution. Texas: Throughout the State, except in region 10 and the northern portions of regions 8 and 9, a weedy species of ditches, field borders, vacant lots and other areas of moist, disturbed soils. General: Possibly native only to Texas but presently distributed from North Carolina, Georgia and Florida westward to Texas and northern Mexico; apparently introduced at Tucson, Arizona, at an early period but there are no recent collections from that state.

Flowering period: Late May to November.

2. **Panicum fasciculatum** Swartz, Prodr. Veg. Ind. Occ. 22. 1788. BROWNTOP PANICUM. Fig. 234. Annual, with tufted or decumbent-creeping culms 30-120 cm or more long, these often rooting at the nodes. *Culm nodes* usually appressed-pubescent, the internodes, especially the uppermost one, often puberulent or hispid also. *Leaves*, at least the lower ones, usually hispid with spreading hairs, the hairs often papillate-based. *Ligule* a dense ring of hairs about 1 mm long from a minute membranous base. *Blades* flat, lanceolate, mostly 4-20 (-30) cm long and 5-15 mm broad, narrowing slightly at base and gradually tapering to a pointed apex. *Panicles* 6-15 cm long, with appressed or erect-spreading, mostly simple branches 1-8 cm long. *Branchlets and the short pedicels* usually scabrous or pubescent and with few to numerous long, stiff, silvery hairs, these occasionally absent. *Spikelets* glabrous, broadly rounded, mostly 2.4-3 mm long, but occasionally shorter, usually yellowish-brown or bronze colored. *First glume* thin, one-third to one-fourth as long as spikelet. *Second glume and lower lemma* usually reticulate with fine cross veins to well below the middle, rounded at apex or slightly pointed. *Lemma of upper floret* rugose, nearly as long as spikelet, the apex blunt, not cuspidate or short-beaked. *Chromosome numbers*, $2n = 18$ and 36.

Distribution. Texas: Reported from all areas of the State except region 1, a weedy plant of low moist sites, often in ditches and along graded field borders. General: Florida, Texas, New Mexico and Arizona, southward at low elevations to northern South America.

Flowering period: Mostly June to November but occasionally flowering in April or May.

Plants of *P. fasciculatum* in Texas are referable to the var. *reticulatum* (Torr.) Beal. The typical variety of *P. fasciculatum* (var. *fasciculatum*) has spikelets 2-2.5 mm long and generally larger, more open panicles.

Fig. 234. *Panicum fasciculatum*. Plant, spikelet and floret. From Gould and Box, 1965.

442   THE GRASSES OF TEXAS

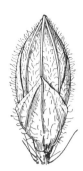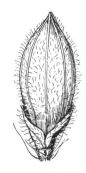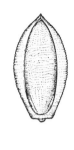

Fig. 235. *Panicum arizonicum.* Two views of spikelet and floret. From Hitchcock, 1935.

3. **Panicum arizonicum** Scribn. & Merr., U.S.D.A. Div. Agrost. Cir. 32:2. 1901. ARIZONA PANICUM. Fig. 235. Tufted annual with erect or geniculate-spreading culms mostly 15-60 cm tall, these freely branched below. *Culms* glabrous or sparsely hispid at nodes and below panicle. *Sheaths* glabrous or coarsely hispid with papilla-based hairs. *Ligule* a minute ciliate membrane, the hairs 0.5-1 mm long. *Blades* narrowly lanceolate, mostly 5-18 cm long and 3-10 mm broad, flat or folded, asymmetrical and somewhat auriculate at base, usually with a few, widely-spaced coarse cilia on lower margins, glabrous or sparsely hispid on surfaces. *Panicles* narrow, mostly 7-15 cm, rarely 20 cm, long, with short, usually simple, erect or erect spreading branches, the main axis and branches sparsely but more or less uniformly pilose with spreading silvery hairs. *Spikelets* pubescent (in Texas plants), mostly 3.3-4 mm long, borne on pedicels mostly 1 mm or less long except for those terminating branchlets. *First glume* one-fourth to one-half as long as spikelet. *Second glume and lower lemma* equal, often somewhat beaked at apex. *Lemma of upper floret* finely reticulate, slightly apiculate at apex, about 3 mm long. *Chromosome number,* $2n = 36$.

Distribution. Texas: Region 10 on open, rocky slopes and dry, sandy flats. General: Texas to southern California and northern Mexico.

Flowering period: Mostly June to September.

4. **Panicum dichotomiflorum** Michx., Fl. Bor. Amer. 1:48. 1803. FALL PANICUM. Fig. 236. Coarse annual with thick, erect or trailing culms commonly 1-2 m long. *Culm nodes* glabrous. *Ligule* a membrane 0.5-1 mm long, ciliate with hairs about 2 mm long. *Blades* flat, glabrous or infrequently puberulent on upper surface, mostly 12-50 cm or more long and 3-12 (-20) mm broad, sharply scabrous on margins. *Panicles* variable in size and general aspect, commonly many-flowered and 12-40 cm long but panicles on lateral branches often smaller. *Panicle axis* glabrous or scabrous. *Spikelets* glabrous, narrowly ovate, mostly 2.4-3 mm long, appressed along the slender but stiff branchlets on short or rather long pedicels. *First glume* broad and short, mostly one-fifth to one-fourth as long as spikelet, truncate, obtuse or broadly

Fig. 236. *Panicum dichotomiflorum*. Inflorescence and spikelet. From Gould and Box, 1965.

444   THE GRASSES OF TEXAS

acute at apex. *Second glume and lower lemma* about as long as spikelet. *Lemma and palea of upper floret* smooth and shiny, the lemma narrow and narrowly pointed. *Chromosome number,* $2n = 54$ ($2n = 36$ also reported but this number needs confirmation).

Distribution. Texas: Regions 1, 2, 3, 4 and 9 and possibly the southern portions of regions 5 and 8, infrequent in central and western portions of the State. Mostly in ditches, low fields and other areas of moist, disturbed soils. General: Throughout the eastern half of the United States and occasional in the western states.

Flowering period: August to October or November.

5. **Panicum capillare** L., Sp. Pl. 58. 1753. *Panicum capillare* var. *occidentale* Rydb. COMMON WITCHGRASS. Fig. 237. Annual. *Culms* mostly 20-80 cm long but much shorter on depauperate plants, usually much-branched and decumbent-spreading at base, pubescent or hairy at least at the nodes. *Culm internodes* hollow. *Sheaths* papillose-hispid with spreading hairs. *Ligule* of short, stiff hairs, these more or less connate and membranous below, 0.7-1.5 (-2) mm long. *Blades* flat, elongate, 5-15 (-25) mm broad, hirsute or hispid on one or both surfaces or occasionally merely ciliate on margins below. *Panicle* large, diffuse, usually one-half or more as broad as long and often one-half or more the entire length of the culm, with spikelets widely spaced and infrequently overlapping and imbricate; *panicle branches* scabrous, widely spreading at maturity, the pulvini in the branch axils well-developed, pubescent; pedicels slender, at least some 1-3 cm or more long. *Panicle* breaking off from rest of plant at maturity. *Spikelets* glabrous 2- (1.8-) 3.5 mm long, the tips of the upper glume and lower lemma rather abruptly extended into an acuminate apex. *First glume* acute to acuminate, one-third to two-thirds as long as spikelet. *Palea of lower floret* typically absent but occasionally developed. *Lemma of upper floret,* smooth and shiny, 1.3-2.3 mm long, 0.5-0.9 mm broad, without scars at base. *Chromosome number,* $2n = 18$.

Distribution. Texas: Occasional in all regions except the South Texas Plains (region 6) but most common in north-central Texas, usually growing as a weed of disturbed soils, often in gardens, flower beds and vacant lots. General: Southern Canada and throughout most of the United States, from coast to coast.

Flowering period: June or July to November.

6. **Panicum hillmanii** Chase, J. Wash. Acad. Sci. 14:345, f. 1. 1934. HILLMAN PANICUM. Annual with thick culms mostly 20-65 cm tall. *Culms* and *leaves* more or less papillate-hispid and pubescent. *Ligules* as in *P. capillare,* 1.7-2.5 mm long. *Blades* firm, typically bluish-green, mostly 9-15 cm long and 5-12 mm broad. *Panicles* large, often as broad or broader than long, with stiffly spreading branches and spikelets on short to moderately long pedicels. *Pulvini* in axils of panicle branches pubescent. *Spikelets* glabrous, 2.4-3 mm long, the second glume and lower lemma abruptly narrowed into an

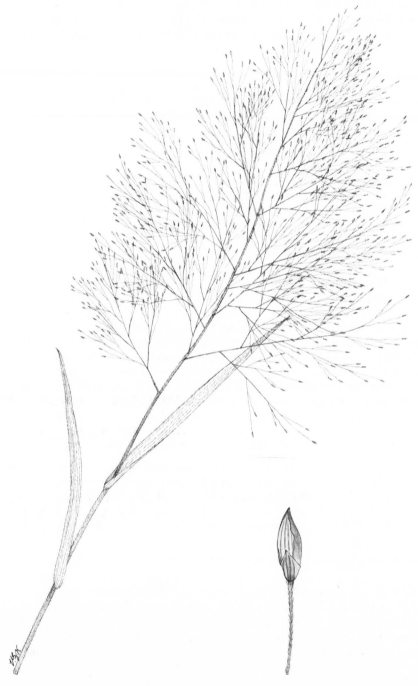

Fig. 237. *Panicum capillare*. Inflorescence and spikelet. From Gould and Box, 1965.

446   THE GRASSES OF TEXAS

acuminate apex. *Palea of lower floret* oblong-ovate, about 1.5 mm long. *Lemma of upper floret* smooth and shiny, 1.1-1.3 mm broad, dark at maturity, with a raised crescent-shaped scar at base. *Chromosome number,* 2n=18.

Distribution. Texas: Regions 5, 8, 9 and 10 in ditches, open roadsides and pastures, not frequent. General: Kansas to Texas and New Mexico and in California.

Flowering period: Mostly July to October.

Panicum hillmanii possibly is not specifically distinct from the widespread and variable *P. capillare.*

7. **Panicum philadelphicum** Trin., Gram. Pan. 216. 1829. PHILADEL-PHIA WITCHGRASS. Tufted annual with slender, usually thinly hispid or hirsute culms 20-50 (-60) cm tall. *Sheaths* papillate-hispid with slender, spreading hairs. *Ligule* a fringe of hairs 0.5-1.5 mm long. *Blades* thin, strongly hispid or hirsute on both surfaces to nearly glabrous, usually ciliate with papilla-based hairs, 5-15 cm long and 2-7 mm broad. *Panicles* open, 7-15 cm long, mostly one-third to one-half as broad as long, with erect-spreading branches; *spikelets* typically short-pediceled and appressed in small clusters at the tips of the slender branches and branchlets; axils of panicle branches glabrous or sparsely hairy. *Spikelets* glabrous, 1.5-2 (-2.2) mm long, acute or slightly acuminate at apex. *First glume* about one-third as long as spikelet. *Palea of lower floret* absent. *Lemma of upper floret* smooth and shiny. *Chromosome number,* 2n=18.

Distribution. Texas: Reported by Correll and Johnston (1970) to be rare in sandy and gravelly soil in eastern and north-central Texas (regions 1, 3, 4 and 5). General: Connecticut to Minnesota, south to Georgia and Texas.

Flowering period: Summer and early autumn.

8. **Panicum flexile** (Gatt.) Scribn., in Kearney, in Bull. Torrey Bot. Club 20:476. 1893. WIRY WITCHGRASS. Tufted annual, the culms occasionally solitary but usually clustered and with few to several very short flowering branches at base. *Culms* 12-75 cm long, hispid on nodes and upper portion of internodes to nearly glabrous; *internodes* hollow, without pith. *Sheaths* hispid to nearly glabrous. *Ligule* a fringe of hairs 0.5-1.5 mm long, the hairs more or less fused together at base. *Blades* 6-25 (4-30) cm long, 2-7 mm broad, glabrous to sparsely hispid or pilose. *Panicles* open, relatively few-flowered, 7-20 (-30) cm long and one-half to one-third as wide as long; *branch pulvini* glabrous or pubescent; *panicle branches* erect-spreading, less frequently widely spreading, most commonly with a single long-pediceled spikelet terminating the branches and branchlets. *Spikelets* glabrous, slender, 3-3.4 (2.7-3.9) mm long. *First glume* acute to acuminate or mucronate, one-half or slightly less as long as spikelet. *Second glume and lemma of lower floret* acuminate, about equal or glume slightly longer. *Palea of lower floret* absent. *Lemma of upper floret* smooth and shiny, narrow, dark brown at maturity. *Chromosome number,* 2n=18.

Distribution. Texas: Correll and Johnston (1970) note that a collection of this species was made at Clarksville, Red River County (region 3) in the past century. Apparently it has not been collected recently in the State. General: Eastern Canada and New York to North Dakota, Florida and Texas, mostly in moist soil of pastures and open woods.

Flowering period: Summer and early autumn.

9. **Panicum hirticaule** Presl, Reliq. Haenk. 1:308. 1830. *P. pampinosum* Hitchc. & Chase. ROUGHSTALK WITCHGRASS. Fig. 238. Annual, culms usually moderately branched at base, hispid or glabrous, 15-80 cm tall. *Sheaths* usually hispid with papillate hairs. *Ligule* a ring of hairs 0.9-3.5 mm long. *Blades* sparsely hispid to nearly glabrous, ciliate on margins, mostly 7-15 cm long and 3-12 mm broad but occasionally longer or shorter and broader or more narrow, the broader blades tending to be auriculate at base. *Panicles* 5-20 cm long, one-fourth to one-half as broad as long; pulvini in axils of panicle branches typically glabrous, rarely pubescent. *Spikelets* appressed to the branchlets on short pedicels, the pedicels of lateral spikelets mostly 1-2.5 mm long. *Spikelets* glabrous, narrowly ovate, mostly 2.3-3.5 mm long. *First glume* acute, from slightly less to slightly more than one-half the length of the spikelet. *Second glume* and *lower lemma* about equal, narrowly acute or acuminate. *Palea of lower floret* present, usually well developed. *Lemma of upper floret* smooth and shiny, with or without a crescent-shaped scar at base. *Chromosome number, $2n = 18$.*

Distribution. Texas: Region 10 on dry, open slopes and in dry, sandy ravines and washes. General: Texas, New Mexico, Arizona and California, south into the drier regions of Mexico and also present in South America.

Flowering period: Mostly August to October, occasionally flowering in July.

10. **Panicum miliaceum** L., Sp. Pl. 58. 1753. BROOMCORN MILLET. Coarse annual. *Culms* erect or decumbent at base, 20-100 cm tall, glabrous or the lower nodes and internodes pubescent or hispid. *Sheaths* pustulate-hispid. *Ligule* a fringed membrane, commonly 1.5-3 mm long including the hairs. *Blades* thin, weak, variously pubescent or hispid to nearly glabrous, commonly 10-20 cm long and 6-15 mm broad but as much as 30 cm long and 20 mm broad. *Panicles* more or less contracted, 5-20 (-30) cm long and one-third to one-fourth as broad, usually somewhat drooping, the spikelets short-pediceled and crowded on the branchlets and branch tips; *panicle branches* never strongly spreading, lacking pulvini and glabrous in their axils. *Spikelets* plump, broadly ovate or elliptic, mostly 4.5-5 mm long. *Glumes* and *lemma* of lower floret thin, strongly-nerved; lower glume 5-nerved, acute or acuminate, one-half to three-fourths as long as upper glume and lower lemma; second glume and lemma of lower floret 9- (7-11-) nerved, acute to acuminate. *Lemma of upper floret* 3-3.5 mm long, smooth and shiny, yellowish- to reddish-brown. *Chromosome number, $2n = 36$.*

Fig. 238. *Panicum hirticaule*. Inflorescence and spikelet. From Gould and Box, 1965.

SUBFAMILY VI. PANICOIDEAE   **449**

Distribution. Texas: Probably not established in the State but occasional as a weed of disturbed soils in the northern and central portions. General: Introduced in the United States and now growing as an escape from cultivation at widely scattered locations in the cooler portions of the country.

Flowering period: July to October or November.

Broomcorn millet is cultivated in Europe and Asia where the grain is used for human food. In the United States it has been grown to a limited extent for human consumption but more commonly has been utilized for animal forage.

11. **Panicum verrucosum** Muhl., Descr. Gram. 113, 1817. WARTY PANICUM. Fig. 239. Annual with slender, glabrous culms 15-120 cm or more long, the culms first erect and little branched, later often becoming decumbent, widely spreading and freely branched at the lower nodes. *Sheaths* glabrous on back, ciliate with fine hairs on margins. *Ligule* a minute fringe of hairs 0.3 mm or less long. *Blades* thin, flat, bright green, glabrous, 5-20 cm long, 4-10 mm broad. *Panicles* few-flowered, with 1-3 spikelets at tips of slender, rather stiffly spreading branches, these bare of spikelets near base; *pedicels of lateral spikelets* mostly shorter than spikelets. *Spikelets* elliptic to obovate, glabrous, 1.7-2.1 (-2.5) mm long. *First glume* greatly reduced, usually one-fourth to one-fifth as long as spikelet. *Second glume* and *lemma of lower floret* roughened with small warts, about equal in length. *Lower floret* neuter, palea absent. *Lemma* and *palea of upper floret* finely reticulate, margins of lemma rather thin, not inrolled over palea. *Chromosome number*, $2n = 36$.

Distribution. Texas: Regions 1, 2 and 3, usually in moist or marshy, sandy soil and often in open woodlands. General: Massachusetts and Michigan south to Florida and Texas.

Flowering period: July to October or November.

12. **Panicum brachyanthum** Steud., Syn. Pl. Glum. 1:67. 1854. PIMPLE PANICUM. Fig. 240. Glabrous annual with slender, wiry culms; essentially similar to *P. verrucosum* but blades 1-3 mm broad, spikelets 3.2-4 mm long and second glume and lemma of lower floret tuberculate-hispid. *Chromosome number* not reported.

Distribution. Texas: Regions 1, 2 and 3 in sandy or clayey soils of open woodlands, forest borders, fence rows and well-drained road right-of-ways. General: Arkansas and Oklahoma to Louisiana and Texas.

Flowering period: Mostly August to October.

13. **Panicum trichoides** Swartz, Prodr. Veg. Ind. Occ. 24. 1788. Annual with short, broad, thin, flat blades and open panicles of minute spikelets on slender, mostly long pedicels. *Culms* freely branched below, often with long, creeping, stoloniferous bases, the erect branches mostly 15-40 cm tall; lower internodes puberulent to hispid. *Sheaths* pubescent or hispid, often with

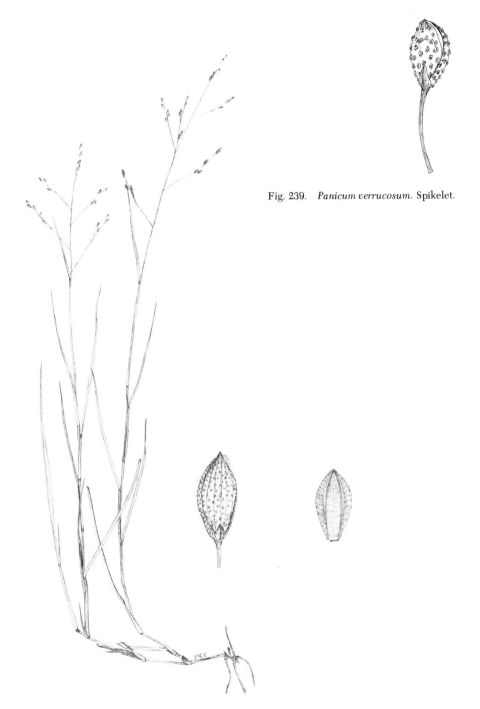

Fig. 239. *Panicum verrucosum.* Spikelet.

Fig. 240. *Panicum brachianthum.* Plant, spikelet and floret. From Gould and Box, 1965.

papilla-based hairs. *Ligule* a ciliate membrane less than 0.5 mm long. *Blades* ovate-lanceolate, glabrous or sparsely hispid, mostly 2-7 cm long and 6-22 mm broad, with a broad, cordate, asymmetrical base and narrowly acute apex. *Panicles* 4-18 cm long, usually two-thirds or more as broad as long, with numerous branches and branchlets. *Spikelets* mostly 1-1.4 mm long, on pedicels as much as 1-2 cm long. *Glumes and lemma of lower floret* usually sparsely strigose, first glume slightly less than one-half as long as spikelet, second glume rounded at apex, slightly shorter than lemma of lower floret. *Lemma of upper floret* light brown and minutely rugose at maturity. *Chromosome number,* $2n=18$.

Distribution. Texas: Collected in vicinity of Brownsville in the southernmost portion of region 2, probably not established. General: Southern Texas, Mexico, Central America and the Caribbean, south to Brazil and Peru; also in Asia and islands of the Pacific.

Flowering period: Mostly late summer and autumn.

14. **Panicum obtusum** H.B.K., Nov. Gen. et Sp. 1:98. 1815. VINE MESQUITE. Fig. 241. Perennial, typically developing erect culms and long, wiry stolons from a hard, knotty or rhizomatous base. *Erect culms* mostly 20-60 cm tall, with glabrous nodes. *Stolons* to 1 m or more in length, with swollen, densely hairy nodes. *Sheaths* rounded, glabrous or hispid, the reduced, basal leaves usually villous. *Ligules* membranous, 1-2 mm long. *Blades* firm, elongate, flat or involute, 2-7 mm broad, light bluish-green, usually with a few long hairs above the ligule but otherwise glabrous. *Inflorescence* a narrow, contracted panicle or raceme, mostly 3-10 (-14) cm long and 5-13 mm broad, with short, appressed, usually unbranched primary branches or the spikelets all short-pediceled on main axis. *Spikelets* oblong or obovate, 3.4-4 mm long, glabrous. *Glumes* broad, rounded at apex, nearly equal and as long as spikelet or slightly shorter. *Lower floret* usually staminate, with a large, well-developed palea that often exceeds lemma in length. *Lemma of upper floret* smooth and shiny, minutely reticulate. *Chromosome number,* $2n=40$ ($2n=20$ in a Mexican collection).

Distribution. Texas: Throughout the State except in region 1, mostly in clayey lowland pastures, swales and ditches that periodically dry out. General: Missouri to Colorado, south to Texas, Arizona and northern Mexico.

Flowering period: May to October.

15. **Panicum coloratum** L., Mant. Pl. 1:30. 1767. Not *P. coloratum* Walt. or *P. coloratum* Cav. KLEINGRASS. Tufted perennial with culms mostly 60-135 cm tall from firm, often knotty bases. *Rhizomes* not developed. *Culm nodes* glabrous or minutely puberulent. *Sheaths* glabrous or hispid with papilla-based hairs. *Ligule* a fringed membrane, 0.5-2 mm long including hairs. *Blades* elongate, 2-6 (-8) mm broad, glabrous or hispid on one or both surfaces. *Panicles* mostly 8-25 cm long, with spikelets short-pediceled on spreading, freely rebranched branches. *Spikelets* 2.8-3.2 mm long, glabrous. *First glume* 1-1.5 mm long, broad at base, abruptly narrowed to an acute apex.

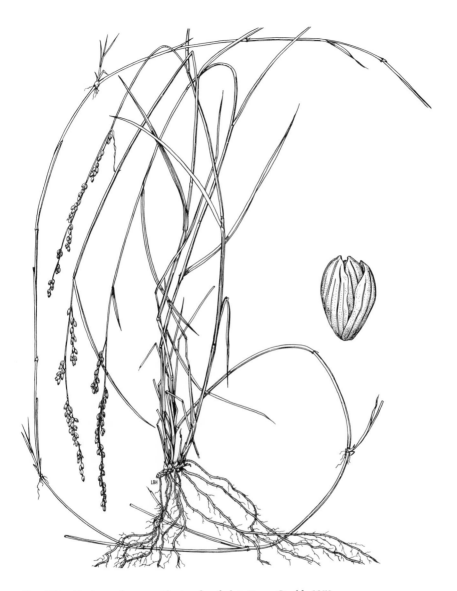

Fig. 241. *Panicum obtusum*. Plant and spikelet. From Gould, 1951.

Second glume and *lower lemma* about equal or the narrowly pointed second glume longer. *Lower floret* staminate, with a broad, thin palea equaling the upper floret in length. *Lemma of upper floret* smooth and shiny, slightly beaked at apex. *Chromosome number*, several reports of $2n=36$ and other records of $2n=18$, 32 and 44.

SUBFAMILY VI. PANICOIDEAE   453

Distribution. Texas: Introduced into southern and central Texas as a forage grass, persisting on the Edwards Plateau (region 7). General: Native to Africa, now widely introduced in the warmer regions of the world.

Flowering period: Mostly May to September.

16. **Panicum virgatum** L., Sp. Pl. 59. 1753. SWITCHGRASS. Fig. 242. Stout perennial with scaly, creeping rhizomes. *Culms* firm, tough, 0.6-2 (-3) m tall, in large or small clumps, usually unbranched above base; nodes glabrous or pubescent. *Sheaths* rounded, glabrous. *Ligule* a fringed membrane 1.5-3 mm long. *Blades* firm, flat, elongate, 3-15 mm broad, commonly glabrous but occasionally pilose. *Panicles* open, broad or rather narrow, many-flowered, 15-55 cm long, with spikelets mostly short-pediceled and clustered on long, slender branches. *Spikelets* glabrous, mostly 3-5 mm long. *Glumes* narrowly acute or acuminate, the first glume two-thirds to three-fourths as long as the second, the second slightly longer than the lower and upper lemmas. *Lower floret* usually staminate, with a large, membranous palea. *Lemma of upper floret* narrowly ovate, smooth and shiny, light-colored. *Chromosome numbers* reported, $2n = 18$, 36, 54, 72, 90 and 108; several aneuploid counts also reported.

Distribution. Texas: In moist lowlands in all regions of the State. General: Southeastern Canada, throughout most of the United States except on the Pacific Coast, Cuba and northern Mexico.

Flowering period: Late August to October.

17. **Panicum amarum** Ell., Bot. S.C. and Ga. 1:121. 1816. *Panicum amarulum* Hitchc. BITTER PANICUM. Coarse perennial with glabrous, glaucous culms in large or small clumps or solitary from stout, creeping rhizomes. *Erect culms* 0.3-2 m or more tall. *Leaves* firm, glaucous, usually glabrous except for the ligular hairs. *Sheaths* rounded. *Ligule* a ciliate membrane, the membrane about 0.5 mm long, the hairs 1.5-3 mm long. *Blades* flat or folded, elongate, mostly 3-15 mm broad. *Panicles* dense, contracted, 10-35 (-50) cm long. *Panicle branches, branchlets* and *pedicels* glabrous, the pedicels short and stout. *Spikelets* mostly 4.5-6 (-6.5) mm long, glabrous. *Glumes* acute, the first glume one-half to two-thirds as long as the second, the second slightly exceeding the lower lemma, usually narrow and appearing somewhat beaked at apex. *Lower floret* staminate, with palea slightly shorter than lemma. *Lemma of upper floret* smooth and shiny, ovate or oblong. *Chromosome number*, $2n = 36$.

Distribution. Texas: Region 2 on sandy beaches and dunes. General: On the Atlantic and Gulf coasts from Connecticut to Florida and Texas, in the West Indies and on the eastern coast of Mexico.

Flowering period: Mostly September to November.

Correll and Johnston (1970) use the name *Panicum amarulum* for the Texas plants of this complex. Chase (1951) reported the presence of both *P.*

Fig. 242. *Panicum virgatum.* Inflorescence, floret and spikelet.

SUBFAMILY VI. PANICOIDEAE 455

amarum and *P. amarulum* on the Texas coast. The two "species," however, seem to represent no more than growth forms or varieties of a single species.

18. **Panicum havardii** Vasey, Bull. Torrey Bot. Club 14:95. 1887. HAVARD PANICUM. Coarse perennial with stout culms from an extensive system of scaly rhizomes. *Culms* glabrous, glaucous, mostly 70-160 cm tall, usually solitary or in small clusters. *Leaves* glaucous, firm and tough. *Sheaths* rounded, glabrous. *Ligule* a minute membrane fringed with hairs mostly 2-4 mm long. *Blades* linear, flat or folded, mostly 5-10 mm broad, usually with a few hairs just above the ligule, the tips long-attenuate and often involute. *Panicles* typically large, open, as much as 40 cm long, the primary branches stiffly spreading at maturity. *Spikelets* 6-8 mm long, glabrous. *Glumes and lower lemma* usually tapering to a long, narrow, somewhat beaked apex, the first glume from less than one-half to about two-thirds the length of the second. *Lower floret* staminate, with a large, well-developed palea. *Lemma of upper floret* smooth and shiny, usually 1.5-2 mm shorter than the second glume and lower lemma. *Chromosome number* not reported.

Distribution. Texas: Region 10 and western portion of region 7, in dry sand, usually in and along dune formations. General: Western Texas, southern New Mexico and northern Chihuahua, Mexico.

Flowering period: Mostly September and October.

Panicum havardii is closely related to *P. virgatum* and *P. amarum*. All are coarse rhizomatous perennials with similar vegetative and inflorescence characteristics.

19. **Panicum repens** L., Sp. Pl. ed. 2. 87. 1762. TORPEDOGRASS. Fig. 243. Perennial with erect culms mostly 35-75 cm tall from stout, scaly rhizomes, these often widely spreading and freely branched. *Culm nodes* glabrous or the lower ones hispid. *Sheaths*, at least the lower ones, commonly hispid with papilla-based hairs, the hairs sometimes restricted to the margins. *Ligule* a minute membrane fringed with hairs 0.5-1 mm long. *Blades* firm, flat or folded, 5-25 cm long, 2-8 mm broad, commonly hispid on one or both surfaces. *Panicles* narrow but open, 7-15 cm long, the spikelets on short, stout pedicels. *Spikelets* plump, glabrous, 2.2-2.7 mm long, with thin, light-colored glumes and lower lemma. *First glume* broadly rounded, truncate, collar-like, mostly 0.6-0.8 mm long. *Second glume and lower lemma* equal, often slightly L·aked at apex. *Lower floret* staminate, at maturity as large as the upper. *Lemma of upper floret* smooth and shiny. *Chromosome number*, the count of $2n=54$ obtained from Texas plants, records from other localities include $2n=36$, 40 and 45.

Distribution. Texas: Region 2 on coastal sands in Jefferson, Chambers and Galveston counties. General: Along the Gulf of Mexico, Florida to Texas, possibly not native; widespread in tropical-subtropical coastal regions of the world.

Flowering period: Late August to October.

Fig. 243. *Panicum repens.* Inflorescence and spikelet.

20. **Panicum antidotale** Retz., Obs. Bot. 4:17. 1786. BLUE PANICUM. Fig. 244. Perennial, with a hard, knotty base. *Culms* firm or hard, often glaucous, mostly 0.5-2 (-3) m tall, becoming much branched and bush-like in age. *Culm nodes* pubescent, conspicuously swollen. *Sheaths* glabrous or the collar puberulent. *Ligule* a fringed membrane, 0.5-1 mm long including the hairs. *Blades* flat, elongate, glabrous or the lower ones puberulent, mostly 4-12 mm broad. *Panicles* open or somewhat dense and contracted, freely branched, mostly 12-25 cm long. *Spikelets* glabrous, broadly ovate, 2.5-3 mm long, borne on short pedicels and at the tips of short branchlets. *First glume* thin, broad, broadly rounded or obtuse at apex, mostly one-third to one-half the length of the spikelet. *Second glume and lemma of lower floret* about equal, broad and thin at apex. *Lower floret* staminate, with a palea as long and nearly as large as lemma. *Lemma of upper floret* smooth, shiny, narrowly pointed, about as long as spikelet. *Chromosome number,* $2n = 18$.

Distribution. Texas: Commonly used in range reseeding and frequent in regions 6 and 7. Also introduced and more or less persistent in regions 2, 3, 4, 8 and 9. General: Native to India, introduced in southwestern United States and elsewhere as a forage grass.

Flowering period: April to November or December.

21. **Panicum gymnocarpon** Ell., Bot. S.C. and Ga., 1:117. 1816. SAVANNAH PANICUM. Fig. 245. Stout perennial with essentially glabrous herbage and erect culms mostly 60-100 cm tall from creeping, stoloniferous bases as much as 2 m long, these rooting freely at the nodes. *Ligule* a membrane 0.6-1 mm long. *Blades* long, broad, flat, mostly 0.8-3 cm wide, auriculate or cordate at base, occasionally sparsely ciliate on the lower margins. *Panicles* mostly 15-40 cm long, with several to numerous stiffly erect-spreading primary branches, these with small clusters of spikelets on short pedicels, many on short, appressed, lateral branches. *Spikelets* 5.5-7 mm long, glabrous. *Glumes* with narrow, usually attenuate tips, first glume 3-nerved, about as long as lemma of lower floret, second glume 5-nerved, 1-1.5 mm longer than first glume and lemma of lower floret. *Lower floret* neuter, with a palea about one-half as long as the lemma. *Lemma of upper floret* narrowly oblong, much shorter than glumes and lower lemma, usually about 2 mm long. *Chromosome number* not reported.

Distribution. Texas: Regions 1 and 3 and wooded portions of region 2, in moist woodland or forest habitats. General: On the Coastal Plain, South Carolina and Florida to Texas and in southern Arkansas.

Flowering period: July to October.

22. **Panicum hians** Ell., Bot. S.C. and Ga. 1:118. 1816. GAPING PANICUM. Fig. 246. Perennial with slender, tufted culms mostly 20-75 cm tall, these strictly erect or more commonly decumbent at base, often freely branched. *Nodes* glabrous or scabrous. *Sheaths* rounded or somewhat compressed laterally, glabrous or ciliate-pubescent on upper margins. *Ligule* a

Fig. 244. *Panicum antidotale*. Plant and spikelet. From Gould and Box, 1965.

Fig. 245. *Panicum gymnocarpon.* Inflorescence, spikelet and floret.

460   THE GRASSES OF TEXAS

Fig. 246. *Panicum hians.* Plant and spikelet. From Gould and Box, 1965.

fringed scale about 0.5 mm long. *Blades* flat or folded, narrow, mostly 6-18 cm long and 2-5 mm broad, often pilose or hispid with long hairs above ligule on adaxial surface. *Panicles* small, few-flowered, variable in branching and general aspect, mostly 6-20 cm long, with spikelets clustered along short or rather long, erect-spreading primary branches and short secondary branches. *Primary branches* slender, usually bare of spikelets on the lower 1.5-3 cm. *Spikelets* glabrous, 1.8-2.6 mm long, at first broadly oblong, later widely gaping at apex between the florets. *First glume* acute, one-third to one-half as long as spikelet. *Second glume* equally or slightly shorter than lemma of lower floret. *Lower floret* neuter, the palea becoming inflated, obovate, often apiculate, much larger and broader than lemma. *Lemma of upper floret* narrowly ovate, pointed, smooth but not shiny. *Chromosome number,* 2n=20.

Distribution. Texas: Regions 1, 2, 3, 4, 6 and 7 in low, moist, often-shaded sites. General: Coastal Plain, Virginia to Florida and Texas and in southern Missouri, Arkansas, Oklahoma and northeastern Mexico. Chase (1951) also included New Mexico in the distribution.

Flowering period: Mostly December through May but occasionally flowering throughout the year.

23. **Panicum purpurascens** Raddi, Agrost. Bras. 47. 1823. PARAGRASS. Fig. 247. Coarse perennial with thick decumbent, trailing culms as much as 4-5 m long. *Nodes* (actually sheath bases) densely bearded. *Sheaths* densely pubescent on collar, rounded and hispid with papilla-based hairs on back or the uppermost glabrous or nearly so. *Ligule* a fringe of hairs about 1.5 mm long from a minute membranous collar or callus. *Blades* flat, mostly 10-30 cm long and 0.5-1.5 cm broad, glabrous, scabrous or hispid with papilla-based hairs. *Panicles* mostly 12-20 cm long, with usually 8-18 widely-spaced, spreading primary branches 2-9 cm long, these simple or the lower ones with short secondary branches. *Basal portion of primary branches* villous-pubescent. *Spikelets* short-pediceled, imbricate and more or less paired on the flattened branch rachis, the pedicels often with a few long silvery hairs. *Spikelets* glabrous, 2.8-3.4 mm long. *First glume* acute, usually 1 mm or less long. *Second glume* and lemma of lower floret about equal. *Lower floret* staminate, with a thin, membranous palea as long as or longer than the lemma. *Lemma and palea of upper floret* finely rugose. *Chromosome number,* 2n=36.

Distribution. Texas: Introduced along the Gulf Coast (region 2) as a forage grass and now rather frequent along waterways and in coastal marshes and pastures at the southern tip of the State. General: Coastal Plain, Florida to Texas; Chase (1951) reports that this species probably was introduced into Brazil at an early date from Africa.

Flowering period: Mostly September to November in Texas.

Paragrass has long been cultivated in the American tropics as a forage grass and was introduced into the United States at an early date. Nealley collected this grass in Texas in 1889, and it was in cultivation at Starkville, Mississippi in 1891.

Fig. 247. *Panicum purpurascens.* Inflorescence and spikelet.

SUBFAMILY VI. PANICOIDEAE   463

24. **Panicum hemitomon** Schult., Mantissa 2:227. 1824. MAIDEN-CANE. Strong perennial with erect culms from creeping rhizomes and stoloniferous bases. *Erect culms* mostly 50-150 cm tall with numerous sterile shoots usually associated with the relatively few floriferous shoots. *Sterile shoots* sometimes with densely hirsute sheaths but the floriferous shoots usually with glabrous sheaths. *Ligule* a short, densely ciliate membrane, mostly about 1 mm long including the hairs. *Blades* of erect culms flat, lanceolate, mostly 12-30 cm long and 7-15 mm broad, typically glabrous. *Panicles* contracted, mostly 10-30 cm long and seldom over 1.5 cm broad, the spikelets closely clustered on erect, short or rather long primary branches and short, appressed secondary branches. *Primary branches* floriferous to base, usually with a tuft of silvery hairs at base and a few long hairs at base of secondary branches. *Spikelets* subsessile, 2-2.6 mm long. *Glumes* scabrous on midnerve and often somewhat beaked at apex, first glume acute, about one-half as long as spikelet, second glume equaling the lower lemma or slightly shorter. *Lower floret* staminate, with a thin palea slightly shorter than lemma. *Lemma and palea of upper floret* shiny, relatively thin, the lemma only loosely clasping the palea above. *Chromosome number*, $2n=40$.

Distribution. Texas: Regions 1 and 2, in ditches and along canals, swales, riverbanks and lake shores. General: On the Coastal Plain, New Jersey to Florida and Texas and in Tennessee; also in Brazil.

Flowering period: Mostly April to September.

25. **Panicum tenerum** Beyr., in Trin., Acad. St. Petersb. Mem. VI Sci. Nat. 1:341. 1834. Perennial with slender, wiry, stiffly erect, tufted culms mostly 40-100 cm tall from a firm, knotty, often subrhizomatous base. *Sheaths* rounded, glabrous or the lower sheaths pubescent above, conspicuously shorter than culm internodes. *Ligule* a minute, densely ciliate membrane. *Blades* narrow, firm, flat or involute, mostly 4-18 cm long and 1.5-3 (-4) mm broad. *Panicles* small, contracted, mostly 4-8 cm long, with spikelets short-pediceled and clustered on few, appressed, simple or nearly simple, primary branches. *Spikelets* glabrous, 2.2-2.8 mm long, not pronouncedly asymmetrical. *First glume* broadly acute at tip, about two-thirds as long as spikelet. *Second glume and lemma of lower floret* equal or nearly so, narrowly acute, somewhat spreading at maturity. *Chromosome number*, $2n=40$.

Distribution. Texas: Regions 1 and 2, infrequent (Tracy Herbarium records from Hardin County only), in wet or moist, usually sandy soil of forests, forest margins and coastal grasslands. General: North Carolina to Florida and Texas and in the West Indies.

Flowering period: May to July in Texas and late summer and autumn in the Southeast.

26. **Panicum anceps** Michx., Fl. Bor. Amer. 1:48. 1803. *Panicum rhizomatum* Hitchc. & Chase. BEAKED PANICUM. Fig. 248. Perennial with tufted culms 30-100 cm tall from stout, scaly rhizomes. *Culm bases* flattened, often keeled; nodes glabrous or somewhat hispid. *Leaves* glabrous,

Fig. 248. *Panicum anceps.* Inflorescence, spikelet and floret.

scabrous or variously hispid or pubescent, in the hairy forms the collar and sheath base usually densely hispid. *Lower sheaths* typically keeled and laterally compressed. *Ligule* a minute membranous collar, 0.4 mm or less long. *Blades* long and narrow, flat or folded, 4-8 mm broad. *Panicles* variable, open or somewhat contracted, 15-40 cm long, with spikelets short-pediceled and clustered on secondary branches, branchlets and tips of primary branches; lower panicle branches mostly 4-15 cm long. *Spikelets* glabrous except for scabrous keel of first glume, 2.8-3.5 mm long, oriented slightly obliquely on pedicel. *First glume* broad, broadly acute at apex, one-third to one-half as long as spikelet. *Second glume and lemma of lower floret* about equal, narrowly acute, rather widely separated at maturity. *Upper floret* usually about 1 mm shorter than second glume and lower lemma, the lemma narrowly oblong, smooth and shiny. *Chromosome number,* $2n=18$ (one report of $2n=36$).

Distribution. Texas: Regions 1, 2, 3 and 4 (a record from Webb County in region 6 may be erroneous), in forest or shaded, grassy pasturelands, usually in low, moist areas. General: New Jersey to southern Illinois and Kansas, south to Florida and Texas.

Flowering period: July through November.

27. **Panicum rigidulum** Nees, Agrost. Bras. 163. 1829. *Panicum agrostoides* Spreng., *P. condensum* Nash, *P. stipitatum* Nash, *P. longifolium* Torr. REDTOP PANICUM. Fig. 249. Tufted perennial with flowering culms and sterile shoots densely clumped from a firm base; rhizomes not developed. *Culms* erect or decumbent below, 40-100 cm tall, often branched at the upper nodes to produce lateral panicles as well as the terminal one; lower culm internodes typically flattened. *Sheaths*, at least the lower, laterally compressed and keeled, glabrous or less frequently hispid, occasionally with a line of hairs on the collar. *Ligule* a ciliate membrane 0.5-1 mm long. *Blades* glabrous or sparsely hispid, long, narrow, flat or folded, mostly 4-12 mm broad and as much as 50 cm long. *Panicles* variable, terminal and axillary, 10-40 cm long, loosely contracted or more frequently open and with slender, spreading branches. *Main panicle branches* usually bare of spikelets near base, the spikelets clustered at the branch tips and on short secondary branches; branchlets and pedicels usually with a few long, spreading hairs. *Spikelets* mostly 1.6-2.5 mm long, glabrous, erect on the short pedicels, not obliquely angled. *First glume* acute, two-thirds or slightly less as long as spikelet. *Second glume* acute, often slightly beaked, usually slightly longer than lemma of lower floret. *Lemma of upper floret* about three-fourths as long as lemma of lower floret, smooth and shiny, narrowly ovate, with or without a short stipe at base. *Chromosome number*, $2n = 18$.

Distribution. Texas: Regions 1, 2, 3, 4 and 7 in moist pastures and open woodlands and along streambanks and ditchbanks, often in partial shade. General: Throughout the eastern United States, westward to Kansas, Oklahoma and Texas; also in the West Indies and introduced in a few scattered localities in the western United States.

Flowering period: August to November.

Spikelet measurements are for Texas plants, some forms in southeastern United States have spikelets to 2.8 mm long.

28. **Panicum bulbosum** H.B.K., Nov. Gen. et Sp. 1:99. 1815. *Panicum plenum* Hitchc. & Chase. BULB PANICUM. Fig. 250. Tufted perennial with plant base firm, knotty and often rhizomatous, culm bases typically but not always swollen and bulbous. *Culms* glabrous, stiffly erect, 50-140 (-180) cm tall, unbranched above base. *Sheaths* glabrous to variously pubescent or hairy. *Ligule* a short-ciliate membrane 0.5-2 mm long. *Blades* flat, elongate, glabrous or variously hairy on both surfaces, usually with long, stiff hairs on upper side above ligule, mostly 2-6 mm broad but as much as 15 mm broad in some forms. *Panicles* open but often narrow, well-exserted, 12-40 (-50) cm long, the spikelets short-pediceled but loosely arranged on slender branchlets. *Spikelets* glabrous, narrowly oblong, mostly 2.8-3.9 mm long. *First glume* from slightly less to slightly more than one-half as long as spikelet, broadly acute at apex. *Second glume and lemma of lower floret* about equal, often slightly beaked at apex. *Lower floret* staminate or neuter, with a large, well-developed palea. *Lemma and palea of upper floret* finely rugose, usually shiny. *Chromosome numbers* reported, $2n = 36$, 54 and 72; one record of $2n = 70$.

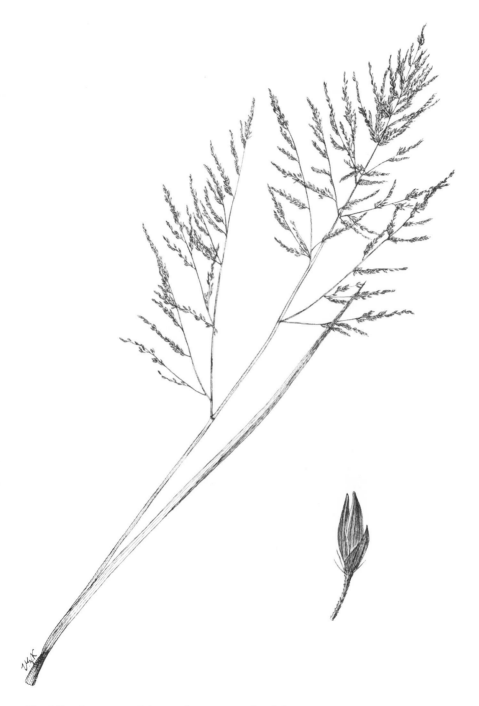

Fig. 249. *Panicum rigidulum.* Inflorescence and spikelet. From Gould and Box, 1965, as *P. agrostoides.*

SUBFAMILY VI. PANICOIDEAE   **467**

Fig. 250. *Panicum bulbosum.* Plant, spikelet and floret. From Gould, 1951.

Distribution. Texas: Region 10, one record from Crockett County in the western portion of region 7, at medium to high elevations, on rocky canyon slopes and in shaded ravines. General: Texas, New Mexico and Arizona, south through the mountainous areas of Mexico to Chiapas.

Flowering period: Mostly August to October but occasionally as early as June.

Panicum bulbosum as presently interpreted comprises populations of extremely diverse aspect. The most common form in Texas, with narrow blades and relatively small spikelets, is referable to *P. bulbosum* var. *minus* Vasey. Large, broad-bladed plants without the cormlike swellings at the culm bases have been referred to *P. plenum* Hitchc. & Chase. Further investigation of the complex is necessary for a satisfactory taxonomic disposition of the populations involved.

29. **Panicum maximum** Jacq., Coll. Bot. 1:76. 1786. GUINEAGRASS. Fig. 251. Stout perennial with thick culms 1-2.5 m tall from a firm, often rhizomatous base. *Culm nodes* typically densely hirsute. *Sheaths* rounded, usually hispid or hirsute, often with papilla-based hairs, the collar densely pubescent. *Ligule* a short membrane densely ciliate with stiff hairs 3-4 mm long. *Blades* long, flat, mostly 0.8-3.5 cm broad, variously hispid or pubescent to nearly glabrous. *Panicles* large, open, broad or narrow, usually 20-50 cm long, with slender, wiry primary branches mostly 8-20 cm or more long. *Spikelets* short-pediceled, glabrous, oblong, widely spaced on the branchlets or somewhat clustered, mostly 3-3.5 mm long. *First glume* usually one-fourth to one-third as long as spikelet, broadly acute or obtuse at apex. *Second glume and lemma of lower floret* subequal, usually 0.75-1 mm longer than lemma of upper floret. *Lower floret* staminate, with a palea as long as lemma. *Lemma and palea of upper floret* transverse-rugose, the lemma often slightly apiculate. *Chromosome number:* The aneuploid number of $2n = 32$ has frequently been reported; other records include $2n = 18$, 36, 44 and 48.

Distribution. Texas: Probably not established in any area of the State, but experimental plantings have been made at Angleton, Kingsville, Austin and elsewhere. General: Widespread in tropical regions of the world, possibly native to Africa.

Flowering period: Mostly September to November.

Guineagrass is one of the major forage grasses of tropical-subtropical pastures. It is widespread and frequent in the American tropics and apparently occurs spontaneously in Florida from early introductions.

30. **Panicum diffusum** Swartz, Prodr. Veg. Ind. Occ. 23. 1788. SPREADING PANICUM. Weak perennial, usually in small dense tufts. *Culms* spreading or rarely ascending, slender, wiry, frequently branching, commonly about 30 cm or less long but occasionally to 100 cm long. *Culm nodes* pubescent with both spreading and appressed hairs. *Ligule* a membrane about 0.5-1 mm long, ciliate with hairs 1-2 mm long. *Blades* mostly flat, glabrous or occasionally spreading-pilose on both surfaces, mostly 5-20 cm long and 1-4.5 mm broad. *Sheaths* mostly shorter than culm internodes, glabrous to papillose hirsute. *Sheath margins*, especially the lower, ciliate with a line of ascending hairs. *Terminal panicles* exserted, pyramidal, 5-25 cm long, the branches scabrous, ascending or stiffly spreading, with few short-pediceled spikelets toward the ends. *Lateral panicles*, for the most part, partially included in the sheath. *Spikelets* glabrous, acute, about 2.1-2.7 mm

Fig. 251. *Panicum maximum*. Plant, two views of spikelet and floret. From Hitchcock, 1935.

long and 1 mm wide. *First glume* acute, one-half the length of spikelet. *Second glume* and *lemma of lower floret* about as long as spikelet. *Lemma* and *palea of upper floret* smooth and shiny, elliptic. *Chromosome number,* $2n=36$.

Distribution. Texas: Regions 2, 3, 4, 5, 6, 7, 8 and 10, mostly in ditches, roadsides, lawns and other areas of loamy or clayey, disturbed soils. General: Texas, eastern Mexico to Brazil, the West Indies, Cuba and the Bahamas.

Flowering period: April through October or November.

Following Nash (1903), most authors have included United States plants of this taxon in *Panicum hallii* var. *filipes* (as *P. filipes*). *P. diffusum* differs from the *filipes* entity in usually having a prostrate growth habit, green, not glaucous leaves and the tetraploid ($2n=36$) chromosome complement.

470   THE GRASSES OF TEXAS

31. **Panicum ghiesbreghtii** Fourn., Mex. Pl. 2:29. 1886. *Panicum hir-tivaginum* Hitchc. GHIESBREGHT PANICUM. Perennial. *Culms* in small tufts, erect or ascending, rather robust, occasionally branching, 50-80 cm tall. *Culm nodes* densely hirsute with both spreading and appressed hairs. *Ligule* a membrane 0.5 mm long, ciliate with hairs to 4.5 mm long. *Blades* flat, papillose-hirsute on both surfaces, occasionally glabrescent, 20-40 (-60) cm long and 8-14 (-18) mm broad. *Sheaths* papillose, ascending-hirsute, densely so for about 10 mm above the nodes, mostly longer than culm internodes. *Sheaths margins* smooth or occasionally ciliate, with a line of ascending hairs as in *P. diffusum*. *Terminal panicles* short-exserted, often nearly equaled by the upper blades, 20-35 cm long, usually less than one-half as wide, the branches scabrous, ascending and naked at base, the branchlets more or less appressed, bearing short-pediceled, approximate but not crowded spikelets. *Lateral panicles* partially included in sheath. *Spikelets* glabrous, acuminate, about 2.8-3.4 mm long and 1 mm wide. *First glume* acute, about one-half the length of the spikelet. *Second glume and lemma of lower floret* about as long as spikelet. *Lemma and palea of upper floret* smooth and shiny, elliptic. *Chromosome number* not reported.

Distribution. Texas: Regions 2 and 6 (Calhoun, Cameron and Hidalgo counties), infrequent in low, moist ground and dense thickets. General: Southern Texas, Mexico to northern South America, the West Indies and Cuba.

Flowering period: June through November, rarely spring.

This species appears closely related to *Panicum diffusum* in having similar pubescence, culm branching and green but not glaucous foliage. It differs in its broader blades, larger spikelets, erect habit and usually greater amount of pubescence.

32. **Panicum capillarioides** Vasey in Coulter, Contr. U.S. Natl. Herb. 1:54. 1890. SOUTHERN WITCHGRASS. Fig. 252. Erect or ascending perennial from a knotty crown. *Culms* stiff, often crooked, 30-60 (-70) cm high. *Culm nodes* densely ascending- or spreading-pubescent. *Ligule* a membrane about 0.5 mm long, ciliate with hairs to 1 mm long. *Blades* rather stiff, flat or occasionally drying somewhat involute, short-pilose on upper surface and sparsely papillose-hirsute on lower, often glabrescent, 20-50 cm long and 2-12 mm broad. *Sheaths* mostly equaling or exceeding the usually short culm internodes, ascending- or spreading-hirsute. *Sheath margins* smooth or partly ciliate with a line of ascending hairs. *Panicles* short-exserted or partially included, usually nearly equaled by the upper blades, few-flowered, 10-30 cm long and often as wide or wider. *Panicle branches* scabrous, ascending or stiffly spreading at maturity, with short-pediceled spikelets near the ends of the branchlets, the axils short-pubescent. *Spikelets* glabrous, long-acuminate, about 5-6.5 mm long and 1-1.2 mm wide. *First glume* acuminate, one-third to one-half as long as spikelet. *Second glume and lemma of lower floret* about as long as spikelet. *Lemma and palea of upper floret* usually 1.6-1.8 mm long, smooth and shiny, elliptic. *Chromosome number*, $2n=36$.

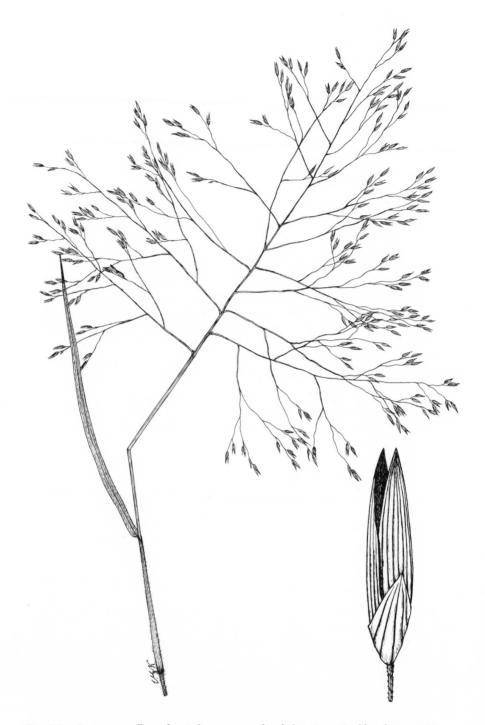

Fig. 252. *Panicum capillarioides*. Inflorescence and spikelet. From Gould and Box, 1965.

Distribution. Texas: Regions 2 and 6, frequent in sandy soils near the coast and around oak motts. General: Southern Texas and northeastern Mexico (Tamaulipas, Nuevo Leon and San Luis Potosi).

Flowering period: April through December.

Panicum capillarioides is readily distinguished by the peculiarly elongated second glume and by the lemma of the lower floret, both of which are much prolonged beyond the fruit, and by the knotty basal crown.

33. **Panicum hirsutum** Swartz, Fl. Ind. Occ. 1:173. 1797. HAIRY PANICUM. Erect, robust perennial. *Culms* as much as 1 cm thick and 1-1.5 m or more high, occasionally branching near base. *Culm nodes* appressed pubescent with hairs to 4 mm long. *Ligule* a membrane about 0.5 mm long, ciliate with hairs to 5 mm long. *Blades* mostly flat or folded, essentially glabrous, 20-60 cm long and 1.5-4 cm broad. *Sheaths* mostly longer than internodes, papillose-hirsute with spreading to ascending prickly hairs, often densely hirsute at summit. *Panicles* short-exserted to included at base, oblong, 20-45 cm long, the many branches scabrous, ascending or spreading and densely-flowered, the spikelets on short, appressed pedicels. *Spikelets* glabrous, acute, about 1.7-2.2 mm long and 1 mm wide. *First glume* acute, one-third to one-half the length of spikelet. *Second glume* and *lemma of lower floret* about as long as spikelet. *Lemma* and *palea* of upper floret smooth and shiny, elliptic. *Chromosome number*, $2n = 36$.

Distribution. Texas: Regions 2 and 6, mostly in low, moist, rich soils, often in shaded habitats, rare or localized in the Brownsville region of south Texas, near the Rio Grande. General: Extreme southern Texas, eastern Mexico to Brazil, the West Indies and Cuba.

Flowering period: May through December.

This is the tallest and most robust species of the *Diffusa* section of *Panicum*. It also has the most compactly-flowered panicles. Spikelet characters and pubescence patterns indicate close affinities with *P. ghiesbreghtii*. It is to be noted that the stiff, spinescent sheath hairs of *P. hirsutum* may cause mechanical irritation to the skin when handled.

34. **Panicum hallii** Vasey, Bull. Torrey Bot. Club 11:64. 1884. Erect or ascending perennial with stiff, glaucous culms 20-80 cm high. *Culm nodes* ascending or appressed-pubescent to glabrous. *Ligule* a membrane about 0.2 mm long, ciliate with hairs to 1.3 mm long. *Blades* glaucous, flat and rather stiff or sometimes lax and curling on drying, sparsely papillose-hirsute to glabrescent, 4-30 cm long and 2-10 mm broad. *Sheaths* mostly equal to somewhat shorter than the internodes, sparsely papillose-hirsute to glabrous. *Panicles* usually well exserted, few to many branches, pyramidal, the spikelets on short appressed pedicels or occasionally spreading on capillary branchlets. *Spikelets* glabrous, acute or acuminate, about 2.2-3.7 (-3.9) mm long and 1-1.5 mm wide. *First glume* acute, one-third to two-thirds the length of the spikelet. *Second glume* and *lemma of lower*

floret about as long as spikelet. *Lemma* and *palea* of upper floret dark brown and shiny, ovate-elliptic. *Chromosome number*, $2n = 18$.

Primary panicle branches mostly less than 15, few-flowered, with spikelets appressed near the ends of stiffly ascending branches; sheaths mostly papillose-hirsute; nodes appressed- or ascending-pubescent
34A. *P. hallii* var. *hallii*

Primary panicle branches mostly more than 15, many-flowered, with spikelets appressed on branchlets or more commonly somewhat spreading on capillary pedicels; sheaths glabrous or sometimes ascending-hispid near summit; culm nodes short appressed-pubescent or glabrescent
34B. *P. hallii* var. *filipes*

34A. **Panicum hallii** Vasey var. **hallii**. HALLS PANICUM. Fig. 253.

Distribution. Texas: Regions 2, 3, 4, 5, 6, 7, 8, 9 and 10, scattered to abundant on sandy to clayey calcareous soils. General: Oklahoma, Texas, Colorado, New Mexico and Arizona and in Mexico, Coahuila and Durango to San Luis Potosi.

Flowering period: April to November.

34B. **Panicum hallii** Vasey var. **filipes** (Scribn.) Waller, Southw. Naturalist 19:105. 1974. *Panicum filipes* Scribn. FILLY PANICUM. Fig. 254.

Distribution. Texas: Regions 2, 3, 4, 5, 6, 7, 8 and 10 (primarily in regions 2, 3, 4 and 6, occasional to frequent along moist roadsides and disturbed sites on clay soils. General: Texas and south through Mexico to Guerrero.

Flowering period: April to November.

Panicum hallii var. *filipes* can usually be distinguished from *P. hallii* var. *hallii* by its taller habit, lax rather than stiff or curled blades, larger panicles with more branches and spikelets, smaller spikelets and lack of overall papillose-pubescence. This variety reaches its most typical expression in southern Texas as a tall, glabrous, glaucous to purplish plant, which has large, many-branched panicles with capillary, spreading branches. Elsewhere the variety is less well-defined. On arid, clayey sites through the central and lower Rio Grande plains, plants of both *P. hallii* varieties frequently are depauperate and with small spikelets. Here they are difficult to distinguish except by the typical pubescence patterns.

35. **Panicum pilcomayense** Hack., Bull. Herb. Boissier II. 7:449. 1907. Erect, robust perennial. *Culms* stiff, 50-100 cm high. *Culm nodes*, at least the lower, appressed-pubescent. *Ligule* a membrane about 0.5 mm long, ciliate with hairs to 2.5 mm long. *Blades* 20 to 60 cm long and 4-10 mm broad, flat or drying involute, essentially glabrous except for some long hairs on upper surface and margins near base. *Sheaths* mostly longer than the internodes,

Fig. 253. *Panicum hallii* var. *hallii*. Plant, spikelet and floret. From Gould and Box, 1965.

SUBFAMILY VI. PANICOIDEAE 475

Fig. 254. *Panicum hallii* var. *filipes*. Plant and spikelet. From Gould and Box, 1965, as
P. *filipes*.

476   THE GRASSES OF TEXAS

glabrous. *Panicles* short-exserted or included at base, broadly pyramidal and diffuse, 20 to 40 cm long, often one-third to one-half the plant height. *Lower branches* in verticils of 3 to 7, as much as 30 cm long. *Upper branches* binate, ternate or solitary, scabrous, naked below, the spikelets near the ends of spreading branchlets. *Lower branch axis* usually short pilose. Panicle disarticulating as a tumbleweed at maturity. *Spikelets* glabrous, acute or abruptly acuminate, 2.4-3 mm long and about 1 mm wide. *First glume* acute, one-third to one-half the spikelet length. *Second glume* and *lower lemma* about as long as spikelet. *Lemma* and *palea* of upper floret smooth and shiny, elliptic. *Chromosome number*, $2n=36$.

Distribution. Texas: Regions 2, 3 and 4, mostly in ditches and depressions of prairie sites and field margins, occasional inland to Brazos and Navarro counties, apparently introduced from South America. General: Southeastern Texas and eastern South America.

Flowering period: April through November.

This species differs from other members of the *Panicum diffusum* group by its verticilled branches, disarticulating panicle and strongly perennial habit. When not fully exserted, the inflorescence bears some resemblance to that of *P. hallii* var. *filipes*.

97. DICHANTHELIUM (Hitchc. & Chase) Gould

Tufted perennials, for the most part with a tuft or rosette of short, broad-bladed basal leaves developed during the cool season. *Culms* stiffly erect, mostly 20-70, infrequently -150, cm tall. *Sheaths* rounded on back, those of the culm leaves typically shorter than culm internodes. *Ligule* a ring of hairs, a short, ciliate or glabrous membrane or absent. *Blades* of vernal (spring) shoots typically flat and broad but narrow and involute in a few species; late-season plants of most species branching at upper nodes, some becoming bushy-branched and with fascicles of short, narrow leaves. *Panicles* of primary shoots typically open, usually well exserted on long peduncles. *Inflorescences* of secondary branches often much-reduced, occasionally with only 2-6 spikelets, these partially hidden in the fascicled leaves. *Spikelets* long- or short-pediceled, ovate, elliptic or obovate, awnless, rounded or somewhat pointed at apex, 1.4-4 mm long, usually puberulent but glabrous in a few taxa; disarticulation below glumes. *First glume* typically thin, broad and short. *Second glume* and *lemma of lower floret* about equal or the glume shorter. *Lower floret* neuter, the palea present or absent, often half or more as long as lemma. *Upper floret* with a shiny, glabrous, hard or coriaceous lemma and palea, the lemma tightly inrolled over the margins of the palea.

Hitchcock and Chase (1910) proposed *Dichanthelium* as a section of *Panicum* and this disposition has been followed in all systematic treatments of North American grasses to the present. Although closely related to *Panicum*, *Dichanthelium* comprises a closely interrelated series of taxa which possess numerous characteristics to delimit the group from *Panicum*. Brown and

Smith (1972) and Smith and Brown (1973) have discussed basic differences between *Panicum* and *Dichanthelium* in respect to the CO_2 fixation aspect of photosynthesis and to related differences in the sheath around vascular bundles of the leaf. Cytologically the genus *Dichanthelium* is unique among the larger panicoid genera in the relatively low incidence of polyploidy. Of over 100 species commonly recognized in the group, all but three for which counts have been reported are diploid ($2n = 18$). The three polyploid taxa all are tetraploid ($2n = 36$). Characteristically, *Dichanthelium* species flower early in the spring and again in the summer or autumn. According to available information, little, if any, seed is set in spikelets of the spring or vernal inflorescence. Most seed apparently is produced in cleistogamous spikelets of the later-developed and reduced lateral inflorescences.

For the most part *Dichanthelium* is a North American genus, with a few species extending southward into South America. In their monograph of *Panicum* (1910), Hitchcock and Chase included 109 species in this group. Chase, in the 1951 revision of Hitchcock's Manual, recognized 111 species for the United States, reporting 53 to occur in Texas. Gould (1969) listed 48 species for the state. In the most recent treatment of Texas grasses, Correll and Johnston (1970) recognized 26 specific taxa for Texas. In preparing the present treatment, further reduction in the number of recognized Texas species was found necessary (Gould, 1974) to delimit definable species and to devise workable keys to the species.

Spikelets 0.9-2.4 mm long   A

Spikelets 2.5-4.3 mm long   AA

A

Blades of basal rosette or tuft 1-4 (-5) mm broad; culm leaves 8-20 cm long, infrequently more than 5 mm broad 17. *D. linearifolium*

Blades of basal rosette or tuft 6 mm or more broad when culm leaves 8 cm or more long

 Ligular hairs, at least of upper leaves, 1.5-6 mm long

  Sheaths pilose, pubescent or lanate on back; culm nodes bearded, internodes pubescent 5. *D. lanuginosum*

  Sheaths glabrous on back, glabrous or pubescent-ciliate on margins; culms glabrous or internodes sparsely pilose 4. *D. lindheimeri*

 Ligular hairs less than 1.5 mm long, absent in some species

  Sheaths of mid-culm leaves villous over back with long, spreading hairs

Blades ciliate on margins to well above middle; ligule a glabrous or minutely fringed rim; culms not branching above base; basal blades long, soft, yellowish-green   6. *D. laxiflorum*

Blades ciliate only below middle if at all; ligule with hairs to 1 mm long; culms bushy-branched in age; basal blades firm, not yellowish-green   2. *D. angustifolium*

Sheaths of mid-culm leaves not villous on back

Cauline blades broad and cordate at base, glabrous except for a few stout, papilla-based hairs on lower margins; blades mostly 7 mm or more broad, often as much as 15-30 mm broad

Spikelets 1.4-2 mm long, broadly oblong or obovate
    8. *D. sphaerocarpon*

Spikelets 2.4-2.5 mm long, narrowly oblong
    14. *D. commutatum*

Cauline blades not cordate at base, with or without cilia on lower margins, glabrous or variously hairy; blades infrequently as much as 8 mm broad; spikelets 1.3-2.4 mm long, narrowly oblong

Blades thin or firm, at least some 6-15 cm long and the basal ones often 5-7 mm broad

Blades thin, glabrous or nearly so; spikelets 1.4-2.2 mm long; panicles open, often many-flowered, spikelets not appressed to the branches; culms glabrous or nodes bearded with spreading hairs   1. *D. dichotomum*

Blades firm, glabrous or variously hirsute or pubescent; spikelets 1.8-2.4 mm long; panicles tending to be small and few-flowered, the lateral spikelets short-pediceled and appressed to the branches; culms glabrous or variously hairy but nodes not bearded with spreading hairs when internodes glabrous
    2. *D. angustifolium*

Blades thin, typically 1-4.5 cm long and 1.5-4.5 mm broad; plants of acid bogs and moist seeps   3. *D. ensifolium*

AA

Blades of vernal leaves never or infrequently as much as 12 mm broad

Spikelets narrowly obovate, gradually tapering to a narrow base, 3.5-4.3 mm long

Blades thick, mostly 3-8 cm long, abruptly pointed, usually coarsely hispid-ciliate on the margins to well above middle

11. *D. nodatum*

Blades thin, mostly 4-15 cm long, tapering above to a narrow, acuminate apex, ciliate on margins only near base

12. *D. pedicellatum*

Spikelets ovate, oblong or slightly obovate, not tapering gradually to a narrow base, 2.5-4.8 mm long

Broadest culm blades 4-5 mm broad and usually 10-20 cm long; plants without basal rosette of broad, short blades

Spikelets 3.2-4.8 mm long, pointed or beaked at apex and with lemma of upper floret considerably shorter than lemma of lower floret and second glume   16. *D. depauperatum*

Spikelets 2.5-3.2 mm long, typically rounded at apex and with lemma of upper floret nearly as long as lemma of lower floret and second glume   17. *D. linearifolium*

Broadest culm blades usually more than 5 mm broad when as much as 10 cm long; plants with basal rosette of broad, short blades

Ligular hairs 1.5-6 mm long

Spikelets 2.5-2.7 mm long

5. *D. lanuginosum* var. *villosissimum*

Spikelets more than 2.7 mm long   10. *D. oligosanthes*

Ligular hairs absent or less than 1.5 mm long

Culms pubescent with long, spreading hairs, the nodes usually densely bearded with spreading hairs; hairs of sheath retrorse or spreading at right angles in age   9. *D. malacophyllum*

Culms glabrous or variously pubescent, the nodes not densely bearded with spreading hairs; hairs of sheath (when present) antrorse

Spikelets 2.8-3.7 (2.5-4) mm long, broadly elliptic to obovate; second glume and lower lemma 5-nerved

10. *D. oligosanthes*

Spikelets 2.5-2.8 mm long, usually elliptic or obovate but not broadly so; second glume and lower lemma 7-nerved

2. *D. angustifolium*

Blades of vernal leaves, at least some, 13-35 mm broad

Blades velvety-tomentose or puberulent on abaxial surface, glabrous or puberulent on adaxial surface

Spikelets 2.5-2.8 mm long; blades not striated   7. *D. scoparium*

Spikelets 3.5-4.2 mm long; blades often striated   13. *D. ravenelii*

Blades not velvety-tomentose or puberulent on abaxial surface, usually glabrous on both surfaces

Spikelets broadly elliptic to obovate, turgid, with heavy, broad nerves
                                        10. *D. oligosanthes*

Spikelets narrowly elliptic to obovate, not turgid or strongly-nerved

Spikelets 3.5-4.2 mm long; culm nodes, at least some, densely bearded
                                        13. *D. ravenelii*

Spikelets 2.6-3.3 mm long; culm nodes glabrous or slightly pubescent

Blades mostly less than 10 cm long; sheaths glabrous or pubescent on the margins   14. *D. commutatum*

Blades mostly 10-20 cm long; sheaths, at least the lower ones, papillose-hispid with spreading hairs   15. *D. clandestinum*

1. **Dichanthelium dichotomum** (L.) Gould, Brittonia 26:59. 1974. *Panicum dichotomum* L. Fig. 255. Culms slender, 20-80 (-100) cm tall, usually tufted from a compact, often knotty crown, glabrous or the nodes bearded with spreading hairs, becoming much-branched and "bushy" with short, reduced and fascicled leafy branches in age (autumnal phase). *Leaves* of basal rosette and lower cauline leaves broad and short, usually broader than those above. *Sheaths* glabrous, rarely sparsely pilose, the hairs usually confined to margins. *Ligule* a glabrous rim or a fringe of hairs 0.2-1 mm long. *Blades* of main culms 4-12 (-15) cm long and 3-10 (-13) mm broad, thin, glabrous on both surfaces or less frequently thinly pilose, often sparsely ciliate on the margins near base, tapering gradually to an attenuate tip. *Leaves* of fascicled "autumnal" branches with narrow, flat or involute blades commonly 3-7 cm long. *Panicles* 3-8 (-10) cm long, well exserted, open, with branches, branchlets and pedicels tending to be spreading, the spikelets not appearing secund on the branchlets. Late-formed panicles greatly reduced on short, fascicled branches. *Spikelets* oblong or obovate, usually narrowly so, 1.5-2.4 mm long, glabrous or less frequently puberulent. *Second glume* and *lemma of lower floret* strongly 7-9-nerved. *Chromosome number*, 2n=18.

Distribution. Texas: Regions 1, 2, 3, 4 and 5 in moist, sandy soils, usually in or along woodlands. General: Maine and Michigan to Florida and Texas; also in the West Indies.

Flowering period: April to June and again in late summer and autumn.

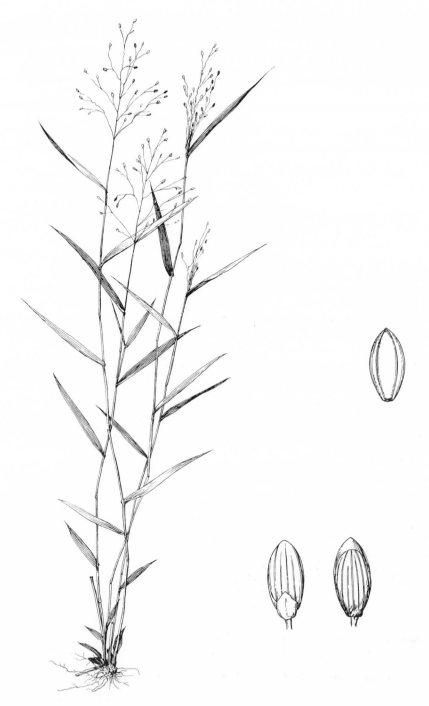

Fig. 255. *Dichanthelium dichotomum*. Plant, two views of spikelet and a floret. From Hitch-cock, 1935, as *Panicum dichotomum*.

482   THE GRASSES OF TEXAS

In its typical form *Dichanthelium dichotomum* has glabrous, wiry culms from a compact, often knotty crown, glabrous, short, stiffly-spreading blades and small (1.5-2 mm long), glabrous spikelets. Other names which have been applied to Texas plants of *D. dichotomum* are *Panicum nitidum* Lam., *P. barbulatum* Michx., *P. microcarpon* Muhl., *P. yadkinense* Nash, *P. lucidum* Ashe, *P. roanokense* Ashe, *P. trifolium* Nash, *P. tenue* Muhl. and *P. albomarginatum* Nash.

2. **Dichanthelium angustifolium** (Ell.) Gould, Brittonia 26:59. 1974. *Panicum angustifolium* Ell. Fig. 256. Plants with basal rosette of short, broad blades. *Culms* densely tufted, mostly 30-75 cm tall, glabrous or variously hairy, occasionally villous; secondary (autumnal) branches with reduced, fascicled narrow leaves developed at the upper nodes in age. *Sheaths* glabrous or variously hairy, sometimes villous, often with long papilla-based cilia on the upper margins and tufts of long hairs at apex. *Ligule* absent or a fringe of short hairs, 1 mm or less long; blades of some plants densely long-hairy in ligular area but the short ligule then usually well-defined. *Blades* of culm leaves variable but typically firm, narrowly lanceolate-attenuate, glabrous to variously hairy, mostly 6-15 (-20) cm long and 2-6 (-8) mm broad. *Panicles* small, few-flowered, with spikelets more or less appressed along short, erect or spreading branches; secondary inflorescences contracted, greatly reduced, often with only 5-10 racemose spikelets. *Spikelets* 2-2.8 mm long, narrowly elliptic or obovate, usually pubescent or puberulent but sometimes glabrous. *Chromosome number*, $2n=18$.

Distribution. Texas: Regions 1, 2, 3 and 4 in and along woodlands and in prairie sites, especially along fence rows and in brushy sites. General: Southeastern United States, from Virginia, Tennessee and Missouri, south to Florida and Texas, southward through eastern Mexico and Central America to northern South America.

Flowering period: April to June and again with late summer and fall precipitation.

As presently interpreted, a highly variable species, adapted to open as well as woodland habitats. Relatively glabrous plants of eastern Texas often are very similar to *Dichanthelium dichotomum* of the same region. For the most part *D. angustifolium* has smaller panicles, larger spikelets and more pubescent herbage than *D. dichotomum*. Included in *D. angustifolium* in the present interpretation are plants referred by previous authors to *Panicum chrysopsidifolium* Nash, *P. arenicoloides* Ashe, *P. consanguineum* Kunth, *P. ovinum* Scribn. & Smith, *P. aciculare* Poir., *P. portoricense* Hamilt., *P. lancearium* Trin. and *P. neuranthum* Griseb.

3. **Dichanthelium ensifolium** (Ell.) Gould, Brittonia 26:59. 1974. *Panicum ensifolium* Ell. Fig. 257. Culms slender, tufted, 20-45 cm tall, glabrous. *Autumnal culms* sparingly branched above base. *Sheaths* essentially glabrous, occasionally with a few hairs on sides of collar. *Ligule* a minute fringe, usually 0.1-0.5 mm long. *Blades* thin, short, spreading and often

Fig. 256. *Dichanthelium angustifolium*. Plant and spikelet. From Gould and Box, 1965, as *Panicum ovinum*.

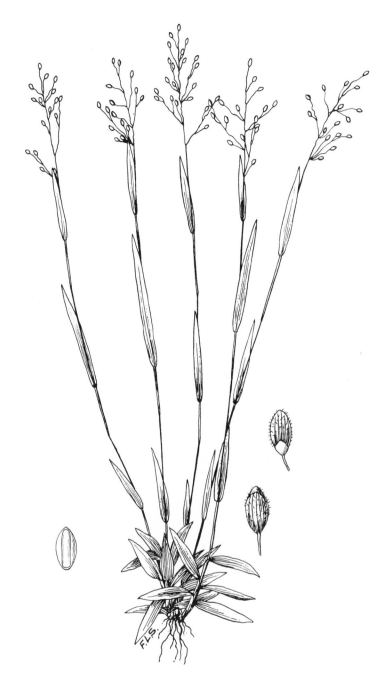

Fig. 257. *Dichanthelium ensifolium*. Plant, two views of spikelet and a floret. From F. Lamson-Scribner, American Grasses-II, 1899.

SUBFAMILY VI. PANICOIDEAE   485

reflexed, usually 1.5-4.5 cm long and 1.5-4.5 mm broad, glabrous or puberulent towards tip on abaxial surface, with a slight constriction at base. *Panicles* 2-6 cm long, the short, spreading branches with few spikelets. *Spikelets* broadly oblong or obovate, turgid, puberulent to glabrous, 1.5-2 mm long. *Chromosome number* not reported.

Distribution. Texas: Regions 1 and 3 in moist, sandy, often boggy areas. General: On the Coastal Plain from New Jersey to Florida and Texas.

Flowering period: April to June and again in late autumn.

The name *Panicum curtifolium* Nash has been applied to Texas plants of this species by most authors. *Dichanthelium ensifolium* frequently grows in association with sphagnum moss, *Drosera, Xyris* and other plants typical of the acid, boggy areas of eastern Texas.

4. **Dichanthelium lindheimeri** (Nash) Gould, Brittonia 26:60. 1974. *Panicum lindheimeri* Nash; *P. lanuginosum* var. *lindheimeri* (Nash) Fern. LINDHEIMER DICHANTHELIUM. Culms slender, 30-70 (-90) cm tall, glabrous or the internodes sparsely pilose. *Culms* soon branching to produce dense fascicles of reduced, leafy branchlets, these bearing few-flowered, non-exserted inflorescences. *Sheaths* glabrous, pubescent or ciliate on margins above. *Ligular hairs* usually dense, 2-6 mm long. *Blades* bright green, glabrous or essentially so on surfaces, occasionally ciliate on margins near base, 3-9 (-15) cm long and 3-11 mm broad. *Primary panicles* open, typically small, 4-7 (-10) cm long and slightly narrower than long. *Spikelets* elliptic or somewhat obovate, 1-2 mm long, puberulent. *Chromosome number*, $2n = 18$.

Distribution. Texas: Frequent in woodlands and along woods borders in regions 1, 2, 3 and 4, occasional in region 7, and westward to region 10 (Trans-Pecos). General: Southeastern Canada, the eastern half of the United States, Arizona, New Mexico, California and northern Coahuila, Mexico.

Flowering period: April to June and again in late summer and fall.

Dichanthelium lindheimeri frequently has been treated as a variety of *D. lanuginosum,* and the two differ basically only in herbage indument. It is probable that average spikelet size in *D. lanuginosum* is greater than in *D. lindheimeri,* but in both species there are forms with very small spikelets. Close relationships also are apparent between Texas plants of *D. lindheimeri* and *D. dichotomum,* both of which have essentially glabrous herbage, thin blades and open panicles of small spikelets. The two differ in the long ligule (ring of ligular hairs) of *D. lindheimeri.*

5. **Dichanthelium lanuginosum** (Ell.) Gould, Brittonia 26:60. 1974. *Panicum lanuginosum* Ell. Culms 20-60 (-90) cm tall, slender or rather stout, the nodes bearded with erect or spreading hairs, with or without

a glabrous ring below, the internodes pilose, strigose-pubescent or villous. In age, culms often branching to produce clusters or fascicles of greatly-reduced leafy branchlets with few-flowered inflorescences. *Leaves* pilose, hispid or villous, the blades occasionally nearly glabrous. *Sheaths* with appressed or spreading hairs on back as well as on margins. *Ligules* usually with a band of short hairs below a ring of long hairs (2-6 mm long), the long hairs occasionally present only on sides of ligule. *Vernal blades* lanceolate, mostly 5-12 cm long and 5-12 mm broad. *Panicles* 4-10 cm long, slightly longer than broad, the late-formed inflorescences of the fascicled branches very few-flowered. *Spikelets* pubescent, narrowly to broadly elliptic, mostly on pedicels as long as to considerably longer than spikelet. *Chromosome number,* $2n = 18$.

Spikelets 1.4-2.1 mm long	5A.	*D. lanuginosum* var. *lanuginosum*
Spikelets 2.2-2.8 mm long	5B.	*D. lanuginosum* var. *villosissimum*

5A. **Dichanthelium lanuginosum** (Ell.) Gould var. **lanuginosum.** *Panicum huachucae* Ashe, *P. tennesseense* Ashe. WOOLLY DICHANTHELIUM.

Distribution: Most frequent in regions 1, 2 and 3 but occasional throughout the State except in region 9 (High Plains).

Flowering period: Mostly April to June and then again in late summer and autumn. In the spring, this taxon often tends to flower slightly later than associated species of *Dichanthelium.*

Plants in the western portion of the range often have less hairy herbage and thus approach *Dichanthelium lindheimeri.* The name *Panicum huachucae* was proposed for thinly pubescent plants that tend to branch early and profusely. Texas plants of *D. lanuginosum* var. *lanuginosum* also have been variously referred to *Panicum auburne* Ashe, *P. thurowii* Scribn. & Merr., *P. praecocius* Hitchc. & Chase, *P. leucothrix* Nash, *P. longiligulatum* Nash and *P. ovale* Ell.

5B. **Dichanthelium lanuginosum** (Ell.) Gould var. **villosissimum** (Nash) Gould, Brittonia 26:60. 1974. *Panicum villosissimum* Nash. WHITEHAIRED DICHANTHELIUM. Plants referable to this taxon have spikelets 2.2-2.8 mm long and pilose culms and leaves, the sheaths with erect-spreading hairs to 3 mm long.

Distribution. Texas: Regions 1 and 3 and also in Parker County of region 5, in sandy woodlands. General: Eastern United States from Massachusetts and Florida to Kansas and Texas and south through western Mexico to Guatemala.

Flowering period: April to June and again in late summer and fall.

6. **Dichanthelium laxiflorum** (Lam.) Gould, Brittonia 26:60. 1974. *Panicum laxiflorum* Lam., *P. xalapense* H.B.K. OPENFLOWER DICHANTHELIUM. Plants with a basal tuft of numerous soft, light green blades, these similar to the culm blades and mostly 7-15 cm long. *Culms* slender, glabrous or internodes below panicle, 15-40 (-50) cm tall, not branching above base. *Nodes* bearded with soft, spreading hairs. *Sheaths* rather uniformly pilose with spreading, often reflexed hairs 2-3 mm long. *Ligule* a minutely fringed or glabrous rim. *Blades* 3-10 mm broad, mostly 7-16 (-20) cm long, glabrous or more or less inconspicuously pilose on the surfaces, usually ciliate on the margins to well above middle. *Panicles of vernal culms* well exserted, mostly 7-12 cm long, typically lax and few-flowered; panicle branches usually hirsute with long, soft hairs. *Inflorescences* developed in late summer and fall compact, more closely-flowered, usually not exserted above the basal clump of leaves. *Spikelets* broadly ovate or oblong, slightly pointed, 1.7-2.3 mm long. *First glume* thin, 0.5 mm or less long. *Second glume* and *lemma of lower floret* pubescent, strongly-nerved. *Chromosome number*, $2n = 18$.

Distribution. Texas: Regions 1 and 3, mostly in sandy soils of woodland sites. General: Southeastern United States, from Maryland and Florida to Missouri, Arkansas and Texas; also Mexico, Guatemala and the Dominican Republic.

Flowering period: April to June and again in late summer and autumn.

A distinctive character of *D. laxiflorum* is the early-formed basal rosette or tuft of numerous, rather long, yellowish-green leaves. This species is one of the first dichantheliums to flower in the spring. Texas plants referred to *Panicum strigosum* Muhl. by Chase (1951) are probably of this species, but no Texas specimens of this type have been examined in the present study.

7. **Dichanthelium scoparium** (Lam.) Gould, Brittonia 26:60. 1974. *Panicum scoparium* Lam. VELVET DICHANTHELIUM. Culms tall, coarse and thick, to 150 cm in height, usually becoming much-branched at the upper nodes in age. *Internodes, sheaths, ligules* and *upper portion of nodes* typically but not always velvety-pubescent; lower portion of node usually with a broad, glabrous, glandular-blotched band or zone. *Ligule* a dense tuft of hairs 1-1.3 mm long. *Basal blades* short but mostly 13-30 mm broad. *Vernal blades* firm, velvety-pubescent to nearly glabrous, 10-25 cm long and 8-18 mm broad. *Blades* of bushy-branched autumnal culms mostly 2-5 cm long and 3-6 mm broad. *Panicles* 8-20 cm long, longer than broad, the spikelets mostly on short pedicels or nearly sessile. *Spikelets* 2.2-2.8 mm long, ovate or oblong, strongly nerved, typically puberulent but occasionally glabrous, broadly pointed. *Chromosome number*, $2n = 18$.

Distribution. Texas: Regions 1 and 3 in sandy soils of woodlands and low, moist areas, apparently infrequent in Texas. General: Massachusetts to Florida, westward to Missouri, Oklahoma and Texas; also in Cuba.

Flowering period: Flowering on vernal culms, May to June, autumnal phase flowering till November.

Texas plants with glabrous or nearly glabrous sheaths have been referred to *Panicum scabriusculum* Ell. and *P. cryptanthum* Ashe.

8. **Dichanthelium sphaerocarpon** (Ell.) Gould, Brittonia 26:60. 1974. *Panicum sphaerocarpon* Ell. Culm 20-80 cm tall, glabrous or the nodes appressed-pubescent, sparingly branching in age (autumnal form) at upper nodes. *Leaves of basal rosette* broad and short, usually with crisped, white, cartilaginous margins. *Sheaths* usually pubescent with fine, soft hairs on one or both margins, otherwise glabrous. *Ligule* typically absent, occasionally present as a fringe of hairs to 1 mm long. *Blades* thick, glabrous on surfaces, ciliate with a few widely-spaced, stout, papilla-based hairs on lower margins, cordate-clasping at base. *Panicles* open, many-flowered, 6-15 (-20) cm long, slightly narrower than long, with glabrous main axis and branches. *Spikelets* puberulent to glabrous, 1.4-2 mm long, broadly oblong or obovoid to nearly spherical at maturity. *Chromosome number*, $2n = 18$.

Mid-culm blades 6-11 (-14) mm broad, the uppermost blade usually 3-9 cm long   8A. *D. sphaerocarpon* var. *sphaerocarpon*

Mid-culm blades, at least some, 15-30 mm broad, the uppermost blade usually 10-15 cm or more long
      8B. *D. sphaerocarpon* var. *polyanthes*

8A. **Dichanthelium sphaerocarpon** (Ell.) Gould var. **sphaerocarpon.** *Panicum sphaerocarpon* Ell. var. *inflatum* (Scribn. & Smith) Hitchc. & Chase. ROUNDSEED DICHANTHELIUM. Fig. 258.

Distribution. Texas: Throughout the State except in the High Plains and Rolling Plains (regions 8 and 9), most common in the eastern and southern portions, infrequent in the Trans-Pecos region, usually in sandy soil and shaded habitats. General: Throughout the eastern United States, west to Michigan, Missouri, Kansas, Oklahoma and Texas and south through Mexico to Venezuela.

Flowering period: Late March to June and again in late summer and autumn.

8B. **Dichanthelium sphaerocarpon** (Ell.) Gould var. **polyanthes** (Schult.) Gould, Brittonia 26:60. 1974. *Panicum polyanthes* Schult. LEAFY DICHANTHELIUM.

Distribution. Texas: Region 1 in woodlands, apparently infrequent. General: Throughout the eastern United States except in Florida, westward to Missouri, Oklahoma and Texas.

Fig. 258. *Dichanthelium sphaerocarpon* var. *sphaerocarpon*. Plant and spikelet. From Gould and Box, 1965, as *Panicum sphaerocarpon*.

490   THE GRASSES OF TEXAS

Flowering period: April to June and again in late summer and autumn.

Dichanthelium sphaerocarpon var. *polyanthes* in its typical form has long, broad culm leaves, a long, broad leaf at the upper culm node and a relatively long, narrow panicle. Plants of var. *polyanthes*, however, seem to intergrade completely with plants of the typical variety of *D. sphaerocarpon*, and there is no clear basis for the separation of the two taxa in some cases.

9. **Dichanthelium malacophyllum** (Nash) Gould, Brittonia 26:60. 1974. *Panicum malacophyllum* Nash. SOFTLEAF DICHANTHELIUM. Culms 30-70 cm tall, in age branching at the upper nodes to produce dense fascicles of short branches and reduced leaves. *Herbage* pubescent throughout, the leaf sheaths and culm nodes and internodes with long, soft spreading hairs, the blades velvety pilose on both surfaces, ciliate on margins. *Ligule* a fringe of hairs 1-1.5 mm long. *Blades* 6-10 cm long, 5-12 mm broad. *Panicles* of vernal culms well exserted, 3-7 cm long. *Panicles* of autumnal branches much reduced and partially hidden in the leaf fascicles. *Spikelets* oblong or obovate, papillose-pilose, 2.6- (2.5-) 3.2 mm long, the upper glume and lower lemma with 7-9 strong nerves. *Chromosome number* not reported.

Distribution. Texas: Reported by Correll & Johnston (1970) to occur in north-central Texas but no Texas specimens have been examined in the present study. General: Tennessee, Missouri and Kansas to Arkansas, Oklahoma and Texas.

Flowering period: April to June and again in late summer and autumn.

10. **Dichanthelium oligosanthes** (Schult.) Gould, Brittonia 26:60. 1974. *Panicum oligosanthes* Schult. Culms in loose to dense clumps, 15-85 cm tall, glabrous to densely puberulous. *Autumnal culms* much-branched above base. *Sheaths* glabrous to densely papillate-hispid, the margins finely to densely ciliate. *Ligule* a dense fringe of hairs 0.1-4.2 mm long. *Vernal blades* 3-14 cm long, 3-12 (-15) mm broad. *Vernal inflorescences* well exserted, 4-13 cm long, about half as wide as long. *Autumnal inflorescences* 2-5 cm long, little if at all exserted, with 1-9 spikelets. *Spikelets* broadly elliptic to obovate, blunt or subacute, 2.9-(2.5-) 4 mm long, 1.2-2.2 mm broad. *Glumes* and *lower lemma* glabrous to papillate-pilose, the first glume 0.8-2.2 mm long, narrowly acute to obtuse. *Chromosome number*, $2n=18$.

Ligule usually 1.6 mm or more long; abaxial leaf surface usually uniformly tomentose, occasionally puberulous

10A.   *D. oligosanthes* var. *oligosanthes*

Ligule usually less than 1.6 mm long; abaxial leaf surface puberulous to glabrous, never tomentose   10B.   *D. oligosanthes* var. *scribnerianum*

10A. **Dichanthelium oligosanthes** (Schult.) Gould var. **oligosanthes.** Culms usually puberulous to villous. *Blades* narrowly acuminate, mostly 5-8 mm broad. *Lowermost internode of panicle axis* usually villous or tomentose.

Distribution. Texas: Regions 1, 2, 3, 4, 5, 6 and 7 in sandy, well-drained but moist sites of woodlands and brushy areas. General: Massachusetts and Michigan, south to Iowa, Texas and Florida.

Flowering period: April to June and again in late summer and fall.

Dichanthelium oligosanthes var. *oligosanthes* is morphologically similar to *D. ravenelii* but has smaller leaves and spikelets and a more slender, less robust growth habit.

10B. **Dichanthelium oligosanthes** (Schult.) Gould var. **scribnerianum** (Nash) Gould. Brittonia 26:60. 1974. *Panicum scribnerianum* Nash, *P. helleri* Nash. SCRIBNERS DICHANTHELIUM. Fig. 259. Culms glabrous to slightly puberulous. *Blades* glabrous to puberulous. *Spikelets* 2.7- (2.5-) 3.3 (-3.8) mm long, mostly 1.4-1.8 mm broad, glabrous to papillate-pilose. *Lowermost internode of panicle axis* glabrous, scabrous or puberulous.

Distribution. Texas: Reported from all regions of the State, usually present in loamy to loamy-clay sites in open or brushy areas. General: Throughout the United States, except in Alabama, Georgia and Florida, and also in Mexico.

Flowering period: Mostly April to June and again in late summer and fall.

Texas plants referred to *Panicum malacon* Nash by some authors belong to this species.

11. **Dichanthelium nodatum** (Hitchc. & Chase) Gould, Brittonia 26:60. 1974. *Panicum nodatum* Hitchc. & Chase. SARITA DICHANTHELIUM. Fig. 260. Culms firm, 20-50 (-65) cm tall, curving-erect from a subrhizomatous base, scabrous or puberulent to short-hispid. *Sheaths,* at least the lower ones, puberulent or short-pilose on back, often with longer hairs on margin. *Ligule* a dense tuft of hairs 1-2 mm long. *Blades* thick and firm, minutely puberulent on both surfaces, mostly 3-9 cm long and 4-9 mm broad, ciliate with papilla-based hairs to well above middle, rather abruptly acute at apex. *Vernal panicles* 4-13 cm long, the branches usually not widely spreading, the slender spikelets appressed along the branches and branchlets. *Spikelets* puberulent, narrowly obpyriform, tapering from above middle to base 3.5-4.3 mm long. *First glume* thin, 1.5-2 mm long. *Chromosome number* not reported.

Distribution. Texas: Sandy grasslands of the South Texas coast and plains (regions 2 and 6). General: Endemic to southern Texas.

Flowering period: April to June and again in late summer and fall under favorable conditions.

Fig. 259. *Dichanthelium oligosanthes* var. *scribnerianum*. Plant (autumnal phase), inflorescence (vernal phase) and spikelet. From Gould and Box, 1965, as *Panicum oligosanthes*.

SUBFAMILY VI. PANICOIDEAE   493

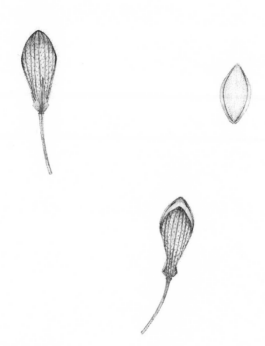

Fig. 260. *Dichanthelium nodatum.* Two views of spikelet and floret. From Gould and Box, 1965, as *Panicum nodatum.*

12. **Dichanthelium pedicellatum** (Vasey) Gould, Brittonia 26:60. 1974. *Panicum pedicellatum* Vasey. CEDAR DICHANTHELIUM. Fig. 261. Culms 20-70 cm tall from a firm, knotty base, puberulent or hirsute, at least below. *Culms* freely branching in age but the secondary branches usually not appearing fascicled. *Sheaths* puberulent, appressed-pilose, scabrous or glabrous. *Ligule* a ring of hairs mostly 0.3-1 mm long, occasionally with a few longer hairs. *Blades* glabrous to sparsely appressed-pilose or puberulent, usually ciliate with a few long papilla-based hairs near base, 4-12 mm long and 3-8 mm broad, narrow at base and gradually tapering above to an acuminate apex. *Panicles* 4-7 (-11) cm long, slightly longer than broad, with the large, slender spikelets short-pediceled and appressed along branches and branchlets. *Spikelets* 3.5-3.9 mm long, narrowly obovate, tapering from above middle to base. *Glumes* and *lemmas* usually minutely puberulent. *First glume* about 2 mm long, thin, acute, often involute at the tip on drying. *Chromosome number,* $2n = 18$.

Distribution. Texas: Edwards Plateau (region 7) and limestone outcrops in regions 4 and 5, in limey soils, usually on well-drained, rocky sites. General: Endemic to Texas and northern Coahuila, Mexico.

Flowering period: Mostly March to June, occasionally late summer and autumn.

Fig. 261. *Dichanthelium pedicellatum*. Spikelet.

13. **Dichanthelium ravenelii** (Scribn.) Gould, Brittonia 26:60. 1974. *Panicum ravenelii* Scribn. Culms stout, mostly 40-75 cm tall, pubescent with erect or spreading hairs, the nodes bearded with spreading hairs, usually with a broad glabrous band below the bearded portion. *Culms* branching in age at the upper nodes to produce clusters of short leafy lateral branches with reduced blades. *Sheaths*, at least of the lower leaves, pubescent with coarse, erect or spreading, often papilla-based hairs. *Ligule* a fringe of hairs, usually 2-4 mm long but occasionally not more than 1 mm long. *Blades* mostly 8-15 cm long and 10-25 mm broad, abruptly narrowing at the base, typically glabrous on adaxial surface and tomentose or puberulent on abaxial surface but occasionally glabrous or puberulent-tomentose on both surfaces. *Panicles* mostly 7-13 cm long, open and usually few-flowered, the axis puberulent at least below. *Spikelets* broadly oblong to obovate, pubescent, 3.7-5 mm long. *Lower glume* mostly 1.8-2.2 mm long. *Chromosome number*, $2n = 18$.

Distribution. Texas: Regions 1, 2 and 3, in sandy woodlands. General: Delaware, Kentucky and Missouri, south to Florida and Texas.

Flowering period: April to June and again in late summer and fall.

Dichanthelium ravenelii appears closely related to *D. oligosanthes* but typically has broader blades, larger spikelets and more conspicuously bearded culm nodes. Texas plants referred by some authors to *Panicum leibergii* (Vasey) Scribn. and *P. boscii* Poir, including the variety *molle* (Vasey) Hitchc. & Chase, are variants of this species.

SUBFAMILY VI. PANICOIDEAE   495

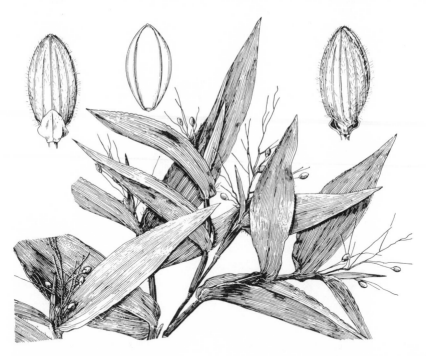

Fig. 262. *Dichanthelium commutatum.* Plant, two views of spikelet and a floret. From Hitchcock, 1935, as *Panicum commutatum.*

14. **Dichanthelium commutatum** (Schult.) Gould, Brittonia 26:59. 1974. *Panicum commutatum* Schult. VARIABLE DICHANTHELIUM. Fig. 262. Culms tufted from a knotty base, 40-75 cm tall, branching in age at upper nodes to produce branchlets with moderately reduced, fascicled leaves; *nodes* and *internodes* typically glabrous, occasionally sparsely hairy. *Sheaths* pubescent-ciliate on margins at least above, occasionally pubescent on collar, otherwise glabrous. *Ligule* absent or a fringe of hairs not over 1 mm long. *Blades* thin, broad, typically glabrous except for a few cilia on the lower margins, mostly 6-9 mm long and 9-25 mm broad but occasionally to 15 cm long and 35 mm broad, the broader blades cordate at base. *Panicles* mostly 6-12 cm long, slightly longer than broad, with spikelets rather distantly spaced on slender pedicels. *Spikelets* narrowly elliptic, slightly pointed, puberulent or glabrous, 2.4-3.3 mm long. *First glume* thin, obtuse or broadly acute, about 1 mm long. *Chromosome number*, $2n = 18$ and 36.

Distribution. Texas: Regions 1 and 2 in sandy woodland soils, often in the deep shade of dense forests. General: Throughout the eastern United States and westward to Michigan, Missouri, Oklahoma and Texas.

Flowering period: April to June and again in late summer and fall.

Included in *D. commutatum* in the present interpretation are Texas plants referred by Chase (1951) and other authors to *Panicum joorii* Vasey.

15. **Dichanthelium clandestinum** (L.) Gould, Brittonia 26:59. 1974. *Panicum clandestinum* L. DEERTONGUE DICHANTHELIUM. Culms rather stout, 40-100 (-125) cm tall, often from a stout rhizome 5-10 cm long, usually forming large clumps; *culm nodes* glabrous or slightly hairy, the *internodes* scabrous to papillose-hispid at least below nodes. *Sheaths*, at least the lower ones, typically papillose-hispid; *collar* pubescent on sides and sometimes across back. *Ligule* a fringed scale 1 mm or less long or absent. *Blades* thin, elongate, glabrous or scabrous, 10-28 cm long and 1-3 cm broad. *Panicles* 8-16 cm long, considerably longer than broad, with slender erect-spreading branches bearing rather widely-spaced spikelets on long or short pedicels. *Spikelets* glabrous or puberulent, narrowly elliptic, slightly pointed, 2.7-3.1 mm long. *Chromosome number*, $2n = 36$.

Distribution. Texas: Northern portions of regions 1 and 3, infrequent, in sandy woodlands. General: Eastern half of the United States from Maine to Florida and westward to Iowa, Kansas and Texas.

Flowering period: April to June and again in late summer and fall.

16. **Dichanthelium depauperatum** (Muhl.) Gould, Brittonia 26:59. 1974. *Panicum depauperatum* Muhl. STARVED DICHANTHELIUM. Basal rosette of broad, short leaves not developed. *Culms* mostly 25-50 cm tall, glabrous or the lowermost nodes and internodes hispid or puberulent; in age the culms not becoming bushy-branched but developing small, reduced panicles in leafy portion of plant. *Leaves* variously pilose or hispid to nearly glabrous, the sheaths commonly thinly pilose, the blades commonly glabrous or nearly so on upper surface. *Ligule* a fringe of hairs 0.3-1 mm long. *Blades* linear or the lower ones lanceolate, mostly 1-5 mm broad and 8-20 cm or more long, gradually tapering to a long, slender tip, often involute on drying. *Panicles* narrow, 4-8 (-10) cm long, with rather widely-spaced spikelets on short, usually erect-spreading, little-rebranched primary branches. *Spikelets* narrowly ovate, pointed, glabrous or sparsely pilose, mostly 3.2-4.8 mm long, with upper glume and lemma of lower floret typically somewhat beaked and noticeably longer than lemma of upper floret. *First glume* about 1 mm long, broadly obtuse or rounded at apex. *Second glume* strongly 9-nerved. *Chromosome number*, $2n = 18$.

Distribution. Texas: Occasional in and along forested areas of region 1; one typical collection from near Giddings (*Silveus 7028*) and records from "north central Texas" indicated by Correll and Johnston (1970). Throughout the eastern United States and westward to Minnesota, eastern Kansas, Oklahoma and Texas.

Flowering period: Tracy Herbarium records April-May but this species probably flowering again in the fall.

17. **Dichanthelium linearifolium** (Scribn.) Gould, Brittonia 26:60. 1974. *Panicum linearifolium* Scribn., *P. perlongum* Nash, *P. werneri* Scribn. SLIMLEAF DICHANTHELIUM. Similar to and probably intergrading

with *D. depauperatum* but sheaths often more densely pilose, spikelets 2.2-3.2 mm long, elliptical, with a rounded apex, the upper glume and lemma of lower floret not beaked and only slightly if at all longer than lemma of upper floret. *Chromosome number* not reported.

Distribution. Texas: Regions 1, 2, 3, 4, 5 and 7, locally frequent on sandy or gravelly soil in woods openings and in open grasslands. General: Widely distributed in the eastern half of the United States and occurring on prairie sites westward to North Dakota, eastern Colorado and central Texas.

Flowering period: Mostly March to June and late August to October.

98. PASPALIDIUM Stapf.

About 20 species, in the warmer parts of the world.

1. **Paspalidium geminatum** (Forsk.) Stapf, in Prain, Fl. Trop. Afr. 9:583. 1920. *Panicum geminatum* Forsk. Perennial with culms in clumps from a firm, often somewhat rhizomatous base. *Culms* and leaves glabrous. *Ligule* a short, ciliate membrane. *Blades* linear, 3-6 mm broad, flat or folded. *Inflorescence* a narrow elongate panicle with spikelets subsessile on 7-17 short, spicate branches. *Inflorescence branches* single at the nodes, widely-spaced below and progressively closer together above. *Spikelets* borne singly in two rows on the flattened branch rachis, oriented with the rounded back of lemma of upper floret turned towards rachis as in *Paspalum*, disarticulating below glumes. *Spikelets* 2.2-3 mm long, ovate or elliptic, glabrous, 2-flowered, the lower floret sterile or staminate, the upper perfect. *First glume* broad, rounded or truncate, one-fourth to one-third as long as spikelet. *Palea of lower floret* well-developed, about as long as lemma. *Lemma of upper floret* finely rugose, acute at apex. *Chromosome number, 2n = 36.*

Spikelets 2.2-2.7 mm long; glumes and lemma of lower floret thin but not papery, the nerves usually conspicuous
1A. *P. geminatum* var. *geminatum*

Spikelets 2.8-3 mm long; glumes and lemma of lower floret pale, thin and papery, the nerves inconspicuous
1B. *P. geminatum* var. *paludivagum*

1A. Paspalidium geminatum var. **geminatum.** EGYPTIAN PASPALIDIUM. Fig. 263.

Distribution. Texas: Regions 1, 2, 3 and 6, mostly along ditches, streams and lakes, often in shallow water. General: Southern Oklahoma to Florida and Texas, south through Mexico to Central and tropical South America and also in the Old World tropics.

Flowering period: April to September, occasionally later in the fall.

498   THE GRASSES OF TEXAS

Fig. 263. *Paspalidium geminatum* var. *geminatum*. Inflorescence and spikelet. From Gould and Box, 1965, as *Panicum geminatum*.

SUBFAMILY VI. PANICOIDEAE   499

1B. **Paspalidium geminatum** var. **paludivagum** (Hitchc. & Chase) Gould, Southw. Naturalist 15:391. 1971. *Panicum paludivagum* Hitchc. & Chase. WATER PASPALIDIUM. Similar to *P. geminatum* var. *geminatum* but the spikelets slightly larger, the glumes and lemma of the sterile floret more papery and with inconspicuous nerves and the plant frequently developing long stolons.

Distribution. Texas: Regions 2 (Galveston County) and 6 (Uvalde County). The Texas specimens examined may not be sufficiently different from the typical variety to warrant segregation into a separate taxon. General: Chase in Hitchcock's Manual (1951) lists the range of this taxon as Florida, Texas, Mexico and Guatemala.

Flowering period: The two Texas specimens examined were collected in August and October.

99. PASPALUM L.

Annuals and perennials, many with rhizomes or stolons. *Ligule* a membrane or ring of hairs. *Blades* usually flat, often thin and broad. Inflorescence with 1 to many unilateral spicate branches, these scattered or, in a few species, paired at culm apex. *Spikelets* 2-flowered, the lower floret staminate or neuter, the upper perfect; spikelets subsessile or short-pediceled, solitary or in pairs on a flattened, occasionally broadly winged rachis, the spikelets with the rounded back of lemma of upper floret turned towards the rachis. Disarticulation at base of spikelet or, in a few species, at the base of inflorescence branch. *First glume* typically absent but irregularly present in a few species. *Second glume and lemma of lower floret* usually about equal, broad and rounded at apex or less frequently acute. *Lemma of upper floret* firm or indurate, usually smooth and shiny, with firm, inrolled margins. *Palea* broad, flat or slightly convex, the margins entirely enfolded by lemma.

A genus of about 400 species distributed throughout the warmer regions of the world.

Rachis broad and winged, usually as wide as the two rows of spikelets; plants of moist or wet habitats

Rachis extending beyond uppermost spikelet; inflorescence branches falling from main axis   1. *P. fluitans*

Rachis not extending beyond uppermost spikelet; inflorescence branches not falling from main axis

Spikelets about 2 mm long   2. *P. dissectum*

Spikelets more than 3 mm long   3. *P. acuminatum*

Rachis not winged, broad or narrow but not as broad as the 2 or 4 rows of spikelets

Inflorescence branches 2, paired or less than 1 cm apart (1-2 additional branches occasionally present below)

Spikelets broadly ovate, elliptic or obovate, obtuse or broadly acute at apex

Spikelets 1.4-1.8 mm long, ciliate on margins; plants with long stolons
4. *P. conjugatum*

Spikelets 2 mm or more long, glabrous or puberulous but not ciliate, rhizomatous or subrhizomatous, without long stolons

Rachis internodes 2.5-7 mm long, the spikelets widely separated, not overlapping
10. *P. separatum*

Rachis internodes less than 2.5 mm long, the spikelets overlapping

Spikelets 2.8-5 mm long
5. *P. notatum*

Spikelets 2-2.5 mm long
6. *P. minus*

Spikelets narrowly ovate or elliptic, tapering to an acute apex

Plants densely cespitose, without creeping rhizomes   7.   *P. almum*

Plants with creeping rhizomes or stolons

Second glume and lemma of lower floret glabrous, the lemma flat
8.   *P. vaginatum*

Second glume and lemma of lower floret pubescent, the lemma convex
9.   *P. distichum*

Inflorescence branches 1-numerous, when 2 then the branches 1-2 cm or more apart

First glume present on some or all spikelets

Plants without rhizomes; spikelets pubescent, less than 3 mm long
11.   *P. langei*

Plants with stout rhizomes; spikelets glabrous, 3 mm or more long

Blades involute, 2 mm or less wide (as folded)
12.   *P. monostachyum*

SUBFAMILY VI. PANICOIDEAE   501

Blades flat, 6-15 mm wide

Inflorescence a single spicate raceme or occasionally with 2 spicate branches   13. *P. unispicatum*

Inflorescence with usually 3-5 spicate branches
                                        14. *P. bifidum*

First glume absent on all spikelets

Margins of spikelets ciliate with long hairs

Inflorescence branches mostly 3-6   16. *P. dilatatum*

Inflorescence branches mostly 12-20   17. *P. urvillei*

Margins of spikelets not ciliate with long hairs

Second glume absent   18. *P. malacophyllum*

Second glume present

Lemma and palea of perfect floret dark brown and shiny at maturity   A

Lemma and palea of perfect floret green, light brown or straw-colored at maturity   AA

A

Plants annual

Spikelets 2-3 mm long

Spikelets glabrous 2-2.2 mm long   19. *P. boscianum*

Spikelets appressed-pubescent, 2.3-3 mm long   20. *P. convexum*

Spikelets more than 3 mm long, appressed-pubescent
                              21. *P. scrobiculatum*

Plants perennial

Culms 0.5-1 m tall; blades mostly 3-7 mm broad; lemma of lower floret usually with transverse wrinkles along margins 22. *P. plicatulum*

Culms 1-2.5 m tall; blades mostly 10-25 mm broad; lemma of lower floret without transverse wrinkles   23. *P. virgatum*

Spikelets elliptic or obovate

Blades involute or folded, 2 mm or less broad (as inrolled or folded); erect culms single or in small clusters from long, stout rhizomes
12.   *P. monostachyum*

Blades flat, at least some 3-15 mm or more broad

Spikelets widely spaced on the rachis, the pairs not or only slightly overlapping; plants with rhizomes   14.   *P. bifidum*

Spikelets closely imbricated on the rachis; plants with or without rhizomes

Spikelets glabrous, 2-2.5 (infrequently 2.7) mm long; inflorescence branches typically 1.5-4 cm long; rachis 1.5-2 mm broad; leaf blades 6 mm or less broad   24.   *P. lividum*

Spikelets glabrous or pubescent, when glabrous then 2.7-3.4 mm long and the inflorescence branches typically 4-10 cm long; rachis 1-1.5 mm broad; leaf blades 2-15 mm broad

Blades lanceolate, flat, mostly 6-15 mm broad
25.   *P. pubiflorum*

Blades linear, often folded or involute, mostly 2-5 mm broad

Spikelets glabrous, borne in 2 rows on rachis   7.   *P. almum*

Spikelets usually pubescent, borne in 4 rows on rachis
26.   *P. hartwegianum*

Spikelets suborbicular, broadly ovate or broadly obovate

Spikelets 3.6-4.8 mm long; plants with stout rhizomes
15.   *P. floridanum*

Spikelets 3.4 mm or less long; plants with or without rhizomes

Inflorescence branches 1-2, occasionally 3-4; spikelets 1.4-2.6 mm long, glabrous or pubescent; inflorescences commonly developed in the axils of upper leaves   27.   *P. setaceum*

Inflorescence branches mostly 3-several; spikelets 2.2-3.4 mm long, glabrous; inflorescences not developed in the axils of upper leaves

Spikelets solitary on either side of rachis   28.   *P. laeve*

SUBFAMILY VI. PANICOIDEAE   503

Spikelets paired or both solitary and paired on either side of rachis   29. *P. praecox*

1. **Paspalum fluitans** (Ell.) Kunth, Rev. Gram. 1:24. 1829. WATER PASPALUM. Fig. 264. Annual with thick, succulent culms, these usually decumbent or creeping below and rooting at the lower nodes. *Culm nodes* puberulent. *Leaves* glabrous or pubescent. *Ligules* 1.5-2 mm long, the margins a continuation of the sheath margins and often forming pointed sheath auricles. *Blades* thin, short, mostly 8-15 (-25) mm broad. *Inflorescence* usually 8-16 cm long, with numerous, scattered branches. *Inflorescence branches* mostly 3-7 cm long, with a thin, broad rachis equaling or exceeding in width the two rows of short-pediceled spikelets and projecting as a point beyond the uppermost spikelet, eventually disarticulating at base. *Spikelets* 1.2-1.7 mm long, oblong or ovate, puberulent, acute at apex. *Chromosome number* not reported.

Distribution. Texas: Regions 1, 2 and 3, infrequent, in moist or marshy soil of ditches, marshes, lakes and streambanks, often with the culms floating. General: Southeastern United States from Virginia and Illinois southward and in South America.

Flowering period: Mostly late summer and fall but one collection made in February (Angelina County, Diboll, *Parks* in 1947).

2. **Paspalum dissectum** (L.) L., Sp. Pl. ed. 2. 81. 1762. MUDBANK PASPALUM. Perennial with usually decumbent, creeping, mat-forming culms, the erect tips 5-50 cm tall. *Herbage* glabrous or sparsely hairy. *Blades* thin, mostly 3-6 cm long and 2-5 mm broad. *Inflorescences* small, numerous, usually of 2-4 branches bearing 2 rows of spikelets. *Inflorescence branches* 1-3 cm long, with a thin, flat rachis 2-3 mm broad, this not extended beyond the uppermost spikelet. *Spikelets* 1.8-2.2 mm long, glabrous, oblong, broadly acute or obtuse at apex. *Chromosome number*, $2n=40$.

Distribution. Texas: Regions 1, 2 and 3, occasional in moist or marshy soil, usually on streambanks and lake shores. General: New Jersey and Illinois, south to Florida, southeastern Texas and Cuba.

Flowering period: July to November.

3. **Paspalum acuminatum** Raddi, Agrost. Bras. 25. 1823. BROOK PASPALUM. Perennial with decumbent, creeping, much-branched culms 30-100 cm long. *Lower culm internodes* and *sheaths* laterally compressed. *Blades* mostly 4-12 cm broad. *Inflorescence branches* 2-5, persistent, 3-7 cm long, the rachis 2.5-4 mm broad, terminating in a spikelet. *Spikelets* in 2 rows, about 3.5 mm long, abruptly pointed. *Lemma of upper floret* 2.8-3 mm long. *Chromosome number* not reported.

504   THE GRASSES OF TEXAS

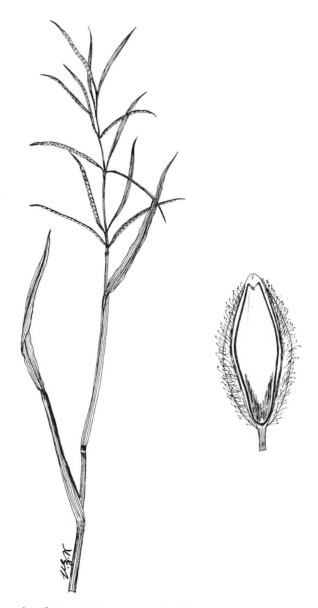

Fig. 264. *Paspalum fluitans.* Inflorescence and spikelet.

Distribution. Texas: Reported from region 6; no Texas collections examined by the author. General: Louisiana and Texas, south through Mexico to
Brazil and Argentina.

Flowering period: Late summer and fall.

SUBFAMILY VI. PANICOIDEAE   505

4. **Paspalum conjugatum** Bergius, Acta Helv. Phys. Math. 7:129. pl. 8. 1762. SOUR PASPALUM. Fig. 265. Perennial with erect culms 25-50 cm tall from long, leafy stolons. *Nodes* of the stolons usually pilose. *Blades* thin, flat, mostly 8-12 cm long and 5-15 mm broad, glabrous or less frequently pilose, with a ring of stiff hairs immediately above the membranous ligule. *Inflorescence branches* 2, paired at culm apex, mostly 5-15 cm long, widely spreading. *Spikelets* elliptic, broadly pointed, mostly 1.5-2 mm long, closely imbricated on rachis. *Glumes* sparsely long pilose on the margins. *Lemma of upper floret* straw-colored. *Chromosome number,* 2n=40.

Distribution. Texas: Southern portion of region 2, all specimens examined from Cameron County. General: Texas, south through Mexico, Central America and the Caribbean to Argentina and also present in the Old World tropics.

Flowering period: Texas collections of flowering specimens made from September to November.

5. **Paspalum notatum** Flugge, Monogr. Pasp. 106. 1810. BAHIAGRASS. Fig. 266. Perennial with erect culms mostly 20-75 cm tall from thick, scaly rhizomes. *Leaves* glabrous or essentially so. *Ligule* a dense ring of short hairs. *Blades* 2-6 mm broad, flat, folded or involute, usually firm and tough in texture. *Inflorescence* typically of 2 spicate branches 4-12 cm long, these paired at culm apex or one slightly below the other, a third branch infrequently present below the terminal ones. *Spikelets* closely imbricated in 2 rows, broadly ovate, elliptic or obovate, glabrous and shiny, 2.8-3.5 mm long. *Lemma of upper floret* straw-colored. *Chromosome numbers* reported, 2n=20, 30 and 40.

Distribution. Texas: Regions 1 and 2, introduced as a pasture grass but occasional on roadsides, along ditches and in other slightly disturbed sites with adequate moisture. General: Native to Mexico and Central and South America, introduced as a forage and erosion-control grass in the eastern and southeastern United States.

Flowering period: June to November.

One of the introduced strains or varieties that has been reported from Texas bears the name *P. notatum* var. *saurae* Parodi. This selection is a large, coarse plant with long blades and small spikelets (mostly 2.8-3 mm long). Not infrequently 1-3 additional branches are present below the terminal pair of inflorescence branches.

6. **Paspalum minus** Fourn., Mex. Pl. 2:6. 1886. MAT PASPALUM. Similar to *P. notatum* but culms infrequently over 30 cm tall, the rhizomatous bases usually forming dense mats, the spikelets 2-2.5 mm long and less shiny than in *P. notatum* and the lower sheaths and blades often hirsute or hispid.

Distribution. Texas: Regions 2 and 6, in open grasslands or along woods borders, infrequent. General: Texas and Mexico, south to Paraguay.

Flowering period: Our records, June and November.

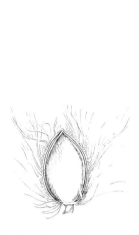

Fig. 265. *Paspalum conjugatum.* Spikelet. From Hitchcock, 1935.

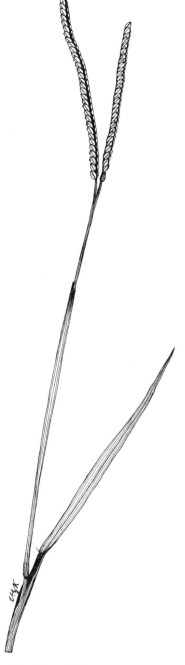

Fig. 266. *Paspalum notatum.* Inflorescence. From Gould and Box, 1965.

SUBFAMILY VI. PANICOIDEAE   **507**

7. **Paspalum almum** Chase, J. Wash. Acad. Sci. 23:137. f. 1. 1933. COMBS PASPALUM. Cespitose perennial with densely clustered culms mostly 25-50 cm tall. *Ligule* membranous, about 2 mm long. *Blades* thin, flat or folded, mostly 2-5 mm broad, ciliate with papilla-based hairs on margins near base. *Inflorescence* variable in aspect, commonly with a terminal branch and a second branch inserted 0.5-1.5 cm below; occasionally 1-3 additional branches scattered below the upper two. *Branches* mostly 4-9 cm long, bearing 2 rows of spikelets on a thin, flattened rachis. *Spikelets* glabrous, narrowly ovate, elliptic or obovate, 2.9-3.4 mm long. *Lemma of upper floret* straw-colored. *Chromosome number* reported, $2n=24$.

Distribution. Texas: Southern portion of region 1 and northeastern portion of region 2 (specimens examined from Hardin, Orange and Jefferson counties). General: Reported by Chase (1951) to occur in Texas, Brazil, Paraguay and Argentina.

Flowering period: Summer and early fall.

8. **Paspalum vaginatum** Swartz, Prodr. Veg. Ind. Occ. 21. 1788. SEASHORE PASPALUM. Perennial with culms mostly 10-60 cm tall from an extensive system of long, slender rhizomes. *Sheaths* large, conspicuous, straw-colored. *Ligule* a minute scale-like membrane. *Blades* (in Texas plants) glabrous or essentially so, mostly 1-4 mm broad, inrolled or folded on drying and seldom appearing more than 2 mm broad. *Inflorescence* generally with 2 more or less paired branches at culm apex, occasionally 1-2 additional branches irregularly developed below. *Inflorescence branches* 2-6 cm long with a broad, triangular rachis and spikelets in 2 rows. *Spikelets* glabrous, 2.6-4 mm long, ovate-lanceolate, acute at apex. *Lemma of upper floret* straw-colored. *Chromosome numbers* reported, $2n=20$ and 40.

Distribution. Texas: Region 2 on coastal sands, infrequent. General: North Carolina to Florida and Texas, south to Argentina; also in the Old World tropics.

Flowering period: Texas records in Tracy Herbarium, August, September, December and January.

9. **Paspalum distichum** L., Syst. Nat. ed. 10. 2:855. 1759. KNOTGRASS.

Lower sheaths glabrous or sparsely hirsute
　　　　　　　　　　　　　9A.　*P. distichum* var. *distichum*

Lower sheaths strongly hirsute with papilla-based hairs
　　　　　　　　　　　　　9B.　*P. distichum* var. *indutum*

9A. **Paspalum distichum** L. var. **distichum** Fig. 267. Similar to *P. vaginatum* but blades mostly 3-6 mm broad and tending to remain flat, the first glume present on many spikelets, the second minutely pubescent, and the lemma of the lower floret typically more turgid and rounded. *Chromosome numbers* reported, $2n=20$, 30, 40, 48 and 60.

Fig. 267. *Paspalum distichum* var. *distichum*. Leafy culm with inflorescence and spikelet. From Gould and Box, 1965.

Distribution. Texas: Throughout the State, in moist or wet soil, frequently along ponds, lakes and rivers. General: Along the eastern and western coasts of the United States and throughout the southern states; widespread in warm temperate, subtropical and tropical regions of the world.

Flowering period: April to November.

SUBFAMILY VI. PANICOIDEAE   509

9B. **Paspalum distichum** L. var. **indutum** Shinners, Rhodora 56:31-32. 1954. Similar to the typical variety but lower sheaths and often the blades strongly hirsute with papilla-based hairs.

Distribution. Texas: Region 4, known only from Dallas County. General: Known only from Texas.

Flowering period: Collected in flower in August and October.

10. **Paspalum separatum** Shinners, Rhodora 56:32. 1954. Tufted perennial, subrhizomatous at the base, with culms to 50 cm tall. *Lower sheaths* pilose, the upper glabrous. *Ligules* about 0.8 mm long. *Blades* ciliate on lower margins, 6-7 mm broad. *Inflorescence* of 2 terminal branches, the spikelets in 2 rows and widely spaced on branches, not overlapping. *Spikelets* plano-convex, elliptic, obtuse, about 2.2 mm long and 1.5 mm broad, puberulent. *First glume* absent. *Chromosome number* not reported.

Distribution. Texas: Region 3, known only from the type specimen collected near Golden, Wood County (*Shinners 15565*, SMU), "in gray silty clay and chalk gravel." General: Known only from Texas.

Flowering period: The type specimen collected in flower in July.

11. **Paspalum langei** (Fourn.) Nash, North Amer. Fl. 17:179. 1912. RUSTYSEED PASPALUM. Fig. 268. Cespitose perennial with culms 30-100 cm tall from a firm, nonrhizomatous base. *Leaves* glabrous or the lowermost minutely pubescent. *Blades* thin, mostly 7-18 mm broad, tapering to a slender point. *Inflorescences* terminating the long shoots and on slender peduncles in the axils of the upper leaves, usually with 2-5 slender, widely-spaced, spicate branches, occasionally with only 1. *Inflorescence branches* mostly 4-8 cm long, with pairs of spikelets on either side of a flat, narrow rachis. *Spikelets* 2.2-2.6 mm long, elliptic or elliptic-obovate. *First glume* present on some or most spikelets, usually one-fourth to one-third as long as spikelet. *Second glume and lemma of lower floret* pubescent and usually with brownish glandular blotches. *Lemma of upper floret* light brown. *Chromosome number*, $2n=60$.

Distribution. Texas: Regions 1, 2, 3 and 6, usually in moist woods and shaded ditchbanks. General: Florida to Texas and south to Venezuela.

Flowering period: April to November.

12. **Paspalum monostachyum** Vasey, in Chapm., F. Southeast. U.S. ed. 2. 665. 1883. GULFDUNE PASPALUM. Fig. 269. Stout perennial with culms 50-120 cm tall, arising singly or in small clusters from long, stout, scaly rhizomes. *Leaves* glabrous except for the long-ciliate ligule. *Blades* involute, 2 mm or less in width (as inrolled), the lower ones mostly 20-30 or more cm long. *Inflorescence* of 1-3, occasionally of 4, densely-flowered spicate branches, the branches mostly 10-25 (occasionally 8-30) cm long. *Spikelets* usually in pairs of one subsessile and one pediceled, the pedicel occasionally replaced by a short

Fig. 268.   *Paspalum langei*. Inflorescence
and a pair of spikelets. From Gould and
Box, 1965.

Fig. 269.   *Paspalum monostachyum*. Inflorescence and a pair of spikelets. From
Gould and Box, 1965.

SUBFAMILY VI. PANICOIDEAE   511

branch bearing 3-6 crowded spikelets. *Spikelets* glabrous, elliptic, 3-3.5 mm long. *First glume* absent or irregularly developed on some spikelets. *Lemma of lower floret* straw-colored or light brown. *Chromosome number* not reported.

Distribution. Texas: Regions 2 and 6 in sandy soils, most frequent on coastal dune formations. General: Southern Florida and Texas.

Flowering period: May to November.

13. **Paspalum unispicatum** (Scribn. & Merr.) Nash, North Amer. Fl. 1912. ONESPIKE PASPALUM. Perennial with culms 50-80 cm tall, arising singly or in small clusters from stout, scaly rhizomes. *Ligule* ciliate with stiff hairs. *Blades* 3-4 mm broad, sparsely hirsute on both margins to scabrous or nearly glabrous, broadly rounded and somewhat cordate at base. *Inflorescence* usually a single, slender, unilateral spicate raceme 7-20 cm long. *Secondary racemes* frequently produced in uppermost leaf axils. *Spikelets* glabrous, elliptic or obovate, 2.9-3.3 mm long. *First glume* commonly absent or very short on sessile spikelets, usually well-developed on pediceled spikelets. *Lemma of upper floret* straw-colored or light brown. *Chromosome number* not reported.

Distribution. Texas: Southern portion of region 2 and region 6, in sandy soils, infrequent. General: Southern Texas and Cuba to Venezuela and Argentina.

Flowering period: Summer and autumn.

14. **Paspalum bifidum** (Bertol.) Nash, Bull. Torrey Bot. Club 24:192. 1897. PITCHFORK PASPALUM. Perennial with culms 60-120 cm tall, stiffly erect from short, scaly rhizomes. *Rhizome scales* densely lanate-pubescent. *Sheaths* and *blades* typically hirsute with long, silvery hairs, the adaxial surface of blade densely long-hirsute just above the large, lacerate, membranous ligule. *Blades* flat, mostly 4-12 mm broad and 15-40 cm or more long. *Inflorescence* with a narrow, flattened, flexuous rachis with usually 3-5 widely-spaced, sparsely-flowered branches 4-16 cm long. *Spikelets* paired (the lower spikelet sometimes aborted), the members of a pair both pediceled and on a common peduncle, the pairs widely-spaced and not or only slightly overlapping. *Spikelets* 3.3-4 mm long, elliptical. *First glume* absent or irregularly present on some spikelets. *Second glume and lemma of lower floret* glabrous, strongly 5-7-nerved. *Lemma of upper floret* light brown. *Chromosome number* not reported.

Distribution. Texas: Regions 1, 2 and 3, usually in sandy woods openings but relatively infrequent. General: Virginia and Florida to eastern Oklahoma and Texas.

Flowering period: June to November.

15. **Paspalum floridanum** Michx., Fl. Bor. Amer. 1:44. 1803. FLORIDA PASPALUM.

Leaves more or less densely hirsute   15A.   *P. floridanum* var. *floridanum*

Leaves glabrous or nearly so except in vicinity of ligule
$\qquad$ 15B.   *P. floridanum* var. *glabratum*

15A. Paspalum floridanum Michx. var. **floridanum.** Culms 1-2 meters tall from short, thick rhizomes. *Sheaths* and *blades*, at least in part, densely hirsute. *Ligules* membranous. *Blades* firm, flat or folded, mostly 4-10 mm broad and 15-50 cm long, with a dense tuft of long hairs immediately above ligule. *Inflorescence* usually with 2-5 branches, these 4-13 cm long. *Spikelets* glabrous, broadly elliptic to suborbicular, 3.6-4.8 mm long, short-pediceled in pairs and closely-placed in 4 rows on branch rachis. *Lemma of lower floret* with a well-developed midnerve. *Lemma of upper floret* light brown, minutely rugose.

Distribution. Texas: Regions 1, 2 and 3 in low, moist, grassy areas, woods openings and cutover woodlands. In Texas, much less frequent than *P. floridanum* var. *glabratum*. General: Maryland and Florida, west to Illinois, eastern Kansas and eastern Texas.

Flowering period: Mostly August to November.

15B. Paspalum floridanum Michx. var. **glabratum** Engelm. *ex* Vasey, Bull. Torrey Bot. Club. 13:166. 1886. Fig. 270. Similar to the typical variety of the species but sheaths and blades nearly or completely glabrous. On many specimens the blade is conspicuously hirsute immediately above the ligule but otherwise glabrous. *Chromosome numbers* of $2n = 120$, 140 and ca. 160-170 have been reported for Texas collections of *P. floridanum*. The count of $2n = 160$-170 was made on a plant referable to the var. *glabratum* (Brazos County, College Station, *Gould 7812*), and it is most likely that the other counts also were made on plants of this variety.

Distribution. Texas: Regions 1, 2, 3, 4 and 5, widespread and frequent in grasslands and open woodlands throughout eastern Texas but never locally abundant. General: About the same as the typical variety of the species. *Paspalum floridanum* var. *glabratum* is much more frequent than var. *floridanum* in the western portion of the species range but is less common in the eastern states.

Flowering period: Mostly August to November.

16. **Paspalum dilatatum** Poir, in Lam. Encycl. 5:35. 1804. DALLIS-GRASS. Fig. 271. Cespitose perennial with culms mostly 50-120 cm tall from a hard, knotty base. *Lowermost sheaths* usually hirsute, the upper sheaths glabrous. *Ligule* a brownish membrane usually 1.5-3 mm long. *Blades* firm, flat, tapering to a narrow point, mostly 3-12 mm broad, glabrous or sparsely ciliate with long hairs near the base. *Inflorescence branches* mostly 2-7, usually widely spaced on a slender axis. *Spikelets* closely imbricated in 4 rows on a broad, flat branch rachis 3-8 cm long. *Spikelets* broadly ovate, tapering to

Fig. 270. *Paspalum floridanum* var. *glabratum*. Plant, spikelet and floret. From Gould and Box, 1965.

514   THE GRASSES OF TEXAS

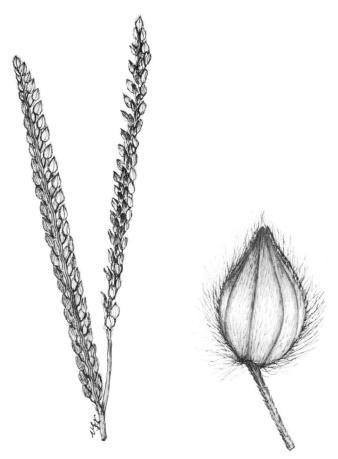

Fig. 271. *Paspalum dilatatum.* Inflorescence and spikelet. From Gould and Box, 1965.

a short, acute apex. *First glume* absent. *Second glume and lemma of lower floret* distinctly 3-5-nerved, 3-4 mm long, pubescent on margins with long, silky hairs. *Lemma of upper floret* light-colored, broadly ovate or suborbicular. *Chromosome numbers* reported, $2n = 20$, 40 and 50 and aneuploid numbers.

Distribution. Texas: Regions 1, 2, 3, 4, 5, 6, 8 and 10, widely seeded as a forage grass, persisting in pastures and as a weed of roadsides, lawns and waste places in the southern part of the State. General: Introduced into the southern United States from Uruguay or Argentina (Chase, 1951), native to South America and widely distributed throughout the warmer regions of the world.

Flowering period: April to November.

17. **Paspalum urvillei** Steud., Syn. Pl. Glum. 1:24. 1854. VASEY-GRASS. Fig. 272. Coarse perennial with culms mostly 1-2 m tall in large, leafy clumps. *Base of plant* firm or hard, subrhizomatous. *Lower sheaths* usually hirsute or villous with long hairs, the upper sheaths glabrous. *Ligule* membranous, well-developed. *Blades* long, coarse, mostly 4-15 mm broad, usually glabrous except for a tuft of hair immediately above ligule. *Inflorescence* of usually 8-30 erect branches, these mostly 4-10, occasionally -14, cm long, with closely imbricated spikelets in 4 rows. *Spikelets* 2.2-2.7 mm long, ovate to obovate, abruptly pointed. *First glume* absent. *Second glume and lemma of lower floret* pubescent with long hairs on margins, the lemma also pubescent on back. *Lemma of upper floret* light-colored. *Chromosome number*, 2n=40.

Distribution. Texas: Regions 1, 2, 3, 4 and 7, usually along lakes, swales and other moist places, frequent as a weed of road ditches. General: Introduced in the United States from South America and now frequent in the Southeast, also present in California.

Flowering period: May to November.

18. **Paspalum malacophyllum** Trin., Gram. Icon. 3. pl. 271. 1831. Perennial from short, scaly rhizomes. *Culms* 0.7-2 m tall, glabrous. *Ligule* about 2 mm long. *Blades* narrow, elongate, 8-35 mm broad, from pubescent on both surfaces to glabrous. *Inflorescence* with usually 10-45 slender branches, these 2-10 cm long. *Spikelets* 1.8-2 mm long, glabrous, narrowly oblong-elliptic, closely placed in pairs on a broad rachis. *First and second glumes* both absent. *Lemma of lower floret* thin, distinctly 3-5-nerved. *Palea of lower floret* absent or rudimentary. *Lemma of upper floret* thin, minutely papillose, distinctly 7-nerved. *Chromosome number*, 2n=60.

Distribution. Texas: *Paspalum malacophyllum* is known only from College Station, Brazos County (region 3), where it has persisted and spread from a garden planting made over 30 years ago in the old Hensel Park nursery. General: Mexico to Bolivia and Argentina, introduced into southern United States as a potential forage grass.

Flowering period: Late summer and fall.

19. **Paspalum boscianum** Flugge, Monogr. Pasp. 170. 1810. BULL PASPALUM. Succulent annual with culms mostly 40-70 cm tall. *Sheaths* broad, loose, glabrous or infrequently hispid. *Ligule* a rounded membrane 1.5-3 mm long. *Blades* long, flat, weak, mostly 6-15 mm broad, usually glabrous except for some long, stiff hairs just above ligule. *Inflorescence branches* 4-12, usually 4-7 cm long, bearing closely crowded spikelets in 4 (infrequently 2) rows on a flat rachis 2-2.5 mm broad. *Spikelets* broadly obovate to suborbicular, 2-2.5 mm long, glabrous. *Second glume and lemma of lower floret* brownish; *lemma of upper floret* becoming dark brown at maturity. *Chromosome number*, 2n=40.

Fig. 272. *Paspalum urvillei.* Plant, two views of spikelet and a floret. From Hitchcock, 1935.

Distribution. Texas: Regions 1 and 2, infrequent, in the moist soil of ditches, field borders and cutover woodlands. Texas collections examined: Jefferson County, south of Fannett, *Silveus 7363*. General: Pennsylvania and Virginia to Florida, Arkansas, Louisiana and Texas and south to Brazil.

Flowering period: September to November.

SUBFAMILY VI. PANICOIDEAE   517

20. **Paspalum convexum** Humb. & Bonpl. *ex* Flugge, Monogr. Pasp. 175. 1810. Cespitose annual with culms mostly 20-40 cm tall from erect or decumbent creeping bases. *Leaf blades* long, flat, soft, mostly 5-12 cm broad, usually conspicuously pilose. *Inflorescence branches* 1-4, mostly 2-4 cm (occasionally -7 cm) long. *Spikelets* closely crowded in pairs on either side of a broad, flat rachis, both spikelets of a pair rather long-pediceled. *Spikelets* broadly obovate to suborbicular, 2.3-3 mm long. *Glume and lemma of lower floret* minutely appressed-pubescent. *Lemma of upper floret* dark brown at maturity. *Chromosome numbers* reported, $2n=30$ and 60.

Distribution. Texas: Region 1, known in Texas from a single collection made on a sandy roadside site 10 miles north of the city of Jasper in Jasper County. General: Texas, northern Mexico and Cuba, south to Brazil.

Flowering period: Late summer and fall.

21. **Paspalum scrobiculatum** L., Mantissa pl. I:29. 1767. Cespitose annual, similar to *P. convexum* but stouter and with unequally biconvex spikelets more than 3 mm long and with lemma of sterile floret loose and wrinkled (Chase, 1951). *Chromosome number*, $2n=40$.

Distribution. Texas: Reported by Chase (1951) to have been collected by Bentley in 1899 at Abilene, Taylor County (region 8). General: An Asiatic species commonly cultivated in India, introduced into the United States at a few localities.

Flowering period: September to November.

22. **Paspalum plicatulum** Michx., Fl. Bor. Amer. 1:45. 1803. *Paspalum texanum* Swallen. BROWNSEED PASPALUM. Fig. 273. Tufted perennial with culms 50-100 cm tall in small or moderately large clumps from firm, often more or less rhizomatous bases. *Culms* slender, stiffly erect, glabrous or the lower nodes puberulent. *Sheaths* keeled, glabrous or less frequently hirsute or pilose. *Ligules* brown, 2-3 mm long. *Blades* firm, folded at base, flat or folded above, mostly 3-7 mm broad, glabrous or more commonly papillose-pilose on the upper surface near the base. *Inflorescence branches* usually 3-10, commonly 3-10 cm long, with pairs of unequally pediceled spikelets closely crowded on either side of the flattened rachis. *Spikelets* broadly elliptic or obovate, 2.4-2.8 mm long, dark brown. *Glume* glabrous or minutely appressed-pubescent. *Lemma of lower floret* thin, usually with transverse wrinkles on the margins. *Lemma of upper floret* dark brown and shiny, minutely reticulate. *Chromosome numbers* reported, $2n=20$, 40 and 60.

Distribution. Texas: Regions 1, 2, 3, 4, 6 and 7, most frequent on sand or sandy loam soils, often in partial shade in open oak woodlands. General: Georgia, Florida and Texas, south to Argentina.

Flowering period: Nearly throughout the year, collected in flower from March to November.

Fig. 273. *Paspalum plicatulum.* Inflorescence and pair of spikelets. From Gould and Box, 1965.

Paspalum texanum Swallen (type from Port Lavaca, Calhoun County, Texas) was described from rhizomatous plants with decumbent culm bases. The spikelets are typified as being non-turgid and with a non-wrinkled lemma of the sterile floret. In view of the great morphological variability of *P. plicatulum* and the wide range of habitats to which it has become adapted, the characters by which *P. texanum* is distinguished do not appear especially significant, and the taxon is not recognized.

23. **Paspalum virgatum** L., Syst. Nat. ed. 10. 2:855. 1759. TAL-QUEZAL. Large, stout perennial with culms 1-2 m tall in large, dense clumps. *Ligule* a short, lacerate membrane. *Blades* long and flat, mostly 1-2.5 cm broad, harshly serrate on the margins. *Panicle* to 30 cm long, with usually 10-16 spreading and usually drooping branches, these 7-15 cm long. *Spikelets* 2.2-2.5 mm long, elliptic to rather broadly obovate, acute or obtuse at the apex, dark colored. *Glume and lemma of lower floret* usually minutely pubescent on the back, occasionally the hairs sparse and present only near apex. *Lemma and palea of upper floret* smooth, dark brown. *Chromosome numbers* reported, $2n=40$ and 80.

Distribution. Texas: Region 6, known in Texas only from collections made near Brownsville, Cameron County. General: Southern Texas through eastern Mexico, Central America and the Caribbean to South America.

Flowering period: September to November.

24. **Paspalum lividum** Trin., in Schlecht., Linnaea 26:383. 1854. LONG-TOM. Fig. 274. Perennial with culms mostly 30-70 cm tall from decumbent or stoloniferous bases, the stolons often 1 m or more in length. *Culms* flattened, usually with many nodes and short internodes at base. *Sheaths* thin, glabrous or hispid with papilla-based hairs, the lower ones sharply keeled, gradually tapering to a narrow apex, soon withering or broken off and exposing the numerous dark-colored stem nodes. *Ligule* a short membrane. *Blades* mostly 3-6 mm broad, glabrous or the adaxial surface sparsely hirsute. *Inflorescence* of usually 3-7 short, spreading-erect branches, these 1.5-4 (occasionally 1-5) cm long. *Branch rachis* 1.5-2 mm wide, with or without a few scattered long hairs, often becoming dark purple. *Spikelets* closely imbricated in 4 rows on the rachis, 2-2.5 mm long, glabrous, elliptic or obovate, broadly pointed. *Glume and lemma of lower floret* thin and papery at maturity. *Lemma and palea of upper floret* finely rugose, straw-colored. *Chromosome number*, $2n=40$.

Distribution. Texas: Regions 1, 2 and 6 in ditches and swales and along muddy coastal flats. General: Florida and Alabama to Texas, south through the Caribbean and eastern Mexico to South America.

Flowering period: May to October.

25. **Paspalum pubiflorum** Rupr. *ex* Fourn., Mex. Pl. 2:11. 1886.

Spikelets pubescent | 25A. *P. pubiflorum* var. *pubiflorum*

Spikelets glabrous | 25B. *P. pubiflorum* var. *glabrum*

25A. **Paspalum pubiflorum** Rupr. *ex* Fourn. var. **pubiflorum**. HAIRY-SEED PASPALUM. Fig. 275. Perennial with culms usually 40-80 cm tall from decumbent, spreading bases, often rooting at the lower nodes. *Sheaths*, at least the lower ones, pilose with pustula-based hairs. *Ligule* a short, often brownish membrane. *Blades* lanceolate, mostly 6-15 mm broad,

Fig. 274. *Paspalum lividum.* Plant and spikelet. From Gould and Box, 1965.

SUBFAMILY VI. PANICOIDEAE   **521**

Fig. 275. *Paspalum pubiflorum* var. *pubiflorum*. Inflorescence and pair of spikelets. From Gould and Box, 1965.

usually glabrous except for a few stiff hairs near base. *Inflorescence* of 2-5, occasionally -7, branches, these mostly 3-10 cm long. *Branch rachis* 1-2 mm broad, bearing 4 rows of spikelets or 2 rows by abortion of the upper spikelet of each pair. *Spikelets* 2.7-3.2 mm long, elliptic or obovate, pointed but not sharply so, pubescent. *Lemma of upper floret* light-colored. *Chromosome numbers* reported, $2n=60$ and ca. 64.

Distribution. Texas: Regions 1, 2, 3, 4, 5, 6, 7, 8 and 10 in ditches and along swales and other low, moist areas, occasionally in partial shade of forest trees. General: Louisiana and Texas to Cuba and Mexico.

Flowering period: Late April to November.

25B. **Paspalum pubiflorum** Rupr. *ex* Fourn. var. **glabrum** Vasey *ex* Scribn., Tenn. Agr. Exp. Sta. Bull. 7:32. pl. 5. f. 18. 1894. Similar to *P. pubiflorum* var. *pubiflorum* but spikelets glabrous and the sheaths commonly less pilose.

Distribution. Texas: Reportedly present in regions 1, 3, 4, 7 and 8 but specimens examined from Parker, Rockwall, Tarrant and Harris counties only. Much less frequent than the typical variety in Texas. General: North Carolina, Ohio and Indiana to Florida, Kansas and Texas.

Flowering period: Tracy Herbarium records, July and October.

26. **Paspalum hartwegianum** Fourn., Mex. Pl. 2:12. 1886. HARTWEG PASPALUM. Perennial, similar to *P. pubiflorum* var. *pubiflorum* but leaf blades narrower (mostly 2-5 mm broad) and usually folded or involute and spikelets slightly narrower, more pointed and less turgid. *Chromosome number* not reported; the records of $2n=60$ attributed to this species by Gould (1958) were based on specimens of *Paspalum pubiflorum*.

Distribution. Texas: Regions 2 and 6 in low pastures, ditches and swales. General: Southern Texas and Mexico.

Flowering period: June to November.

27. **Paspalum setaceum** Michx.*, Fl. Bor. Amer. 1:44. 1803. Tufted, short-lived perennial with culms mostly 30-80 cm tall from knotty bases or short rhizomes. *Ligule* a minute membrane. *Blades* flat, soft or rather firm with long, silvery hairs just above ligule. *Inflorescences* commonly both terminal and axillary, the spikelets in a single spicate raceme or on 2-5 spicate branches. *Raceme* or *inflorescence branches* slender, 3-17 cm long, the lower axillary inflorescence often partially hidden in the leaf sheaths. *Spikelets* elliptic to orbicular, 1.4-2.6 mm long, glabrous or pubescent.

Populations of widely variable but intergrading plant types are herein included in *Paspalum setaceum*. The complex for the most part is distributed throughout the eastern half of the United States, with perhaps the greatest concentration of plants and the greatest variability along the Atlantic Coastal Plain. In Texas these plants flower mainly from May to October.

Leaf blades 2-7 mm broad, villous; spikelets 1.4-1.9 mm long
                                    27A. *P. setaceum* var. *setaceum*

Leaf blades 3-20 mm broad, glabrous or variously pubescent; spikelets
    1.6-2.6 mm long

*This concept of *Paspalum setaceum* is based on the treatment by Banks (1966), and the writer has borrowed freely from the descriptions of the species and its varieties as presented by Banks.

Leaf blades pilose

Midnerve of lemma of lower floret usually absent
27B. *P. setaceum* var. *stramineum*

Midnerve of lemma of lower floret usually present
27D. *P. setaceum* var. *muhlenbergii*

Leaf blades glabrous or essentially so

Herbage yellowish-green to dark green; leaf blades 3-15 mm broad; spike-lets 1.6-2.2 mm long; midnerve of the lemma of lower floret usually absent   27B. *P. setaceum* var. *stramineum*

Herbage dark green to purplish; leaf blades 3-20 mm broad; spikelets 1.7-2.6 mm long; midnerve of lemma of lower floret present or absent
27C. *P. setaceum* var. *ciliatifolium*

27A. **Paspalum setaceum** Michx. var. **setaceum,** *Paspalum debile* Michx. THIN PASPALUM. Culms erect to spreading. Herbage grayish-green. Leaf blades 2-7 mm broad, villous. Spikelets elliptic to suborbicular, 1.4-1.9 mm long, glabrous or pubescent, pale yellow to light green, some-times spotted. Midnerve of lemma of lower floret often absent. *Chromosome number,* $2n = 20$.

Distribution. Texas: Region 1, infrequent, usually in moist ditches, woods borders or sandy pastures. Along the Coastal Plain, Massachusetts to Florida and westward to Texas.

Flowering period: Summer and early autumn.

27B. **Paspalum setaceum** Michx. var. **stramineum** (Nash) D. Banks, Sida 2:276. 1966. P. *stramineum* Nash. Fig. 276. Culms erect to spreading. Herbage yellowish-green to dark green. *Leaf blades* 3-15 mm broad, glabrous to puberulent or pilose. Spikelets mostly suborbicular, 1.6-2.2 mm long, glabrous or pubescent, pale yellow to light green, sometimes spotted. Midnerve of lemma of lower floret usually absent. *Chromosome number,* $2n = 20$.

Distribution. Texas: In all regions but absent from the far western counties, frequent along ditches, open woodlands, pastures and woods borders. General: Throughout the central United States, Michigan to Minnesota and south to Arkansas, Texas and southeastern Arizona. Also scattered along the Atlantic Coastal Plain from Massachusetts to Florida and Louisiana and ranging southward through the West Indies, the Caribbean, Mexico and Central America to Panama.

Flowering period: Summer and early autumn.

Fig. 276.   *Paspalum setaceum* var. *stramineum.* Inflorescence and spikelet. From Gould and Box, 1965.

SUBFAMILY VI.   PANICOIDEAE   525

27C. **Paspalum setaceum** Michx. var. **ciliatifolium** (Michx.) Vasey, Contr. U.S. Natl. Herb. 3:17. 1892. *Paspalum ciliatifolium* Michx., *Paspalum propinquum* Nash. FRINGELEAF PASPALUM. Culms erect to spreading. Herbage dark green to purplish. Leaf blades 3-20 mm broad, glabrous or essentially so. Spikelets elliptic to suborbicular, 1.7-2.6 mm long, glabrous or pubescent, light green to green, sometimes spotted. Midnerve of lemma of lower floret present or absent. *Chromosome number,* $2n=20$.

Distribution. Texas: Regions 1, 2 and 3, not on the immediate coast or further south than Harris County, in open woodlands, ditchbanks and pastures. General: New Jersey to Florida and westward to Oklahoma and Texas and in the West Indies.

Flowering period: Summer and early autumn.

27D. **Paspalum setaceum** Michx. var. **muhlenbergii** (Nash) Banks, Sida 2:280. 1966. *Paspalum muhlenbergii* Nash, *Paspalum pubescens* Muhl. Culms mostly erect. Herbage light to dark green. Leaf blades 3-10 mm broad, pilose. Spikelets suborbicular, 1.8-2.5 mm long, usually glabrous, light green to green. Midnerve of lemma of lower floret usually present. *Chromosome number,* $2n=20$.

Distribution. Texas: Regions 1, 2, 3, 4, 5 and 7 in open woodlands, ditchbanks and pastures. Throughout the eastern United States and west to eastern Iowa, Kansas, Oklahoma and Texas.

Flowering period: Summer and early autumn.

In discussing this variety, Banks (1966) stated, "This variety closely resembles var. *ciliatifolium* except for its pubescent foliage."

28. **Paspalum laeve** Michx., Fl. Bor. Amer. 1:44. 1803. Tufted perennial with culms 40-100 cm tall from a firm base. *Sheaths* glabrous to pilose. *Ligule* membranous, 1-3 mm long. *Blades* flat, linear, 3-10 mm broad, as much as 30 cm long, variously pubescent to nearly glabrous. *Inflorescences* usually developed at apex of main shoots only, axillary inflorescences characteristically absent. *Inflorescence branches* typically 4-10 cm long, 3-5 (occasionally 2-6) per panicle. *Spikelets* glabrous, broadly ovate, oval, obovate or orbicular, 2.4-3.4 mm long and two-thirds as broad to fully as broad as long, typically borne singly and often widely spaced on either side of a flattened rachis. *Pedicels* mostly 0.7-2 mm long. *Lemma of lower floret* 5-7 nerved, the lateral nerves crowded to the margins. *Lemma of upper floret* light brown to straw-colored. *Chromosome number,* $2n=20$.

Flowering period: July to October.

Spikelets ovate, oval, obovate, conspicuously longer than broad, 2-2.5 mm broad

Lower leaf sheaths and blades glabrous or sparsely hirsute
28A.   *P. laeve* var. *laeve*

Lower leaf sheaths and often the blades strongly pilose
                                                28B. *P. laeve* var. *pilosum*

Spikelets orbicular or suborbicular, about as long as broad, 2.7-3.2 mm broad   28C. *P. laeve* var. *circulare*

28A. **Paspalum laeve** Michx. var. **laeve.** FIELD PASPALUM. Fig. 277.

Distribution. Texas: Regions 1 and 3 and northern portion of region 2. General: New Jersey to Florida and westward to Illinois, Missouri and Texas.

28B. **Paspalum laeve** Michx. var. **pilosum** Scribn., Tenn. Agr. Exp. Sta. Bull. 7:34. 1894. *Paspalum longipilum* Nash, N. Y. Bot. Gard. Bull. L:435. 1900.

Distribution. Texas: Regions 1 and 3. General: New York and Pennsylvania to Florida and westward to Tennessee, Arkansas and Texas.

28C. **Paspalum laeve** Michx. var. **circulare** (Nash) Fern., Rhodora 36:22. 1934. *Paspalum circulare* Nash.

Distribution. Texas: Region 1 and northern portion of region 2. General: Massachusetts to Georgia and Mississippi, west to Kansas, Oklahoma and Texas.

29. **Paspalum praecox** Walt., Fl. Carol. 75. 1788. *Paspalum lentiferum* Lam. EARLY PASPALUM. Perennial with culms 50-100 (rarely -150) cm tall from short rhizomes. *Sheaths* more or less keeled, glabrous to hirsute or villous. *Ligules* mostly 2-2.5 mm long. *Blades* 15-25 cm long, 3-7 mm broad, glabrous to hirsute or villous on both surfaces. *Inflorescences* on long shoots only, axillary inflorescences not developed. *Panicle* with usually 3-6 slender, racemose branches, these 2-7 cm long. *Spikelets* short-pediceled and paired or some single and some paired on either side of a flattened branch rachis, the pedicels puberulent, mostly 0.2-1 mm long. *Spikelets* obovate, oval or suborbicular, glabrous, 2.2-3.2 mm long. *Lemma of lower floret* 3-5 nerved, the lateral nerves near margins. *Lemma and palea of upper floret* light brown, minutely papillose. *Chromosome numbers* reported, $2n = 20$ and 40.

Distribution. Texas: Regions 1 and 3 and northern part of region 2 in moist woodlands and pastures. General: Along the Coastal Plain, North Carolina to Florida and west to Texas.

Flowering period: May to September.

Chase, in Hitchcock's Manual (1951), recognized *Paspalum lentiferum* as distinct from *P. praecox* on the basis of a tendency towards larger plants, larger spikelets and more often villous leaf sheaths. Relationships within these populations and between *P. praecox* and *P. laeve* need further study.

Fig. 277. *Paspalum laeve* var. *laeve*. Plant, two views of spikelet and a floret. From Hitchcock, 1935.

528   THE GRASSES OF TEXAS

100. OPLISMENUS Beauv.

A genus of about 10 species in the tropics and subtropics of both hemispheres, none native to the United States.

1. **Oplismenus hirtellus** (L.) Beauv., Ess. Agrost. 54, 168. 1812. BASKETGRASS. Fig. 278. Annual with stoloniferous, trailing culms and thin, broad, short blades. *Erect flowering shoots* mostly 15-25 cm tall. *Culm nodes and sheath margins* hirsute. *Ligule* a ciliate membrane. *Blades* scabrous and sparsely hispid or hirsute, ovate to ovate-lanceolate, mostly 1.5-7 cm long and 5-13 mm broad, widely spreading and often reflexed at maturity. *Inflorescence* a panicle of usually 3-7 widely-spaced, spicate branches, these mostly 1-6 mm long and with 2-9 sessile or subsessile spikelets in 2 rows. Disarticulation usually below glumes but occasionally just below perfect floret. *Glumes* about equal, awned from a minutely notched apex, the awn of first glume mostly 0.5-1 cm long, much longer than that of second glume. *Lemma of lower floret* about as long as second glume, mucronate or short-awned. *Lemma of upper floret* smooth, indurate, elliptic, acute at apex, the margins almost completely enclosing the palea. *Chromosome number, $2n=72$.*

Distribution. Texas: Regions 1, 2, 3 and 6 and southern portion of region 4 in shade of shrubs or trees, usually in moist soils. General: Tropical and subtropical areas of the New World, introduced or adventive in the United States.

Flowering period: Flowering throughout the year under favorable conditions of moisture and temperature.

Most or possibly all plants of this species growing in Texas are referable to *Oplismenus hirtellus* subsp. *setarius* (Lam.) Mez. (*Oplismenus setarius* (Lam.) R.&S.). Hitchcock (1935) and Chase (1951) reported the occurrence of *O. hirtellus* var. *hirtellus* in Cameron County (southern portion of region 6), but this record may be based on robust plants of the subsp. *setarius* with slightly longer blades and longer inflorescence branches than is typical for the subspecies.

101. ECHINOCHLOA Beauv.

Coarse annuals and perennials, mostly with weak, succulent culms and broad, thin, flat blades. *Ligule* a ring of hairs or absent. *Inflorescence* a panicle with few to numerous, simple or rebranched, densely-flowered branches. *Spikelets* subsessile, in irregular fascicles or in regular rows, disarticulating below the glumes. *Glumes and lemma of lower floret* variously scabrous or hairy, less frequently glabrous. *First glume* present, acute or short-awned, much shorter than second glume. *Second glume and lemma of lower floret* about equal, awned or awnless. *Lemma of upper (perfect) floret* indurate, smooth and shiny, with inrolled margins and usually an

Fig. 278. *Oplismenus hirtellus*. Plant and spikelet. From Gould and Box, 1965.

530   THE GRASSES OF TEXAS

abruptly pointed apex. *Palea of upper floret* similar to lemma in texture but narrowing to a pointed tip that is free from lemma margins.

About 20 species, throughout the warmer regions of the world, often growing as weeds.

The following treatment is based on the revision of the United States species of *Echinochloa* by Gould, Ali and Fairbrothers (1972).

Ligules of stiff hairs present at least on lower leaves; plants perennial
1.   E. polystachya

Ligules absent; plants annual

Leaf sheaths hirsute or hispid, usually with papilla-based hairs
3.   E. walteri

Leaf sheaths glabrous

All or some spikelets with awns 15 mm or more long

Coriaceous apex of lemma of perfect floret narrowly acute or acuminate, with gradual transition to a stiff, membranous, usually mucronate tip

Lemma of perfect floret broadly ovate; spikelets usually with at least some papilla-based hairs   2.   *E. muricata*

Lemma of perfect floret narrowly ovate or oblong; spikelets typically without papilla-based hairs   3.   *E. walteri*

Coriaceous apex of lemma of perfect floret obtuse or broadly acute, with a sharply differentiated, withering, membranous tip; lemma of perfect floret broadly oblong or ovate   5.   *E. crusgalli*

All spikelets awnless or with awns less than 15 mm long

Primary inflorescence branches simple, usually 2 cm or less long; spikelets small (2.5-3 mm long), awnless, arranged in 4 regular rows on branch rachis; palea of lower floret well-developed; hairs of inflorescence axis, branches and spikelets not papilla-based   6.   *E. colona*

Primary inflorescence branches often rebranched, the lower branches commonly more than 2 cm long; spikelets small or large, awnless or awned, in regular rows or not; palea of lower floret present or absent, when present then papilla-based hairs present on spikelets or on inflorescence branches

SUBFAMILY VI. PANICOIDEAE   531

Coriaceous apex of lemma of perfect floret narrowly acute or acuminate, with gradual transition to a stiff, membranous, usually mucronate tip; palea of lower floret well-developed
2. E. muricata

Coriaceous apex of lemma of perfect floret obtuse or broadly acute, with a sharply differentiated, withering membranous tip

Palea of lower floret absent or vestigial; spikelets awnless or with awns 1 cm or less long; setae of inflorescence branches absent or much shorter than spikelets
4B. E. crus-pavonis var. macera

Palea of lower floret well-developed

Lemma of perfect floret narrowly ovate or oblong; setae as long as or longer than spikelets not developed on inflorescence branches; panicle axis long, densely-flowered, with numerous branches

Spikelets with awns 2-9 mm long, these uniformly developed on all spikelets; lemma of perfect floret mostly 2.5-2.8 mm long; panicle axis curved or drooping, the branches more or less obscured by the crowded spikelets
4. E. crus-pavonis

Spikelets with awns 2-14 mm long, these often irregularly developed; lemma of the perfect floret usually 3 mm or more long; panicle axis erect, the branches not obscured by the spikelets
3. E. walteri

Lemma of perfect floret broadly ovate or oblong; setae as long as or longer than spikelets present, at least on lower inflorescence branches; panicle axis long or short, stiffly erect, with few or numerous branches
5. E. crusgalli

1. **Echinochloa polystachya** (H.B.K.) Hitchc., Contrib. U. S. Natl. Herb. 22:135. 1920. Coarse perennial with stout culms 1-2 m tall, these frequently decumbent at the base and rooting at the lower nodes. *Culm nodes* glabrous or minutely puberulent. *Leaves* glabrous or the lower sheaths hirsute or hispid. *Ligule* a ring of stiff yellowish hairs, present at least on lower leaves. *Blades* flat, to 3 cm broad and as much as 40 cm long. *Panicle* contracted, usually 15-30 cm long. *Main inflorescence axis and branches* sharply angled, with stout papilla-based setae on the ridges. *Spikelets* 4.5-6.5 mm long to base of awn. *Second glume* acuminate

or short awn-tipped. *Lemma of lower floret* with an awn 2-15 mm long. *Lower floret* with large, well-developed stamens and palea. *Lemma of upper floret* narrowly ovate or elliptic, the coriaceous apex obtuse, with a well-differentiated, thin, membranous, withering tip. *Chromosome number* not reported.

Distribution. Texas: Southern portion of region 2 in wet ditches and swales near coast. General: Southern Louisiana and Texas, south through the West Indies to Argentina.

Flowering period: Fall.

A specimen collected along the intercoastal canal in Jefferson County, Texas [*Williams* in June, 1950 (US)] appears to be the Mexican species *E. holciformis* (H.B.K.) Chase. This is similar to *E. polystachya* in being a perennial with well-developed, hairy ligules and large spikelets, and with stamens in the lower floret. Characteristically, *E. holciformis* has longer awns than *E. polystachya*. The specimen from Jefferson County, Texas, has puberulent culm nodes and awns to 20 mm long. The puberulent culm nodes would make this specimen referable to *E. spectabilis* (Nees) Link, in the interpretation of Swallen (1955).

2. **Echinochloa muricata** (Beauv.) Fern., Rhodora 17:106. 1915. Based on *Setaria muricata* Beauv. Plants annual, mostly 80-150 cm tall. *Culms* many-noded, erect or occasionally spreading from base. *Culm nodes* glabrous, slightly swollen. *Sheaths* glabrous, the basal sheaths prominently distichous in some plants. *Ligules* absent. *Blades* mostly 1-2.5 mm broad, glabrous, the margins minutely serrate. *Panicles* mostly 10-30 cm long, occasionally longer, typically with spreading, somewhat distant branches 2-8 cm long. *Spikelets* green or purple, broadly ovate, awned or awnless, usually conspicuously echinate with stout, papilla-based hairs. *Second glume and lemma of lower floret* about equal in length and both usually hispid with papilla-based hairs. *Lemma of lower floret* awnless or with an awn to 25 mm long. *Lower floret* neuter, with a well-developed, whitish or purplish palea. *Lemma of upper floret* broadly ovate, abruptly narrowing to an acuminate, non-withering tip. *Anthers* mostly 0.5-1 mm long. *Caryopses* broadly oblong or orbicular, whitish or brownish at maturity, 1.2-1.9 mm long. *Chromosome number*, $2n = 36$.

Spikelets 3.5 mm or more long to base of awn or mucronate tip of lemma of lower floret; lemma of lower floret usually with an awn 6 mm or more long, infrequently all spikelets awnless
2A.   E. muricata var. muricata

Spikelets less than 3.5 mm long to base of awn or mucronate tip of lemma of lower floret; lemma of lower floret awnless or with an awn to 6 (infrequently to 10) mm long
2B.   E. muricata var. microstachya

2A. **Echinochloa muricata** (Beauv.) Fern. var. **muricata.** *Echinochloa pungens* (Poir.) Rydb.

Distribution. Texas: Regions 1, 2, 3, 4, 5, 7 and 10 on open roadsides and ditchbanks and along swale areas. General: New Brunswick and Quebec, south to Florida and west to Minnesota, Oklahoma and Texas; a few records from New Mexico and north-central California.

Flowering period: Mostly July to November, occasionally flowering earlier.

2B. **Echinochloa muricata** (Beauv.) Fern. var. **microstachya** Wiegand, Rhodora 23:58. 1921. *E. microstachya* (Wiegand) Rydb. *E. occidentalis* (Wiegand) Rydb., *E.. crusgalli* (L.) Beauv. var. *mitis* (Pursh) Peterm. Fig. 279.

Distribution. Texas: Occasional in all regions in moist, open habitats, usually along swales, ponds and ditches. General: Quebec and Alberta, Canada, south to Florida, Texas and California and also in Chihuahua, Sonora and Durango, Mexico. Infrequent in the eastern United States but more common in the Midwest and the western states. In the eastern United States the separation of this variety from var. *muricata* is somewhat arbitrary, but west of the Mississippi var. *microstachya* is the only representative of the species in most regions.

Flowering period: Mostly July to November.

3. **Echinochloa walteri** (Pursh) Heller, Cat. N. Amer. Pl. ed. 2, p. 21. 1900. Fig. 280. Coarse annual with culms usually 1-2 m tall and forming large clumps but depauperate plants flowering when culms 50 cm or less tall. *Culm nodes* glabrous or sparsely hirsute. *Sheaths* typically hirsute or hispid with papilla-based hairs, especially towards apex, but sheaths frequently glabrous or merely rough-scabrous with antrorse spicules. *Blades* flat, glabrous or scabrous, mostly 0.8-3 cm broad. *Inflorescence* typically large and many-flowered, 10 to over 40 cm long and as much as 10 cm thick, with usually numerous, erect-appressed branches. *Inflorescence branches* bearing short, stout often papilla-based hairs or merely scabrous. *Spikelets* narrowly ovate or oblong, 3-5 mm long excluding the awn. *Glumes and lemma of lower floret* scabrous or hirsute, the hairs not or inconspicuously papilla-based. *Lemma of lower floret* typically with an awn 1.5-6 cm long but occasionally short-awned or awnless. *Lemma of upper floret* coriaceous, narrowly oblong, variable in size but commonly 3-4 mm long, tapering to an acute, usually mucronate tip. *Chromosome number,* $2n = 36$.

Distribution. Texas: Regions 1, 2, 3, 4 and 7. General: Ontario and Quebec, Canada, south through the eastern United States to Florida, westward to Minnesota, Arkansas and Texas; also in Cuba, eastern Mexico and Guatemala.

Fig. 279. *Echinochloa muricata* var. *microstachya*. Spikelet.

Fig. 280. *Echinochloa walteri*. Inflorescence. From Gould and Box, 1965.

SUBFAMILY VI. PANICOIDEAE   **535**

Flowering period: Mostly July to November.

Echinochloa walteri appears closely related to *Echinochloa crus-pavonis*, and the range of the two species overlap in Mississippi, Louisiana and Texas. Texas plants of *E. walteri* tend to have sparsely hirsute to nearly glabrous leaf sheaths.

4. **Echinochloa crus-pavonis** (H.B.K.) Schult., Mantissa 2:269. 1824. *Echinochloa crusgalli crus-pavonis* (H.B.K.) Hitchc. Large, coarse annual, to 1.5 m tall. *Culms* glabrous, many-noded, the nodes often slightly swollen. *Leaves* glabrous, green or purplish. *Ligule* absent. *Blades* mostly 0.7-2 cm broad. *Panicles* 10-30 cm long, densely-flowered. Long setae present or absent on main panicle axis and branches. *Spikelets* 2.8-3.1 mm long to base of awn (when present). *Lower floret* neuter, the lemma awnless or with an awn to 11 mm long. *Awns,* when developed, present on all spikelets and uniform in size. *Lemma of upper floret* grayish, narrowly elliptic, with an acute or obtuse, coriaceous apex and a well-differentiated, withering, membranous tip. *Embryo* about 0.7 as long as caryopses. *Chromosome number,* $2n = 36$.

Palea of lower floret present, well-developed
4A.   E. crus-pavonis var. crus-pavonis

Palea of lower floret absent or rudimentary
4B.   E. crus-pavonis var. macera

4A. **Echinochloa crus-pavonis** (H.B.K.) Schult. var. **crus-pavonis.** Plants frequently 1-1.5 m tall. *Leaf blades* typically 1-2 cm broad. *Panicles* large, commonly 15-30 cm long, densely-flowered, usually nodding and curved at maturity. *Spikelets* usually with awns 2-9 mm long.

Distribution. Texas: Not known definitely to occur in the State but its occurrence is indicated. General: In the United States, southern Florida, Mississippi, Louisiana and (?) Texas; also present in California where it appears introduced; a common grass in eastern Mexico and Central and South America.

Flowering period: Mostly late summer and fall.

4B. **Echinochloa crus-pavonis** (H.B.K.) Schult. var. **macera** (Wiegand) Gould, Southw. Naturalist 15:391. 1971. Plants mostly 60-100 cm tall, with leaf blades usually 7-15 mm broad. *Panicles* usually 10-20 cm long, stiffly erect on a relatively stout central axis. *Spikelets* usually awnless or lemma of lower floret minutely awn-tipped, infrequently the spikelets with awns 6-9 mm long. *Lemma of lower floret* absent or minute.

Distribution. Texas: Throughout the State except in region 1, probably the most common and widespread *Echinochloa* in Texas, growing in ditches, field borders, vacant lots and other semi-disturbed habitats. General: Mississippi to Texas, Arizona and California and south into the border states of Mexico.

Flowering period: Mostly July to November.

5. **Echinochloa crusgalli** (L.) Beauv., Ess. Agrost. 53:161. 1812. Plants annual, with stiffly erect or decumbent-spreading culms, these mostly 30-100 cm tall but occasionally as much as 2 m in length. *Culms* glabrous, many-noded, the nodes slightly swollen. *Sheaths* glabrous. *Ligule* absent. *Blades* mostly 0.5-2.5 cm broad and to 40 cm long, scabrous or sparsely hirsute, the margins finely serrate. *Panicles* mostly from 10-25 cm long, with usually 5-25 appressed or spreading branches, the longer branches rebranched. *Spikelets* mostly 2.8-4 mm long and 1.1-2.3 mm broad, ovate or elliptic, awned or awnless, variously scabrous and hirsute or hispid to nearly glabrous. *Lower floret* neuter, the lemma awnless, short-awned or with an awn to over 5 cm long in the typical variety, the palea large, well-developed. Coriaceous apex of the lemma of upper floret obtuse or broadly acute, with a sharply differentiated, withering, membranous tip. *Anthers* 0.5-1 mm long. *Caryopses* ovate or elliptic, 1.3-2.2 mm long and 1-1.8 mm broad. *Embryo* 0.7-0.8 as long as caryopsis. *Chromosome number,* $2n=54$.

Panicle branches erect or spreading, with awnless or awned spikelets, these not densely crowded on the branches; spikelets straw-colored or greenish, often purple-tinged   5A. *E. crusgalli* var. *crusgalli*

Panicle branches erect-appressed, densely-flowered with plump, awnless, usually grayish-purple spikelets   5B. *E. crusgalli* var. *frumentacea*

5A. Echinochloa crusgalli var. crusgalli. BARNYARDGRASS. Fig. 281.

Distribution. Texas: Occasional throughout the State as a weed of roadways, ditchbanks and field borders and along trampled or otherwise disturbed swale areas. General: Apparently not native to North America but now widespread throughout the United States and southern Canada. It also is occasional in Mexico.

Flowering period: July to November.

Chromosome records of $2n=36$, 42, 48 and 54 have been reported for plants identified as *E. crusgalli*. Most counts, and all those made in the present study, have been $2n=54$. It is believed by the writer that counts other than $2n=54$ for North American plants of *E. crusgalli* are inaccurate, the result of misidentification or possibly based on aneuploid hybrid plants. Mexican specimens upon which counts of $2n=36$ were based (Gould, 1966) have been reidentified as *E. crus-pavonis*.

In the treatments of Hitchcock (1935) and Chase (1951) all plants herein referred to *E. muricata* var. *muricata, E. muricata* var. *microstachya* and *E. crus-pavonis* var. *macera* were included in *E. crusgalli*.

Fig. 281. *Echinochloa crusgalli.* Inflorescence and spikelet. From Gould and Box, 1965.

5B. **Echinochloa crusgalli** var. **frumentacea** (Roxb.) F. W. Wight, Cent. Dict. Sup. 810. 1909.

Distribution. Texas: Region 2. General: Native to southeastern Asia but widely cultivated in the United States and southern Canada as Japanese millet or "billion-dollar grass." This coarse, succulent annual has been collected at widely scattered localities in the United States but apparently does not persist out of cultivation.

Flowering period: Late summer and fall.

6. **Echinochloa colona** (L.) Link, Hort. Berol. 2:209. 1833. JUNGLE-RICE. Fig. 282. Annual with slender, weak, freely-branching culms 10-70

538   THE GRASSES OF TEXAS

cm long. *Leaves* glabrous, without ligules, the blades thin and flat, 3-6 (infrequently -9) mm broad. In the "zonale form," the blades having purple bars, "v's" or blotches. *Inflorescence* short, few-flowered, with usually 3-7 unbranched primary branches, these 1-2 (infrequently -3) cm long. *Nodes of main inflorescence axis and branches* glabrous or with a few short to moderately long hairs, these never papilla-based. *Spikelets* 2.5-3 mm long, awnless, usually inconspicuously pubescent with fine, short hairs, these never papilla-based. *Palea of lower floret* well developed. *Lemma of upper floret* elliptic, usually 2.6-2.9 mm long, the firm portion rounded at apex. *Chromosome number*, $2n=54$.

Distribution. Texas: Throughout the State and in all regions. An adventive weed that thrives in disturbed soils and is frequent in gardens, fields and waste places. General: Frequent in the southeastern and southern states, where it is adventive. Widespread in tropical and subtropical regions of both hemispheres.

Flowering period: Mostly late summer and fall.

102. SACCIOLEPIS Nash*

A genus of about 30 species in the tropics and subtropics of both hemispheres.

1. **Sacciolepis striata** (L.) Nash, Bull. Torrey. Bot. Club 30:383. 1903. AMERICAN CUPSCALE. Fig. 283. Perennial with culms 1.5 m or more tall from erect or more often decumbent or stoloniferous bases that root freely at the nodes. *Sheaths* glabrous to hispid with papilla-based hairs, the upper margins usually ciliate or puberulent. *Ligule* a minute, fringed membrane. *Blades* thin, flat, mostly 8-20 cm long and 6-15 mm broad, often ciliate on the lower margins. *Inflorescence* a contracted, elongate panicle mostly 8-25 cm long, with spikelets borne on short, slender pedicels. Disarticulation below spikelet. *Spikelets* glabrous, awnless, asymmetrical at base, 3.5-4.3 mm long, relatively narrow. *First glume* acute, greatly reduced and usually one-fourth or less as long as second. *Second glume* with 7-11 strong, parallel nerves, inflated-saccate at base. *Lemma of lower floret* usually 3-5-nerved, about as long as second glume. *Lemma and palea of upper floret* indurate, smooth and shiny, rounded at apex, much shorter than second glume and lemma of upper floret. *Chromosome number*, $2n=36$.

Distribution. Texas: Regions 1 and 3, growing in moist soil along ponds, ditches and streams. General: Throughout the southeastern states, from New Jersey and Florida to eastern Oklahoma and eastern Texas; also in the West Indies.

Flowering period: Mostly late August to November.

*After this publication had gone to press, the presence of a second *Sacciolepis* species in Texas was brought to the attention of the author. *Sacciolepis indica* (L.) Chase, native to Asia, recently was collected at two localities in Newton County (region 1). This species typically has leaf blades 3-6 mm broad and a tightly contracted inflorescence 5 mm or less broad and 2-5 (-7) cm long.

Fig. 282.   *Echinochloa colona*. Plant and spikelet. From Gould and Box, 1965.

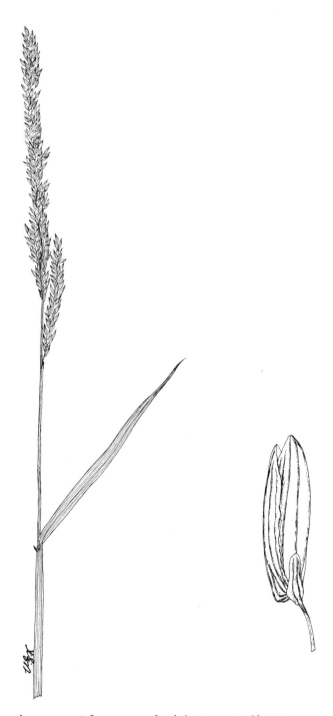

Fig. 283. *Sacciolepis striata*. Inflorescence and spikelet. From Gould, 1968.

SUBFAMILY VI. PANICOIDEAE   541

103. RHYNCHELYTRUM Nees

A genus of 35 to 40 species, mostly native to Africa.

1. **Rhynchelytrum repens** (Willd.) C. E. Hubb., Kew Bull. Inf. 1934: 110. 1934. NATAL GRASS. Fig. 284. Tufted perennial with geniculate-erect culms mostly 0.7-1 m tall. *Culm nodes* puberulent. *Herbage* variously hispid to nearly glabrous. *Ligule* a fringe of hairs 0.5-1 mm long. *Blades* narrow, flat or folded, mostly 8-18 cm long and 2-5 mm broad. *Inflorescence* a loosely contracted panicle mostly 6-20 cm long, with slender, curving, secondary branches and pedicels and villous, purple spikelets. Disarticulation at base of spikelet. *First glume* minute, the second glume and lemma of lower floret about equal, silky-villous with fine hairs, notched and minutely awned at apex. *Lemma of upper floret* much shorter than second glume and lemma of lower floret, narrow, membranous, glabrous, the margins thin and not in-rolled over palea.

Distribution. Texas: Region 6 along roadways, ditchbanks and other areas of moderately disturbed, well-drained soils. General: An African species that has become well established in the warmer regions of the Americas. Reported in the United States from Florida, Texas and Arizona.

Flowering period: Throughout the year under favorable temperature and moisture conditions.

104. SETARIA Beauv.

Cespitose annuals and perennials with stiffly erect or geniculate culms. *Ligule* a short membrane fringed with hairs. *Blades* thin, flat, narrow to broad. *Inflorescence* a usually contracted, densely-flowered, bristly panicle, the spikelets subsessile on main axis and on short branches. Some or all spikelets subtended by 1 to several persistent bristles (reduced pedicels or branches), the spikelets disarticulating above the bristles. *First glume* present but short. *Second glume* equal to or shorter than lemma of the lower floret. *Lemma and palea of upper floret* indurate, rounded at apex, usually finely to coarsely transverse-rugose.

A genus of about 125 species, mostly in Africa but some in the warmer parts of all the continents. In a monographic treatment of the genus, Rominger (1962) listed 43 species for North America, about half of which occur in the United States.

Bristles usually present only at base of terminal spikelet of each branchlet, as an extension of the branchlet axis

    Blades long, narrow, frequently involute, mostly 1-3 (-4) mm broad and at least some blades 13-20 cm or more long; blades tapering to an extremely narrow base   1. *S. reverchonii*

Fig. 284. *Rhynchelytrum repens*. Inflorescence and spikelet. From Gould, 1968.

SUBFAMILY VI. PANICOIDEAE   **543**

Blades narrow or broad, flat, mostly 5-10 (-13) cm long; blades not or only slightly narrowing towards base

Blades 4 mm or less broad; inflorescence bristles shorter than spikelets
2. *S. ramiseta*

Blades, at least some, 4.5-7 mm broad; inflorescence bristles often longer than spikelets
3. *S. firmula*

Bristles present below all or nearly all spikelets

Bristles 4-12 below each spikelet; lemma of upper floret coarsely transverse-rugose; inflorescence contracted, spikelike

Plants perennial, with hard culm bases and usually short, knotty rhizomes
4. *S. geniculata*

Plants annual, the culm bases not hard and wiry
5. *S. glauca*

Bristles 1-3 below each spikelet

Bristles retrorsely scabrous

Margins of upper sheath hyaline, glabrous; leaf blades conspicuously hispid with papilla-based hairs on both surfaces
6. *S. adhaerans*

Margins of upper sheaths pilose; leaf blades scabrous or occasionally with scattered hairs on upper surface
7. *S. verticillata*

Bristles antrorsely scabrous only

Plants annual though often coarse and robust

Lemma of upper floret coarsely transversely wrinkled and rugose
8. *S. corrugata*

Lemma of upper floret finely rugose or smooth

Panicle contracted but relatively loose, the main axis visible for most of its length
11. *S. grisebachii*

Panicle dense, cylindrical and spicate, the primary panicle usually not visible except below

Panicle mostly 3-13 cm long; culms mostly 25-100 cm tall
9. *S. viridis*

Panicle mostly 18-40 cm long; culms mostly 1.5-4 m tall
10. *S. magna*

Plants perennial

Spikelets 2.9-3.4 mm long

Panicles 2-4 (-6) cm long; culms usually branching at upper nodes; spikelets 1.9-2.1 mm long; herbage dark green
12. *S. texana*

Panicles 6-20 cm or more long; culms seldom branching at upper nodes; spikelets 2.0-2.6 mm long; herbage dark or light green

Palea of lower floret nearly as long as palea of upper floret; spikelets mostly 1.9-2.1 mm long at maturity, strongly inflated and appearing globose; blades, at least some, 7-15 mm broad   14. *S. macrostachya*

Palea of lower floret usually one-half to three-fourths as long as palea of upper floret; spikelets mostly 2.1-2.7 mm long at maturity, not strongly inflated and appearing globose; blades narrow or broad

Blades typically 2-5 (-7) mm wide, flat or folded, rarely pubescent; panicle usually columnar; bristles usually appressed, 4-15 mm long; culms mostly stiffly erect, infrequently geniculate, herbage light green or glaucous
13. *S. leucopila*

Blades typically 9-20 mm wide, flat, commonly pubescent; panicle usually tapering from base to apex; bristles spreading, 10-35 mm long; culms usually geniculate and curving-erect; herbage dark green   15. *S. scheelei*

Spikelets 2.7 mm or less long   16. *S. villosissima*

1. **Setaria reverchonii** (Vasey) Pilger, in Engl. & Prantl, Pflanzenfam. ed. 2. 14e. 72. 1940. *Panicum reverchonii* Vasey. REVERCHON BRISTLE-GRASS. Fig. 285. Tufted perennial with stiffly erect culms mostly 35-70 cm tall from a hard, often somewhat rhizomatous base. *Basal scale leaves*

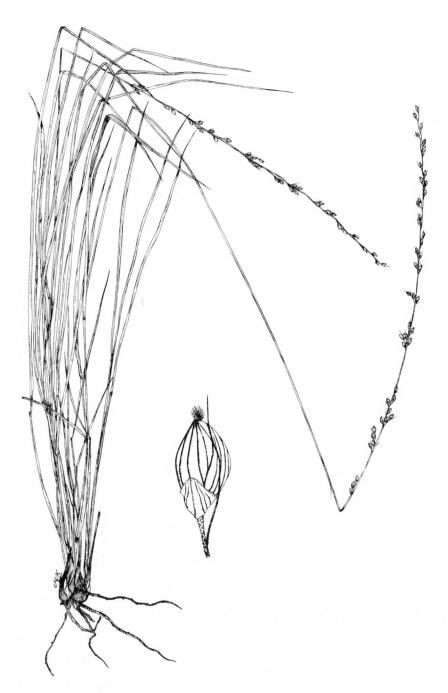

Fig. 285. *Setaria reverchonii*. Plant and spikelet. From Gould and Box, 1965.

546   THE GRASSES OF TEXAS

hirsute or villous, the lower sheaths also more or less hairy, at least on margins. *Ligule* a minute membrane fringed with soft hairs 1-2 mm long. *Blades* long and narrow, flat or more frequently involute on drying, usually narrower at base than sheath apex. *Inflorescence* a narrow, contracted, spikelike panicle 6-20 cm long, the spikelets short-pediceled on short, appressed branches and on upper portion of main axis. *Branchlets and main axis* terminated by a short bristle which subtends the terminal spikelets. *Bristles* shorter to considerably longer than spikelets but rarely exceeding 6 mm in length. Disarticulation at base of spikelet, the bristles persistent. *Spikelets* mostly 3-4 mm long but occasionally only 2.5-2.6 mm in length. *First glume* about one-half or slightly less as long as second glume and lemma of lower floret. *Lemma of upper floret* conspicuously rugose. *Chromosome numbers* reported, $2n = 36$ and 72.

Distribution. Texas: Reported from all regions of the State except regions 1 and 4, probably most frequent on the rocky, well-drained limestone soils of the Edwards Plateau. General: Southern Oklahoma and Texas.

Flowering period: Apparently flowering year-long under favorable growing conditions but most herbarium collections made March-June.

A variable species, closely related to *S. ramiseta* and *S. firmula* which tend to replace it on the semi-arid, sandy plains of southern Texas.

2. **Setaria ramiseta** (Scribn.) Pilger, in Engl. & Prantl, Pflanzenfam. ed. 2. 14e:72. 1940. *Panicum ramisetum* Scribn. Fig. 286. Perennial with culms 30-60 cm tall, tufted from a hard, knotty, rhizomatous base, the short rhizomes and culm bases usually with closely imbricated scale-leaves, these often villous-pubescent. *Lower sheaths* usually sparsely hirsute. *Ligule* a short membrane with soft hairs 1-2 mm or more long. *Blades* flat, mostly 2-4 mm broad and 4-10 (-13) cm long, not or only slightly narrowed at base. *Spikelets* mostly 2.5-3 mm long, exceeding in length the bristles terminating the branchlets. *Lemma of upper floret* rugose. *Chromosome number*, $2n = 36$.

Distribution. Texas: Regions 6 and 7 and the southern portions of regions 2, 5 and 8. General: Texas and northeastern Mexico (northern Tamaulipas, Nuevo Leon and Coahuila).

Flowering period: Mostly January to June and occasionally in the late summer.

Setaria ramiseta is closely related to *S. reverchonii* from which it differs in the shorter, consistently flat blades, broader blade base, consistently short bristles and small spikelets, more pronounced rhizome development, adaptation to non-limey soils and more southerly general distribution. It also is closely related to the broad-bladed *S. firmula*.

SUBFAMILY VI. PANICOIDEAE   547

Fig. 286.   *Setaria ramiseta*. Plant and spikelet. From Gould and Box, 1965.

548   THE GRASSES OF TEXAS

3. **Setaria firmula** (Hitchc. & Chase) Pilger, in Engl. & Prantl, Pflanzen-fam. ed. 2. 14 e:72. 1940. *Panicum firmulum* Hitchc. & Chase. Fig. 287. Tufted perennial with culms mostly 25-40 cm tall from a hard, knotty, rhizomatous base. *Ligule* with a ring of hairs 1.5-2 mm long. *Blades* mostly 3-10 (-12) cm long and at least some 4.5-7 mm broad, abruptly constricted and appearing truncate at base. *Inflorescence* a contracted, spikelike panicle 6-15 cm long, the short branchlets and tip of main culm terminating in a bristle. *Spikelets* mostly 2.8-3.5 mm long, the terminal spikelets usually much exceeded in length by the bristle. *Lemma of upper floret* rugose. *Chromosome number*, 2n=36.

Distribution. Texas: Region 6 and the southern portion of region 2. General: Reported only from southern Texas but to be expected in northeastern Mexico.

Flowering period: Throughout the year under favorable growing conditions, most records January-June.

A species closely related to both *Setaria reverchonii* and *S. ramiseta* from which it is most readily distinguished by the short broad blades. For the most part the culms are shorter than in *S. reverchonii*, the plant base is more rhizomatous and the blades are much shorter. The spikelets of *S. firmula* generally are larger than those of *S. ramiseta*, and the bristle subtending the terminal spikelets is longer.

4. **Setaria geniculata** (Lam.) Beauv., Ess. Agrost. 51, 178. 1812. KNOT-ROOT BRISTLEGRASS. Fig. 288. Perennial with tufted culms 30-100 cm or more tall from short, knotty rhizomes. *Nodes* glabrous. Leaves typically glabrous or inconspicuously scabrous, sometimes with long hairs in vicinity of ligule. *Sheaths* usually keeled, at least the lower ones. *Ligule* a short fringed membrane. *Blades* flat, 2-8 mm broad, mostly 6-25 cm long. *Panicles* densely-flowered, cylindrical, mostly 3-8 cm long. *Panicle axis* puberulent, obscured by the spikelets. *Bristles* 4-12 below each spikelet, antrorsely scabrous, yellow, tawny, green or purple in color, variable in length but mostly 5-10 mm long. *Spikelets* 2.5-3 mm long, elliptical, turgid. *Glumes* thin, shorter than spikelet, the first about one-third as long as spikelet, the second two-thirds to three-fourths as long. *Lemma of lower floret* about as long as lemma of upper floret. *Lemma of upper floret* transversely rugose, acute to slightly beaked at apex. *Chromosome numbers* reported, 2n=36 and 72.

Distribution. Texas: Reported from all regions of the State, usually growing in moist habitats along streams, ditches and lake borders. General: Apparently native to the Western Hemisphere and widely distributed throughout the United States, Mexico, Central America and South America. Rominger (1962) stated that this probably is the most widespread species of *Setaria* in North America.

Flowering period: Flowering almost throughout the year under favorable growing conditions.

Fig. 287. *Setaria firmula*. Plant and spikelet. From Gould and Box, 1965.

550   THE GRASSES OF TEXAS

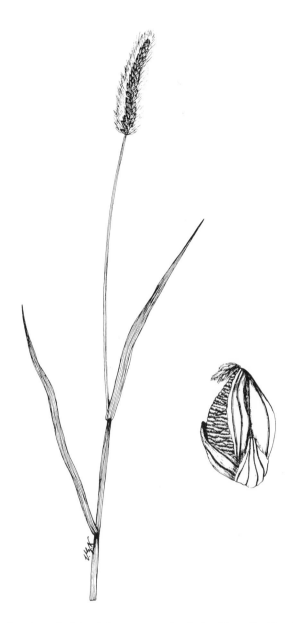

Fig. 288. *Setaria geniculata.* Inflorescence and spikelet. From Gould and Box, 1965.

Despite its frequent occurrence, *S. geniculata* seldom is abundant in any particular locality. Considerable morphological variation is exhibited by populations of this species throughout its range, and numerous names have been applied to segregates from different regions.

SUBFAMILY VI. PANICOIDEAE   551

5. **Setaria glauca** (L.) Beauv., Ess. Agrost. 51, 178. 1812. *Setaria lutescens* (Weigel.) F. T. Hubb. YELLOW BRISTLEGRASS. Tufted annual with culms 20-120 cm tall, usually geniculate below and branching at lower nodes. *Nodes* glabrous. *Sheaths* glabrous, compressed-keeled. *Ligule* a short ciliate membrane. *Blades* 4-10 mm broad, to 30 cm long, loosely twisted, scabrous on upper surface and with long hairs near throat. *Panicle* densely-flowered, cylindrical, mostly 3-15 cm long, the closely-placed spikelets and bristles obscuring the puberulent or hispid main axis. *Bristles* usually 4-12 below each spikelet, antrorsely scabrous, yellow at maturity, mostly 3-8 mm long. *Spikelets* mostly 2.7-3.3 mm long, conspicuously turgid but otherwise similar to those of *S. geniculata*. *Lemma of upper floret* strongly rugose in fine, transverse lines. *Chromosome numbers* reported, $2n=36$ and 72.

Distribution. Texas: Occasional on disturbed soils throughout the State except in region 6. General: Native to the Old World, this species is now frequent throughout temperate and subtropical regions of North America as a weed of cultivated fields.

Flowering period: Mostly June to September.

Setaria glauca is very similar to *S. geniculata* in most characteristics. Its annual habit is the best distinguishing characteristic, but for the most part it also has slightly larger, broader spikelets and panicles with relatively fewer spikelets in each verticil of branches.

6. **Setaria adhaerans** (Forssk.) Chiov., in Nuovo. Giorn. Bot. Ital. 26:77. 1919. Fig. 289. Annual with weak, often geniculate or trailing culms 25-70 cm tall. *Nodes* glabrous, dark colored. *Leaf sheaths* glabrous on the margins. *Ligule* a ring of white hairs 1-2 mm long. *Blades* thin, flat, 5-13 mm broad and 5-20 cm long, hispid on both surfaces with short, papilla-based hairs and also often strigose with longer hairs. *Inflorescence* a dense, spikelike panicle 2-6 (-8) cm long, with a hispid main axis and spikelets clustered on short, verticilled branchlets. *Bristles* typically 1 below each spikelet, the bristle retrorsely scabrous-hispid, usually equaling or greatly exceeding the spikelet in length. *Spikelets* 1.5-1.8 (-2) mm long, oblong-elliptic. *First glume* thin, rounded, one-half or slightly less as long as spikelet. *Palea of lower floret* less than one-half the length of the lemma. *Lemma and palea of upper floret* finely transversely rugose. *Chromosome number*, $2n=18$.

Distribution. Texas: Regions 6, 7 and 10; one collection from College Station in region 3. General: Throughout tropical-subtropical regions of the world. In North America known from southern Bermuda, Cuba, the United States, Mexico and Central America.

Flowering period: Mostly February to July.

A weedy annual of disturbed habitats, often present in the shade of trees or tall weeds. United States plants of this species were referred to *Setaria verticillata* (L.) Beauv. by Chase in Hitchcock's Manual (1951).

Fig. 289. *Setaria adhaerans.* Spikelet. From Gould and Box, 1965.

7. **Setaria verticillata** (L.) Beauv., Ess. Agrost. 51, 178. 1812. HOOKED BRISTLEGRASS. Annual, generally similar to *Setaria adhaerens* but differing in the pilose sheath margins, the absence of papilla-based hairs on both surfaces of the blades and in having spikelets 2-2.3 mm long rather than usually less than 2 mm long as in *S. adhaerens. Chromosome number,* $2n = 36$.

Distribution. Texas: The collection *McCart 9281* from Brownwood, Brown County (region 5), is the only Texas record of this species known to the author. General: Native to the Old World, now established as a weed throughout the cool and temperate regions of North America.

Flowering period: Summer.

8. **Setaria corrugata** (Ell.) Schult., in Roem. & Schult. Syst. Veg. Mant. 2:276. 1824. Coarse annual with culms mostly 30-100 cm tall, the culms usually decumbent or geniculate at base and often rooting at lower nodes. *Lowermost nodes* often scabrous or hispid. *Sheaths,* at least the lower, hispid or strigose. *Ligule* with a ring of hairs 1-2 mm long. *Blades* thin, flat, mostly 4-7 (-10) mm broad and 15-30 cm long. *Panicle* densely contracted, cylindrical, 3-15 cm long, the main axis scabrous and hispid, obscured by the bristles and spikelets. *Bristles* antrorsely scabrous, mostly 7-15 mm long, usually 1-3 below each spikelet. *Spikelets* 1.8-2.5 mm long. *First glume* one-third to one-half as long as spikelet. *Second glume* about two-thirds as long as mature spikelet. *Lemma of lower floret* about equal to that of upper floret. *Palea of lower floret* about two-thirds as long as lemma. *Lemma of upper floret* coarsely transversely ridged and rugose, apiculate at the apex. *Chromosome number* not reported.

Distribution. Texas: Infrequent, known from Jasper and Walker counties (region 1) and Harris County (region 2). General: Sandy, usually disturbed soils from North Carolina to Florida and west along the Gulf of Mexico to eastern Texas.

Flowering period: Summer.

9. **Setaria viridis** (L.) Beauv., Ess. Agrost. 51, 171, 178, pl. 13. fig. 3. 1812. GREEN BRISTLEGRASS. Annual with erect or geniculate culms mostly 25-100 cm tall; nodes glabrous or the lower hirsute. *Sheaths* pilose on margins. *Ligule* a membrane fringed with hairs 1-2 mm long. *Blades* flat or folded, mostly 3-10 mm broad and 8-20 cm long, glabrous or scabrous. *Panicle* narrow, cylindrical, 2-15 cm long, typically densely-flowered and with the scabrous-hispid main axis obscured. *Bristles* antrorsely scabrous, green or infrequently purple, 5-10 mm long, 1-3 below each spikelet. *Spikelets* 1.8-2.6 mm long. *First glume* one-third to one-half as long as spikelet. *Second glume* slightly shorter than lemmas of lower and upper florets at maturity. *Palea of lower floret* variable in development, from vestigial to two-thirds as long as lemma of lower floret. *Lemma of upper floret* finely rugose, not wrinkled. *Chromosome number,* $2n = 18$.

Distribution. Texas: Regions 4, 5, 6, 7, 8, 9 and 10, absent or rare in the eastern portion of the State and present only in the northern portion of region 6. General: Throughout temperate regions of the world and to a lesser extent present in subtropical regions. Apparently introduced in North America where it grows mainly as a weed of fields and waste places.

Flowering period: Mid April to October.

Closely related to *Setaria viridis* and possibly not specifically distinct is the cultivated foxtail millet, *S. italica* (L.) Beauv. Characteristically, plants of *S. italica* differ from those of *S. viridis* in being larger and coarser and with larger, lobed panicles. The grain of *S. italica* is smooth and large, generally about 3 mm long, and disarticulation characteristically is above the glumes. Foxtail millet occasionally is planted in Texas but does not persist in nature. Depauperate, weedy plants often are generally similar to *S. viridis*.

10. **Setaria magna** Griseb., Fl. Brit. W. Ind. 554. 1864. GIANT BRIS-TLEGRASS. Coarse annual with culms mostly 1.5-4 m tall and 1-2 cm thick at the base. *Sheaths* pubescent on the margins. *Hairs of ligule* mostly 2-3 cm long. *Blades* long, broad, flat, mostly 20-40 cm long and 1-3 cm broad, scabrous, especially on adaxial surface. *Panicles* contracted, densely-flowered, usually 14-45 cm long and 1.5-3 cm in diameter, the main axis scabrous and densely villous. *Bristles* 1-2 cm long, yellowish, usually 1-2 below each spikelet. *Spikelets* 2-2.5 mm long, with a well-developed lower floret that is staminate or occasionally perfect and developing a fertile caryopsis. *Lemma of upper floret* smooth and shiny. *Chromosome number,* $2n = 36$.

Distribution. Texas: Region 2, infrequent. General: Along coastal marshes, canals and ditches from New Jersey to Florida and eastern Texas, in saline marshes of Arkansas and introduced in Bermuda, Puerto Rico, Guadeloupe, Jamaica, Yucatan and Costa Rica.

Flowering period: Late summer and fall.

This is the largest *Setaria* in North America. It is restricted to brackish coastal sites except for inland saline marsh locations in Arkansas and Florida.

11. **Setaria grisebachii** Fourn., Mex. Pl. 2:45. 1886. GRISEBACH BRISTLEGRASS. Annual with erect or geniculate-spreading culms mostly 40-80 cm tall but occasionally taller. *Nodes* hirsute. Sheaths pilose on the margins. *Ligular hairs* about 1 mm long. *Blades* sparsely short hispid on both surfaces, mostly 6-20 cm long and 5-13 cm broad but variable and occasionally much larger. *Panicles* variable but mostly 3-18 (-25) cm long, usually sparsely-flowered, contracted and with essentially no elongate branches or with numerous spreading, widely-spaced branches 2 cm or more in length. *Panicle axis* sparsely hispid, usually visible for most of its length. *Bristles* minutely antrorsely scabrous, 0.5-2 cm in length, usually single below the spikelets. *Spikelets* 1.6-2.2 mm long. *Palea of lower floret* usually about one-third as long as the lemma. *Lemma and palea of upper floret* minutely rugose. *Chromosome number* not reported.

Distribution. Texas: Regions 6 and 10 and the western portion of region 7. General: Southwestern Oklahoma and Texas to Arizona and south through Mexico to Central America, usually at elevations above 750 m altitude (Rominger, 1962). One collection from near sea level in Cameron County, Texas (*Shiller G-1113,*), appears referable to this species.

Flowering period: Mostly September and October.

12. **Setaria texana** W.H.P. Emery, Bull. Torrey. Bot. Club 84:97. 1957. Fig. 290. Tufted perennial with strictly erect or decumbent-based, wiry culms 15-70 (-90) cm tall. *Culms* freely branched at and above base. *Nodes* glabrous. *Sheaths* ciliate on margins. *Ligules* ciliate with hairs to 1 mm long. *Blades* thin, mostly flat, 5-15 (-20) cm long and 2-4 (-5) mm broad, scabrous above, smooth or slightly scabrous below, dark green. *Panicles* contracted, spikelike, tapering above, 2-4 (-6) cm long and 5 mm or less broad. *Panicle axis* puberulent. *Bristles* 3-10 mm long, usually solitary below spikelets. *Spikelets* 1.8-2.1 mm long. *First glume* less than one-half as long as spikelet. *Second glume* about two-thirds as long as mature lemma of upper floret. *Palea of lower floret* rudimentary to slightly more than one-half the length of lemma. *Lemma and palea of upper floret* finely rugose in transverse lines. *Chromosome number*, $2n = 36$.

Distribution. Texas: Region 6, southern portion of region 7 and southeastern portion of region 10. General: Southern Texas and the adjacent portions of northern Mexico.

Flowering period: Apparently flowering throughout the year under favorable growing conditions.

This Texas-northern Mexico endemic is closely related to forms of *Setaria leucopila*, and *S. texana* plants are distinguished from depauperate plants of *S. leucopila* with difficulty. For the most part, *S. texana* grows in partial shade and is particularly well adapted to growth in the sandy-soiled oak motts of southern Texas.

Fig. 290. *Setaria texana*. Inflorescence. From Gould and Box, 1965.

556   THE GRASSES OF TEXAS

13. **Setaria leucopila** (Scribn. & Merr.) K. Schum., in Just, Bot. Jahresb. 28:417. 1902. PLAINS BRISTLEGRASS. Fig. 291. Strong perennial with usually pale or glaucous herbage and stiffly erect or geniculate culms mostly 25-100 cm tall. *Culms* infrequently branched above, scabrous and often somewhat pubescent below the nodes. *Sheaths* villous along upper margins. *Ligule* fringed with hairs 1-2 mm long. *Blades* flat or folded, 8-25 cm long, typically 2-5 mm broad but occasionally broader, glabrous, scabrous or infrequently pubescent. *Panicles* densely-flowered, at least some 6-15 cm long but shorter in some forms, 0.7-1.5 cm in diameter. *Panicle axis* scabrous and more or less villous. *Bristles* mostly 4-15 mm long, usually solitary below each spikelet. *Spikelets* 2.1-2.7 mm long at maturity. *Palea of the lower floret* one-half to three-fourths as long as lemma. *Lemma and palea of upper floret* finely rugose and with transverse wrinkles, the palea flat or slightly convex, not gibbous. *Chromosome numbers* reported, $2n=54$, 68 and 72.

Distribution. Texas: Throughout the drier portions of the State, reported from all regions except regions 1, 3 and 4. General: Southern Colorado, Texas, New Mexico and Arizona, south to central Mexico.

Flowering period: May to November.

An important native forage species, usually not occurring in large or dense stands but frequent throughout its area of distribution. Plains bristlegrass primarily is adapted to open sites and is most frequent on well-drained soils along gullies, stream courses and other areas occasionally with abundant moisture.

Setaria leucopila is a highly variable species, formerly included in *S. macrostachya*. Emery (1957, 1957a) investigated this complex and determined the basic differences between the two species. He also described *S. texana* of southern Texas from plants previously referred to *S. macrostachya*. Relationships within populations referred to *S. leucopila* and of plants intermediate in characteristics between this species and *S. macrostachya*, *S. texana* and *S. scheelei* still are poorly understood. Hybridization probably is not infrequent.

14. **Setaria macrostachya** H.B.K., Nov. Gen. & Sp. 1:110. 1815. Cespitose perennial with stiffly erect or geniculate culms mostly 60-120 cm tall. *Ligules* densely hirsute with hairs 2-4 mm long. *Blades* flat, mostly 7-15 mm broad, strongly scabrous above. *Panicles* densely-flowered, 10-30 cm long, 1-2 cm thick and with a scabrous, sparsely hirsute axis. *Bristles* mostly 10-20 cm long, usually solitary below each spikelet. *Spikelets* small, globose at maturity, seldom over 2 mm long and with a strongly inflated and rather coarsely rugose lemma of upper floret. *Palea of lower floret* narrow but about equaling palea of upper floret in length. *Chromosome number*, $2n=54$.

Distribution. Texas: Region 6 and southern portion of region 2. General: Southern Texas and Arizona, south through the highlands of northern and central Mexico.

Fig. 291. *Setaria leucopila*. Plant and spikelet. From Gould and Box, 1965.

Flowering period: May to November.

As interpreted by Hitchcock (1935) and Chase (1951), *Setaria macro-stachya* included all plants herein referred to S. *texana* and S. *leucopila*. Plants of the entire complex were referred to as "plains bristlegrass," a name now being applied to the common species of the southwestern United States, S. *leucopila*.

15. **Setaria scheelei** (Steud.) Hitchc., Proc. Biol. Soc., Wash. 41:163. 1928. Fig. 292. Coarse, cespitose perennial with stout, usually geniculate-spreading culms mostly 70-130 cm tall. *Culm nodes* often puberulent. *Ligule* with hairs 1-2 mm long. *Blades* thin, flat, dark green, mostly 15-30 (-50) cm long and 5-18 mm broad, scabrous and usually finely pubescent. *Panicles* mostly 15-35 cm long but shorter on secondary shoots, typically tapering from base to apex but not infrequently columnar. *Panicle branches* all short and contracted or more commonly the lower ones 1-4 cm long and spreading. *Panicle axis* visible for most of its length or obscured by the spikelets. *Bristles* usually solitary below each spikelet, mostly 15-35 mm long but occasionally shorter. *Spikelets* 2.1-2.6 mm long, ovate or ovate-oblong. *Palea of lower floret* one-half to two-thirds as long as palea of upper floret. *Lemma of upper floret* conspicuously rugose. *Chromosome number*, 2n=54.

Distribution. Texas: Regions 6, 7, 8, 9 and 10 and the southern portions of regions 2 and 4. General: Texas and Arizona (?), south to northern Mexico.

Flowering period: Mainly May to November.

A shade-tolerant grass, usually growing in shaded canyons and open woodlands and frequently abundant.

16. **Setaria villosissima** (Scribn. & Merr.) K. Schum., in Just, Bot. Jahresb. 28:417. 1902. HAIRYLEAF BRISTLEGRASS. Loosely cespitose perennial. *Culms* mostly 50-100 cm tall, usually geniculate below and branching at lower nodes. *Nodes* glabrous or sparsely pubescent. *Sheaths* hirsute on margins, at least above, and usually with long hairs on margins of collar. *Hairs of ligule* 1-2 mm long. *Blades* sparsely to densely pilose on both surfaces, mostly 10-25 cm long and 6-14 mm broad, narrowing gradually both to apex and base. *Panicles* mostly 8-20 cm long, the larger ones with short, spreading branches below and narrowing from base to apex, the smaller ones more compact and with only short, appressed branches. *Bristles* typically solitary below each spikelet, mostly 1.2-2.5 cm in length. *Spikelets* light green, 2.9-3.4 mm long, narrowly ovate, acute at apex. *Palea of lower floret* narrow, one-half to two-thirds as long as lemma. *Lemma of upper floret* finely but conspicuously transverse-rugose. *Chromosome number*, 2n=54.

Distribution. Texas: Regions 7 and 10 and one collection (the type) from San Diego in region 6; apparently restricted for the most part to soils derived from granitic rocks, infrequently collected but reported by Correll and Johnston (1970) as locally common in regions 7 and 10. General: Southwestern Texas, Arizona and northern Mexico (Coahuila and Sonora).

Flowering period: Summer and autumn.

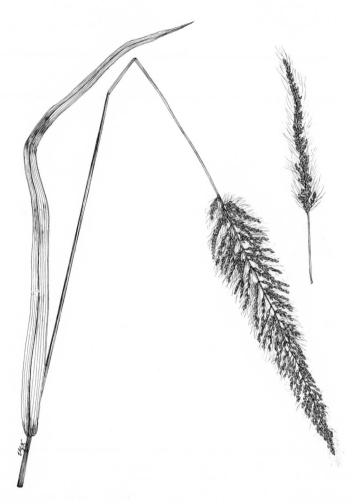

Fig. 292. *Setaria scheelei*. Two types of inflorescence. From Gould and Box, 1965.

105. PENNISETUM L. Rich.

Annuals and perennials, mostly with tall, stiffly erect culms but one species decumbent-prostrate with stout, creeping stolons. *Ligule* a short membrane densely ciliate with long hairs. *Inflorescence* a dense, bristly, elongated, tightly-contracted panicle, the spikelets solitary or in groups of 2-several in fascicles of numerous bristles. *Bristles* separate to the base, not connate. *Spikelets* falling together with the bristles at maturity. *First glume* small or vestigial. *Lemma and palea of upper floret* thin, firm, smooth and shiny, the lemma margins thin and flat.

560   THE GRASSES OF TEXAS

A genus of about 80 species in the tropics and subtropics of both hemispheres. The species of *Pennisetum* and of *Cenchrus* form a more or less continuous series in respect to morphological characteristics, and some authors, including Correll and Johnston (1970), do not recognize *Pennisetum* as a distinct genus. DeLisle, however, in his monographic treatment of *Cenchrus* (1963), maintained both *Pennisetum* and *Cenchrus*.

Long bristles about 1 cm long   1. *P. nervosum*

Long bristles 4-5 cm long   2. *P. villosum*

1. **Pennisetum nervosum** (Nees) Trin., Acad. St. Pétersb. Mém. VI. Sci. Nat. 1:177. 1834. *Cenchrus nervosus* (Nees) Ktze. BENTSPIKE PENNISETUM. Stout perennial with culms to 3 m tall from a hard, knotty base, the lower culm nodes swollen. *Blades* long, mostly 6-10 mm broad, scabrous. *Panicle* usually purple, 10-20 cm long and mostly 12-18 mm thick, the fascicles erect-spreading or reflexed. *Bristles* scabrous, the inner about 10 mm long and the outer shorter. *Spikelets* solitary in each fascicle of bristles, 5-6 mm long. *Chromosome number, 2n=36.*

Distribution. Texas: Region 6 in moist, open or brushy sites along the Rio Grande River near Brownsville, apparently introduced. General: Native to South America and widely introduced elsewhere.

Flowering period: Summer and fall.

2. **Pennisetum villosum** R. Br. *ex* Fresen., Mus. Sechenberg 2:134. 1837. *Cenchrus longisetus* M. C. Johnston. FEATHERTOP. Fig. 293. Cespitose perennial mostly 30-70 cm tall. *Culms* somewhat rhizomatous at base, the nodes not swollen. *Ligule* a ciliate membrane, the hairs about 1 mm long. *Blades* linear, mostly 10-25 cm long and 2-5 mm broad, flat or folded, glabrous. *Panicles* mostly 4-10 cm long, with spreading fascicles of long, tawny-white bristles, the longer bristles 4-5 cm or more in length. *Inner bristles of the fascicle* long-plumose with silky hairs and basal stipe of fascicle also with silky hairs. *Spikelets* one per fascicle, 8-9 mm long. *Chromosome numbers reported, 2n=18, 27, 36, 45 and 54.*

Distribution. Texas: Rather commonly grown as an ornamental and occasionally persisting for a short time as an escape from cultivation. General: Native to Africa but widely distributed elsewhere as an ornamental.

Flowering period: June to November.

106. CENCHRUS L.

Annuals and perennials, mostly with weak, geniculate culms. *Ligule* a short membrane, densely ciliate with short or long hairs. *Spikelets* enclosed in burs, with 1-8 in each bur. *Burs* formed by bristles and/or flattened spines (modified branchlets) fused together at least at base,

Fig. 293. *Pennisetum villosum.* Inflorescence and spikelet. From Gould, 1968.

the bristles and spines usually retrorsely barbed; burs subsessile on a short, angular, unbranched rachis. Disarticulation at base of bur. *Glumes* thin, membranous, unequal. *Lemma of lower floret* thin, equaling or exceeding the second glume. *Palea of lower floret* about equaling the lemma. *Lemma of upper floret* thin, membranous, tapering to a slender, usually acuminate tip, the margins not inrolled. *Caryopses* elliptic to ovoid, dorsally flattened.

In his monograph of *Cenchrus*, DeLisle (1963) recognized 20 species. Most species are native only to the Americas, but a few are distributed throughout the warmer parts of the world.

Burs lacking stiff spines with flattened bases; plants perennial

Bristles conspicuously ciliate-pubescent 1. *C. ciliaris*

Bristles retrorsely scabrous 2. *C. myosuroides*

Burs with stiff spines with flattened bases; plants annual or weakly perennial

Burs with 1 whorl of united, flattened spines, subtended by 1-several whorls of bristles   3. *C. echinatus*

Burs with more than one whorl of flattened spines, the spines projecting at irregular intervals throughout the body of the bur

Burs mostly with 8-40 spines, the base of the larger ones frequently to 1.5 mm broad; upper floret 3.4-5.8 mm long   4. *C. incertus*

Burs mostly with 45-75 spines, the base of the larger ones seldom over 1 mm broad; upper floret 5.8-7.6 mm long
                                        5. *C. longispinus*

1. **Cenchrus ciliaris** L., Mant. 302. 1771. *Pennisetum ciliare* (L.) Link. BUFFELGRASS. Fig. 294. Perennial with culms 50-100 cm tall, erect or geniculate-spreading, branched and "knotty" at base. *Sheaths* laterally compressed and keeled, glabrous to sparsely pilose. *Ligule* a short, ciliate membrane, the hairs mostly 1-1.5 mm long. *Blades* thin, usually flat, scabrous or slightly pilose, mostly 8-30 cm long and 2.5-8 mm broad. *Inflorescence* dense, cylindrical, mostly 4-10 (-13) cm long and 1-2 cm thick. *Bristles* 4-10 mm long, purplish, long ciliate on inner margins, terete, connate only at base or slightly above. *Fascicles* with 2-4 spikelets, the fascicle with a minute, pilose peduncle. *Spikelets* 2.2-5.6 mm long. *Lemma of upper floret* 2.2-5.4 mm long. *Caryopses* turgid, ovoid, 1.4-1.9 mm long, about 1 mm in diameter. *Chromosome numbers* reported, $2n=32, 34, 35, 36, 40, 44, 52$ and 54.

Distribution. Texas: Introduced as a forage grass and now common in sandy soils on rangelands and semi-disturbed sites throughout a region 6 and of occasional occurrence in regions 2, 3, 7 and 10. General: Native to India and Africa and widely introduced elsewhere.

Flowering period: Flowering from early spring till late autumn under favorable growing conditions.

2. **Cenchrus myosuroides** H.B.K., Nov. Gen. et Sp. Pl. 1:155. t. 35. 1815. BIG SANDBUR. Fig. 295. Coarse perennial with stout culms in large clumps. *Culms* more or less woody, mostly 0.7-2 m tall, with slightly swollen nodes, little-branched above the base. *Ligule* a ciliate membrane, the hairs 1-3 mm long. *Blades* scabrous at least on the adaxial surface occasionally slightly pilose, mostly 12-40 cm long and 4-13 mm broad, flat or somewhat folded. *Inflorescence* mostly 8-20 cm long and 6-12 mm thick. *Spikelets* with usually only one spikelet per bur. *Spines and bristles* of bur not flattened, retrorsely scabrous or barbellate, the inner ones about as long as the spikelet, the outer ones shorter, irregular in length. *Bristles* fused below into a hard,

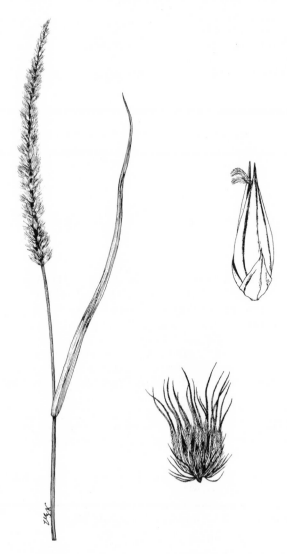

Fig. 294. *Cenchrus ciliaris*. Inflorescence, spikelet cluster (bur) and spikelet. From Gould and Box, 1965.

conical base with disarticulation at the lower, narrow end. *Spikelets* mostly 4-5 mm long. *Chromosome numbers* reported $2n = 54$, ca. 68 and 70; most records, $2n = 70$.

Distribution. Texas: Region 6 and southern portion of regions 2, 7 and 10, most frequent in brushy ravines, ditches and along stream courses. General: Florida, the West Indies, Mexico, the Caribbean Islands and numerous countries of South America.

Flowering period: May through November.

564   THE GRASSES OF TEXAS

Fig. 295. *Cenchrus myosuroides.* Spikelet cluster (bur). From Gould and Box, 1965.

3. **Cenchrus echinatus** L., Sp. Pl. 1050. 1753. SOUTHERN SANDBUR. Fig. 296. Annual with culms geniculate or trailing, the erect tips mostly 15-40 cm tall, the trailing culms to 85 cm long. *Sheaths* laterally compressed, pilose on margins. *Ligule* a ciliate membrane, the hairs 0.6-2 mm long. *Blades* thin, flat or loosely folded, glabrous to variously pubescent, mostly 5-25 cm long and 3-12 mm broad. *Inflorescence* mostly 3-8 (-10) cm long and 0.8-1.2 mm broad, the spikelets in spiny burs 5-10 mm long. *Burs* with one whorl of united, flattened spines subtended by 1-several whorls of shorter, finer bristles. *Spines and bristles* retrorsely barbed. *Spikelets* 5-7 mm long, 2-3 per bur. *Lemma of upper floret* slightly longer than second glume and lemma of lower floret. *Chromosome numbers* reported, $2n=34$, 68 and 70.

Distribution. Texas: Regions 1, 2, 3, 4 and 6, growing as a weed of disturbed soils. General: Throughout the warmer parts of the United States, especially along the East Coast and the Gulf of Mexico. Also frequent throughout the West Indies, the Caribbean, Mexico, Central America and much of South America. Introduced in the Hawaiian Islands, Australia and many Pacific islands.

Flowering period: Throughout the year but mostly late spring through autumn.

4. **Cenchrus incertus** M. A. Curtis, Boston. J. Nat. Hist. 1:135. 1837. *Cenchrus pauciflorus* Benth., *C. parviceps* Shinners. SANDBUR, GRASS-BUR. Fig. 297. Annual or short-lived perennial. *Culms* erect or more commonly geniculate-spreading or stoloniferous at base, mostly 8-80 cm long. *Sheaths* laterally compressed, glabrous or sparsely pilose. *Ligule* a short, ciliate membrane, the hairs 0.5-1.5 mm long. *Blades* thin, flat, typically glabrous, mostly 2-18 cm long and 2-6 mm broad. *Inflorescence* 1.5-8 (-9) cm long, with internodes 2-5 mm long. *Burs* variable, ovoid to globose, with clefts on two sides. *Spines* 8-40 per bur, irregularly protruding from body of bur, variable in shape from long and slender to short and broad, retrorsely barbed, 2-5 mm long, 0.7-2 mm broad at the usually flattened base. *Spikelets* 2-4, usually 3, per bur, mostly 3.5-5.8 mm long. *Chromosome number*, $2n=34$; $2n=32$ and 36 also reported.

Fig. 296. *Cenchrus echinatus.*
Spikelet cluster (bur). From
Gould and Box, 1965.

Fig. 297. *Cenchrus incertus.* Plant, bur and spikelet. From Gould and Box, 1965.

566   THE GRASSES OF TEXAS

Distribution. Texas: Throughout the State, a common weed of pastures, roadsides, ditches, vacant city lots, weedy lawns and other areas of disturbed soils. General: In the United States, frequent throughout the southern and southeastern states, but only occasional on the west coast. Also common throughout Mexico, the West Indies, the Caribbean region, Central America and the central portion of South America.

Flowering period: Mostly summer and fall but occasionally as early as April.

5. **Cenchrus longispinus** (Hack.) Fern., Rhodora 45:388. 1943. LONG-SPINE SANDBUR. Coarse annual with culms in large clumps, tufted and geniculate or decumbent-spreading below, mostly 10-90 cm long. *Sheaths* laterally compressed and keeled, pilose on margins and at throat. *Ligule* a minute fringed membrane, the hairs 0.7-1.7 mm long. *Blades* thin, flat, scabrous to sparsely pilose, mostly 6-20 cm long and 3-7 mm broad. *Inflorescence* of 6-18 burs, usually 4-10 cm long and 1-2 cm thick. *Burs* pubescent, 8-12 mm long, 3.5-6 mm broad. *Spines* numerous, usually more than 50, slender, retrorsely barbed, 3.5-7 mm long, at least some flattened and 0.7-1 mm or broader at base. *Spines* at base of bur numerous, pointing downward, shorter than those on body of bur. *Spikelets* 2-3 (-4) per bur, 6-8 mm long. *Upper floret* 5.8-7.6 mm long, 2.1-3.3 mm broad. *Chromosome numbers* reported, $2n = 34$ and 36.

Distribution. Texas: Regions 3, 4, 5, 7, 8, 9 and 10 and possibly the northern portion of region 6, growing as a weed of disturbed soils but much less common in the State than *Cenchrus incertus*. General: Most frequent in the central and northeastern United States but reported by DeLisle (1963) as occurring in all states except Montana, Idaho, Washington, Alabama and Mississippi. The range extends north to southeastern Canada, and this species also occurs infrequently in the West Indies, Mexico, Central America and Venezuela. It is adventive in Western Europe, South Africa and Australia.

Tribe 21. Andropogoneae

107. IMPERATA Cyrillo

About 8 species, in the warmer parts of both hemispheres.

1. **Imperata brevifolia** Vasey, Bull. Torrey Bot. Club. 13:26. 1886. *Imperata hookeri* Rupr. *ex* Hack. SATINTAIL. Fig. 298. Tall, stout perennial with culms mostly 1-1.5 m tall from thick, creeping rhizomes. *Leaves* glabrous except for a tuft of long hairs in vicinity of ligule. *Ligule* a short, fringed, truncate membrane, this often extended laterally as thin sheath auricles. *Blades* linear, flat, mostly 6-12 mm broad, gradually narrow to both base and apex. *Inflorescence* a dense, contracted, elongate panicle mostly 10-30 cm long, the spikelets for the most part obscured by long, silky hairs. *Spikelets* all alike, awnless, mostly 3-4 mm long, with a tuft of silky hairs at the base, in

Fig. 298. *Imperata brevifolia*. Inflorescence and spikelet. From Gould, 1968.

unequally pediceled pairs on a continuous branch rachis. *Disarticulation* below the spikelet, the long-hairy callus falling with the spikelet. *Glumes* thin, as long as spikelet, the second with a slightly narrower and longer tip. *Lemma of lower floret and lemma and palea of upper floret* thin and hyaline. *Chromosome number* not reported, the basic number for the genus, $x = 10$.

Distribution. Texas: Infrequent in region 10 and the western portion of region 7. One record from Edna, near Victoria in region 2, may have been from a cultivated plant. General: Dry, mostly desert regions of southern Utah and Nevada, south to Texas, New Mexico and southern California. Also present in Sonora and probably Chihuahua, Mexico.

Flowering period: Late summer and autumn.

108. ERIANTHUS Michx.

Stout perennials with culms mostly 1-4 m tall. *Ligule* a glabrous or ciliate membrane. *Blades* elongate, usually flat and broad. *Inflorescence* a large, dense panicle. *Spikelets* all alike and perfect, in pairs of 1 sessile and 1 pediceled. Disarticulation in rachis, the pedicel falling attached to the sessile spikelet. *Glumes* large, firm, subequal, usually with a tuft of long hairs at base. *Lemma of lower floret, and lemma and palea of upper floret* thin and hyaline. *Lemma of upper floret* with a long, straight or loosely twisted awn.

About 25 species, in temperate-subtropical regions of the world, mostly in moist or marshy habitats.

Lemma awn terete, straight

    Callus hairs (at base of spikelet) absent or sparse, when present then much shorter than spikelet; panicle glabrous or nearly so
                                        1. *E. strictus*

    Callus hairs conspicuous, densely tufted and about as long as spikelet; panicle conspicuously hairy   4. *E. giganteus*

Lemma awn flattened at least at base, loosely twisted and geniculate or in loose spirals, at least below middle

    Callus hairs about as long as spikelet, rarely over 8 mm long; lemma awn loosely twisted and geniculate below the middle, the upper half usually straight   2. *E. contortus*

    Callus hairs 1 cm or more long; awn of lemma not geniculate, loosely twisted and in loose spirals to well above middle
                                  3. *E. alopecuroides*

1. **Erianthus strictus** Baldw., in Ell., Bot. S.C. and Ga. 1:39. 1816. NARROW PLUMEGRASS. Fig. 299. *Culms* mostly 1-2.2 m tall from a hard, knotty base. *Nodes of young culms* usually hispid with long, stiff, deciduous hairs, the nodes of mature flowering culms glabrous. *Ligule* a firm, short, minutely ciliate membrane, often continued laterally as short, stiff sheath auricles. *Blades* flat, glabrous, linear, to 80 cm or more long, mostly 6-12 mm broad, gradually tapering to an attenuate tip. *Panicle* usually 20-40 cm long with stiffly erect, usually appressed branches to 15 cm long, these unbranched or branching near base. *Culm internode below panicle* glabrous or sparsely hirsute. *Hairs of panicle* not prominent, the hairs at the base of the spikelets sparse, 1.5-2 mm long. *Spikelets* 8-11 mm long. *Glumes* about equal, glabrous or scabrous-hispid, brownish. *Lemma awn* terete at base, 14-20 mm long, straight or slightly undulant, not twisted, minutely scabrous. *Chromosome number* not reported.

Fig. 299. *Erianthus strictus*. Inflorescence and pair of spikelets. From Hitchcock, 1935, in part.

570   THE GRASSES OF TEXAS

Distribution. Texas: Regions 1 and 2 in moist soil of swales and pond, lake and river borders. General: Virginia, Tennessee and southern Mississippi, south to the Gulf states from Florida to eastern Texas.

Flowering period: Mostly September to November.

2. **Erianthus contortus** Baldw., in Ell., Bot. S.C. and Ga. 1:40. 1816. BENTAWN PLUMEGRASS. Fig. 300. *Culms* mostly 1.5-2.5 m tall from a firm, knotty base. *Culm nodes* appressed-hispid when young, glabrous at maturity. *Ligule* a stiff membrane fringed with stiff hairs 1-3 mm long. *Blades* flat, to 80 cm or more long, mostly 8-18 mm broad. *Panicle* 20-50 cm or more long, mostly 4 cm or more thick. *Culm internode* below panicle glabrous. *Spikelet callus* with a dense tuft of white or tawny, spreading hairs about as long as spikelet. *Spikelets* 6-8 mm long excluding awns. *Glumes* about equal, brownish, narrow at the apex, the first glume often sparsely long-hispid on margins. *Lemma awn* 15-22 mm long, slightly flattened at base, loosely twisted and geniculate below middle, the terminal half usually straight. *Chromosome number* not reported.

Distribution. Texas: Regions 1, 2 and 3, in moist soil of swales, ditches and lake and stream shores. General: Maryland, Tennessee, eastern Oklahoma to Florida and the Gulf Coast west to eastern Texas.

Flowering period: Mostly September to November.

3. **Erianthus alopecuroides** (L.) Ell., Bot. S.C. and Ga. 1:38. 1816. SILVER PLUMEGRASS. Tall, stout perennial, similar to *E. contortus* but hairs at base of spikelets 1 cm or more long and more copious, the main panicle axis and branches more or less obscured by the silky hairs. *Lower internode of panicle axis and internode below panicle* typically appressed-hairy but usually becoming glabrous in age. *Awn of lemma* flattened, loosely twisted and in loose spirals to well above middle. *Chromosome number*, $2n=60$.

Distribution. Texas: Reported by Chase (1951) and Correll and Johnston (1970) to occur in eastern and southeastern Texas (regions 1 and 2) but no Texas collections seen by the author. General: New Jersey, southern Illinois and southern Oklahoma, south to Florida and the Gulf Coast states to eastern Texas.

Flowering period: Late summer and fall.

4. **Erianthus giganteus** (Walt.) Muhl., Cat. Pl. 4. 1813. *Erianthus saccharoides* Michx. SUGARCANE PLUMEGRASS. Fig. 301. *Culms* 1.3-3 m tall, in dense clumps from a hard, knotty base. *Nodes* densely bearded with hairs 2-6 mm long, at least some hairs usually persistent in age. *Sheaths* hispid, at least near the apex, glabrate in age. *Ligule and collar region of leaf* densely villous. *Blades* mostly 0.8-20 mm broad and to 90 cm or more long, appressed-hispid on one or both surfaces but glabrate in age. *Panicle* mostly 15-50 cm long and as much as 8 cm thick, conspicuously hairy. *Axis of panicle*

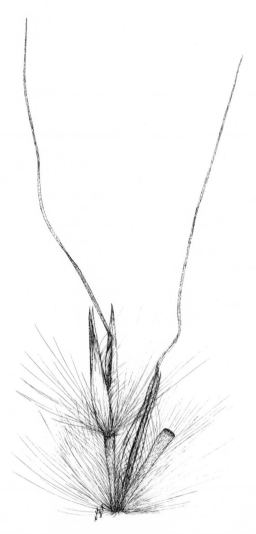

Fig. 300. *Erianthus contortus.* Sessile and pediceled spikelets attached to section of rachis.

and culm internode below panicle villous with appressed or slightly spreading hairs. *Hairs of spikelet callus* copious, brownish, slightly shorter to considerably longer than spikelets. *Spikelets* brownish, mostly 6-8 mm long. *Awn of lemma* straight or slightly curved, terete and untwisted, 12-25 mm long. *Chromosome number* not reported.

Distribution. Texas: Regions 1, 2, 3 and 4, mostly in wet soils of bogs, swales or swamps. General: Southern New York, south to Kentucky, Missouri and the Gulf region from Florida to eastern Texas and also in Cuba.

Flowering period: September to November.

Fig. 301. *Erianthus giganteus*. Plant and spikelet. From Hitchcock, 1935.

109. SORGHUM Moench

Annuals and perennials, many with tall, stout culms. *Ligule* a ciliate membrane. *Blades* long and flat, usually broad. *Inflorescence* an open or contracted panicle, the spikelets clustered on short, racemose branchlets. *Spikelets* in pairs of one sessile and perfect and one pediceled and staminate; at branch tips each sessile spikelet associated with two pediceled spikelets. Disarticulation below sessile spikelet, the rachis section and pedicel or pedicels falling attached to sessile spikelet. *Glumes* coriaceous, about equal in length. *Lemma of lower floret and lemma and palea of upper floret* thin and hyaline, the lemma of the upper floret usually with a geniculate, twisted awn.

A genus of about 35 species, mostly in the warmer parts of Africa, two species native to Mexico and Central America.

Plants annual, without rhizomes   1. *S. bicolor*

Plants perennial, rhizomatous

Pediceled spikelet disarticulating cleanly at node; plants rarely more than 2 m tall; rhizomes long, the rhizome system extensive
2. *S. halepense*

Pediceled spikelet falling with a portion of pedicel attached; plants as much as 3-4 m tall; rhizomes short, the rhizome system not extensive   3. *S. almum*

1. **Sorghum bicolor** (L.) Moench, Meth. Pl. 207. 1794. *Sorghum vulgare* Pers. SORGHUM. Large succulent annual with culms mostly 0.8-2.5 m tall and with long, thin blades 1-5 cm or more broad. *Inflorescence* highly variable, usually a compact panicle 10-20 cm long, with thick, short branches and pedicels, and with awnless spikelets 4-6 mm long. *Glumes* pubescent, usually with a glabrate, shiny spot or area on back. *Chromosome number*, $2n=20$.

Distribution. Texas: Cultivated in many areas of Texas and occurring as a weed of roadside ditches and other disturbed sites. General: Probably of African origin, many varieties of this species have been widely cultivated throughout the warmer parts of the world.

Flowering period: Summer and autumn.

Sorghum bicolor commonly has gone under the name of *S. vulgare* in this country. The numerous cultivated varieties or races, including sorgo, kafir, durra, milo, shallu and broomcorn, have been recognized as separate species by some workers. Sudan grass, commonly cultivated in the United States as a hay and pasture grass, has a loose, open panicle similar to that of *S. halepense,* and the lemma of the perfect spikelet has a persistent, geniculate and twisted awn about 1 cm long. Sudan grass has been given the name *S. sudanense* (Piper) Stapf but probably is no more than a cultivated variety of *S. bicolor*.

2. **Sorghum halepense** (L.) Pers., Syn. Pl. 1:101. 1805. JOHNSON-GRASS. Fig. 302. Coarse perennial with extensive, creeping rhizomes. *Culms* mostly 1-2 m tall but much shorter in dry or otherwise unfavorable sites. *Culm nodes* glabrous or finely pubescent. *Ligule* a truncate, ciliate membrane. *Blades* large, linear, usually glabrous, mostly 0.8-1.5 (-2) cm broad. *Panicle* typically large, open and freely branched but extremely variable, mostly 15-35 cm long. *Spikelets* in pairs of one sessile and perfect and one pediceled and staminate or neuter, at branch tips the sessile spikelet is associated with 2 pediceled spikelets. *Sessile spikelets* 4.5-5.5 mm long, awnless or with a delicate, geniculate, readily deciduous lemma awn. *Glumes of sessile spikelet* broad, coriaceous, nerveless and shiny except at tip, pubescent at least on margins. *Lemma awn*, when present, 1-1.5 mm long, with a twisted lower segment. *Pediceled spikelets* usually staminate, awnless, lanceolate, as long as or longer than the sessile ones but narrower and thinner and with more conspicuously veined glumes. *Caryopses* 2-3 mm long. *Chromosome number*, $2n=40$.

Distribution. Texas: Throughout the State, cultivated as a forage grass but more common as a weed of low roadsides and ditches. General: Massachusetts to Iowa, south to Florida, Texas and southern California, introduced in the United States. Common throughout the temperate and warmer regions of the world, apparently native to southern Europe.

Flowering period: Flowering throughout the year under favorable growing conditions. Early spring flowering plants for the most part are infected with smut.

Johnsongrass has become a serious weed pest of irrigated croplands in some areas. Although frequently grown for forage, this succulent perennial develops cyanogenetic compounds under certain conditions of growth and can be the cause of prussic-acid poisoning in grazing animals.

3. **Sorghum almum** Parodi, Revista Argent. Agron. 10:361. f. 1-3 and pl. 31-34. 1943. Rhizomatous perennial, similar in general aspects to *S. halepense* but with a less extensive and aggressive rhizome system, often taller culms, usually larger (5-6.5 mm long) sessile spikelets and larger (3-3.8 mm long) caryopses. *Chromosome number*, $2n=40$.

Distribution. Texas: Seeded in pastures of regions 6 and 7 and reseeding naturally to an extent. General: An Argentina species believed to be of hybrid origin with one of the parents probably being *S. halepense*.

Flowering period: Summer and autumn.

Fig. 302. *Sorghum halepense*. Inflorescence and spikelet pair. From Gould and Box, 1965.

576   THE GRASSES OF TEXAS

110. SORGHASTRUM Nash

Slender, mostly tall perennials. *Ligule* a stiff, ciliate membrane. *Inflorescence* a loosely or tightly contracted panicle. *Spikelets* basically in pairs of one sessile and perfect and one pediceled and rudimentary, in Texas species the pediceled spikelets usually completely reduced and represented only by the slender, hairy pedicel (2 pedicels at the branch tips). *Spikelets* disarticulating with a section of the rachis and the pedicel or, at the branch tips, with two pedicels. *Glumes* firm, subequal. *Lemma and palea of lower floret* absent or rudimentary. *Lemma of upper floret* thin, hyaline, the well-developed midnerve extending as a stout, geniculate and twisted awn.

A genus of about 15 species in the warmer regions of the Americas and Africa.

Awns mostly 12-17 mm long, once-geniculate; spikelets light brown or straw-colored .... 1. *S. nutans*

Awns mostly 25-35 mm long, twice-geniculate; spikelets dark brown at maturity .... 2. *S. elliottii*

1. **Sorghastrum nutans** (L.) Nash, in Small, Fl. Southeast. U. S. 66. 1903. *Andropogon nutans* L., *Sorghastrum avenaceum* (Michx.) Nash. INDIANGRASS. Fig. 303. Culms stiffly erect from short, stout, scaly rhizomes, mostly 0.8-2.3 m tall. *Culm nodes* hispid with stiffly erect hairs. *Sheaths* glabrous or infrequently slightly hispid, continued at the apex as a stiff membranous ligule 2-5 mm long, this usually developed marginally as thickened, pointed sheath auricles. *Blades* long, linear, flat, mostly 5-10 mm broad, tapering to a narrow base and an attenuate apex. *Inflorescence* a loosely contracted panicle 15-30 cm long. *Uppermost branchlets, pedicels and glumes* hispid with silvery hairs. *Spikelets* 6-8 mm long, the glumes light brown or straw-colored. *Awn of lemma* mostly 12-17 mm long, geniculate, tightly twisted below the bend, loosely twisted and slightly spiralling above the bend. *Chromosome numbers* reported, $2n=20$, 40 and 80.

Distribution. Texas: Reported from all regions but most frequent in the tall-grass prairie areas of central and coastal Texas. General: South-central Canada and throughout the United States east of the Rocky Mountains to northern Mexico.

Flowering period: Mostly September to November.

Sorghastrum nutans together with *Andropogon gerardii*, *Schizachyrium scoparium* and *Panicum virgatum* comprise the "big four" tallgrass prairie grasses of the central U.S. True Prairie Association. All are important range forage species and indicators of range in good condition.

Baum (1967) studied Linnaeus's type description of *Andropogon nutans*, upon which *Sorghastrum nutans* is based, and concluded that the name S.

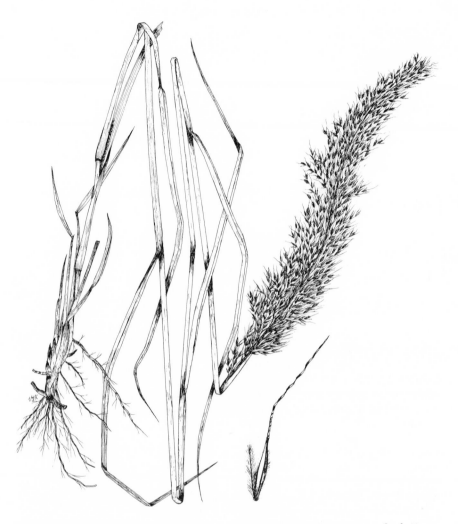

Fig. 303. *Sorghastrum nutans.* Inflorescence and spikelet attached to empty pedicel. From Gould and Box, 1965.

nutans is a synonym of *Stipa avenacea* L. Both *Andropogon nutans* and *Stipa avenacea* were described in the first edition of Species Plantarum (1753). If the name combination *Sorghastrum nutans* is invalid, then *Sorghastrum av- enaceum* (Michx.) Nash is the correct name for indiangrass. However, despite the vague and somewhat confusing descriptions of Linnaeus and the fact that he listed one and possibly two incorrect references for the species, it is quite possible that he had the proper plant in mind and that his basic description is adequate to justify the recognition of *nutans* as the specific epithet. This matter needs further study.

2. **Sorghastrum elliottii** (Mohr) Nash, N. Amer. Fl. 17:130. 1912. SLENDER INDIANGRASS. Tufted perennial with slender culms mostly 0.8-1.8 m tall. *Base of plant* not rhizomatous. *Ligule* firm, membranous, truncate or variously lobed, 2-4 mm long, thickened laterally to form stiff sheath auricles. *Blades* long and narrow, flat or folded, mostly 3-8 mm broad, narrow at base and attenuate at apex. *Inflorescence* a narrow, loosely-and sparsely-flowered panicle 15-25 cm long. *Spikelets* dark brown on slender, flexuous, often recurved pedicels. *Glumes* and pedicels of the reduced spikelets hirsute with brownish hairs. *Spikelets* mostly 5.5-7 mm long. *Lemma awn* dark brown, 23-35 mm long, twisted and usually twice-geniculate.

Distribution. Texas: Regions 1 and 2 and the eastern portion of region 3, usually in sandy soil and in or along the margins of woodlands. General: Maryland, Tennessee and Oklahoma to the Gulf Coast from Florida to eastern Texas.

Flowering period: September through November.

A third species of *Sorghastrum*, *S. secundum* (Ell.) Nash, is reported by Chase (1951) to occur in eastern Texas. This is very similar to *S. elliottii*, and both are widely distributed in the southeastern United States. Correll and Johnston (1970) do not list *S. secundum* for Texas, and the author has not seen Texas collections of the species.

111. ANDROPOGON L.

Cespitose perennials with stiffly erect culms, rounded or flattened and keeled sheaths, membranous ligules and flat or folded blades. *Flowering culm* much-branched and "broomlike" in some species, unbranched or little-branched above base in others. *Inflorescence* a panicle with 2-several racemose branches. *Spikelets* in pairs of one sessile and perfect and one pediceled and staminate or neuter, sometimes rudimentary or absent. Disarticulation in rachis, the sessile spikelet falling attached to the associated pedicel and rachis section. Spikelets 2-flowered, the lower floret neuter, often vestigial. *Glumes* large, firm, awnless. *Lemmas* of lower and upper florets thin and hyaline, the lemma of the upper (perfect) floret awned or awnless.

As presently interpreted, a relatively large group of primarily tropical-subtropical grasses, represented in the warmer regions of all continents; about 17 species in the United States.

Pediceled spikelets large, well-developed, usually staminate

1.   *A. gerardii*

Pediceled spikelets rudimentary, vestigial or absent and represented by the pedicel alone

Sessile spikelets 5-7 mm long; rachis of inflorescence branches stiff
and straight   2.   A. *ternarius*

Sessile spikelets 4 mm or less long; rachis of inflorescence branches
slender and flexuous

Flowering culm profusely branched and rebranched, broom-like, the
terminal sheaths and peduncles greatly reduced and crowded;
main culms stout, tall and coarse   3.   A. *glomeratus*

Flowering culms moderately rebranched, not broom-like; main culms
slender, moderately tall

Sheaths subtending the inflorescences not conspicuously inflated
4.   A. *virginicus*

Sheaths subtending the inflorescences conspicuously inflated
5.   A. *elliottii*

1. **Andropogon gerardii** Vitman, Summa Pl. 6:16. 1792. Stout, cespitose perennial, with or without rhizomes. *Culms* glabrous, often glaucous,
mostly 0.8-2 m tall. *Leaves* green or glaucous, usually glabrous. *Ligule*
a short, stiff, fringed membrane. *Blades* long, linear, flat, rather firm,
mostly 5-10 mm broad. *Inflorescence* of 2-7 spicate branches, these typically 4-11 cm long and unbranched. *Sessile spikelets* 7-11 mm long, usually scabrous and often glaucous, more or less "boat-shaped," with a 2-
keeled, concave first glume and a single-keeled second glume of equal
length. *Lemma* thin, mostly hyaline, deeply cleft and with setaceous lobes
on either side of a stout awn. *Lemma awn* glabrous, geniculate and twisted
below. *Pediceled spikelet* usually about as large as the sessile one, awnless,
staminate. *Chromosome number,* $2n=60$.

Sessile spikelet with an awn 8-20 mm long; rachis internodes ciliate with
usually long hairs, the nodes with a tuft of hairs

Hairs of rachis internodes copious, typically 3-4 mm long and usually
yellow or golden in color; rhizomes well-developed
1C.   A. *gerardii* var. *chrysocomus*

Hairs of rachis internodes sparse to copious, mostly 1-2 mm long; rhizomes absent or short
1A.   A. *gerardii* var. *gerardii*

Sessile spikelet awnless or with awn rarely more than 5 mm long; hairs
of rachis internodes variable, typically short and sparse; rhizomes
well-developed   1B.   A. *gerardii* var. *paucipilus*

1A. **Andropogon gerardii** Vitman var. **gerardii.** *Andropogon provincialis* Lam. *Andropogon furcatus* Muhl. BIG BLUESTEM. Fig. 304.

Distribution. Texas: Throughout the State, usually associated with other tall grasses in prairies and woods openings having sandy or loamy soils. General: Southern Canada and throughout the United States from Montana, Colorado and Arizona; infrequent in the northern and central highlands of Mexico. The type specimen of *A. gerardii* is from Provence, France.

Flowering period: Mostly August through November.

Big bluestem is one of the four most widespread and important forage grasses of the North American tallgrass prairie regions. It usually is associated with one or more of the other three, *Schizachyrium scoparium* (little bluestem), *Sorghastrum nutans* (indiangrass) and *Panicum virgatum* (switchgrass).

1B. **Andropogon gerardii** Vitman var. **paucipilus** (Nash) Fern., Rhodora 45:258. 1943. *Andropogon hallii* Hack. SAND BLUESTEM.

Distribution. Texas: Regions 8, 9 and 10 in sand or sandy soils, often growing with forms of *A. gerardii* var. *gerardii* and apparently intergrading. General: North Dakota and eastern Montana, south on sandy soils to western Texas and Arizona.

Flowering period: Mostly August to November.

In western Texas, the inflorescence of sand bluestem most commonly consists of a pair of short, dark-colored branches with large awnless spikelets and moderately hairy rachis margins. In the dune areas of Ward County, near Monahans, typical plants of *Andropogan gerardii* var. *paucipilus,* with awnless spikelets and inconspicuously short-hairy inflorescence branch rachis margins grow associated with typical plants of *A. gerardii* var. *chrysocomus,* with long-awned spikelets and rachis margins densely villous with long, yellowish hairs. All *A. gerardii* plants of this area develop long, stout, creeping rhizomes.

1C. **Andropogon gerardii** Vitman var. **chrysocomus** (Nash) Fern., Rhodora 45:258. 1943. Fig. 305. *Andropogon hallii* sensu Chase (1951) and Gould (1969) in part.

Distribution. Texas: Regions 8, 9 and 10 in sandy soils. General: Kansas, south to northwestern Texas, New Mexico and northeastern Arizona.

Flowering period: August to November.

2. **Andropogon ternarius** Michx., Fl. Bor. Amer. 1:57. 1803. SPLIT-BEARD BLUESTEM. Fig. 306. Cespitose perennial with culms mostly 70-120 cm tall. *Culms* entirely glabrous or with a tuft of long, silvery hairs just

Fig. 304. *Andropogon gerardii* var. *gerardii*. Plant, spikelet pair and spikelet. From Gould, 1951.

below uppermost leaf- or bract-bearing node. *Basal leaves* with broad, glabrous, hispid, or densely villous sheaths and long, narrow blades. *Ligule* a minute, fringed membrane. *Blades* mostly 2-4 mm broad, glabrous or the lower ones sparsely hispid, the basal ones frequently 20 cm or more long. *Inflorescence* usually with 2 densely villous, paired branches 3-6 cm long, these commonly well exserted above uppermost leaf or bract, less frequently partially included in an enlarged, spathe-like sheath. *Inflorescences* often developed on lateral shoots at all upper culm nodes. *Inflorescence branch rachis* and *pedicels* densely villous with silvery hairs mostly 6-9 mm long.

Fig. 305. *Andropogon gerardii* var. *chrysocomus*. Inflorescence and spikelet pair.

Fig. 306. *Andropogon ternarius*. Inflorescences and spikelet pair. From Gould and Box, 1965.

SUBFAMILY VI. PANICOIDEAE   583

Sessile spikelet 5-7 mm long excluding the lemma awn. *Glumes* glabrous. *Lemma of upper floret* with a hyaline, membranous body and a slender, loosely twisted and somewhat geniculate awn 1.5-2.5 cm long from a deeply bifid apex. *Pediceled spikelet* reduced to a slender, awnless rudiment usually 2 mm or less long and not wider than the pedicel. *Chromosome number*, 2n=40.

Distribution. Texas: Regions 1, 2, 3, 4 and 5, commonly on sandy woods borders and cutover woodland pastures. General: Southeastern United States, from Maryland and eastern Kansas to Florida and eastern Texas.

Flowering period: Mostly September to November but occasionally as early as June.

3. **Andropogon glomeratus** (Walt.) B.S.P., Prel. Cat. N.Y. 67. 1888. BUSHY BLUESTEM. Fig. 307. Perennial, culms densely cespitose, stiffly erect, mostly 75-150 cm tall. *Sheaths* usually glabrous, less frequently hispid along margins and dorsally near collar, the lower sheaths broad, overlapping, strongly compressed laterally and keeled dorsally. *Ligule* a stiff membrane to 1 mm long, ciliate with hairs to 2 mm long. *Blades* elongate, frequently folded, mostly 2.5-6 (occasionally -8) mm broad, usually much narrower than sheaths. *Flowering culms* profusely branched and rebranched, the ultimate branches with their reduced, villous inflorescences broom-like. *Uppermost branchlets* silky-villous, at least just below nodes. *Bracteate sheaths of the terminal branchlets* narrow, typically reddish-brown or bronze-colored. *Inflorescence branches* usually 2, each 1.5-3 cm long, slightly shorter than the subtending sheath and partially enclosed by it. *Branch rachis* delicate, not or only slightly flattened, villous with long, silvery hairs. *Sessile spikelets* usually 3-4.5 mm long, the glumes glabrous. *Awn of lemma* straight or undulant, not geniculate, 1-2 cm long. *Pedicel* slender, terete or slightly flattened, villous with long hairs. *Pediceled spikelets* vestigial or completely absent. *Chromosome number*, 2n=20.

Distribution. Texas: Reported from all regions of the State, usually present in low, moist sites with moderately disturbed, relatively sterile soils. General: Eastern United States, from Connecticut south to Florida, westward to Kentucky, Oklahoma, southern Nevada and southern California and southward into Mexico.

Flowering period: Mostly September to November but occasionally throughout the year.

4. **Andropogon virginicus** L., Sp. Pl. 1046. 1753. BROOMSEDGE BLUESTEM. Fig. 308. Perennial with slender culms in small tufts or clumps. *Culms* mostly 50-100 cm tall, stiffly erect, branching above to produce several inflorescences but not profusely branched and with a dense mass of inflorescences. *Culm nodes* glabrous. *Herbage* glabrous or sheaths and blades variously hispid, the hairs when present usually sparse and along margins. *Sheaths* usually broader than blades, laterally compressed and sharply keeled on midnerve. *Ligules* ciliate. *Blades* elongate, flat or folded, mostly 2-5 mm

Fig. 307. *Andropogon glomeratus*. Mass of inflorescences at culm apex. From Gould and Box, 1965.

Fig. 308. *Andropogon virginicus*. Culm tip with three inflorescences and spikelet with attached pedicel of vestigial spikelet.

SUBFAMILY VI. PANICOIDEAE 585

broad. *Inflorescences* numerous on each flowering culm, characteristically with 2-5 slender, flexuous, spicate branches 2-3 cm long and partially enclosed in slightly inflated, yellowish, straw-colored or slightly bronze-tinged bracts. *Bracts* mostly 3-6 cm long and 2-5 mm broad. *Nodes and upper portion of internode below terminal sheath* most frequently glabrous or with a few long hairs, occasionally with a tuft of hairs. *Rachillas* and *pedicels* slender, villous with long, silky hairs. *Sessile spikelets* mostly 2.5-4 mm long, the lemma with an awn 1-2 cm long. *Pediceled spikelets* vestigial or absent. *Chromosome number,* $2n = 20$.

Distribution. Texas: Regions 1, 2, 3 and 4 and the eastern portions of regions 5, 6 and 7, mostly on loose, sandy and moist soils. General: Throughout the eastern United States, from Massachusetts, Michigan and Iowa, south to Florida and eastern Texas.

Flowering period: Mostly September through November.

Andropogon virginicus frequently grows intermingled with A. *glomeratus* but for the most part occupies higher and drier sites. In the field it can be readily distinguished from A. *glomeratus* by its more slender habit, shorter and less densely-flowered culms and lighter-colored (usually straw-colored) herbage and inflorescence bracts. In Texas, the culms of A. *virginicus* are glabrous or nearly so below the spathe-like inflorescence sheaths, whereas in A. *glomeratus* there is a tuft of long hairs below the sheath.

5. **Andropogon elliottii** Chapman, Fl. Southeast. U.S. 581. 1860. ELLIOTT BLUESTEM. Fig. 309. Tufted perennial, similar in general habit and habitat adaptation to A. *virginicus* but with greatly enlarged bracteate sheaths subtending the inflorescences, the sheaths commonly 6-10 mm broad and 7-15 cm or more long, the bracteate leaves with vestigial or well-developed blades. Further, the inflorescences of A. *elliottii* tend to have shorter peduncles and are more enclosed by the subtending sheaths. *Chromosome number,* $2n = 20$.

Distribution. Texas: Regions 1 and 3 and possibly the upper woodland portions of region 2, usually in partial shade of forest trees. General: Eastern United States, from New Jersey to Florida and westward to Illinois, Oklahoma and eastern Texas; reported from Central America and possibly occurring in Mexico.

Flowering period: Mostly September through November.

112. DICHANTHIUM Willemet

Low to moderately tall perennials, mostly cespitose but some with extensive creeping stolons. *Ligules* membranous. *Inflorescence* a panicle, a few to several spicate primary branches, these sparingly rebranched in a few species. *Branch rachis and pedicels* thick, flattened or rounded. *Lower pair of spikelets of the inflorescence branches* usually awnless and

Fig. 309. *Andropogon elliottii.* Culm apex with several inflorescences and sessile spikelet with attached empty pedicel.

not seed-bearing. *Pediceled spikelet* large, broad, staminate or neuter. Disarticulation in rachilla, the sessile spikelet falling attached to the associated pedicel and rachilla joint immediately above.

A small genus of Asiatic, Australian and African species, none native to the Americas.

First glume with an irregular line of hairs below tip; plants not developing stolons   1. *D. sericeum*

First glume not with a line of hairs below tip; long stolons usually developed

Inflorescence axis and branches just below spikelets finely pubescent
2. *D. aristatum*

Inflorescence axis and branches just below spikelets glabrous
3. *D. annulatum*

Fig. 310. *Dichanthium sericeum.* Inflorescence and spikelet pair. From Gould and Box, 1965, as *Andropogon sericeus.*

1. **Dichanthium sericeum** A. Camus, Bull. Mus. Hist. Nat. 27:549. 1921. *Andropogon sericeus* R. Br. SILKY BLUESTEM. Fig. 310. Tufted perennial, with erect culms mostly 50-100 cm tall. *Culm nodes* densely bearded with silvery, spreading hairs 1-5 cm tall. *Leaves* commonly glabrous or nearly so but infrequently the sheath and both blade surfaces villous with spreading hairs. *Ligule* an erose membrane 1-2 mm long. *Blades* mostly 5-25 cm long and 2-5 mm broad. *Inflorescence* with 2-7 conspicuously villous branches 2.5-6 cm long, these densely clustered and erect at culm apex. *Branch rachis and pedicels* narrow, densely villous, slightly flattened. *Sessile* spikelets 2.5-3.5 mm long, with dark-colored, twisted and twice-geniculate lemma awns 2-3.5 mm long. *Outer glume of sessile spikelet* with a thin rounded apex, this delimited by a line of long, usually papilla-based hairs, the hairs continuing down both sides of dorsal surface. *Pediceled spikelets* about as large as sessile ones but awnless, the outer glume often with a line of hairs across tip and down sides. *Chromosome number,* $2n=20$.

588   THE GRASSES OF TEXAS

Distribution. Texas: Regions 2 and 6, mostly from Corpus Christi southward to Cameron County. General: Native to Australia and introduced in Texas as a potential forage grass.

Flowering period: Mostly May to September but occasionally flowering in late autumn.

2. **Dichanthium aristatum** (Poir.) C. E. Hubb., Kew Bull. 1939:654. 1939. *Andropogon nodusus* (Willem.) Nash, *Andropogon aristatus* Poir. ANGLETON BLUESTEM. Perennial, commonly with both erect and prostrate, stoloniferous culms 2 m or more long; erect culms mostly 70-100 cm tall. *Culm nodes* at first densely bearded but frequently glabrous in age. *Sheaths* glabrous, shorter than the internodes, often only half as long. *Ligule* a truncate, erose hyaline membrane about 1 mm long. *Blades* mostly 6-25 cm long and 3-6 mm broad, glabrous or sparsely hispid with papilla-based hairs. *Inflorescence* well exserted, with 3-5 (2-8) spicate branches mostly 4-7 cm long crowded at the culm apex, the branches loosely erect or erect-spreading. *Branch rachis and pedicels* slender, terete or only slightly flattened, hispid, infrequently villous. *Spikelets* greenish or purple-tinged, 4-5 mm long, the sessile and pediceled spikelets similar in appearance but only the sessile ones awned. *First glume of sessile spikelet* often laterally keeled and slightly winged on upper margins, typically broad and obtuse at apex, sparsely hairy at least on margins and base, the hairs often papilla-based. *Lemma of perfect floret* with a twisted, weakly twice-geniculate, brownish awn 1.5-2.5 cm long. *Chromosome number*, $2n=40$.

Distribution. Texas: Regions 2 and 6, introduced as a forage grass on the lower Texas coast and South Texas Plains and now occasional as a weed of roadsides, ditches and other areas of moderately disturbed soils. General: Native to subtropical Asia, sparingly introduced elsewhere. The type collection is from Mauritius, India.

Flowering period: September to December.

3. **Dichanthium annulatum** Stapf, in Prain, Fl. Trop. Afr. 9:178. 1917. *Andropogon annulatus* Forsk. KLEBERG BLUESTEM. Fig. 311. Perennial with both erect and stoloniferous culms, the latter to over 1 m long. Plant habit and inflorescence very similar to *Dichanthium aristatum* but spikelets, awns and inflorescence branches tending to be shorter. The key character, that of the glabrous inflorescence axis and branch bases, as opposed to the pubescent axis and branch bases of *D. aristatum*, is the only consistent morphological difference between the two species. *Chromosome number*, $2n=40$.

Distribution. Texas: Regions 2 and 6, introduced as a forage grass and occasionally as a grass of roadsides, ditches, pasturelands and vacant city lots, from Brazoria County, south along the coast to Cameron County and at locations through the southern half of the South Texas Plains. General: Native from Africa to India and China, in tropical-subtropical regions.

Flowering period: Flowering throughout the year under favorable growing conditions.

SUBFAMILY VI. PANICOIDEAE   589

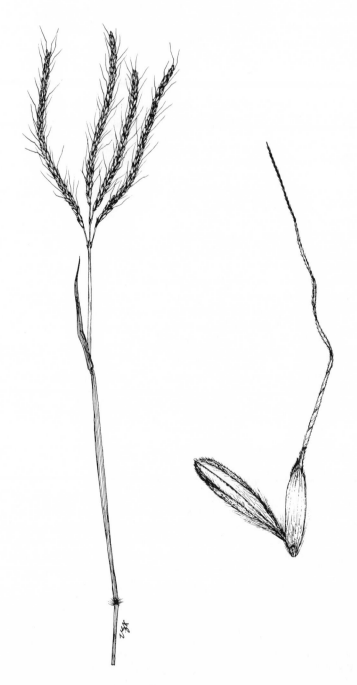

Fig. 311. *Dichanthium annulatum.* Inflorescence and spikelet pair. From Gould and Box, 1965, as *Andropogon annulatus.*

590   **THE GRASSES OF TEXAS**

113. BOTHRIOCHLOA Kuntze

Perennials and annuals; the native Texas species cespitose perennials with stiffly erect culms. *Ligules* membranous. *Blades* long, narrow, flat. *Inflorescence* a panicle, the spikelets in pairs on few to numerous primary branches, these rebranched in a few species. Disarticulation at base of spikelets, the rachis joint and pedicel falling with the awned, sessile spikelet. *Pedicels and upper rachis internodes* with a central groove or broad, membranous area. *Sessile spikelets* perfect, usually awned, more or less triangular in outline, the first glume dorsally flattened, the second glume with a rounded median keel. *Lemma of upper floret* reduced to a thin, hyaline body and a stout midnerve, this usually extended as a geniculate and twisted awn. *Pediceled spikelets* well-developed, neuter or staminate, awnless.

A genus of about 30 species distributed throughout the warmer regions of all continents.

Pediceled spikelets neuter, smaller and narrower than the sessile ones

Sessile spikelets less than 4.5 mm long; awn of lemma 18 mm or less long; first glume of sessile spikelet never with a glandular pit

Awns 8-18 mm long   1. *B. saccharoides*

Awns 0-6 mm long   2. *B. exaristata*

Sessile spikelets 4.5-7.3 mm long; awns 20-33 mm long

Panicle axis less than 5 cm long; panicle branches mostly 2-7, rarely more than 8

Culm nodes glabrous or puberulent; first glume of all sessile spikelets pitted

Upper culm nodes glabrous; primary panicle branches never rebranched; first glume of sessile spikelet 5.5-7 mm long, glabrous on back, with a relatively large and deep glandular pit; leaves mostly in a basal tuft, the culm leaves reduced; blades rarely over 2 mm broad   3. *B. edwardsiana*

Upper culm nodes glabrous or puberulent; lower 1-2 panicle branches frequently rebranched; first glume of sessile spikelet 4.5-5.7 mm long, usually sparsely hispid on back near base; glume pits relatively small and shallow; culm leaves well-developed; blades 2-5 mm broad   4. *B. hybrida*

Culm nodes pubescent with long, spreading, silky, white hairs; first glume of some or all sessile spikelets pitless
5. *B. springfieldii*

Panicle axis usually 5-20 cm or more long; panicle branches mostly 9-30 or more

Panicles of the larger culms 14-25 cm long; culms stout, stiffly erect, little-branched above base, 1.2-2.5 m tall, bluish-glaucous below nodes; culm nodes bearded with spreading hairs 3-6 mm long; panicle axis and branches often remaining "kinked" from compression in sheath; pollen averaging 39-40 microns in diameter
7. *B. alta*

Panicles mostly 7-13 cm long; culms tending to be decumbent and much-branched below in age, mostly 1.2 m or less tall, not bluish-glaucous below nodes; culm nodes bearded with appressed hairs less than 3 mm long; panicle axis and branches not "kinked"; pollen averaging 45-52 microns in diameter
6. *B. barbinodis*

Pediceled spikelets neuter or staminate, about as large and broad as the sessile ones

Panicle axis usually longer than branches   8. *B. bladhii*

Panicle axis shorter than branches

First glume of sessile spikelet never with a large, glandular pit
9. *B. ischaemum*

First glume of sessile spikelet with a large, glandular pit
10. *B. pertusa*

1. **Bothriochloa saccharoides** (Swartz) Rydb., Brittonia 1:81. 1931. *Andropogon saccharoides* Swartz. Cespitose perennial with culms erect or somewhat geniculate below, never developing rhizomes or stolons. *Herbage* glaucous or green, usually maturing with a bronze or reddish tinge. *Leaves* glabrous except for a few long hairs in vicinity of ligule. *Ligule* an erose, hyaline membrane 1-3 mm or more long. *Blades* linear, firm, flat or irregularly folded, mostly 3-6 (-8) mm broad, tapering to a long, attenuate tip. *Inflorescence* a densely-flowered, contracted panicle, the branches erect or loosely erect-spreading in age. *Panicle branches* numerous, shorter than the main axis; branches and pedicels with a medial, membranous groove, fringed on the margins with long, silky hairs. *Pediceled spikelet* neuter, much narrower and usually shorter than the sessile one. *Glumes of sessile spikelet* firm, the first larger than the second and clasping it by the margins below apex. *First glume* flat dorsally and rounded or loosely

keeled on margins. *Second glume* broadly keeled. *Awn of lower floret* mostly 8-18 mm long, geniculate below the middle, with both segments loosely twisted.

Panicles 6-10 (-13) cm long; glumes ovate, relatively broad and blunt, dull green, commonly glaucous with a whitish, waxy bloom; pollen averaging 32-38 microns in diameter; present throughout the Texas range of the species   1A.   *B. saccharoides* var. *torreyana*

Panicles of the larger culms 10-20 cm long; glumes narrowly ovate, shiny green; pollen averaging 39-42 microns in diameter; present in southeastern and southern Texas
                                     1B.   *B. saccharoides* var. *longipaniculata*

1A. **Bothriochloa saccharoides** var. **torreyana** (Steud.) Gould, Southw. Naturalist. 3:212. 1959. SILVER BLUESTEM. Fig. 312. Plants with a conspicuous basal cluster of leaves. *Culms* mostly 50-80 mm tall. *Herbage* and *spikelets* commonly glaucous. *Chromosome number,* $2n=60$.

Distribution. Texas: In all regions of the State but less common in the eastern and coastal areas than the variety *longipaniculata.* In northern and western Texas this is one of the most common perennial roadside grasses. General: Alabama, Missouri and southern Colorado, south to northern Mexico. Silver bluestem is restricted to relatively dry, usually sandy soils. On clayey soils it only grows on well-drained sites, such as railroad and road embankments and dry banks of ditches and gulleys.

Flowering period: Mostly May to November.

1B. **Bothriochloa saccharoides** var. **longipaniculata** (Gould) Gould, Southw. Naturalist. 3:212. 1959. *Andropogon saccharoides* var. *longipaniculatus* Gould. LONGSPIKE SILVER BLUESTEM. Fig. 313. Plants usually without a conspicuous basal cluster of leaves. *Culms* commonly 60-130 cm tall. *Herbage and spikelets* usually not glaucous. *Chromosome number,* $2n=120$.

Distribution. Texas: Regions 1, 2, 3, 4 and 6, mostly in woods openings, well adapted to clayey soils and quite shade-tolerant. General: Southeastern and southern Texas to northeastern Mexico. Plants of Guatemala, Salvador and Panama are not entirely typical but also may be referable to this taxon.

Flowering period: Mostly May to November.

Longspike silver bluestem appears to have arisen through hybridization of *Bothriochloa saccharoides* var. *torreyana* and *B. exaristata* and the subsequent doubling of the chromosome number. The variety appears to be genetically stable and to have normal sexual reproduction.

Fig. 312. *Bothriochloa saccharoides* var. *torreyana*. Inflorescence and spikelet pair. From Gould and Box, 1965, as *Andropogon saccharoides* var. *torreyanus*.

594   THE GRASSES OF TEXAS

Fig. 313.   *Bothriochloa saccharoides* var. *longipaniculata*. Plant and spikelet pair. From Gould and Box, 1965, as *Andropogon saccharoides* var. *longipaniculatus*.

2. **Bothriochloa exaristata** (Nash) Henr., Blumea 4:520. 1941. *Andropogon exaristatus* (Nash) Hitchc. AWNLESS BLUESTEM. Fig. 314. Cespitose perennial with culms mostly 70-130 cm tall. *Sheaths and blades* glabrous except for a few hairs in the vicinity of the ligule. *Ligule* membranous, truncate, 1-2 mm long. *Blades* long, flat or folded, 3-8 mm broad. *Inflorescence* a silvery-pubescent, contracted and densely-flowered panicle mostly 9-15 cm long. *Panicle branches* numerous, much shorter than the main axis. *Sessile spikelets* narrow, about 3 mm long, awnless or the hyaline lemma of the perfect floret with an awn 1-4 mm long. *Pediceled spikelet* neuter, much narrower than the sessile one, 2-4 mm long, awnless. *Chromosome number*, $2n=60$.

Distribution. Texas: A relatively rare species, known only from the upper Texas coast (region 2), from Brazoria and Fort Bend counties northward. This species is adapted to heavy, moist, black, clayey soils of the coastal prairie. General: Coastal Louisiana to the northern one-third of the Texas coast and reported from Brazil and Paraguay where it has gone under the name of *Andropogon hassleri* Hack.

Flowering period: Apparently flowering throughout the year under favorable growing conditions.

3. **Bothriochloa edwardsiana** (Gould) L. R. Parodi, Gramin. Bonaer. (ed. 5) 116. 1958. *Andropogon edwardsianus* Gould, Field & Lab. 19:183-185. 1951. MERRILL BLUESTEM. Fig. 315. Tufted perennial. *Culms* slender, stiffly erect or somewhat geniculate-spreading on the margins of large clumps, mostly 35-65 cm tall; upper culm nodes glabrous or glabrate, the lower nodes glabrous to densely short-hairy, the hairs not over 1 mm long. *Leaves* mostly in a basal tuft, with a waxy bloom during the growing period. *Ligules* membranous, 1-1.5 mm long. *Blades* filiform, ciliate on the margins below middle, mostly 1-2 (infrequently -3.5) mm broad, those of the basal tuft 10-25 cm long. *Panicle* of 3-6 simple racemose branches, these mostly 6-10 cm long. *Panicle axis* short, not over 1.8 cm long, with 1-3 nodes. *Sessile spikelet* 5-8 mm long excluding the awn. *First glume* narrow, tapering to a narrowly acute or slightly bifid apex, glabrous and shiny, with a deep, cylindrical, glandular pit 2-2.5 mm from apex. *Lemma of sessile spikelet* with a geniculate awn 20-28 mm long. *Pediceled spikelets* neuter, glabrous or scabrous, narrow, about 3 mm long. Pedicels averaging 4.7-5 mm long, with a deep medial groove and ciliate on margins with long hairs. *Chromosome number*, $2n=60$.

Distribution. Texas: Region 7, known only from Edwards, Kerr and Menard counties, where it grows in fertile, rocky soils over limestone. General: Texas, Argentina and Uruguay.

Flowering period: Flowering specimens have been collected in May, June and July.

An attractive native species of limited distribution but rather abundant in the areas of occurrence.

Fig. 314. *Bothriochloa exaristata*.
Spikelet pair.

Fig. 315. *Bothriochloa edwardsiana*. Plant and spikelet pair.

4. **Bothriochloa hybrida** (Gould) Gould, Southw. Naturalist. 3:212. 1959. *Andropogon hybridus* Gould. HYBRID BLUESTEM. Fig. 316. Perennial with stiffly erect culms in small to medium-sized clumps. *Culms* 30-80 cm tall, moderately branched and leafy above base, with glabrous or puberulent nodes. *Leaf sheaths* green or glaucous, glabrous. *Ligule* a fimbriate membrane 1-2 mm long. *Blades* linear, mostly 2-4, rarely 5, mm broad, usually sparsely ciliate on lower margins and often with a few hairs on the surfaces. *Panicles* hairy but not villous, 6-11 cm long, usually with 3-8 branches on an axis 0.6-3.5 (-4.5) cm long, the lower branches often simply rebranched. *Rachis joints and pedicels* about equal, with a broad, membranous, often dark-colored central groove and thick, hairy margins, the hairs 5-7 mm long at apex but much shorter at base. *Sessile spikelets* 4.5-6.5 mm long, with awns 18-25 mm long. *First glume of sessile spikelet* shiny, with a moderately deep glandular pit above middle and usually with a few stiff hairs on the lower one-third to one-half of back. *Pediceled spikelets* neuter, much narrower than the sessile ones, mostly 2.2-3.6 mm long. *Chromosome number*, $2n=120$.

Distribution. Texas: Regions 2, 6 and 7 in open pastures and on road right-of-ways, often abundant along mowed road ditches and other moderately disturbed sites. General: South-central Texas and northern Mexico.

Flowering period: Mostly April through October but flowering at all months of the year under favorable growing conditions.

5. **Bothriochloa springfieldii** (Gould) L. R. Parodi, Gramin. Bonaer. (ed. 5) 120. 1958. *Andropogon springfieldii* Gould. SPRINGFIELD BLUE-STEM. Fig. 317. Cespitose perennial with culms 30-80 cm tall. *Culm nodes* densely bearded with silvery, spreading hairs 3-7 mm long. *Ligules* short-ciliate, lacerate, 1-2 mm long. *Leaf blades* 2-3 (-5) mm broad, glabrous or sparsely hispid with papilla-based hairs on adaxial surface and with long hairs in vicinity of ligule. *Panicles* densely white-villous, with 2-9 primary branches 4-7 cm long, these infrequently once rebranched. *Rachis joints and pedicels* about equal, densely long-villous on margins, with a broad, thin membranous central area. *Hairs of inflorescence* branches 5-10 mm long. *Sessile spikelets* mostly 5.5-7.3 (-8.5) mm long. *First glume* hairy on lower one-third or one-half of dorsal surface, occasionally with a faint glandular pit or depression above middle. *Lemma awns* 20-26 mm long. *Pediceled spikelets* neuter, much narrower than the sessile ones, mostly 4-5 mm long. *Chromosome number*, $2n=120$.

Distribution. Texas: Regions 9 and 10 on rocky slopes and along ravines, frequent on road right-of-ways. General: Western Texas, New Mexico and northern Arizona.

Flowering period: Mostly July through October.

Bothriochloa springfieldii commonly has been identified as *B. barbinodis* from which it differs typically in the smaller habit, narrower blades, longer spreading nodal hairs, panicles with fewer branches, shorter central axis, more densely white, villous pedicels and rachis joints and a *chromosome number* of $2n=120$ rather than $2n=180$.

Fig. 316. *Bothriochloa hybrida*. Inflorescence and spikelet pair. From Gould and Box, 1965, as *Andropogon hybridus*.

Fig. 317. *Bothriochloa springfieldii*. Two inflorescences and a spikelet pair.

SUBFAMILY VI. PANICOIDEAE   599

6. **Bothriochloa barbinodis** (Lag.) Herter, Revista Sudamer. Bot. 6:135. 1940. Cespitose perennial, the culms often in large clumps. *Culms* erect or geniculate at base, tending to become decumbent and much-branched below in age, mostly 60-120 cm tall. *Culm nodes* bearded with hairs mostly 1-3 mm long (occasionally longer), these typically erect and not widely spreading. *Leaves* essentially glabrous except for few to numerous long hairs on upper sheath margins and in vicinity of ligule. *Ligule* 1-2 mm long, becoming erose and lacerate. *Blades* firm, linear, 2-7 mm broad, often 25-30 cm or more long but the upper culm blades greatly reduced. *Panicles* mostly 7-13 cm long, often partially included in upper sheath, with a straight main axis and numerous primary branches mostly 4-9 cm long, these erect or loosely spreading at tips, the basal ones moderately rebranched. *Internodes of panicle branches and pedicels* more or less densely villous on the thickened margins, with a broad, membranous central region. *Sessile spikelet* 4.5-7.3 mm long excluding awn. *First glume* usually sparsely hairy below the middle. *Lemma awn* 20-30 mm or more long, geniculate and twisted. *Chromosome number*, $2n = 180$.

First glume of sessile spikelet on most or all spikelets without a glandular
   pit or depression   6A.   *B. barbinodis* var. *barbinodis*

First glume of sessile spikelet on most or all spikelets with a glandular
   pit or depression at or above the middle
                                   6B.   *B. barbinodis* var. *perforata*

6A. **Bothriochloa barbinodis** (Lag.) Herter var. **barbinodis.** *Andropogon barbinodis.* Lag. CANE BLUESTEM. Fig. 318.

Distribution. Texas: Regions 2, 5, 6, 7, 8, 9 and 10, mostly on loose, limey soils. General: Central and western Texas, southern Colorado, Utah and California, south through the highlands of Mexico and also in Argentina and Uruguay.

Flowering period: Mostly May to October but flowering throughout the year under favorable growing conditions.

Despite the extremely high chromosome number ($2n = 180$), populations of *B. barbinodis* var. *barbinodis* exhibit a wide range of variation in respect to morphological characters. It is assumed that this species has evolved through hybridization of taxa with $2n = 60$ and $2n = 120$ chromosome complements and the doubling of chromosome numbers. It is possible that populations referable to this species have arisen several times and from different combinations of parental species (Gould, 1953).

6B. **Bothriochloa barbinodis** (Lag.) Herter var. **perforata** (Trin. *ex* Fourn.) Gould, Southw. Naturalist. 3:212. 1959. *Andropogon perforatus* Trin. *ex* Fourn. PINHOLE BLUESTEM.

Fig. 318. *Bothriochloa barbinodis* var. *barbinodis.* Inflorescence and spikelet pair. From Gould and Box, 1965, as *Andropogon barbinodis.*

Distribution. Texas: With the same general distribution and habitat preference as the typical variety. General: Texas and New Mexico, through the highlands of Mexico and in Argentina and Uruguay.

Flowering period: Same as for the typical variety.

Plants referable to the var. *perforata* are not known to differ from those of the typical variety in any characters other than the presence of the glandular glume pit. It is probable that this character indicates a relationship with *B. edwardsiana.*

7. **Bothriochloa alta** (Hitch.) Henr., Blumea 4:520. 1941. *Andropogon altus* Hitchc. TALL BLUESTEM. Stout, cespitose perennial with stiffly erect culms mostly 1.2-2.5 m tall. *Culm internodes* bluish-glaucous below nodes, the nodes bearded with spreading hairs 3-6 mm long. *Panicles* usually 14-25 cm long, the main axis and branches often remaining "kinked" from compression in sheath. *Pollen* grains averaging 39-40 microns in diameter. *Chromosome number,* 2n = 120.

Distribution. Texas: Known only from a few collections in the southern portion of region 10. General: Western Texas and southern New Mexico to west-central Mexico and also reported from Bolivia and Argentina.

Flowering period: Mostly August through November.

A species closely related and similar to the more widespread *Bothriochloa barbinodis,* differing primarily in the key characters and the chromosome number of 2n = 120.

8. **Bothriochloa bladhii** (Retz.) S.T. Blake, Proc. Royal Soc. Queensland 80(6):62-63. 1969. *Bothriochloa intermedia* (R.Br.) A. Camus, *Andropogon intermedius* R. Br. AUSTRALIAN BLUESTEM. Fig. 319. Cespitose perennial, not developing rhizomes or stolons. *Culms* strictly erect or decumbent at base, mostly 50-110 cm tall. *Nodes* bearded with appressed hairs 1-2 mm long, glabrate in age. *Sheaths* glabrous. *Ligule* a short, truncate membrane, becoming erose and lacerate in age. *Blades* glabrous except for a few hairs in vicinity of ligule, linear, attenuate, 3-6 (-8) mm broad, the lower ones 20-30 cm or more long. *Panicles* 8-15 cm long, with numerous slender, erect-spreading branches mostly 4-7 cm long, these simple or the lower ones sparingly rebranched, none as long as panicle axis. *Panicle branch and pedicel internodes* ciliate on margins with inconspicuous hairs, at least those near the branch tips with a narrow medial groove. *Sessile spikelets* mostly 3.5-4 mm long. *First glume* glabrous, scabrous or hairy below middle, usually broadest slightly above middle, with an obtuse or broadly acute apex and with or without a glandular pit or depression (occasionally 2) at or above middle. *Lemma awn* geniculate and twisted, mostly 1-1.5 mm long. *Pediceled spikelets* staminate, similar to sessile one in size, shape and general appearance. *Chromosome numbers* reported, 2n = 40, 60 and 80.

Distribution. Texas: Introduced as a forage grass in southeastern and southern Texas, regions 2, 3 and 6, and occasional as a roadside grass in these areas. General: Native to tropical-subtropical Asia, Australia and islands of the Pacific, introduced in Texas and elsewhere.

Flowering period: Mostly September to November.

9. **Bothriochloa ischaemum** (L.) Keng, var. **songarica** (Rupr.) Celerier & Harlan, J. Linn. Soc. London 55:758. 1958. *Andropogon ischaemum* L. var. *songaricus* Rupr. *ex* Fisch. & Mey. KING RANCH BLUESTEM. Fig. 320. Tufted perennial, with slender, strictly erect or decumbent culms, these becoming somewhat stoloniferous or rhizomatous under close grazing or

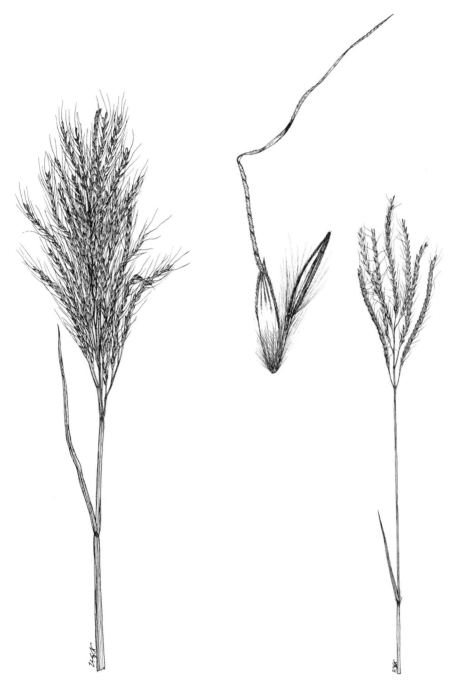

Fig. 319. *Bothriochloa bladhii.* Inflorescence. From Gould and Box, 1965, as *Andropogon intermedius.*

Fig. 320. *Bothriochloa ischaemum* var. *songaricus.* Inflorescence and spikelet pair. From Gould and Box, 1965, as *Andropogon ischaemum* var. *songaricus.*

SUBFAMILY VI. PANICOIDEAE   603

cutting. *Culms* mostly 30-50 cm tall but occasionally over 100 cm long when decumbent or trailing at base. *Culm nodes* bearded with short hairs, glabrate in age. *Sheaths* glabrous. *Ligule* a short, truncate membrane. usually 1 mm or less long. *Blades* linear-attenuate, mostly 2-4 mm broad and 4-20 cm long, the uppermost greatly reduced, usually sparsely hispid with long papilla-based hairs, at least in vicinity of ligule. *Inflorescence* well exserted above uppermost leaf, mostly 4-10 cm long and with 2-(1-) 8 primary branches 3-9 cm long, these infrequently rebranched. Branches slender, terete below the spikelets. *Internodes of branch rachis and pedicels* ciliate on margins, at least the terminal internodes and pedicels with a narrow medial groove. *Sessile spikelets* 3-4.5 mm long, narrowly ovate. *First glume* never with a glandular pit or depression, usually scabrous on margins and hispid on back below middle, the apex acute. *Lemma awn* geniculate and twisted, mostly 1-1.5 mm long. *Pediceled spikelet* staminate, awnless, about as long as sessile one but usually narrower. *First glume* glabrous or hairy below middle. *Chromosome numbers* reported, 2n=40, 50 and 60.

Distribution. Texas: Regions 2, 3, 4, 5, 6 and 7, a common roadside grass throughout the area of distribution and persisting as a pasture grass in central Texas, mostly from range seedings. General: Frequent throughout southern and central Europe and Asia and introduced in Texas, Mexico and elsewhere.

Flowering period: Mostly July through November but flowering throughout the year under favorable growing conditions.

10. **Bothriochloa pertusa** (L.) A. Camus, Ann. Soc. Lyon. N. Ser. 76:164. 1931. *Andropogon pertusus* (L.) Willd. PITTED BLUESTEM. Tufted perennial with culms mostly 20-60 cm tall but often decumbent or stoloniferous at base and as much as 100 cm long. *Nodes* usually bearded, glabrate in age. *Sheaths* glabrous. *Ligule* a short, ciliate membrane. *Blades* usually sparsely hirsute, often with papilla-based hairs, mostly 10-20 cm long and 2-5 mm broad, the upper blades greatly reduced. *Panicles* well exserted, 2-7 cm long, with usually 2-7 loosely erect-spreading branches, these mostly 2.5-6 cm long and simple or rarely rebranched. *Internodes of branch rachis and pedicels* ciliate on margins and, at least those at branch tips, with a dark-colored medial groove. *Sessile spikelets* 3-4 mm long, narrowly oval, acute at apex. *First glume* shiny, hairy below middle with a deep medial glandular pit or depression. *Lemma awn* geniculate and twisted, mostly 1-1.7 mm long. *Pediceled spikelets* neuter, as long as the sessile ones but usually narrower, the first glume with or without a central pit or depression, occasionally with 2 pits. *Chromosome numbers* reported, 2n=40 and 60.

Distribution. Texas: Introduced in experimental pasture seedings in southern Texas (region 6) and sparingly established in pastures and as a casual grass of roadsides and ditches. General: Northern Africa to India and China, introduced by experiment stations at several locations in the United States but apparently persisting spontaneously only in southern Texas.

Flowering period: Mostly August through November but flowering at all times of the year under favorable growing conditions.

114. SCHIZACHYRIUM Nees

Annuals or perennials (Texas plants perennial), with or without rhizomes. *Leaves* with rounded or compressed and keeled sheaths, membranous ligules and flat or folded blades. *Flowering culms* much-branched above, each leafy branch terminating in a single spicate raceme. *Spikelets* appressed to rachis or divergent. *Rachis joints and pedicels* thick, more or less flattened, the rachis joints with a cup-shaped or irregularly lobed or toothed appendage at apex. Disarticulation at base of sessile spikelets, the rachis section and pedicel falling attached to spikelet. *Sessile spikelets* perfect, with large firm glumes and thin, membranous, hyaline lemmas in both lower and upper florets. *Lemma of upper floret* awned or awnless. *Stamens* usually 3 but occasionally 2 or 1.

Internodes of rachis thick, not flexuous, glabrous or ciliate at base and apex only (except in S. *scoparium* var. *neomexicanum*); spikelets remaining appressed to rachis

First glume of sessile spikelet pubescent on back   3. S. *hirtiflorum*

First glume of sessile spikelet glabrous on back

Rachis of raceme densely villous; western Texas
                           5.   S. *scoparium* var. *neomexicanum*

Rachis of raceme not densely villous

Sessile spikelet about 4 mm long; blades about 1 mm wide; eastern Texas   1. S. *tenerum*

Sessile spikelet usually 6-9 mm long; blades mostly 2-3 mm wide; western Texas   2. S. *cirratum*

Internodes of rachis relatively thin and flexuous, ciliate throughout or nearly so   4. S. *scoparium*

1. **Schizachyrium tenerum** Nees, Agrost. Bras. 336. 1829. *Andropogon tener* (Nees) Kunth. SLENDER BLUESTEM. Tufted perennial with slender, usually much-branched culms mostly 60-100 cm tall. *Culm nodes and leaf sheaths* glabrous. *Ligules* less than 0.5 mm long, minutely ciliate. *Blades* 0.5-1.5 mm broad and 5-15 cm long, involute or flat, glabrous or sparsely hairy above ligule, with a broad central zone of bulliform cells sharply delimited on adaxial surface. *Racemes* slender, mostly 2-6 cm long and 1-1.5 mm broad,

developed at all upper culm nodes. *Rachis and spikelets* glabrous, the pedicels glabrous except for a few hairs on one side near apex. *Sessile spikelets* narrow, mostly 3.5-4.5 mm long, the lemma with a delicate, geniculate awn 0.6-0.8 mm long. *Pediceled spikelets* narrow, awnless, usually as long as or slightly longer than sessile ones. *Chromosome number*, $2n = 60$.

Distribution. Texas: Region 1 and 2, infrequent in sandy soil of pine forest openings and coastal prairie. General: Georgia and Florida, west to Oklahoma and eastern Texas and also in Central and South America.

Flowering period: August through November.

2. **Schizachyrium cirratum** (Hack.) Woot. & Standl., New Mexico Coll. Agr. Bull. 81:30. 1911. TEXAS BLUESTEM. Fig. 321. Tufted perennial with slender culms mostly 40-80 cm tall. *Culms* strictly erect or, in the larger clumps, decumbent at base, moderately branched above. *Culm nodes* glabrous. *Sheaths* glabrous, rounded on the back or slightly keeled above. *Ligule* hyaline, 1-2.5 mm long. *Blades* glabrous or sparsely ciliate on margins, linear-acuminate, 1-4 mm broad, the basal ones mostly 6-15 cm long, the upper ones reduced. *Racemes* slender, stiffly erect, mostly 2-3 mm thick and 3.5-8 cm long; lateral racemes usually developed at upper 1-2 nodes in addition to terminal one. *Rachis joints* glabrous except for a line of short hairs on nodes at point of disarticulation. *Pedicels of staminate spikelets* ciliate with long hairs on one side near apex. *Sessile spikelets* 7-10 mm long, glabrous on back, glabrous, scabrous or short-ciliate on the margins above middle. *Lemma awn* twisted and once-geniculate, 12-15 mm long. *Pediceled spikelets* usually staminate, awnless, as long as but usually narrower than the sessile ones. *Chromosome number*, $2n = 20$.

Distribution. Texas: Mountains of Jeff Davis, Brewster and Presidio counties in region 10 on rocky slopes, mostly at elevations of 5,000 feet or higher. General: Western Texas to southern California and south in the mountains of Coahuila, Chihuahua and Sonora, Mexico.

Flowering period: June to November.

Similar to *S. scoparium* var. *neomexicanum* in the stiffly erect rachis and pedicels but with larger pediceled spikelets and much less hairy racemes.

3. **Schizachyrium hirtiflorum** Nees, Agrost. Bras. 334. 1829. *Andropogon hirtiflorus* (Nees) Kunth, *Andropogon feensis* Fourn., *Schizachyrium feense* (Fourn.) A. Camus. Fig. 322. Cespitose perennial with culms stiffly erect and in small clumps. *Culms* mostly 50-100 cm tall, glabrous and usually glaucous, branching at the upper nodes to produce 1 or 2 erect lateral racemes as well as the terminal raceme. *Sheaths and blades* glabrous, scabrous, or sparsely hispid with long, often papilla-based hairs. *Ligule* 1.5-2.5 mm long, erose at apex. *Blades* thin, linear-acuminate, mostly 1.5-4 mm broad. *Racemes* mostly 3-4 mm broad and 5-8 cm long, the rachis and pedicels straight, erect, typically hispid on back as well as on margins. *Sessile spikelets* 5-9 mm long, the first glume commonly villous to sparsely hispid,

Fig. 321. *Schizachyrium cirratum*. Spikelet pair on rachis. From Gould, 1951, as *Andropogon cirratus*.

Fig. 322. *Schizachyrium hirtiflorum*. Plant and inflorescence tip with one sessile and two pediceled spikelets. From Gould, 1951, as *Andropogon hirtiflorus*.

SUBFAMILY VI. PANICOIDEAE   607

usually rugose or papillate. *Lemma of sessile spikelet* with a geniculate, twisted awn 0.8-1.5 mm long. *Pediceled spikelets* staminate or neuter, narrower and usually considerably shorter than sessile spikelets. *First glume* sparsely hispid or scabrous, the lemma awnless or more commonly with a short, straight awn. *Chromosome numbers* reported, $2n = 60$ and 100.

Distribution. Texas: Region 10 on mountain slopes at medium to high elevations. General: Georgia and Florida, western Texas to eastern Arizona, highlands of Mexico and Central America.

Flowering period: Mostly August to October but occasionally earlier.

Populations of *Schizachyrium hirtiflorum* in western Texas were referred to *Andropogon hirtiflorus* var. *feensis* by Chase in Hitchcock's Manual (1951) and to *Schizachyrium feense* by Correll and Johnston (1970). The characters upon which *feensis* entity is distinguished from *S. hirtiflorum* do not appear sufficiently consistent to warrant taxonomic separation. Further investigation of these populations and their relationships to *S. cirratum* and the tropical *S. semiberbe* Nees is needed. Cytological records indicate that the *S. hirtiflorum* of western Texas with a $2n = 100$ chromosome number may have arisen through hybridization of *S. cirratum* and a closely related species. In the mountains of Texas, New Mexico and Arizona, *S. hirtiflorum* frequently grows intermingled with *S. cirratum*.

4. **Schizachyrium scoparium** (Michx.) Nash, in Small, Fl. Southeast. U. S. 59. 1903. *Andropogon scoparius* Michx., Fl. Bor. Amer. 1. 57. 1803. Cespitose perennial, with or without rhizomes. *Culms* 50-200 cm tall, green or glaucous, freely branching above to produce numerous floriferous branches. *Sheaths* strongly keeled and laterally flattened, to 10 mm broad on some plants but usually much narrower, glabrous to villous-pubescent. *Ligules* firm, 1-3 mm long. *Blades* linear-acuminate, the basal ones mostly 1.5-4 (rarely -6) mm broad and 25 cm or more long, glabrous or sparsely hispid to villous. *Racemes* mostly 2.5-5 cm long. *Rachis joints and pedicels* ciliate with long, silvery hairs, at least on the upper two-thirds. *Sessile spikelets* mostly 6-8 mm long, the first glume glabrous or scabrous, the lemma 8-15 mm long. *Pediceled spikelets* staminate or neuter, as long as the sessile ones to much shorter, awnless or with a short, straight awn. *Chromosome number*, $2n = 40$.

Lower sheaths and blades villous; southeastern Texas
                         4B.   *S. scoparium* var. *divergens*

Lower sheaths and blades glabrous or sparsely pubescent

    Plants rhizomatous; culms and sheaths strongly compressed and sharply
         keeled; rachis joints and pedicels more or less densely villous;
         plants of southeastern and southern Texas
                         4D.   *S. scoparium* var. *littoralis*

Plants not rhizomatous; culms and sheaths moderately compressed, the sheaths weakly or strongly keeled

Rachis and pedicels villous, nearly straight at maturity; western Texas
4E. S. *scoparium* var. *neomexicanum*

Rachis and pedicels ciliate but not villous; rachis more or less zig-zag and pedicels spreading at maturity

Pediceled spikelets 1.5-5 mm long, consisting of a single empty glume; central, western and southern Texas
4A. S. *scoparium* var. *frequens*

Pediceled spikelets 4.5-7 mm long, at least some consisting of two glumes and often a lemma and stamens; eastern Texas, in pine and oak woodlands   4C. S. *scoparium* var. *virile*

4A. Schizachyrium scoparium var. **frequens** (C. E. Hubb.) Gould, Brittonia 19:73. 1967. *Andropogon scoparius* Michx. var. *frequens* C. E. Hubb. LITTLE BLUESTEM. Fig. 323. Plants not producing creeping rhizomes. *Leaves* glabrous or sparsely hispid. *Inflorescence axis and pedicels* hairy but not densely villous. *Pediceled spikelets* narrow, shorter than the sessile ones.

Distribution. Texas: Throughout the State except in region 1, a dominant of tallgrass prairies, frequent in woods openings and on rocky slopes of moderate to lightly grazed pastures and rangeland. In western Texas this variety is less frequent than variety *neomexicanum* with villous rachis joints that are straight or nearly so at maturity.

Flowering period: August to December.

4B. Schizachyrium scoparium var. **divergens** (Hack.) Gould, Brittonia 19:73. 1967. *Andropogon divergens* (Hack.) Anderss. *ex* Hitchc. EASTERN LITTLE BLUESTEM. Sheaths and blades, at least in part, villous with long shaggy hairs. Pediceled spikelets well-developed, often as long as sessile ones and with two well-developed glumes.

Distribution. Texas: Regions 1 and 2, a shade-tolerant variety of S. *scoparius* that is frequent in open pine forest and pine-hardwood woodlands of eastern Texas. General: Arkansas and Mississippi to eastern Texas.

Flowering period: August to December.

Plants of *Schizachyrium scoparium* var. *divergens* frequently grow intermingled with plants of the variety *virile* and, to a lesser extent, variety *frequens*. The character of herbage pubescence does not appear to be of great taxonomic significance.

4C. Schizachyrium scoparium var. **virile** (Shinners) Gould, Brittonia 19:73. 1967. *Andropogon scoparius* var. *virilis* Shinners, Rhodora 56:36. 1954.

Fig. 323. *Schizachyrium scoparium* var. *frequens*. Plant and spikelet pair. From Gould and Box, 1965, as *Andropogon scoparius* var. *frequens*.

610   THE GRASSES OF TEXAS

VIRILE LITTLE BLUESTEM. Plants strictly cespitose, relatively tall and coarse and with broad blades. *Rachis joints and pedicels* only moderately hairy on margins, not villous. *Pediceled spikelets* equaling or only slightly shorter than sessile ones, often staminate.

Distribution. Texas: Regions 1, 3 and 4, mostly in open woodlands and along forest borders. General: Arkansas and Oklahoma to eastern Texas.

Flowering period: August to November.

4D. **Schizachyrium scoparium** var. **littoralis** (Nash) Gould, Brittonia 19:73. 1967. *Andropogon littoralis* Nash. SEACOAST BLUESTEM. Plants with well-developed rhizomes, strongly compressed and keeled sheaths, glaucous herbage and densely villous rachis joints and pedicels.

Distribution. Texas: Regions 2 and 6, typically in deep sand and common on coastal sands near sea level in southern Texas. General: Reported by Chase in Hitchcock's Manual (1951) as *Andropogon littoralis*, occurring along the northeastern U. S. coast, along the shore of Lake Ontario and Lake Michigan in Ohio and Indiana and in Texas.

Flowering period: Mostly August to December but occasionally as early as June.

4E. **Schizachyrium scoparium** var. **neomexicanum** (Nash) Gould, Brittonia 19:73. 1967. *Andropogon neomexicanus* Nash. NEW MEXICO LITTLE BLUESTEM. Plants tufted, without rhizomes. *Herbage* usually glaucous. *Rachis of raceme* densely villous. *Pedicels* relatively stiff and straight, not or only slightly curving outward at maturity.

Distribution. Texas: Regions 8, 9 and 10, mostly on open, rocky slopes. General: Western Texas to Arizona.

Flowering period: August to November.

115. EREMOCHLOA Buese

About 10 species, native to tropical and temperate Asia.

1. **Eremochloa ophiuroides** (Munro) Hack., in DC., Monogr. Phan. 6:261. 1889. CENTIPEDEGRASS. Decumbent, mat-forming perennial with erect culms from leafy stolons, these often long and much-branched. *Culms* mostly 10-30 cm tall. *Herbage* glabrous except for a few hairs on sheath and blade in vicinity of ligule. *Sheaths* laterally compressed and sharply keeled. *Ligule* a short, ciliate membrane. *Blades* flat, mostly 1-4 mm broad and 3-8 cm long. *Inflorescence* a slender raceme 2-5 cm long; the spikelets in pairs of one sessile and one pediceled, the pediceled spikelet greatly reduced and sometimes absent. Disarticulation in rachis, at base of sessile spikelet. *Sessile spikelets* dorsally compressed, broadly oblong, 3-4 mm long, awnless, imbricated along one side of a slender rachis. *First glume* large, glabrous, shiny,

nearly flat, 7-nerved, winged above, the rounded wings about 0.5 mm broad. *Second glume* 3-nerved. *Chromosome number,* $2n = 18$.

Distribution. Texas: Occasional as an escape from experimental plantings, Tracy Herbarium records are from regions 1 and 3, in Cherokee, Leon and Brazos counties. General: Native to southeastern Asia.

Flowering period: Mostly September to November but occasionally flowering at other times of the year.

116. TRACHYPOGON Nees

A genus of about 12 species in tropical-subtropical regions of the Americas and Africa.

1. **Trachypogon secundus** (Presl) Scribn., U.S.D.A. Div. Agrost. Cir. 32:1. 1901. CRINKLEAWN. Fig. 324. Cespitose perennial with culms 60-120 cm tall. *Culm nodes* densely bearded, glabrate in age. *Sheaths* rounded on back or slightly keeled, those of the lower and middle leaves continued at apex into a brownish, membranous ligule 1-10 mm long, the upper leaves with a short, fringed ligule. *Blades* 1-6 (-8) mm broad, the narrow ones often involute. *Blades of lower leaves* 20-30 cm long. *Inflorescence* a spikelike raceme 10-18 (-28) cm long. *Spikelets* in pairs on a continuous rachis, one subsessile and awnless and one with a slightly longer pedicel and long-awned. *Disarticulation* at base of the longer-pediceled, perfect spikelet. *Subsessile spikelet* staminate, 6-8 mm long. *First glume of subsessile spikelet* strigose-pubescent, rounded on the back. *Longer-pediceled spikelet* about the same length and same appearance as subsessile one but the lemma with a stout awn 4-6 cm long. *Lemma awn* loosely twisted and contorted, densely plumose below with hairs mostly 2-5 mm long. *Chromosome number,* $2n = 20$.

Distribution. Texas: Regions 2, 6 and 10, mostly in loose, sandy soils. General: Southern Texas, New Mexico and Arizona, south through Mexico and also in Argentina.

Flowering period: Mostly September to November.

117. ELYONURUS Humb. & Bonpl. *ex* Willd.

Cespitose perennials with slender, moderately tall culms and narrow, flat or involute blades. *Ligule* a short, ciliate membrane. *Inflorescence* a spikelike raceme, with disarticulation in rachis. *Spikelets* awnless, in pairs of one subsessile and perfect and one pediceled, the pediceled one similar in size and appearance to the subsessile one but staminate. *First glume of perfect spikelet* firm, moderately coriaceous, the second glume thinner. *Lemmas of both florets* thin and hyaline, the paleas absent.

A genus of about 15 species in tropical and subtropical regions of both hemispheres.

Fig. 324. *Trachypogon secundus*. Plant and spikelet. From Gould and Box, 1965.

Culms glabrous below nodes; first glume glabrous on back, ciliate towards
the apex   1.   *E. tripsacoides*

Culms pubescent below nodes; first glume densely woolly
       2.   *E. barbiculmis*

SUBFAMILY VI. PANICOIDEAE   613

1. **Elyonurus tripsacoides** Humb. & Bcnpl. *ex* Willd. Sp. Pl. 4:941. 1806. PAN AMERICAN BALSAMSCALE. Fig. 325. *Culms* glabrous, mostly 60-120 cm tall, in small clusters from knotty, rhizomatous bases, branching at upper nodes to produce stiffly erect, floriferous branches. *Leaves* hispid with papilla-based hairs in vicinity of ligule and often on upper portion of sheath. *Sheaths* rounded at base. *Ligule* a fringed membrane to 1 mm long. *Blades* mostly filiform, flat or more commonly involute, 1-2 (rarely -4) mm broad, the basal ones 16-30 cm or more long. *Racemes* 6-15 cm long. *Rachis* broad, flat, ciliate on margins. *Pedicels* broad and flattened but thick, hispid or pilose on back, at least on lower half, slightly shorter than pediceled spikelets. *Subsessile spikelets* mostly 6-8 mm long, the pediceled spikelets slightly shorter. *First glume of sessile spikelet* broadly rounded and usually glabrous on back below apex, ciliate on margins, irregularly lobed or cleft and hispid at apex. *Chromosome number,* $2n=20$.

Distribution. Texas: Regions 2 and 6 on sandy soils in coastal grasslands and woods openings. An *Elyonurus* collection (*Silveus 228*) reported to be from near Fort Davis in Jeff Davis County (region 10) definitely is *E. tripsacoides,* but the occurrence of this species in western Texas needs verification. General: Georgia and Florida, southern Mississippi to southern Texas, the Gulf coastal region of Mexico and south to Argentina.

Flowering period: May to November.

2. **Elyonurus barbiculmis** Hack., in DC., Monogr. Phan. 6:339. 1889. WOOLSPIKE BALSAMSCALE. Fig. 326. Tufted perennial, without rhizomes. *Culms* mostly 40-90 cm tall, unbranched or less frequently branched above, pubescent on upper portion of internodes, the nodes glabrous. *Leaves* as in *Elyonurus tripsacoides* but thicker and with conspicuously raised and thickened nerves. *Racemes* mostly 5-10 cm long. *Peduncle* densely villous below raceme, raceme axis and pedicels. *Subsessile spikelets* 4.5-7 (-8) mm long, the pediceled ones slightly shorter. *First glume of subsessile and pediceled spikelets* pilose on back. *Chromosome number,* $2n=20$.

Distribution. Texas: Region 10 on rocky slopes, mostly at elevations of 4,000 feet or higher. General: Western Texas to southern Arizona and northern Mexico.

Flowering period: June to November.

118. HETEROPOGON Pers.

A genus of about 8 species distributed in the warmer parts of both hemispheres.

1. **Heteropogon contortus** (L.) Beauv. *ex* Roem. & Schult., Syst. Veg. 2:836. 1817. TANGLEHEAD. Fig. 327. Cespitose perennial. *Culms* 20-80 cm tall, much-branched at the base and also freely branching at upper nodes, glabrous. *Leaves* glabrous except for a few long hairs on sheath and blade margins in vicinity of ligule. *Sheaths* laterally compressed and sharply keeled.

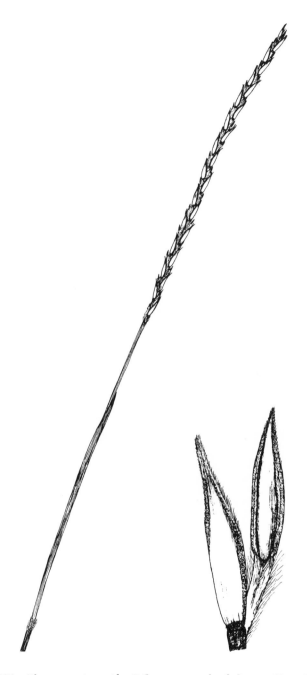

Fig. 325. *Elyonurus tripsacoides*. Inflorescence and spikelet pair. From Gould and Box, 1965.

SUBFAMILY VI. PANICOIDEAE   615

Fig. 326. *Elyonurus barbiculmis*. Plant and spikelet pair. From Gould, 1951.

Fig. 327. *Heteropogon contortus*. Inflorescence and spikelet. From Gould, 1951.

SUBFAMILY VI. PANICOIDEAE   617

Ligule a short, fringed membrane. *Blades* flat, mostly 4-6 (rarely -10) mm broad and 6-20 cm or more long. *Racemes* mostly 4-7 cm long excluding awns. *Spikelets* in pairs, one sessile and one pediceled, both of the lower few to several pairs staminate or neuter and awnless, the remainder of the sessile spikelets perfect, with a sharp-pointed bearded callus and a dark-colored, geniculate and twisted awn. *Staminate or neuter spikelets* 7-10 mm long, with broad, thin, green, many-nerved glabrous or sparsely hispid glumes. *Perfect spikelet* 5-8 mm long with narrow, rounded, dark-colored, several-nerved, brownish-hispid glumes. *Awn of lemma of perfect floret* commonly 5-12 cm long, hispid, weakly twice-geniculate. *Chromosome number*, most reports, $2n=60$.

Distribution. Texas: Regions 2, 6, 7 and 10, frequent both in grasslands of lower Gulf Coast and in mountains of western Texas, usually in sandy soil. General: Tropical and subtropical regions of both hemispheres; in the United States, present in southern Texas, New Mexico and Arizona.

Flowering period: March through December, mostly June through November.

Numerous chromosome numbers have been reported for this species, including euploid counts of $2n=20$, 40, 50, 60, 70 and 80.

Correll and Johnston (1970) report the occurrence of *Heteropogon melanocarpus* (Ell.) Benth. in southeastern Texas but note that it is rare and probably not persistent. *H. melanocarpus* in an annual, with a medial row of large, depressed glands on the first glume of the staminate spikelets.

119. HEMARTHRIA R. Br.

Twelve species, native to tropical-subtropical regions of the Old World, introduced in the Americas.

1. **Hemarthria altissima** (Poir.) Stapf & Hubbard, in Kew Bull. 1934:109. 1934. *Manisuris altissima* (Poir.) Hitchc. *Rottboellia altissima* Poir. Fig. 328. Coarse perennial with culms mostly 40-100 cm long. *Culms* glabrous, with numerous nodes and short internodes. *Sheaths* thin, keeled or not keeled, glabrous or sparsely hairy on margins above. *Ligule* a short, ciliate and lacerate membrane. *Blades* thin, flat or folded, 3-8 mm broad. *Inflorescence* a glabrous spikelike raceme 3-5 (-10) cm long, with thick, tough, dorsally compressed clavate internodes. *Racemes* usually produced at all upper culm nodes, enclosed at base by the subtending sheaths. Disarticulation at nodes of rachis. *Spikelets* in pairs of one sessile and perfect and one pediceled and staminate or neuter, both more or less sunken in the corky rachis. *Sessile spikelets* elliptic-oblong, awnless, with a triangular callus. *Lower glume* 4-7 mm long, flattened on back, not pitted, with or without a constriction near apex, obtuse to notched at tip; upper glume obtuse to acute. *Pediceled spikelets* about as long as the sessile ones, usually acute. *Pedicels* flattened, broadly linear, more or less fused to rachis internodes. *Chromosome number* not reported.

Fig. 328. *Hemarthria altissima*. Inflorescence and spikelet pair. From Gould and Box, 1965, as *Manisuris altissima*.

Distribution. Texas: Regions 2, 6 and 10, infrequent in the State. General: Throughout the warmer parts of the world, adventive in the United States.

Flowering period: Mostly June to October but one Texas collection made in December.

SUBFAMILY VI. PANICOIDEAE   619

120. COELORACHIS Brongn.

Tufted perennials with or without rhizomes and with narrow, flat blades. *Ligule* a short ciliate membrane. *Inflorescence* a cylindrical or flattened spikelike raceme with short, stout, clavate internodes. *Racemes* well exserted or enclosed at base in the subtending sheaths. Disarticulation at the rachis nodes. *Spikelets* awnless, in pairs of one sessile and perfect and one pediceled and neuter (in Texas species). *Sessile spikelets* convex on back. *Lower glumes* firm or hard, usually winged, 2-keeled below, rugose or pitted on back at least on margins (in Texas species). *Lemmas of both lower and upper florets* thin, hyaline, awnless.

Nineteen species throughout the tropics and subtropics of the world.

Sheaths rounded or only slightly keeled; first glume more or less pitted
1. *C. cylindrica*

Sheaths compressed-keeled; first glume with irregular transverse ridges
2. *C. rugosa*

1. **Coelorachis cylindrica** (Michx.) Nash, N. Amer. Flora 17:85. 1909. *Rottboellia cylindrica* Michx. *Manisuris cylindrica* Kuntze. CAROLINA JOINTTAIL. Fig. 329. *Culms* mostly 30-100 cm tall, single or in small clumps from short, knotty rhizomes. *Culms and leaves* glabrous. *Sheaths* rounded or only slightly keeled. *Ligule* truncate, 0.5-1 mm long. *Blades* flat or folded, mostly 8-30 cm long and 1.5-4 mm broad, with few to several strongly and uniformly developed nerves. *Racemes* glabrous, 6-15 cm long, about 3 mm thick, the spikelets occasionally spreading in age, making the raceme 5-6 cm wide. *Sessile spikelets* 4-6 mm long, only slightly shorter than the pedicel and pediceled spikelet, with a flattened, leathery first glume, this shallowly pitted on back between nerves, at least along margins. *Pediceled spikelets* greatly reduced, less than one-half the length of pedicel. *Chromosome number*, $2n = 18$.

Distribution. Texas: Regions 1, 2, 3, 4, 5, 6, 7 and 8, widespread in tallgrass prairies and woods borders but infrequently abundant. General: North Carolina to Missouri and south to Florida, Louisiana and Texas.

Flowering period: Mostly May to July but occasionally in summer and autumn.

2. **Coelorachis rugosa** (Nutt.) Nash, N. Amer. Flora 17:86. 1909. *Manisuris rugosa* (Nutt.) Kuntze. WRINKLED JOINTTAIL. Course perennial with stout culms mostly 75-130 cm tall, branching and rebranching above, the numerous, slender ultimate branches all raceme-bearing. *Culms and leaves* glabrous. *Sheaths* keeled, at least near apex, the lower sheaths as much as 2 cm broad at base. *Ligule* a short, truncate, lacerate membrane. *Blades* 2-8 mm broad and to 35 cm or more long, usually folded on midnerve. *Racemes* glabrous, 4-8 cm long and 2-2.5 mm thick. *Sessile spikelets* 3.5-5 mm long.

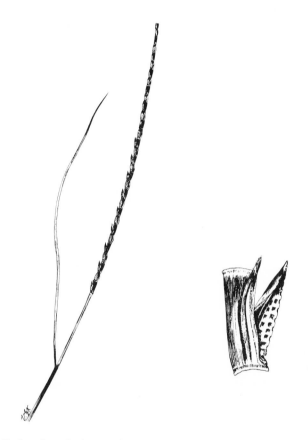

Fig. 329. *Coelorachis cylindrica.* Inflorescence and spikelet pair. From Gould and Box, 1965, as *Manisuris cylindrica.*

First glume coarsely and irregularly transversely ridged. *Pedicels* thickened above, bearing a much reduced, rudimentary spikelet. *Chromosome number* not reported.

Distribution. Texas: Regions 1 and 2, mostly in moist soil along streams, swales and lakes, infrequent. General: Along the Atlantic Coastal Plain, New Jersey to Florida and west along the Gulf of Mexico to eastern Texas and also reported from Missouri.

Flowering period: Mostly July to October.

SUBFAMILY VI. PANICOIDEAE   621

121. TRIPSACUM L.

A genus of 7 species native to the warmer parts of the Americas.

1. **Tripsacum dactyloides** (L.) L., Syst. Nat. ed. 10. 2:1261. 1759. EASTERN GAMMAGRASS. Fig. 330. *Culms* 1.5-3 m or more tall, in large clumps from thick, knotty rhizomes. *Culms and leaves* glabrous. *Sheaths* rounded, smooth and shiny. *Ligule* a short, ciliate or lacerate membrane. *Blades* thin, flat, mostly 10-25 mm broad and 30-75 cm or more long. *Inflorescence* a single spicate raceme 12-25 cm long or of 2-3 erect, spikelike, racemose branches. *Raceme or racemose branches* with staminate spikelets above and pistillate spikelets below. *Staminate spikelets* awnless, 2-flowered, mostly 6-10 mm long, in pairs on one side of a continuous rachis. *Glumes of the pistillate spikelets* membranous, flat, several-nerved. *Pistillate spikelets* subsessile, usually solitary, hard and bony, awnless, mostly 6-8 mm long, the glumes indurate, fused with the rachis and tightly enclosing the other spikelet parts. *Lemmas of sterile and perfect florets of pistillate spikelets* thin and hyaline, often reduced. *Pedicels and pediceled spikelets* usually absent, a rudiment occasionally present. *Staminate portion of inflorescence* deciduous as a whole, the pistillate portion breaking up at the nodes into hard, shiny, beadlike units. *Chromosome numbers* reported, $2n=36, 54, 72, 90$ and 108; aneuploid numbers also reported.

Distribution. Texas: Throughout the State but most frequent in the eastern portion, mostly in low, moist, little-disturbed grassland sites. General: Throughout the eastern half of the United States, west to Nebraska, Kansas, Oklahoma and Texas; also in the West Indies and northern Mexico.

Flowering period: April to November.

122. ZEA L.

As interpreted by Reeves and Mangelsdorf (1943), a genus of 3 species. Included with *Zea mays* are two Mexican species, *Z. mexicana* (Schrad.) Reeves and Mangelsdorf (*Euchlaena mexicana* Schrad.) and *Z. perennis* (Hitchc.) Reeves and Mangelsdorf (*Euchlaena perennis* Hitchc.). *Zea mays* has been grown in the New World from prehistoric times and is known only from cultivated plants. The other two species are native to Mexico.

1. **Zea mays** L., Sp. Pl. 971. 1753. CORN or MAIZE. Monoecious annual with thick, succulent culms mostly 1.5-3 m tall. *Ligule* short, membranous. *Blades* elongate, broad, flat. *Spikelets* unisexual. Staminate spikelets 2-flowered, in unequally pediceled pairs on spikelike branches of a terminal inflorescence. *Glumes of staminate spikelets* broad, thin, several-nerved. *Lemma and palea of staminate spikelets* thin, hyaline. *Pistillate inflorescences* lateral, enclosed in numerous foliaceous sheaths, the spikelets paired in rows on a thickened, woody or corky axis (cob). *Pistillate spikelets* consisting of one perfect floret (upper) and one reduced floret (lower), the latter sometimes developed as a second perfect floret. *Glumes of pistillate spikelets* broad, thin, rounded at apex, much shorter than the mature caryopses. *Lemma of lower*

Fig. 330. *Tripsacum dactyloides.* Inflorescence with pistillate spikelets below the staminate ones. From Gould and Box, 1965.

floret and lemma and palea of upper floret membranous and hyaline. *Caryopses* large, thick, with an embryo three-fourths to four-fifths as long as the endosperm. *Chromosome number,* $2n = 20$.

Distribution. Texas: Cultivated throughout the State and occasional as a roadside escape. General: Grown throughout the United States and widespread as a crop plant on all continents.

Flowering period: Late spring and summer.

LITERATURE CITED

Anderson, D. E. 1961. Taxonomy and distribution of the genus *Phalaris*. Iowa State Coll. J. Sci. 36:1-96.

Avdulov, N. P. 1931. Karyosystematische Untersuchung der Familie der Gramineen. Bull. Appl. Bot. Pl. Breed. 44:1-428.

Banks, D. J. 1966. Taxonomy of *Paspalum setaceum* (Gramineae). Sida 2:269-284.

Baum, B. R. 1967. Kalm's specimens of North American grasses: their evaluation for typification. Can. J. Bot. 45:1845-1852.

Bentham, G. 1881. Notes on Gramineae. J. Linn. Soc. Bot. 19:14-134.

Boyle, W. S. 1945. A cytotaxonomic study of the North American species of *Melica*. Madroño 8:1-26.

Brown, R. 1810. Prodomus florae novae Hollandiae, vol. I. R. Taylor, London, pp. i-viii, 145-590.

Brown, W. V., and B. N. Smith. 1972. Grass evolution, the Kranz syndrome, $^{13}C\big/C^{12}$ ratios and continental drift. Nature 239(537):345-346.

Chase, A. 1951. Rev. of Hitchcock's manual of the grasses of the United States, 2d ed., U.S.D.A. Misc. Publ. 200.

Church, G. L. 1929. Meiotic phenomena in certain Gramineae. *I. Festuceae, Aveneae, Agrostideae, Chlorideae,* and *Phalarideae*. Bot. Gaz. 87:608-629.

Church, G. L. 1936. Cytological studies in the Gramineae. Amer. J. Bot. 23:12-15.

Church, G. L. 1940. Cytotaxonomic studies in the Gramineae-*Spartina, Andropogon* and *Panicum*. Amer. J. Bot. 27:263-271.

Church, G. L. 1967. Taxonomic and genetic relationships of eastern North American species of *Elymus* with setaceous glumes. Rhodora 69:121-162.

Clayton, W. D. 1965. The *Sporobolus indicus* complex. Kew Bull. 19:287-293.

Clayton, W. D. 1967. Studies in the Gramineae: XIII, Kew Bull. 21:99-110.

Clayton, W. D. 1968. The correct name of the common reed. Taxon 17:157-158.

Correll, D. S., and M. C. Johnston. 1970. Manual of the vascular plants of Texas. Texas Research Foundation, Renner, Texas. 1881 p.

Covas, G. 1949. Taxonomic observations on the North American species of *Hordeum*. Madroño 10:1-121.

DeLisle, D. G. 1963. Taxonomy and distribution of the genus *Cenchrus*. Iowa State Coll. J. Sci. 37:259-351.

Ebinger, J. E. 1962. Validity of the grass species *Digitaria adscendens*. Brittonia 14:248-253.

Emery, W. H. P. 1957. A cytotaxonomic study of *Setaria macrostachya* (Gramineae) and its relatives in the southwestern United States and Mexico. Bull. Torrey Bot. Club 84:95-105.

Emery, W. H. P. 1957a. A study of reproduction in *Setaria macrostachya* and its relatives in southwestern United States and Mexico. Bull. Torrey Bot. Club 84:106-121.

Erdman, K. S. 1965. Taxonomy of the genus *Sphenopholis*. Iowa State Coll. J. Sci. 39:259-336.

Fernald, M. L. 1950. Gray's manual of botany. 8th ed. American Book Company, New York. 1632 p.

Gould, F. W. 1951. Grasses of southwestern United States. Univ. of Arizona Biol. Sci. Bull. 7.

Gould, F. W. 1953. A cytotaxonomic study in the genus *Andropogon*. Amer. J. Bot. 40:297-306.

Gould, F. W. 1957. Texas grasses, a preliminary checklist. Tex. Agr. Exp. Sta. MP-240.

Gould, F. W. 1958. Chromosome numbers in Southwestern grasses. Amer. J. Bot. 45:757-767.

Gould, F. W. 1962. Texas plants—A checklist and ecological summary. Tex. Agr. Exp. Sta. MP-585.

Gould, F. W. 1963. Cytotaxonomy of *Digitaria sanguinalis* and *D. adscendens*. Brittonia 15:241-244.

Gould, F. W. 1968. Grass systematics. McGraw-Hill Book Company, New York. 382 p.

Gould, F. W. 1968a. Chromosome numbers of Texas grasses. Can. J. Bot. 46:1315-1325.

Gould, F. W. 1969. Texas plants—A checklist and ecological summary. Tex. Agr. Exp. Sta. MP-585/Revised.

Gould, F. W. 1974. Nomenclatural changes in the *Poaceae*. Brittonia 29:59-60.

Gould, F. W., and Z. J. Kapadia. 1962. Biosystematic studies in the *Bouteloua curtipendula* complex. The aneuploid, rhizomatous *B. curtipendula* of Texas. Amer. J. Bot. 49:887-891.

Gould, F. W., and Z. J. Kapadia. 1964. Biosystematic studies in the *Bouteloua curtipendula* complex II. Taxonomy. Brittonia 16:182-208.

Gould, F. W., and T. W. Box. 1965. Grasses of the Texas Coastal Bend (Calhoun, Refugio, Aransas, San Patricio and northern Kleberg counties). Texas A&M Univ. Press, College Station, Texas. 189 p.

Gould, F. W., G. O. Hoffman and C. A. Rechenthin. 1960. Vegetational areas of Texas. Tex. Agr. Exp. Sta. L-492.

Gould, F. W., M. A. Ali and D. E. Fairbrothers. 1972. A revision of *Echinochloa* in the United States. Amer. Midl. Naturalist 87:36-59.

Griffiths, D. 1912. The grama grasses, *Bouteloua* and related genera. Contr. U. S. Natl. Herb. 14:343-428.

Hitchcock, A. S. 1920. The genera of grasses of the United States with special reference to the economic species. U.S.D.A. Bull. 772, Rev. ed. 1936.

Hitchcock, A. S. 1935. Manual of the grasses of the United States. U.S.D.A. Misc. Publ. 200.

Hitchcock, A. S., and A. Chase. 1910. The North American species of *Panicum*. Contr. U. S. Natl. Herb. 15:1-396.

Kapadia, Z. J., and F. W. Gould. 1964a. Biosystematic studies in the *Bouteloua curtipendula* complex III. Pollen size as related to chromosome numbers. Amer. J. Bot. 51:166-172.

Kapadia, Z. J., and F. W. Gould. 1964b. Biosystematic studies in the *Bouteloua curtipendula* complex IV. Dynamics of variation in *B. curtipendula* var. *caespitosa*. Bull. Torrey Bot. Club 91:465-478.

Linnaeus, C. 1753. Species plantarum. Holmiae, impensis Laurentii Salvii. 2 vols.

McClure, F. A. 1963. A new feature in bamboo rhizome anatomy. Rhodora 65:134-136.

Mobberly, D. G. 1956. Taxonomy and distribution of the genus *Spartina*. Iowa State Coll. J. Sci. 30:471-574.

Nash, G. V. 1903. Poaceae, p. 48-161. *In* J. K. Small, Flora of the Southeastern United States. Publ. by the author (Small), New York.

Nicora, E. G. 1962. Revalidacion del genero de Gramineas *Neeragrostis* de la flora Norteamericana. Revista Argent. Agron. 29:1-11.

Pinson, J. N., Jr., and W. T. Batson. 1971. The status of *Muhlenbergia filipes* Curtis (Poaceae). J. Elisha Mitchell Sci. Soc. 87:188-191.

Pohl, R. W. 1969. *Muhlenbergia*, subgenus *Muhlenbergia* (Gramineae) in North America. Amer. Midl. Naturalist 82:512-542.

Prat, H. 1932. L'épiderme des Graminées: étude anatomique et systématique. Ann. Sci. Nat. Bot. 14:117-324.

Prat, H. 1936. La systématique des Graminées. Ann. Sci. Nat. Bot. 18:165-258.

Raven, P. H. 1960. The correct name for rescue grass. Brittonia 12:219-221.

Reeves, R. G., and P. C. Mangelsdorf. 1943. A proposal taxonomic change in the tribe *Maydeae* (family Gramineae). Amer. J. Bot. 29:815-817.

Rominger, J. M. 1962. Taxonomy of *Setaria* (Gramineae) in North America. Ill. Biol. Monogr. 29.

Sauer, J. D. 1972. Revision of *Stenotaphrum* (Gramineae: Paniceae). Brittonia 24:202-222.

Shinners, L. H. 1958. Flora of the Dallas - Fort Worth area. Publ. by author, Dallas. 514 p.

Silveus, W. A. 1933. Texas grasses. Publ. by author, San Antonio. 782 p.

Smith, B. N., and W. V. Brown. 1973. The Kranz syndrome in the Gramineae as indicated by carbon isotopic ratios. Amer. J. Bot. 60(6):505-513.

Soderstrom, T. R. 1967. Taxonomic study of subgenus *Podosemum* and section *Epicampes* of *Muhlenbergia*. Contr. U.S. Natl. Herb. 34:75-189.

Stebbins, G. L., and B. Crampton. 1961. A suggested revision of the grass genera of temperate North America. Recent Advances in Bot. 1:133-145.

Swallen, J. R. 1955. Flora of Guatemala. II. Grasses of Guatemala. Fieldiana: Botany 24:1-390.

Swallen, J. R. 1964. Gramineae, p. 70-145. *In* T. H. Kearney and R. H. Peebles, Arizona flora, 2nd ed.

Terrell, E. E. 1967. Meadow fescue: *Festuca elatior* L. or *F. pratensis* Hudson? Brittonia 19:129-132.

Texas Agricultural Extension Service. 1958. Land resource areas of Texas. Tex. Agr. Ext. Ser. L-400. 4 p.

Tharp, B. C. 1952. Texas range grasses. Univ. of Texas Press, Austin. 125 p.

Wagnon, H. K. 1952. A revision of the genus *Bromus*, section *Bromopsis*, of North America. Brittonia 7:415-480.

Wilson, F. D. 1963. Revision of *Sitanion* (Triticeae, Gramineae). Brittonia 15:303-323.

Yates, H. O. 1966. Revision of grasses traditionally referred to *Uniola* II. *Chasmanthium*. Southw. Naturalist, 11:415-455.

GLOSSARY

Abaxial. Located on the side away from the axis.

Aciculate. Needleshaped.

Acuminate. Gradually tapering to a point.

Acute. Sharp-pointed, not abruptly or long-extended but making an angle of less than 90°.

Adaxial. Located on the side toward the axis.

Adherent. Sticking; clinging; adhering.

Adnate. Grown fast to, grown together.

Adventive. Introduced by chance or accidental seedlings and imperfectly naturalized.

Aneuploid. Having a chromosome number that is not an exact multiple of the basic haploid number.

Annual. Of one season's or year's duration from seed to maturity and death.

Anther. The pollen-bearing part of the stamen.

Anthesis. The period during which the flower is open and functional.

Antrorse. Directed forward or toward the apex; the opposite of retrorse.

Apex (pl. *apices*). The tip of an organ.

Apical. Situated at or forming the apex.

Apiculate. Terminating abruptly in a small, short point.

Appressed. Pressed closely against or fitting closely to something.

Arcuate. Bent or curved like a bow.

Aristate. Awned.

Articulation. A joint or node.

Ascending. Rising or curving upward.

Asymmetrical. Without symmetry.

Attenuate. Tapering gradually to a narrow extremity.

Auricle. An ear-shaped appendage; name applied to pointed appendages that occur laterally at the base of the leaf blade in some grasses and laterally at the sheath apex in others.

Awn. A bristle or stiff, hairlike projection; in the grass spikelet, usually the prolongation of the midnerve or lateral nerves of the glumes, lemmas or palea.

Axil. The upper angle formed between two structures such as the culm axis and a branch or a spikelet pedicel.

Axillary. In an axil.

Axis (of culm, inflorescence, etc.). The central stem or branch upon which the parts or organs are arranged.

Barbellate. Having short, stiff hairs.

Beaked. Ending in a firm, prolonged tip.

Bearded. Bearing stiff, usually long hairs.

Bifid. Deeply two-cleft.

Bilateral. Two-sided, arranged on opposite sides.

Blade. The expanded portion of a flattened structure such as a leaf or flower petal. The blade of the grass leaf is the usually flattened, expanded portion above the sheath.

Bloom. In reference to grass herbage or spikelets, a waxy or powdery covering.

Bract. A modified leaf subtending a flower or belonging to an inflorescence; the glumes, lemma and palea of the grass spikelet are bracts.

Bracteate. Having bracts.

Bristle. A stiff hair or hairlike projection.

Bulliform cells. Usually large, thin-walled, highly vacuolated, colorless epidermal cells present in the intercostal zones of the leaf blade. These are most commonly present at the base of furrows on the adaxial surface but may also be present on the abaxial surface.

Bur (burr). A rough or prickly covering around seeds, fruits or spikelets, as the bur of the grassbur or sandbur, *Cenchrus.*

Callus. The hard, usually pointed base of the spikelet (as in *Heteropogon,* *Andropogon* and related genera) or of the floret (as in *Aristida* and *Stipa*) just above the point of disarticulation. In the spikelet, the callus is a portion of the rachis; in the floret, it is a portion of the rachilla. In *Eriochloa* the callus is the thickened node and remnant first glume; in *Chrysopogon* it is part of the pedicel.

Capillary. As applied to hairs, very slender and fine.

Capitate. Head-shaped; collected into a head or dense cluster.

Capitellate. Bearing a minute globular swelling at the apex.

Cartilaginous. Firm and tough but flexible; like cartilage.

Caryopsis. A dry, hard, indehiscent, one-seeded fruit with the thin pericarp adnate to the seed coat; the characteristic grass fruit. This differs from the achene only in the fusion of the pericarp and seed coat.

Cauline. Belonging to the stem, of the stem.

Cespitose (caespitose). In tufts or dense clumps.

Chaffy. With thin, dry scales.

Chartaceous. With the texture of stiff writing paper.

Cilia. Marginal hairs.

Ciliate. Fringed with hairs.

Ciliolate. Furnished with minute cilia.

Cinerous. The color of ashes; light gray.

Clavate. Club-shaped, thickened or enlarged at the apex from a slender base.

Cleft. Cut or divided into lobes.

Cleistogamous spikelet. Spikelet in which fertilization takes place within the spikelet.

Collar. The outer side of a grass leaf at the junction of the blade and sheath.

Concave. Hollowed out; opposite of convex.

Connate. Fused together; firmly united.

Continuous rachis. A rachis that does not disarticulate at the nodes at maturity.

Cordate. Heart-shaped; with a broad, notched base and a pointed tip.

Coriaceous. Leathery in texture.

Corm. The enlarged, fleshy base of a stem.

Culm. The stem of a grass.

Cuneate. Wedge-shaped; narrowly triangular and broadest at the tip.

Cuspidate. Tipped with a short, sharp, rigid point.

Deciduous. Falling, as the leaves from a tree.

Decumbent. Applied to stems that curve upward from a reclining or horizontal base.

Decurrent. Extending downward from the point of insertion.

Dentate. Having a toothed margin or toothlike projections or processes.

Depauperate. Impoverished, stunted.

Dichotomous. Dividing or forking into 2 equal parts; dichotomous branching is repeatedly branching into pairs.

Diffuse. Scattered; dispersed; spreading.

Digitate. Radiating from a common point or base, as the fingers (digits) of the hand; common bermudagrass, *Cynodon dactylon,* has an inflorescence of digitately arranged spicate branches.

Dioecious. Unisexual, with staminate and pistillate flowers on separate plants.

Diploid. With respect to polyploid chromosome series, having twice the basic (x) number of chromosomes.

Disarticulate. To separate at the joints or nodes at maturity.

Distichous. Distinctly two-ranked, in two rows.

Divaricate. Widely spreading or divergent.

Dorsal. The back side or surface; the surface turned away from the central stalk or axis; abaxial surface.

Echinate. Prickly, provided with prickles.

Ellipsoidal. An elliptic solid, twice as long as broad and rounded at the ends.

Elliptic. In the form of a flattened circle, more than twice as long as broad.

Endemic. Indigenous or native in a restricted locality.

Endosperm. Nutritive tissue arising in the embryo sac of most angio-
sperms following the fertilization of the two fused polar nuclei (primary
endosperm nuclei) by one of the two male gametes. In most organisms
the cells of the endosperm have a 3n chromosome number.

Entire. Undivided; in reference to leaves or bracts, the margin continuous,
without teeth or lobes.

Ephemeral. Lasting for a day or less.

Erose. Irregular and uneven, as if gnawed or worn away.

Euploid. With a chromosome number that is an exact multiple of the basic
(x) complement.

Excurrent. Extending out, as the nerves of a leaf or bract; in grasses
the midnerve of the lemma is extended out (excurrent) as an awn
in many cases.

Exserted. Projecting beyond the surrounding parts, as a stamen or stigma.

Fascicle. A cluster or close bunch, usually used in reference to culms,
leaves or branches of the inflorescence.

Fibrillose. Composed of or furnished with small, fine fibers.

Filiform. Threadlike; filamentous.

Fimbriate. Fringed with coarse hairs or narrow segments of tissue.

First glume. Lowermost of the two glumes.

Flabellate. Fan shaped, broadly wedge-shaped.

Floret. As applied to grasses, the lemma and palea with the enclosed flower.
The floret may be perfect, pistillate, staminate or neuter.

Floriferous. Flower-bearing.

Fusiform. Spindle-shaped; rounded and tapering from the middle toward
each end.

Geniculate. Abruptly bent, as at the elbow or knee joint.

Gibbous. Swollen on one side; with a pouchlike swelling.

Glabrate. Becoming glabrous; somewhat glabrous.

Glabrous. Without hairs.

Glaucous. Covered or whitened with a waxy bloom, as a cabbage leaf or
a plum.

Globose. Spherical or rounded; globelike.

Glomerate. In densely contracted, headlike clusters.

Glumes. The pair of bracts usually present at the base of the spikelet, below the floret or florets.

Grain. In respect to grasses, the unhusked or threshed fruit; used in reference to the mature ovary alone or the ovary enclosed in persistent bracts (palea, lemma, glumes).

Herbage. The stems and leaves of an herbaceous plant.

Hirsute. Provided with rather coarse and stiff hairs, these long, straight and erect or ascending.

Hispid. Provided with erect, rigid, bristly hairs.

Hispidulous. Minutely hispid.

Hyaline. Transparent or translucent.

Imbricate. Overlapping, as the shingles of a roof.

Imperfect. Unisexual flowers or florets; with either male or female reproductive structures but not both.

Indument. The hairy covering.

Indurate. Hard.

Inflorescence. The flowering portion of a shoot; in grasses, the spikelets and the axis or branch system that supports them, the inflorescence being delimited at the base by the uppermost leafy node of the shoot.

Innovations. The basal shoots of a perennial grass plant.

Internode. The portion of the stem or other structure between two nodes.

Involucre. A circle or cluster of bracts or reduced branchlets that surround a flower or floret or a group of flowers or florets.

Involute. Rolled inward from the edges.

Joint. A culm, rachilla or rachis internode together with a portion of the node at either end; term generally used in reference to the units of a disarticulating culm, rachis or rachilla axis.

Keel. A prominent dorsal ridge, like the keel of a boat. Glumes and lemmas of laterally compressed spikelets are often sharply keeled; the palea of some florets is two-keeled.

Lacerate. Irregularly cleft or torn.

Lanate. Woolly; covered with hairs resembling wool.

Lanceolate. Lance-shaped; relatively narrow, tapering to both ends from a point below the middle.

Lemma. The lowermost of the two bracts enclosing the flower in the grass floret.

Ligule. A membranous or hairy appendage on the adaxial surface of the grass leaf at the junction of sheath and blade.

Linear. Long and narrow and with parallel margins.

Membranous. Thin, soft and pliable, with the character of a membrane.

Monoecious. Flowers unisexual, with male and female flowers borne on the same plant.

Monotypic. Having a single type or representative, as a genus with only one species.

Mucro. A short, small, abrupt tip of an organ, as the projection of a nerve of the leaf.

Mucronate. With a mucro.

Muticous. Blunt; without a point.

Nerve. A simple vein or slender rib of a leaf or bract.

Neuter. Without functional stamens or pistils.

Node. Region of culm, branch or spikelet axis at which leaves, bracts or branches are produced.

Nodulose-roughened. Roughened with rounded protuberance or knobs.

Obconic. Cone-shaped, with attachment at the narrow end.

Obdeltoid. Inversely triangular, attached at the narrow end.

Oblanceolate. Inversely lanceolate, attached at the narrow end.

Oblong. Two to three times longer than broad and with nearly parallel sides.

Obovate. Inversely egg-shaped (as in longitudinal section), with the broader end near the apex.

Obpyriform. Inverted pear-shaped.

Obtuse. Blunt or rounded, making an angle of 90° or more.

Oval. Broadly elliptic.

Ovary. The enlarged lower part of the pistil in angiospermous plants, enclosing the ovules or young seeds.

Ovate. Egg-shaped (in longitudinal section) with the broadest end toward the base.

Palea. The uppermost of the two bracts enclosing the grass flower in the floret; the palea usually is two-nerved and two-keeled.

Panicle. As applied to grasses, any inflorescence in which the spikelets are not sessile or individually pediceled on the main axis.

Papilla (pl. *papillae*). A minute, nipple-shaped projection.

Papilla-based hairs. Hairs arising from papillae.

Pectinate. With narrow, closely set and divergent segments or units like the teeth of a comb.

Pedicel. The stalk of a single flower; in grasses, the stalk of a single spikelet.

Pedicellate. Having a pedicel.

Peduncle. The stalk of a flower cluster; in grasses, the stalk of a spikelet cluster.

Pedunculate. With a peduncle.

Pendent, pendulous. Suspended or hanging.

Perennial. Living for more than one year.

Perfect. A flower or floret with both male and female functional reproductive structures.

Pericarp. The fruit wall developed from the ovary wall.

Persistent, persisting. In reference to rachis or rachilla, one that does not disarticulate.

Petiole. A leaf stalk.

Pilose. With soft, straight hairs.

Pistil. The female (seed-bearing) structures of the flower, ordinarily consisting of the ovary and one or more styles and stigmas.

Pistillate. Having a pistil but not stamens.

Plumbeous. Lead-colored.

Plumose. Feathery, having fine, elongate hairs on either side.

Polyploid. A plant with three or more basic sets of chromosomes; any ploidy level above the diploid.

Primary inflorescence branch. Branch arising directly from the main inflorescence axis.

Prophyll. The first leaf of a lateral shoot or vegetative culm branch. The prophyll is a sheath, usually with two strong lateral nerves and numerous fine intermediate nerves; a blade is never developed.

Puberulent. Minutely pubescent.

Pubescent. Downy or hairy.

Pulvinus (pl. *pulvini*). A swelling at the base of a leaf or of a branch of the inflorescence.

Pungent. Terminating in a rigid, sharp point.

Pustulate. With irregular, blisterlike swellings or pustules.

Raceme. As applied to grasses, an inflorescence in which all the spikelets are borne on pedicels inserted directly on the main (undivided) inflorescence axis or in which some spikelets are sessile and some pediceled on the main axis.

Rachilla. The axis of a grass spikelet.

Rachilla joint. See *joint.*

Rachis. The axis of a spike, raceme or spicate inflorescence branch; also applied to the axis of a compound leaf.

Reduced floret. A staminate or neuter floret; if highly reduced, then termed a rudimentary floret.

Reticulate. Having the veins or nerves disposed like the threads of net.

Retrorse. Pointed downward or toward the base; the opposite of antrorse.

Rhizome. An underground stem, usually with scale leaves and adventitious roots borne at regularly spaced nodes.

Rosette. A whorl or cluster of basal leaves.

Rudiment. In the grass spikelet, one or more rudimentary florets.

Rugose. Wrinkled.

Scaberulous. Minutely scabrous.

Scabrous. Rough to the touch, usually because of the presence of minute prickle-hairs (spicules) in the epidermis.

Scarious. Thin, dry and membranous, not green.

Second glume. The uppermost of the two glumes of a spikelet.

Secund. Arranged on one side only, unilateral.

Semicircular. Partially circular.

Serrate. Saw-toothed, with sharp teeth pointing forward.

Sessile. Inserted directly, without a stalk.

Seta (pl. *setae*). A bristle or a rigid, sharp-pointed, bristlelike organ.

Setaceous. Bristly or bristlelike.

Sheath (*of leaf*). In grasses and sedges, the basal portion of the leaf, the part that encloses the stem.

Somatic cells. Body cells, with $2n$ chromosomes, as opposed to reproductive cells, or gametes, with n chromosomes.

Spathe. A large bract enclosing an inflorescence.

Spicate. Spikelike.

Spicule. Short, stout, pointed projection of the leaf epidermis; spicules often grade into prickle-hairs.

Spike. An inflorescence with flowers or spikelets sessile on an elongated, unbranched rachis.

Spikelet. The basic unit of the grass inflorescence, usually consisting of a short axis; the rachilla, bearing two "empty" bracts; the glumes, at the basal nodes; and one or more florets above. Each floret consists usually of two bracts, the lemma (lower) and the palea (upper), and a flower. The flower usually includes two lodicules (vestigial perianth segments), three stamens and a pistil.

Spine. A stiff, sharp-pointed projection or tip.

Spinescent. Becoming spinelike; ending in a spine; bearing spines.

Stamen. The male organ of the flower, consisting of a pollen-bearing anther on a filiform filament. Collectively, the stamens of a flower are referred to as the androecium.

Staminate. Having stamens but not pistils.

Stigma. The part of the ovary or style that receives the pollen for effective fertilization.

Stipe. A stalk.

Stipitate. Having a stalk or stipe, as a fruit or an elevated gland.

Stolon. A modified horizontal stem that loops or runs along the surface of the ground and serves to spread the plant by rooting at the nodes.

Stoloniferous. With stolons.

Stramineous. Straw-colored; yellowish.

Striated, striate. Furrowed; striped; streaked.

Strigose. Set with stiff bristles or hairs; sparsely hispid.

Style. The contracted portion of the pistil between the ovary and the stigma.

Sub. Latin prefix meaning "almost," "somewhat," "of inferior rank," "beneath."

Subtend. To be below and close to.

Subterranean. Below ground.

Subulate. Awl-shaped.

Succulent. Fleshy or juicy.

Tawny. Dull brownish-yellow.

Taxon. Any taxonomic unit, as species, genus or tribe.

Terete. Cylindrical, round in cross section.

Terminal. Growing at the end of a branch or stem, as a bud, inflorescence, etc.

Tertiary branches. With branches branched and rebranched.

Tesselate. Checkered, in small squares or blocks, either as elevations, depressions or color patterns.

Tetraploid. Having four of the basic (x) sets of chromosomes.

Throat. The adaxial portion of the grass leaf at the junction of sheath and blade.

Tomentose. Covered with short, soft, densely matted, woolly hairs.

Translucent. Allowing the passage of light rays, but not transparent.

Transverse. Lying or being across or in a cross direction.

Trifurcate. Having 3 forks or branches.

Trigonous. Three-angled.

Truncate. Terminating abruptly as if cut off transversely; appearing "chopped off."

Tuberculate. Covered with tubercles or warty protuberances.

Turgid. Swollen, tightly drawn by pressure from within.

Type, type specimen. The specimen upon which the name of a plant species, subspecies or variety is based and to which it is permanently attached.

Undulant, undulating. Gently wavy.

Unilateral. One-sided; developed or hanging on one side.

Unisexual. With either male or female sex structures but not both.

Vernal. Growing in the spring.

Verrucose. Covered with warty protuberances.

Verticil. A whorl; having three or more members or parts attached at the same node of the supporting axis.

Verticillate. Having flowers, etc., arranged in verticils.

Vestigial. Rudimentary and almost completely reduced, with only a vestige remaining.

Villous. Bearing long, soft, unmatted hairs.

Viscid. Sticky; glutinous.

Whorl. A ring of similar parts radiating from a node.

INDEX TO PLANT NAMES

Latin names and the page number of the primary reference to each name are in boldface. Names considered to be synonyms are in italics.